CONTENTS

Contents

Girls
LIKE US

Girls LIKE US

CAROLE KING,

JONI MITCHELL,   782.4

CARLY SIMON—

and the Journey of a Generation

SHEILA WELLER

EBURY
PRESS

To the women of the
1960s generation
(Were we not the best?)

1 3 5 7 9 10 8 6 4 2

Published in 2008 by Ebury Press, an imprint of Ebury Publishing
A Random House Group Company

The Random House Group Limited Reg. No. 954009

Addresses for companies within the Random House Group can be found at
www.randomhouse.co.uk

A CIP catalogue record for this book is available from the British Library

The Random House Group Limited supports The Forest Stewardship Council (FSC),
the leading international forest certification organisation. All our titles that are printed
on Greenpeace approved FSC certified paper carry the FSC logo. Our paper
procurement policy can be found at www.rbooks.co.uk/environment

Mixed Sources
Product group from well-managed
forests and other controlled sources
www.fsc.org Cert no. TT-COC-2139
© 1996 Forest Stewardship Council
FSC

Printed in the UK by CPI Mackays, Chatham, ME5 8TD

ISBN 9780091899240

To buy books by your favourite authors and register for offers visit www.rbooks.co.uk

PART ONE

"we can only look behind
from where we came"

three women,
three moments,
one journey

spring 1956: naming herself [*]

One day after school, fourteen-year-old Carole Klein sat on the edge of her bed in a room wallpapered with pictures of movie stars and the singers who played Alan Freed's rock 'n' roll shows at the Brooklyn Paramount. She was poised to make a decision of grand importance.

Camille Cacciatore, also fourteen, was there to help her. The girls had done many creative things in this tiny room: composed plays, written songs, and practiced signing their names with florid capital *C*'s and curlicuing final *e*'s—readying themselves for stardom. But today's enterprise was larger. Camille inched Carole's desk chair over to the bed so both could read the small print on the tissue-thin pages of the cardboard-bound volume resting on the bedspread between them. Carole was going to find herself a new last name, and she was going to find it the best way she knew how: in the Brooklyn phone book.

---

[*] The dating of this day has been estimated to the best of Camille Cacciatore Savitz's memory.

Camille Cacciatore envied her best friend. "Cacciatore is much worse than Klein! I wanna change my name, too!" Camille had wailed—gratuitously, since both girls knew Camille's father would blow his stack if his daughter came home with a new appellation. Mr. Cacciatore, a transit authority draftsman, was stricter than Mr. Klein, a New York City fireman who, having retired on disability, now sold insurance.

Not that Sidney Klein still lived with Carole and her schoolteacher mother, Eugenia, whom everyone called Genie, in the downstairs apartment of the small two-story brick house at 2466 East Twenty-fourth Street, between Avenues X and Y, in Sheepshead Bay. Carole's parents had recently divorced—a virtual first in the neighborhood—but Sidney came around frequently, and Carole's friends suspected that her parents still loved each other.

So Carole alone could change her name, just as Carole alone was allowed to attend those magical Alan Freed shows (Camille's parents disapproved of "that jungle music"), often making the pilgrimage to the Paramount *both* weekend nights to soak up the plaintive doo-wop of the Platters, Frankie Lymon and the Teenagers, and Queens's very own Cleftones, as well as the dazzling piano banging of Jerry Lee Lewis. Freed had coined the term "rock 'n' roll" three years earlier, when, as a white Ohio deejay affecting a Negro style and calling himself Moondog, he was spinning discs after midnight for a black audience that grew to include a swelling tide of white teenagers starved for the powerful honesty of "race music." Now, in his Brooklyn mecca, Freed drew hordes of fans—and fans destined to be heirs. Carole was among the latter.

The two girls hunched over the phone book and paged past the front matter—the sketch of the long-distance operator, in her tight perm and headset, ready to connect a Brooklynite to Detroit or St. Louis or even San Francisco; the *Warning!* that it was a misdemeanor to fail to relinquish a party line in an emergency. They flattened the book at page 694: where the J section turned into the K section. Carole wanted a name that sounded like Klein: *K,* one syllable. "We were very systematic," Camille recalls. Line by line, column by column, they looked and considered and eliminated.

Kahn . . . Kalb . . . Kamp . . . : Somewhere between Kearns Funeral Home and Krasilovsky Trucking, there had to be the perfect name (or, failing that, an okay one that didn't sound ethnic) to transport the young tunesmith to her longed-for destiny.

Best friends for two years now, Carole and Camille had walked the four blocks to Shellbank Junior High every day. Now they made the longer trek to James Madison High School, where the sons and daughters of lower-middle-class Jews (Italian families like Camille's were a distinct minority) roiled with creative energy. So did the kids from Madison's rival, Lincoln High, and those from another nearby high school, Erasmus Hall. The cramped houses from which these students tumbled each morning were the fifty-years-later counterparts of the tenements of the Lower East Side, where hardworking parents had sacrificed to give their offspring the tools to make culture—musical culture, especially. In fact, so alike were the two generations that, today, Camille Cacciatore Savitz's most lasting impression of the interiors of those small houses—"Every house had a piano! To not have a piano . . . it was like not having a *bed* in those houses!" she marvels—uncannily echoing what a Lower East Side settlement-house worker wrote in a 1906 report: "There is not a house, no matter how poor it be, where there is not . . . a piano or a violin, and where the hope of the whole family is not pinned on one of the younger set as a future genius."

But there was a difference: those young Lower East Side pianist-songwriters had romanticized high-society top-hatters and New England white Christmases. Their World War II–born Brooklyn counterparts, Carole and her peers—with their opposite sense of romance—would soon be extolling the humanity found within the very kinds of tenements those earlier songwriters had struggled to escape.

The piano in the small Klein living room was always in use, by Carole. The commercial tunes that sprang from her fingers combined the rigor of the classical music she'd studied with the wondrous Negro sounds she was absorbing at the Freed shows and on the radio. Carole's father helped her record them onto "demos," but aiding his daughter's career dream didn't make him any less proprietary toward her. Carole was expected to steer a clear path from high school to college, where she would stay four years, obtain her teaching credential, and get married—no crazy surprises. In civil-service Jewish families, people were *menschen:* substantial, sensible.

This was 1956. Mr. and Mrs. Ricky Ricardo had separate beds on *I Love Lucy.* Dissemination of information about birth control to married women was a crime in some states. Every word of *Seventeen* magazine was vetted by a pastor. In garment factories, union inspectors checked skirt lengths before job lots were shipped to department stores. Elvis may have been singing, Jack Kerouac writing, and James Dean's movies still being shown even after his fatal car accident, but there were few female analogues. Doris Day pluckily kept wolves at bay; the Chordettes crooned like estrogened Perry Comos. The 1920s had their flappers; the 1930s, their fox-stole-draped society aviatrixes, cheerfully trundling off to Reno for divorces; the 1940s had Rosie the Riveter. But the deep middle of the 1950s had both the most constricted images of women and (until just recently) the worst popular music of all the previous four decades: a double punch that could be considered a privation—*or* a springboard.

In 1956 girls weren't agents of their sexuality, much less gamblers with it. No girl would have dared sing about how she'd weighed the physical and emotional (*not* the moral) drawbacks of sex—getting pregnant, feeling used—against the greater pull of the act's transcendent pleasure, or how she'd wondered, in the midst of sex, if the boy would drop her afterward. You couldn't get such a song on the radio, even if one existed. In a few years, however, Carole would write that song, based on events in her own life, and the resulting record would be the casual opening salvo of a revolution.

Karl . . . Kass . . . Katz . . . : Carole and Camille were getting hungry. That meant a trip to Camille's house on Twenty-sixth Street. Genie Klein didn't cook much; sometimes she just laid out a jar of borscht and an entrée of "dairy" (cottage cheese, sour cream, cucumbers, scallions) with rye bread and shav, a bitter drink that made Camille almost puke when she tasted it. Mary Cacciatore, on the other hand, cooked like Mario Lanza sang: passionately. Carole would raid the Cacciatores' icebox for peppers and onions or spaghetti and meatballs.

One bond between Camille and Carole was their self-perceived beauty deficiency. Although she had fetchingly upturned eyes, Carole's narrow face was unremarkable; she rued her too-curly hair, and, as Camille says, "she really didn't like her nose." Carole may have suspected that the boys at Madison did not regard her as a beauty. "She was a plain-looking girl with messy hair and ordinary clothes," says then Madison High upper classman Al Kasha, who also became a songwriter. "But at the piano, in the music room, playing Rachmaninoff and Tchaikovsky, she was a different person—she came alive." She had an internal compass, and she hung her self-esteem squarely on her talent.

Though this would be hard to imagine in 1956, when standards of feminine beauty were at their most unforgiving, in fifteen years Carole would represent an inclusive new model of female sensuality: the young "natural" woman, the "earth mother." The album that would afford her this status would, five years after its release, stand as the biggest-selling album in the history of the record industry; would settle out as one of the biggest-selling albums of the 1970s; and then and for years after, would remain the biggest-selling album written and recorded by a woman. It would singularly define its several-years-slice of the young American experience.

Carole's album's historic success would raise the stock of other singer-songwriters (a concept she would help establish) who were women, and it would constitute a Cinderella story with a moral: a behind-the-scenes songwriter and simple borough girl becomes a pop star without changing herself in the slightest. She would have come a long way from those grim negotiations with her teenage mirror. Yet her success was so enormous and early that every subsequent effort would be measured negatively against it. The unpretty girl who'd earned her fortune through hard work and talent would, ironically, find her fate mimicking that of the too-pretty girl who'd dined out a bit too long on early-peaking beauty.

Kaye . . . Kean . . . Kehl . . . : Maybe this weekend the girls would catch a flick at the Sheepshead Bay theater: Carole with Joel Zwick, Camille with Lenny Pullman. Then they'd hit Cookie's, near the Avenue H train station. The luncheonette's booths would brim with talk of who'd cruised Kings Highway in whose souped-up car the night before (and made out in Dubrow's Cafeteria afterward), and who was lucky enough to have gotten on *Ted Steele's Bandstand,* New York's local precursor to *American Bandstand.* Stanzas of mock-Broadway-songs-in-progress would be excitedly test-marketed for Madison's *SING!* competition, which pitted the freshmen against the sophomores and the juniors against the seniors and was as big a deal as the school's football games.

Kehm . . . Kern . . . Kerr . . . : From the vantage point of 1956, it might seem that Carole would never leave Brooklyn, so deeply enmeshed was she in its provincial vibrance. Her future seemed preordained. In the eras before Carole and her peers reached young adulthood, middle-class women had one man in their lives—one husband (and an "appropriate" one), or in the case of his premature death or the rare divorce, two. A woman's life was set within the grid of that one early life decision; there was little room for movement. But in the late 1960s and early 1970s, a new idea evolved: *A woman is entitled to an experiential quest—yes, even a crazy one; it is part of her nature to seek one.* She could Live Large. She had many verses in the song of her life, and a different partner for each one of them.

Carole would end up marrying four times—each marriage a different hidden melodrama underlying her seemingly pragmatic, work-focused life. "The people she loved, she loved *deeply,*" says a female friend who knew her just before and through the height of her fame. Carole's last two marriages would spring from her infatuation with a mythical type of man, a regional subculture, and a way of life as foreign to the streets and stoops of Brooklyn, and the boys therein, as any that existed in America—yet she would sing of it, "And with all I'm blessed with I am certain: I'm where I belong." "Carole has lived at least three lives," her friend Danny Kortchmar says. In fact, she wasn't unusual:

many midlife women Carole's age would end up *so* far off their birth-right paths, it was as if they'd *gone looking* for Alice's rabbit hole to tumble down. Which is exactly what many of them had done.

Ultimately, Carole would settle down—for a while, anyway—not atypically, with the man who, as her friends put it, she "should have been with" in the first place. But as any woman in her generation would know: without that long detour into the dangerous and the for-bidden, such a choice would have been an unimaginative capitulation, not a happy ending.

Kick . . . Kiel . . . Kilp . . . King: "Hey, what do you think about King?" Carole asked.

Camille said, "I don't know anybody named King."

"Me neither," Carole admitted.

"Well—there's a lot of them," Camille said, pointing to page 731: a half page . . . then a full page . . . another full page . . . another half page—*three whole pages* of Kings.

King. The *K* and the *n*, same as Klein. The exclamatory, percussive sound. The tried-and-true stage-name quality. What was not to like?

And thus Carole Klein of Sheepshead Bay became Carole King of America. As casually and proactively as she did everything, she chose the name she would live under for the rest of her life. Then, with that first big decision out of the way, she went off with Camille to concen-trate on a second one. So, spaghetti and meatballs? Or peppers and onions?

october 21, 1964: exposing herself

"Good evening, ladies and gentlemen, welcome to the Half Beat," the young man greeted the tables of patrons, their faces strobed by candle flames spouting from Chianti bottles. There were more than a dozen cof-feehouses like this one in Yorkville Village, Toronto's folk music quarter. On any given night the mournful Scottish and English ballads, rousing work songs, and angry protest anthems (courtesy of the Dylan imitators) soared from the lungs of young performers who were hoping to get their breaks—and hoping to purge themselves of the bourgeois primness of their parents in the provinces. These were the years when folk music was providing the rebellion and authenticity commercial rock 'n' roll had stopped supplying. One of these "folkies" was the delicate-featured, high-cheekboned twenty-year-old in the wings, with feather-banged blond hair curled up in a flip just past her ears and long legs terminating in go-go boots. A Gibson guitar was strapped over her miniskirt, but she also carried a small, mandolin-type instrument, the *tiple* (tee-pleh).

"Tonight we have for your entertainment . . . Joni Anderson!" the emcee announced.

Joni had loved pop music before it had gotten so bubblegum. One of her favorite songs from high school—indeed, for decades to come, she would call it her favorite song of all time—was the Shirelles hit of four years before, "Will You Love Me Tomorrow." It was written by Carole King and Gerry Goffin, a married couple who were among a group of barely-out-of-their-teens New York songwriters who mixed a deep infatuation with Negro church music and R&B with a Broadway songwriting style, and turned the results into Top 40 radio. "Will You Love Me Tomorrow" had been the first pop song to address the risks of sex in a woman's life—which was now, as she stood in the wings of the Half Beat, precisely Joni Anderson's dilemma. Carole King had solved the dilemma the way girls always had—she married the boy who had gotten her pregnant in a big traditional wedding. Joni Anderson was dealing with her pregnancy in a brand-new way: unmarried and alone. She was extremely afraid her parents would find out about her pregnancy, yet she refused to let it stop her life or curb her dreams.

"Joni's been appearing here for the last two weeks and will be for the next three weeks," the emcee continued. "Starting next Monday, we have her under contract. We hope she'll stay here. We hope you'll enjoy her as much as we have."

Yorkville was Canada's version of Greenwich Village and Cambridge, Massachusetts, where six years earlier, three Boston University coeds, in spontaneous protest, had thrown off their freshman beanies and had become best friends and soul mates. The three—a Boston Brahmin named Betsy; a Staten Island lawyer's daughter named Debbie; and a California physicist's kid named Joanie—were one of any number of cliques of folkie girls then asserting their nonconformist sensibility, playing English ballads on their Gibsons and Martins and reinforcing in each other an adventurousness that was otherwise hard for girls to pull off; guys could at least pretend to be romantic wanderers, while rebel girls could just get pregnant. ("There were tears over boys, and a harrowing trip to a doctor who was supposed to be able to 'fix' things," the Betsy of the threesome—Betsy Minot Siggins—says today. "It felt like we were both the initiators of *and* the victims of the sexual revolution.") But this clique turned out to be *the* clique: the one that advanced the narrative. The Joanie of the threesome, Joan Baez, didn't just achieve stardom; her stardom constituted the first time in the United States that an arcane musical genre was lofted to commercial popularity on the strength of a *female* performer. Now, four years after her rise to fame and two years after she graced the cover of *Time* magazine, Joan Baez remained the gold-standard embodiment of the sensitive girl curled over her guitar. It was Baez's bell-clear soprano that Joni Anderson was emulating.

"Let's give her a little bit of a welcome now—Miss Joni Anderson!"

Through a round of applause, Joni strode to the chair, sat down, and, in a breathless, Canadian schoolgirl's voice, said: "It's sure refreshing to have a mic to work with for a change"—a giggle—"after some of the places I've been in." Sympathetic laughter from the audience. What they (and she) didn't know was that this moment would be one of her last singing songs meant to *sound like* traditional ballads. In less than a year, she'd begin to offer audiences the original songs of vulnerability, wit, wonderment—and only retroactively understood sadness—that she was starting to write. On the heels of those first compositions of hers would come a new wave of songs that, as she put it, were "beginning to reveal feminine insecurities, doubts, and recognition that the old order was falling apart"—songs that "depicted my times." With that eventual torrent, in six years she would set the bar for emotional self-exposure—"confessional" songwriting—just about as high as it would ever be set by anyone. But tonight her self-exposure concerns were literal: She was single and at slightly over five months, visibly pregnant. Already, the small tiple was much easier to manipulate than the guitar.

"The first song I'd like to do is a song about when a man becomes so involved in almighty liquor that he begins to think of it as a woman," she said, with a smile in her voice. "And he calls his bottle 'Nancy Whiskey.'"

Her real name was Roberta Joan Anderson, and her family hailed most recently from Saskatoon, Saskatchewan, eighteen hundred miles north of the North Dakota border. She had come to Toronto several months earlier, taking the train across the prairie with her art school boyfriend. Then he'd split, leaving her a painting of a moon as a good-bye-and-sorry-I-got-you-pregnant gift. She had recently moved to a room-with-shared-bath in a rooming house on Huron Street. It was from this extremely modest base that she was trying to make her way as a folksinger, without money or connections and in deep secrecy about her pregnancy.

But if she was self-conscious, she hid it, as she strummed her tiple and gaily sang the traditional Scottish song—

> *Whiskey, whiskey, Nancy Whiskey*
> *The more I kissed her, the more I loved her*

After the audience applauded her final bars of "Nancy Whiskey," Joni announced: "In 1961 a man named Ewan MacColl wrote a song and entered it into a song contest in England. It wasn't much of a surprise to anybody when it won." What's significant is that she would choose—of *all* songs, *now*—this violent faux-Child Ballad about the anticipation, birth, and *loss* of a baby. "It has very, very dramatic lyrics," she warned as she began singing the song.

Joni's neighbor across the hall at her rooming house was a young poet from the Ojibway tribe named Duke Redbird. They'd squeeze past each other in the hall—Duke with his long black braids, Joni with her flaxen hair. He could see that she was pregnant, but he sensed from her attitude not to mention it. "Joni had a stoicism that reminded me of the Indian women I grew up with," Redbird recalls. "When we'd walk by each other's open doors, she never acknowledged her difficulties." Inside her small room, pungent with incense, she showed him her scrapbook, proudly turning the pages and explaining the newspaper clips of her performances at coffeehouses in Calgary, a few in Edmonton, and her real-live TV debut, singing on a Saskatchewan hunting and fishing show.

Still, Duke Redbird worried about his neighbor, who was living on pizza and donuts. He mentioned his concern to his brother so much that one day his brother arrived at Duke's door with a bag of apples and said, "Let's give them to that pregnant girl." The two young men knocked on Joni's door and held out the fruit. "They're *root,* from nature; *good* for you now," Redbird's brother said awkwardly. Joni gratefully—and hungrily—took the bag. There were other signs of her vulnerability. "Late at night," Redbird says, "when Joni's door was closed, I'd hear her playing her guitar and singing: not words, just sounds, like she was using her voice to meditate. I was struck by her melancholy."

That same melancholy was in her voice now as she continued to sing what she had identified as the MacColl song (it was actually written by Sydney Carter) to the Half Beat patrons:

> *Rock-a-bye, baby, the white and the black*
> *Somebody's baby is not comin' back . . .*

After covering a Woody Guthrie number, among other songs, Joni packed up her instruments and exited the club, perhaps stopping to jam at the crash pad of her friend Vicky Taylor, with whom she would soon form a duo. Then it was back to the Huron Street room and her meditative strumming and vocal yodeling. Listening from the hall one such night—maybe it was even *this* night—Redbird was moved to pick up a pen and write a poem, which, though never published, he has kept to this day: A "woman with the cornsilk hair and sweetgrass [incense] in her hand" is on a water journey, navigating a river's "invisible shoals" and "silent rapids"–the poem was explicitly about Joni's pregnancy, her circumstances. Redbird understood both the risk (those "shoals" and "rapids") *and* the lack of acknowledgment of and respect for that risk: its "silent," "invisible" nature. Indeed; male folksingers might boast of riding the rails, but few of the young ones, including Dylan, ever did. (Dylan hadn't even hitchhiked to New York–he was given a ride by a friend.) For girls, the tougher though completely unacknowledged and unsung rite of passage was being pregnant, alone, penniless, and court-ing scorn in a rented room far from a home that you couldn't return to. Sometimes Duke Redbird would knock on Joni Anderson's door and ask if she was all right. She never said she wasn't.

Over the next three years, Joni's life would be typical of many North American women's when the early to mid-1960s–that Jack-and-Jackie-influenced era of glamorized traditional marriage–slowly turned into the later 1960s, and a new culture was spawned, both by the neo-Edwardian style of the English groups and by the softer offshoots of psychedelia. Just as some of Joni's counterparts attending college would marry young professors, Joni would marry a man eight years her senior who was al-ready living the life she thought she wanted. But as she pulled ahead of her husband in talent and ambition, she would realize–as other girls would–that young marriage to a sophisticated man was *not* the start of Real Life but, rather, an impediment to it. She would write her prema-turely wise song about the cycles of age in part to lambaste *Esquire*'s claim, during those years, that, as she put it, "a woman was all washed up after 21," and she would move to New York in 1967, just when single women were starting to live in cities in a new way: eschewing the old regulating supports–roommates, day jobs–for solitary, emotion-driven, night-based experience. Sex was then newly immediate–an innocent generosity, a basic communication–but romance was rough and ready laissez-faire capitalism, the only rules of the game being men's rules. Joni's cactus tree metaphor would be a secret playbook and shared record for the relatively few young women who lived in that then vul-nerable manner.

Joni would leave for L.A. when California dreaming was becoming a reality, and she would become both the It Girl and anthropologist of her newly coined female archetype, a rusticated American version of Left Bank femininity. She would write the haunting national anthem of her generation's most emblematic gathering, and she would play Wendy to three choirboy-voiced Lost Boys powwowed from equal tribes, and with one of them she would legitimize the gallantry of a new kind of intimacy. She would leave this ideal love to set off as a vagabond, living in a cave with a self-made outlaw who "kept [her] camera to sell." Young women who liked "clean white linen and fancy French cologne" had never toured Europe like this before. In 1970 it was the *only* way many of them would want to do so.

Throughout the next decades, the 1970s through mid-1990s—years when young women would push the limits of independence, ambition, and self-fulfillment as never before—Joni would compose the bumpy epic poem of that exploration. She would choose the title of the signal album *Hejira* because she liberally interpreted the Arabic word to mean "to run away, but honorably," something that women were starting to do: even when the After was no better than the Before, when the destination was worse than the starting point.

Those songs would echo Joni's own life journey: solitary cross-country road trips and even more solitary months in the woods; a fan-shearing turn to jazz; an almost unceasing, night-crawling workaholism, yielding twenty-one original albums and a "crop rotation" of paintings, as well as a self-assured choice of long-term lovers. These were men who—since they "mirrored [her] back simplified" and were far less wealthy and celebrated than she—stood in almost intentionally pointed contrast to her male *friends*, who were the most successful and glamorous men in Hollywood. In all of this she would turn a new twist on an old type, the "dame," the tough, cranky, boastful woman living for her craft. But where previous versions (Lillian Hellman, Gertrude Stein) were masculinized, *she* would remain, illuminatively, feminine.

In 1980, Joni would do something familiar to single women then turning forty—women wearying of the historically unprecedented time they'd logged as battle-scarred free agents, at the same moment that mating shibboleths were loosening: She would meet a wholesome younger man who was awed to be her lover, and she would marry him, with the male becoming the nurturer of the couple. Then, after a ten-year run, she'd end the marriage with *I am who I am; I am not changing.* Here was the cactus tree, a quarter century later.

Over these last twenty years her puzzling-out of her life and career would feature the same hurt, anger, and heightened self-regard shared by female age mates whose elevated expectations had left them unwilling to be pushed aside in the same "due course" of life that had bound earlier generations of women. Her "An angry man is just an angry man [but] an angry woman? 'Bitch!'"—sung in a lifetime chain-smoker's raspy alto—would be a back page of the well-shared hymnal she wrote, whose psalms to ice cream castles in the air had been chorused in trilling soprano.

But all of this would come years in the future.

Meanwhile, in late 1964, Joni Anderson scraped by in Yorkville. She would perform a few weeks longer; then, in increasing desperation, she'd move into Vicky Taylor's crash pad and later to the closet-sized attic room of a male platonic friend, in a building marked for demolition. Finally, when her labor pains started, two weeks past her due date, she would check herself into the charity ward of Toronto General Hospital—and there confront what she was singing about tonight: she was having a baby she could not keep and would not keep.

Hundreds of accidentally pregnant girls made that decision every day, for the sake of the baby's well-being, their reputations or their parents', and their own desired freedom. But how could they experience the decision without guilt—or fail to internalize society's judgment of their relinquishment as selfishness? The burden of both judgments, the internal one *and* the societal one, would resonate incalculably over two-thirds of Joni's lifetime. As a close confidante of Joni's says, "*Everything in Joni's emotional life has been about the baby.*"

During their time on Huron Street, neither Joni Anderson nor Duke Redbird could have any idea that, thirty years later, by multiple coincidences, *he* would be the one to lead Joni's long-relinquished grown daughter to her.

But that was decades down the road. So much of life would be lived in the interim.

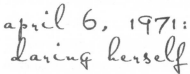

april 6, 1971:
Daring herself

When Steve Harris knocked on the door of Carly Simon's Hyatt Continental House room, he wasn't surprised at the fear he saw in her face. Harris, an A&R man at Elektra Records, had spent two months cajoling Carly, an unknown who had extreme stage fright, into consenting to a live concert, so necessary to promote the single, "That's the Way I've Always Heard It Should Be," from her self-titled debut album. The record had sold only 2,000 copies, but it had ignited water-cooler talk among the special group of record company secretaries and receptionists that Elektra president Jac Holzman had sent it to; word-of-mouth had started, and Holzman was determined to maximize it.

Carly and Steve had flown out to L.A. the other day, on one of those brand-new 747s, their mutual fear of flying blunted by old-fashioneds and Valium in the first-class cabin. They were determined to have fun and forget that the Big Night was looming. Since landing, Carly—an unreconstructed East Coast girl—had been playing the enchanted naïf. Despite her highly sophisticated upbringing (her father, Richard Simon, was the cofounder of Simon & Schuster), she had never been to California before, a poor-little-rich-girl-ism that amazed her. In between dates with Michael Crichton (she and Steve had nicknamed the very tall doctor-novelist "Big Boy"), she'd been marveling at the tropical L.A. colors, at the hotel's rooftop pool, and at the platform beds in their rooms—Steve's had a crown over it! She kept repeating the mantra "I can't get nervous because this is a foreign country; I'll be performing to *foreigners.*" In fact, though, she would be performing—opening for Cat Stevens at the Troubadour—*not* to foreigners but to

L.A.'s music elite. And here was her fun-loving chaperone, Steve, come to deliver her to her Waterloo.

Carly collapsed on Steve's chest, "shaking and trembling, like a scared puppy," Steve recalls. She was also stuttering; her long-extinguished childhood tic had resurfaced.

She was a tall, once chubby, now slim, leggy young woman in her mid-twenties wearing a floppy hat, a diaphanous skirt, and high boots. Her strong features—very full lips in prognathic face, low-bridged nose, sloe eyes—all cushioned in the remnants of baby fat, gave her a startling sensuality and made her ethnicity an enigma. (Her father was Jewish; her mother was half-German, part-Spanish, and, so the cherished family story went, part black.) As they got in the elevator, Carly told Steve that, as a child, she'd made up a special language to overcome her stammer. If only she could remember it!

That childhood of hers had been straight out of *The New Yorker*. Luminaries were guests in the Simons' living room. Carly and her siblings had attended the nearby private schools favored by wealthy, intellectual families, and the second generation replicated the first one. One of Carly's best friends, Ellen Wise Salvadori, was studying to be a Jungian therapist, while her husband was poised for deanship of a college art department. Her other best friend, Jessica Hoffmann Davis, was becoming a cognitive developmental psychologist. Carly's oldest sister, Joey, was an opera singer; middle sister Lucy married a psychiatrist. It was from this talk-rich world that Carly's song had percolated.

Rendered in her emotional contralto, the elegant ballad she'd written with her friend, *Esquire* writer Jake Brackman, presented a sophisticated woman struggling with a decision. She is in her thirties, but even though her friends have settled down, she's in no hurry to do so. Her boyfriend is the sentimental idealist about marriage; *she's* the hesitating cynic: "But soon you'll cage me on your shelf." This song was the first antimarriage pop ballad written and sung by a woman.

Real-life personifications of the song—young women criticizing marriage, ending their marriages, and writing about it—were popping up all over New York now. Women's liberation had been the work of female civil rights and antiwar activists in collectives in Berkeley, Boston, New York, and elsewhere, for three years, but now it was fully entrenched in the young mainstream intelligentsia. Women in the media, arts, and academe—Carly's crowd—had come to view society and their personal histories through this powerful new lens that was supplanting all others. The movement relied on the intimate sharing of experiences: "consciousness raising." As they pooled their stories about, among other facets of their lives, love (with a new, tough analysis replacing yesterday's commiseration), women came to view men's put-up-or-shut-up rules of romance in the same way that newly unionized nineteenth-century factory workers viewed "If you don't come in Sunday, then don't come in Monday" signs: *Two can play that game, baby.*

This movement was about to get its own national publication. Right at this moment, as Carly and Steve Harris were stepping onto the curb at Santa Monica and Doheny, back in New York, a memo marked "Confidential: Some notes on a new magazine" was being circulated among *New York* magazine writer Gloria Steinem and a half-dozen other women; for its title, *Sister* and *Everywoman* vied with the odd-sounding *Ms.* And in law firms around the country, handfuls of attorneys were reframing as offensive and unjust practices that just a year before were regarded as unremarkably normal: separate newspaper job listings for men and women, rape victims' need for corroborating witnesses, banks' refusal to give women credit cards.

This new idea that was taking hold in the media and being argued in the courts—that young women had integrity—was having its echo in music. Carole King and Joni Mitchell had just arrived at the pinnacles of their careers, at twenty-nine and twenty-seven years of age, respectively. They were months away from achieving, for the former, commercial success unequaled in the recording industry; for the latter, respect unparalleled among her musician peers—by way of very different albums, *Tapestry* and *Blue,* that had this in common: neither had one false note in it. These triumphs would be clouded with pain. Carole's marriage to the one husband her friends would later wistfully call "the normal one" would end, leading her to a next marriage, in which the consequences of her husband's insecurity were infinitely more destructive. As for Joni, her "living on nerves and feelings," as she'd later describe in a lyric on *Court and Spark,* would lead to a bottoming out, in the course of which she would issue a self-harming cry for help (she has referred to it as a "suicide attempt") after being rejected by a famous boyfriend.

Carole and Joni were in many ways opposites. Carole was Everywoman; Joni, the Bohemian. Carole was a craftsman, a tunesmith; Joni, a poet, an artist. Carole was a comforting, accessible friend; Joni, the object of women's awe and men's infatuation. Carole (now pregnant with her third child) was maternal; she lived by adding. Joni was solitary; she lived by relinquishing. Carole's songs celebrated easy-to-grasp feelings in an optimistic spirit by way of clear, infectiously rhythmic expression. Joni's songs described complex needs and emotional states; they did not skirt pessimism; and—like the astonishingly original Laura Nyro, the only other female singer-songwriter Joni respected—she had begun to use her voice like a jazz instrument, with abrupt shifts of tempo, octave, mood, and volume.

But Carole and Joni were also alike: both were raised in lower-middle-class households. Neither was a sister (Joni, literally; Carole, functionally), and neither *had* a sister; the idea of confiding in women—that brand-new coin of the realm—was *not* second nature to them, nor was the inclination (Joni's "exposed nerve endings" and confessional songs notwithstanding) to bare their souls to friends. They shared a vague distrust of the chattering classes' "talking cure" and, in different ways, were self-directed. Both were instilled with traditional morality and had paid the price for defying it: Carole, bearing her first child at barely past seventeen; Joni, giving up a baby at twenty-one. Both were naturally ambitious; neither had sought to submerge her talent in a traditional female role.

As if each of these three women's lives represented one-third of a larger story—each, so to speak, a single-hued transparent gel, which when superimposed resulted in a full-color picture—Carly Simon's experience and work filled in the breaches of Joni's and Carole's, for she represented vulnerabilities the other two did not have. When woven together, the strands of their three separate lives, identities, and songs tell the rich composite story of a whole generation of women born middle-class in the early to middle 1940s and coming of age in the middle to late 1960s.

Unlike Carole and Joni, Carly came from a big family awash in estrogen. Carly, her two older sisters, and their sometimes-sisterlike mother (Andrea Simon loved not just to gossip with her daughters but also to flirt with their boyfriends) filled the house with grandiose female dramas and set up Carly's lifetime comfort with and appreciation of female friends. "More than Joni and Carole, Carly is a woman's woman—the notes and gifts, the concern, the phone calls," says Betsy Asher, then wife of James Taylor's manager, Peter Asher, and a woman who was the chief hostess (and secret keeper) to L.A.'s rock world. But the solicitousness wasn't mere etiquette. A lifelong analysand in a therapy-worshiping subculture, Carly believed in the value of intimate confession (and she listened raptly as others poured their hearts out), and she confided with great, incautious gusto. "Carly doesn't have a privacy barometer—it *all* comes out," says Jessica Hoffmann Davis. "Carly doesn't bring her defenses forward from one moment to the next; she doesn't give herself that buffer, that solace," Mia Farrow agrees. Ellen Wise Questel (Carly's friend who in 1971 was Ellen Wise Salvadori now goes by her remarried name, Questel)* explains, "A mystic once said, 'You have two eyes; one says yes to the world, the other says no. You need to see with *both* of them.' Carly sees more with the eye that says yes, and that makes her so vulnerable. She belongs in

---

* Here and throughout, a woman who uses one name in her current life but as a character in this book was known by a different name may be referred to in two, or more, ways. Some women married, divorced, and remarried and changed names at each juncture, making the process of identifying them both as characters at any given point in the narrative *and* as quoted sources slightly more complicated. Apologies to the reader for the sometimes confusing last-name-shuffle.

another century, the era of grand feelings and penned love letters. Carly would be perfect in a Tolstoy novel." Stuck in New York (eight months pregnant) on the night of Carly's Troubadour opening, Ellen mentally replayed a defining moment from their teen years: "Carly's sitting on the school steps with her guitar, playing 'When I Fall in Love,' and she's singing the '. . . it will be for-*ev*-er . . .' with *such* passion." Neither Carly nor Ellen could know that, through an introduction tonight, the prophecy of that lyric—the inability to stop loving someone even after one *can* and *wants* to—would be set in motion in Carly's life.

In contrast to Carole's and especially Joni's family, Carly's was extremely modern about sex. Sex was a *wonderful* thing, Andrea Simon made clear—sometimes a bit too abundantly. But if sex had not carried for Carly the price it had for Carole or the consequences represented in Joni's youth, the conflict Carly felt between love and ambition (which Carole and Joni did *not* share) was equally limiting. There was also the matter of her charismatic older sisters; *they* were the ones who were supposed to be stars, *not she*. This single of hers, this solo album, this Troubadour gig: if something came of it, it would destroy the God-given hierarchy in Carly's family.

The Troubadour busboys were setting a red rose in a bud vase on every table—a gift from Carly to her audience. Tonight she'd be wooing the L.A. rock community (many, recently transplanted New Yorkers), which was like the cool kids' table in the school cafeteria. Carole and Joni were the popular girls on that bench, and here *she* was, the interloper: about to wander over with her tray in her hands to see if she could join them. "Carly was completely unnerved when we got to the dressing room, like, 'How can I get out of this?'" Steve Harris recalls. He was getting a crash introduction to her intense neuroticism, which made even those who loved her describe her as a little "crazy."

Carly asked Steve if she could take a short walk in the alley to clear her head. He wouldn't let her go by herself, so down the stairs they loped together. Carly would have to dare herself to get on that stage.

But she was good that way, always daring her heart to be broken to pieces; rarely shirking from the sexually exhibitionist gesture other women wouldn't *think* of undertaking. As they circled the block, Steve saw the huge effort Carly was making to calm herself. He vowed to think of some reward once the show was over.

Carole King and Joni Mitchell had someone in common: James Taylor. Taylor was now, officially (courtesy of last month's *Time* magazine cover), the biggest male rock hero in the country and the touted culture-changing avatar of a new intimate, thoughtful ballad style that was muscling loud rock offstage. James was a deeply close musical friend of Carole and, until recently, Joni's lover.

Everyone thought Joni and James had split up. But here they were, gliding into the Troubadour together. Carly loved James's music. In a bit of faux diva-ness intended to stanch this feared engagement, she'd insisted that Steve find her a drummer who sounded "just like" Taylor's drummer, Russ Kunkel, or else she wouldn't perform. (Steve booked in-demand Kunkel himself so she'd have no out.) Now Russ walked into Carly's dressing room, excitedly reporting that James Taylor would be watching her. "Why'd you have to tell me that?" Carly wailed.

But when she took the stage, the microphone saved her. It kept sliding. Her constant need to steady it as she sang made her forget her terror, and she delivered, as the critics would rave, a star-is-born performance.

After Cat Stevens finished his set, Steve Harris strode over to James—the two had met before, and James looked like he'd enjoyed the show—and invited him "to come up and say hello to Carly." James, who'd played the Troub, had been in its dressing room before, scoring his preperformance hit of smack (encased in knotted balloons, in case you had to swallow it) from a young dealer who happened to be a Beverly Hills doctor's son and who always had the best stuff. Joni came along, close by James's side. In a bit of quick thinking, Steve said to Joni: "Cat's over there," steering Joni to Stevens's dressing room as James entered Carly's—"looking like a country boy," Steve recalls. "Carly could barely contain her excitement."

When Steve left the room, Carly was seated on the couch; James, at her feet on the floor with his legs crossed. "They were deep in conversation," Steve recalls. "I could see the intensity between them."

Over the next eight months Carly Simon would spin off on romances with an array of rock and movie stars, while writing and recording two hit albums, the second delivering a monster hit that is generally considered the first, and most defiant, feminist rock song of the mainstream second-wave feminist era. (The song also sparked a still-in-play guessing game about who its subject was.) But through that whirlwind, the face of the man she met that night would beckon, as if the old saying *A woman loves only one man in her life* had crankily invaded her psyche to thwart the enormous distance she and other young women were hurtling from it. As Timothy White put it in *Rolling Stone:* "Carly was the brainy beauty, the ultimate catch. But while everyone was chasing [her], she was running after the one guy who just kept on walking."

Carly's marriage to James Taylor in November 1972, and the family they would create, would be a kind of skeptical urban woman's test case. At a moment in time when marriage was grandly suspect and wanting a baby was something smart women were embarrassed to admit, Carly would be among those who, in doing both, bore the burden to *not* be backsliding. But, having married in an era when the tortured boy was the only one worth having, yet before codependency entered the lexicon, Carly would learn the difficulty of making a family man of an addict. And, like countless women crowding suddenly numerous female therapists' offices, she would, against her better judgment, feel the need to downplay her success around her husband. In that season of feminism's deepest, most glamorous reach, Carly's next three album covers—demure pregnant glow; soft-porn heat; writhing sensuality—would reassure her wary cohort that domesticity *could* be reinvented (well, sort of . . .), even beyond her own family's secretly decadent model. Her marriage would wind down during a stridently idealistic time when a movie starring her Sarah Lawrence classmate Jill Clayburgh would complete the thought her own first song had helped push into the zeitgeist eight years earlier: *Escaping a flawed marriage = liberation*. But Carly and others would learn that it wasn't that simple. If only feminist fortune cookie sentences could, as ordered, change the heart. They couldn't.

Carly would "come around again," marrying a man whose solicitude corrected his predecessor's distance, only to face serial monogamy's irony: behind every solved problem lies a fresh one you hadn't anticipated. Crises would come to this woman of the charmed childhood. In the wake of her unique mother's death, she would write a universal song about the mother-daughter bond, reemploying her favored symbol of femaleness—the river—which also inspired Joni. She would become one of the one in eight American women to be diagnosed each year with breast cancer; she'd undergo a mastectomy. Depression would leave her challenged to learn to trim the sails of her neediness, "to travel alone and lightly." She would encounter, with Joni and Carole, the loophole in the Constitution of their egalitarian generation: Women get "older"; men are "ageless."

But she was good at dares. She would have one of her biggest-selling albums in late middle age, a feat simultaneously shared by Carole in the wake of a season of veneration for Joni (with one music executive declaring, "Joni Mitchell is simply one of the most important and influential songwriters in the history of popular music"). Carly would now be taking her cues from her "wise woman at the end of the bar," and all three would by now have coursed along the winding, glamorous, but, as Carole had put it, definitely "rutted" road of the prime of their lives. And in the process—because, yes, songs *are* like tattoos—they would write, in music, a history of how that life really was, for them and so many girls like them.

After James Taylor left Carly Simon's dressing room (and exited the club with girlfriend Joni), Carly walked onto the Troubadour fire escape with her guitar and serenaded the fans who'd gathered on the sidewalk. A stone's throw northeast, up the hill in Laurel Canyon, Carole was at home with her husband and children on Appian Way, near Joni's place on Lookout Mountain. This year, 1971, the media would soon essentially declare, was both the Year of the Woman and the Year of Women in Music. Under those banner headlines stood a generation of females who'd been little girls in one America—a frantically conventional, security-mad postwar nation, without rock 'n' roll or civil rights, and with an anxiously propagandized, stultifying image of women—and who'd created their own Dionysian counter-reality, which was now yielding an even more revolutionary chapter.

Carole King's, Joni Mitchell's, and Carly Simon's songs were born of and were narrating that transition—a course of self-discovery, change, and unhappy confrontation with the *limits* of change, which they, and their female listeners, had been riding.

Here is the story of their lives, and of that journey, from the beginning.

PART TWO

*"i'm home again,
in my old narrow bed"*

carole

Carol Klein was born in Manhattan on February 9, 1942 (some-where, early on, she added the *e* to her first name) but lived almost her entire youth in the borough to which her parents would soon move: Brooklyn. "You know the *New Yorker* magazine map, where the whole country drops off after Manhattan? That's what we were with Brooklyn," says Camille Cacciatore Savitz whose family, like Carole's, moved to the end-of-the-alphabet avenues of Sheeps-head Bay at the cusp of the 1950s. The neighborhood was still semirural then, with fields abutting houses and the occasional goat in an adjacent backyard, tied up so as not to get to the neighbors' clotheslines. In short order, the grid of streets filled up with rows of semidetached redbricks—their sidewalk-to-second-floor staircases as steep as rescue chutes, in order to make room for ground-floor ga-rages. Predating these inelegant buildings was the Kleins' brick, two-family house (another family lived upstairs), with its small front lawn and backyard. From there Carole walked to P.S. 206 every day, in Harry S. Truman's America: "a little Howdy Doody girl, with blue eyes and freckles and a smile on her face and a ponytail," her best friend from those years, Barbara Grossman Karyo, recalls. She was already taking piano lessons, sitting down with a teacher to play scales the year that "Tenderly," "Come Rain or Come Shine," and "Zip-a-Dee Doo-Dah" were heard on the radio and Victrola. The mainstay of her piano education, however, was classical (the Russian romantics, her favorites) and the Broadway songbooks of Rodgers and Hart and Rodgers and Hammerstein. She *loved* Richard Rodgers.

Barbara and Carole's friendship started the way many friendships started back then: "in line." Both were small, so they were placed next to each other at the front of the organ-pipe-like rows of girls that assembled in the schoolyard each morning. Reticent Barbara admired feisty Carole, who got in trouble for chewing gum and passing notes.

Carole graduated from grammar school in 1952, when great American literature was still consumed (Ralph Ellison, Ernest Hemingway, and Bernard Malamud had brand-new offerings); when everyone flocked to Gene Kelly musicals; when the highly regionalized country (interstate highways would be the project of the *next* president, Eisenhower) was just beginning to be united by way of Dave Garroway's *Today* show, which could be seen on rabbit-eared black-and-white television sets. Ten-year-old girls read comic books about Little Lulu and Sluggo and Archie and Veronica, where the characters spouted freshly postwar jargon—*Babs; Chum; Well, I'll be a monkey's uncle; Pow! Right in the kisser!*—that set the tone for the epistolary etiquette—

> *To Babs,*
> *Your loving chum is sad to go*
> *But we will meet in* [*P.S.*] *14, I know*

—that Carole imparted in Barbara's yearbook.

At Shellbank Junior High, Camille Cacciatore joined Carole and Barbara's best-friendship. Each of the girls had a distinction that made her feel "different." Camille was one of the rare non-Jewish children in the neighborhood. Barbara had lost a father not to the war but to a disease, encephalitis. Carole had *two* emotional melodramas to weather, and in the face of what might have been grief, insecurity, and even guilt, she turned to music as release and comfort.

Carole had a little brother, Richard, who was born deaf and severely mentally retarded. Genie and Sidney Klein sent him to live at the nearby Willowbrook State School on Staten Island, an institution of last resort for families with mentally disabled children. Sometimes Richard came back for a weekend, but it was clearly unworkable for the boy to live at home. Yet Willowbrook was a frightening place—a silent, 350-acre campus of hidden-away children. Even fifteen years before a television exposé uncovered scandalous abuse and neglect (young patients sleeping in cages in their own feces, among other horrors), there was enough suspicion of ill treatment for parents to do their own investigating.

But Carole, Camille says, seemed girded. "She didn't cry. She didn't talk about it"—not about the institution, or her brother. Still, years later it would seem that she put those feelings into her tender "Brother, Brother," about a fortunate person's sympathy toward a luckless sibling cut off from the world: "And though you didn't always talk to me / there wasn't much my lovin' eyes could not see."

Carole's parents' divorce, so novel in that traditional world, had, to her friends, a haunting irresolution to it. "I remember once, when Carole and I were about eleven, Sidney came to the house to pick up Carole for his visitation time with her, and I saw this wistful, romantic scene at the door: Carole's divorced parents hugging and kissing," Camille says. "It was as if they really loved each other but couldn't figure out how to make it work." On the surface, the elder Kleins were as ordinary as other Brooklyn parents; their working lives rendered them not at all bohemian, and with their (in Barbara's memory) "shabby, dingy house," they'd never be called glamorous. Still, there was something romantic about them, in the eyes of their daughter's young friends. Camille recalls Sidney Klein as "a tall, gorgeous man

with a mustache—he looked a little like Clark Gable. Sidney was *vital*.
He wasn't one of those disappearing-into-the-woodwork fathers, of
which there were plenty. At a cottage they took every summer on
Lake Waubeeka in Danbury, Connecticut, he even took me for a ride
on a motor scooter. It scared and thrilled me." Barbara recalls Genie
Klein as "a beautiful, fragile, ethereal, flighty, slightly *eccentric* woman,
with perfect diction. She wasn't like the other mothers." Later friends
have noted that Carole's eschewal of artifice—which blossomed in
Tapestry—is in marked contrast to her mother. "She seemed to be her
own person very early," says Camille. Leslie Korn Rogowsky, a friend
from their teen years, adds, "She had a sense of who she was and
what she wanted to do; that was unusual—you *felt* it."

The children of city utility and service workers (Barbara's father
worked for the gas company and Camille's for the transit authority,
while Carole's dad was a fireman), the three friends were thrifty: babysitting for fifty cents an hour; stopping for five-cent pickles and dime
knishes on the way home from Shellbank; occasionally splurging on
lunch at the Chinese restaurant, ninety-nine cents for a four-course
meal, leaving a tip of pennies. But beyond humble Brooklyn, there
shimmered an elegant media ideal of womanhood. Broken only by the
pluckiness of Debbie Reynolds, a serene, pedestaled femininity was radiated by the young actress Grace Kelly, by the older actress Loretta
Young (thrusting open the French door on her weekly TV show), by
models Jean Patchett and Suzy Parker, and by the soft-portraitured
Breck Girls in *Life* magazine. Advertisements and commercials of
women in cocktail dresses kissing their kitchen appliances drove home
a schizophrenic mandate: Lure men with elegant wiles and *then* become
a cheerfully addled serial procreator. Carole wrote in Barbara's ninth-
grade autograph book:

> *May your blessings be many, may your troubles be few.*
> *May your boyfriends be many, and your children, too.*
> *But don't come crying when your hair is in curls.*
> *I told you to try for only girls.*

As "extremely theatrical" (that's the expression many use) as Genie Klein was, neither she nor Sidney seemed to Carole's childhood friends to be particularly musical. Carole was the only one they saw at the piano, and she showed talent immediately. In a competitive field of musically gifted students, Carole won the Shellbank talent show and requested as her prize a baritone ukulele. Soon after, she appeared on the national TV talent show, Ted Mack's *Original Amateur Hour*, strumming that uke through a rousing rendition of the hit parade–topping "Shrimp Boats." Carole avidly listened to what she'd later call that "Patti Page era" music. "I used to listen to the radio and tear every song apart and try to figure out why it was what it was, even if it wasn't a hit," she has said.

Carole gave parties in her family's basement–"and they were packed," remembers Barbara, especially during rounds of Spin the Bottle. Carole's date was her boyfriend, whom she met in Shellbank's advanced math class: smart, creative–and tiny–Joel Zwick. "I was the most unthreatening boyfriend you can imagine," says Zwick (who went on to become a successful director; among his credits are the TV sitcom *Laverne & Shirley* and the film *My Big Fat Greek Wedding*). "I don't think I weighed 100 pounds soaking wet or cleared five feet until I graduated high school. Genie Klein had such a dramatic way and she was so protective of Carole, she was intimidating. But I was too harmless for her to worry about. In fact, my nickname was Only Joel, as in (when the girls were having a pajama party and I'd ring the bell): 'You can open it; it's *only Joel*.'"

"Eventually, these parties Carole and other kids gave had lots of touchy-feely going on," Barbara remembers. To "get felt up" in the ninth grade was a first step to three or four years of fending off the pull of sex, a tension made all the more fraught by the new sleeper hit by an L.A. group, the Penguins, to which everyone was slow-dancing. The sensual, pleading song–so different from those genially corny white hit parade staples–sounded like nothing these Brooklyn girls had heard before:

Ear-ear-ear-ear-ear-earth angel. Ea-earth a-an-gel . . .
Will you be mi-ine?

"On Monday there was this other music; on Tuesday there was rock 'n' roll." That's how The Band's Robbie Robertson once described the seemingly overnight mid-1954 shift in popular music. One day middle-aged white writers were cranking out saccharine pop songs like "How Much Is That Doggie in the Window?," "Mr. Sandman," and the trusty "Shrimp Boats," which were presented, by way of live skits, on TV's Lucky Strikes–sponsored *Your Hit Parade* . . . and the next day the world changed. White teens started listening to, and demanding, an alternative: black music. (This overnight change can also be illustrated by the fact that in January 1954 an unknown Elvis Presley was recording Joni James covers; just a few months later, his raw, plaintive "That's All Right, Mama" was making good on his producer Sam Phillips's dream of finding "a white man who had the Negro sound and Negro feel.")

So unquestionedly segregated was the popular record industry after World War II that, as late as 1953, no less a suave hipster than Ahmet Ertegun (the son of Turkey's ambassador to the United States who became a blues fanatic and founded Atlantic Records in 1947, recording, among others, Big Joe Turner and Ray Charles) didn't think to market his beloved Negro groups to white audiences. These groups played a genre of music that the industry was newly calling "rhythm and blues." (The term had actually been coined in 1949 when Jerry Wexler, then a *Billboard* writer and soon to be Ertegun's partner, wrote a *Saturday Review of Literature* essay decrying the then-standard term "race music" as not only insensitive but also, since it implied only *one* race, inaccurate. Wexler's term "rhythm and blues," or R&B, finally gained traction in the early 1950s.)

Instead, the crossover demand came from white teenagers. By early 1954 A&R men in New York were hearing about "cat music": records by black performers, made for black customers, which were secretly being purchased by white teenagers in the South and Southwest—the newly available transistor radio having enabled teens to listen to music out of their parents' earshot. A disparate smattering of R&B-loving white deejays, who in some sense "passed" for black—Dewey Phillips, out of Memphis; Greek-American Johnny Otis (a musician as well as the host of a TV music-variety show), out of Los Angeles; and Alan Freed, out of Cleveland—who had previously been serving black audiences, turned on the tap for these soul-starved white kids. In the culture-jolting synthesis that emerged, blacks did the innovating while whites got the credit. Though Bill Haley and the Comets' 1955 "Rock Around the Clock" officially put the new genre on the map, that jitterbug-paced hit by the white rockabilly performer had none of the fluidity of Jackie Brenston's 1951 "Rocket 88," which most scholars date as the *real* first rock 'n' roll song. And although Alan Freed got the credit for coining the term "rock 'n' roll," he appropriated Delta blues singer Wynonie Harris's sex euphemism "good rockin'."

Rock 'n' roll in 1954 and early 1955 consisted of white singers trying to sound black (Elvis on "That's All Right, Mama") and black singers trying to whiten their sounds (Chuck Berry's hillbilly "Maybellene," "Johnny B. Goode," and "Sweet Little Sixteen"; Little Richard's "Tutti Frutti"), but most of those songs—while highly danceable—were not emotionally affecting. Instead, being frenetic, they were safely *un*sensual. By contrast, the slow, languid "Earth Angel" *was* sexual. When Alan Freed moved to New York in 1954 and started broadcasting on WINS and presenting his concerts at the Brooklyn Paramount, he featured these songs—variously called street-corner, a cappella, or doo-wop—by the Penguins, the Willows, the Spaniels, the Flamingos, the Platters (with their classic "Twilight Time" and "The Great Pretender"), the Moonglows (who gave the new genre one of its first national hits, "Sincerely"), the local-hero Cleftones (whose "You Baby You" was a proudly borough-born national seller), which had a sweet, pleading urgency.

Often that pleading urgency was leavened by the humor of the lowest basso "answering" the highest falsetto, the farcelike vocal

contrast handily erasing the threatening sexuality. But when that humor
was absent, as it was in "Earth Angel," and all you heard *was* the poignance ("I'm just a fool . . . a fool in love with you-ou-ou . . ."), the result
was a high-voiced longing—a linking of vulnerability to carnality—that
was highly appealing to girls. "'Earth Angel' was the breakthrough for
us," Barbara Grossman Karyo remembers, expressing a widespread feeling among girls about the song, which, after various releases, became a
hit in 1955 and 1956. "Slow dancing to 'Earth Angel' was the beginning
of our sexual awakening." And so the year before the decade-long battle
for civil rights began in the South by way of Rosa Parks's refusal to give
up her bus seat to a white man, and the year that fourteen-year-old
Emmett Till was violently murdered in Mississippi for supposedly whistling at a white woman (his killers enjoying a kangaroo-court acquittal),
white girls were getting in touch with their sexuality with the help of
black male voices.

Two things, however, were absent from this music. One was girls. The
tight harmonics of doo-wop were perfected at night on street corners, and
it was neither feminine nor safe for girls to be hanging out at night on
street corners; they were indoors, minding their younger siblings and
washing the family's dishes. The Royaltones had Ruth McFadden and the
Platters had Zola Taylor (whom they recruited from a—rare—all-girl doo-
wop group, Shirley Gunter and the Queens), but, in the mid-1950s, that
was about it. Still, for the white girls in the audience at the Freed shows,
these two young singers modeled a new way of being female: moving
their bent arms in and out at waist-level as their hips bobbed so effortlessly it seemed as if they had an extra joint.

The other thing that was absent was strings. Violins and cellos gave
a song a classical feeling and a melodrama that might make it accessible, and, with the right soloist, could lend it pathos. In a few years this
formula would be struck upon by an unlikely young pair of composer-
producers—"unlikely" because melodrama was the last thing any acquaintance would associate with them. Though Jewish, they considered
themselves twelve-bar-blues-writing Negroes at heart: New York–born
Mike Stoller and Baltimore-raised Jerry Leiber. Right now Leiber and

Stoller were in Los Angeles, the quiet capital of R&B recording, using their wit, their commercial instincts, and their adulation of Negro life to lob a new genre of black music into the Top 40.

Genie Klein encouraged Carole to audition for the famous, and famously selective, High School of Performing Arts. Carole was accepted, and she braved the long daily commute to and from the uppermost tip of Manhattan. (A later recording colleague would say of Genie, "I think she would have loved to have been an actress and a star" and that, ironically, Carole ended up achieving "many things"–like fame–"that Carole didn't even value as much as Genie did." Another later friend says: "Genie was a 'cope'–a very strong-willed and difficult woman, and she pushed Carole, to make up for what Richard couldn't be.") After only a semester at the specialized school, she quit and rejoined her friends at local Madison High, where she resumed her close friendship with Camille–the two of them now fighting off despair about their looks. Camille says, "Carole and I thought everything was wrong with our faces, but we had no idea how to change it. We had no options, no money–where would we even start?" True, they both wore the fashionable cinch-belted straight skirts and blouses with the collars turned up, under which scarves were jauntily knotted to the side of their necks, but their versions were knockoffs of the better-labeled ones worn by Madison High's style queens, like the pretty, wealthy Nancy Tribush, whose social ease and confidence they coveted. Hair was a problem. "We despaired of our hair," Camille recalls. "The ideal was the WASPy straight blond hair in a flip or a pageboy. Carole and I would look in the mirror and there was *nothing* we could do with our curly hair! Our hair had a mind of its own!" Then there was the issue of their facial imperfections. "Do any teenage girls like how they look? Think they're pretty? We didn't."

But you didn't need a mirror when you had a piano. When she wasn't at the Freed shows, Carole was trying out her compositions–her first one was called "Go Steady with Me"–for Joel after school. He'd sit on a stool in her living room while she played and sang, and she'd ask him, as soon as she'd plunked the last note, "So whaddya think? Whaddya think?" "She was very driven to become a success," Joel remembers. She talked almost exclusively about music to Joel. She never mentioned her parents' divorce. He was her boyfriend, but he never met her father and didn't even know she had a brother.

Sometimes on weekends Carole would go to her friend Leslie Korn's house for slumber parties, with another group of girls who were, as Leslie puts it, "just on the edge of being goody-goody. We all had ponytails and poodle skirts and fuchsia and chartreuse sweater sets, and whoever didn't have a boyfriend wanted one, badly." They were racy enough to sometimes sneak a cigarette and pose for a picture on New Year's Eve in nothing but their bras and panties, album covers hiding their faces. "And all of us were virgins." A whole week of this crowd's telephone talk time was once devoted to the question of whether Sandy, a seriously good athlete, should, on her bowling date with Danny, throw the game she could easily win. Boys *had* to win at sports.

Despite such thinking—so much a part of life for girls that no one noticed—Carole didn't think twice about asserting herself over boys, not in sports but in that part of her life that mattered to her, pop music. In junior year she formed a doo-wop group specializing in her own compositions and covers of popular white doo-wop hits, like Danny and the Juniors' "At the Hop" and the Del Vikings' "Come Go with Me." "She was the unquestioned leader, and she ran a tight ship," doing "lots of the writing and all the arranging," recalls Joel, whom she'd selected ("more because I was her boyfriend than anything") as tenor. Camille's boyfriend Lenny Pullman was made baritone, and Carole chose Iris Lipnik, a policeman's daughter, as soprano. "Every day after school we would go over to Iris's apartment and rehearse from three to five p.m.," Joel remembers. "Carole would write out lead sheets—my lyrics for 'Go Steady with Me' were, literally, 'Doo wot da doo wat da doo wat da doo wat, ooh, ooh, ooh . . .' For all Carole's talent, she couldn't keep up with the fast rhythm of 'At the Hop,' so another friend of ours, Richie Suma, would be brought in, just to play piano on that one song."

They named their group the Co-Sines for their advanced math class at Shellbank, and they played local Sweet Sixteen parties, sometimes teaming up with a group from Brighton Beach, the Tokens, to perform at USO halls in the New York area. The Tokens' lead singer was a talented, enthusiastic cabdriver's son who had an unrequited crush on Carole. His name was Neil Sedaka. By senior year, Sedaka had arranged for the Co-Sines to audition for Ahmet Ertegun. "Ertegun offered us a contract," says Joel Zwick. "But because we were minors, our parents had to sign it. *One* parent held out, and we were all pretty sure it was Carole's mother, Genie. Which makes sense: Carole was the only real talent among us, and if she got a record contract, that would be the end of school for her." The other Co-Sines didn't dream of objecting to Mrs. Klein's presumed putting the kibosh on their prized Atlantic contract. Emotional and theatrical, "Carole's mother," Joel says, "scared the bejesus out of us."

So the Co-Sines remained amateur, and Carole got through her last year at Madison with a big role in the group-written *Senior SING!* musical. Its plot had the class of 1958 escaping their humdrum lives to live in so-near-yet-so-far Greenwich Village.

One young borough man who *was* spending his days in Greenwich Village coffeehouses during this time was a quietly passionate but frustrated nineteen-year-old Brooklyn Tech graduate named Gerald Goffin. Gerry had had a complicated, partly traumatic childhood. His conservative Jewish parents had divorced when he was young, and he had lived with his salesman father, Jack, for five years, while his younger brother, Alvin, remained with their mother, Anne. Sometimes Jack, an untrustworthy man and a womanizer, would disappear for weeks at a time, leaving a bewildered and insecure Gerry in the care of relatives. Gerry eventually returned home to his mother, but home was a depressing place—a cramped Jamaica, Queens, apartment that was shared with Gerry's stern, old-world Orthodox grandfather, a furrier, who put Gerry to work doing scut work on the fur pelts in the basement.

He escaped those confines by spending a year at another regimented place, Annapolis. Needing to earn his college tuition, he'd joined the Marine Corps National Guard, had scored 158 out of a top score of 160 on the academy entrance test, and had gained admission. But he was expelled for demerits. He was now back in the cramped apartment with his mother, grandfather, and brother, commuting to Queens College, and attending Marine Corps Reserves meetings. Greatly gifted at math, he'd been pushed by his mother to declare a chemistry major, though he dreamed of being a playwright.

To escape from all of these strictures, and failure, he took to sitting in Village coffeehouses—the only racially integrated part of the city. He had a fascination with African Americans—like many over-monitored, life-cramped white kids, especially in areas where progressive politics was the norm, he romanticized that population as a vicarious key to his own liberation. He appreciated a nervy, soulful life to which he felt drawn and yet unequal. "I wasn't really a beatnik, but I read a lot about beatniks," he says. Gerry was a voyeur of sorts—and he made a good one, being so inarticulate as to be almost monosyllabic. Yet beneath a personality that could erupt in temper, he observed deeply, and he was empathic—he had a talent for absorbing someone's essence. That inarticulate intensity—together with his lean, dark good looks—made him appealing to girls.

Still, for a nineteen-year-old would-be rebel, he possessed surprisingly conventional taste in music. He didn't listen to folk, rock 'n' roll, or R&B, or even jazz. Rather, after his father had taken him as a young teenager to a Rodgers and Hammerstein play, he used those literate scores—*Carousel, Oklahoma!, South Pacific*—as his standard. These, of course, were also the foundation of Carole's musical curriculum. Gerry loved these songs—he could hum them and feel them, but he could not play them. When Laurents, Bernstein, and Sondheim's *West Side Story* opened in September 1957, a startlingly high new bar was set—musical theater could now romanticize issues (intergroup love affairs;

the anger of disenfranchised populations) so fresh they were almost
more incipient than current. Gerry was moved to imitate the breakthrough musical. He started writing a serious, urban musical, which he
named *Babes in the Woods,* about Beat generation dreamers in Greenwich
Village.

While this boy she didn't know was writing hipster dialogue on ta-
bletops at Bleecker and MacDougal, Carole was writing a more conventional—but uplifting—essay, "You're a Senior," for the Class of 1958
Madison yearbook. She described the excitement of making one's
mark on the future, in musical terms: "The baton rises . . . You wait ap-
prehensively. There it is—the downbeat. You're a senior . . . your note is
different from any other: *you are an individual.*"

After graduating in June 1958, at age sixteen (because of advanced
placement early on, Carole, Barbara, Camille, and Joel all graduated
young), Carole now tried in earnest for a record contract, not with the
Co-Sines but on her own. Over the summer and at the beginning of
her first semester at Queens College, she regularly rode in to visit the
publishers and producers who had offices in the Brill Building at 1619
Broadway, and at nearby 1650 Broadway, both edifices comprising the
revived latter-day counterpart to Tin Pan Alley, that long-demolished
block of brownstones on West Twenty-eighth Street where, during the
first two decades of the century, tunesmiths had hawked their catchy
songs to player piano roll and sheet music publishers.

"Carole would come in by herself, this very cute little girl in bobby
sox and schoolbooks under her arm," recalls Jerry Wexler, Ahmet Ertegun's partner at Atlantic. "She would bring a demo, or she'd sit down
at the piano and play. I loved her voice, and I thought her music was
very unusual, very soul-inspired. The fact that she had classical train-
ing enabled her to play popular music very well, bordering on blues
and jazz, but not quite—it was her own mixture. She had a sense of purpose, but she also seemed a little intimidated. One time she was playing
a record she'd made and it kept skipping. Something was wrong with
its manufacture. She got so upset she started crying."

Wexler, at 1619 Broadway, worked with fellow R&B purist Ahmet

Ertegun. In music appreciators' style, they hunted out talent in obscure clubs and far-off roadhouses, then presented those acts in such a way that commercial concerns didn't overpower their authenticity. A block north, at 1650 Broadway, the brand-new Aldon Music was alive with a different brand of ambition. Aldon aimed to crank out commercial hits for the burgeoning teenage audience. It was the joint enterprise of an odd couple. Al Nevins (the "Al" in the Aldon) was a hit parade writer who'd made the transition to the new pop—he'd written the Platter's "Twilight Time." He was a polished, mature insider. Donny Kirshner (the "don" in Aldon) was the high-strung young upstart, but he had a golden gut, as well as the idea of running his place like a racetrack, filled with talented writers kept hungry and roaring by being forced into daily competition with one another.

Like so many in the music business, Kirshner was working-class Jewish. His father was a Bronx tailor, just as Wexler's father had been a Bronx butcher. But, atypically, Kirshner was conventional. He would eschew drugs all his life and stay married to his high school sweetheart for half a century. He was a proud square ("I was a devout coward, a very cautious guy who didn't want any aggravation," he says) in an industry of real and faux hipsters, but his nasal voice, unrepentant domestic stability, and neurotic demeanor were offset by a disarming physical confidence: he was six feet two, and his basketball talent had won him the only athletic scholarship that Seton Hall, a Catholic college, had ever awarded to a Jewish student. When you weren't mad at Kirshner for overworking or hocking you, you could rely on him, as you could on few others.

After trying to write songs for the singers, such as Frankie Laine, whom he'd waited on during his days as a Catskills resort waiter (a common career path for pop music professionals of the era), Kirshner had landed his first break with a bit of serendipity. Two and a half years earlier, on a freezing winter day, he'd run into a budding singer he knew named Natalie Quirsky in a Bronx candy store, and she almost bodily dragged him upstairs ("Have I got a talent for you!") to her fifth-floor walk-up to see a friend. The slightly built, pale Italian boy, bent over a mop, guarding against the cold in a wool cap and scarf, cleaning Natalie's apartment in exchange for the use of her piano, was unprepossessing. But as soon as Kirshner heard him sing, he decided to drop everything he was trying to do and become his manager. The boy's name was Walden Robert Cassotto. Renaming himself Bobby Darin, he virtually moved in with Donny, and the two set off to conquer the music world, for a long time getting no further than writing jingles for Orange Furniture Store in New Jersey and being kicked out of the Franconero home in nearby Bellville by hot-tempered George Franconero, who didn't approve of Darin's infatuation with his daughter Concetta, who was Kirshner's friend from his Seton Hall days. By 1958, Concetta Franconero, now known as Connie Francis, had a #1 hit in "Who's Sorry Now?" and Bobby Darin and Donny Kirshner were preparing for Bobby to record a song called "Splish Splash" (this was the era of the shameless novelty song). That's when Kirshner talked Al Nevins into going into business with him.

No sooner were the white tile letters *ALDON MUSIC* affixed to the black felt under the glass near the top of the alphabetical directory on 1650 Broadway's lobby wall than "two little nebbishy kids come to see me," Kirshner recalls. They were Carole's friend Neil Sedaka and his songwriting partner, Howie Greenfield. Kirshner sat Neil and Howie down at Aldon's piano and got an infectious earful. Later, Kirshner took the song the two had played—an upbeat ditty called "Stupid Cupid"—to his friend Connie Francis, who promptly made a Top 10 hit of it. Donny signed up Neil and Howie, gave them a cubicle with a piano, and started casting around for other hungry young writing teams.

Carole was commuting to Queens College from home every day in that fall of 1958, but home was now a tract house in Rosedale, Queens, inhabited by a reconfigured family. In a touching act of midlife romance, Genie and Sidney had remarried. (They would eventually divorce a second and final time.) Although Genie insisted that Carole go for her teaching credential, it was music Carole wanted, of course—and at Queens she quickly found other pulsingly ambitious young talents.

One was a short, thoughtful boy from Forest Hills named Paul Simon. Paul had an equally music-obsessed friend named Artie Garfunkel, a tall boy whose thick, frizzy hair and serious demeanor called to mind the young classical pianist Van Cliburn. The two had renamed themselves Tom Graph (Artie chose "Graph" for the graph paper on which he charted Top 40 hits) and Jerry Landis ("Landis" was Paul's girlfriend's last name), and as Tom and Jerry, they'd had a small hit, "Hey, Schoolgirl." Now, with Paul, Carole recorded demos of other people's songs, and played piano and drums on these recordings.

Meanwhile, Gerry Goffin—also living at home, in the "oppressive" apartment with his mother and grandfather—was back at Queens College as well. By February 1959, he'd completed the book for *Babes in the Woods* and was starting to write the lyrics. But since he couldn't write music or play an instrument, he needed a partner for the score's melodies. "I had been dating another girl," Gerry remembers, "and I asked her, 'Do you know anybody who can write music to my play?'" Gerry's girlfriend knew of the Carole-Paul crowd of songwriters. "And so she told me, 'Carole Klein, whose work name is Carole King.'"

Gerry and Carole first got together in the Queens College lounge. It was strictly "a work thing," Gerry says, but Carole was taken by the wiry, unsmiling, slow-to-talk young man whose dolorous eyes, almost-black curls, and rosebud lips made him look a little like Sal Mineo. During that meeting the two made a deal: she would write the melodies to his *Babes in the Woods* songs if he wrote lyrics for her pop compositions.

As Carole quickly started carrying out her part of the deal, Gerry came to realize that his Beat play was "uninformed—a bad play," he says now—and he shelved it. Instead, this musical dynamo of a girl took over. Under Carole's energetic tutelage, Gerry switched his radio dial from Broadway music to rock 'n' roll stations. "And once I listened to it, I liked it," Gerry says. "She introduced me to Alan Freed."

In Carole's Rosedale living room one day after classes, Carole and Gerry wrote their first song together—Gerry recalls it as "a so-so song called 'The Kid Brother.'" Sidney was in the house a lot now—the retired fireman had a small insurance business. He distrusted this sullen, too-handsome, twenty-year-old Annapolis reject who was sitting too close on the piano bench to his virginal seventeen-year-old daughter. "Carole's father was very tough, very right wing," Gerry recalls.

After Carole and Gerry polished "The Kid Brother," they drove into Manhattan and presented the song to Jerry Wexler. Wexler had always been a fan of the charmingly confident *and* intimidated "saddle-shoed" girl, and now, with this new boy, the effect was doubled. Wexler thought Carole and Gerry were "very earnest," and he gave them a $25 advance for the song. As they left, Wexler remembers musing, "These terrific kids are going to come up with great songs—songs that are most adaptable to black voices."

By now Gerry had broken off with his girlfriend, and Carole and Joel's relationship had returned to its more natural state as a friend-ship—and "Carole and I," Gerry says, "were boyfriend and girlfriend." They had much in common: parents who'd divorced at a time when few parents did, mothers who wanted them to be something they didn't want to be, and trauma within their families—Gerry's father taking him away from his mother and then disappearing for periods of time; Car-ole's institutionalized brother. But according to a close friend in whom Carole would later confide, Gerry had actually had much more to bear. His emotional intensity had veered into psychological problems serious enough for his parents to have sought medical treatment for him. By contrast, Carole was a rock. Whatever the burdens of her family, "Carole was not emotional," Gerry says; she kept her feelings in. Gerry was innately conflicted. He was a family- and religion-bound boy who yearned to be independent; a white Jewish kid infatuated with Ne-groes; a science student who couldn't read or play music but wanted to write it; a person with artistic ambition pumping out pop songs.

Early in the relationship, Carole introduced Gerry to Joel Zwick. When Joel met his replacement, he sensed that "she was the brains behind the operation" with Gerry. "Later, I even had the feeling that she might have attributed to Gerry lyrics that *she* had written." While neither part of this assumption proved true (Gerry would soon domi-

nate their songwriting sessions and come to be considered one of the
best lyric writers in popular music), a larger point is implied: Carole
had made her talent and ambition a central part of her appeal to men.
These qualities were to her what beauty was to other girls. She enveloped Gerry with her musical energy, and her drive gave direction to
his previously aimless writing. Joel's assessment was correct in another
sense, too: in years to come, Carole—emotionally the stronger of the
two—would protect Gerry.

As spring turned to summer and Carole continued seeing Gerry,
Sidney Klein decided to take his disapproval public. How better to
keep his daughter from an untrustworthy suitor than to impose a sanc-
tion in the sphere of her life that mattered most? Jerry Wexler opened
his mail one day in the summer of 1959 and found a threatening letter
from Sidney Klein. "He wanted to put the trade on notice: nobody was
to do *any* business with songs involving Gerry Goffin and Klein's minor
daughter, or else there would be a restraining order," Wexler recalls. "In
no uncertain terms: '*You will not* do *any* business with this young man!'
However, as far as I could see, the letter had no legal force—it didn't
come from a judge. It was just a parent trying to impose his will on his
daughter, so I paid no attention to it."

Sidney's hunch proved accurate. At just about the time he shot off
that letter, Carole discovered she was pregnant. Nervously, Carole
and Gerry confronted her parents with the news. "Carole's parents
asked me, Did I want Carole to get an abortion?" Gerry says. "And
we both agreed we didn't want an abortion. I said I wanted to marry
Carole." But Gerry also says, of why he married so young, "I wanted
to get out of the apartment with my grandfather." And—speaking several months before his death in April 2005—melodist Jack Keller
(soon to begin writing with Gerry twice a week), remembered that
Gerry felt Carole's pregnancy had sealed his fate. "When she said,
'I'm pregnant,' that was it. He was a regular Jewish guy from Brooklyn—she's pregnant, you get married."

A traditional wedding was planned for as soon as possible, just
before Labor Day, Camille recalls. "I must have told Carole a hundred

times, 'I can't believe your father is being so nice and giving you this big wedding! *My* father would *kill* me—my *sweet little mother* would kill me!—if I said I was pregnant.' And Carole told *me,* many times: 'What if one day my child does the math and figures it out?!' That worried her so much—that her child would find out she'd been pregnant when she got married."

The wedding was held on August 30 at a social hall on Long Island, with a Reform rabbi officiating, and it was attended, Gerry recalls, "by a lot of firemen and a lot of teachers." Seventeen-and-a-half-year-old Carole, in white, walked down the aisle on Sidney's arm. They took their vows under the *chuppah.* Gerry smashed the glass; bride and groom were raised aloft in their chairs by the guests; and during his dancing of the traditional Russian dance, "Sidney crossed his arms across his chest," Camille recalls, "and he was leaping and crouching so much, my mother thought he'd have a heart attack."

Finishing college was out of the question now. After settling into a small apartment on Brown Street in Sheepshead Bay, Gerry got an assistant chemist's job at Argus Chemicals in nearby Red Hook, while Carole became a secretary at an office in Manhattan. "I made $5,000 a year and she made $5,000 a year, and that was enough for us to go out for a turkey dinner in the neighborhood after work, before coming home and writing," Gerry says. Every night they wrote—Carole at the piano, Gerry standing next to her, the ashtray overflowing. "Nobody knew not to smoke while you were pregnant then," says Camille, who visited them. Sometimes they had backyard barbecues with fellow Brooklyn music world couples like Brooks and Marilyn Arthur. "Burgers—they couldn't afford steaks," says Marilyn. "We were all broke," Brooks adds. "We chipped in and brought the Hebrew Nationals, burgers, and potato salad."

By now, Carole and Gerry had signed up with Aldon. Neil Sedaka had had a hit with a song "Oh! Carol" (Carole and Joel concluded it *had* to have been about Carole), and, with Gerry's help, Carole had written a novelty "answer" song, "Oh! Neil," bringing Donny Kirshner into her and Gerry's lives. (Carole herself sang "Oh! Neil," and Sidney

Klein played the shotgun-wielding father at the end of the record, a humorous reenactment of his early anger at Gerry.) The young couple's workaholism was just what Kirshner was looking for. He paid them $1,000 for the coming year. They started to write, but "one song after another, Donny couldn't do anything with them," Gerry says.

On March 23, 1960, Carole went into labor, was admitted to a hospital in Brooklyn, and had a baby girl. Fathers weren't in the delivery room with their wives back then; they paced or, if they were broke and barely out of their teens, stayed with their buddies, then entered the maternity wing in a mixed state of excitement and fear. "I went with Gerry to the hospital—he was nervous; they were *kids,* and now they were parents," Jack Keller remembered. "They *needed* things—they needed a couch, they needed a car. I think Al Nevins gave them a couch." The baby was named Louise Lynn—Louise, for Gerry's deceased paternal grandfather, Louis. They called her Lou Lou.

Carole went back to writing songs with Gerry almost immediately after giving birth. For his $1,000 investment, Donny Kirshner was eager to use all her time, day and night. One day, she was in the Aldon office when another young female songwriter, Cynthia Weil, presented herself. As Cynthia recalls the first meeting: "In walks this little girl, who looks about twelve, with no makeup and a Band-Aid on her knee." Cynthia, by contrast, was a Manhattan-raised, Sarah Lawrence–educated fashion plate who had only been to Brooklyn a couple of times in her life—accompanied by, and visiting the family of, her German nanny. Cynthia recalls, "Donny said, 'Her husband is working as a chemist and he writes lyrics with her, but they can only write at night. She should be writing during the day. So she can write with you during the day.' Then Carole sat down and played something for me, and she was amazing. Just to see this little girl sit down at that piano and pound with that voice—amazing!"

Soon after that first meeting, Cynthia took two subways to the unknown depths of Brooklyn to meet with Carole, who had month-old Louise in a bassinet as she delivered a catchy melody. Cynthia agreed to write lyrics for it, and she took the lead sheet home on the long trip back to Manhattan. An hour later, Cynthia was turning the key in the lock of her apartment door when she heard her phone ring. It was her brand-new partner, apologetic. "Carole says, 'I know this is not the right way to start a good writing relationship, but Gerry came home from work and he was very angry that I gave you that melody, because he likes it and has a great idea for it.'" Cynthia had no choice but to give the melody back to Carole for Gerry to work with. The incident underscored the relationship of the newlywed parents. Carole might have been the dynamic instigator of songwriting, but Gerry was the possessive husband, and he called the shots.

For eight months—through spring, summer, and fall of 1960—the young parents lived the life of frenetic hack songwriters. In the small apartment with its budget furniture, amid the baby's cries, they wrote one mediocre song after another. "Thirty, forty, forty-five songs—none any good," Gerry recalls. "They were derivative. They were novice. They weren't melodic, and the lyrics were poor." Barbara Grossman visited Carole. "I was a college cheerleader, still living with my parents. Carole had quit college, was married with a baby, paying her own rent, and writing songs at night with Gerry after he came home from work. It seemed unbelievable, the distance between my life and her life." Late 1950s rock 'n' roll was themed on working-class melodrama: stanched dreams, grueling work, two kids against the world—the existence that Carole was living.

In 1959 a new "Earth Angel" had risen to the top of the pop charts. If you were a suburban girl of thirteen or fourteen and heard the Drifters' "There Goes My Baby," you stopped in your tracks, drew a breath, and realized: "This is a song I could go 'all the way' to." The urgent ballad with its booming doo-wop intro and its sexual narrator, desperately wailing

"There goes my baaa-by / Movin' o-on down the line . . ."

was enveloped in a classical string section. The lead singer—who lost his girl because he "made her cry" and is now beside himself wanting her back—had a phlegmy-from-wailing-so-hard voice; his dropped verb endings ("There go' my baby"; "I want to know if she love' me") suggested some intriguing neighborhood that little white girl radio listeners didn't know; and his every utterance was bathed in Carnegie Hall–like strings, giving his anger and pain a haunting ennoblement. Virginal middle-class girls imagined sex in big-R romantic terms—like Shakespeare, like the Brontë sisters—and here it was, in this bodice-ripping ballad by this Othello.

His name was Benjamin Earl Nelson (soon to be self-renamed Ben E. King: like Carole, he'd added a "King" to his name), and he'd only gotten the lead singing job because the intended lead, Charlie Thomas, froze up in the studio. The writing and production were done by Jerry Leiber and Mike Stoller, who had spent their youths writing as black as they desperately wanted to be (their first R&B hit, in 1951, was Charles Brown's "Hard Times," which was later recorded by David "Fathead" Newman for Ray Charles and was more authentically bluesy than two teenage white boys could ever be expected to be); who had been recently adapting for Elvis their songs, like "Hound Dog," that had originally been recorded by black blues singers; and who had been for the last few years burnishing the safely unsensual and humorous side of the doo-wop tradition to a commercial high gloss with their series of snarky hits for the Coasters, like "Yakety Yak," "Charlie Brown," and "Poison Ivy"—all following the bold "Searchin'." Now the pair had taken the Drifters, a fallen-on-hard-times pet group of Ertegun's and Wexler's (Ertegun had proudly discovered the original Drifters lead singer, Clyde McPhatter, whom he and Wexler considered one of the best R&B singers ever), who had a new, default lead singer (Nelson)—and brazenly reversed course. They worked up an operatic strings arrangement on a slow-dance lament ("What can I do? What can I-I do-o-oo?"). Wexler was so angry when Mike and Jerry played him the violin-filled arrangement, he wanted to hurl the tape recorder at the wall. But Wexler was not a fourteen-year-

old suburban girl. Carole and Gerry got it immediately: the new Drifters sound was *West Side Story*.

By now, black a cappella–based popular music had finally gained
some female voices. In 1957 four schoolgirls at St. Anthony of Padua
High School in the Bronx—girls who'd harmonized together on Grego-
rian chants in chapel for years and improvised secular music in the
gym and the halls—named themselves the Chantels (after their basketball rival school, St. Francis de Chantelle) and recorded a song called
"Maybe." "Maybe" was not the kind of song—coy, upbeat—that some
record companies thought that girls should like and that black girls
should deliver. (When a Bronx group, the Bobbettes, wrote vengefully
about a teacher they hated, a man named Mr. Lee, the record company
made them rewrite the angry song as a bouncy paean to him. It was recorded in that latter, insincere form.) "Maybe," by contrast, was a serious blues-and-gospel-flavored plaint: "Ma-ay-be, if *I* cry *e*-very night,
you'll come back to-o-o me . . ." What's more, it was written by one of
the girls, the group's lead singer, Arlene Smith. Pioneeringly, in early
1958 (when black male groups didn't score as often as white male
groups, and black *female* groups almost never charted), "Maybe"
became a pop hit.

Across the river in Passaic, New Jersey, four teenage girls had taken
heart at the Chantels' earned fortune. They were Shirley Owens, Addie
Harris, Beverly Lee, and Doris Coley, a foursome who called themselves the Poquellos. Like the Chantels, they had harmonized in the
high school gym, had made up their group name in school ("One day
in Spanish class, we just made up the word 'the Poquellos'; it sounded
flighty and pretty, like birds," says Beverly Lee), and had long listened
to New York's premier R&B station, WWRL, which represented the
real black-music sound, not the Negro-music-for-white-kids presentation
by Alan Freed on WINS. Mary Jane Greenberg, a fellow student in the
racially integrated Passaic High, saw her classmates perform a self-
written novelty song called "I Met Him on Sunday" at the school talent
show and virtually begged them to meet her mother, Florence Greenberg, who owned a small record label with the feminine name Tiara

(later renamed Scepter). After brushing off several of Mary Jane's entreaties, the Poquellos finally agreed. During the living room audition Florence Greenberg was floored: the material's mediocrity couldn't hide lead singer Shirley Owens's distinctive voice: deep, low, carelessly nasal, occasionally flat, as confidently relaxed as a jazz singer's. But Greenberg knew they had to have a more commercial name. So, taking the "Shir" from their lead singer's first name and the "els" from their admired Chantels, Greenberg anointed them the Shirelles.

The group's first efforts (including the song they'd sung at the talent show, and two songs with "boyfriend" in the title, with Shirley's voice inexplicably relegated to background) never gained traction, and they were dropped from the label that, through Shirley's efforts, had adopted them. When respected R&B A&R man Luther Dixon entered the picture to help them stage a "comeback" six months later, he used Shirley to sing lead on "Tonight's the Night," which announced a girl's intention to abandon her virginity. But the title was the only thing revolutionary about the mild hit. It had a leaden, monotonous melody and robotic non-lyrics. Still, the thoughtful ambivalence that Shirley expressed ("I don't know, oh I don't know right now . . .") in her breaking, vinegary alto—early in the first year, 1960, of a brand-new decade (and during the season that the Food and Drug Administration had quietly approved the sale of the first birth control pill)—can be seen, in retrospect, as a kind of run-up to something. But a run-up to *what?*

Carole King was an eighteen-year-old mother of a six-month-old when she sat down at the Brown Street piano one late afternoon in the fall of that same year. In a couple of hours she'd be off to play mah-jongg with Genie. Gerry was at Argus Chemical, completing a day of testing polymers and epoxies; he had a Marine Corps Reserves meeting afterward. Carole and Gerry had given *fifty* songs to Donny. In their tight, two-person universe—small apartment, no-sleep schedule, paycheck-to-paycheck existence, demanding baby, pump-'em-out songwriting—they had almost become one person. With his voyeur's knack, Gerry could intuit the feelings of his young wife, who kept her emotions hidden.

Kirshner worked by pitching to one or two artists' managers or A&R men at a time. He knew he could get to Florence Greenberg, so he told Carole to think of the Shirelles as she wrote. Still, Florence was too easy a sell—*she* had come to *him*—and Donny wanted what he couldn't have; he was secretly obsessed with selling songs to Guy Mitchell, who, having engineered Johnny Mathis's string of hits, was the hottest A&R man on the street. Carole didn't know this. She thought of the Shirelles as she sat down at the piano.

Carole stretched her hands over the keys. She produced an elegant semiclassical ballad, its third bar containing an emotional chord (called the "major III" or "secondary dominant of VI") that George Gershwin might have used but that was never heard in current pop songs. She had trouble finding a melody for the bridge, so she left that incomplete. After finishing the song as best she could, she pushed the "on" button on the big Norelco tape recorder that sat on the piano next to the full ashtray, and she *da-dah-dah*'d her wordless melody while she played it. As she grabbed her coat to go meet Genie, she wrote a note to Gerry: "Donny needs a song for the Shirelles tomorrow. Please write"—and propped the note against the tape recorder.

When Gerry came home to the empty apartment and listened to the tape, he was euphoric. "I had never heard a melody like that from Carole before! It was *melodic*!" he recalls. "It was structured better musically than anything she'd written before—it was AABA; the others had been: verse, chorus, verse, chorus. I listened to it a few times, then I put myself in the place of a woman—yes, it was sort of autobiographical. I thought: What would a girl sing to a guy if they made love that night? It wasn't a great lyric, but it was very simple: Will you love me in the morning, *after* we've made love?"

Gerry showed the lyric to Carole when she walked in the door around midnight. He'd begun the song with decorous metaphors for lovemaking, arranged in a tight, alliterative, conversational two bars ("Tonight you're mine completely / You give your love so sweetly"); and he'd filled her Gershwin-like third-bar melody with a triple rhyme— "To*night* the *light* of love is in your *eyes*," to reinforce the urgency of its quickened last six beats. He'd also written the bridge melody (with a yearning third bar) and its lyric about heartbreak with the morning sun. Carole picked it out on the piano, following along as he sang it. Working until two a.m., they nailed it.

The song (which they temporarily called, simply, "Tomorrow") was about a young woman sleeping with a boy despite no promise of commitment. Channeling the sensibility of the matter-of-fact, emotion-hiding girl who fell in love with him a year and a half earlier, Gerry wrote a whole character. The words tell us the singer is a cut-to-the-chase person who, despite her vulnerability, possesses restraint—she's not demanding constant reassurance. She also accepts responsibility for her freedom; it's *her* job to manage the emotional ambiguity and the risk of pregnancy. It's not a supplicant's "*Please* tell me now" or an arm-twisting "*Just* tell me now." It's "*So* tell me now," implying, I'll take it from here; the burden is now on me. Because it reflected them so effortlessly, Gerry says, "We just thought it was another song."

Donny Kirshner helped Carole and Gerry fortify the hook and shorten the song from five to three minutes. They made a demo, with Carole singing (*sans* strings arrangement). Even though it was a woman's song, Donny brought the demo to Guy Mitchell. Mitchell listened and told Kirshner he loved the song but was committed to the composers of Mathis's "Wonderful, Wonderful" and "Chances Are." Kirshner left the meeting dejected and only then let Florence Greenberg hear the demo. Greenberg gave it to Luther Dixon and he played it for the Shirelles. Beverly Lee recalls, "We looked at each other like, 'Is this a *joke?*' It sounded like a country-western song, real twangy." The girls' consensus: it was too white. But Dixon, who is black and whom they trusted, said, "You're *gonna* record this song," Beverly says. The Shirelles begrudgingly agreed to show up at the studio.

Carole and Gerry knew their song had to be bathed in violins and cellos. Gerry was "dying to steal from the Drifters," as he puts it; he and Carole had written a song for the group ("Show Me the Way") that got shelved, and he loved the cellos in "This Magic Moment" and "Dance with Me." If anyone admired two Jewish boys who seemed black, wrote black, and successfully produced black groups, it was Gerry. But it was Carole who was determined to write the string arrangement. As soon as she knew the Shirelles had agreed (however reluctantly) to show up for the session, she approached Al Kasha, Jackie Wilson's A&R man (and a Madison High alum). As Kasha recalls, she said, "You write with Luther Dixon. Do you think he would be upset about using strings?" Not waiting for an answer from Dixon through Kasha, she started the arrangement, undaunted by her ignorance of the instruments. "I came over to Carole's house and she was sitting at the kitchen table, writing the score," Camille remembers, "using a book she checked out of the library, *How to Write for Strings*. She taught herself from a *library* book!"

Luther Dixon wasn't sure he wanted Carole's arrangement, but Gerry pushed on her behalf. "I kept asking Luther if she could write it," Gerry says. "He resisted at first. Then he said, 'All right, I'll give her a shot.'" The next issue was: How *many* cellos, how *much* of a Drifters sound? "We wanted four cellos," Gerry recalls. "Luther gave us two." Carole and Gerry schemed to double the two to four in the studio—and they did so.

When the Shirelles got to the studio and heard the arrangement, they were stunned, says Beverly Lee. "The song was completely different than the one on the demo. It was *beautiful*. All those *strings*! It blew our minds! I thought: *Thank God* for Carole King, for this."

With Carole on kettle drums, they recorded: Shirley taking most of the song alone, her low, nasal voice, with its catch in the throat, fading on the long notes and straining on the high ones with amateurish humanity; the violins soaring rapturously; the cellos grinding anxiously; Addie, Doris, and Beverly chanting *"sha da DOP shop, sha da DOP shop"*—but all of that receding on Shirley's two "So tell me now, and I won't ask again"s.

By the end of the first week of December 1960—just as the brand-new Enovid birth control pills were rolling off Klein Pharmaceuticals' assembly lines lab in Skokie, Illinois, and reaching their first customers; and three weeks after John F. Kennedy won the election (he and his beautiful, subtly ironic, and Europeanized young wife changing American culture with a jolt, overdue/overnight, just as rock 'n' roll had), the Shirelles had become the first African-American female group in American history to have a #1 hit. And a song that reflected a concept so new—a young single woman's declaration of herself as an emotionally and sexually independent and responsible person—that it didn't have a name, was the song all America was singing.

CHAPTER TWO

A world away from the second-generation Jewish New York pop-culture realm of Carole King lay the deep plains, Northern European Protestant milieu that Roberta Joan Anderson was born into on November 7, 1943, in Fort Macleod, Alberta, Canada.

Fort Macleod was a barely populated town in the foothills of the Canadian Rockies (a fifty-mile straight shot north from Montana's western border) that had been, sixty years earlier, a snowbound, wind-mauled Mounties outpost in Blackfoot territory. Raised as an infant in that 2,000-resident town, in wartime conditions of quaintness (mail and water coming in open wagons) and privation (soap scarce enough that when you got it, "You washed your dishes and your hair and your clothes with it, whether it was detergent or shampoo," Joni has said), then moving northeast with her parents to a succession of towns on the flat, wheaty plains of midwestern Canada, Roberta Joan took her entertainment the old-fashioned way: from family stories. Those about her parents' mothers stood out most. She heard aunts' accounts of her Grandmother Anderson and Grandmother McKee, and she made these women into supporting characters in her own life narrative, turning their unfulfilled talent into her legacy and their frustrated ambition into her obligation. "There must [have been] some kind of genetic thrust," she's said, of the career that both her grandmothers had desired. "I'm the one who got the musical gene; it landed in a female, and it had to be taken home for the sake of these women."

As a fourteen-year-old Norwegian farm girl, Joni's paternal grandmother had longed to be a pianist, but she knew that dream was out of the question, so she'd "wept . . . behind [the] barn," Joni has said, then ordered herself, "'Dry your eyes, you silly girl! You will never have a piano.' She became a stoic." She and her family moved to New Norway—a newly incorporated but primitive village in Alberta that attracted Scandinavians and Scandinavian Minnesotans looking for cheap, fertile land—in the first decade of the twentieth century. There she met and married a fellow Norwegian émigré, a young man named Anderson, who was, as Joni has called him, "a nasty drunk"; with him she had "baby after baby," Joni has said. "She raised eleven children and lived a horrible life: giving, giving, giving—a self-sacrificing animal to her many children." Still, "through all the hardship, *she never wept*." Such reining-in of emotion seemed to Joni a heroic refusal of weakness.

One of those eleven children was William, a good-natured boy who liked to play the trumpet and who inherited his mother's rectitude. Bill escaped the chaos of home by joining the Royal Canadian Air Force and by avoiding marriage throughout his twenties.

On Joni's mother's side was Canadian-born Sadie McKee, descended from a man who, in Scotland, had worked on the estate of Sir Walter Scott. Unlike Grandmother Anderson, Sadie McKee wasn't an old-world peasant; she hailed from a long line of classical musicians. She didn't tearfully jettison her musical gifts as a young adolescent; she played the organ, wrote poetry, and listened to opera on the gramophone well into her years as a frontier farm wife. She wasn't a baby-making doormat but rather a snob. (She married "an oxen-plowing prairie settler and thought she was too good for him," Joni has said.) And she most definitely wasn't a stoic; she was "a spitfire, a tempest, the *opposite* of long-suffering [and] good-natured. She was always having fiery fits [and she felt] that she was too good [for her fate]—a poet and musician stuck on a farm." In the midst of one fight with the tempestuous Sadie, her husband threw his wife's treasured gramophone records to the floor; Sadie retaliated by kicking a door off its hinges. If Joni inherited from her father's mother the stoicism that Duke Redbird would be so struck by in the Huron Street rooming house, then she inherited from her *mother's* mother what she has called "the Irish blood: fight before you think." (Joni never kicked a door off the hinges, but she did once throw a drink in *Rolling Stone* publisher Jann Wenner's face when he supposedly smirked at the sight of her struggling to enter an awards show, unaided, through a mass of fans. And in the midst of separate emotional fights with two women close to her—one was her housekeeper, Dora—Joni slapped them both on the face.) The lesson that any ambitious, talented girl in the Canadian prairie might draw from these matriarchs seems clear: having babies in poverty and desperation, and remaining in the provinces, will destroy your dreams almost before you can dream them.

Sadie's daughter Myrtle McKee was raised on the farm that her mother disdained, and she was as proud and particular as her mother was—determined to move up and out. She passed up offers to marry common men—farmers, policemen—biding her time as a teacher in a rural school and feeling so superior to the materials she had to work with, she often made her own schoolbooks. When she was still unmarried at thirty, Myrtle took a job in a bank in the big city of Regina, Saskatchewan. After expressing her frustration at the lack of eligible men in town (it was 1942 and they were all in wartime military service), she was introduced by a friend to Bill Anderson. They married on his two-week air force leave; their only child, a daughter, was born within the year. She was named Roberta, but almost immediately everyone called her by her middle name: Joan.

The young family moved around a lot, as Bill advanced—from butcher-grocer to manager—in his work for a regional supermarket chain. They lived in Fort Macleod until Roberta Joan was a year and a half, then moved to Maidstone, Saskatchewan, a village of just over four hundred residents, where the family entertained itself by listening to the Andrews Sisters' and the McGuire Sisters' mellifluous close-harmony, piped through the console radio. Myrtle was a controlling mother. "I have a very early memory of being walked on a leash," Joni has said. "You know, they used to put children on these leashes." Hearing Victrola music tin-speakered out the front of a Woolworth's, "I stopped on my leash and began to bounce up and down and sing with great enthusiasm. My mother gave me a tug, and I remember thinking that was very insensitive of her."

When Joan was five, the family moved again, to nearby North Battleford, a town with a three-block-long downtown, of about 7,000 residents. Joan made friends with two children on the street: red-haired, freckle-faced, classical-music whiz Frankie McKitrick, the son of a school principal, and short-blond-haired Sandra Stewart, the daughter of a road contractor and a nurse. Sandra, who was called Sandy, remembers first meeting her new neighbor Joan—"this very, very fair-complected girl with wispy, shoulder-length white-blond hair." All three children were in strict Mrs. Thompson's first-grade classroom at the Alexander School. In a town of robust boys who threw rocks and sticks, Frankie was a hopeless misfit, so unathletic that he was excused even from volleyball, in love with the sonatas and rhapsodies he was learning to play (he would later become a choir director). Similarly, in a town where girls played with dolls (which Joan eschewed, though Myrtle did make her sparkly princess costumes), Sandy, to Joan's approval, disdained the company of girls, "and I messed up a lot of playtimes by gathering up the boys and crashing the party," Sandy recalls. Add Peter Armstrong, a mammoth boy with a glorious voice (he went on to have a singing career in Europe), and an Our Gang was formed: Frankie, the pianist; Joan, the artist; Sandy, the tomboy; and Peter, the fat boy with the celestial tenor.

The foursome put on circuses in Sandy's garage, and Joan was the choreographer of these efforts. "Joan always had to be the lead character—it had to be done *her* way; she always played the ringmaster, so she could be the boss, and a lot of the acts she came up with were *not* well received by those of us who had to do them," Sandy remembers. Frank agrees: "Joan was unflinching. She and I would have serious arguments about how we would present a backyard circus. Her artistic temperament wouldn't yield to mine, and I usually gave in." Sandy wasn't so good-natured. "Joan and I would have fights. We were both headstrong, but Joan liked to rule the roost." When they weren't playing circus, they were singing and dancing. Joni has recalled, "I danced around the room while Frankie played the piano, and we all did the hula on the lawn in the sprinklers."

Older than all the other children's parents, exotically possessed of but a single child (in a neighborhood of medium-sized families) and a "house full of very nice things," as Sandy says, the senior Andersons trained a startling, almost glamorous attention on their daughter—"Joan was totally indulged"—and displayed a notable gentility and decorousness. "Both of them were proper," Sandy says. "It's not that they were strict. Mrs. Anderson was a lovely mum, with the gentlest voice, but you felt you always needed to mind your p's and q's around them and be on your best behavior. Joan's dad was very, very quiet—a gentleman to the nth degree: very proper." Big band horn playing was his release. Frankie would come over to the Anderson house after school and play piano while Mr. Anderson tooted his trumpet (Leroy Anderson's "A Trumpeter's Lullaby" was a favorite duet for the two of them) and Joan made her paintings. "No one at school could hold a candle to Joan's ability to blend color and draw; she absolutely excelled in art," Frank says. Myrtle served juice—soda pop didn't darken her door—and Joan would run around after her pet rabbit, nervously picking up the pellets it left outside the cage before her mother noticed. (Myrtle considered even *cats* barn animals and wouldn't let Joan keep a kitten.)

Perhaps in compensation for the fact that their Queen Street home was a "wartime house"—one of many identical, inexpensively built houses for veterans—Myrtle was doubly determined to make it an impeccable one. She vacuumed the garage daily and sniffed at neighbors' housekeeping deficits. ("Mrs. Dawson across the street keeps a very, very dirty home, you know . . . ," Joni would paraphrase later.) Joni grew up in an atmosphere "almost Victorian, in the sense of such an emphasis on what neighbors would think, and on those relatively strict codes of what is proper," says her second husband, Larry Klein, of the stories Joni told him about her childhood. But if Myrtle knew what her daughter must *not* be, she also guided her to what she should—and would—be: a lover of the arts and beauty. She trained her Joan to press flowers in scrapbooks and recite Shakespearean sonnets. And when Joan was eight, Myrtle and Bill and Harold and Katie McKitrick were the only parents who wrote permission notes to have their children excused from school to see the art film *Tales of Hoffman,* a sequel to *The Red Shoes.* "In strict, proper Canada, in 1951, to be released from school because your parents thought it was important for your development to see a movie—well, it just wasn't done! And it was thrilling!" Frank recalls. The movie—with its ballets and romance (the male protagonist has love affairs with a mechanical doll, a Venetian courtesan, and a Greek singer)—captivated Joan. "I remember standing on the street with her afterward: she was reliving one of the characters, making an emerald appear in his hand," Frank says.

That Myrtle would want her young daughter to see a culturally uplifting movie doesn't surprise Chuck Mitchell, whom Joni married when she was twenty-one. "From what Joni said, Myrtle was constrained in her own life, and she didn't want her daughter to be constrained," Chuck says. "She knew she had a gifted daughter, so she gave Joni her all—she was 140 percent mom, and an *assertive* mom—and she made it very clear that the only way Joni could escape the prairie was to go with her talents." "Joan was *completely* different from her parents; she got a different gene somewhere" is how drummer John Guerin, one of the most significant men in her life, described Joni and her parents, in an interview he gave for this book, shortly before his January 2004 death. Guerin wore a puzzled smile and shook his head as he said, "I don't know *where* she got it. 'Cause her mother and father are very straight-ahead, middle-class midwestern people." Graham Nash remembers: "Myrtle! Oh, God! I once went to Joni's parents' house; I think it was 1970. Downstairs in the spare bedroom, which is where I slept. I'd been living with Joni for two years, but no, no, no, we couldn't stay in the same room at Myrtle's! I'm talking to Joan, I've got my hand on the door. I said to Joan: 'What's your mother like? Give me a clue here.' And she said: 'I'll tell you what my mother's like: run your finger on top of the door.' Now this is downstairs in the *spare* bedroom. I run my finger across the top of the door. Not a *speck* of fucking dust *anywhere*! I said, 'Wow!' She said: 'Myrtle.'"

Myrtle's exacting standards, fierce control, and faith in her daughter's artistic gifts probably combined to keep Joan emotionally beholden to her. A mother who underestimates a little girl can eventually be written off as unsupportive, but a mother who sees her daughter's best self even before *she* does is harder to disengage from. "When I knew Joni, her mom could upset her," says Dave Naylor, a record producer who was involved with Joni in the 1970s. "A couple of times I'd be talking to her and then she'd get a call from her mother, and by the time I got over to her house she was a mess. I always wondered how this little old lady sitting in a rocking chair in Saskatchewan could reach out and grab her and still pull the chain. It amazed me."

When Joan was in fourth grade, a new minister, Reverend Allan Logie, arrived in town to take over the pulpit at Third Avenue United Church. The minister's older daughter, Anne, became Joan's new close friend. The same-aged girls were similarly dreamy and creative (under her subsequently adopted name Bayin, Anne would become a well-regarded photographer) and, like their friend Sandy Stewart, secretly rebellious. ("I found a kindred spirit in that one-stoplight town," Anne would later write in a memoir about her friendship with Joni, published in the Canadian magazine *Elm Street*.) Both were ballasted by the same combination of propriety and artistic expressiveness: Anne's mother, the minister's wife, directed the community theater. Like Myrtle Anderson's pressed-flower scrapbooks and Shakespeare quoting, Laura Logie's trunks full of Elizabethan clothes fueled the girls' drama lust. In the same way that proper Bill Anderson belted the trumpet to release his inhibitions, Allan Logie, when not sermonizing from the pulpit, wrote witty poetry. Unlike Sandy, who was as stubborn and willful as Joan, Anne had a more cautious spirit and let herself be led by her new friend's charisma. "Joan was a force of nature, more daring than me," Anne Bayin said, in the *Elm Street* memoir, adding: "She turned brooms into batons, she had a nose for fashion, she wore stars on her shoes and her dad's ties to school. She was a trendsetter. Kids copied her."

Inspired by the royal domestic doings in the motherland (Princess Elizabeth bearing Prince Charles in 1948 and Princess Anne in 1950—and, upon her father's death, ascending the throne as Queen Elizabeth II in 1952), Anne and Joan cut old curtains into wedding veils and held mock weddings and other ceremonies in their backyards. They also had a Wild West infatuation. Anne dressed up as Annie Oakley, while Joan—who adored Roy Rogers (and whose favorite TV show was *Wild Bill Hickock*)—decked herself out like Dale Evans. A photograph of Joan—standing on the wooden porch of her house in a cowboy hat and cowboy vest, one cuffed-jeaned ankle crossed over the other, arms akimbo, her left hand on the handle of her toy gun—exhibits a self-possession rare for a nine-year-old. She even dared ask her Sunday school teacher—and Reverend Logie himself—a question about an apparent incest suggestion in the book of Genesis: If Adam and Eve were *all alone* in the Garden of Eden, and had two sons, Cain and Abel, and then Cain had a child—well, *who* did Cain have the baby *with*? No elder could answer the question to young Joan's satisfaction.

Joan, Sandy, and Anne sang in the church's junior choir, for which Frankie played the organ, under the direction of Mrs. Girling, whose loud voice thundered with vibrato. Singing star Peter was also the cutup; Sandy, Joan, and Anne got in trouble for laughing at him mid-hymn. During province-wide music festivals they'd wait their turn in the rear pew while junior choir after junior choir filed to the front, shuffled into neat rows, and, pigtails bobbing, sang "Hey, Nonny, Nonny, on yonder hill there was a maiden . . .'" while a stout woman sternly judged the entrants.

At seven, Joni started piano lessons, "with a real rush, with a thrill to play; I wanted to jump immediately into playing the piano beautifully," she's said. But her teacher, Miss Trevellen, rapped her knuckles with a ruler when she improvised. Joni has blamed the place and times for curbing self-expression, and while that may have been true, even the more straitlaced teachers appreciated her spirit. Drab Miss Bready, who taught fourth grade at King Street School (to which the neighborhood children had transferred and of which Frankie's father was principal), wrote that Roberta Joan was "original."

Into this churchly, small-town primness strode a villain: the polio virus. One morning in early November 1953, a week before her tenth birthday, Joan got out of bed for a normal day in Miss Fulford's fifth-grade class at King Street, but something was not right. She put on her pegged gray slacks, red-and-white gingham blouse with sailor collar, and blue sweater—but the dressing took some doing. As she has remembered it, "I looked in the mirror, and I don't know what I saw—dark circles or a slight swelling under my face." *Something* was wrong. Was this a flu? Walking to school, Joan felt achy, but she managed to get through the day. The next morning she had *no* energy. When, at Myrtle's prodding ("Get up! Come!"), Joan couldn't rouse herself, Myrtle yanked her daughter out of bed—and Joan collapsed. She ended up being airlifted on a "mercy flight" to St. Paul's Hospital in Saskatoon, the capital of the province. She was diagnosed with polio, a highly contagious viral disease that, in its rare bulbar manifestation (where the lower brain stem is affected, damaging the interior horns of the spinal cord), could cause paralysis.

This was the height of the Canadian polio epidemic, which was well on its way to afflicting 8,878 people, mainly children, out of a national population of less than 15 million. While polio cases in the far more populous United States had *decreased* by a third (from 58,000 to 35,000) over the previous year's figures, polio in Canada had almost doubled, from its 1952 tally of 4,755. (The wide availability, in 1955, of the polio vaccine created by Jonas Salk would virtually extinguish the disease in both countries.)

The higher impact of the disease in clean, uncrowded Canada made sense. At the turn of the twentieth century, the polio virus had circulated endemically. Children in then typically large families were exposed to it as a matter of course and developed immunity, which was reinforced by the maternal antibodies they'd acquired from having been breast-fed by immune mothers. But as the practices of breast-feeding and having large families came to be eschewed as "low class," these ostensibly better-nurtured children were deprived of an indemnifying brush with the virus. This is what made polio so horrific and ironic. Here were civilized families: small, clean, orderly. Yet, as if being punished for virtue, they were ravaged by this paralyzing virus. The poster child for postwar progress—a coddled only child raised in a home kept spotless by a class-conscious mother, in a roomy, clean-aired town—was a prime candidate for this nightmare.

When her classmates, almost none of whom had ever been on a plane, heard that Joan had been *flown* to the hospital, a pall of tragic glamour hung over her in her absence. "It was so dramatic, *so Joni,* it took my breath away," recalls Anne. "I confess, my first unforgivable reaction was one of envy, before reality and fear set in." As for Joan's parents, they "were devastated—you could read it in their faces—but they never cried. Oh, no! No crying from Joan's mother," says Sandra. "She was very strong."

The polio unit at St. Paul's was run by the locally legendary Canadian order the Sisters of Charity, also known as "Grey Nuns." Well before the caseload doubled, the Grey Nuns had been scrambling worriedly to accommodate the glut of new patients who were rolled into the ward daily with high fevers, throbbing headaches, and the virus racing toward their nervous systems. On August 25, 1952, a Grey Nun had written in the group's log: "The polio epidemic is at its full . . . We pray Mary to protect the youngsters from this sickness," only—less than a month later—to have to amend the assessment: "Polio cases are multiplying. To help our overworked nurses, the public health department is sending six additional nurses . . . . Nine iron lungs are working all the time; eight of which are borrowed from other hospitals in the province." (Iron lungs were tank respirators into which polio victims were slid on large trays with only their heads exposed. The loudly hissing tanks pushed air pressure into the patients' diaphragms and chests, doing their breathing for them.) At year's end the hospital had treated 358 polio patients; 15 died.

As 1952 had turned to 1953, bad had turned to worse, and by April

20, 1953, plans were made to enlarge the polio ward to a polio department, with a separate entrance, so that the highly contagious new patients "would not pass through the main part of the hospital," as the
nuns put it. It was through that new quarantine entrance that Joan Anderson was wheeled—past the mortifying phalanx of iron-lunged children—and settled into a bed in the full children's ward. As if the terror,
the fever, and the isolation weren't punishment enough, the ten-year-old
was subjected to a torturous-seeming regimen: she was wrapped in
almost scalding hot compresses several times daily—this treatment pioneered by a World War I–era Australian military nurse nicknamed Sister
Kenny, who had devised the method after she'd observed Aboriginals
successfully treating their polio victims that way.*

Joni has said that her back muscles were affected by the polio ("It
ate muscles in my back" is how she put it), and that for a while, as
she lay in the hospital and submitted to the scalding compresses, she
didn't know if she would walk again. Fortunately, she would not be
left with a limp or a shortened leg, which were common effects of the
illness ("She ran all over the place! She ran up and down stairs; she
didn't complain," says Chuck Mitchell, of Joni eleven years later), although she would complain, in the 1980s, of vague effects of post-
polio syndrome. The real effect was emotional. Her second husband,
Larry Klein, says, "Joni's bout with polio at a young age was probably the one crisis—well, that, and the baby—that sculpted her inner
resolve and sensitivity into the form that led to her strong talent as
an artist. She certainly talked about polio as the thing that changed
her: she had been a very outgoing child, and that illness was a huge
experience that forced her inward." As Joni has said: "I think the creative process was an urgency then. It was a survival instinct."

---

* Sister Kenny had fought the European medical establishment (which advocated a different treatment: immobilization, splinting, and casting), eventually finding more open-
mindedness in the U.S., where her technique was partially supported by the National
Foundation for Infantile Paralysis and taught in a Minnesota hospital. Sister Kenny-
trained therapists then fanned north to Canada.

"Survival" is apt; young Joan *fought* her polio. She has said, "I remember, the boy in the bed next to mine was really depressed. He didn't even have polio as bad as I, but he wasn't fighting it—he wasn't fighting to go on with what he had left . . . I had to learn to stand, and then to walk [again]. Through all of this, I drew like crazy and sang Christmas carols. I left the ward long before that boy, who had a mild case of polio in one leg [and] lay with his back to the wall, sulking." She has also said that she made a promise to the Christmas tree in the ward that if she recovered, she would "make something of myself."

Selfless though the Grey Nuns may have been, even in tending severely ill children they did not relax their unforgiving moral code. One of them excoriated Joan for moving in such a way on her bed that her bare legs were visible to that sulky little boy while she was singing him a Christmas carol. "I was nine years old . . . and he was pouting and picking his nose and . . . telling me to shut up, when a nun rushed in and practically beat me up for showing my legs. A nine-year-old to a six-year-old!" Joni would later say. (On the other hand, she got along well with the ward's charismatic Sister Mary Louise, who eventually became mother superior and whose charity Joni admired. After she became famous, Joni sang at events at the sister's behest. "She grabbed me by the ear and put me to work," Joni has recalled. "She wanted me to join the order and write my memoirs.")

Joan was discharged from the hospital after six weeks, and her recovery was supervised by Myrtle, who homeschooled her for a year—blackboard, homework, and all. It was during this intense bonding between punctilious mother and convalescing daughter that an exchange occurred that, Joni has told friends, was central to her life. One of a number of those to whom Joni has recounted this incident says, "Joni never really put this together in her mind until much later, in her adult life, but then she started seeing it as so central—as the crux of things." It involved an incident where her mother was called to defend her, but her mother took the other person's side and humiliated Joni. Joni felt she'd lost her mother's trust. Then she started thinking, maybe her mother was right. "She's confronted her mother about it, and her mother says, 'Poppycock! I never did that.' But whatever was said that day, it affected Joni. She said, many times, that she didn't want to be a mother—not [in 1965], not ever—because she didn't want to be *her* mother."

Joan began wrestling with the good girl/bad girl duality provoked by that upsetting accusation of the doctor. She rejoined the church choir, but one night, after all the pious singing, she slipped around to a frozen pond with a friend who possessed a purloined pack of Black Cat Cork, Canada's version of Camels. While the cigarette-dispensing friend and several other ten-year-olds were choking and gagging from the inhaled nicotine, Joan *liked* the experience. "I took one puff and felt really smart," she has said. "I thought, 'Whoa!' I seemed to see better and think better." She became a secret preteenage smoker—initiating a habit that, over fifty years later, she still has not defeated.

Something even more significant happened in her tenth year: she fell in love with the idea of writing beautiful music. It was the majestically romantic "Rhapsody on a Theme of Paganini" that did it. Composed in 1934 by Sergei Rachmaninoff at a make-or-break time—his Fourth Piano Concerto had been a failure and he'd been blocked for five years—the composition's almost over-the-top emotionality made it a favorite for movie soundtracks. One movie that utilized it, *The Story of Three Loves,* arrived in the North Battleford theater in 1953. Joan was in the audience. Set on an ocean liner (an exotic site for a girl thousands of miles from any ocean), the movie consisted of three melodramas. As a kind of fantasy stand-in for transgression in the ultraconformist decade, melodrama was a cinematic staple aimed at women (director Douglas Sirk perfected the genre) and this trio was no exception. The first story essayed forbidden love: a boy (Ricky Nelson) becomes magically transformed into a man, only to fall in love with his female governess (Leslie Caron); in the second, a ballerina (*Tales of Hoffman* and *The Red Shoes* star Moira Shearer) has a fatal heart attack while auditioning for a choreographer (James Mason), who then stages the ballet she inspired for her to view from heaven. In the third, a trapeze artist (Kirk Douglas) who is agonizing over his partner's death rescues from suicide a woman (Pier

Angeli) who blames herself for her husband's murder by Nazis. These two fall in love, of course.

Joan left the movie intent on tracking down the music. She went to Sallows and Boyd Furniture Store, which stocked 78s and let customers listen without buying. Joan asked for "Rhapsody on a Theme of Paganini" and listened to its fevered twenty-three minutes. "It was the most beautiful melody I'd ever heard," she has said. She returned to the store's listening booth again and again, "and I would just go into raptures over it—it was the melody; it killed me, *killed* me." She'd already had a memorable brush with the emotive possibilities of the female voice—when she was seven, she'd heard an Edith Piaf record at a French-Canadian girl's birthday party. At the point in the song when Piaf's voice plaintively soloed and then joined the male chorus, "I had goose bumps," she has said. "I dropped my cake fork." The hours at Sallows and Boyd furthered that impact. Voice, melody: two of songwriting's three elements were now lodged in her subconscious.

With Bill Anderson's next promotion, the family made its final move, to Saskatoon, a hundred miles south of North Battleford, a real city at last. They purchased a new green house, at 1905 Hanover Avenue, the nicest of the Anderson homes, right next to Lathey's Swimming Pool. It was 1954—James Dean, Elvis Presley, and Chuck Berry were just about to sharpen the idea of the teenager as rebel. Joan was eleven years old and loosened from the sweet grip of her family's church-centered life in the smaller town.

For a girl who was considering rebellion, midwestern Canada in the mid- to late 1950s was fertile territory. At a time that was already the peak of anxious traditionalism everywhere, that region (more Britishly proper and "more 'nosegay' than America," as Joni has put it) was filled with women like Myrtle: newly middle-class, distancing themselves from farm childhoods through an almost exaggerated respectability. Between 1955 and 1957, the women's pages of one of the Andersons' main local papers, *The Leader-Post,* brimmed with notices of social events both festive ("Mrs. S. C. Atkinson entertained at an evening party in honor of Mrs. C. Hay. Mrs. W. B. Ramsay poured from a table centred by pale mauve tulips and tall white tapers") and functional ("A demonstration of various kinds of sewing machines will be a feature of a tea, sponsored by the Regina Home Economics Club"). These pages also called for a harder line on children. Opinion pieces lashed at the "permissive" parenting that had virtually redefined child rearing since the 1946 publication of Benjamin Spock's *The Common Sense Book of Baby and Child Care*. One Fred Rawlinson called it a "joy to hear recently in Regina that every parent and every teacher said 'no' to a child at least once a day." "Mrs. Muriel Lawrence, the Mature Parent," ridiculed lenient mothers. Psychologist A. E. Cox said parents who drove their kids everywhere were abetting "a pattern of evolution that might result in a physically useless, big-headed human race."

Yet amid all the self-conscious refinement and the keeping of children in their places was an inspiring paean, by local poet Ella Davis, to a tougher heroine of a former era. The poem was simply called "Amelia," as if that first, distinctive name alone were enough to describe the brave aviatrix who had gone alone across the Atlantic Ocean. Davis praised her "high dreams" in "all out altitudes."

Did thirteen-year-old Joan Anderson (who was now defying Myrtle by sneaking out to the jazz-and-burlesque tent at the Mile Long Midway carnival) notice that poem in the newspaper on that summer 1957 day and feel a stab of romantic identification? "Amelia": the intimacy of that first-name-alone as a title. "Dreams." "Altitudes." One wonders.

Starting junior high at Queen Elizabeth School in Saskatoon provided Joan with the third key to her future as a songwriter: a mentor—a taskmaster, really—for poetry writing. Within weeks of starting school, she'd established herself as the class artist, just as she had in North Battleford. She was hanging up paintings she'd made for an evening PTA meeting when a teacher she remembers as "a good-looking Australian came up to me and said, 'You like to paint?' I said, 'Yes.' He said to me, 'If you can paint with a brush, you can paint with words. I'll see you next year.'"

The teacher was fifty-year-old Arthur Kratzmann, who had previously noticed, as he would later say, "how beautifully she could paint" when he walked into another class and watched her dabbing watercolors.

Next year, in seventh grade, Joan Anderson did indeed have Arthur Kratzmann for English. By now, she was fascinated by the man, whose background was somewhat romantic. Kratzmann, the son of an Australian sharecropper, had been a track star in Australia and had taught on Canadian Indian reservations. For his part, Arthur Kratzmann viewed Joanie Anderson as a "slim, blond-haired, blue-eyed, respectful, obedient, quiet, responsive student." Kratzmann prided himself on being able to *really* teach English composition—to see his students as "artists who put down words and phrases and sentences that nobody else ever had in the world," he has said. "The kids rise to the challenge. Joni Mitchell was one of them. She didn't strike me as the most outstanding person I've ever had in the field, but she wrote well."

But first he had to shake her up. He'd observed that she was derivative. "She'd see a painting of a landscape and she'd duplicate it, and when we'd be writing poetry, she'd have a tendency to, say, pick Wordsworth's daffodils and write a poem about tulips but use the same rhyme scheme and style." He was determined to push imitation out of her.

For her first assignment, Joan wrote a poem about a stallion. She went riding at a nearby stables, so she knew something about horses. Seeking to impress her teacher, she looked in *Reader's Digest* for verbal images. Kratzmann handed the poem back to her, with "Cliché," "Cliché," "Cliché," "Cliché" scrawled in the margins and lines drawn to the many words he'd circled. "He marked me harder, I think, than American college professors mark," she later opined. When she approached him after class to talk about it, Kratzmann grilled her: "How many times have you seen *Black Beauty*?" She answered, "Once." "What do you know about horses?" She told him about her riding. He shot back: "The things that you've told me that you've done on the weekends are more interesting than this." Then he said: "You must write in your own blood." He's later explained, "At the time I was studying Nietzsche, who used to tell people that they must do things in their own blood, so I turned the quotation on her." Arthur Kratzmann's exhortation had the same effect as Rachmaninoff and Piaf. The phrase "Write in your own blood" became a motto for the preteenager and triggered her lifelong love of Nietzsche. "She picked up on that and started to write about her life," Kratzmann has recalled.

In fall of 1957, Joan entered Nutana Collegiate High School, while the school in which she would spend the balance of her high school years—Aden Bowman Collegiate—was being built. Gifted art students at Aden Bowman took art classes at Saskatoon Technical Collegiate, and it was here that Joan studied—and argued—with the Abstract Expressionist painter Henry Bonli. The Bonlis kept a studio in Toronto, but he and his wife, Elsa, had spent time in New York, where they'd befriended the most authoritative critic, Clement Greenberg. Bonli's sophistication leapt out at Joan, but she was as stubborn with painting as she had been with backyard circuses, and as forthright with her art teacher as she had been with her Sunday school teacher. "I know she objected to the way I was teaching, and she didn't like my colors," says Bonli. "She didn't like putty; she liked bright colors." But Bonli indirectly gave her something else: permission to spruce up her name. At a time when Susans were becoming Susi, Barbaras Barbi, and Pattys Patti, Joan Anderson, beguiled by the jaunty final *i* of her teacher's last name (and, possibly, by the hit parade singer Joni James), became Joni Anderson.

At Aden Bowman Joni's best friend was another tall, thin, blond Joan, Joan Smith, who lived on nearby Cumberland Avenue. A third friend, Marie Brewster Jensen, says, "The two Joans looked so much alike they could have been sisters." (Joan Smith Chapman disagrees: "Joni's features were more severe than mine; she had high cheekbones.") Joan Smith was even-keeled and conventional; she would marry her high school beau at nineteen. Joni Anderson was looking for something more. "Neither of us were very absorbed in school," Joan Smith Chapman says. They lived for the weekends, when they'd go to the YMCA dances at the Spadina Crescent and dance: first, to Elvis, Chuck Berry, and Little Richard and then—with less enthusiasm on Joni's part—to the late-1950s *American Bandstand* regulars like Frankie Avalon, Fabian, and Donny Kirshner's friends Connie Francis and Bobby Darin. "Nobody knew Joni Anderson had polio; she loved to dance," says a boy in their crowd, Bob Sugarman, whom everyone called "Sugie," and who was friends with Tony Simon, the "nice, smart fellow" Sugarman says Joni "bummed around with, but I don't remember Joni hooking up with anybody in particular. I wouldn't say Joni was in the popular group; she was too reserved and individual. She was going by the beat of her own drummer."

Those endless weekends of Y dances "were pretty innocent, mellow evenings. You got a ride down with your parents and got a ride home from them; there was no alcohol and certainly no drugs," says Joan Chapman. But Marie Jensen remembers a bit more teenage angst, which was released during Joni-Joan-and-Marie slumber parties at Joan's house, where the girls' heads rarely touched the pillows unmediated by "those big round plastic rollers with the big clips in them," Marie recalls. Marie lived in another community, Prince Albert, two hundred miles north, and knew the two blond Joans from their vacations there, on Lake Waskesiu (pronounced Wask-ah-soo), with their parents. She was less like the contented Joan than the restless Joni. "We were 'finding' ourselves, trying to understand that we didn't have to do things like our mothers had, to exist," Marie says. "Joni was beautiful, and she always looked so well put-together, in those little Jackie Kennedy kinds of coats and a hair band. But she was reserved and withdrawn and she had her insecurities, like I did, like we all did: Were we pretty? Who *were* we? Where were we 'going'? We had strong separation and approval issues with our mothers—more than the next generation of girls, I think." Marie believes this is because prairie-Canadian mothers of that era had themselves experienced distant mothering from hardworking farm women who hadn't doted on them. So, to compensate, "*our* mothers," Marie says, "said to themselves, 'We're going to fix our relationships with our daughters.' Maybe they fixed them too much." Joni, the lone only child in the crowd—Myrtle's masterpiece-in-progress—may have suffered this overcompensation most intensively. Toward the end of high school, she started rebelling—drinking too much; frequenting the "rowdy" west side of town, where the Indian and Ukrainian kids lived; slacking off in her classes (they bored her, she's said; she drew pictures on math assignments). She had entered a turbulent period. A current close friend of Joni's says, on the basis of how Joni has described these years, "Joni was always at odds with Myrtle, who was opinionated and critical of her. Myrtle was a straight cat. 'You're going to school! You're going to be educated! You're going to be a *good* girl!'"

"I saw that tension in Joni when she was a teenager," says the woman who, as a girl, probably did more than anyone else to model rebellion for Joni. Her name was D'Arcy Case. She was Marie Brewster's friend from Prince Albert, and her parents ran an inn on Lake Waskesiu where the Saskatoon kids hung out on vacations. Petite, brunette, and strikingly pretty, D'Arcy was a flamboyant, passionate baby beatnik, and her exaggerated persona threw down the gauntlet at, as she puts it today, that "fucking dainty little culture" of late-1950s Canada. One day, for example, D'Arcy dyed her hair red, green, and blue, to match a plaid skirt. She was so obsessed with Edith Piaf (whose voice Joni had been so moved by) that one night, on impulse at a party, she took a blunt scissors and chopped her past-shoulder-length hair off to a boy's length—"just like Edith had done during the French Resistance, identifying with the German women who'd been shamed," D'Arcy says. But for all her wildness, D'Arcy maintained sobriety and a don't-you-put-your-hand-under-my-blouse sense of propriety. Her parents were alcoholics; having seen how liquor could ruin a life and having to be a kind of parent to her parents, she herself never drank. She became a kind of sober companion to the rowdy but innocent, pent-up Saskatoon kids who invaded the lake on holidays.

D'Arcy would look after the inebriated Saskatoon kids at wiener roasts, and Joni Anderson quickly became her favorite. "She got really drunk, a lot," D'Arcy says. But D'Arcy felt there was something deeper behind Joni's drinking than the simple rebellion and delight in excess that powered the other teenagers. "There was something tragic there. You have to drink when you have something like I felt Joni had—so much inner fire, in contradiction to her perfect little only-child life [created] by a mother who is essentially saying, 'Here's your life, dear; all arranged for you.' Joni got lots of attention from her parents. She was privileged—she had nice clothes and sweater sets, where some of the others of us had to earn our own money—but that came at a price. She was very tightly looked after. I think she really wanted to break out. She was really screwing up in school; still, it was so hard for her to do so. She had her parents' expectations to deal with."

One night Joni looked up at the stars and started reciting her poetry for D'Arcy. "It wasn't the coolest thing to do, back then and there, to be writing or reciting poetry. But Joni looked at the sky, which on the prairie is so expansive—it goes on for miles. There's a sense that you can get *out,* that you can go *anywhere.* I viewed Joni as a tortured rebel; her drinking, a reaction to the fact that she was *way* too smart for this little-mind town she was in, where they sent the message: 'Don't dream beyond this.'"

Around Joni's junior year she bought herself a $38 baritone ukulele and a Pete Seeger songbook. In truth, though, folk music wasn't inspiring her as much as 1950s scat singing. She had discovered Lambert, Hendricks and Ross, and "they were," as she has said, "my Beatles." (Despite the general impression that Joni moved from folk to jazz only later in her career, serious musicologists—listening to the syncopation, three-plus-three-plus-two rhythms, and sophisticated swing rhythms found in some of Joni's earliest recorded songs—believe that, in a way, she was *always* a jazz artist.) She was in love with performing, but she had what people considered a "weird" (as several called it) squeaky voice, and she played the ukulele so much at the sleepovers at Joan Smith's house that, as Marie Brewster Jensen recalls, "I wanted to say, 'Please, Joni, take your ukulele and *go home!*" One day Frankie McKitrick came to visit her from North Battleford. The two old friends sat in the Andersons' basement recreation room, "and Joni took out the ukulele and she said, 'You gotta see what I'm doing! I'm so excited about it!'" Frank says, "And I'm thinking, 'Wait here, *I'm* the musician; *you're* the artist.' She started singing and playing, and I really thought she wasn't very good at it. I said, 'Joan! Stick to the art!' But she wasn't listening. She had her own idea, and she wasn't about to let go of it."

From that point on, Joni would begin to (to use her own words) "bring home" the musical talent and ambition that both her grandmothers had urgently passed on to her.

CHAPTER THREE

carly

Born in New York City—*Current Biography* gives June 25, 1945, as her birthdate—Carly Simon received her unique first name to honor her parents' close friend Caroline "Carly" Wharton, the grand-dame-like wife of theatrical lawyer John Wharton. Carly Elizabeth Simon's family was distinctive, and not just because it was wealthy and cultured in the venerable New York tradition of first-night theatergoing, literary-lights friends, and glorious country houses. Rather, it was unusual because a thread of highly unconventional romance ran through the pasts of both of her parents and penetrated their marriage, with powerful complications. "Issues of deception and betrayal are tremendously central to the Simon family," Carly's close friend Jake Brackman says. Carly's second husband, Jim Hart, puts it this way: "Carly grew up with no boundaries, other than the boundaries of sophistication. That's what I was there for—to give Carly the idea of boundaries." (Boundaries were something that Hart, having trained for the Catholic priesthood, was in a very good position to impart.)

But both men's somewhat stern assessments miss something. Daring to love across lines of inappropriateness provides a vision of living by one's passions, a not-unuseful lesson in the 1950s, a decade that offered girls much more soul-flattening messages. The melodramas that Joanie Anderson watched in North Battleford movie theaters to counteract her family's and her milieu's stifling propriety, Carly Simon witnessed not on a movie screen but *within* her home. In her twenties Carly would personify a fusion of traits and inclinations—classiness *with* sexual voracity; almost soft-porn-like self-display *and* conscientious motherhood; tidy privilege *plus* ragged longing—that had previously been thought dichotomous but which, during the sparks-flying juncture of second-wave feminism with the sexual revolution, were suddenly seen as powerful, real, and *acceptable* for middle-class women. And the precedent for this all-too-human contradiction shimmered in the sad, bright air of a series of book-lined, Chopin-filled living rooms.

Carly's father, Richard Leo Simon, was the eldest of five children of prosperous German-Jewish feather-and-silk manufacturer Leo Simon and his wife, German-born Jew Anna Meier. The family was assimilated "almost to the point of being anti-Semitic; there was a lot of snobbery, and I don't think they ever set foot in a synagogue," says Jeanie Seligmann, whose mother, Elizabeth Simon Seligmann, was Richard's younger sister. (Brothers Henry, Alfred, and George were born in between the two; Leo and Anna named all five of their children for British monarchs.) "'Compat,'" the grandchildren's nickname for Leo Simon, since first-grandchild Joanna could not pronounce "Grampa," "would say things to his [own] children, while they were growing up, like, 'Don't act like a kike.'" Despite the crude jargon and a message that sounds self-loathing to today's ears, in the assimilationist era of the first two decades of the twentieth century, that sentiment was shared by other socially ambitious German Jews for whom even Reform Judaism felt too ethnic. The Ethical Culture movement, formed in 1870 as an alternative spiritual body to Reform Judaism, called for (in the name of idealistic universalism) an abandonment of all traces of Jewish ethnicity; then as now, the movement stood for progressive politics. The elder Simons joined the group, even though its intellectual tone was unmet by the somewhat rough-hewn Leo. Richard Simon attended Ethical Culture School—Carly and her sisters would later briefly attend its other campus, Fieldston—then Columbia University. Eventually growing so tall (six feet four) that he towered over every man in a room, Richard had long fingers that enhanced his gift for piano. His brothers would become experts in music—loving, respectively, opera, American musical theater, and jazz—but only Richard was capable of a serious performing career. Still, after his World War I service, he would fall into work as a piano salesman and then become a successful book publisher, relegating his daily hours at the keyboard to the realm of private solace.

While Richard was growing up in his parents' proper West Eighty-sixth Street home, a frequent visitor was a German-speaking Swiss-born professional nurse named Jeannette "Jo" Hutmacher, who was Richard's mother's close friend and a helper with the children. Even before he was twenty, Richard, who had his pick of girls in his circle, grew infatuated with this uneducated woman eighteen years his senior. Ultimately, the two embarked upon a love affair and Richard Simon's first sexual experience. When Richard was in his late twenties, his mother died, and Jo immediately moved into the Simon house to care for the youngest children. Richard had long since moved out, and had formed with motor-trade magazine editor Max Schuster their eponymous publishing company. They'd started with crossword puzzles and hadn't yet made the great leap to literature and major nonfiction. It wasn't exactly as if the young man was in love with his own mother-substitute, but, even by liberal standards, Richard's ongoing involvement with Jo yielded an eyebrow-raising pairing. He even proposed marriage to her. But the older, service-class immigrant understood what her young lover was too privileged, and too romantic, to grasp. "Jo knew their marriage would be unacceptable," Jeanie Seligmann says. "She was eighteen years older and of 'inferior' social class; she didn't even have a high school education. She said, 'I won't marry you because it won't be good for you—I'll hold you back.' Uncle Dickie was heartbroken; Jo made him very, very happy."

Meanwhile, in Philadelphia, the young woman who would be Carly's mother, Andrea Louise Heinemann, was growing up alongside her brothers, Fred ("Dutch") and Peter. Their German-born father had abandoned the family, and their Spanish-born Catholic mother, Asunción María Del Río Heinemann, was raising them on her own in a state of near-poverty but with an aura of glamour and culture. María, whom everyone called Chibie (pronounced Shee-bee), was one of those magical creatures of an earlier, self-made America. Exotic, intentionally cloaked in mystery, Chibie told people that she had been Thomas Mann's secretary (and maybe more than that . . .) and hinted that she'd had affairs with Fiorello La Guardia and perhaps even with Franklin Delano Roosevelt. Bravado and illusion were her arts; "When I die," she frequently warned her wider family, "you will know *nothing*." She was definitely a boundary crosser. One day Andrea came home from school to find her mother in bed with one of her own boyfriends. Still, Chibie was a person of substance—intellectual, multilingual, literary; a perfect speller, always giving her grandchildren and nieces books of poetry—and despite that powerful breach of trust, mother and daughter were very close.

Chibie called herself "Moorish" and said she had African blood. (The Moors, from northwest Africa, invaded Spain in 711 and didn't leave until 1492.) Those who knew Carly's uncles, Peter Dean and Dutch Heinemann, say they possessed African features; in her youth, curly-haired Andrea was likened to Lena Horne. Carly enthusiastically believes Chibie's assertion about her lineage.

In 1934, Andrea, a switchboard operator at the now-thriving Simon & Schuster, caught her boss's eye. "Hello, little woman," Simon said one morning, tipping his hat. She responded, flirtatiously, "Hello, big man." Carly later wrote an evocative song about her parents' courtship, back when Manhattan was "carriage rides and matinees."

Andrea was quite beautiful—with high cheekbones and a delicately sculpted nose, she resembled Katharine Hepburn—and she was tactile and captivating, touching people's hands, calling them "darlingest." Simon proposed when he learned that his competition was circus impresario John North Ringling. (Carly would similarly use Mick Jagger to hasten her marriage to James Taylor.) She and Richard Simon married in 1935. The groom had immediate regrets. From his European honeymoon, he wrote to Jo Hutmacher, "I've made a terrible mistake." But when the new husband visited his first love after he returned to New York, Jo, on moral grounds, refused a rekindling of their physical relationship; she would stay in Richard's life in the sidelined way to which she was accustomed. Richard's feelings for Jo were left to be expressed in nonsexual but powerful imprints: when his and Andrea's first child turned out to be a girl, she was named Joanna—the final two syllables for Richard's mother, Anna, and the first syllable in honor of Jo. "I must say, Andrea was a good sport to go along with that," Jeanie Seligmann says. After Joanna (nicknamed Joey) came Lucy, Carly, and the sole boy, Richard Peter, always called Peter. During these years Simon & Schuster would invest in Pocket Books and pioneer the mass-market paperback, publishing Dorothy Parker, Agatha Christie, Emily Brontë, and Thornton Wilder in inexpensive form, as well as hardcover literature and nonfiction.

Jo Hutmacher became "Auntie Jo" to the Simon children, and Auntie Jo and Andrea's mother, Chibie, became roommates. They lived for many years in an apartment owned by the Simons—the wise, simple Swiss nurse who'd turned down marriage to Richard Simon and the divalike intellectual whose daughter was making a glamorous life with him. This female Odd Couple had a fine old time watching *The Honeymooners* in their bathrobes at night. Richard Simon visited Jo often; she was his confidante. Most families don't start with such melodrama: rivals living as roommates, de-eroticized ex-lovers close at hand, wives so ripe for anger. It was within this nest of potentially explosive emotions—all wrapped up in taste, wealth, intelligence, and enterprise—that Carly Simon was nurtured.

Andrea's detractors (and there were several in the Simon family) looked askance at what they considered her slipshod attention to maternal detail. She was often mysteriously dashing off somewhere (without telling her husband, she drove an emergency ambulance during World

War II), forgetting to wash her daughters' hair and sew errant buttons on their coats. But Joey, Lucy, and Carly today believe that Andrea was a good mother; latter-day defenders of Andrea Simon contend that her new husband's immediate outreach to Jo had placed her at a disadvantage right from the start, justifying whatever private-space-carving was necessary to keep her in emotional fighting form to manage, with aplomb, the increasingly large family. Jim Hart, who became close with Andrea through marriage to Carly (Andrea never bypassed the chance to charm a handsome man), says, "Andi tried hard to remake what was unacceptable"—the fact that her husband retained affection for another woman—"by suppressing it, and in whatever way she could. Otherwise, she couldn't have proceeded to become this incredibly positive force in her children's lives." Radio personality Jonathan Schwartz, who as a teenager spent a great deal of time with the Simons, describes in his memoir, *All in Good Time*, Andrea moving with "joy and energy" about the kitchen in the weekend house in Stamford, Connecticut (a magical estate of nineteen rooms on sixty-four acres, with gardens, pool, and tennis court; frequent guests included Jackie and Rachel Robinson, Random House editor Bennett Cerf, and Benny Goodman). Andrea was "a mother-director-chef: a hummingbird, tasting, sipping, laughing with delight," Schwartz recalled. "In her hair a hibiscus, . . . her blouse often a white ruffled peasant garment. She marveled at what the children said, her deep voice rising in appreciation. She was easy to thrill. Children in wet bathing suits did it. A thunderstorm did it. Strawberries, tomatoes, apples . . . did it."

But underneath Andrea's joie de vivre lay a steely discipline, the same steely discipline shared by Carole's and Joni's mothers. Like theatrical, emotional Genie Klein—who grilled her mentally disabled son about abuse he may have suffered at Willowbrook, who intimidated the members of her daughter's first singing group, and who seemed to have wanted to have been the star that Carole became—and like proper, proud Myrtle Anderson, who vacuumed her garage daily and who, in the mid-1990s, called her middle-aged daughter's sharing of a hotel room with her boyfriend "disgrace[ful]"—Andrea Heinemann

Simon was the dominating linchpin of the family. "She was a fireball—controlling, very bright, very organized," says Tim Ratner, who became Carly's first boyfriend when she was fifteen.

For Carly's first six years, home was two fused apartments comprising the top floor of a gray six-story doorman building at 133 West Eleventh Street. Only twelve families shared it, including Elizabeth Simon Seligmann, her physician husband, Arthur, and their daughters, Mary and Jeanie. The building was a block away from the private school, City & Country, that the Seligmann girls and Simon girls attended. (Pete Seeger guest-taught in Carly's kindergarten class, leading the children in the rousing folk songs that, since he was blacklisted, he could perform only *off*stage.) The five girls were always in each other's bedrooms: cutting out paper dolls; bunched around Elizabeth as she read them *Mary Poppins*; being led by Andrea in rounds of charades; trading library books—Carly loved spunky Francie Nolan of *A Tree Grows in Brooklyn*—while eating the chocolate and vanilla ice cream cups, with pictures of Roy Rogers and Dale Evans on the inside lids, they'd buy at nearby Rosie's. There were so many girls in this Simon generation that upon the birth of a sixth to another brother, Alfred Simon quipped, referring to the ladies' luncheon spot, "Congratulations on the latest daughter—what a boon for Schrafft's."

"Because the men were always off working by day and sound asleep at night, it was a very girl-oriented household—especially in the summer, at Carly's parents' weekend house in Stamford," says Jeanie Seligmann, "where one of those closets contained a stash of Andrea's discarded evening gowns, mantillas, and high heels that we played dress-up in. All our mothers and aunts were around. It was a household *so* full of strong women, so nurturing and earth-motherly that, come to think of it, it's a wonder none of us turned out to be lesbians." But there was one sadistic woman in the household, Carly's Scottish nanny, Nancy Anderson, who, in an effort to get her to stay put after lights out, "put stuffed animals under my bed and said they'd come out and bite me if I tried to get out of bed," Carly recalls. Still, as was typical of prosperous Jewish-lite families of the time (on both coasts), someone was always at the living room piano, and Carly would go off to bed singing the love ballads of Richard Rodgers (also a favorite of Carole's) and family friend Arthur Schwartz, father of Jonathan.

Just after the turn of the decade, the family of six moved to a grand Georgian home on a high mound of lawn at 4701 Grosvenor Avenue, in the Fieldston neighborhood of Riverdale, a kind of suburb within the city. They also retained the Stamford estate. So there were two grand homes, in two leafy neighborhoods, forty-five minutes away from each other. Both houses overflowed with lived culture—"there were books everywhere, manuscripts everywhere, photo albums everywhere, records everywhere," the youngest Simon sibling, Peter, recalled recently—and with the makers of culture, including Irwin Shaw, Will and Ariel Durant, bridge master Charles Goren, poet Louis Untermeyer, myriad other writers and scholars, and once, even, Albert Einstein. Each of the children got his or her own room in the Grosvenor house. Carly's was small and low-ceilinged with a single bed, in contrast to Lucy's larger one, which was watched over by two grizzled mutts that the family called their "Manchester Guardians," after the English newspaper.

The early 1950s was the era of three-martini-lunching Manhattan warriors: sleek, well-bred men, train-commuting from the suburbs to do battle in the world of advertising and publishing by day, kings of their castles at night. Dick Simon discovered and published the novel that defined that era—Sloan Wilson's *The Man in the Grey Flannel Suit*—and Simon himself lived an only slightly more bohemian version of the life the book described, a life in which only men, give or take a few brittle "career women," powered the media business; in which wives were highball-proffering, Claire McCardell–clad soother-hostesses; in which children were bathed and in their pajamas (Dr. Dentons and flowery nightgowns, for the Simon kids) promptly after dinner. "Dick made it understood that he was to receive certain attentions," Andrea Simon once said, "and one of them was: no children around when he came home from the office. He went to the library and closed the door." Lucy Simon says today, "We were not heiresses. We grew up more with a sense of abandonment than privilege."

Carly was so sensitive to the precise amount of alone time she was able to wrest from this preoccupied man that, years later, she would be able to name the seasons of their singular closeness: spring and summer of 1952 and 1953. "We used to drive out to Ebbets Field almost every day the Dodgers were home, and watch them play," she has recalled. "We'd sit and talk about RBIs, Texas Leaguers, and Carl Furillo's batting average." Andrea coached her in this talk. Carly sensed her mother felt insecure because of her high-school-only education—when Bernard Baruch or the Durants were over, she would race into the kitchen on some invented errand to avoid an intimidating conversation. But Andrea felt authoritative on matters of social charm, a confidence she imparted to her youngest daughter. Becoming the baseball expert for her father was something, Carly has said, that she did "to cultivate a relationship with [him] . . . I felt he didn't love me. People have told me I'm wrong, but I didn't *feel* it."

One night, in an act of daughterly coquetry—and during her obsession with *Gone with the Wind*—Carly asked her father, "Daddy, do you have any good-looking friends who could come to the house?" She was doing her very best Scarlett O'Hara (whom she idolized so much, relatives started calling her "Scarly"). Her father answered, "There's a man coming today who, in fact, looks just like Clark Gable!" Taking him at his word, "I got so excited and got all dressed up, put on makeup—the works. When the dinner guest showed up, I came down the stairs Scarlett O'Hara style, and he was just a little old man with glasses. I saw my father laughing at me."

The pecking order among the Simon girls was clear. The two older sisters were the beauties, and each in her own distinct way: "Joey the glamorous and Lucy the lovely," says Ellen Wise Questel. Joey, with her perfectly coiffed pageboy and her precociously made-up face, was elegant, queenly, headed for a career in opera and already acting the diva. Lucy was "almost comic-book beautiful," Carly's friend Jessica

Hoffmann Davis recalls; "the most conventionally pretty of the sisters," says Tim Ratner, who would soon be Carly's boyfriend. But Lucy was so nice, you couldn't hate her for her beauty. She was "saintly," says Jeanie Seligmann; "demure," Carly has said. Lucy "please[d] people," Jonathan Schwartz noted, and, he observed, Lucy was "their father's favorite."

"It's hard to overstate how much Carly was the 'leftover' sister, next to exotic, chic, interesting Joanna and perfect Lucy," says Jessica Hoffmann Davis. "Carly was skinny and lanky and wore her sisters' clothes. She never thought she fit in anywhere, a feeling that led to this deep longing to be an *insider,* something that, despite all outward appearances, she never thinks she achieved." "I [was] the gawky, awkward stutterer, which is how I sometimes see myself still," Carly says today.

In a photo of all four children, taken by their father, eight- or nine-year-old Carly—all limbs and angles—leans in, boyishly splay-legged in sleeveless shirt and shorts: smirking, front-toothless, the hand of her jackknifed right arm smacking the air in a goofy salute. Her gawkiness is in striking contrast to her poised, feminine sisters. This was the Carly that Sloan Wilson saw on his many evenings at the Simons'. He wrote a memoir in which he called all the Simon women—*except* Carly—extremely attractive, which *crushed* her.

One evening during the time that Carly felt closest to her father by way of those Ebbets Field afternoons, Richard Simon was raced to the hospital with a heart attack. Alarmed and desperately worried (would her father die?), Carly performed a ritual she'd heard was supposed to work: she knocked on wood for good luck. When her father survived the night, she interpreted that ritual as the difference between his life and death, and so for the next five years she knocked on her headboard, night table, and bedroom wall—500 knuckle-whacking times—every night before going to bed. Already stuttering, Carly was soon visited by the first of a lifelong string of neuroses: she became agoraphobic, her stomach knotting up and her throat constricting when she left for school each morning. Panic attacks left her shaking. Andrea sent her to a psychiatrist, which meant being excused from class at Fieldston

School for two hours every Tuesday and Thursday. (The teacher told her classmates her absences were because she was "complicated.")

Richard Simon's heart attack led to progressive cardiovascular disease. Increasingly disabled—and eventually subject to delirium—he retreated to the shadows, playing his Chopin (sometimes easing onto the piano bench next to Carly while she was practicing a Schubert sonata and expertly taking over the piece). "Joey and Lucy got more of the vivid, attentive Uncle Dickie; by the time Carly was ready to perceive him, he was much less functioning," Jeanie Seligmann says. "Carly's relationship with him was never totally established" by the time he started fading into ill health, Lucy Simon has said.

Despite Carly's phobias, her deep worry for her father's health, and her sense of being overshadowed by her dazzling sisters—or perhaps in reaction to those things—she seized on and burnished two personal assets. The first one was performing. "Joey and Lucy had nice singing voices, but Carly was amazing; Carly was lit from within—she was a performer from day one," says Jeanie. In her small bedroom, Carly would sing songs into her small handheld mirror, imagining herself performing a movie score. At the family recitals that Andrea endlessly staged, Carly (inspired by her Uncle Peter's girlfriend, singer Betty Ann Grove, who was often around) would belt out the bouncy Teresa Brewer hit "Music, Music, Music" ("Put a-noth-er nick-el in, in the nick-el-o-de-on . . .") and Rosemary Clooney's vampy, suggestive "Come on-a My House"—singing both songs "with demonic energy," Jeanie recalls, "but like a grown-up, despite the fact that she was missing two teeth. Everybody thought she was a very special talent. On our drives up to Martha's Vineyard, where my parents had a house, Carly would tell such funny stories from the backseat, my father almost drove off the road, he was laughing so hard."

Carly's other offensive line was sexuality. Preadolescent Carly loved the word "sexpot" even before she knew what it meant; and she was so curious about menstruation that one day, enlisting Jeanie as her partner in crime, she rummaged through the maids' rooms at the Stamford

estate, rooting in the wastebaskets for their soiled sanitary napkins—
"and there was something exciting when we found them," admits
Jeanie. But nothing matched the celebration that occurred—at Andrea's insistence—on that sparkling summer day when Carly got her
own long-awaited period. As if taking the coded term "I fell off the
roof" to new literalness, Andrea grandly announced a rooftop toast to
the moon. Champagne bottle and three flute glasses in hand, Andrea
rustled Carly and Jeanie up to a flat area atop the Stamford house,
gazed into the heavens, and raised her goblet to the celestial clock of
the menstrual cycle—Carly had become a woman!—after which the
girls took sips of the bubbly alcohol.

In seventh grade, Carly transferred to Riverdale Country Day Girls'
School, a half mile up the leafy, mansion-lined road from Fieldston.
Jessica Hoffmann was the other tall girl at the back of the line there.
She had transferred from the nearby private school her mother owned
and ran, the Hoffmann School; Jessica and her family lived in the
apartment above the classrooms. Who, Jessica wondered, on that first
day of seventh grade, was this "very tall, very skinny girl, her clothes a
little too small," lined up next to her? "She looked like she would trip
over her hundred-feet-long legs; she looked like she was wearing
somebody's hand-me-downs, which she probably was. Her teeth were
fabulous—big, wonderful front teeth with a space in between," which
meant, at lunch, "when she laughed, she would spit her milk across
the room. She would start laughing and—*pshew!!*—it would be a foun-
tain." Jessica viewed this "very funny, very cool and offbeat" girl as
being as out of place as she was.

Where Fieldston had been liberal, Riverdale in the 1950s was
starchy and pious. The girls—who wore pale, circle-pinned Shetlands
over Oxford shirts tucked into gray pleated skirts—took their lunch at
small tables, and when the teacher sat down (the better to monitor
manners that were expected to be impeccable), a dozen penny-loafered
feet slapped the floor as the girls stood at attention—the same way
they popped up from their school desks whenever a teacher entered a

classroom. At assemblies the girls sang the school anthem: "It is the spirit that quickeneth, thus sayeth the Lord . . . and thus sayeth Life, confirming the Word. This truth, O Riverdale, help us live!"

Both Carly and Jessica had a Christian mother and a Jewish father; in the mid-1950s that latter fact mattered to society gentiles on guard against a perceived stealth invasion by Jews who might "pass." So when Jessica and Carly were the only girls in the class not invited to a dance at Riverdale's Christ Church, Andrea Simon, now a civil rights activist, was quietly outraged. So was Jessica's mother. Both women goaded the head of the school to complain to the church; Jessica and Carly were invited to its *next* dance.

Once the school dance hurdle was crossed, dancing *school* became the girls' shared bête noire. They were both so tall that none of the boys asked them to dance, so every week Carly and Jessica were left to dance with Mr. Yule and Mrs. Yule, the near-geriatric instructors. "Dancing with *Mrs.* Yule was the *deepest* humiliation," Jessica recalls. Carly was still stuttering (in a year or two she'd have conquered it)— and "with the stuttering, and her spitting milk through her big-spaced teeth, and her curly hair and too-small dresses, she was almost a match to me, with my too-short Buster Brown bangs and terrible skin and braces." Both girls were obsessed with keeping their hair straight— "Carly kept two brushes in her coat pocket; we ironed our hair, we used big rollers . . ." Carly dealt with her awe at her older sisters' beauty through gossip: she passed notes to Jessica about who Lucy was dating and whether or not they made out.

Next to Jessica's apartment, Carly's house was a castle—a castle full of music. "I remember walking up the path to Carly's house and hearing this beautiful, incredible music . . . her father playing. I sat on the step, listening. The door opened, it was him. I was embarrassed to be sitting there. Like my father, he was very tall. Of all the daughters, Carly looked the most like him." From Richard's classical piano, to Joey's opera, to the after-dinner standards and light-opera songfests, "the musicalness of Carly's home was a standout," Jessica says. "There was always someone singing instead of speaking in the house, and everyone knew all the words to Eugene Field's poems and everyone had a great voice—harmony singing was a group activity, like sports in other families."

Jessica was impressed that Carly's mother was an activist; Andrea had started a campaign to force the town of Stamford to sell a house to her friends Rachel and Jackie Robinson, an ambitious goal at a time when adjacent Darien still had anti-*Jewish* covenants. When the legendary Brooklyn Dodger and his wife couldn't find anything in Stamford "available" for purchase, Andrea announced to the real estate agents that she would assemble a group of clergymen to picket their offices. A home for the Robinsons materialized.

Somewhere between Carly's tenth and twelfth birthday—as her father, who had never relinquished his emotional closeness to Auntie Jo, slipped into seriously ill health—Andrea hired a young Columbia University scholarship student named Ronnie Klinzing to be a companion and baseball and tennis coach for Peter. Her son was awash in a sea of women, and Andrea believed he felt at least passively neglected by his infirm father. ("I can count on one hand the number of times we did anything together," Peter Simon, today a photographer specializing in landscapes after an eclectic photography career, recently said of him.) Ronnie Klinzing had a husky, chiseled handsomeness, reminding Carly of Rock Hudson. When Jeanie Seligmann saw Ronnie on the relatively recent occasion of Peter Simon's birthday, she was reminded of how "really very magnetically sexy he was," a quality that must have been much more intense when he was a college student. He also had a robust voice. Sometimes he stood at the Simon piano, during the family musicales, singing Kurt Weill. Ronnie lived at the Columbia dorms and commuted to the Riverdale house on weekdays. He had his own room at the Stamford house on weekends and in the summer.

But was Ronnie's true purpose merely role modeling for Peter? One day, Carly's older sisters discovered not. Behind a dresser in a bathroom next to Ronnie's bedroom was a passageway that led to a closet in Andrea's bedroom. When Joey confronted her mother with the suspicion that Ronnie was her lover, Andrea did not deny it.

So here was Andrea Simon—whose mother had slept with her boyfriend and whose husband had fallen in love with the older woman who had been his siblings' surrogate mother—implanting in her house a lover young enough to be the beau of any of her daughters. It was at once stunning and unsurprising. "Carly was very confused and troubled by the revelation of her mother's affair with Ronnie," remembers Jessica. "She didn't understand it." For her part, Jessica—upon hearing the true nature of the relationship—earnestly reported to her school-principal mother, "Mrs. Simon has a . . . *paramour*," to which Mrs. Hoffmann bemusedly huffed, "You're not supposed to know what a paramour *is!*" Jeanie Seligmann remembers that, at age twelve, "Carly hated Ronnie with a *passion*." She devised a code name for him— "Hark"—after the wicked duke/henchman in James Thurber's fable *The Thirteen Clocks*. One day, the girls ceremonially recited, "Hark, Hark, the dogs do bark / The duke has found a kitten," as Carly pulled Jeanie into Ronnie's room, closed the door, and opened his dresser drawers. She rummaged around until she found what she was looking to sabotage: Ronnie's jockstrap! She whipped it into the air. The bedroom door sprang open. Ronnie caught Carly red-handed. He made a mock-lunge for both girls but treated the incident with good humor.

Ronnie Klinzing would remain in the household for several years. In the family's complex equation of affection and need, hurt and compensation, Andrea now had, through her young lover, both a means of revenge against an emotionally unfaithful husband and a carnal reward for being the sole truly present parent. The musicales, sumptuous dinners, civil rights activism; the visits by the crazy uncles—Uncle Peter, Sam Cooke's early manager, would lead everyone in camp songs like "Down by the Riverside" and once took a whipped-cream-topped pie off the dinner table and smashed it in his face to get a laugh—all of this continued. But underneath this wholesome joie de vivre, Carly has said, the household vibrated "an atmosphere of erotica," a "sexual haze . . . so thick you could cut it."

It was another girl at Riverdale—Ellen Wise—to whom Carly drew close as third form turned to fourth form (Riverdale used the English nomenclature for junior high to high school matriculation), who most mirrored her feeling of being the neglected sibling. Small, blond Ellen, the daughter of worldly parents—a very wealthy father and a beautiful actress-turned-arts-benefactor mother—had a brother who was charismatic and manic depressive. He was the focal point of the family, leaving her emotionally marooned, just as Carly's glamorous sisters, her father's remoteness and illness, and, now, the riveting issue of Ronnie left Carly feeling sidelined. "I was aware that it felt chilly in the family for Carly—she felt neglected; I felt pain for her," Ellen Wise Questel says. Ellen was tiny and Carly was tall, "so when we'd walk arm in arm, we looked like Mutt and Jeff, but we were very, very close—soul mates, best friends the way teenage girls need to have best friends. Those were not easy years for us.

"We were both a little adventurous in those years, in terms of our interest in boys—we were precocious. I remember Carly always being called sexy." (Carly would later say, "People always said I had a kind of raw sexuality. Maybe it was my big mouth; maybe it was my long legs.") The school had a dress-code enforcer, a Southern woman named Mrs. Rorbach who called everyone "honey chile" and stood by the school bus door and made all the girls close their eyes to see if they'd snuck on any verboten eyeliner or mascara. Mrs. Rorbach would often point to Carly's straight skirt and say, "Now, *this* is *too* tight, honey chile." "Carly wasn't at all inhibited about her clothing," Ellen says.

Carly was one of the first in her crowd to get birth control—to have it *offered* to her, by her mother. In 1958 and 1959, the fourth form girls at Riverdale Country Day School, who were otherwise so privileged— with their after-school trips to Bonwit's (which had a malt shop in its juniors department just for them and their fellow private-school girls); with their parents dashing out at night to benefits and Broadway openings—weren't any more liberated than the Madison High girls in Brooklyn or the Aden Bowman girls in Saskatoon. Officially, at least, "sex was an absolute taboo; it could ruin a girl's reputation. 'Going all the way' was talked about, but nobody was very open about it and it wasn't clear who did what and who didn't," says Ellen. Jessica recalls, "Mrs. Simon had gotten Carly a diaphragm—it was a *big* thing to have a diaphragm in high school—and Carly could give you the name of a gynecologist [who would fit a girl with a diaphragm], if you were one of the few girls in the class who were having relationships. Carly's mother was so ahead of her time: wanting to help *prevent* pregnancy, rather than ignore the risk. Mrs. Simon's progressive attitude helped Carly help the girls whose mothers were more 'pristine' about [sex]." Andrea was, so to speak, Carly's friends' very own Margaret Sanger.

During her sophomore year, Carly acquired her first real boyfriend, a senior named Tim Ratner. Their romance bloomed during Riverdale's production of Gershwin's *Girl Crazy* (featuring "Embraceable You" and "I Got Rhythm"), in which he was the male lead and she, a chorus soloist. "She was beautiful in her own quirky way," Tim Ratner recalls. "And she had a great, self-deprecating sense of humor—she could make fun of herself." Tim had been flirting with a "beautiful blond senior" in the play, he recalls, "and I was also occasionally distracted by the other pretty girl in the show." But Carly, employing her lessons from Andrea, fastened on Tim, and Ellen recalls that "an incredible passionate young romance" ensued. "It was a romantic play, so it was an era of heady romance—of newness—for us." The girls had moved from their Shetlands-and-Oxford-shirts to a more sophisticated look featuring dance clothes from Capezio and flats from Pappagallo. All of a sudden, awkward Carly became "Betty in *Archie and Veronica*—the *popular* girl," Jessica laughs, adding that the next year Carly would be a cheerleader, chanting "Maroon and white! Fight! Fight!" for the football team. "Tim and Carly were a campus couple. Here was Timmy, so popular and handsome—tall, athletic, ruddy complexion, aquiline nose, great smile—and Carly, the best singer in the lower school. It was our own version of a *People* magazine story about two stars in a film who fall in love making a movie."

Carly had just started taking guitar lessons; she and Jessica traveled to the Manhattan School of Music for them. Although Lucy, now in nursing school, had her ear tuned to the folk music that was suddenly replacing jazz as the cool music, Carly was still mostly in love with the classical music and standards that had long filled the family living room, and she regularly bought $1.50 balcony seats at Broadway theaters to hear it. Jonathan Schwartz, her big-brother figure, was now spinning standards as a disc jockey on WBAI. It was during the run of *Girl Crazy,* and the first weeks of her romance with Timmy, that Ellen saw Carly sitting on the school steps, playing and singing "When I Fall in Love" with such feeling, especially on the "It will be for-*ev*-er." Ellen realized something that decades of being close with Carly has cemented: she was uncommonly, almost dangerously, romantic, this woman who "has read *Anna Karenina* about ten times."

Carly and Tim's spring and summer romance was full of music, "mainly American standards, which we were getting to love, through the show," Tim says. "Carly had a wonderful, true alto, even though she'd never taken a singing lesson. She just had natural pipes." They'd stay up long into the night, call Jonathan Schwartz at the station, and request dedications for each other. Then, wrapped in each other's arms, they'd listen as Jonathan's smooth voice announced the dedication and segued into the lush, thoughtful music. They improvised duets of "Blue Skies"; they harmonized over Andre Previn, Eydie Gorme, and Frank Sinatra records. Tim says: "I remember being with her at two in the morning, listening to 'In the Wee Small Hours of the Morning' for the first time."

Visiting Carly often at the Stamford house over the summer of 1959, Tim saw the complexity of her home life—the "highly matriarchal atmosphere, the strong older sisters, a mother both very organized and also cut off and not available, a father growing progressively less functional." Ronnie's relationship with Andrea was never explicit, "but any observer could tell what it was. There was sadness for Carly. A few years later I'd hear the Beatles' 'She's Leaving Home' and think it captured the sadness I felt in Carly."

Tim went off to Dartmouth in the fall of 1959. Carly began to play the guitar in earnest, finding her voice in the folk music whose popularity had, in a year's time, swept like a brushfire from college to high school. Now the sounds of "John Henry" were more likely to be heard from guitar-strumming Carly than "When I Fall in Love." Carly and Ellen and Jessica got deeper into a bohemian look: black turtlenecks and bottle-green skirts. They subwayed down to the Café Wha? on MacDougal Street. Carly loved Odetta. She was the most privileged of white girls, but she wanted to sing like the Alabama-born, L.A.-raised Negro opera-singer-turned-folksinger who had wowed Pete Seeger and inspired the unknown Bob Dylan. (A few years later, Carly and Lucy were playing a coffeehouse. When Carly saw Odetta in the audience, she was so intimidated, she walked off the stage and fainted.)

In Stamford at the beginning of the summer after Carly's fifth form year, Richard Simon was being nursed by Jo Hutmacher while Ronnie Klinzing remained with Andrea. During this time, an MIT boy, Paul Sapounakis, who'd had one of the now-common unrequited crushes on Lucy Simon, suggested to his friend Nick Delbanco, who had just finished his freshman year at Harvard, that the two visit the Simon house—"and you," Paul said, "can date the younger sister." Delbanco had grown up in a Westchester County suburb of New York after a childhood in London; his parents were Jews who'd fled Germany for London on the eve of the Holocaust. Their name, Italian for "moneylender," literally described what the family had been until they'd left Italy for Germany in 1630. Nick's father was a businessman-painter; the household retained a cultured, somber European feeling—heavy woods, sacher tortes, a stunning art collection—and the shortish, intense-featured Nick conveyed an old world gravitas. He had an almost theatrically formal voice; he was dashing. A lover of James Joyce and Malcolm Lowry (the "proud modernists," as he puts it), he was writing serious fiction and, even as an undergraduate, was thought of within Harvard's English department as a likely candidate for renown.

Nick Delbanco entered the Simon house with Paul Sapounakis and took in the scene: the "stony-faced" infirm Richard Simon, sitting (as Nick would later put it, in an essay in his *Running in Place: Scenes from the South of France,* in which he pseudonymed Carly as "Dianne") "in an armchair . . . wearing pajamas and a bathrobe, hands folded in his lap." The evening family recital, around the grand piano, was about to begin. Like other family visitors, Nick watched, that night and subsequent nights, the performing Simon girls "offe[r] show tunes, operetta, opera, folksongs, torch songs, the blues. The three girls took turns . . . joined in duets and trios; their brother photographed them all. Then a guest would play Chopin or Lizst and [Carly] would return to my side," eliciting praise. "She was perfect, better than ever, the best. Play 'John Henry' again, I would ask her, or 'Danny Boy.'" She obliged, in her "deep, strong, throaty voice" with "erotic abandon."

Carly unfurled her ample insecurities at Nick—"She had the remnants of a stammer and a forthright anxiety," he would later write. "She said that her family left her feeling insecure, unloved, and that her comic antics were a ploy to gain attention. . . . She had clamored for applause . . . to make her father smile at her." Her father's infirmity felt like a "reproach to her."

On July 30, Richard Simon suffered a fatal heart attack. "I showed up at Carly's father's funeral, and that's the first time she took me seriously," recalls Delbanco. "It was a dark and complicated time for her." Soon enough Carly and Nick were locking themselves into attic rooms in the secret-filled house.

Lucy Simon sees their father's death as being pivotal for Carly. "*My* relationship to our father was very stable; I always felt loved; there was nothing I had to prove to him. Carly didn't have the comfort of that kind of relationship with him." It was the start of decades of unfinished business.

But the comforting attention of Nick Delbanco enabled Carly to avoid confronting it. Her romance with Nick continued when she entered Riverdale's sixth form and he went back to Harvard for his sophomore year. Even though Carly had to bend at the knees when she stood next to Nick to hide the fact that she was considerably taller, her friends thought it terribly glamorous that she was going with this debonair Harvard novelist. Actually, all the girls had artistic boyfriends— Jessica's, a sensitive, poetic would-be jazz musician (her mother referred to him as "Heathcliff"); Ellen's, every Riverdale girl's crush— handsome Vieri Salvadori, half Jewish, half Italian, on his way to becoming an art critic. Carly's once-difficult-to-tame hair was now long and lustrous; she tossed it, boho-vampishly, behind her right ear; it flowed down her shoulder. Next to her senior class yearbook photo—a sexy, wide-smiling sideways shot—is written: "There are always crowds around Carly: admiring younger girls, distressed seniors, and bewitched lads. They know she is sincere, that her emotions are free, and that she can feel and appreciate more deeply than many. Carly cares." It would prove to be an enduringly accurate description.

Fueled by the pain of her father's death and the blush of new romance with an intense young writer, Carly threw herself into folk music—Odetta, Baez, Ian and Sylvia, Cynthia Gooding. She wrote songs, once attaching the Robert Burns poem "Ye Flowery Banks" to the ever-romantic melody of "Greensleeves," another time writing with Jessica a faux–Child Ballad with phallic lyrics. "We loved the 'bonnie, bonnie banks' songs and the 'turtle dove' songs," says Jessica. "Not for us fair maidens" AM rock 'n' roll.

For her application to Sarah Lawrence, Carly and Jessica composed an essay about a book that "changed my life": Daniel Defoe's *The Fortunes and Misfortunes of the Famous Moll Flanders.* The only thing was, neither girl had read the novel. They laughed until they wept as they wrote, "Moll faced adversity with the kind of courage I'd like to have in my life" and "In Moll I find the inspiration to be a confident woman." It was a grand put-on.

Put-on or not, Carly was accepted at Sarah Lawrence. One night at the Stamford house just before Carly started packing for the dorm at the nearby campus, Uncle Peter watched Carly and Lucy harmonizing on a folk song and said, "You two should form a group." The thought registered more strongly with Lucy than Carly. It would soon be Lucy, the secure older sister, who would drag Carly, the younger one frenetically proving herself, into the modest beginning of a career that would—for a deceptively long stretch of time—seem mostly unpromising.

PART THREE

"and the sun poured
in like butterscotch"

carole

1961–1964

By John F. Kennedy's inauguration—January 20, 1961—Carole King was close to slipping the bonds of adolescence. At two weeks shy of nineteen years old, she was a wife, a mother, and she had written the #1 pop song. On the bright, cold day that the handsome new president announced, "Let the word go forth that the torch has been passed to a new generation of Americans," Carole was changing eleven-month-old Lou Lou's diapers at Brown Street and was probably refining the chord changes of what would be—in eight months—her and Gerry's second #1 hit, the bouncy and catchy (if significantly less weighty) "Take Good Care of My Baby."

The Bobby Vee hit had started with the rudimentary melody that Carole had taken back from Cynthia Weil that April 1960 night because Gerry had not wanted Carole to write with another partner. But the song had really developed when the two new parents started working at 1650 Broadway (Gerry had just quit his job at Argus Chemicals), cramped in what Carole would later recall as a "little cubbyhole with just enough room for a piano, a bench, and maybe a chair, if you were lucky," where "you'd sit there and write and you could hear someone in the next cubbyhole composing some song exactly like yours." On any given day in the early 1960s, a tour through the cacophonous halls of Aldon would yield Carole and Gerry (perhaps working up "One Fine Day" or "Oh No Not My Baby") mere yards away from Neil Sedaka and Howie Greenfield (maybe knocking out "Calendar Girl" or "Breaking Up Is Hard To Do"), close by Cynthia Weil and her husband, fellow Madison High alum Barry Mann (who might be composing "On Broadway"—or "You've Lost That Lovin' Feelin'" for the Righteous Brothers, which became the song most played on the radio of the next four decades, outplaying even the Beatles). Rounding out the group was Doc Pomus (his real name was Jerome Felder), a disabled polio survivor who, though white and Jewish, had been a blues and R&B singer. Pomus now wrote melodies with the much younger Mort Shuman, a Lincoln High alumnus, including "A Teenager in Love," "Save the Last Dance for Me," and "This Magic Moment." Eventually a third young married couple, Ellie Greenwich and Jeff Barry, joined the stable, specializing in songs for the young Phil Spector's "wall-of-sound" girl groups, the Crystals and especially the Ronettes, who, in the mid-1960s, kicked the Shirelles' and the Chantels' decorousness up a good notch with their pale-lipsticked, thick-eyelinered, teased-haired, sob-in-the-throat foxiness. Greenwich and Barry wrote "Be My Baby" and "Da Doo Ron Ron (When He Walked Me Home)."

"The pressure was really terrific," Carole has said, "because Donny would play one songwriter against another. He'd say, 'We need a smash hit!' and we'd all go back and write a song and the next day we'd each audition [for example] for Bobby Vee's producer." Al Kasha, who, as Jackie Wilson's A&R man, observed the process closely, says, "Kirshner would pit writers against each other, so you were constantly writing. He'd say, 'The Drifters are up for a date' or 'Bobby Vee is up for a date'—and they'd all be writing, day and night, trying to outdo each other."

Cynthia Weil remembers that a frequent gambit was to try to ambush Donny at his office door when he came out to go to the men's room ("Sooner or later he'd *have* to go," she reasoned), the better to find out who he was cooking up a deal with—what group to try to write a hit for. Donny "created this family of competitive siblings who all wanted to please him, and the way to please him was to write hit songs," Cynthia has said. "We were always, 'Donny, d'you like this? Donny, d'you like *this?*'" "I wasn't much older than they were, but they were like my kids," Donny says. "I was their father, mother, psychiatrist."

Between late-1950s early rock 'n' roll (Chuck Berry, Fats Domino, Elvis before the army) and the British Invasion and ascent of Bob Dylan, the songwriters Kirshner had collected essentially wrote the pop soundtrack for young America, yielding some 200 chart hits in a five-year period. Carole had a signature style now. As she would later describe it, "I loved taking simple melodies [influenced by] classical [compositions] and Rodgers and Hart and Rodgers and Hammerstein—taking those melodic influences and putting [them] in the context of rhythm and blues's styling, phrasing, and rhythm."

Life for Carole now was round-the-clock songwriting and mothering. She and Gerry would often take Lou Lou to Aldon, a major ordeal in the days before strap-on baby carriers and folding, lightweight strollers, when mothers of young children were essentially restricted to their homes and neighborhoods. In her memoir, *How I Became Hettie Jones,* the young poet Hettie Cohen, who married the noted young Beat poet LeRoi Jones (later to be known as Amiri Baraka), recounts arduously maneuvering a big, heavy baby carriage up steep loft stairs to get to a poetry reading. Carole, with her heavy stroller, like Hettie with hers, didn't let the supposedly dominating vocation—and the unwieldy accoutrements—of motherhood keep her from creating. "I didn't let the fact that I had a child slow me down. I just brought her with me," Carole would later say. "I [was] like: 'Okay! Feed the baby and then go to the piano!'" She sat at the piano with Lou Lou on her lap. Lou Lou, it is said, once slammed the piano lid on Carole's fingers to demand attention from her work-focused mother.

"I used to walk into Aldon, and the baby would be in a playpen in the middle of the office, and Carole would be at a demo session—it's just the way it was; we never thought about it," says Cynthia, adding,

"I had no idea why people wanted to have these noisy things anyway; I didn't get having babies at all." Donny Kirshner remembers "my secretary was babysitting and diapering" Lou Lou while, in the smoke-filled songwriting cubicles, the young writing teams plunked out and hummed out and argued out a string of three-minute wonders. Being an infant and child in a home of constant, fevered songwriting "was really not an environment where [my parents] could have a family responsibility," the adult Louise Goffin once bluntly told an interviewer. "I was like a kid with other kids, and it's been a long road figuring out how grown-ups actually function in the world."

"These kids!" Kirshner marvels today. "Nobody in America knew who they *were*! But look at all this talent—these ethnic Jewish kids from Queens and Brooklyn, coming up with these universal lyrics!" Whether by way of a kibbitzy warmth that harkened to vaudeville or a serious melancholic literacy that suggested Gershwin, many of "the kids'" songs were also subtly Jewish. At a time when elite colleges still listed "Religion:____" on application forms and enforced anti-Jewish quotas, and when country clubs, fraternities, and sororities rejected applicants on the basis of faith and ethnicity, young Jewish-Americans were incorporating their country's optimism and fairness into eager-to-please records that contributed to a looming spirit that would soon quash the remnants of institutional anti-Semitism.

But it was the far greater injustice of racism that the best of these songs really addressed. Being Jewish, the writers had an understanding of discrimination and an inclination toward social justice, and in some cases (Pomus and Shuman's, Leiber and Stoller's) a serious immersion in, or (Goffin's) an earnest infatuation with, the black experience. And they happened to be writing during one of the most dramatic and heroic periods of American history, just as Martin Luther King Jr. was emerging as America's Gandhi, helping to lead and endure the violent struggles comprising the civil rights movement. The Freedom Rides throughout the South; the lunch counter sit-ins in Greensboro, North Carolina, Nashville, Tennessee, and over a dozen other cities; the brutal fire-hosings and dog attacks ordered by Birmingham police chief Bull

Connor, and the church bombing in that same city that killed four pre-teenage girls; the violent resistance to the enrollment of a single black student, James Meredith, to the University of Mississippi; and the murders of voter registration workers Michael Schwerner, James Chaney, and Andrew Goodman in that state's Neshoba County—all these events transpired during the time that Carole and Gerry were pounding out songs at their Brown Street piano and in their Aldon cubicle. A string of hits the Aldon writers produced—Carole and Gerry's "Up on the Roof," sung by the Drifters; Mann and Weil's "Uptown," sung by the Crystals; and Jerry Leiber and Phil Spector's "Spanish Harlem," sung by the Drifters' Ben E. King as a solo artist—presented the struggles of people of color, not in the South, but in the place the writers knew and loved, New York, through a kind of pop companion-narrative to the civil rights movement. In this pieced-together canon there's an oppressed protagonist ("Everyone's his boss and he's lost in an angry land") who's pushing against almost impossible odds, yet with humanity intact ("It's growing in the street, right up through the concrete")—and, finally, trudging to high ground for a spiritual epiphany: "I climb way up to the top of the stairs, and all my cares just drift right into space." White teenagers in suburban ranch houses may not have been closely watching the struggle in the South, but hints of its essence and grandeur were being laced into their driving-to-school and beach music, and something was rubbing off on them: a taste of the romance of multiethnic urban life and of a concept—"soulfulness"—that was taking hold as a cultural ideal beyond its core group.

Those early days at Aldon were so halcyon, sometimes Donny Kirshner couldn't believe his own life. How did this hard-hocking self-admitted coward from Washington Heights get so lucky? One day in early 1961, for example, he'd just gotten off the bus (he never learned to drive), in South Orange, New Jersey, walked the few blocks home, and picked up the ringing phone. It was his friend Bobby Darin, imploring Kirshner, on behalf of himself and his fiancée, to "get us a rabbi, a priest—*anybody* who can marry us; we'll be there by eight," Kirshner recalls. A week earlier the pair had secretly taken their wedding-license blood tests in the Kirshners' living room; now, here was beautiful blond Sandra Dee (née Douvain)—local girl turned Hollywood star—"in a gorgeous purple coat-dress," walking in and reclining on Donny and Sheila's white Barcalounger, waiting for the clergyman—"and I'm standing there, pinching myself," Kirshner says.

As for the life that Carole tumbled into, it was unique. She and Gerry *had* to become close friends with Barry Mann and Cynthia Weil because, as Cynthia says, "nobody else *lived* like us"—very young, married to their professional partners (with whom they often passionately quarreled), working all the time, and so competitive that when the two couples drove up to the ski house Cynthia and Barry had rented in New Hampshire, they made bets on which couple's songs would be played more on the radio. Carole and Gerry had discovered an exotic new food that few Americans knew about in 1961 (and most wouldn't discover for another twenty years), and they turned their colleagues on to it. After sessions, Mike and Jerry and Carole and Gerry, or Carole and Gerry and Cynthia and Barry, would go to a little Japanese restaurant in Times Square and talk arrangements and demos over the odd, tasty delicacy the Goffins ordered for them: raw fish pressed atop thumb-sized rice blocks—sushi.

Carole and Cynthia's bond, much more than Gerry and Barry's, had a two-against-the-world quality. For although the music industry was full of slightly toughened older women in counterintuitive roles (Jewish women in their forties were frequently managers of male black R&B singers, for example), most *very* young middle-class women did not behave the way Carole and Cynthia did. It was embarrassingly unfeminine in 1961 to be a piano-banging, moon/June rhyming, argumentative workaholic. The ideal was the whispery-voiced, wry-smiling Jackie or the aloof mascot-coquette. A September 1961 *Life* magazine, with Jackie on the cover, ran a long pictorial on the new rage, surfing (which would help spark a fascination with hitherto-boondock Southern California that would, a few years later, draw the music industry there), featuring a photo of a pretty girl with a board. It bears a caption that begins with two sentences that were *not* considered insulting then:

"Most girls lack the strength required of good surfers. Some try hard; others mostly decorate the shallows." *Decorating the shallows* was exactly what cool girls were supposed to do, and do well, and *want* to do. In most late-teen, young-adult circles, Carole and Cynthia would be considered uncool.

Still, if you jumped from the peer to the historical context, Carole and Cynthia were actually filling large—if little-remembered—shoes. The 1920s and 1930s had been a kind of unacknowledged Golden Age of women tunesmiths. There was Dorothy Fields, with her lyrics for "I Can't Give You Anything but Love," "On the Sunny Side of the Street," "A Fine Romance," and "The Way You Look Tonight"; Dana Suesse, who wrote "The Night Is Young and You're So Beautiful" and "You Oughta Be in Pictures"; and Ann Ronell, of "Willow, Weep for Me" and, thumbing its nose at the Depression through Disney cartoon characters, "Who's Afraid of the Big Bad Wolf?"

But for all their historically ballasted success as women songwriters—and their equal if not superior contribution to hit-making with their husbands—Carole and Cynthia reflexively yielded to their men's egos. Their songs were always listed as being written by "Goffin and King" and "Mann and Weil"—guys' names first, period. Both loved their men more than their men loved them. Cynthia, who had been writing theater songs for Frank Loesser's publishing company and who'd then gone to work writing with Teddy Randazzo, had caught sight of Barry Mann—Brooklyn-macho, high-strung, in cowboy boots—when he walked in with Howie Greenfield one day to try to sell a song to Randazzo, and she was so taken by him ("I *had* to know him") that she asked the receptionist where he worked, was told "Aldon"—and applied there simply to meet him. "I got signed by Donny," she admits, "because I was stalking Barry." (They married just about a year later.)

As for Carole and Gerry, the men in and around Aldon saw an unmistakable dynamic between them. Jack Keller, who wrote songs with Gerry two days a week for six years, put it bluntly and forcefully: "Carole was madly in love with Gerry—just *totally* in love with him. It was obvious. There was no doubt. And Gerry? Gerry was probably

not so sure. He was, in my opinion, immature and young." Says Al
Kasha, "I don't want to put Carole down, but she was the unpretty girl
and Gerry, back then, was very handsome. Carole was madly in love
with him; you could see it. But to Gerry, Carole was the girl he got
pregnant." Kasha also noticed something else: "Gerry seemed to vener-
ate black women. If you look at the titles of the songs he wrote–'What
a Sweet Thing That Was,' 'Don't Say Nothin' Bad (About My Baby)'–
they were black titles; they were a black woman speaking."

While "Will You Love Me Tomorrow" was still riding the charts, in
February 1961, Carole and Gerry got their first song recorded by the
Drifters, "Some Kind of Wonderful." After that came another placement, "When My Little Girl Is Smiling," with the group whose strings-
suffused majesty they had "stolen" (as Gerry put it) so profitably. Both
songs were elegiac, lightly soulful love ballads. Mike Stoller remembers
that "Carole and Gerry would come up and play songs for us for the
Drifters. I thought Carole was extremely talented, and I was taken by
how young she was. I liked the way she played her songs, and I *loved*
the way she sang them."

In the sessions, Carole would unself-consciously exert control–her
enthusiasm and confidence simply took over. Just as she had with the
Co-Sines and just as she had with the cellos on "Will You Love Me Tomorrow," she'd proffer her arrangement, instruct in key and phrasing,
play drums or piano, and sing backup. "Carole used to hang in there
with us tough," Drifter Charlie Thomas told author Ken Emerson, in
Always Magic in the Air: The Bomp and Brilliance of the Brill Building Era,
with bemused admiration. "She used to pound down. She wasn't no
hard woman–a girl at her age!–but, Jesus, this woman couldn't sing at
all, and she's going to give *me* the key? But she played the piano, and it
was amazing the songs that she'd give us." Brooks Arthur, who was the
production engineer on Carole and Gerry's demos, also remembers
Carole's "commanding" confidence. "She was very, very strong in her
opinions–she always had a grand vision in her head of a song; she
didn't have to use words; within the piano playing she was spelling the
arrangements out for whoever would cover her songs. And when she

sat down at the piano, it was drop-dead great. Oh, my God—everything sounded like a hit!"

Still, for all Carole's natural assertiveness with singers and musicians—and for all the admiration it inspired—it was Gerry's will and his temper that dominated their sessions together. "Gerry was the boss—the husband: that was clear," said Jack Keller. "They were both very excitable about writing, and it was fun. We were, all of us, intense: me, Barry Mann—we were very intense, very cocky. Howie Greenfield was the kind of guy who would lock the door so Neil couldn't get out until he got that hit. Gerry with Carole, it was the same thing, only Gerry would go in the room with Carole and you could hear Gerry *screaming* at her: 'What's the *matter*?! Are you *crazy*?! Can't you *hear* that chord?!' We would fall on the floor, laughing." Barry Mann says, "It was very frustrating for Gerry to get across to Carole what he wanted to say in a song. He'd try to express himself"—Mann, flailing his hands, pantomimes an agonized attempt to make a point. "He really had a *vision* of a song," but he couldn't play an instrument or read music, so "it would be, 'No, no! *That* chord!' He would get angry—at Carole."

With Gerry the intense partner, Carole was viewed as the lighter. Says Al Kasha, "Carole was more commercial, she wanted hits, and she was so fluent it was scary. Gerry was very deep—almost monosyllabic, but brilliant. He was a very slow writer. Sometimes you write through your head, quickly, or you write through your heart. Everything that Gerry ever wrote, he wrote through his heart; they were feeling-full lines. Richard Rodgers said if melodies don't come fast, they're not going to be good—they have to come intuitively. But lyrics, you have to take time with. Oscar Hammerstein spent a month on the lyrics of 'Oh, What a Beautiful Morning,' and Richard Rodgers wrote the melody in minutes. Hammerstein was Gerry and Rodgers was Carole." Carole's straightforward tradecraft and lack of angst left her open to being somewhat underestimated by others—as well as underestimated *and* taken for granted by Gerry.

* * *

At the time, rhythmic, infectious songs that also invented new dances were deemed to have instant hit potential, thanks to the success of the dance craze known as the Twist. Based on a song of that name, the Twist was conceived in an Atlanta roadhouse in late 1958, courtesy of Hank Ballard and the Midnighters, but popularized by Chubby Checker. By early 1962, it had become the symbol of the "with-it" style of the young upper middle class. Couples in their twenties and early thirties—mover-and-shaker men affecting the rakish air of Sinatra's Rat Pack and the Kennedy brothers; their pretty wives in Courrèges-inspired chemise dresses, with teased-crowned flips mounding up behind matching headbands—were Twisting up a storm at Washington and New York parties and at nightclubs like Manhattan's Peppermint Lounge. The song was hokey even by Top 40 standards. Checker—born Ernest Evans—just repeated the same phrase over and over, in his pleasantly raspy voice. And the dance—elbows out; feet, boxer-stationary on the floor; upper torso and lower torso rhythmically gyrating in opposite directions—wasn't sensual.

But the dance wasn't the point. Rather, the "craze," as it was called, was a pretext for the expression of a rock 'n' roll–born desire. Establishment young marrieds wanted to do something new instead of graduating from youth to some pre-positioned Real Adulthood like their counterparts in the 1940s and 1950s had done. ("What's it *like,* being married?" a friend of the young newlywed Diane Arbus had asked, in awe, in 1941; even for Ethical Culture girls, going from girl to wife had then signaled a piously regarded instant transformation to maturity.) They wanted to take a little of their youth *with* them—to hold on to their freshly obtained rhythms and prerogatives even after they started families, joined country clubs, and entered the halls of power. The Twisting young wives who basked in the Kennedy glow—and the even-younger women who couldn't help but feel drizzled by the stardust sparked by Jack and Jackie's immediate smashing of the template of First Couple dowdiness (Ike and Mamie, Bess and Harry, Eleanor and FDR)—had married right after college and were busy producing their 2.5 children. Their husbands were ambitious and often idealistic, and the women's standards, intelligence, and politics were also expressed in their husbands' vocations; it was understood that the man was achieving for both of them. The women "were holding it all together," as the narrator in Lois Gould's *Such Good Friends,* a novel that reflected this cohort a decade later, put it. They were running the family, acquiring and burnishing social connections, creating a *chic* (that brand-new Jackie word) couple front: Marimekko instead of chintz; fondue pots, not pressure cookers. They were too young for "the problem that has no name" that an older woman, magazine writer Betty Friedan, was now writing a book about—working daily in the New York Public Library, to get away from her children—and they would eventually be the early ones to work, through Friedan's NOW, to change things.

Early marriage and motherhood remained glamorous and appealing. Indeed, many within this cohort of women—which Barbara Raskin would bring to life in her 1987 novel, *Hot Flashes*—would, decades and divorces after the fact, still regard their time of being wives and mothers of young children, during the Kennedy/civil rights years, as their peak experience and the capstone of their identity. The Twist trumpeted the early years of this glamorized youthful domesticity.

Hot on the heels of the Twist came namesake dance songs like Dee Dee Sharp's "Mashed Potato Time," which landed on the charts in 1962. At Aldon, the race was on to create the next dance craze, spurred by Donny's frantic dictate, "We gotta get a smash! We gotta get a smash!" Carole and Gerry came up with "The Loco-Motion." "Everybody's doin' a brand-new dance now / Come on, baby, do the Loco-Motion": These were the kinds of cheerfully inane lyrics Gerry hated to write. Nevertheless, "The Loco-Motion" was pop-perfect, and the Goffins found its saxophone-powered sound in their usual way, with Gerry the dependent visionary and Carole the trusty facilitator. Gerry heard a compelling sax riff while they were watching Bobby Darin at the Copa, and he asked Carole to re-create it. She did so, and they plugged the sound into the demo.

To record "The Loco-Motion," they looked around for a black girl singer who had a voice that sounded as much like Dee Dee Sharp's as possible. They found one—except she wasn't exactly a singer; she was a girl in the neighborhood who had done a bit of backup singing for Carole and Gerry, and whom Carole had recently hired to be Lou Lou's babysitter. Her name was Eva Boyd, and she was nineteen, one year younger than Carole. In the recording studio, Eva Boyd was re-named "Little Eva," and Carole sang background harmonies with her babysitter on the tight, powered song. In weeks—in August 1962—the song reached #1.

Eva Boyd had come into Carole and Gerry's life by way of another nineteen-year-old singer and new mother who lived in Brooklyn, Jeanie (her real name: Earl-Jean) McCrea Reavis. Eva had been visiting her brother in Coney Island one day, and her brother happened to live a couple of doors down from Jeanie and her young husband. Eva and Jeanie became friends, and fledgling-singer Jeanie encouraged Eva to try to sing as well. Jeanie knew that Carole and Gerry needed a baby-sitter because she was a new member of the Cookies, a black girl group that did a lot of Aldon session work. The Cookies had an illustrious history; they had predated even the Chantels. The original Cookies had had a record contract as far back as 1954, had won the highly com-petitive Apollo Amateur Night in 1955, and were then signed by one of Ahmet Ertegun and Jerry Wexler's top A&R men, Jesse Stone, to Atlantic.

On Atlantic, Jeanie's older sister, Darlene McCrea, and Margie Hendrix and Pat Lyles had a top R&B hit, but something more impor-tant happened: Ray Charles saw them and transformed them into his Raelettes, with Margie Hendrix becoming his call-and-response queen (belting out "What kind of man are you?" "Bay-beeee, oh bay-beeee," and "Hit the road, Jack, and don't you come back no more"), as well as his partner in heroin addiction and his lover. In a certain status hier-archy, which would encompass the aspirations of Leiber and Stoller—and Gerry Goffin—the Raelettes were female R&B royalty. So too by extension were the reconstituted Cookies, one of whom was Darlene McCrea's younger sister, Jeanie.

Jeanie McCrea was born in Brooklyn, but the McCrea family had moved back down to North Carolina when she was two. When Jeanie, her sister, Darlene, and their mother—lured by the better factory jobs and the lack of Jim Crow—returned to Brooklyn when Jeanie was a young teenager, they settled in Coney Island. "We were one of only four black families on our block," Jeanie recalls, among "a mixture of Jewish and Christian—mostly Italian—families. We were used to being the minority. But we all played together, the black kids and the Jewish and Italian kids. The kids' parents may not have visited each other, and my parents warned me not to be a 'nuisance' around the white families—'Don't be running in and out of people's houses'—but we *kids* got along fine." Jeanie attended Lincoln High, one of a handful of African American students there in the late 1950s, during which time President Eisenhower expressed a then-prevalent mood about the rights of Negroes in the segregated South by declining Martin Luther King's call for civil rights legislation with the remark, "You can't legislate morality."

Jeanie's mother died; she spent the end of her Lincoln High days living alone with Darlene. Jeanie was painfully shy, and although Darlene and Darlene's friend and fellow Cookie Dorothy Jones thought Jeanie had a fine singing voice—and she did sing in church—Jeanie didn't think her voice was good at all. In fact, she was so self-conscious that another friend, Margaret Williams, "had to hold my hand in glee club at Lincoln, just to give me confidence," Jeanie recalls. Right after graduating Lincoln, Jeanie chose marriage as a way to assert her adulthood. As soon as she turned eighteen, in 1960—"the day that I could sign the papers by myself"—Jeanie married a fellow North-Carolina-to-Brooklyn transplant, nineteen-year-old Grandison Reavis, known as Grant, a construction worker. Jeanie was excited when John Kennedy won the presidency. During the Nixon-Kennedy campaign, black voters, who had traditionally eschewed the Democratic Party because of the segregationist Southern Democrats and stuck with the party of Lincoln, turned to Kennedy when the candidate's brother Bobby Kennedy supported, with ummistakable sincerity—and implored his brother to support—efforts to get Dr. King released from his Georgia jail cell. To

Jeanie McCrea Reavis, as for Carole King, Kennedy's election felt like a new day for America.

Jeanie gave birth to a baby boy, Grandison Jr., and when Jeanie's sister, Darlene, left the Cookies to join the Raelettes, Darlene—and Margaret Williams, who was also now a Cookie—talked Jeanie into joining the group. Jeanie pushed past her shyness, found her pipes, and did so. The Cookies played at Aldon sessions; the men at Aldon found her a welcome addition. "Jeanie was," remembers Al Kasha, "especially pretty." Carole and Gerry wrote a song for the Cookies, "Chains"; between Jeanie's resonant alto, Carole's gospel-plus-Tin-Pan-Alley melody, and Gerry's lyrics combining, as they did, Broadway and black talk ("Chains . . . My baby's got me locked up in chains / But they ain't the kind that you can see"), the song was not only a hit but was seized upon by a then-unknown singer-guitarist in England named John Lennon. (The Beatles later recorded it.)

Carole was pregnant again ("Carole seemed to *always* be pregnant," Cynthia Weil says). In fact, she was so pregnant when she and Gerry attended the BMI Awards ("Will You Love Me Tomorrow" was honored as the Song of the Year of 1961), her acute physical condition, coupled with the very apt meaning of the words of the song she had won for, provided mirth at the festivities. Jerry Wexler watched Carole's father proudly hugging Gerry, while Carole beamed. Remembering the threatening letters Sidney Klein had written him in the summer of 1959, Wexler smiled to himself at how a son-in-law's success could turn a father's disapproving fury into *"schepen nachas"*: a proud, good feeling in the pit of one's stomach. However, though Sidney Klein did not know this, his original suspicion of Gerry Goffin as an unreliable suitor was not without merit.

Carole's desire to please Gerry was evident to their friends. A demo she'd made of a song she and Gerry originally wrote for Bobby Vee, "It Might As Well Rain Until September," was released as a single. It was Carole's own, solo vocal, and it rose to #22. But having his wife as a recording artist displeased Gerry. According to Jack Keller, "Gerry told her, 'That's it—no more records.'"

By now, Gerry had redeemed himself after the cheerful inanity of "The Loco-Motion" with one of the most beautiful songs he and Carole ever wrote—and for the Drifters, to boot. Carole had conceived the elegiac melody in the car one day. The title that the over-busy young songwriter, mother, and wife chose for it was "My Secret Place," signifying an elusive privacy; but Gerry, as homage to his beloved *West Side Story,* renamed it "Up on the Roof." The song employs harmonic twists as the narrator scales the stairs to his tenement's tarred top, which is also his emotional balm, his protection, and ("the only place I know / where you just have to wish to make it so") the launch-site of his fantasies. This couple who in their own lives had resolved the issues of commitment, parenthood, and vocation with such sweeping prematurity now wrote a love song to *irr*esolution: to aching, pining, dreaming. From their anguish-free life they romanticized the flight from anguish—which of course is another way *of* romanticizing anguish. "Up on the Roof" is Gerry Goffin's favorite of the songs he has written, perhaps because it taught him a way out. If he craved some risky melodrama to come along and rescue him from his crushingly old-too-soon life, then he would "just have to wish to make it so." Maybe it was just that simple.

"Up on the Roof" reached #5 in February 1963; Sherry Goffin was born a month later. When Carole went into labor, Cynthia Weil—ever her best friend *and* chief songwriting rival—was happy. Only seventy-two hours of being forcibly removed from the vicinity of a piano would slow Carole down and enable Cynthia to get a jump on her, Cynthia says, only half-jokingly. (Carole's next hit with Gerry, "One Fine Day," for the Chiffons, reached #5 three months after she delivered. The melody of the song—like that of a hit she would write a year later, "Oh No Not My Baby," for Maxine Brown—is plaintive and rapturous, a cut above standard pop fare.) Also soon after Sherry's birth, Carole and Gerry wrote what would be the Cookies' biggest hit, "Don't Say Nothin' Bad (About My Baby)," on which Jeanie McCrea uttered a memorable warning—"So, girl, you better *shut your mouth!*" coining an enduring bit of jargon. This was the season—late summer 1963—of the

March on Washington, when Martin Luther King's "I Have a Dream" speech rang in the air in the space between the Lincoln Memorial and the Washington Monument during what *The New York Times* called "the greatest assembly for a redress of grievances that this capital has ever seen"; and the year that, by some activists' counts, 930 separate civil rights demonstrations took place in 115 cities in the South. The ideals of the movement were effortlessly in place in the smoky, laughter- and argument-filled Goffin-King-Cookies sessions. "Our music world was a little world of its own—everyone was like family," Jeanie recalls. "We related to one another as people; there were no racial issues." Jeanie observed Carole and Gerry's arguments, "but they were *good* arguments; they made the song *work*," and she also saw how "frustrated Gerry would get, trying to express what he wanted to hear in the music."

In early fall the Cookies went on tour. Gerry went with them. Carole stayed home with the children. Barbara Grossman Karyo remembers visiting Carole at Brown Street at this time, "and Carole was upset with Gerry," for reasons she didn't spell out to her old school friend. What Carole might have been hesitant to say is that she suspected that Gerry was having a love affair with Jeanie McCrea. Jack Keller, sounding cornered when approached on the subject, sputtered: "They were *kids*—practically teenagers! Gerry was a kid, in the music business. And a guy may go on the road, producing, while his wife is home. You get what I mean? It's normal. Everybody does it—it's no big deal. All I know, there was an affair and whatever happened after, I don't know." And yet it was what happened after that was notable. For starters, Carole—ever the professional—continued to work with Jeanie, and with Jeanie and Gerry together, even after getting wind that they were romantically involved.

Carole, Gerry, and the Cookies were all back in New York, recording one afternoon toward the end of November. "I don't even remember what we were recording," says Jeanie. "But I was with Carole and Gerry at the time, and we were in the middle of the session—and somebody ran in and said, 'President Kennedy has been shot!' We all went into a state of shock. I can't remember who cried and who didn't, but for all of us, it was like the earth stood still. Everything stopped. We were in suspension. It was like ice thrown at us. There was such sadness. We loved him! He was such a loved president. How could he be dead? How could someone have killed him?"

Further complicating the intense emotions in the recording studio that fateful day was this fact: Jeanie was newly pregnant with Gerry's baby. There was no way that Gerry Goffin was *not* going to claim paternity of this love child, born to this beautiful black woman singer. Such parenthood would transform Gerry into what he yearned to be: soulful, rebellious, black by proxy—in some parts of the country, an outlaw.* Gerry loved *West Side Story;* now he and Jeanie were, symbolically, a version of the musical's forbidden lovers Tony and Maria, singing "Somewhere."

Far from being skittish about the baby, both parents were apparently anticipating the birth, even though they were married to others. The fact that Jeanie and Gerry's baby was welcomed, and perhaps even planned, is confirmed by the "baby" herself. Dawn Reavis Smith says, "I always knew Gerry was my father, and from the time I was five, he always told me I was 'planned.' He said, 'You were wanted, from the beginning.' Later, when I was going off to college, I talked to my mom about it; she said they [she and Gerry] *did* plan to have me. I thought, 'This is opening a can of worms,' since she was married to my stepfather [Grant Reavis] at the time." So, Dawn says, she didn't pursue the subject further with her mother.

As early 1964 turned to middle 1964, Jeanie's pregnancy grew undeniably apparent.

What a state of affairs for Carole! Into her already eventful twenty-two years (two daughters, eight top hits including—once you added Steve Lawrence's saccharine rendition of "Go Away Little Girl" in the

* In 1964 Richard and Mildred Loving could still be jailed if they returned to Virginia, where they had been indicted in 1958 for "miscegenation"; they had recently filed a lawsuit that would lead to the 1967 U.S. Supreme Court decision declaring unconstitutional the ban against interracial marriage in over a dozen other states.

spring of 1963–four #1 hits) was thrown this stunner: The husband
she was madly in love with was proudly having a baby with another
woman. "Did Carole feel betrayed?" a woman who learned of the story
later rhetorically asks. "Well, wouldn't *you* feel betrayed?" Through it
all, however, Carole kept her young marriage intact and continued
working with Gerry–familiarly playing the prolific melody writer to
Gerry's tortured lyricist. Carole even sat by while Gerry–with another
composer, Russ Titelman–wrote a beautiful love song, "I Never
Dreamed," for the Cookies, geared to Jeanie's voice. What today seems
like complacence, even masochism, was then just bad luck with a man.
A woman could leave a man who'd strayed and humiliated her, but
clergymen, marriage counselors, and advice columnists pragmatically
did not recommend it.*

Jeanie gave birth to Gerry's baby, Dawn, in July 1964, while still
married to Grant (they would remain married for years, until his
death). Although this complicated turn of events was a secret to most of
the record industry, and even to many at Aldon (and has remained unknown to the public), those close to the Goffins knew about it. When a
friend from those days mutters, with anger toward Gerry, "Carole was
insecure [about her attractiveness] and Gerry didn't help much," it's a
good bet that the affair with Jeanie is the backstory. Astonishingly (by
today's values), Carole cowrote with Gerry a song specifically for
Jeanie, as a solo artist, "I'm Into Something Good" (which Jeanie recorded and which only later achieved hit status, through Herman's
Hermits). Writing music was what Carole *did;* writing it with *Gerry* was
what she did. Her talent and work energy had always been her calling

---

* There were a lot worse things than infidelity and humiliation, and they weren't con-
demned or illegal. "Domestic violence" didn't exist in the penal code. A man's violence
toward his wife was considered a "family matter" that the police could not be faulted
for not interfering with, and it wasn't even much of a social shibboleth. In fact, it was
so taken for granted that a man's violence to his woman could be a sign of passion that
when Eva Boyd told Carole and Gerry that her boyfriend had struck her during an argument that then turned conciliatory, they wrote a song–impossible to imagine being
written today–called "He Hit Me (and It Felt Like a Kiss)." The Crystals recorded it.
Many radio stations, however, refused to play the record.

card with men, her most comfortable and effective mode of bonding. So, she would stay with Gerry and write songs with him, even songs for Jeanie.

Still, what must it have been like to have your colleagues watch you being cuckolded? In *Superior Women,* her *The Group*–type effort about five women who come of age in the early 1940s, the novelist Alice Adams (whose finest work, *Listening to Billie,* virtually defined midcentury American female bohemia) creates a character named Janet Cohen, a smart, feisty Brooklyn girl married to, and very supportive of, a charismatic playwright named Adam Marr. One night, at a dinner party the couple are hosting after he becomes famous, Marr sadistically lets it be known to the highly discomfited guests that the woman he is infatuated with, and with whom he is forming some significant liaison, is not his wife, Janet, but rather one of the guests, a shy, beautiful black model named Sheila. As Janet's friends ache on behalf of their humiliated friend, "Adam is looking at [Sheila] . . . with the most evident delight, with obvious lust, and absolute admiration, and his look is observed by all his guests, none of whom quite dares to look back at Janet," who is trying to maintain her dignity with her steely pragmatism. Janet would seem a stand-in for Carole in 1964.

Before year's end, Carole and Gerry moved to a tract ranch house in West Orange, New Jersey, one town away from Donny. Cynthia and Barry and Carole and Gerry had recently confronted Donny for better contracts. Kirshner had, without telling them first, sold Aldon—and their contracts—to Columbia/Screen Gems (for the even-then low sum of $3 million) and become head of its music division. But while Cynthia and Barry had made a stand against Donny, Carole and Gerry had not. There was some inexplicable pull between the young couple and the song publisher; the successful Goffins could certainly live without Kirshner and yet not only did they remain in his stable, they put themselves in his geographical locus. Their instinctive need to live near Donny would eventually prove providential.

Also moving to New Jersey at this time were Jeanie and Grant Reavis and their children—or rather, their son and Jeanie's baby daughter with Gerry. Carole and Gerry purchased a house for the family. "They had a lot of money and the Reavises were poor; it was a simple decision for them," says Gerry's next wife, Barbara Behling Goffin, who heard the story from Gerry later. "Carole's attitude was, Gerry was responsible for the baby, so they would do this," says a close friend of hers.*

Carole's tolerance of Gerry's love child and her financial generosity to the baby's mother were not immediately karmically rewarded. The rest of 1964 found her struggling to write decent songs with Gerry, even though Aldon had clearly crested. Its girl groups were being outshone by Motown's Supremes, Marvelettes, and Martha and the Vandellas. And Berry Gordy deftly read the nation's mood, in which the idealization of racial harmony and the love affair with soul music were best served up with tear-wiping buoyance—and with a rhythm section that matched, like the beat of an implanted heart, the bounce of freeway driving and the pulse of young bodies on a dance floor. The services of all those earnest young Alan Freed Show alums were needed no more. As author Ken Emerson puts it, "Berry Gordy's 'Sound of Young America' . . . proved that black artists did not need white writers

---

* "Carole has been wonderful to me," Dawn Reavis Smith says today. Dawn—whose relationship with her father was able to flower once he and Carole divorced, in 1968—was "always" included in postdivorce Gerry's assemblage of his daughters, she says. "Whenever Louise and Sherry were visiting Gerry, Gerry would send for me, too. His brother would pick me up and drive me to him, or I was flown out [to California]. I always felt secure and supported. I never had to search for my father. Louise always knew that we were sisters. Sherry didn't understand it until she was much older; Louise tells a funny story about how for a long time Sherry thought I was her 'soul sister,' not her biological one." Dawn moved with her mother to North Carolina for high school. Jeanie got a degree as an early childhood specialist and opened a day care center; Dawn attended the University of North Carolina at Chapel Hill. Majoring in journalism, she became a TV news reporter for CBS in Greenville, South Carolina, and then for ABC in Little Rock. She married UNC basketball star Kenny Smith, who became a star player for the Houston Astros; they had two children, then amicably divorced. Dawn has remained close with her half sisters, Louise and Sherry, and she was a bridesmaid at Louise's wedding.

carole

Carole and her parents, Sidney and Genie Klein, during their postdivorce reunification, on the steps of their summer cabin at Lake Waubeeka in Danbury, Connecticut, circa 1957. *(Camille Cacciatore Savitz)*

Carole Klein and best friend Camille Cacciatore graduate from James Madison High School in Brooklyn, June 1958. *(Photo by Mary Cacciatore, from collection of Camille Cacciatore Savitz)*

Hardworking teenage young marrieds in love, Carole King and Gerry Goffin take a break from an Aldon recording session in late 1959. She is seventeen, a few months away from giving birth to Louise, and they are about a year away from writing "Will You Love Me Tomorrow." *(Michael Ochs Collection/Getty Images)*

Carole's new life in Laurel Canyon was marked by marriage to Charlie Larkey (far right), and a musical family that included Danny Kortchmar (in front), Connie Falk O'Brien (under Danny's cigarette), Joel O'Brien (smiling, behind Danny), and Ralph Schuckett (far left). *(Richard Corey)*

Carole's new lyricist, Toni Stern, the Sunset Strip–raised bohemian whom all the guys wanted, brought irony and sophistication to Carole's melodies, resulting in *Tapestry*'s biggest hit, "It's Too Late." *(Courtesy of Toni Stern)*

It was Danny Kortchmar's best friend, James Taylor, who, in persuading Carole to play piano for his concert tour, got Carole over her fear of performing. Here, in 1970, Carole and James sing "Up on the Roof" at her alma mater, Queens College. *(© Sherry Rayn Barnett)*

A star-studded moment at the *Tapestry* recording session: James Taylor and his girlfriend, Joni Mitchell, sing backup on Carole's "Will You Love Me Tomorrow." In its original release by the Shirelles, the song had meant a lot to Joni; now Carole was reprising it in her own voice. (© *Jim McCrary, 1971*)

After the huge success of *Tapestry*, Carole tried to hide her fame by playing the role of the classical music student's dowdy wife. Here, she and her husband, Charlie Larkey (far left), join best friends Stephanie and John Fischbach for dinner in Las Vegas in the early 1970s. *(Courtesy of John Fischbach)*

When, in the mid-1970s, Carole fell for Rick Evers, a young Idaho man who'd spent time in prison, her friends worried. He would insist on being pictured on her albums *Simple Things* (shown) and *Welcome Home*, which he influenced. *(Photos by Roy Reynolds for Capitol/EMI, with the permission of Capitol/EMI)*

To Carole's urban friends, fourth husband Rick Sorensen was "Rick Two." In Idaho, he was known as "Teepee Rick." From the late 1970s to the mid-1980s, they raised livestock and fought their neighbors, Custer County, and the federal government over property rights. *(Photo by Dave Brookman for* The Idaho Statesman, *with the permission of* The Idaho Statesman)

When Carole fell in love with screenwriter/director Phil Alden Robinson in the early 1990s, her friends felt she'd finally found the right guy. At a 2002 New York State Writers symposium at which he was speaking, they look happy. *(Judy Axenson)*

Environmentalist and political activist as well as musical legend, Carole campaigned for John Kerry for president in 2004. Here, they're in Missouri. *(Getty Images)*

to reach a broad pop audience." Writing now for a desultory roster consisting of Columbia/Screen Gems TV teen idols Paul Petersen and Shelley Fabares, Carole would remain the unfussy pro while Gerry's mood would darken. At Brown Street Gerry had repeatedly lamented to Jack Keller, "I can't keep writing songs for Bobby Vee; I don't want to do this in five years." His complaint would now grow more desperate. Two events in late 1964—the Beatles' arrival in New York and Bob Dylan's revolutionary supplantation of pop lyrics with poetry—would push Gerry to the brink, putting Carole in danger.

Again, from Alice Adams's *Superior Women:* watching Janet Cohen's dinner-table humiliation at the hands of her husband, and understanding the divorce it portends, one of Janet's friends imagines a silver lining. Freed from her obsession with her husband, "[M]aybe now Janet can go to med school," the friend hopefully muses. Eventually, there would be a similar liberation for the real-life young woman whom Alice Adams's character coincidentally resembled: Carole.

CHAPTER FIVE

joni

1961 – early 1965

Joni had had a style tips column, "Fads and Fashion," in the Aden Bowman Collegiate paper, and she had been the school fashion plate, with her color-coordinated outfits and headbands. So it stood to reason that she would get a job in fashion after high school, while saving for the $800 yearly tuition required by the College of Art within the Southern Alberta Institute of Technology, to which she'd been accepted. A job in fashion in Saskatoon meant selling better junior sportswear at the local department store while doing freelance modeling. (Wholesale clothiers hired models to come to a suite at a local hotel, where the girls became, as Joni has said, "quick-change artists, exhibiting clothes for retail buyers. You wore a black slip and changed behind a screen because you were a young woman working in a hotel room with a traveler.") She had generous employee discounts at the department store, which allowed her to dress to the nines, in stylish ensembles complete with hats and gloves.

Sandy Stewart, Joni's old neighbor from North Battleford—the tomboy with whom she had frequently locked horns over the backyard circuses—had moved to Saskatoon, and at night the friends hung out with the post-high-school/young college crowd at the popular Commodore Café. "We would sip Cokes in the big high booths in the back," Sandy recalls. "It was a neat place where all our friends came—Sugie [Bob Sugarman], Tony Simon, Joan Smith and her fiancé Barry Chapman. We traveled as a group." Joan Smith was planning her wedding; Joni would be an attendant. The senior Andersons—with whom Joni was still living, of course—were welcoming to the crowd. Give or take a few things (immediate college, say), this was the life Joni was supposed to be living.

Sometime in the early autumn of 1962, however, Joni reconnected with D'Arcy Case, the wild child from Lake Waskesiu, now living in Saskatoon. D'Arcy had seen Joni around town in the intervening year, wearing, as she recalls it, "little Jackie Kennedy, princess-line coats. She had a model-y, tight-assed persona, but I *knew* she wasn't that." D'Arcy remembered Joni's poetry, drunkenly recited while D'Arcy had steadied the wobbly Joni on the golf course under the prairie sky.

"I can't remember if I called Joni at the store or at her house," D'Arcy says. "Or maybe she just came into the coffeehouse on her own." The coffeehouse was the Louis Riel, Saskatoon's only folk club, housed in a former library on Saskatoon's Broadway Avenue and named after a Métis (pronounced May-tee: part-European, part-Indian) hero; D'Arcy and her boyfriend, Rudy Hinter, were its managers. "I told Joni, 'All these people come here and sing their poetry. *You* could sing *your* poetry.'"

Walking for the first time into the dark room with its twinkling wall lights, Joni might have felt as if a curtain had just been slashed open on her future. There was D'Arcy in hipster mufti: black, thick-ribbed Dalkeith sweater, dark sheath skirt, and black tights. At top volume, the record player blared Edith Piaf singing "Non, Je Ne Regrette Rien" followed by a Lenny Bruce album. As coffee boy Ralph Martin manned the noisy grinder, the rich aroma of espresso mingled with the pungent hashish snaking up from the performers' lounge in the basement. On the small stage Mickey O'Nate might be trying to vary a stand-up routine that, when heard three nights in a row by the same audience in that one-club town, drew laughs the first night, grimaces the second, and boos the third. Featured singer Karen James would arrive, her twelve-string strapped on her shoulder, her dog, Blue, at her side. Earl, the sandwich man, would drunkenly slice the meat and cheese for his Reubens and hot turkeys. At his corner easel

Rockney McKay brush-stroked his hallucinogenic masterpiece *Nun in Purgatory.* Elsewhere Rene Gold—a bespectacled, Oxbridge-accented young doctor who co-owned the club, drove a Jaguar XKE, and lived in Saskatoon's poshest penthouse—would be hitting on one or both of the waitresses. But the Louis Riel's central melodrama was D'Arcy's. Her coworkers suspected that Rudy had a mean temper. "Poor D'Arcy," the staff would whisper when she'd arrive at work, her face dappled with bruises. This serving of underground life could seduce a tortured rebel. So Joni became a Louis Riel waitress, consigning her Jackie Kennedy suits, gloves, and pillbox hats to the darkest depths of her Hanover Street closet.

Waitressing at a coffeehouse, a jazz club, or an "underground" restaurant was the way girls of the 1960s transformed themselves from onerously middle-class to instantly cool. Such labor was a mark of honorable rebellion, of class-transcendent wisdom—the female version of rich boys doing construction work. (Plus there were always men—*uncorny* men—to tell you you were beautiful.)

By 1962 coffeehouses with folksinger entertainers could be found in most major North American cities. The Louis Riel was owned by four men—three doctors (Ted Tulchinski, Michael Smith, and Rene Gold) and the club's interior designer turned shareholder Colin Holliday-Scott. Indeed, club ownership seemed a man's game by definition: Doug Weston owned L.A.'s Troubadour; Manny Rubin, Philadelphia's Second Fret; in Chicago Albert Grossman's Gate of Horn had prefigured Grossman's management of all the newly minted folk sensations, from Peter, Paul and Mary to Dylan. Yet these early-1960s clubs that proffered Viennese java, plucked chords, and earnest voices were (as opposed to the coffeehouses linked with Beat poetry, Lenny Bruce, and *jazz*—Los Angeles's 1955-opened Unicorn, for example) the heirs of seminal clubs that had been launched by four proprie*tresses.* In 1956 a generous but tough-minded woman named Liz (last name, lost to history) opened the Caricature on Greenwich Village's MacDougal Street, where hungry folkies (whom Liz fed, gratis) strummed and sang when the cops chased them out of Washington Square Park; elegant, blond Tulla Cook founded the Coffee Grinder, which was, in 1957, a haven for Harvard Square's amateur musicians; and two twenty-three-year-old Brandeis graduates, Paula Kelley and Joyce Kalina, bought a nearby antique store and, doing the electrical wiring themselves, turned it into Club 47. Within a year Kelley and Kalina showcased a girl who was everything a female entertainer in the late 1950s was not supposed to be—somber, drably dressed, not conventionally beautiful—yet she drew an SRO crowd of tweed-jacketed Harvard men. Her name was Joan Baez.

The 1960 mainstream ascendance of folk music, by way of Baez (hit album, *Time* cover, thousands of young girl clones all over America) was actually two years in the making. The Big Bang had been the Kingston Trio's 1958 surprise #1 hit, "Tom Dooley," a reworking of a Civil War-era ballad about the hanging of a man who'd killed his love (the last folk hit before *that* had been the Weavers' version of "Goodnight, Irene," which had reached #10 in 1948). It was through the congenial, wholesome trio that a whole generation of college students began singing "Michael, Row the Boat Ashore" and "Kumbaya" at fraternity campouts and incorporating a watered-down version of the folk ethos into their sensibility.

Of course, the emerging folk sensibility for which the Kingston Trio served as unthreatening appetizer was actually quietly revolutionary. One of its two founding fathers, Pete Seeger (from whom Trio founder Dave Guard had bought his first guitar in 1954), was blacklisted for his membership in the Communist party and had served as a self-styled "Johnny Appleseed of protest music," publishing instruction books (Joni had bought one) that taught young people how to appropriate the musical genre that he was banned from performing. Well before that—in 1939—in the communelike Almanac House on West Tenth Street in Greenwich Village, Seeger, sometimes the revered Woody Guthrie, and others wrote new songs that sounded like real Southern and rural working-folks' plaints. Writing respectfully faux "people's songs" was the closest that many folksingers got to the Appalachian hollows, road gangs, and steel mills. (Bob Dylan spent many weeks looking at nineteenth-century newspapers at the New York Public Library to inspire his own writing.) The music Seeger's followers made popular eventually pushed left-wing social protest—against the bomb, the blacklist, the arms race, and particularly for civil rights—in from the red-diaper-baby margins of society to the center of youthful concern, popularizing an aesthetic that valued the unpolished and handmade over the mass-produced and the commercial.

Most histories of the folk resurgence stress its political import and gloss over the fact that its dramas were vicarious. And they bear a masculine imprint. The Kingston Trio were male. Pete Seeger and Woody Guthrie were male. So was Huddie Ledbetter, a.k.a. Lead Belly, who thrilled young white middle-class folk devotees by being the genuine article: a black man whose voice carried the pain of the Jim Crow South and who'd done real time on prison chain gangs. (He was a convicted murderer.) And, of course, the artist who eventually vaulted folk music into the social and cultural epicenter, essentially inventing the American counterculture—Bob Dylan—was male. Other than Lead Belly, these folk avatars got their material from their sympathetic imaginations and old newspapers. Yet for all the masculine icons and political themes, what was so quietly significant about the rise of folk music among North American youth in the late 1950s was that it kicked wide the door to *female* storytelling—and storytelling based on an exaggerated version of *real*, not imagined, experience (family treachery, mating and pregnancy, all larded with troubling consequences). Folk, in the 1950s, allowed young women to use deceptively ultratraditional vessels (high, pure, trilling voices; long skirts and hair; imagery of hearth, heart, and childbirth) to test social and cultural limits and to mine an antique lode of tough-minded songs about emotional wars and reproductive perfidies.

This lode was the Child Ballads, the group of Scottish and English topical tales that had been handed down on the Scottish moors since the sixteenth century. Nineteenth-century English folklorist Francis James Child had collected and codified these antique story-songs—hence their name—and they became a substantial part of the playlist of the new American folksingers, many of whom, in the mid-1950s, were women: Jean Redpath, Judy Henske, Bonnie Dobson, Jo Mapes, Peggy Seeger, and breakthrough artist Carolyn Hester, a Texan who moved to the Upper West Side of Manhattan early in the decade to perform at Greenwich

Village's folk clubs, and whose sensual good looks paved the way for the phenomenon that was Joan Baez. In voices clear as running brooks, with a pious-sounding sorrow that camouflaged their sometimes violent messages, these women sang Child Ballads such as "Greensleeves," "Barbara Allen," "Maid of Constant Sorrow," "Geordie," and "Mary Hamilton."

Although the Child Ballads were anonymous, Drake University historian Deborah A. Symonds recently unearthed the fact that their nameless writers were overwhelmingly—ten to one—female. Employing the mayhem of the earlier male battle ballads, the women of the Early Modern Age wrote of their own battles, which were every bit as bloody as the crashing clank of sword on chain mail: murders of lovers, murders of spouses, murders of sisters. Then, as feudal life in Scotland and northern England gave way to the agricultural revolution of the eighteenth century, the ballads became obsessed with a single subject: these hard-pressed women's abandonment of their infants and, in the frequent extreme, their desperation-bred acts of infanticide (as in "Mary Hamilton").

The intense refocusing of the ballads' subject matter reflected events in the changing society. In feudal days, a woman's pregnancy would trigger a betrothal, and the newly married couple would live on the family's land. But with the buying up of small farms in the eighteenth century by the emerging bourgeoisie, the poor were left landless—you couldn't marry without land to live on—so the young poor *stopped* marrying. While the shamed, land-poor menfolk ran away to join the army, the shamed pregnant women were left to bear out-of-wedlock children in vast number. A novel, *The Heart of Midlothian,* was written about the phenomenon—as it happened, by the man that an ancestor on Joni Anderson's mother's side had worked for, Sir Walter Scott. Probably out of reader-friendliness, Scott made the heroine ladylike, wealthy, and sympathetic: her midwife, not she, kills the baby. But when scholar Symonds embarked on her research on the real stories behind the Child Ballads (culminating in *Weep Not for Me: Women, Ballads, and Infanticide in Early Modern Scotland*), she discovered that the actual woman upon whom Scott based his novel was not a wronged noblewoman but a poor commoner, and she was not innocent but guilty. Terror at giving birth unmarried had led her to smother her child rather than abandon it to inevitable slow death by cold, starvation, and scavenging animals. Yet, Symonds found, after the mother did the deed, she virtually begged to be found out. She interred the newborn in a shallow grave, along with a clue: a half-buried remnant of her own easily identifiable garment. With this boldly self-indicting gesture, she announced to her village that her guilt and her sorrow were painfully real but were devoid of shame or dishonesty.

To bear a baby out of wedlock during a time of social revolution when young people, in large number, had stopped getting married; to "cold-heartedly" relinquish the infant while leaving clues of your guilty act; to sing about it and your life, somewhat transforming the culture in the process: this antiquated pattern of the Scottish moors, which gave birth to so many songs, would be repeated. By Joni Anderson Mitchell.

Unsupportable pregnancy leapt the centuries and the ocean as a pressing issue for women in folk music. Betsy Minot, who worked in the Boston/ Cambridge folk clubs and formed the folkie-girl best-friendship with Joan Baez and Debbie Green, remembers how dangerous and harrowing it was to get a safe abortion in the late 1950s and early 1960s, even if, as she was, you were privileged and connected. Dave Van Ronk, whom Dylan had anointed the "king" of MacDougal Street, remembers, during that time, the girls who hung out at the Caricature pulling each other aside for nervous "consultations" about, Van Ronk rightfully inferred, pregnancy worries.

But to be pregnant and unmarried in midwestern Canada in the early 1960s incited far more terror than to bear that burden in worldly Boston or Manhattan. In the early months of 1963, Joni Anderson and the other women at the Louis Riel watched stridently bohemian D'Arcy lose her cool and start to grow panicked and flustered over her imminent fate as an unwed mother. "It was all shame, shame, shame, *double* shame, to be pregnant and not married," D'Arcy recalls. "It was just awful to 'get caught' by pregnancy. Somehow we thought, with the wishing and pull-it-out method, we'd never get caught. Abortions were too danger-ous. You'd hear stories from girls in our circle—a couple of them had frightening illegal abortions: you'd go in and there'd be this dirty old cot. Three doctors owned our coffeehouse—and they were from more-forward-thinking England—but even *they* weren't going to help me! Al-though one of them did give me a bottle of saline solution and said, 'This might do something,' and I remember standing in the bathroom and then, in a flash, thinking, 'I can't handle this!' and flushing it down the toilet." As the weeks went by, the young women in the Riel—Joni in-cluded—noticed, with anxious sympathy, D'Arcy growing more desperate and struggling into pregnancy-disguising girdles, a sight that drove home the mores of their provincial community. In Canada in the early to mid-1960s, Joni would later say, "the scandal [of unwed pregnancy] was so intense. The main thing at the time was to conceal it. A daughter could do nothing more disgraceful. It ruined you in a social sense. You have no idea what the stigma was. It was like you murdered somebody."

During these months Joni was changing her persona. She was now wearing her hair long and straight—"She was a very nice little waitress who looked like a hippie; she wore furry hats and what I thought of as bag-lady clothes," the club's co-owner Colin Holliday-Scott recalls. "She had contempt for me because I was so straight and conservative, a Perry Como fan. She had attitude." In this freshly bohemian guise, "Joni used to come to my apartment, which was above a plumbing shop," D'Arcy recalls, "and once she painted a whole wall with a tree with triangle leaves, each with a different poetic saying."

But Joni was more eager to express her creativity through music than through art—and publicly. So one day she strode up to the mic at the Louis Riel's Sunday night hootenanny.* She started strumming her uku-lele, she opened her mouth to sing—"and she sounded unlike anything

---

* Weekly hootenannies—anyone who wanted to could sing—harkened back to Seeger's Almanac House and became a tradition in clubs, in coffeehouses, and on college cam-puses everywhere.

we'd been used to hearing," D'Arcy recalls, "Everybody thought she sounded very weird and off-key. People were raising their eyebrows, like, 'This isn't folk music—this is really odd.'"

Still, Joni was committed to performing, and she made her case to D'Arcy's boyfriend, the club's co-manager Rudy Hinter. Hinter asked Colin Holliday-Scott and Rene Gold if they would give Joni a chance to pinch-hit in an emergency. The two owners agreed to listen to the pretty waitress sing and then consider it.

Joni's audition yielded sharply divergent opinions. Holliday-Scott recalls, "I thought, 'Oh my God, she's awful. She's a laughingstock, this girl with this ridiculous voice.' It was so different, not mainstream; she would change her pitch a lot." But Rene Gold vehemently disagreed. He said, "Colin, I think this girl has got something." Within weeks, featured entertainers Sonny Terry and Brownie McGhee sent word through their manager that they would be one week late for their scheduled engagement. Rudy and D'Arcy pushed to allow Joni to fill in, and Rene Gold was in their corner. Holliday-Scott recalls, "I said, 'You're all mad!' but Rudy was so keen on it. So, though I had great reservations about Joni, I ended up saying, 'All right, if you think so, I'll let her sing for the two weeks.'" To his surprise, during the November 5 to 14 engagement, "the crowd received her much better than I thought they would. Those young people *really* liked her." From then on—spring and summer 1963—when a featured performer couldn't make it, either Joni Anderson, paid in tips alone, or a local group called the Nomads would substitute.

Through these sporadic evenings in which she doubled as entertainer, Joni was developing a following, and she was determined to improve her musicianship. "Joni wanted to play better," recalls Shawn Phillips, a featured performer at the Riel. "I distinctly remember telling her that anything she could do at the lower end of the guitar neck she could do higher up. I think she was intrigued by my use of nonstandard chords" on his signature "The Bells of Rhymney," in which Pete Seeger embellished and set to music the words of a coal-miner friend of Dylan Thomas, yielding a song—

Oh what will you give me
Say the sad bells of Rhymney . . .

—that was typical of the romantic, half- or faux-archaic songs that were
then so popular.

Joni has said she was fascinated by Phillips. "He was the first person
I'd ever known who had written a song. For some reason that was really
intriguing to me, really exotic." Joni's awe at the new world she was in
was not lost on Phillips. "Joni was curious," Shawn says. "There was that
glint in her eye—she wasn't asleep at the wheel, like most inhabitants of
a small town are. She had the sense that many young people who grow
up in the stifling ambience of rural communities have—that there was
certainly something *more* to the world than Saskatoon."

Wearing a veil, a long white wedding gown—and an extremely tight
girdle to hide her three-month pregnancy—D'Arcy Case married Rudy
Hinter in a proper ceremony in a high-vaulted local Anglican church on
May 11, 1963. Joni was a wedding guest. A special entertainment was
built into the ceremony. Just before D'Arcy walked down the aisle, from
the balcony two soaring-voiced young male Negro singers stood and delivered a stirring hymn in the formal timbre and phrasing that recalled
Paul Robeson but with a folk and gospel undertone. The singing wedding
guests were Joe Gilbert, a tenor, and Eddie Brown, a baritone—two very
handsome young men in the Harry Belafonte mold, from California's Bay
Area. They were wearing, as they did in their performances at the Riel
and other clubs, matching small-shouldered jackets with skinny lapels.
In the elite world of black folksingers (of which Josh White was king) the
pair—billed as Joe & Eddie and possessed of a chart hit, "There's a Meetin'
Here Tonight"—were the strongest comers. For years they had been favorites at campus parties at the University of California in their native
Berkeley; then they had played San Francisco's legendary Hungry i. As
their discoverer and producer Gene Norman, of Crescendo Records, put it
in the liner notes to their first album, "They appeal to every age and musical preference group . . . The teenage 'Top 40' fan, the college crowd,
the ethnic folknik, the gospel fan, the old-timers who simply enjoy good

old two-part harmony—Joe and Eddie reach them all." They had just appeared on television's *The Danny Kaye Show.*

Of the two, Joe—compact, honey-skinned, particularly handsome—was the ladykiller. With his furrowed brow and his sensual lips, set in a generous jaw, he radiated intensity. Joni turned her head up to the balcony as they sang and noticed him. Afterward, at the reception, she and Joe moved toward each other and began talking. They made a striking pair—two beautiful, trim, poised young people of counterpoint complexions. They did more talking at the Louis Riel that week, between Joni's bobbing and weaving among the tables with her trays full of steamed coffee and sandwiches, and Joe's spirited duetting with Eddie on "[They Call the Wind] Mariah" and "Children, Go Where I Send Thee."

Joe and Eddie were staying with D'Arcy and Rudy, who now had a large home with a pool. The Hinters played host to the club's black singers, who felt uncomfortable in the nearly milk-white outpost. (When, originally, D'Arcy had driven Sonny Terry and Brownie McGhee to the best hotel in town, the medieval-castle-like Bessborough, where she expected them to check in, the two snapped at the naïve little white girl, "You don't know *nothing.* We can't stay *here.*" "They looked like they were about to be lynched," recalls D'Arcy. After that, Terry and McGhee stayed at D'Arcy and Rudy's house whenever they played the Riel. So did folksinger Len Chandler, who came to Saskatoon with his white wife, Nancy, and didn't want to be hassled.)*

Joe and Eddie stayed with the newly married Hinters, but not out of fear of standing out in an all-white hotel. "They had none of that old-school attitude: acting so polite, being scared of the white authorities,"

---

* Folk-world mixed couples were routinely set upon, even in relatively sophisticated Los Angeles; and, as a measure of the violent disapproval for interracial unions, even white girls who were simply socializing with friends who happened to be mixed couples were "sent a message" by the authorities. Around this same time Tamar Hodel, the young white wife of black folksinger Stan Wilson, and her best friend, teenage Michelle Gilliam—soon to be Mama Michelle Phillips of the Mamas and the Papas—had been rounded up by cops who had burst into a social gathering. Tamar and Michelle were driven to an L.A. station and booked. Tamar, being married to a black man, was *a priori* in jeopardy. But Michelle's "crime"? According to the angry sergeant: being "at that party with all those niggers."

says D'Arcy. Rather, they did so for comfort and camaraderie. "Both of them were married, but their wives didn't come with them on the road"; staying at a private home and getting home-cooked meals was a perk. The two were different. "Eddie was a big softie, but Joe was arrogant— *very* arrogant," D'Arcy recalls. "So arrogant he was almost mean. That Joe, he could break any girl's heart."

D'Arcy noticed that Joni Anderson was falling for Joe. A romance seemed to be blooming between them—either that or, D'Arcy hastens to add, it may have been "just a meeting of the minds" or a case of "love of the person and the musical sounds they were producing." Whatever the scope of the infatuation, one night D'Arcy took Joni aside and, in an effort to protect her, said, "Look, Joni, it will never work—Joe's married!" But the warning seemed to fall on deaf ears. "I think she fell in love with him," D'Arcy says.

In the fall of 1963 a very pregnant D'Arcy Case, despondent in her marriage to her abusive husband, tried to throw herself off a building. After the failed suicide attempt, D'Arcy was hospitalized with "situational depression"; out of concern for the health of her unborn baby, she refused medication—and then, faced with the likelihood that the baby (a girl, born in November 1963) could be legally snatched away from her, she "got sane, real fast," as she puts it.* The lesson implicit in D'Arcy's near-tragedy—that serious misery could ensue when panic and shame forced a pregnant girl to marry the wrong man, just for respectability—would soon prove a useful cautionary tale to Joni Anderson.

The Southern Alberta Institute of Technology—SAIT, as it was called— was a pair of buildings: a modern one of brick and glass and a stately Gothic counterpart, both set on a wide-lawned campus in Calgary, Alberta. There—engulfed by the institute's main student body (one thousand slide-rule-wielding crew-cut males majoring in aeronautical

---

* D'Arcy went on to have a successful career as a UN-affiliated international forestry consultant. She now owns a bed-and-breakfast in western Canada with her daughter.

engineering, aircraft maintenance, agricultural mechanics, commercial radio, diesel mechanics, power plant engineering, and a half dozen similar fields)—as if air-dropped from a separate planet, were 160 *other* students. Most of them were sporting goatees, growing out their own crew-cuts into greasy ponytails, donning T-shirts with holes in them, and inwardly smiling triumphantly as—in a touché to their farm-raised parents' puzzled disapproval of their career choice—they charcoal-sketched every curve of the nude models in life drawing class. These were the students in SAIT's College of Art. Although the engineering students probably thought, as one art student surmised, "Who *are* these kooks?" the art students were proud of their individualism and thrilled to be drawn together like kindred needles culled from the vast haystack of central Canada. As one of them, Bruce Sterling, says, "We were all small-town country kids trying to be Jackson Pollock."

The other thing that distinguished the College of Art from most of the rest of SAIT was women—something the industrial students took note of, by way of gauntlets of wolf whistles. Every third art student was female and, judging from the 1964 yearbook, many of them were lovely, stylish girls—girls with gamey smiles and teased bubbles and flips ("We were still back-combing our hair, but we were hippies," says Joni's classmate Beverly Nodwell DeJong) and some with long, Left Bank–worthy tresses and serious, penetrating gazes. Among the loveliest was Joni Anderson, whose class photo shows her with a bouffant-topped, thick-banged "shelf pageboy," the popular hairstyle that year, attained by setting the rollers vertically. Joni was still assuming that art, not music, would be her calling.

Although she'd come from a year of sophisticated coffeehouse life—and, just as college was starting, had traveled north to take the stage with her guitar at the Yardbird Suite and the Depression, two coffeehouses in Edmonton—she had the same "quiet country girl" way about her as the other students, Bruce Sterling recalls. "But she also seemed driven, and equally so about art and music." Beverly DeJong remembers "a presence about Joni, a *strength*." Sterling adds something else: while many of the girls switched from skirts to pants as the freshman year wore on, "Joni continued wearing skirts all year. And she always smelled good. She maintained a straitlaced, ladylike air with the administration and the teachers, and she became one of their favorites."

As a freshman art student, Joni took the required curriculum—two drawing courses: one expressive, the other analytical; the history of art; an English course; elements and principles of art (composition in second semester); and an elective: introduction to painting or printmaking, textiles, or ceramics. Joni was talented; fellow student Doug Bovee recalls her paintings were "very poetic—she was not someone who handled high realism very well, but they always had a lyrical quality—the figures were elongated"; Beverly DeJong cites her "beautiful drawings: flowers and self-portraits." Most of the young women in her class were also talented—showing one's work was a prerequisite for enrollment. But while women comprised a third of the art school, the prevailing sentiment was that important artists were, by definition, male. Not one of the 2,300 artists cited in H. W. Janson's *History of Art* (the seminal text at the time) was female. On New York's Abstract Expressionist/Color Field scene—the students' lodestar—amid Pollock, Still, de Kooning, Motherwell, Rivers, Rothko, Twombly, and Noland, there were very few women, chiefly Helen Frankenthaler and an American named (coincidentally) Joan Mitchell, who moved to Paris. This Cedar Tavern/Tenth Street galleries crowd was high-testosterone; its females were either gallery owners like Betty Parsons, or artists-turned-husband-managers like Lee Krasner, or molls, like Larry Rivers's mate Maxine Groffsky, a literary agent in her inconspicuous nonloft life, and Ruth Kligman, the crowd's Elizabeth Taylor in both appearance and romantic appetite, who quickly went from mourning her lover Jackson Pollock (dead in the drunken car crash she'd survived) to romancing Willem de Kooning. In this two-fisted set it helped that a woman artist be beautiful, like Eva Hesse, or beautiful *and* towering, like Marisol.

That gender assumption was alive and well at SAIT. Beverly DeJong, who today makes large architectural installations, remembers that shortly after she arrived there, "a male guidance counselor told me, 'You should go into crafts. My wife did that and she always had fun, teaching children.' And there were discussions with male students about it; a friend was absolutely *certain* he should be paid more for an art job than me. A few years

later I joined the staff of the art college—I was the only female among fifty
instructors from 1969 to 1976—and, sure enough, I got paid less than the
men." Of the many art instructors in 1963-64, all were men, DeJong recalls, except Marion Nicholl, an Abstract Expressionist and a large woman
"who wore muumuus and always seemed angry that she had to be teaching rather than painting, but that made her more endearing."

Joni has said that the school's emphasis on Abstract Expressionism
turned her off, though George Mihalcheon, a painter and painting
teacher who was on its faculty, says that, though Ab-Ex prevailed in
painting, "the college had ten different disciplines at the time; it's hard
to say there was a common direction." Whatever the reason, "music was
part of Joni's life in that school, from day one. She used to sit in the
hallway and pluck her guitar," recalls classmate Doug Bovee. "She played
the guitar in the washroom—the bathroom," Beverly DeJong says. Then
she started performing at lunchtime—on a little raised platform, in the
foyer of the auditorium, which was right across from the cafeteria, so all
the students could hear it. "She was pretty good," remembers ceramics
teacher Walter Drohan. "We thought she was leaning more toward enter-
taining than art." "Many, many lunch hours, Joni would be in the foyer,
or in the auditorium itself, singing," Bruce Sterling recalls. "Songs like
'Kumbaya.' We were all very political. The day Kennedy was assassinated
everyone congregated together. A lot of us felt very close to him—he
was going to save the world for *us,* too. Except there were also anti-
American Canadians, who were mad at Kennedy for antagonizing the
Russians during the Cuban missile crisis and who figured the Russians
would come down from the north on *us,* not the U.S. They figured he got
what was coming to him. The school was polarized when Kennedy was
assassinated. I don't remember which side Joni was on, but she was very
vocal and political in favor of the civil rights movement, so she probably
mourned Kennedy, like most of us did."

Soon hootenannies were set up in the auditorium at lunch hour and
after classes, and Joni—in her shelf pageboy and her proper skirt and
blouse—was the main performer, seated before a dramatic, Bosch-like stu-
dent-painted mural of Viking dragon slayers. A teacher from the indus-

trial drafting department who was also an amateur folksinger—a man in his thirties named Eric Whittred—formed a duo with her. "Ours was a strictly off-the-cuff presentation, but she certainly had talent and a lovely voice," Whittred recalls. "Joni did a beautiful job on a Kingston Trio song, 'Oh, Sail Away'—it moved me, and many of us. We would sing 'Sloop John B' and 'Jamaica Farewell,' songs by the Kingston Trio and Harry Belafonte. 'Tom Dooley' was at the height of its popularity"—actually, it had been a hit five years earlier—"so we definitely did that." As SAIT students gathered around and sang and swayed in unison, Joni Anderson and Eric Whittred sang "Michael, Row the Boat Ashore," "The Whiffenpoof Song," "Lemon Tree," and Bob Dylan's "Blowin' in the Wind," which had been a hit for Peter, Paul and Mary the previous summer. Joni was aware of Dylan by now (and in her earliest appearances in Canada, in the coming year, her look would be compared to Mary Travers's), though it would not be until he blared out "You got a lot of nerve, to say you are my friend . . ." in the opening bars of "Positively 4th Street" in September 1965 that it came to her, like a lightning bolt, that "you could write about *anything*. It was a different kind of song than I had ever heard."

On weekends Joni played the local clubs—mainly the Fourth Dimension— "singing long, tragic songs in a minor key," as she puts it. Joni's eminence as the campus folksinger, her beauty, and her growing self-possession made her extremely popular. "There were lots of suitors at her door—and, unfortunately, I wasn't one of them, not that I didn't try," says Bruce Sterling, adding that Joni's popularity could make her "aloof" and argumentative. "One day she would be going on, with her social consciousness, about the poor bum on the street, and the next day she'd walk right by him; but if you called her attention to her inconsistency, she'd snap at you." But she also exuded kindness. "She was very patient and compassionate to Doug Bovee," Sterling remembers. Bovee had had polio as a child—even before the great epidemic of 1953, to which Joni had fallen victim—and he had been irreversibly affected. He got around campus in long-arm braces and sometimes in a wheelchair. "Our lockers were near each other's, and Joni would help me get things out of mine if I couldn't reach them" Bovee says. "I think she respected me— or maybe she feared me. Maybe it was 'There but for fortune go I.'" Joni never told Bovee that she, too, had had polio; he learned this only after she was famous and the polio story became a dramatic, character-revealing part of her biography. No one at the art school knew. The symptoms of the childhood brush with the disease were gone, and, plunging into adulthood, she was keeping the frightening past *in* the past.

Joni, who had spent her post-polio girlhood negotiating the fine line between the "good girl" and "bad girl" dichotomy that existed in middle-class society, had now found a way to master it. Safely far from home, she developed a dual persona, alternating the department-store-model propriety with the coffeehouse freedom. Off campus, "she was a bit of a party gal," says Doug Bovee. "There was a restlessness on her part; she was in the fast lane of the fast group." Bruce Sterling says, "For all her straitlaced appearance in school, when she was down at the clubs she drank hardy, and she was kind of an animal, making sexual innuendos [sic] at the guys. She was picking up guys and letting them pick her up, putting out signals and spending time in cars and going places. She had lots of boyfriends at the time, boyfriends in the real sense"—at least from what he *heard*. How did he know? Reliably or unreliably: "Guys talk."

In school, however, she took care to keep the alternate image burnished. SAIT had a beauty contest for queen of the school every year, and since the vast majority of the females in the school were in the art school, the pressure was on the pretty art students to enter. One of the most respected art teachers, George Anglis, told the women in his class they shouldn't yield to that pressure. "He said, 'Don't run for queen, it will take too much time away from your work,'" recalls Beverly Nodwell DeJong, who at the time was an extremely fetching brunette who could easily have been a contender. Beverly took the teacher's advice and didn't toss her hat in the ring. Joni Anderson did, however.

The six queen candidates lined up for a photo in virtually identical dark, below-knee-length suits, black pocketbooks looped on their arms. They looked like a ladies' luncheon group or a sextet of dowdy stewardesses. Joni stands out: her expression, professionally camera-friendly; her suit, chic and youthful; her stance model-like; her accessories (long black gloves, arty brooch), cutting-edge. Unlike the others, she knew how to present herself in public, even in this conventional guise. The campaign poster she made for herself (a vertical, doubled "JOAN" next to a horizontal "Anderson," with action-painter splotches over a self-portrait) was more sophisticated than the others. The student body voted. Joni was runner-up to Queen Sheila Dalgarno, a thick-eyebrowed brunette with chiseled features who'd had the advantage of being not in the art college but in lab tech.

At some point in the middle of the school year, Joni moved out of her rented room in a private house and formed what was, in early 1964, an avant-garde arrangement: she took a second-floor loft in an old warehouse in town with her boyfriend, a tall, thin, goateed fellow art freshman, Rick Williams. Joni kept the cohabitation secret from her parents.

Rick Williams hailed from a small town in British Columbia and had a warm laugh. Their loft, Doug Bovee recalls, "had a mattress thrown on the floor, a few drapes, and a lot of paintings against the wall—a great place for a party, and they had them. People would drift in and out on the weekends. There was booze, and someone might bring in some pizza. They played 'heavy' stuff: Dylan, jazz, maybe some early Beatles. No Motown. We were 'deep.' Everyone went to see Ingmar Bergman's *The Seventh Seal* and *The Virgin Spring* at the local film festival. We were hippies." The word *hippie* was one year shy of coinage, but the concept was emerging. "We wore casual clothes, our ratty hair tied back. And acid was the drug of choice."

Acid, of course, was LSD (lysergic acid diethylamide), which was openly traded in class for $2 a tab, having freshly become available through a rapid-fire underground grapevine of psychology and art students all through North America. At a time when many long-distance phone calls were still made through an operator and Special Delivery was the fastest—and emergency-only—means of travel for messages exceeding telegram length, the speed of the news about consciousness-expanding drugs (and the dissemination of those drugs themselves), even to the hinterland likes of Calgary, Alberta, spoke volumes about an inchoate readiness for a new sensibility: a deeper window into mind and body, spirit and human connection.

LSD was first created in 1938 in a chemical lab by adding compounds to a base of lysergic acid (which is found in a grain fungus, ergot). In the 1950s, extra-medical interest in it and natural sister compounds was revived by Aldous Huxley's reports of his experiments with mescaline and then later in the decade stoked by a *Life* magazine article that described the use of psilocybin mushrooms in indigenous Mexican religious ceremonies. Harvard psychology lecturer Timothy Leary and professor Richard Alpert soon began conducting research on psilocybin and LSD with graduate students; the professors' pro-ecstatic bent ("[W]e are attempting to create a new paganism and a new dedication to life as art," Leary wrote) resulted in their dismissal from Harvard, whereupon their mystique intensified. While Joni was living with Rick Williams in their painting-strewn party loft, to the west and down the coast in northern California Augustus Owsley Stanley III was perfecting the mass manufacture of LSD, opening the way for its more efficient dissemination, which would, along with other forces, spark the psychedelic era. Riding the toggle switch of her high good girl/bad girl life, Joni Anderson in 1964 could probably not imagine that the earmarks of the gentler, pensive side of psychedelic style (verbal free association; emotional depth and bravery; flowing hair and raiment; serpentine graphics) would be her ticket to the success that she was only now beginning to actively desire.

Increasingly, Joni spent weekends in nearby Edmonton, where she performed at the Yardbird Suite. Sometimes she ventured to coffeehouses in Regina and Winnipeg. "So I was leading this dual life, half in art and half in music," she has said. Her insecure first efforts at the Louis Riel, where everyone had thought her voice "weird," had given way, through these months of hootenannies and club performing, to a developed vocal style and a confidence at the microphone. Folksinger Chick Roberts first saw her in the Regina and Winnipeg clubs, "doing covers of others' songs," of course—"and she knocked me out. She was very gorgeous, very ethereal, lovely, with her blond hair." Her voice tone had modulated. "She sang great."

With her folksinging career modestly launched, Joni was growing frustrated by the strictures of art college. "You wouldn't touch color until semesters of black and white; you had to have a lot of basic aesthetic and skeletal understanding of anatomy," says Beverly DeJong. Joni has told interviewers that she became "very disillusioned that there were people around me getting C's because their technical ability was only average, even though their creative ability and originality was greater than mine. This was something I recognized, so at the end of the year I quit art college and began a search through music."

True enough, to a point. Joni did leave at the end of the first year, and to pursue music. But she had an additional motive.

At some point in the second semester Joni and Rick Williams broke up, and another first-year art classmate with whom Joni had been friends became her boyfriend. His name was Brad MacMath. He was from Regina, and he was very handsome: extremely tall with piercingly deep-set, up-slanted eyes and high cheekbones. Like Joni, he switch-hit straight and wild, though on campus he, too, cut a deceptively clean-cut figure. "He seemed more Ivy League, button-down," Bruce Sterling says. Yet he was such a freeloader and a cigarette bummer that, Joni would later wryly recall to friends, for his birthday, she bought him a glass-bottomed pewter mug, with the endearment "The Mooch" engraved on it. And in their subsequent hitchhiking, Brad's reluctance to bathe left him with, as her friends say she reported, "the worst BO she ever smelled."

Joni has told the media and even confidantes (who believe the story, which she imparted with great conviction) that Brad MacMath was her first lover and that, as she put it to a reporter as recently as 2001, "I lost my virginity and got pregnant all in the same act." It's striking that she felt the need to present herself this way. Did the panic felt by D'Arcy Case and other girls "caught" pregnant, and Myrtle's stern moralism all weigh on her so heavily that, decades and a counterculture later, she *still* had to see herself as the Good Girl, paying for her first lapse from grace?

In the summer of 1964, Joni and Brad MacMath boarded a train east, for Toronto. The two were headed for the Mariposa Folk Festival, a three-year-old, three-day event held in the nearby town of Orillia. But the almost-cross-country trip had a second purpose. Whether knowingly or just out of instinct and common sense, Joni was following the current Canadian practice for unmarried pregnant young women: going far from home to bear her child in secrecy. She just wasn't doing it in the traditional–protected–way.

At the time, there were dozens, if not hundreds, of secret maternity homes for Canadian girls who had gotten themselves "in trouble." Parents of girls who were lucky enough to secure placement (waiting lists had lengthened with the beginning of emboldened sexual activity) sent their daughters 3,000 miles, from Vancouver to Toronto, or vice versa– or two-thirds of that distance across the country–to live in the private maternity homes that sprouted up in every Canadian city and sizable town.* There, as Canadian TV journalist Anne Petrie (a 1967 alumna of one such home) recalls, in her book *Gone to an Aunt's: Remembering Canada's Home for Unwed Mothers,* the rule was "No last names–ever." "[T]he girls just disappeared" from their own communities, Petrie writes. "The cover stories were vague. 'Gone to visit an aunt' was typical." Until Petrie wrote her book in the late 1990s, her own siblings never knew of their sister's secret baby, born and given up for adoption thirty years earlier. Parents eager to protect the "family name" were key in the process. Says Sandra Jarvies, president of the main organization, Canadian Birth Mothers United, of those women who gave up their babies for adoption: "Of the about 300 single mothers who gave birth in the mid-1960s and gave up their babies for adoption whom I've talked to, almost *all* used their parents to help them; if you couldn't tell your parents, you were *really* in trouble."

Canadian girls who decided to forgo, or *had* to forgo, the help of their parents–who wanted or needed to hide their pregnancies *from* them–could still get into these secret maternity homes, with their hot meals and dorm-style beds, by traveling to another province and registering confidentially. But in mid-1964–in addition to the girls whose parents helped them, and in addition to the girls who got into the

---

* In the United States, approximately 1.5 million young women gave birth in similar homes from 1945 to 1972.

pregnancy homes by themselves—there began to appear a *third* type of pregnant, unmarried Canadian girl: the bohemian girl who rejected the hypocrisy and constriction (and the coddling) of being hidden away. Many of these girls were making a statement—"I'm pregnant and unmarried and *not* ashamed of it." Joni Anderson was one of these girls, but only up to a point. She rejected the idea that she should feel shame, and yet family disgrace was not a concept she was thumbing her nose at, by any stretch of the imagination. She was going far from home, but no one—neither her parents nor a proprietress of a protective maternity home—would be helping her. She would be out in public and self-supporting, even though she had no plan for how she'd make money, yet manage to conceal the pregnancy from her parents at all costs. In short, she was choosing the path of greatest risk and least protection.

What help Brad might provide was questionable from the outset. The help that Joni wanted from Brad was also questionable. Unlike D'Arcy, who'd desperately wanted to marry Rudy (and did so, to disastrous results, divorcing him soon after their daughter was born), Joni was *not* in love with Brad MacMath.

The unwanted pregnancy seems to have spurred Joni to take new creative risks—to write her own songs; she wrote her first, what she called a feeling-sorry-for-myself song, "Day by Day," on the train ride to Toronto. The closer she got to delivering her baby (in increasingly desperate circumstances), the more her work—singing and starting to write—seemed to preoccupy her, perhaps both to distract from the frightening inevitability of imminent birth and possibly to set up an emotional and moral bargain: if I give up this unsought baby, then I'm not going to do so for nothing. If I make this serious relinquishment, I will use my reclaimed life to "give birth," as it were, to something else. In the months after she had her baby, who was put temporarily into foster care and then put up for adoption, Joni would write a flood of songs so beautiful and original, no one who'd heard her covering the folk standards at those midwestern Canadian coffeehouses or hootenannies could have anticipated their volume or virtuosity. It was as if she heard her grandmothers say: "We had babies in provincial poverty and we never reached our creative potential. If you heed our warning by refusing the first path, then when you go the second path, make it worth it—put your whole heart into it."

Joni herself seems to have believed that the loss of the baby equaled the beginning of the songs. Though she has today firmly settled on a narrative that blames her first husband, Chuck Mitchell, for the adopting-out of the baby (something Chuck Mitchell adamantly disputes), she spontaneously reacted differently the very first time an interviewer (for Greater London Radio, in June 1990), playing "gotcha" journalism, outed her airtight secret. After the setup, "Do you miss having a close-knit family?" to which Joni replied, "Well, we [she and her second husband Larry Klein] have cats and also I have a lot of godchildren. I haven't had children by choice, really," the interviewer pounced: "You *did* have a child, didn't you, when you were very young? Do you know what happened to him or her?" Seemingly stunned, Joni confessed [emphasis added]:

> "I do and I don't. Maybe I do. Maybe I know a little. Maybe I don't know anything. I'll tell you by that I think I've done my—people are too possessive about their children, too ego-centric with their children, anyway. I reproduced myself. I made a beautiful child, a girl. When—but at the time I was penniless. There was no way I could take—she would have been—I was not the right person to raise this child. There was no indication that I would—I don't have a good education, I couldn't keep her. It was impossible under the circumstance. I had no money when she was born, none. *Imagine, I mean—none of the music could have come out.* We would just have been—I would have been waitressing or something. It wouldn't have been—fate did not design this to occur."

Once they disembarked the train in Toronto. Joni and Brad took a bus to Orillia, but there they discovered that the Mariposa Festival was hastily being moved to Toronto—"at the last minute," recalls festival organizer Martin Ornot, "the township's council ruled that we could not present the show because a lot of people were hanging out." Ornot turned to three youngsters who had just traveled to the concert, sleeping bags under their arms—Joni, Brad, and a third person—and asked them to help load the trucks. "Joni was very attractive and really sweet," Ornot recalls. "Brad was tall and good-looking, and she introduced him as her boyfriend. They were a nice couple, and definitely affectionate. Joni and her friends helped load things on the truck, and I made arrangements for them to get passes for the festival, which was held at an old baseball stadium, in exchange."

Joni and Brad remained in Toronto, living at a rooming house. Calling back her post–high school experience, she got a job at Simpson's Department Store to save enough money for the $150 musicians' union dues, and she and Brad fell into the hippie life. ("Brad was the original hippie—proud that he never had a job for more than four months," says one who heard the story from both Brad and Joni.) In the early autumn weeks after Mariposa, Martin Ornot would see Joni around Yorkville Village, the charming eighteenth-century neighborhood of cul-de-sacs and one-way streets bounded by Yonge Street, Avenue Road, the Toronto Museum, and the University of Toronto, which was the spawning ground for folk clubs: the Purple Onion, the Mousehole, the Riverboat, the Cellar Club, the Gates of Cleeve, the Penny Farthing, the Night Owl, and many others, perpetually opening and closing. "I didn't notice that she was pregnant," Ornot says, "and I would have noticed, if it was visible, because I was myself thinking about pregnancy—my wife had just given birth." Joni had a fetching look—"she wore long gowns or jeans, leather jackets, holding her guitar, she had long hair"—and a compelling way about her. "She seemed quiet. If vulnerability can be translated into people wanting to do things for her, then she was vulnerable. You really wanted to be around her and help her, if you could. It wasn't that she was needy; it was that she was so nice." Joni had apparently begun writing, though not playing, her songs. "When we spoke, it was usually about her songs," Ornot recalls. Toronto was the big league—established artists like Ian and Sylvia, Gordon Lightfoot, and Buffy Sainte-Marie played the Toronto clubs. "I assisted her," Ornot says—in recommending clubs to seek work in, in giving her repertoire advice—"in any way I could."

Eventually, Brad left for Regina (he would later journey to Haight-Ashbury and be one of the original residents in that quintessential hippie community) and Joni moved into the Huron Street and Avenue Road rooming house, across the hall from young Ojibwa Indian poet Duke Redbird. "We were all like flower children," Redbird recalls. "Dylan and Baez were saying that things should change, and we in Yorkville felt that way. We were kids; give peace a chance." While Joni never talked about her increasingly visible pregnancy—and Redbird "assumed she was getting through a difficult period"—she talked about "spirituality," Redbird recalls. "Because I'm a native person, we talked about earth and spirituality. She was from the prairie; she brought an innate amount of spirituality with her. She was composing. The conversations we had were about her music and her lyrics," none of which Redbird can remember. Redbird, in speaking of the plight of his fellow First Nations people, as Native Canadians call themselves, experienced the same kindness that Joni had visited on polio-stricken Doug Bovee. "She had this immense reserve of feeling for people who were having difficulty—the downtrodden and unaffiliated." His friendship with her "represented a bridge between the WASP world, which she belonged to, and the world of the disenfranchised."

As the weather grew colder, the population of Yorkville shrunk. Gone were the thousands of tourists who'd swarmed around all summer, primed as they'd been by "beatnik" cartoons in the Toronto *Telegram*, such as one showing a suited young man bearing a milk bottle, a loaf of white bread, and an oven-ready fowl, approaching a couple—bearded, sandaled guy and long-haired, capri-pants'd girl—entwined under a dangling bare bulb, and saying, with puzzlement: "But I thought you said to bring a chick, a bottle, and some bread." Now only a couple of hundred people—club owners, folksingers, students, and shopkeepers—remained. Without Brad around to help at all, Joni played as many gigs as she could, in a variety of coffeehouses. Folksinger Jeanine Hollingshead remembers a visibly pregnant Joni at the Sunday and Monday night hootenannies. "She was showing—we all knew—but, gosh, she kept working." The women on the scene wore short mod dresses with swirly paisley prints and high go-go boots, or longer skirts, but whatever you wore, getting on six and seven and eight months, you couldn't hide a pregnant belly. "The question" among the folksingers, Hollingshead recalls, "was always, who was the daddy? And would she keep the baby? But it was nobody's business and nobody asked. We had all left our small towns to get away from that gossip, that judgment."

Joni was by no means the only pregnant unmarried girl in Yorkville. "There were many, many," Hollingshead remembers. Some were folk-singers—a girl named Cathy Young, for example. "But not all were folk-singers. Some of them probably came here because they were pregnant and didn't want to be at home." Joni herself has said that she met fif-teen-year-old pregnant girls living lives of precocity, risk taking, and abandon that shocked her. Still, Joni stood out; her dignity and beauty made her an unbidden focus of attention. "Joni was shy," Jeanine Hol-lingshead recalls, "and she seemed very sad to be going through it alone." Yet despite the apparent melancholy, the poverty, the conspicu-ous pregnancy, and her aloneness (or perhaps *because* of these things), Joni exuded charisma. The whole last year and a half—of watching per-formers at the Louis Riel and of performing, there and at SAIT and at the coffeehouses in Calgary, Edmonton, and Regina—had given her a sense of herself as a show-woman. Along the way, she had acquired a real guitar. "When she introduced her song, you would lean in and listen," Hollingshead says. "That gorgeous, bell-like voice would take you away. She would say, 'This is a song for my friends . . .'"

Joni had lots of friends—chief among them, a funny, freeloading young, wire-specs-wearing American guitar player named David Rea, who was one of the trickle-turning-into-a-flood of American males coming north to escape the draft during these early months of the Viet-nam War; and the "den mother" of Yorkville, singer Vicky Taylor. Jet-black-haired, freckle-faced, Vicky Taylor was the classic hipster girl, taking her cues from a slightly earlier era. She was in psychoanalysis; she was madcap (given to dancing on tables in a leopard-print bikini); and, in Tom Lehrer fashion, as Jeanine Hollingshead recalls, "she would sing a naughty little song she'd written about the birth control pill." Vicky had an apartment that was an all-purpose crash pad for destitute folksingers, where she ladled out a poor-man's porridge that she called "gunk." Looking back on that time, Joni has said, "Vicky was the only person on the folk scene that was nice to me. Every time she went out on an audition, Vicky would insist on dragging me along."

Among Vicky's (and Jeanine's) friends was a rangy boy from Winnipeg, a rock 'n' roller who had only turned folkie when he'd aged out of the local rock club at nineteen and had written a song, "Sugar Mountain," bewailing the injustice. He was a novelist-sportswriter's son; he had a classically handsome, chiseled face, an intense expression, and a ragged, bleating, provocatively unmusical voice. He had suffered polio during the same epidemic that had felled Joni. His name was Neil Young.

As Joni soldiered on through the last months of 1964, she and Vicky Taylor briefly formed a duo, named—for their opposite hair color—Black and White, and they performed at such clubs as the Mousehole, where Vicky was already a bit of a star. Then Joni got her own solo engagement at the Half Beat, charming the customers not just with her singing voice and her loveliness, but with the breathless, talkative sincerity of her presentation. When she sang "Crow on the Cradle"—the faux–Child Ballad song about the loss of a baby—her ambivalence and confusion about her own imminent maternity rang out, albeit in a code the listeners couldn't divine, in her quavering voice: "Crow on the cradle, tell me: What shall I do?"

Joni has said that her prenatal diet was "atrocious," something that Duke Redbird recalls as true for all of the Yorkville rooming house dwellers. "It's not even so much that we didn't have money; we were, all of us, too excited being on our own and creating art to think about eating until we had to." But he and his brother were worried enough about Joni's health to give her the gift of apples. Not thinking about eating, not having money to eat well, never talking about her pregnancy or even admitting its existence: Redbird saw, and admired, all these things as the calm resolve of the girl who sadly sang and strummed her guitar through her closed door at night. "Joni had a very strong presence of being centered. I'm sure she had fears, but her demeanor was one of stoicism," he says. But author Anne Petrie, who spent months in a secret Canadian unwed-mothers' home in the 1960s, might look at what Redbird admired as stoicism and—empathetically—call it something different: "massive denial." As Petrie wrote in her memoir, "I was pretending nothing was happening . . . I ignored the evidence of my body. Here it was changing by the day. I was doing what a woman is at least partly made for, growing and carrying a baby that was mine, made of me. I would feel it kick, I would even watch my stomach change shape as a baby fist or foot moved across it, but emotionally I was completely detached."

As December wore on, Joni's pregnancy was too pronounced for her to play her guitar. The large, inflexible wooden instrument lay literally too high atop her belly for her to get a good grip on the strings. "That big old guitar!" Jeanine Hollingshead says. "Ask any pregnant woman how hard it is to play a guitar when you're seven months pregnant—it starts to get away from you! That's when Joni started to really use the tiple"—a small instrument, on the order of a ukulele or mandolin.

Duke Redbird left the boardinghouse around Christmas; Joni was still there, and six weeks away from her due date. As the new year, 1965, loomed, Joni's lugubrious eight-months girth rendered her unable to perform. Penniless, she went to live in Vicky Taylor's aerie over the Lickin' Chicken restaurant.

There Vicky played Joni her friend Neil Young's song "Sugar Mountain," and the song's premise—that the Winnipeg boy felt so unhappily "old" at nineteen—led Joni to begin to write a kind of "answer" song about the value of age. Months later, she would pick up the song again and complete it. This blue-note-filled song—with its emotional turn on the ninth and tenth syllable of the third bar—seems suffused with a sense of premature longing for something lost. It would be called "The Circle Game," and she began writing it in the last weeks before she went into labor.

The baby was two weeks late. (How Joni came by this information is unknown.) In the middle of the second week of February 1965 she entered the charity ward of Toronto General Hospital. Children's Aid Society social workers visited her. According to what she, decades later, told her daughter (in the company of a friend), there was a "glut' of babies of

unwed mothers in Toronto at this time; the local paper had just published an article on the subject. But Sandra Jarvies of Canadian Birth-
mothers says that the social work establishment, government, and media
all "exaggerated the number of unwed mothers—there weren't as many
as they said—because they were busy promoting adoption." Jarvies adds,
"Social workers were in the hospitals, counseling girls that it 'wasn't
really your baby,' that it was in the 'best interests of the baby' to have it
adopted, that 'if you love your baby,' you'll give it up; the baby will be
'illegitimate' if you keep it." Joni has said she was fiercely judged by the
staff. "The time of her birth was traumatic for me. That's why I could
identify with the women who were sent to the Magdalene Laundries"—
the punitive Irish home for "wayward" girls that she wrote about so stirringly in her song of that name, included on her Grammy-winning
mid-1990s album *Turbulent Indigo*.

On February 19 Joni gave birth to a healthy baby girl. She wrote on
the birth certificate: Kelly Dale Anderson. "Kelly" (the first of the last-
names-as-girls'-first-names) was popular with bohemians at the time
(Hettie and LeRoi Jones named a daughter Kellie). More, as she explained
in the wrenching song "Little Green" (sometimes, early on, she forthrightly sang the words as "*Kelly* Green"), written about the birth: "Call
her green for the children who've made her." She used the name Anderson because, again from the song, "You sign all the papers in the family
name. You're sad and you're sorry but you're not ashamed."

Immediately after giving birth, Joni's breasts were bound, to stop her
breast milk supply. Having decided that the baby would, at least for now,
go into foster care while she sorted out her options, she told the nurses
not to bring the baby to her. But they did. Two weeks post-due, Kelly
Dale was a beautifully formed, pink-cheeked baby. At that point a friend
says, "She realized she had a baby and was going to give it up.""

early
1961 – late 1965

In the early '60s, when Ivy League schools were all-male and Seven Sisters schools all-female, scattered clusters of eminences-in-the-bud were springing up at elite colleges. The men who would one day shape their generation were dog-earing copies of Blake and Kierkegaard or Marcuse and C. Wright Mills; shaving irregularly; cutting lectures to sleep off hangovers in clothes-strewn rooms. At Cornell were experimental novelists Thomas Pynchon and Richard Fariña—the latter soon to marry Joan Baez's sister, Mimi, and become close friends with Bob Dylan—as well as Peter Yarrow, imminently of Peter, Paul and Mary. At Harvard Albert Gore Jr. was rooming with Tommy Lee Jones, while Erich Segal, studying for his Ph.D. (at the same time that Daniel Ellsberg was acquiring his), envyingly noted the handsome Tennessee senator's son's courtship of Southern ladies' college beauty Mary Elizabeth "Tipper" Aitcheson. At Yale, Bob Woodward—just out of military service; his Illinois accent porterhouse-thick—was sharpening his sleuth's rapier while Yankee Texan George W. Bush was pulling ample strings to not flunk out; working-class Brooklynite Alan Dershowitz was editing the law review; and Gary Hart-né-Hartpence, a fundamentalist Christian from Kansas, was graduating from divinity school.

In contrast to these later-famed male clusters, what mostly sprung up, in 1961 to 1964, at the elite *women's* colleges were cliques of smart, talented, opinionated girls who were on their way to becoming the *wives* of those young men. Such was the cultural dictum, for even the smartest daughters of wealthy, educated families. The very recent year 1960 would prove to have marked the all-time youngest age of first marriage for American women for the entire prior one hundred years—more than half of women married by age twenty—affirming the gut sense that decades' most "typical" characteristics emerge at their sunsets. "Girls' identities were very much about the man you were with," recalls Carly's best friend, Ellen Wise Questel, now a psychotherapist, who went off to Sarah Lawrence, along with Carly. Despite privilege and culture and high expectations, Ellen says, "We were still not whole." Carly—only slightly facetiously—remembers imagining her future thus: "I was going to live in the kitchen and serve little pouffy mousses with demitasses to my husband, the poetry professor at a small New England college, and his terribly intellectual friends, around an old farm table where no napkins matched." In Carly's Andrea-modeled version, it was the man who would *do* the interesting thing; the woman—wittily, flirtatiously, creatively—who would be his muse, the power behind his throne, and a thinking-woman's version of a socialite. Still, the Riverdale girls were expected to finish college before getting married, and not to have children immediately. But be major creators in their *own* right? That wasn't necessarily part of the agenda.

However, adds Ellen, "If there was *one* women's college that got the few women who *did not* think in that conventional way—who believed in their own talent and expected to be artists in their own right—then that was our college, Sarah Lawrence." "It was a magic time to be at Sarah Lawrence," says award-winning filmmaker Helen Whitney, who was a student there during those years.

Strolling the campus flanked by graystone Tudor halls; grabbing lunch at the Caf in Reisinger after coming from dance or theater upstairs; underlining Proust or Talcott Parsons, Malinowski, or Quine and Strawson in the library beneath McCracken; sprawling on the steps of Westlands or Titsworth—*everywhere* strode ballerina-postured students (not a square inch of bleeding madras on their collective torsos) whose then-unknown names would soon define the American female cutting edge.

There was disciplined, taut-bodied Meredith Monk, already making avant-garde dances, and soignée Hope Cooke, eyes kohl-smudged, trench coat thrown over her mud-hemmed sari—engaged to some older guy she'd met in a Darjeeling bar, who just happened to be the king of Sikkim (soon making her the only American queen of a Himalayan kingdom, not to mention the only *bohemian* one). Spelman transfer student Alice Walker, eighth child of sharecroppers, scoped out the tricky terrain (passionately liberal, yet land-mined with status hierarchies) of the white northeastern intellectual elite during her 1963-to-1965 tenure there. After graduating, she'd return South as a civil rights activist, in 1968 becoming the black member of the first interracial marriage in Mississippi—all this before emerging as one of the defining female writers of her generation.

Then there was Jill Clayburgh, wild child from a proper Upper East Side family (in a decade and a half, she'd put a face on feminism by way of *An Unmarried Woman*), who palled around with one of the very few male students, Brian De Palma ("who was screwing everyone," a female alum recalls) and also with fellow drama major Jennifer Salt, the daughter of blacklisted screenwriter Waldo Salt. Jennifer's lifelong best friend was Janet Margolin, who had just debuted as the deep-and-alienated Lisa in *David and Lisa*, an American film that miraculously provided starved non-philistines with an *un*imported antidote to *Gidget*. Sally Kempton, daughter of newspaper columnist Murray, had serious late-night, dorm-room talks with future La Mama dancer-actress Lanny Harrison (whose Jewish father had owned a Harlem radio station, whose mother had been a suffragette, and who herself had been almost kicked out of Asbury Park High for having a black boyfriend) about "who we were to men, and what men were to us, and how we loved to flirt but we wanted to be completely strong and yet still have relationships," Lanny recalls. Sally would go on to marry Harrison Starr, the producer of the late-1960s zeitgeist film *Zabriskie Point* (directed by Michelangelo Antonioni); then she'd publish a bombshell personal essay in *Esquire* to help take feminism mainstream, and after *that,* disappear into an ashram, as Swami Muktananda's top aide, for thirty years. There was wickedly funny Sybil Littauer, already getting her own show at the Betty Parsons Gallery; acting student Pepa Ferrer, whose stepmother was Audrey Hepburn; and sardonic Jane Barnes, who danced on tables to John Lee Hooker records. "We were all boy-crazy," says Lanny Harrison. "We would go down to parties in New York—parties near Columbia, parties in the Village, wherever we heard there were parties—and dance until we dropped, to Motown and to bluesy folk artists like Jesse Fuller and Reverend Gary Davis. Then we'd climb over the wall and sneak back, long after curfew."

It was into this rich stew of swaggering, culturally snobbish femininity that the not-un-like-minded Carly Elizabeth Simon was plunked in late 1961. She loved her Russian literature class, taught by a female Russian professor, and she was praised for an oral report on Gogol, a triumph to her, since, as she says, "I was still living in fear of having to speak aloud in class." She felt vulnerable around her old fourth-grade Fieldston teacher, who was now a college English instructor, Joseph "Pappy" Papaleo, because at Fieldston she'd been the phobia-beset nine-year-old, fearful of attending school in the morning, and he used to cajole her into class with yo-yo tricks. She feared that her craziness, though tamped down, still showed, even now in college, where she was a "woman," not a "pupil."

Carly was one of the two folksingers on campus; the other was Helen Rheinhold. "Carly was the more showbizzy folksinger," says Lanny Harrison, "while Helen, who was from Brooklyn, was more the Fred Braun sandals, frizzy hair parted down the middle, very *folky* one. Everyone loved them both; they were just different."

Along with her prized Odetta records, Carly had brought some of her large collection of classical Nonesuch albums to her Gilbert Hall dorm room. She was also beginning to admire Judy Collins, the former

teenage pianist who'd switched from piano to guitar and had just released *A Maid of Constant Sorrow* in the mold of Joan Baez singing
Child Ballads, and especially Judy Henske, the self-described "tall,
foot-stomping beatnik" from Wisconsin who'd sung with the Whiskey-
hill Singers and opened for Lenny Bruce before becoming a solo act.
Carly heard in Henske's belting voice a hint of her own potential.
"[Henske] was just kind of solidly earthy—amazing," Carly felt, especially on "Wade in the Water"; over the next few years, Carly "emu-
lated" her and "copied her songs," which alternated a folk repertoire
with the art songs of Jacques Brel.

Carly's cachet within the highly discriminating campus status hier-
archy was inched upward by her boyfriend, Nick Delbanco, who was
the young novelist at Harvard, courted by serious publishers, destined
for literary fame and glamour. "He was very smart, witty, and sexy. I
thought they were a great couple," says Lanny Harrison. Typical of the
time, "I always had the feeling Nicky had more power in the relationship," remembers Ellen, who notes that among even the most confidently creative girls at Sarah Lawrence "there was still that little piece
missing, that had to do with men." And Carly—reaching for attention
but riddled with insecurities—was *not* one of the most confidently
creative girls at Sarah Lawrence. Nick had come into her life at her
most vulnerable moment, as her father was dying, and he filled the
role of knight in shining armor. Carly saw Nick as her "protector," her
"warrior," she says today, adding (with a dash of Andrea-like drama)
that he was "my caretaker and my lover and my handsome darling."

One of the things that impressed the Sarah Lawrence girls was
how *European* Nick seemed. Nick had taken his parents' old-world
gravitas and fashioned a contemplative suavity. Students at Sarah Lawrence and Harvard—and many elite colleges—avidly read Bosley
Crowther's film reviews in *The New York Times* and devoured the European cinema. Truffaut's *Jules and Jim* and *The 400 Blows* and Vit-
torio de Sica's *The Bicycle Thief,* Godard's *Breathless,* Fellini's *La Dolce
Vita:* college students in the early 1960s longed for that weary Continental decadence in their own lives. Carly was as intrigued by foreign

films as any self-respecting Sarah Lawrence girl; she especially loved Ingmar Bergman. (Years later—in the mid-1970s—when her friend Mia Farrow was dating Bergman's cinematographer Sven Nykvist, Carly asked Nykvist, "What do you think happened to the people in *Scenes from a Marriage* after the movie ended?" Nykvist said he had no idea. "The next weekend," Mia says, "Carly came back to my house with pages and pages of description she'd written about what she thought would happen to the characters; it was breathtaking.")

From the movies came the infatuation with European life. The motor scooters; the baguettes and bunches of flowers in those randy flats near crumbling edifices; the droop of Simone Signoret's eyelids, the tilt of the Gauloises from Jean-Paul Belmondo's lip, the transformation of Jean Seberg from Iowa girl to French New Wave movie star married to Parisian leftist intellectual: all of this seemed salvation from the banality of suburban, even *wealthy* suburban, America. It had begun with the coffeehouses where Joni waitressed and performed and with the romanticization of tight-quartered city life in Carole's songs—European ideas, both. Soon would come other ideas from the history-rumpled mother continent (and the British Isles)—long hair and dandy clothes for men; a jaded attitude toward romantic exclusivity; boutiques, whose fashion put a piquant innocence (and, hence, a permission) into sexuality—that would help push the culture in a new direction. Women in their twenties and early thirties, following Jackie Kennedy's lead, were already living Frenchified lives (even in their roles of luncheon-going, baby-producing wives to rising-star alpha men). Coq au vin, runny cheeses, croissants: in 1961 through 1963, these were the domestic appurtenances of an elect who might in some ways still *live* like but would never *be* like their mothers.

Nicky had spent the summer of 1961 traveling to Athens and Rhodes with his friend Paul Sapounakis, soaking up local color for the novel he was starting. When, during that trip, he got the news that Ernest Hemingway had shot himself to death, Nick "took it as a private grief and personal injunction," as he put it, and proceeded to toast the literary lion at Le Select, Les Deux Magots, Brasserie Lipp, and

Café de Flore. After he returned home and the college year wore on, he talked to Carly about their living together in the south of France, where family friends could rent them a farmhouse. Carly signed on to the plan. While her classmates were planning their majors, "I was planning a major in getting the hell out of there and going to Europe with Nick."

Meanwhile, during the summer of 1962, Carly and Nick lived together on Martha's Vineyard, where Nick drove a fish truck (a suitably macho job for a Hemingway-in-training). Playing house with one's boyfriend was a bold move in 1962. "It was a little bit shocking to my parents' friends for us to be shacking up together," Carly recalls. But for the Sarah Lawrence girls who visited—Lanny Harrison was one— it was oh, so sophisticated.

Lucy Simon proposed to Carly that they embrace the idea Uncle Dutch had originally suggested and form a sister singing duo. "Carly did not have an ambitious edge," Ellen recalls, but she did have an exhibitionist streak, that yearning to perform. Lucy worked up a folklike arrangement for the nursery rhyme "Wynken, Blynken and Nod" by Eugene Field. The older sister's soprano close-harmonized over the younger's contralto—"Carly's voice was developing into something low, unique, and more commercial than mine," Lucy says. With this and a few other self-written songs under their belts, "we said, 'Let's go to Provincetown!'—with one guitar," recalls Lucy. "We had little matching red dresses and matching red heels. We roomed in a rooming house for $50 a week and went around to the various bars, calling ourselves the Simon Sisters. We got a job in a place called the Moors—it was about a mile away from our little room—and we would thumb a ride to the Moors in our matching dresses."

The P-town audiences were charmed by the Simon Sisters—lovely Lucy, with her long hair and big hoop earrings; strong-featured Carly, with her big, sensual mouth. By summer's end the young women had written more songs—Nick helped on lyrics—and played Village clubs: the Gaslight on MacDougal, the Bitter End on Bleecker.

Given her new downtown performing schedule, Carly, during her sophomore year, was now being castigated by the dorm mother for signing in so often postcurfew, and she was begging her professors for extensions on her papers. The Simon Sisters got a contract with Kapp Records; they recorded their own songs and some folk standards on *Wynken, Blynken and Nod,* with the title song released as a single.* (The girls got elite treatment from producer John Court and arranger Gary McFarland. When a still-unknown young keyboard player named Al Kooper arrived at the studio to play on the session, "half of Count Basie's band was in the studio," he recalls. "I was pretty terrified when I recognized them.") With flute accompaniment as well as guitar and banjo, the album had the fairy-tale-recast-as-folk-song quality that had paid off for Peter, Paul and Mary on "Puff the Magic Dragon." "Wynken and Blynken and Nod one night sailed off in a wooden shoe," the Simon Sisters sang. "They sailed on a river of crystal lights, into a sea of dew . . ." It sounded virginal, feminine, and melodious.

The summer of the album's release, 1963, Carly and Nick again played house on Martha's Vineyard, this time renting in rustic Menemsha. Carly and Lucy sang at the popular hangout the Mooncusser, and one of the young patrons who'd stop by and watch her sing was fourteen-year-old Jamie Taylor, the third of five children of Dr. Isaac (Ike) Taylor, dean of the University of North Carolina's medical school, and Ike's strong-willed and stunning wife, Trudy Woodard Taylor.

In an America where the concept barely existed, the Taylors were genuine bluebloods. Ike was of old Yankee and North Carolina stock— his family had sailed over from Scotland in the late 1700s—and his wife's New England roots reached even deeper; the Woodards had left England in the late 1600s. Together, Ike and Trudy had become eccentric southerners: Trudy, a civil rights advocate in a segregated state; Ike, a drinker, womanizer, and adventurer (once, going off on a long medical mission to Antarctica); all the children, musical and rebellious (*none* of

---

* On some Web sites and reissues, the spelling has been changed to "Winken, Blinken and Nod."

them, despite their parents' erudition, finishing college). Their summers at their Vineyard home were full of sailing; Ike, who hailed from a long line of seafarers, instilled a love for the sport and for the island itself into his brood. Son James was on the brink of a stormy adolescence that would include drug taking and emotional breakdown at the elite prep school Milton Academy; after being heard musing about attempting suicide, he would finish the term in the safety of McLean psychiatric hospital. James was a palpably privileged boy—his breakdown was occasioned, he'd later say, while he was starting the process of applying to "colleges like Reed, Harvard, and Swarthmore" and realizing "I couldn't do it because I didn't want to." But it was precisely that touch of throwaway aristocracy that would leaven his darkness (intensified by his eventual heroin habit) and make him irresistible to young women.

On the Vineyard James began to play guitar and sing, along with his summer best friend, a Westchester County boy named Danny Kortchmar, whose parents, Emil and Lucy—a businessman and writer, respectively—kept a house on the island as well. James was tall and skinny, classically "American"-handsome, wry and langorous. Danny Kortchmar—short and wiry and ethnic-looking; quick on the draw—was coming into an appearance and manner that would eventually have him frequently mistaken for Al Pacino. Danny had grown up regarding the youngest Simon daughter, Carly, as "a weird, gawky kid."

But Danny was quicker to recognize what he says now was the "tremendous charisma" in the often melancholic James. "James was always an unhappy kid," Danny told a reporter, right after James became a star, and "he always had the same profound effect on people, especially girls. They always say he's the most honest, sensitive guy they've ever met. They make out he's some kind of messiah, with special wisdom." James's subsequent stay at McLean would add to the mystique, but even then he operated above his pay grade as a ladykiller: at fifteen, he was, as Danny would put it, "dating twenty-year-old chicks." Danny—"Kootch," as he was starting to call himself—was also drawn to James's talent. "We used to hitchhike on the Vineyard. Once, James burst into a Ray Charles song, and I said, 'Man, *you* can *sing!*'" Two years older than James, Danny taught him a great deal about the guitar; and Danny's strong personality—and heavier, R&B-style guitar playing—dominated the group they would eventually form, the Flying Machine.

Meanwhile, the single "Wynken, Blynken and Nod" was taking off, and Lucy had talked Carly into dropping out of Sarah Lawrence before the start of her junior year so the Simon Sisters could gain a following through touring. Jessica Hoffmann Davis believes that Carly didn't want to drop out of college but did so for Lucy's sake. Lucy and the newly disenrolled Carly were in a plane one November morning, on their way to one of their concerts, when Carly's already significant fear of flying was exacerbated by the voice over the intercom: "This is your captain speaking." As dreaded as the expected warning of turbulence would be, the actual news was worse: the president had been shot.

The confirmation of Kennedy's death came soon after a trembling Carly and Lucy touched down in Massachusetts. Their concert was canceled, of course, and they took the next flight home. An emotional Nick picked the distraught sisters up at the airport, and everyone watched the unfolding events at the house in Riverdale, flanking despondent Andrea, who had viewed John Kennedy as a friend to the civil rights movement. Watching newly widowed Jackie stoically exiting the plane that carried her husband's body—her husband's bloodstains on her pink suit—Carly could not have imagined that in two decades she and the First Lady would form a deep and playful friendship.

Now that Carly was no longer encumbered by college, Nick moved ahead with renting a house in the village of Châteauneuf de Grasse in the south of France. He had just finished a graduate fellowship at Columbia University and procured an advance from the publisher Lippincott for his first novel, ambitiously set in Greece, which he would title *The Martlet's Tale.** He'd brought the Simon Sisters' record on his trip

---

* Upon his novel's release, twenty-three-year-old Delbanco would be greeted with unqualified praise from high quarters. Mark Van Doren hailed the novel as "a tale of great richness, told with superb economy"; *Saturday Review* extolled its "lyrical intensity" and "characterizations . . . that glitter with the awesome truth of human anguish"; and *The New York Times* called it "a true work of imagination."

to Europe, along with the press photos of Carly and Lucy, looking tawny and twinlike with beads over Mexican blouses, open-mouthed at the microphone; but the record, Nick has recalled, was already "worn thin with use, smooth with repetition." Nick "yearned for . . . the actual skin of my darling instead of promotional photos." (Not that he wasn't also happily screwing around in Europe, according to Carly.)

When the plan was set for Carly to join him, Carly's friend Jessica Hoffmann, now a student at St. John's College in Maryland, thought it was "over-the-top romantic" that Carly was dashing off to live in a remote French village with her writer-lover.

Carly flew to London on a winter day in early 1964. Nick met her at the airport and they took a train to Milan, where she bought a tape recorder for any new songs she might compose, and they rented a midnight-blue Alfa Romeo convertible and headed for the Riviera: Nick wielding the stick shift, Carly's long hair blowing in the breeze, her sunglasses properly sophisticated, her guitar on her lap. But they were still American barely-postadolescents in a foreign country: Nick, nervous about the speeding *autostrada* drivers; Carly, full of phobias and, thanks to Nick's recent activity, the imminent recipient of, as she wryly recalls, "three different kinds of venereal diseases."

Carly was homesick and confused, and would be every night of their six-month stay. First of all, Chibie—the grandmother to whom she felt so close, the fount of all that Heinemann-woman charisma— had recently died. Second, she was skipping out on a career opportunity; "Wynken, Blynken and Nod" was proving to be a surprise hit, quickly climbing to #76 on the *Billboard* chart and inching even higher in a few markets. The Simon Sisters' manager, Harold Leventhal— who had managed the Weavers (virtually becoming blacklisted along with them), was a close friend of Woody Guthrie, and just the past year had presented Dylan in his first Town Hall concert—wanted Carly to be able to fly home if touring or promotion were in order. But to Carly, love mattered more. The romantic dream of supporting a creative man was supposed to be the signal aspiration of women of her station. But did that shoe fit?

On their way to the south of France, Carly and Nick managed to find a village hotel whose proprietor did not frown suspiciously at the different last names on their passports. The next morning they drove the Grand Corniche, and then through a long olive grove, to their ter-racotta-tile-roofed, wood-shuttered stone farmhouse. The landlady—a stooped, elegant Joan of Arc scholar—served them tea and handed them the house key. They walked around the drafty abode, locating nooks and pulleys and provisions ("two children playing house," as Nick put it), and from the second-floor windows glimpsed Provence's undulating hills and the twinkling lights of Cannes in the distance.

Aside from the embarrassment of getting her VD antibiotics pre-scriptions noisily translated into French and filled at the local phar-macy, "it was wonderful," Carly recalls. "You had to boil water on the stovetop just to take a bath, and there was a mimosa tree right outside the door and a pool, all covered with leaves, where I tried to get a tan in March, sitting there reading *The Red and the Black*." While Carly read Stendhal and sang new melodies into her tape recorder, Nick worked on his novel, intuiting the feelings of his fictional dying Greek matriarch, with her secret cache of money near her house in Rhodes. In their life together, the couple appropriated the intensity of Nick's prose. Nick photographed a pensive Carly in a sweater and Courrèges-style skirt, her back-combed long hair riffled by the breeze in the field, braced by spindly winter trees. And every night they toasted each other with the local red wine. Once in bed, however, Carly's anxiety attacks would descend like clockwork—night shakes so intense that she was certain she was having a nervous breakdown. Today Carly be-lieves the shaking attacks were a combination of a later-proved allergy to the wine *and* the enormous dose of estrogen in her daily Enovid.

Every woman who took Enovid back then was, by today's standards of drug approval, a guinea pig. Enovid had been approved by the FDA during the last naïve and lax moment in the agency's history—two years *before* the dangers of thalidomide (an anti-nausea agent for pregnant women that turned out to cause severe physical malformations in babies) forced a tightening of clinical trial standards. Not only had

Enovid essentially slipped through that approval crack (in fairness, been *pushed* through because women *wanted* a birth control pill, desperately), but no one knew exactly what the side effects might be if, for the first time in history, so many people—7.5 million by 1969—ingested a medication daily, for so long, for something *other than* to treat a disease. When it came to drugs for women, the medical establishment, including obstetrics and gynecology, was overwhelmingly male, and women were not included in clinical trials for medications appropriate for both sexes, so there was no reliable data on how such drugs would affect female bodies. This solipsism led to naïveté at best—for years, drug companies didn't believe women would even *want* to take a pill to not have babies—and, at worst, it led to danger. High-dose Enovid was thought to cause thromboembolism and obstructions of blood vessels leading to crucial organs, a risk substantially reduced by lower-dosage versions of the Pill in the early 1970s. But a possible link to the early Pill and breast cancer has never been disproved, and this would later prove significant for Carly.

Still, despite Carly's night shakes (and her VD), day-to-day life was romantic. Carly picked the tulips, irises, and anemones in the fields and watched the fruit trees ripen. She and Nick entertained their—*très* impressed—school friends who flew over to visit; they strolled to town for baguettes and cheese, the *International Herald Tribune* and *Nice Matin,* and were soon on gossiping terms (who in town was a drunk and who wasn't?) with the post office matron and the grocer.

Nick worked on his novel every day, but Carly grew confused about what exactly she was doing there. She wrote to Jessica letters that combined "a sort of adolescent angst, on the one hand—she was far away from her all-time-favorite vanilla milk shakes—with this luscious, brave woman in love on the other," Jessica recalls. She slept late, descending from the bedroom "catlike," Nick has said, turning the radio to France-Musique as page after page of the saga of Orsetta Procopirios and her grandson Sotiris issued forth from Nick's Olivetti roller. While there was plenty for a novelist to do in this secluded house, for Carly "there was no one to listen to her sing," Nick says, "except the occasional shepherd." Nick had planned the trip according to his own needs and agenda, and he expected Carly to fit into it. Was it petulant for her to feel disaffected? Nick could see Carly the performer chafing for an audience. "A career like hers doesn't happen by accident," he says today. "She worked very hard for it." He now sees the idyll to France as "the beginning of the end for me and her."

Jaunts to St. Tropez, Cannes, and Cap d'Antibes were pleasant distractions. Carly loved that the villagers mistook her for actress Françoise Hardy, whom she indeed resembled (and consciously tried to dress like), so much so that "I started giving my autograph as such," she says, "just as my mother had succumbed to signing, 'Katharine Hepburn.'" But a trip to Barcelona reminded Carly of Chibie, who'd often talked of her Spanish youth. Carly broke down in tears there and was still crying when she and Nick returned to the farmhouse. Over the next days they argued, about everything and nothing.

In the midst of this tension Carly got word that "Wynken, Blynken and Nod" was doing very well in San Francisco. Everyone—Lucy, Andrea, her managers—was calling her home. In Nick's lightly fictionalized recounting of a key exchange, she says her career is on the line. "Where does that leave me?" he asks. "You could come, too," she says. "And carry your guitar again? And sit there in the Bitter End until the bitter end again? No thanks," he huffs. In 1964 even nurturing men not only thought but *talked* this way.

Carly decided to return home. Jake Brackman, soon to become Carly's best friend and collaborator, says, "There's a certain kind of woman who either has to *have* a great man* or who achieves greatness herself. If Carly had stayed with Nick, she would have had a Martha Stewart kind of creativity." Instead, she got on the plane for New York without Nick, on the first step toward the previously not-consciously-desired latter.

---

* Today Nicholas Delbanco is the author of twenty-four books, mostly highly regarded fiction, and directs the MFA program in creative writing at the University of Michigan at Ann Arbor. He is considered one of the most significant writers of fiction in America. The character in Delbanco's 2006 novel, *Spring and Fall,* about the forty-years-later resumed romance of college lovers, is at least partly based on Carly.

Dionne Warwick happened to be on Carly's flight; her "Walk On By" had just become an enormous hit. Carly approached the singer and gave her a tape of one of the songs she'd just composed. It would be the beginning of many such fruitless solicitations.

Carly reentered psychoanalysis, but she didn't return to Sarah Lawrence.

Over the next year, she and Lucy continued singing at the clubs—no longer with matching dresses—in the role of opening act. They were teamed up with "intellectual" cabaret performers: rising comics Woody Allen, Dick Cavett, Joan Rivers, and Bill Cosby; writer-singers Shel Silverstein and Theodore Bikel, and a folk group, the Tarriers, that included Marshall Brickman (who would later write *Annie Hall* and *Manhattan* with friend Woody Allen) and actor Alan Arkin. Carly's cousin Jeanie Seligmann, who was then attending Bryn Mawr, caught their now-polished act at the Second Fret in Philadelphia and remembers thinking that however plagued with self-doubt she knew Carly to be, "she was destined for stardom—she was just that outstandingly talented and creative."

Carly and Lucy recorded a second Kapp album, *Cuddlebug,* that featured a song of Carly's, "Pale Horse and Rider," which one reviewer called an "Ian-and-Sylvia-like up-tempo troubadour gallop," along with folk standards like "Motherless Child" and Pete Seeger's "Turn, Turn, Turn," soon to become the vehicle for the Byrds' introduction of folk rock to a primed young public, and a French version ("Ecoute dans la Vent") of "Blowin' in the Wind."

Carly and Nick had begun the long process of disentangling. The feeling Nick had had in Grasse, that Carly craved an audience, was borne out when they'd go to Arthur, the discotheque of the Manhattan elite, which was a bridge between the Kennedy-era Twist couples and the worlds of Andy Warhol and Leonard Bernstein. Danny "Kootch" Kortchmar, James Taylor's friend, who'd known Carly as the "weird" kid from the Vineyard, played there occasionally with a band he'd formed, and he noticed "she was turning into this rowdy kind of party chick. I'd hear about her, 'Oh, man, Carly was in there, tearin' up the place!' I thought: Well, I guess she's not gangly and gawky anymore. She's a fox now."

Nick says they broke up because their next step would have had to be marriage, and they both felt too young for that. Still, Nick was probably more upset than Carly: His novel, *Grasse 3/23/66*, with the photo he'd taken of Carly as the cover, was a stream-of-consciousness prose-poem about heartbreak. A flyleaf running together quotes from the book reveals its essence: "My wife and I drove from Milano to Grasse; in the foothills behind Valbonne we found a house and stayed. A year after arrival, our marriage broke; she left. *I am gone mad with words, with grief* [emphasis added]." With its passionate prose and Mediterranean setting, it resembles other novels of the era: *Second Skin* and *The Blood Oranges*, by John Hawkes, and *Beautiful Losers*, by Leonard Cohen, who would soon prove significant in Joni's life.

It was Carly who wanted most to move on—and that wish set her apart from her closest female peers. Lucy was falling in love with young psychiatrist David Levine. Jessica had fallen in love with fellow St. John's student Will Davis, whom she married in a wedding so thoughtfully planned (bride photo by Bachrach, silver pattern from Tiffany, dress from Bergdorf's, two hundred guests at the black-tie nuptials, personalized vows featuring snippets of e. e. cummings), one might never have guessed it had been a hastily assembled affair, for Jessica was pregnant. And that June—1965—Ellen married Vieri Salvadori; Carly, in a cap-sleeved pink satin dress, was a bridesmaid. One of the reasons Ellen and Vieri were marrying young was so that the groom could serve his country without being sent to Vietnam.* Right after the wedding, Vieri headed off for a year in the Air National Guard, while Ellen moved in with her other best friend, actress Jennifer Salt. A few days later, Carly picked up the handsome young English shoe salesman who sold her a

---

* Carly's high school boyfriend, Tim Ratner, joined the U.S. Air Force, active duty, and flew reconnaissance flights in Vietnam. And, two years before the hit music of ex-101st Airborne member Jimi Hendrix would help turn Vietnam into America's first rock 'n' roll war, Tim sang his and Carly's beloved show tunes and standards in the air force chorus, which performed in shooting distance of the rice paddies.

pair of Charles Jourdan pumps at Bloomingdale's. When her salesman returned to England, Carly followed him there. The Simon Sisters had some British bookings, so, she figured, why not go early? Plane-phobic Carly *sailed* over on the U.S.S. *United States* in late July, but after their brief fling, Carly parted ways with the salesman. With time on her hands, she called the man who was set to be her and Lucy's manager for their English tour, Willie Donaldson. Donaldson would give Carly her first taste of genuine adult love, and she would never forget him.

Donaldson, then thirty, already had quite a reputation in decadent English circles. He was a charismatic, slightly perverted literary and theatrical figure, described by the *Guardian Unlimited* as "avowedly chaotic but blessed with a formal manner." Raised on a proper country estate by wealthy parents who had died when he was a young man, he had read English at Cambridge University in the early 1950s, and, while there, had spent some of his very considerable inheritance underwriting the student literary magazines that published the early work of two acquaintances, Ted Hughes and his American wife, Sylvia Plath. After that, Donaldson joined what was known as "the Princess Margaret crowd." By 1965, he had freshly coproduced the satirical revue *Beyond the Fringe,* starring Peter Cook and Dudley Moore, which Carly had seen in New York and had loved.

When Carly called him to say she was in town, Donaldson invited her over. A tall man with plump lips, very white skin, bad teeth, and colorless eyebrows and lashes, he was no Casanova on the surface. He favored baggy suits, under which lay a body that Carly would soon see had an "old man's look." Still, Donaldson's pastiness and deshabille belied his extraordinary appeal to—and self-confidence with—women. He'd broken off with his debutante girlfriend for a journalist's wife, then had an affair with a dancer, and had just been stormed out on by his current lover, the actress Sarah Miles, when she'd found another woman's shoe under the bed of their town house. So he was technically unattached when the younger Simon Sister pressed his London doorbell.

Donaldson showered Carly with flattery, and she was smitten by his attention and his brilliance. The aristocrat's son and the publisher's daughter seemed to speak their own language. "From the beginning, I got Willie's joke—he planted something and I picked it right up," Carly says, of that magical first meeting. "We took a walk in Trafalgar Square, and we felt a very unnerving immediate intimacy." Days later, after Lucy arrived for the booking Willie had arranged for them at a club called the Rehearsal Room on Sloan Street, "the three of us—Lucy, Willie, and I— had our first tea together at Fortnum and Mason's. I realized that every time he turned to Lucy, I was really jealous."

Carly fell into "a very passionate, ardent" summer-long love affair with Donaldson. "With Willie, I became the girl I'd always wanted to be—older, very witty, really funny—*English*-funny, as if I had *always* been English." The love affair was "a solid, six-week-long *kill* for both of us," Carly says, "so intense" it was as if "we both died. I don't think either of us recovered." Years later, Donaldson would write, in his memoir, *From Winchester to This,* that Carly was "the answer to any sane man's prayers: funny, quick, erotic, extravagantly talented."*

Willie was that fundamental step in a young woman's romantic prog-ress: the dark corrective who welcomely destroys the innocence and pro-vinciality of a girl's bubble world with her college beau. Willie's intense, casual amorality** was antipodal to Nicky's dependable reverence. "Nick had always taken care of me," Carly says, "but Willie was the opposite. I

---

*   However, he wasn't always so nice. In his 1987 novel, *Is This Allowed?*, Donaldson wrote what Carly calls "an unflattering, ball-busting scene"—with real names used—in which she and her husband, James Taylor, are sitting with Willie during a trip to London "and I'm making signs to Willie behind James's back."

**   Soon after his breakup with Carly, he lived in a brothel and wrote a novel. From 1985 to 1995 he was a crack addict and a pimp, while continuing to write—novels, plays, newspaper columns. He invented a character, right-winger Henry Root, whose phony letters incited credulous response from Margaret Thatcher, among others. His last book, the satirical *Brewer's Rogues, Villains and Eccentrics,* was called "fiendishly en-tertaining" by the *Guardian Unlimited.* When he died in 2005, at seventy, the *London Daily Telegraph* eulogized him as "a pimp, crack fiend . . . a lazy, self-indulgent sex addict and a comic genius."

felt *I* was taking care of him." She also found him "the funniest man I had ever met. And he had a humor that was just on the verge of being the most flattering and yet was delivered with a killer's instinct." Thinking about another decadent, charismatic young British man with whom she would later have a significant flirtation, she adds, "Mick would have *loved* him," explaining that, metaphorically, Willie "strode the stage with his own microphone and quietly sang the songs of the deep and sick recesses of his mind. Most people would have advised me, 'Stay a thousand miles away from Willie Donaldson. He's dangerous.'"

Willie plied Carly with telegrams—"Come home, Little Frog Footman!" (his nickname for her) as she and Lucy were boarding the U.S.S. *United States* for the voyage home. Also boarding the luxury liner, the girls noticed, was Sean Connery. As soon as they checked into their stateroom, Carly sent Connery a letter through a steward, who delivered it while the actor was on the massage table. He arrived at the Simon sisters' stateroom door ten minutes later, his hair greasy from the massage oil; and as the ship lumbered across the Atlantic, he would pursue both sisters. As they talked literature in the velvet-rope-rung first-class lounge, he tried "to persuade Lucy and me to do things we had never heard of," says Carly. On the voyage's last night, Carly had half-decided that if Connery called the stateroom she would—Willie or no Willie—go up to his suite, which happened to be the ship's deluxe penthouse. But Carly was busy rolling her wet hair over beer cans "so it would be straight, like Julie Christie's"—she didn't reach the ringing stateroom phone in time. *Lucy* answered the phone. What happened next, Carly says, is lost to history.

Arriving back in the Riverdale house on September 8, Carly announced that she and Willie Donaldson would marry; their shipboard telegrams had firmed up their plans. She and her fiancé wrote letters almost daily—"Willie's letters were dazzling." Then they petered out. "I got more and more frantic," Carly recalls. On October 24 a letter postmarked London finally landed in her mailbox. Carly tore it open and took in the news: Willie and Sarah Miles had reconciled. Alas, dear Little Frog Footman, it was ever-so-lovely, but it was over.

Carly was devastated.

Over the years—indeed, the decades—Carly's brief, passionate love affair with Willie Donaldson has remained incandescent to her. She says, even today, "I can't seem to get back that sense of myself that [Willie] was bound to and found attractive." "Willie! Do you know how often I hear his name with her?" marvels her friend and former manager Arlyne Rothberg; "You'd think he saved her life!"

Lucy became engaged to David Levine. Carly, rejected by the man she loved madly, remained alone, all the more so after the Simon Sisters disbanded. She had dropped out of Sarah Lawrence; she was jobless; she had spent all her money on psychotherapy. It was a lost, aimless time for Carly—and things would get worse before they got better.

carole
1964 – early 1969

In the telescoped lens through which we tend to view the 1960s, the Beatles' arrival in the States in February 1964 looks like the match that lit the youth revolution—the moment when popular music shifted from a commercial diversion to a conduit for social change, in one great love-fest punctuated by *Yeah! Yeah! Yeah!* But those early Beatles were actually somewhat frostily received by young self-defined sophisticates. Though the mop tops incited teary passion when their *Ed Sullivan Show* debut beamed onto millions of Zenith and Sylvania screens, the scream-ers were mostly aged nine to sixteen. By contrast, the peers of Carole, Joni, and Carly had already staked out a "higher" native-born, musical loyalty—to Dylan and Baez or to secularized gospel music, from Aretha Franklin, whose brilliance shone through even her ill-produced Colum-bia albums, and the Genius, Ray Charles. Though the February 1964 Beatles were appealingly cocky and boldly fey—an intriguing new com-bination for insular U.S. youth—they registered, to many post-teen music snobs, as novel background noise to a change already begun. And though Dylan had excitedly demanded, "What was *that?*" when he'd first heard "I Want to Hold Your Hand," he soon cautiously down-graded his assessment, decreeing the Liverpool boys "bubblegum," though his girlfriend, Greenwich Village–bred union activist's daughter Suze Rotolo, who'd been mentoring her beau in political consciousness, presciently called them "fantastic."

It wasn't until 1965's *Rubber Soul* that many of the young early skeptics would reverse their original opinions and fall madly in love with the Beatles, and that the bowl-haircutted boys in the collarless suits—now long-haired and oracular, the brilliant Lennon-McCartney synergy in full swing—would emerge as the blinding countercultural avatars we regard them as today. But with their maiden voyage, from that presumed-dowdy country beyond the wide ocean, they lobbed the grenade of a superior, fully formed youth culture across the fruited plain of Frankie Avalon and Annette Funicello movies: clothing designers (Mary Quant, Ossie Clark), photographers (David Bailey, who coined the image of the fashion photographer as rebel), and models (Jean Shrimpton, Twiggy); as well as actors (Terence Stamp, Albert Finney, Michael Caine, David Hemmings) and actresses (Jane Birkin, Jane Asher, and, especially, Julie Christie, whom thousands of young American women, Carly Simon among them, were suddenly dying to look like). Mainly, the British Invasion would be about other rock stars: performers who (Mick Jagger, Keith Richards, and—baddest of all—Brian Jones) trounced the Beatles' own skiffle-band-based geniality with their effortless decadence, and who (Erics Clapton and Burdon) knelt at the altar of the Delta blues more deeply than any white boy in America, or who (Stevie Winwood) sang with a plaintive blackness that startlingly contradicted their wispy, white appearance.

The British Invasion was the second blow (Motown having been the first) to Carole and Gerry, and they humbly swallowed this bitter pill in their West Orange home. It was a tract house, with a doorbell that rang with the eight-bar hook of "Will You Love Me Tomorrow." Inside, Carole—along with her live-in household majordomo, Willa Mae Phillips—cared for Louise and Sherry. She and Gerry had a black Cadillac, and when she drove it into Manhattan, she invariably got towed, like some befuddled Lucy Ricardo. While many of her contemporaries were turning their faces to a new sun, Carole remained under the old one: a housewife-mother in a dull suburb, who played mah-jongg with Donny Kirshner's wife, Sheila, and Brooks Arthur's wife, Marilyn, evincing the taste of an older woman. She was living her life from the inside out, according to her responsibilities and her character, admirably oblivious to image.

Her lack of pretense was rewarded—she and Gerry were the ob-jects of the Beatles' fascination. "In England, Goffin and King were huge—they were legends," says Peter Asher, who was the Peter of the pop duo Peter and Gordon as well as the brother of Paul McCart-ney's soon-to-be fiancée, Jane Asher. "We were crazy about Goffin and King. We didn't know who they were, just the names. But they wrote all the songs we loved—'Crying in the Rain'; we were huge Everly Brothers fans." Well before their own stardom, the Beatles had covered Carole and Gerry's songs, treating their Hamburg audiences to "Will You Love Me Tomorrow," as well as to more obscure Carole-Gerry compositions, and playing "Take Good Care of My Baby" at their audition for Decca Records. When the Beatles' "Love Me Do" was inching up the British charts, it met competition from Carole's own rendition of "It Might As Well Rain Until September," a bigger hit in England than in the United States. Finally, they'd just recorded Carole and Gerry's "Chains" on their debut album, *Introducing the Bea-tles* (since then, re-issued as *Please Please Me*). Peter Asher recalls: "When the Beatles first came to America, *that's* who they wanted to meet: Goffin and King."

Entrusted with the task of introducing Carole and Gerry to the Beatles was *New York Post* writer Al Aronowitz, who lived near them in New Jersey. Aronowitz had met the Goffins when *The Saturday Evening Post* assigned him a piece on girl groups. The bearlike jour-nalist was insecure and prickly; he both adulated genuine hipsters and feared they'd find him lacking, a sensibility that found an un-canny mirror in Gerry. Gerry Goffin and Al Aronowitz inevitably became close friends, *best* friends. Yet it was Carole who would most be changed by Aronowitz's clamorous entry into the Goffins' life.

The chain of melodramas Aronowitz incited and the people he delivered to them would lead Carole to remake her personal and musical destiny.

Aronowitz had befriended the Beatles' chief roadie, Neil Aspinall, when the Fab Four landed at Idlewild Airport on a cold February day in 1964. To ingratiate himself to the group he was assigned to cover, he ferried Carole and Gerry to the Beatles' suite at the Warwick Hotel. "John made come-ons to Carole," Gerry later said, "but in a kidding way." While the media and teenyboppers lusted for John and Paul, it was Carole Klein from Sheepshead Bay upon whom their idols showered awe.

Aronowitz had a knack for befriending musical legends. Bob Dylan wrote "Mr. Tambourine Man" at Aronowitz's house: "sitting," the journalist recalled in his memoirs, "with my portable typewriter at my white Formica breakfast bar in a swirl of chain-lit Camels cigarette smoke, his bony, long-nailed fingers tapping the words out on my stolen canary-colored *Saturday Evening Post* copy paper" and playing Marvin Gaye's "Can I Get a Witness" over and over for inspiration. And it was Aronowitz who brokered the musical introduction of a generation, bringing Dylan to meet the Beatles—an evening that also turned the Beatles on to marijuana, setting their work on the path from playful and tuneful to profound and culture-changing.

Aronowitz's friendship with Dylan and his keys to the kingdom of "deep" songcraft made him a kind of life coach for Gerry. "Aronowitz thought Gerry was a genius," Barry Mann says, and Al used that admiration—plus drugs—to help push Gerry out of his rut of three-minute wonders to the Other Side. "I thought Gerry's lyrics were beautiful," is how Aronowitz put it, in an interview for this book a year before his 2005 death. "I considered marijuana a wonder drug; it gave me my greatest epiphanies. The first time I smoked it, I felt free." Like scores of jazz musicians over the decades, and like the imminent entire panoply of rock musicians, Gerry made dope smoking a key part of his creative life.

Gerry's mission had a kind of remedial urgency. America was changing, with astonishing speed and intensity, and the change was being led by its youth. The Vietnam War was tapping into an even wider vein of outrage than had the civil rights movement, whose earliest, hardest battles had been shrouded by the Deep South's violent barricades mentality at a time when national television news had yet to achieve its ultimate power and reach. The idealistic, euphoric energy that massed around Dylan and the Beatles was something that Gerry and Carole felt a part of, but their music didn't match. Dylan's headlong rush of poetic, free-associative lyrics made Gerry feel "like a dwarf." He'd *thought* that he and Carole had been writing meaningful songs with the likes of "Up on the Roof," but now Dylan's songs made him, and to some extent Carole, realize despondently, "We weren't even close." When Gerry met Dylan backstage at the latter's Carnegie Hall concert and offered kudos that concluded, "You've got a right to be very proud of yourself," Dylan's sarcastic rejoinder—"I *do*?"—was a slap on Gerry's already-humiliated face. The knife was plunged deeper when Carole, walking down MacDougal Street with Aronowitz in 1965, ran into painter-musician Bobby Neuwirth. Aronowitz, perhaps naïvely, was proud to show Carole off to someone in Dylan's inner circle. But Neuwirth's greeting to Carole was aggressive. "You're the chick who writes songs for bubblegum wrappers, right?"

Friends of Carole's and Gerry's worried about Aronowitz's influence on Gerry. Though Aronowitz had always claimed that he never gave Gerry LSD, Barry Mann, for one, believes that Aronowitz not only plied Gerry with the hallucinogen, but that some of the acid he supplied may have been laced with dangerous substances, like PCP. "Gerry got very involved with Al Aronowitz," says Mann. "With the acid, he prodded him on: 'Expand your mind.' I hated Aronowitz. There are intelligent people who don't use their intelligence for good, just for evil. That's Al Aronowitz." Others disagree. Jerry Wexler says, "Al Aronowitz was a brilliant guy" who never received credit for his musical matchmaking or his journalism.

Carole, Gerry, and Al Aronowitz formed a partnership, Tomorrow Records, to try to write and produce Beatles- and Dylan-sounding music from talent that Aronowitz would scout for them. Aronowitz scoured north Jersey for a promising act, and he found one in a young group that played at high school and CYO dances and called itself the Myddle Class. It featured a brilliant guitarist, Rick Philp (who would, within a few years, be beaten to death by a psychotic roommate), and a gifted singer and writer, Dave Palmer. But the group's star, by virtue of his calm, thoughtful air and arresting handsomeness, was its only moderately talented Fender bass guitar player, a lanky boy from a well-off Jewish family in the town of Mountainside, New Jersey: Charlie Larkey. Charlie was eighteen in 1965 when, as he recalls, "Al came to see us and wanted to be our manager. He said he would bring us to his new partners, Carole King and Gerry Goffin." To Charlie, who was five years younger than Carole, the names Goffin and King rang no bells. "I was familiar with their songs on the radio, but I couldn't tell you who wrote them," he says.

The Myddle Class (faux-medieval vowels were in vogue: the Byrds, the Cyrkle) had originally called themselves the King Bees, after an old blues song, "I'm a King Bee," which the Rolling Stones had covered. But there was *another* group called the King Bees—also from upper-middle-class families, working a similar tri-state circuit. *Those* King Bees included drummer Joel O'Brien, from Great Neck, whose mother was an actress and whose father was a well-known disc jockey, and a Larchmont boy named Danny Kortchmar—the same Danny Kortchmar who happened to be James Taylor's summers-on-the-Vineyard best friend. "They got their record out first, so we had to change our name," Charlie says. But the meeting of Charlie and Danny was the crucial beginning of a nexus, pinioned by Danny. As his best friend, James Taylor, once remarked, using Danny's nickname, "Kootch is like Wompater in Vonnegut's *Cat's Cradle*"—Wompater being the character who unintentionally got everyone else together.

The circle would include the cultured, hipster-like Joel, who was obsessed with Jean Renoir and Charlie Parker, and whose younger brother was on his way to becoming an art critic; Joel's gentle, intelligent childhood-sweetheart-turned-wife, Connie Falk O'Brien; Connie and Joel's best friend from Great Neck, the antic, emotional would-be painter Richard Corey, the son of humorist and social critic Professor Irwin Corey; and Richard's older sister, Margaret, a tiny, charismatic Carnegie Tech drama student. A photo of Margaret that Richard had magneted to the refrigerator of his Village apartment—"looking very dramatic, in a great, tight dress; her hair pulled back in a chignon," as Connie O'Brien Sopic remembers it—had led James Taylor, when visiting Richard one day, to be struck by her sad-eyed, imperious beauty. James demanded of Richard: "Who *is* that girl? I *have* to meet her." Radiating from her face was James's mother Trudy Taylor's hauteur and strength, Jewish rather than high-WASP version.

The group also included Danny Kortchmar's close friend from Mamaroneck, Stephanie Magrino, a petite brunette who'd graduated high school early and moved into Manhattan to attend the School of Visual Arts; and, later, John Fischbach, the tall, lanky scion of Madison Avenue's Fischbach art gallery, who'd been a Riverdale schoolmate of Carly's and was a novice record producer. Rounding out the cadre would be the fiercely witty Abigail (née Gale) Haness: like Carole, a lower-middle-class Brooklyn girl and community-college dropout, now go-go dancing on Murray the K's TV show, on which Charlie Larkey played bass guitar.

Aronowitz brought the Myddle Class to Gerry and Carole, and they all got down to work, making demos. "The whole time we were working with the Myddle Class, Carole and Gerry were fighting like cats and dogs," Aronowitz recalled. Given the emotional load Carole was shouldering—Jeanie Reavis and her husband living with Gerry's baby in the nearby house Carole had helped purchase—the potential for conflict was rife. Carole took comfort by confiding in her new best friend, Sue Palmer, the wife of Myddle Class singer Dave.

Against such stressors, Charlie Larkey must have appeared to Carole as quite a vision. He had a privileged kid's absence of a chip on the shoulder and a suburbanite's lack of angst. He was handsome in a smart-boy way: rangy, with sensual lips, heavy-lidded eyes, and long, thick hair. Al Aronowitz said, "He was a beautiful kid, and all the girls in high school were after him." Says Abigail Haness: "Charlie was a hot guy; he had a way about him. He was tall and quiet with dark hair and white skin; he wore tight jeans; he was a dazed and bewildered kid from the suburbs—very sexy." So appealing was Charlie that when the Myddle Class played a party given by noted magazine photographer Carl Fischer, Fischer picked the young bass guitar player to embody the anti-draft movement on the cover of *Esquire*. Charlie's long hair spilled out under a soldier's helmet and grazed the shoulders of his pea-coat, and his blue eyes gleamed in his sensual face, under the cover line: "You think war is hell? You should see what's happening on campus." Young women were supposed to pass newsstands, look at Charlie, and think, I don't want this cute guy killed in Vietnam! Many of them did just that.

Meanwhile, Gerry nursed grandiose visions. During one two-week period, he placed frenetically inspired phone calls to Cynthia and Barry. The crumbling of the superego seemed necessary to access one's artistic core. Wanting Gerry to *break through,* Carole cheerled his creative growth and balmed his ego. Similarly, Joan Baez had doted on her then-less-established boyfriend, Bob Dylan, making him breakfast at her Carmel Highlands home, tiptoeing around as he composed, raving about how brilliant he was.

But Carole had not been immune to the quiet charms of handsome Charlie Larkey, and increasingly isolated from Gerry, the songwriter and the bass guitar player had time to get to know each other. "She fell hard for him," a friend says. The two embarked upon what an observer describes as "this really torrid love affair." But it wasn't uncomplicated: Abigail Haness, whom Charlie knew from their work on the Murray the K show, was having a fling with him herself. Charlie was *very* appealing.

The Myddle Class played second or third bill at the quintet of three-and-four-bands-a-night clubs on MacDougal Street—the Café Wha? and Cafe Bizarre, the Gaslight, the Au Go Go, and the Night Owl (where Danny Kortchmar, Joel O'Brien, and James Taylor's new group, the Flying Machine,* held forth). One night Charlie brought his secret, married girlfriend, Carole, into Manhattan to see the reconstituted, renamed group that had, in the recent long ago, won the coin toss to call itself the King Bees. Danny recalls, "When we heard that Charlie had Carole King in the audience, boy, did we feel: Carole King's a legend! She wrote all those great songs! She was the real thing. I had tremendous respect for her before I even met her.

"She heard us play and she was *very* encouraging," Danny continues. "And of course she immediately loved James. She recognized that he had it." James and Joel were now shooting heroin, a habit that had them speaking a private junkie language, making Kootch, who wasn't about to get *near* a hypodermic needle, feel excluded, hurt, and square. James was crashing at Joel and Connie's Charles Street apartment, sleeping in a chair in the living room, usually either drugged out, playing his guitar, or both. "Music is a language, and that's what it was for James. He used to say that songs 'streamed through' him," says Connie. A few years later, James said of this time and the times he was institutionalized that such darkness was "an inseparable part of my personality, as innate and incurable as having a size 10D shoe. I don't know what I would do if I didn't have music to totally engross me. I need it desperately." Connie adds, "James was always layered, and he was always charismatic. And he was really, really smart—smart in the way that you know you're smart and you don't talk about it."

---

* The house band at the Au Go Go was the Blues Project, whose members Joni would get to know at around this same time. Both the Flying Machine and the Blues Project were blues-based bands of coddled white boys (a fact mocked by James Taylor in his introductory patter to his "Steamroller"), but there was a difference: the Blues Project boys were middle class while the Flying Machine were the sons of the cultural and intellectual elite. Aside from James (whose father was the dean of the college of medicine at the University of North Carolina), Joel (whose "Cole Porter world" parents, as Joel's wife, Connie, viewed them, socialized with Broadway eminences), and Danny (whose mother was a prolific novelist), bass player Zach Wiesner's father, Jerome, had been President Kennedy's main nuclear science advisor and would soon become the president of MIT.

The band on the street at the time—the one to beat—was the jug band turned rock band, the Lovin' Spoonful, soon to produce the infectious hits "Do You Believe in Magic" and "Summer in the City."

When Carole invited Danny/Kootch to play on the demos she and Gerry were producing for Charlie and his group, Danny was "more thrilled than I'd ever been in my life"—and once he got to those sessions he was wildly impressed. He'd never been in a recording studio before, and Carole radiated the same dominating surety that she had exhibited in the Drifters sessions. "Such skill!" Kootch recalls. "She knows so well how to make a record, how to pull the parts together, how to arrange for a rock band. She'd say, 'Play the chinks here—*chink! chink! chink!*' 'Play this line; one, two, *play* with me!' Working with Carole was like going to Harvard." Yet the veneration was part of the problem: Carole's studio craft made her register to slightly younger guys like Kootch not as the groovy chick she would have liked to be seen as but as an awesome professional.

At some point Carole experienced what would be the first of several breakups with Charlie over the course of their ten years together—all of which she took hard. "She was madly in love with him," says a friend, and she was insecure about her attractiveness. Charlie quickly took up with Danny Kortchmar's friend Stephanie Magrino, whose tiny frame, large eyes, and cascading dark hair made her very attractive to men; Charlie and Stephanie became a couple, moving into an apartment together in Manhattan's Yorkville while Carole returned to her familiar role as the helpmeet of the unpredictable genius. Still, Carole couldn't quite stay away from Charlie and from the free, young life that seemed possible with him. The distance from 1965 to early 1967—years she had spent in her New Jersey tract house—had been millennial. It was impossible to be a young adult during that time and not feel the world changing—and changing *for you,* to your rhythms, by your peers, according to your idealism. It was, as the Byrds* sang in Pete Seeger's song, a "turn, turn, turn" of the culture.

---

* One day in late 1964, Roger (then Jim) McGuinn (who'd recently been playing with Bobby Darin) picked up his twelve-string guitar and, because his Byrds needed an introduction to "Mr. Tambourine Man," set eight notes inspired by Bach's "Jesu, Joy of Man's Desiring" to a nonfolk beat he says he got from the Beatles' appropriation of a Phil Spector beat. McGuinn chose the Dylan bar that had the most new-hipster appeal: "the 'boot heels to be wandering' were like Beatle boots, Kerouac boots." The revolutionary genre of "folk rock" was born.

Much of this movement started in San Francisco. Its psychedelic culture seemed to have popped out of the oven fully baked one magical day, with the same suddenness as the Beatles-borne stealth British Invasion and, before that, the youthfulness and idealism validated by President Kennedy's election. The Diggers, who dispensed free food in San Francisco, and Ken Kesey's Merry Pranksters, with their cross-country bus rides, are today given credit for the burst of LSD felicity–that sense of living in an ecstatically affectionate, private-joke reality, on a chemically tinged plane above the plodding pathos of the straight world. But the goofy-macho air of (the considerably older) Kesey and his infamous psychedelic Trips Festivals were *not* what attracted middle-class girls in the Bay Area and, increasingly, all over the country. Rather, they sensed a feminine coloration from the start, beginning with the graphic designs of the suddenly flowering posters for the Fillmore and Avalon Ballroom rock concerts, for Jefferson Airplane, the Grateful Dead, the Sopwith Camel, Big Brother and the Holding Company, and other groups of art students, folkies, ex-Beats, and assorted musicians who had mystically synergized a sensual, LSD-heightened hard rock. Although the graphic artists were all male (Wes Wilson, Rick Griffin, Stanley Mouse, Alton Kelley, Victor Moscoso), the style was baroquely feminine in the extreme–everything swirled or sinewed. The dancing style, too–which was actually a near-simultaneous import from L.A.*–was sensual and

---

* It had been created in mid-1965, during the culture-changing Byrds concerts at Ciro's (the once iconically glamorous Sunset Strip nightclub, reopened under new ownership), by sculptor Vito Paulekas and dancer Carl Franzoni. Paulekas was a wild-eyed guru who (though few of his acolytes knew this) had spent four years in prison in Massachusetts in the 1940s before moving to L.A. for self-reinvention. Paulekas and Franzoni trained a troupe of young "freakers" in the sensual body movement that soon became synonymous with late-1960s dancing. When you walked into Ciro's in 1965, heard the music, and saw the (stoned) dancing, you were jolted by its radical fluidity, gentleness, and introspection. "You knew a new world had arrived," says one habitué. The Byrds took the Paulekas-Franzoni dancers on tour with them later that year, but they were too ahead of their time. The group got beat up in the Midwest. But, as with so much from that era, gross irresponsibility and tragedy lay on the flip side of the ecstasy. An acid-tripping Paulekas set his young son atop a high ladder in his art studio one night, and the child fell to his death. It is unlikely that Paulekas was prosecuted for the fatal negligence.

langorous, a welcome replacement for the corny, thumping Twist-era dances that had prevailed for seven years.

To them, too, San Francisco previewed a Renaissance princess way of being a young woman: the long velvet dresses, the mastery of tarot and astrology, the Tiffany lamps, the thrift shop antiques, the Beardsley prints. This persona would be eventually represented by Joni (after she got out of her miniskirt phase), who was right now stage-pattering about a new kind of poor but classy bohemian maiden to a growing circle of fans in folk clubs from Detroit to Philadelphia, New York to Florida.

San Francisco's psychedelia—frivolous on its own—was lent gravitas by the historic bohemia of nearby Carmel and Big Sur and, especially, by the ballooning political consciousness of Berkeley, across the Bay. The university had been animated by a compelling activism, sparked by 1963's Free Speech Movement, which in turn had been preceded by protests against the House Un-American Activities Committee. And in a pattern that had also flourished on other campuses over the past five years, Berkeley had turned into a glamorous incubator of radicalism. By the sheer weight of the new mood's seductive embrace and the hurtling events of the times, penny-loafered freshmen had been flipped into ardent politicos with what seemed like a 75 percent conversion rate. The same students who, lavaliered and madras'd, had lofted beer mugs in Larry Blake's Rathskeller in 1964 were, by 1967, sipping espresso at the small marble tables at the Forum and Café Mediterranean: leafing through Student Nonviolent Coordinating Committee and Students for a Democratic Society pamphlets and copies of the *Berkeley Barb* and the *Oracle*. Few girls who went through Berkeley as the mid-1960s turned to the late 1960s didn't have at least one friend who'd started out as an A-student goody-goody and ended up on an FBI list.

All over the country, young women Carole's age were shopping at new boutiques, some of which—lodestarred by New York's Paraphernalia, and its designers Betsey Johnson and Michael Mott—took the Mary Quant look one novel step further (paper dresses, neon dresses), but all of which put forth a look of sexuality-*with-innocence*. Young women Carole's age were growing their hair long, shifting the facial emphasis from the mouth, which now went pale and invisible, to the window-of-the-soul eyes, which became in some (like Rudi Gernreich's model Peggy Moffitt) hauntingly aggressive but mostly (English model Twiggy, American model-of-the-hour Cathee Dahmen, and Andy Warhol superstar Edie Sedgwick) Keane-painting waifish and full of wonder. In concert with the widened availability of the new, slightly lowered-dose birth control pill,* this *winsomeness*—the jaunty miniskirts and boots, the big, wide eyes—repelled adjectives like "cheap" and "tramp," words that seemed relics of a recent-but-long-ago Dark Age. An act (casual sex among unmarried people) that had always been shameful and tragic now acquired a butterfly-winged lightness. Add to all this the now fully realized version of the sexy intellectual that Carly's circle at Sarah Lawrence had pioneered. Its archetype was a polished young woman from a family of means, who wore an expensive suede jacket and hoop earrings, with the sides of her shiny long hair gathered at the back of her head by a wooden-chopstick-clasped leather thong. This kind of woman, who was suddenly seen on so many campuses, had dashing, Gauloises-smoking boyfriends (in the plural) in rumpled tweed jackets, professors or freelance hipsters who roosted on the fringes of campus. Girls who had started college when "I'm here to get my MRS degree" was still unembarrassedly quipped in sorority bedrooms now looked at these role models—graduate students, TAs—and saw a sophisticated, intellectual, single-or-not questing womanliness. The message was *Why stop now?*

In the harbor of ideas, a big ship was turning. If you were, in 1966–67, a female college senior at an elite private college or a top-tier progressive university—Michigan or Berkeley or Northwestern or Wisconsin—you saw a forked road. Some of your friends were planning postgraduation weddings, while others were secretly rebelling against those first boys they'd had sex with. One day, on a break between classes, a girl of the second sort might pick up a stranger, bring him back to her apartment,

---

* Although the Pill was still not legal for unmarried women in many states, many doctors prescribed it to them anyway.

and crisply sever her long- (if indifferently) held belief in love as a prerequisite for sex in one half hour. As she slipped afterward into her lecture
hall seat, she would realize *I can do this*. But *this* wasn't sex per se. That
would have been cheap. What she had done was all about sophistication
and risk. As Sara Davidson paraphrased her and her Berkeley roommates' thinking in her time capsule 1977 memoir, *Loose Change,* "We decided we were going to be like [D. H.] Lawrence's women. We would not
marry for security or be hampered by convention . . . It's almost as if we
took vows then: we were going to make life as interesting a journey as
possible and were willing to suffer pain if necessary."

A young woman in the spring and summer of 1967 was walking
toward a door *just* as that door was springing open. A stage was set for
her adulthood that was so accommodatingly extreme—so whimsical,
sensual, and urgent—that behavior that in any other era would carry a
penalty for the daring was shielded and encouraged. There was safety
in numbers for every gorgeous madness; good girls wanting to be bad
hadn't had so much cover since the Jazz Age. San Francisco—glowing
with psychedelic mystique, the whole city plastered with Fillmore and
Avalon posters of tangle-haired goddess girls—was preparing for a con-
vocation (of hapless runaways from provincial suburbs, it would turn
out), the Summer of Love, through which the term "flower children"
would be coined, while in harsh, emotion-sparking contrast, helicopters
were dropping thousands of U.S. boys into the swamps of Vietnam.

At the nearby Monterey Pop Festival the Mamas and the Papas were
passing the baton to Big Brother and the Holding Company's Janis
Joplin: sweat drenching her bell-bottomed white rib-knit pant suit as she
wailed in bluesy angst. The festival, which featured Jimi Hendrix's first
filmed guitar immolation, drew a glamorous young elite that seemed to
have just materialized one day. This was the New Hip, and D. A. Pennebaker's footage soon displayed it in all its envy-stoking splendor: almost
uniformly beautiful young people, wafting to the music in slow motion
while radiating that essential property of any ascendant new cultural
scene—they were your high school "in" crowd in fresh costume.

The music world's function as stand-in to the high school cafeteria was also, cruelly, served by the stinging rejection experienced* by the most talented new artist there, Laura Nyro, an overweight, shrill, and seemingly possessed writer-pianist whose brilliant, original songs were as American as Stephen Foster's and Irving Berlin's. ("*That* should be the National Anthem," the Blues Project's Steve Katz said of "Stoned Soul Picnic," while Stephen Sondheim declared: "In economy, lyricism and melody, it is a masterpiece.") Nyro's dazzling word soup mixed imagery from antebellum plantation life with Damon Runyon and Stagolee, yielding a white girl's reverent obsession with soul. Joni considered Laura Nyro her only female peer, and Carole's hits had influenced Laura, just as Carole would be influenced by Laura's first album.

In spring 1967, if you walked down the street as the Young Rascals' "Groovin'" drifted from one of the brand-new head shops, you had to agree with that dreamy song: there *wasn't* "*any*thing that's *bet*-ter" than this golden moment.

All this shimmering possibility knocked at the cage of Carole's troubled marriage.

Morally disciplined and long-suffering with Gerry, Carole now began to follow her instincts. Even though she and Charlie had broken

---

* Nyro and her backup singers had arrived at the festival in long, black nightclub gowns, and she, a rare bird from another planet, was overtaken, confounded, and outnumbered by the psychedelia of Jefferson Airplane, Hendrix, and Joplin, and by the SoCal hipness of the Mamas and the Papas, who had recently made electric folk rock sybaritic and glamorous. Laura bombed at the festival and as she sang, she heard, or *thought* she heard, the audience booing her. "Laura walked off the stage crying," Michelle Phillips recalls, and as both Michelle and festival coproducer (with John Phillips) Lou Adler attest: "Laura carried that baggage all her life." But, almost three decades later, Adler and Pennebaker carefully watched and (with the aid of sound amplification that had been unavailable in 1967) listened to the original footage of Laura's performance, and they made an astonishing discovery: the booing was something Laura had imagined. "Those *weren't* boos!" Adler says today. "It was a person saying, 'We . . . love . . . you'!" Lou Adler and Michelle Phillips were eager to get the tape to Laura to reverse her pain. Laura died, of ovarian cancer, in April 1997, before she was able to hear it.

up, she continued to rendezvous with him, in the apartment he shared with his new girlfriend, Stephanie Magrino. Stephanie knew Carole had been to see Charlie because she, a dark brunette, had found a strand of Carole's light-brown hair in their bed, and Charlie had confessed.

Charlie and Danny Kortchmar were now members of the Fugs, the local-legend group headed up by poets Ed Sanders, Tuli Kupferberg, and Ken Weaver. As Charlie describes them, "The Fugs were a link between the Beat generation and rock 'n' roll." The group's Peace Eye Bookstore had a hand in turning the sleepy, ethnic and poor Lower East Side into the newly renamed soon-to-be-hippie haven, the East Village. Stephanie was working at the Fillmore East, assisting Joshua White, who'd perfected a newly essential component of psychedelic music: the light show. This world that Charlie and Stephanie had effortlessly fallen into was a planet away from Carole's bourgeois New Jersey. Carole was not too old for this new world; rather, the life she was living was too old for *her*. She'd gotten on the elevator when young adult life had meant responsibility and sober idealism. Now it meant playfulness, politics, and sensuality.

Through it all, Carole and Gerry continued writing together. Though their marriage was crumbling, the greater bond of their musical collaboration was in overdrive. Now that the new Dylan- and Beatles-led forms of music were dominant, it was natural that they, nothing if not competitive, would pound on the door of that rejecting new order, demanding to be included. They would be awarded entrance by way of their "Wasn't Born to Follow," a folk-rock-like melody with airily poetic lyrics ("You may lead me to the chasm where the rivers of our visions flow into one another") that attracted the hipness-gatekeeping Byrds, who eventually chose to record it. But it was not this out-of-character song that endured. Rather, a very different song, perfecting the pop-soul idiom they had pioneered, would constitute their pre-divorce masterpiece.

Gerry had run into Jerry Wexler outside of Grand Central Terminal one day, and from his limousine window Wexler had shouted: "You and Carole should write a song called 'You Make Me Feel Like a Natural Woman.'" A few weeks later the pair showed up at Wexler's Atlantic office and, he recalls, "they said, 'Here's 'Natural Woman.' You told us to write it.'" After everyone laughed at how literally the two had taken the suggestion, Carole sat down at the piano. It was a spiritual song—full of gospel blue notes and blue harmonies—disguised as a love song, in three-four time with a swing feel. Wexler recalls, "I thought: Oh, my God, is this wonderful, or what?! It was a hit, I *knew* it."

Wexler wanted to get it to Aretha Franklin, who was at the peak of her fame with young white listeners. She had been dubbed the Queen of Soul, largely as a result of her biggest hit to date, Don Covay's "Chain of Fools," in which Wexler's respect for her gospel genius was tweaked by a Brill Building touch: Ellie Greenwich, who with her husband, Jeff Barry, had written latter-day girl-group songs ("Da Doo Ron Ron," "Leader of the Pack"), added the irresistible "chain, *chai*-ain, *chaiiin*"s in the background. Still, Wexler knew "Aretha could be picky." Recently Paul McCartney had sent her a beautiful song called "Let It Be," with churchly cadences that seemed tailor-made for her. "Aretha said, 'I can do that,'" Wexler recalls. "She cut the song, but for whatever reason didn't okay a release on it." Eventually—tired of waiting for Aretha's release, and dismayed that the Queen of Soul had acted so dismissively—the Beatles cut their own version, more Anglican choirboy than Baptist congregation. Would the same fate befall "Natural Woman"?

It didn't. The Queen not only recorded and released it, but "[t]he song has become part of Aretha's . . . persona, a product of her own soul," Wexler wrote in his autobiography, *Rhythm and the Blues*. For young women in the fall of 1967, "Natural Woman" was a watershed—a hymn to female sexuality right after the Summer of Love. From being worried that your heart might "be broken when the night meets the morning sun" to wailing, "Oh, baby, what you done to me, you made me feel so good inside . . ."—now *there* was a sea change. With its gospel melody's sanctified, tender fatigue, "Natural Woman" didn't express dewy love or even happy love; rather, it romanticized that very "willing[ness] to suffer pain if necessary" on life's "journey" that Sara Davidson, her friends, and countless young women now yearned to

pursue. In a moment of passionate political protest and kaleidoscopi-
cally dazzling cultural change, sex and independence were now part of
a young woman's quest: a beatific road to character.

Charlie and Stephanie broke up, and Charlie and Carole got back
together. Then Charlie broke up with Carole again.

In late 1967 Carole officially separated from Gerry and set out to reinvent herself. Alone, without much more than an introduction to Mamas
and Papas producer Lou Adler to write songs for the Monkees movie
Head, she took seven-year-old Louise and four-year-old Sherry and
moved across the country to a city she did not know: Los Angeles. She
was seeking "a new identity," she would say. The music business was
relocating there. Many of its bellwether artists perched in Laurel
Canyon, a bosky tangle of steep, winding, gladed West Hollywood
streets shooting off at Crescent Heights above Sunset. Chris Hillman
and Roger McGuinn of the Byrds lived there (David Crosby had a
house in Beverly Glen Canyon, to the west); Cass Elliot, who was becoming, in the words of Graham Nash, "the Gertrude Stein of the
Canyon," had a home on Woodrow Wilson Drive. (John and Michelle
Phillips had just moved into Jeanette MacDonald's elegant mansion in
Bel Air. The first Rich Hippies and the first rock stars to "go Hollywood," they gave huge and frequent parties, drawing everyone from
Marlon Brando to Warren Beatty to, of all people, Zsa Zsa Gabor.
They kept peacocks in their backyards, and they dismayed their proper
neighbors by wafting around the gated streets in glittery robes fit for
Moroccan royalty. When the Phillipses sold the house to an unknown
man with a reassuringly stuffy-sounding first name–Sylvester–their
neighbors were relieved . . . until that new neighbor, Sylvester–Sly–
Stone, moved in: a *black* rich hippie who, when he couldn't find his
house key, got impatient and *shot* the door open.)

Record producer Paul Rothchild resided on Ridpath, a narrow
ledge of road accessed by one of the Canyon's main streets, Kirkwood.
Rothchild was a glamorous figure–he drove a Porsche and wore a

velvet Borsalino hat—"these were the things that denoted one's station in the canyon," Jackson Browne would later say, of the man who housed and mentored him—and a dozen other talented virtual runaways from Sunny Hills High in Orange County—in the finer points of French art songs. Browne, the almost-too-beautiful boy with the Prince Valiant hair, was a few years from coming into his own. Rothchild was the producer of the Doors, who had had the summer's most explosive hit, "Light My Fire," anointing Jim Morrison—recently the pudgy-faced UCLA film student son of an army officer—as a satanically poetic rock god.* Rothchild's house and the adjacent houses—of hipster-like manager Billy James and record producer Barry Friedman—were an enchanted commune of crash pads for the enchanted almost-famous.

Carole moved into a nearby house on a street with an appropriate name for the break with the past on which she was embarking: Wonderland Avenue. She let her hair, which she'd previously teased and sprayed, grow free—the natural ripples she'd long despaired of she now appreciated. She took to wearing long, clingy, scoop-necked "granny dresses." With her neighbor Fred Hoffman, a Canyon wild child who would later become an art historian, she started attending yoga classes downtown at the Integral Yoga Institute. She'd get on the mat in the incense-perfumed room and savor the physical grace and the spiritual peace as Swami Satchidananda's image beamed down from the wall in approval. She stopped eating red meat (though she still smoked) and started to cook vegetarian. She enrolled Lou Lou and Sherry in the Laurel Canyon School, and drove them there and back daily, inhaling

---

* A year earlier Morrison had been spending his days sunbathing spread-eagled on State Beach (but rarely getting wet) with a crew of Beverly High surfers who'd grown up in glamorously dysfunctional families, and who cheerfully committed petty thefts with their hero, dashing outlaw surfer Miki Dora. Morrison wrote poetry by day ("terrible" poetry, according to his best friend, Robbie Freeman), while, at night, high on acid, he dazzled people with his "deep" metaphysical apocalyptic rants—and horrified them by gleefully stamping out lit cigarettes on his pliant girlfriend Mary's bare stomach. *Now* Morrison, basically untamed, was the FM airwaves' charismatic bad boy, soon to be called the Lizard King.

the menthol of the eucalypti through the open car window. She and Fred and another neighbor, Michael Schwartz, a regular on a TV dance show, played volleyball down the street, calling themselves the Wonderland Wonders. She bought last-minute grocery items at the Canyon Country Store, which topped a hillock just off Laurel Canyon Boulevard, and which was festooned with slouching, sexy hippie boys—just as, fifteen years earlier, the same site had been festooned with bearded "nature boys" with names like Gypsy Boots, who'd descend to Beverly Hills for day jobs, digging swimming pools. "Carole found herself when her marriage to Gerry was over," says Cynthia Weil. "I think Carole was always a hippie at heart, but she'd been living that life in New Jersey because she wanted to please Gerry. She was disconnected from her core there. In California, she began to live who she really was."

Danny Kortchmar's crowd was moving to California, close on Carole's heels. Abigail Haness came out first. She was involved with a musician named Michael Ney, whom she'd followed out to L.A. when he joined a new band called Clear Light, which Paul Rothchild was producing. After Abigail had told Danny about the band, he contacted Rothchild and was signed as guitarist. So Danny and his wife, Joyce, flew out and moved into the heart of the action: Barry Friedman's house on Ridpath. "People were coming and going all the time: musicians, dope dealers," Danny says. "Everyone was on the same street, hanging out. In New York it was, 'Rehearse? *Where?*' *Here* it was, 'Hey, you need a guitar? Borrow mine!' It was all those now-cliché things—mellow, laid-back, do your own thing. It was hard not to dig it." "We all came out here to reinvent ourselves," says Abigail.

When Carole knocked on Barry Friedman's door one day, Danny was thrilled and surprised to see her. Carole King! The Brill Building pro and suburban mom, in funky Laurel Canyon! Danny says, "I said, 'Jam with us, man! You play the piano and we'll groove!' She said that no one had ever asked her to jam before."

Then, just after New Year's 1968, Stephanie Magrino flew out to

San Francisco to visit friends. On impulse she stopped off in L.A. and crashed with Danny and Joyce. Reveling in the warm January weather, she decided to stay. Carole came over one morning while Stephanie was making breakfast, and Danny, who knew Carole had stolen time with Charlie during Stephanie and Charlie's time as a couple, suggested she cook Carole *one* skimpy egg, as punishment. Stephanie did, but what was supposed to have been a touché led to everyone collapsing in hilarity. Despite their past competition for the absent Charlie, Stephanie says, "We felt a kinship right away," and, over several days, they came to view each other as sisters.

In late-night talks after Carole put the girls to sleep, Stephanie ran down her biography to Carole–she had left home early, fleeing a harshly critical mother–and Carole in turn described the challenges of life with Gerry. "Just sharing our stories gave us the strength to see our lives more clearly; Carole and I buoyed each other," Stephanie says. The difference in age (five years) and accomplishment was a boon to their friendship. Carole had come to L.A. to break from the world she knew, that peculiar hothouse of same-aged, married songwriting couples like Cynthia and Barry.

Stephanie moved in with Carole. "Here we were–young, free, independent women who'd come out to California, where it was sunny, 'peace and love' all around. We weren't limited to the preconceived notions our parents had for us. Carole's mind-set was: She was coming into her own. She wasn't in her father's house and she wasn't in her husband's house. She was her own woman. But she was still a little apprehensive."

Carole flew back to New York and convinced her indispensable nanny, Willa Mae Phillips, to move to L.A. as well. Willa Mae came out, living with Carole during the week, then repairing to her own rented apartment on weekends. Stephanie says, "Willa Mae had no children of her own and, oh, did she mother us: me, Carole, Louise, and Sherry. She made us make up when we fought. I have a sister named Carol; Willa Mae would say, '*That* Carol isn't your sister; *this* Carole is your *real* sister!'"

Stephanie and Carole hit the produce stalls at Farmer's Market; they took yoga classes together; they'd get their sushi fix at a little Japantown restaurant named Haruna. And they shared their single-woman adventures. To Stephanie, Paul Rothchild was just the best kisser ever. And though Carole was still in love with Charlie, if he wasn't there—well, he wasn't there. One day she picked up a handsome, strange hippie hitchhiking near the Canyon Country Store. He had long, black, curly hair and he looked like a yogi. Carole and Stephanie took to calling him Weird Harold behind his back. And then as quickly as Weird Harold materialized, he was gone—that was cool, too. Living in California, and especially in Laurel Canyon, Carole said, around that time, "enabled me to take things as they come a lot more, without going into the type of thing that many New Yorkers will do, and as I used to do: intellectualizing everything, saying, 'Why did I do this?' and 'I wonder what he meant by that?' You just don't get into that out here." "But I was so much older then; I'm younger than that now," the Byrds had sung, interpreting Dylan's "My Back Pages" with quavering emotion. Like the song's narrator, Carole was dusting off the premature responsibility she'd rolled into at seventeen. Men had always had the option, even if behind their wives' backs. Now, over the next years—when, within the grand bacchanal of the new culture, staying monogamous to one's first love seemed almost life-denyingly monastic—young women with children were doing so, too.

But this "free" life wasn't *entirely* free. She and Gerry still had their Velcro-like relationship. He had moved to L.A., too, ostensibly for the same musical fresh start, but also because he couldn't really let go of Carole. Her years of adoration and their seemingly irreplaceable writing fit were, as his friend Jack Keller pointed out, the binding his fragile psyche had depended on; he homed in on her, reflexively.

Gerry rented a house in Beverly Glen Canyon, and his new girlfriend moved in. She was none other than Sue Palmer, Carole's recent best friend. "It was awkward for Carole to be around Gerry and Sue while Charlie wasn't there, and the awkwardness reflected the times,"

Stephanie says. "We acted differently, but we still had our old emotions." Carole had been trying to persuade Charlie to move to L.A., but he was resisting. More than the move itself, he was resisting commitment. Stephanie was encountering similar resistance from her boyfriend, John Fischbach, with whom she now sometimes lived, in another Canyon house. John had parlayed a relationship with his University of Colorado friends, the group Lothar and the Hand People, into a position managing the group, and now his ambitions ran even higher: with family money, he was building his own recording studio. "The guys wanted to have their girls, but they wanted to be free, too," Stephanie says. It was coming to be understood—not just in Laurel Canyon, but everywhere—that the new values benefited young men more than young women. In most cases, girls in love might want to *feel* free, but their lovers wanted to *be* free.

Carole's emotional Achilles' heel—men—became evident one day when she briefly returned to New York; she saw Charlie and it didn't go well.

How could you learn to be the new woman you were pretending to be?

Returning to Laurel Canyon after the trip back east, Carole got a lesson by way of a new collaborator, Toni Stern. Strikingly pretty, with a mane of golden, frizzy hair, twenty-three-year-old Toni "was a total bohemian—she lived alone; she didn't take crap from anyone; she did what she wanted to do," says Danny Kortchmar. "She was tall and lanky and *all* the guys wanted her." Toni had grown up on the Sunset Strip; her mother was a nightclub manager. "As a teenager, I used to get into Sneaky Pete's, the Whisky a Go Go, and PJ's," Toni recalls. "I thought of myself as a mixture of Eloise and *Inside Daisy Clover*." Toni had rolled into a relationship with tall, handsome, and slightly older producer Bert Schneider. A few years earlier, Schneider had been a wealthy and very conventional guy. Now, given the presto!-change-o! times, he was a sexy, long-haired, drug-savvy groover king in the New Hollywood, soon to produce *Easy Rider* and, eventually, the anti–Vietnam War documentary *Hearts and Minds*. Schneider paid the rent on Toni's Laurel Canyon cottage, seeing her when they both chose, and otherwise leaving her to her freedom.*

Just before Carole moved to L.A., Toni had visited Paris, where a film director suggested she try writing song lyrics. She wrote some and mailed them to Bert, who liked them—and who had a partnership with Lou Adler. Schneider arranged for Toni to meet Carole at the Screen Gems apartment on Sunset. At issue: in Carole's and Gerry's divorce a "baby" was being split. Carole got custody of the melody to a song ("As We Go Along"), while Gerry got the words. Finding a new lyric for the song (which ultimately went nowhere) was the occasion for the meeting between the two women.

Toni recalls: "One of the first things Carole did was hand me a bunch of Motown albums—Marvin Gaye was one—and say, 'Listen to these; these are *real* songs.'" The two began to write together—at Screen Gems, then at Toni's cottage on Kirkwood, or at Carole's house, just up the block. Opposites, they played off each other. "There was a practicality in Carole that was comforting—I would hand her a whole lyric, neatly written out, and she would sit down and we'd have a song within hours," says Toni. "Working with her made me feel validated, like I *wasn't* a wild child." For her part, Carole was faced with a young woman who trod with a lighter step than she had ever tried. "I'm sure there was a California quality in me that appealed to Carole," Toni says. "She was moving from a familial, middle-class lifestyle to Laurel Canyon, where she started to let her hair down, literally and figura-

---

* Soon after he and Toni broke up, Schneider would divorce his wife and become involved with Candice Bergen. By now he was ragingly political, a close friend of Abbie Hoffman's at the height of Hoffman's Yippie mischief, and a friend and avid patron— one might say acolyte ("What can I say? He's my hero," Schneider had said)—of Black Panther Huey Newton, who had been convicted of manslaughter in the 1967 shooting of a police officer. During this time—as Bergen recalls in her autobiography, *Knock Wood*—Abbie Hoffman excitedly suggested that Bergen use Henry Kissinger's presumed crush on her (he had asked her for a date) to "put acid in his Tab." Bergen declined to send Nixon's Secretary of State on an acid trip, but, urged by Schneider not to pass up the opportunity to "confront" Kissinger about the war, she did go on the date with him.

tively. We worked off our contrasts." Toni's sophisticated take on love dropped a touch of vinegar into Carole's melodic wholeheartedness. Among the three songs they wrote together in early 1968 was the jazz-flavored, acerbically worded "Now That Everything's Been Said," about a woman whose boyfriend has left her, with no warning signs, "to work it out, all on my own."

On the afternoon of April 4, word spread like wildfire through the Canyon: on a hotel balcony in Memphis, Martin Luther King Jr. had been shot and killed by a Southern white man. "The shooting was such a shock to us—how could this have *happened*?" remembers Stephanie. "There was such sadness, with this underlying feeling of embarrassment—how could this racist violence still be happening in this day and age? Who were these people who were threatened by such goodness? It was heartbreaking for all of us." For Carole the assassination held special resonance. Her songs with Gerry had done their modest part in running alongside the civil rights moment; the Aldon-sessions world had been, as Jeanie Reavis had said, a little color-blind family; and, by virtue of Carole's daughters' half siblinghood with Jeanie and Gerry's daughter, Carole's own family was what very few families in 1968 were: biracial.

The night of King's assassination, Bobby Kennedy, who had tossed his hat in the ring of the Democratic presidential primary, made a direct, heartfelt plea for calm to the black community—in the most natural of ways, invoking his own brother's murder. Before that tragic evening, Kennedy had been viewed within his party as a kind of political spoiler, angling in, late in the game, on Eugene McCarthy's carefully built antiwar perch and threatening to divide the constituency. Now all of that changed. Kennedy's impromptu remarks forged a bond between the former attorney general and America's urban blacks and rural Hispanics. The spring of 1968 saw Kennedy flower: touring the country, pressing brown and white flesh, visiting crowded ghettos and sun-parched migrant worker camps, sometimes in the company of farmworkers' organizer César Chávez. "Bobby," as people called him now, was greeted with tremendous emotion, and he returned it: hanks of his longish hair falling over his forehead, face flushed, smiling that abashed, toothy smile of his as ecstatic onlookers tugged at his garments. As March turned to April and April to May, Bobby Kennedy was being transformed into a political messiah. People started to believe that he could take the country's shocked and wounded soul and deliver it, deliver *everyone,* to the same idealistic mirage world that all the young people were singing about and marching for.

By now, Charlie had made plans to move to L.A. "It took me a while to get it together," he remembers, but he booked a flight for early June. Carole was eager to add a male presence to her four-female household. Then, two days before his flight, the news flashed onto TV screens: a man had stepped up to Bobby Kennedy at L.A.'s Ambassador Hotel, right after his California Democratic primary win, and shot him. He was gravely injured.

"It was unbelievable; we were just in shock," Charlie remembers. And there he was, about to move to L.A. "I was afraid for a while," Charlie says. "I thought maybe I shouldn't go. I didn't know if there was going to be a riot, even a war. I felt something cataclysmic was going to happen."

The day after he was shot—June 6, 1968—Bobby Kennedy succumbed from his injuries. "That period of assassination was so unreal, so dark and heavy for all of us," Stephanie says. "I remember being huddled with John in our house, stunned, crying, glued to the television. We'd had such high hopes. We had marched for so many things we believed so strongly about. Now it seemed like everyone who had inspired us to think as we did, to *hope* as we did: they were just picked off, one after another."

The day after the assassination, Charlie Larkey conquered his fears and boarded a plane for Los Angeles, to move into the Wonderland house with Carole, Willa Mae, Louise, and Sherry. Even though he was just twenty-one, his quiet, serious manner served him well as unofficial stepfather to the girls. It felt natural for him—"it was a role I wanted to jump into," he says.

With Charlie around, jazz was in the air. The cool jazz of Miles Davis and the spiritual jazz of John Coltrane, Pharoah Sanders, and

McCoy Tyner rang through the house now, along with Carole's favorites, Aretha and Otis and Stax and Motown. Carole was very happy. But then, in the last days of August 1968, the streets of Chicago exploded after the Democratic National Convention. Thousands of antiwar protestors marched, demonstrated, listened to rally speeches (by Allen Ginsberg, Norman Mailer, Tom Hayden, Abbie Hoffman, Jerry Rubin, and others), and—especially the tight, brand-new extremist cadre, the Weather Underground—tumultuously clashed with an overpowering army of tear-gas-and-billy-club-wielding police (under orders of Mayor Richard Daley), yielding hundreds of injuries and arrests. Charlie—who had performed with the Fugs on a flatbed truck at the huge antiwar March on Washington the previous winter, who'd been *Esquire*'s poster boy for the antidraft movement, and who, until his recent birthday, had been one of millions of American males eligible to be drafted while unable to vote—stared at the violence on the TV screen and angrily thought: This is going to expose America to what the powers-that-be are capable of. As well as being outraging, it seemed tragic. Bobby Kennedy's murder had, as Tom Wicker had written in *The New York Times,* "added sorrowful emphasis to one of [his own] political themes—the necessity for orderly and just redress of grievances, in place of violent action." Now there seemed *nothing but* violence, everywhere.

The L.A. émigrés coped with the outrage the only way they knew how—through music. As a tribute to the hometown they'd abandoned but would always love, Carole, Charlie, and Danny created a band called The City, with Carole on piano and vocals, Charlie on bass guitar, and Danny on rhythm guitar. They found a temporary drummer in the excellent Jim Gordon.

Carole's determination was the guiding force, says Danny. "Her attitude was: 'We're gonna write a song today, now!' while the rest of us were, 'Uh, do I . . . *feel* like it?' She would sit down and—*BAM!*"—a song or arrangement emerged. The City found a welcoming listener in Lou Adler, a star within L.A.'s lustrous hip-istocracy. "Lou Adler was the coolest guy I ever met," Danny says. "His laconic style, his insouciance, his not taking it too seriously. He was a great dresser, and he was living with [*Mod Squad's*] Peggy Lipton." (Later he would have a love affair, and a baby—the first of his eventual seven sons, by various women—with Britt Ekland.)

The four of them—Charlie on bass, Danny on guitar, Carole pumping the piano, Jim Gordon on drums—put a sophisticated gloss on a raft of new Carole-Gerry songs, three Carole-Toni songs, and two songs Carole wrote with Dave Palmer. Later critics would cite her trademark "hook 'n' riff heavy arrangements," evident on this album.

During the sessions that led to The City's album, *Now That Everything's Been Said,* "Carole would sing or play parts to Charlie and [me]," Danny has said, "and once we got it right, we could hear how great this record was going to be." At the demo sessions a young organ player, Ralph Schuckett, had been enlisted to help. Schuckett was so excited he was nervous. Here was "Carole King, the famous Brill Building hit maker," as Danny had hyped her—her songs had been Ralph's "favorite songs in elementary school and junior high"—sitting at the piano, writing the chord charts when Ralph walked in. "She said, 'You must be Ralph,' and introduced herself to me with that wonderful smile, intent on putting me at ease." This would be a template for her integration into a younger group of L.A. musicians. Many of them would view her, barely past twenty-five, as a legend of a *bygone* era that had dovetailed with their early adolescence; she would disarm them with her warmth and approachability, earning a role for herself. That role would have a name: earth mother.

The album cover shows three characters—Charlie (with his huge, sad eyes; long-limbed, in paisley shirt); hipster Danny, in banded broad-brimmed hat; and an intense and earthy-looking Carole in a white Indian shirt—squatting on the grass in front of an old car. In a breakthrough for her, Carole sang solo on almost every one of the twelve tracks. But the album's most compelling cut was "A Man Without a Dream," with Danny singing Gerry's lyrics ("It was such a good song," Danny says, "even my singing couldn't diminish its power") and with Carole's melody echoing the infectious plaintiveness of Curtis Mayfield and the Impressions.

Now That Everything's Been Said was the first album Danny had ever played on, so it seemed like a big accomplishment. But meanwhile, over in England, Danny's friend James Taylor was one-upping him.

James, nineteen, had crossed the ocean some months earlier with the idea of being a "street musician" in London. As shambly as he seemed, he left behind a local reputation, in Chapel Hill, North Carolina, as a young "remarkable virtuoso folk guitarist and singer," says novelist Russell Banks, who had played big brother to the tormented young James. Once in London, James dug into his jeans pockets and pulled out an address that Danny had given him: that of singer and Beatles intimate Peter Asher. Danny had met Peter several years earlier, when Danny's King Bees were touring with Peter and Gordon, Peter's duo with Gordon Waller. Toward the end of the duo's pop reign, they'd played L.A., and Peter had stayed with newly arrived Danny and Joyce at their Canyon home; Peter offered to reciprocate, should Kootch ever find himself in London. Now Peter beheld, at the front door of his London maisonette, not Kootch, but Kootch's friend—a handsome, rangy young man bearing a demo tape. Peter's wife, Betsy, coming out of the bathroom in flannel bathrobe and hair rollers, was struck by the young stranger's paradoxes. "He was like a big, goofy guy, but he was all Southern grace and charm." Peter played James's tape and—Betsy recalls—"both of us immediately knew how gifted James was; it was obvious." "I heard great music, great talent," Peter says.

Peter agreed to bring James to Paul McCartney, his friend and once near-brother-in-law (Paul had been engaged to Peter's sister, actress Jane Asher). James Taylor would be the first non-Beatle produced on Apple Records, and Peter soon came to know James as "a mass of contradictions: a thoroughly shy, self-effacing person *and* an extremely straightforward person. He was very smart, but," as he would learn later, "he was also a junkie."

Peter not only obtained an Apple deal for James; he and Betsy put him up. The willowy Betsy Doster Asher, the daughter of a Kentucky Secret Service officer, was affecting a British accent and eagerly growing into her new status-by-marriage as part of a family—the Ashers—so cultured, they'd awed the lowly pre-fame Beatles. Peter's psychiatrist father and oboe professor mother had opened working-class Paul McCartney's eyes to the finer things in life when, four years earlier, he'd come courting Jane and had moved in. But, in truth, if Betsy had been a few years younger, she might have crossed paths with James Taylor on MacDougal Street: she'd been a waitress at the Café Wha? and had worked in the office of the Cafe Au Go Go; she'd met Peter while she was working for a publicist and he was singing with Gordon. Now, here she was: playing the beleaguered hostess to this "big kid who was in some ways mature beyond his years" but was untroubledly, and seemingly indefinitely, freeloading on them. Betsy started leaving newspapers open to the "Flats to Let" pages, as a hint that James ought to find his own place. "I thought of James as a kind of nuisance younger brother," says Betsy.

The crowbar that pried James out of the Ashers' maisonette was Margaret Corey, the girl with whom James had engineered a meeting through her brother Richard. She had come to London to study acting (and to link up with James), and, funded by her father, Professor Irwin Corey, she leased a Belgravia apartment, where James joined her. Tiny Margaret ("James would pick her up, she would jackknife her legs up, and he would bounce her up and down like a basketball," Richard says) was so outspoken and madcap, she seemed to have enough assertiveness for both of them, which was very appealing to James.* She had once insisted so loudly on putting her feet up on an airplane seat, she was bodily ejected before takeoff. Margaret would walk around the Village in short skirts and see-through blouses; a dancer herself, she was forever developing crushes on beautiful male ballet stars (just before James, she'd pursued and, to her rapture, finally bedded dashing Bol-

---

* "The women James goes for are strong, and he turns his power over to them," says one who's known Taylor since virtually the beginning of his career, adding, "James marries women so he doesn't have to make another decision."

shoi Ballet choreographer Yuri Vladimirov); and she was sophisticated—she knew Lenny Bruce through her father, and she cultivated a
friendship with photographer Richard Avedon. As James prepared to
record *James Taylor* at Apple, he found familiar solace in heroin. Being
game for any new experience and eager to bond with her boyfriend in
the ultimate way, Margaret shot up along with him.

James Taylor would turn out to be overproduced, an imperfect show-
case for this complex young singer-writer who would prove capable of
exuding darkness, thoughtfulness, and intimacy in equal measure. Peter
Asher, convinced of James's talent, would vow to get it right the next
time. He and Betsy were planning to join the musical diaspora and settle
in L.A., where he would concentrate on producing and managing James
to best effect. Still, all the best producing and managing couldn't do what
one just-right song could do, as Peter Asher knew better than anyone. It
was to his mother's basement music room that Peter had been summoned one day in 1963, to hear a new song by the still-unknown Paul
McCartney, who was practicing there with the unknown John Lennon.
Peter descended the stairs—and heard "I Want to Hold Your Hand."

Now, in the summer of 1968, James and Margaret welcomed house-
guests—Joel and Connie O'Brien and Richard Corey—bearing unhappy
news. There was a girl, Susan Oona Schnerr, from Long Island, whom
they all knew. James had had a brief romance with her when both were
psychiatric patients at McLean; James and Joel had hung out with her
in the Village during their Flying Machine and scag-shooting days; and
she'd reentered their life as a State University of New York at Stony
Brook friend of Joel's brother Geoffrey. Susie Schnerr was a beautiful
brunette with what Richard Corey calls "Brigitte Bardot lips." The
severe depression that had landed her in McLean had over the years
gone unabated. Richard had met and had a shipboard romance with
her on a youth tour ship to Europe, during which she'd unnerved him
by walking the deck near the railings, talking about how much she
wanted to kill herself. Richard had been greatly relieved when they'd
made it to port without her having jumped overboard. But now Susie
Schnerr *had* killed herself, by overdose. Joel, Connie, and Richard had

known this for a while, but had not told James—Richard and Connie
had felt the news would dampen their friend's mood at a critical
moment: the acquisition of his record contract. But Joel, the group's
hipster-sage, felt James deserved to know. He informed James.

James absorbed the shock of the news. Then, in a brooding, reflective
mood, he used the unsettling fact that they'd delayed telling him to craft
the opening bars (changing "Susan" to "Suzanne" for rhythm)—"Just yesterday morning they let me know you were gone . . ."—of a ballad he
would complete over the course of months in various locations, the last
being Austen Riggs Psychiatric Hospital in Stockbridge, while getting addiction treatment. He called the song "Fire and Rain." The loss of the
doomed "Suzanne," James's struggle to stay straight, and his cry for help
("Look down upon me, Jesus, you gotta help me make a stand"*) all
gave the song *earned* white-boy soul. In two years, the song—and James—
would usher in a musical sea change.

Now That Everything's Been Said was released at the beginning of 1969,
but with no tour (Carole was afraid to go onstage, for one thing) or
promotion, it sold abysmally. Carole, whose expectations for the album
had been sensibly low—"I'm a songwriter, not a singer," she would tell
people—easily steeled herself against the album's lack of airplay and
notice. But Charlie had been banking on the album, of which he was
inordinately proud. "It didn't occur to me that it wouldn't be a success;
it was a big surprise when it wasn't," he says. He was twenty-one,
barely more than an amateur, and he was living with a successful songwriter five years his senior. He didn't want to be swallowed up; he
needed to find and prove himself as a musician in his own right. He
broke up with Carole, rented an apartment over a garage on nearby

---

* According to Richard Corey, James had originally written "Maggie" (Margaret's
nickname), not "Jesus," but Paul McCartney had told him he couldn't have two girls'
names in one song.

Stanley Hills Drive, and, to support himself, got a job as a busboy at the new vegetarian restaurant Help! on Fairfax.

Around the country, other young women for whom the new times had brought divorce and freedom were negotiating the same conflict. They were responsible parents (now, functionally, *single* parents) who put their children first, but they were also in the position of being, once again, teenagers in love. The *need* for complete control in one's maternal life and the complete *loss* of control in affairs of the heart: it was a tough push-pull. "All the people I'm friends with now are four and five years younger than I," was the seeming non sequitur that Carole would volunteer to a reporter in two years' time. Perhaps her proffering of that self-conscious detail was a way of expressing not just the new lightness she felt but also the heaviness, unique in her new circle, that she carried, as well.

Finally, there may have been a sense of familiar failure. Carole consistently succeeded at her work. But love was a different story. "Since she had 'failed' with Gerry," says a friend, "she was going to make this [relationship with Charlie] ideal. But it wasn't ideal."

Meanwhile, a new young woman had moved to the Canyon, "and she was all anybody could talk about," says Danny. "She was so dramatically talented, so beautiful, so utterly charismatic." David Crosby brought her to Danny and Barry Friedman's house one day. "She was shy," recalls Danny. "Oh, I was *round-shouldered* shy!" is how she–Joni Mitchell was her name–would describe herself during those weeks. The shyness was an element of that "gosh-golly" propriety that had served her well, obscuring her innate toughness. But the shyness may have also been something else–a self-girding, against a looming irony: receiving the reward that her work deserved would actually be more painful than *not* receiving it, given what she had gone through, and then decided to do, two fraught years earlier.

joni

march 1965—december 1967

When twenty-one-year-old Joni Anderson walked out of the Toronto General Hospital maternity ward in February 1965, she was in a "sort of numb and half-awake period," as she would later recall to intimates. Her newborn daughter was in foster care, and she was recovering from the nurses' fierce disdain, which she has labeled as "traumatic." "She was one of the walking wounded. She'd been chastised both tangibly and passively by the nuns in the place—it was just tremendous," says her second husband, Larry Klein, of what she told him fifteen years later. "She felt she was going to stigmatize her parents, that she would be relegated to the dungeon of existence" if it were revealed that she'd had a child out of wedlock. "She felt ostracized, with no hope for a job, and then [a couple of months later], here was this guy who wanted to be with her. She thought: That's the strongest way the wind's blowing."

That last line reflects Joni's bitterly flippant memory of meeting, in March 1965, Detroit-based Chuck Mitchell, a blond, clean-cut folksinger eight years her senior. For many years, Joni has demonized her first husband, who, as she put it (in the song she wrote about him, "I Had a King"), "carried me off to his country for marriage too soon." Especially since her reunification with her grown daughter, Joni has said that, racked with time-pressured "desperation" about the baby ("I couldn't leave her too long in a foster home—either I had to find a job so that I could support her or give her up for adoption before she was too old"), she told Chuck Mitchell about the birth, and that they made plans to save money to (as she referred to it vernacularly) "get the baby out of hock." When he asked her to marry him, she has said, he agreed to "take us both." Then (as Joni's account, which she's shared with friends and given to the media, continues), after they were married Chuck turned around and said, "I'm not raising another man's child."

Chuck Mitchell strongly denies he uttered that sentence, and he says, "I have no recollection—none—of agreeing to keep Little Green, and I think I would if I did. For absolute certain, I did not Indian-give. I did not say, 'Sure [let's get the baby]' and then 'No, we can't.'" Rather, "I said a very effective thing. I was no dummy. I didn't know a lot of things at thirty, but I knew when I looked at this woman—this feral girl: whoa! there was so much life in her!—that all she talked about were her songs, her writing, her drawings—I knew what she wanted, and how do you take care of a child and have a career? There was no way! My recollection was that, even though she talked about the baby—'What should we do?' 'We have to make a decision'—she never seriously considered [reclaiming her]. So I said, 'It's your choice. I'll go along with whatever you want.'" Chuck didn't want the baby; by leaving the decision to Joni, he avers, he predicted things would work out the way both of them wanted. Chuck felt "reasonably sure" Joni's priority was her songwriting and singing; that, absent anyone urging her otherwise, she'd stay the course she'd tentatively set in the hospital: surrender and adoption.

If Chuck Mitchell is remembering things correctly, then Joni may well be angry at him not because he fought her inclination but, rather, because he didn't.

That Joni came to understand that the decision was providentially made is suggested in a 1978 interview, in which she said—apropos of recalling a recent conversation she'd had with Georgia O'Keeffe—"after 1965 was really the first opportunity that women had in history" to be accepted as creative artists; therefore (she continued, in the interview), given that fresh opening, she *had* to make use of the musical genes passed on by her grandmothers. In 1978 no one but her close friends knew about the baby, yet in that interview she specifically cited the year 1965 (not 1966, when well-known folksingers began singing her songs, or 1967, when she acquired a manager and a champion, or 1968, when her first album was released) as the springboard, as if 1965 was a personal marker for her. She seemed to have made peace with the thirteen-year-old bargain, a peace that the two men closest to her during the late 1970s, John Guerin and Don Alias, both say she exhibited to them.

The piercing quality of Joni's songs, from the faintly panicked earnestness in her first two albums to the defenselessness of *Blue,* was the aftertaste of her decision, one that is so unnecessary to today's young female performers that its very historical existence has almost been forgotten. Today, it's a career boon for an edgy young performer to be with child; today, magazines burst with expensively acquired photos of unmarried stars: pregnant, pushing toddlers in strollers, or both. This was not the case in 1965.

Chuck and Joni met in March 1965 at the Penny Farthing, one of the higher-profile Toronto folk clubs. Joni Anderson was booked in the upstairs room, as the minor act; Chuck Mitchell had star billing downstairs. This was his first Canadian appearance; his repertoire consisted of Bertolt Brecht and Kurt Weill songs as well as historical folk music of the "Greensleeves" variety. The pair met cute—someone at the club knew Joni had been fiddling with "Mr. Tambourine Man" and said, "That song you've been trying to learn? There's an American downstairs and he's singing it." Chuck and his accompanist, Loring Janes, caught Joni's act—Chuck said, "Great legs"; Loring—more high-mindedly—said, "Great left hand." Joni took Chuck to task for mangling Dylan's work. "He'd rewritten some of it, and badly, too," she said, "and so we immediately got kind of into a conflict." Still, she consented to take a walk with him in a nearby park. It was a "raw, late-winter day," Chuck recalls. Although Joni has preferred to call what developed "an odd friendship," Chuck says, "We got together after the stroll, in Joni's narrow, cramped room, with its single bed by the window." Joni was—she would soon use this term on a Beatles-song character with whom she identified—"poverty-stricken." By contrast, Chuck, who'd recently quit a good job writing promotional material for the Detroit Board of Education, was comfortable; he exuded a certain polish. "Joni was certainly proud of Chuck, and she was happy for him to meet her friends," says Yorkville folksinger Jeanine Hollingshead, who'd admired Joni's grace during her pregnancy. "Chuck was American and really self-confident. We Canadians were very—I won't say 'insecure,' but Americans' national pride was much stronger and made for more outgoing citizens. We didn't [gain that confidence] until Trudeau became prime minister" in 1968.

Very soon after their meeting Joni took the train across the Canada-U.S. border; Chuck met her at the station and drove her to his home. He proposed within thirty-six hours. They fixed a June wedding date, setting out for club engagements and to meet each other's parents in the interim. Chuck wanted them to sing as a duo; Joni assented. He had a calm, literate, flauntingly knowledgeable air that she would soon find condescending. He also had what he admits is a "snide, confrontational" sense of humor, causing Joni to bristle when he made fun of her "big teeth" by remarking, "When you don't wear makeup and you smile, you look like a rhesus monkey." Their edgy sparring; Chuck's paternalism; Joni's anxiety about the baby, counterpoised with the flowering of her talent: all this would animate their fractious yet functional two-year-long relationship.

She called him Charlie. She was Joni—"and with a circle over the *i* when she wrote it; that was very important," he says. The practice of intimates calling her Joan came later; "If I called her 'Joan'—or especially 'Roberta Joan,' which I did when I wanted to piss her off—she'd say, 'Cut that shit out!'" Joni never talked about her polio to Chuck. "She did what she had to do. There's a line from a David Blue song: 'So Lucy, so easy she goes by, she moves on earth and sky . . .': that was Joni. She not only looked great, she moved well."

Chuck was something of a snob, and he took pride in being from a "pedigreed" Midwestern family. His paternal grandfather had been an editor at the Duluth *Herald;* an aunt had an apartment in the exclusive

River House in New York; his mother and father had attended Mills and Antioch, respectively. A graduate of Principia, a Christian Science–affiliated college in Illinois, he viewed his art college dropout fiancée as a "prairie girl" from a "rube place, and this was the days before big-time television; there wasn't a sense of everybody being homogeneous. I mean, she liked to go bowling—talk about your kitsch!—and with those little balls, like they do in Canada!" (The bluntness with which Chuck Mitchell—who has remained on the folk and small-theater circuit and also restores historic houses along the Mississippi River—makes these provocative remarks seems to acknowledge that his ex-wife's enormous renown makes his years-ago snobbery meaningless and ironic.) Joni once said: "My husband had a degree in literature. He considered me an illiterate, and he didn't give me a great deal of encouragement regarding my writing"—a view expressed in words she wrote after the end of her marriage, in "I Had a King": "He's swept with the broom of contempt." (At other times, feeling less the victim, she's said: "He liked Cape Cod and English furniture and was more cultured; I was just a rampant adolescent.") Escaping small-town Canada seemed urgent to Joni. "Her attitude was, 'I don't want to have to answer to those people [back home]; I don't want to live in that tight little society; I want to be free!' It was a powerful motivation for her," Chuck recalls.

Joni and Chuck were married on a June afternoon in 1965 in a small ceremony in the tree-dotted front yard of Chuck's parents' home in the countryside north of Detroit, by an Episcopalian preacher standing on an elm stump they'd rolled into place for the occasion. Joni made her own dress. On a radio show on which they appeared a year and a half later (when their marriage was fraying but they were pretending it wasn't), Joni—in her sweet, eager-to-please voice with its distinct Canadian oo's—described the wedding, with a happy giggle: "There were trees and birds and streams and folksingers and baroque trios hiding in the bushes." "It was sort of a Versailles wedding, only it was rural and rustic," Chuck picked up, "with the birds singing and violins and flutes—" "From the Detroit Symphony Orchestra," Joni cut in, proudly. From 1965 to 1967 many young couples had such weddings—on mountaintops, in meadows, with homemade gowns and self-written vows. (Joni and Chuck recited the standard wedding vows.) These sensitive, arty nuptials expressed the shift in zeitgeist from helmet-teased-haired Twist dancers to the gentler, just-precounterculture world of Peter, Paul and Mary songs, of Charlie Brown's Christmases, and of plays (*Barefoot in the Park*) and films (*A Thousand Clowns*) celebrating the sweet spontaneity that up-scale young adults were now starting to romanticize. This was the world of the long-haired playground moms in Robert Hemenway's story "The Girl Who Sang with the Beatles," in which lovers—quite like Carly's friend Jessica Hoffmann Davis and her groom—quoted e. e. cummings lines in their wedding vows and etched them on their wedding bands, and of the sometimes steelier version of these women in Grace Paley's short stories, Anne Roiphe's early novels, and Mary Cantwell's memoirs (which helped usher in the current return of the memoir genre). These latter young heroines were opinionated and nonconformist, yet they were *a priori* coupled. Despite the proud contrariness of this wedge of time, the idea of young marriage lay unchallenged. And marriage to a man more advanced in the glamour fields of the arts or media, politics, or academia enabled a dewy bride to leap several game-board squares ahead in worldliness. In 1965 people still advanced from youth to adult-hood. Two years later, that natural progression would be confounded, that value nullified.

After a honeymoon night spent in a Port Huron hotel and then a per-forming engagement in London, Ontario, Joni and Chuck settled into the "tenement castle" of "I Had a King": Chuck's three-bedroom fifth-floor walk-up, with its bay windows and octagonal dining room, at 93 West Ferry Street, adjacent to Wayne State University. By day, newlywed Joni, wearing jeans and chain-smoking dual-filter Tareytons, refinished the dark, ornate woodwork that Chuck had stripped, and filled the apartment with Indian quilts from J. L. Hudson's and thrift store antiques, eventu-ally turning the heavy, depressing lair into a green-hued fantasyland straight out of the imagery of J. R. R. Tolkien. Joni had picked up Chuck's ardor for *The Lord of the Rings;* both were swept up in the world of Middle Earth. At night Joni hosted Chuck's best friends—folksinger-comic Cedric Smith and his wife, Joan, one night; lawyer Armand Kunz and his fashion writer wife, Marji, the next. Roast beef and Yorkshire pudding was Joni's specialty. After dinner the Mitchells and Smiths would have raucous, all-night poker games; on the nights the Kunzes were over, Joni and Marji might talk fashion (both were stylish beauties of opposite coloring—Marji had black hair—who knew their way around a sewing machine) and, as the months went on, Armand and Chuck would talk about Armand's setting up the Mitchells' music publishing company.

In these early weeks after her marriage, Joni would often go with Chuck to the Chess Mate, the main folk club in Detroit—on McNichols (also known as Six Mile) and Livernois, next to the University of Detroit campus. The club was owned by Morrie Widenbaum, an unkempt inveterate gambler who was the Michigan state chess champion, and, along with another Detroit club called the Living End, it was a hinterland bright light in the still-vibrant acoustic folk circuit. Quiet, watchful Joni did not perform—at least that's how Eric Andersen perceived her. "She was just a fan in the audience: hanging out and listening, and impressed by all these people from New York, wanting to meet them," says Andersen, who was a highly regarded young singer-songwriter from Greenwich Village by way of San Francisco by way of Pittsburgh, and who had been Tom Paxton's protégé. (Chuck's memory is different. "The idea that she might spend more than five minutes without going on the stage is a little bit silly; she didn't have much of a shy bone," he says.) Eric was a tall, classically handsome man—his chiseled features not unlike Neil Young's and James Taylor's—and Joni listened avidly to his "Miss Lonely, Are You Blue," her own songs-in-progress brewing in her mind. She admired Eric's open tunings, a form of playing that was often used on pedal steel guitars and blues slide guitars and which gave Eric's song a swollen, resonant sound.

At about this time, rising to a head was the issue of the baby.

The more Chuck Mitchell is prodded to recall his conversations with Joni, the more it emerges that—for all his emphasis on her apparent career-mindedness—her early talk of the baby was indeed frequent, even persistent. "She had a concern," he says. She would bring up the subject "in a number of places, wherever we talked. The conversation may have been when we drove around, because we were always driving someplace. Initially it was, 'We have this issue, Chuck. What should we do? What should I do?' [I said,] 'Joni, make your choice and we'll live with it.'" Joni has said, "There was a desperation about me" at the time on the subject. But Chuck says that "the baby wasn't the central thing in our conversation—but then, it may have been that I wasn't that sensitive." Still, "there were no long silences followed by tears, although what was going on in her inner self, I don't know. She may have agonized, but I saw no sign of it. It was, 'I don't know what to do; should I keep the baby or not?'" Thinking hard about those long-ago conversations, Chuck says, "It could have been that I said, 'Oh, Christ, I don't want to hear about that!'"—then he thinks better of it—"but, no, I don't think so." From this remove, it's not hard to imagine a young woman more obsessed with the subject than she feels is welcome by her new husband. Significantly, Chuck adds, "We didn't call the baby Kelly Dale or by any name. We called the baby 'it'; not to be cruel, but for distance."

Chuck and Joni traveled to Canada frequently in those early months, playing small clubs in Regina and Moose Jaw in Saskatchewan, as well as Toronto, sometimes joining the Smiths at the Black Swan coffeehouse in Stratford, Ontario, home of the Shakespeare Festival, where Chuck's parents, Scott and Mary, were often in attendance. (Joni has said that Chuck used his parents' likely disapproval as a reason to disfavor their taking the baby. Chuck denies this. He was, however, close with his parents.) En route to one such Canadian engagement Joni and Chuck made a momentous stop—at the foster home.* This was Joni's chance to claim the baby.

Today Chuck says, "I remember it being a discomfiting situation." In later conversations Joni would say that the baby seemed well cared-for,

* Chuck, admitting his memory is fuzzy, says he believes they visited the foster home "before we got married," but Joni has consistently said that (in her view) Chuck told her he would take the baby and that is why she married him—and then he *didn't* take the baby; so her memory puts the trip to the foster home after the marriage.

as if measuring this stability against the peripatetic life that she and Chuck were living. She held her infant in her arms, and Chuck cradled the baby, too. All he remembers of that moment is "I didn't feel the way I would later feel, holding my own two children." Was Chuck's diffidence toward the baby the sole zero-hour decider? Or were other factors—the months of mother-baby separation after a lack of bonding in the hospital; Joni's unabated fear of her parents' reaction and the shame they might bear in their community over the timing and circumstances of the birth; her blossoming talent—did *all* these things, in the aggregate, lead to an almost preordained outcome? It's unknowable.*

Joni signed the surrender papers. She was asked to disclose information that, though she did not know it at the time, was filed in a folder marked "Non-Identifying Background Information" that eventually became part of the Canadian Ministry of Social Service's Parent-Finders Match Program, through which adoptees, at age eighteen, could obtain information about their birth parents without learning their names. Kelly Dale Anderson's "non-identifying background information" consisted of this: her birth father was very tall; her birth mother was of Northern European descent, had had polio, and hailed from the province of Saskatchewan. Then came these words, based on what Joni spoke, or wrote, at the surrender: "Mother left Canada for U.S. to pursue career as folksinger."

At some point after this final farewell to the baby, Joni headed with Chuck for Toronto, to perform. Joni had remained in touch with her high school art teacher Henry Bonli, who'd become a fairly well known painter, and his wife, Elsa. Over the next year and a half, when Joni

---

* The events directly leading to relinquishment of the baby are something Joni has talked about over the decades with friends, in different versions. Her conversation with a close friend about that day in the foster home yields a credible summation. According to the friend, "From what she told me, I don't think she had enough gumption to stand up to Chuck and say, 'No! I want this baby. I have to have this baby. I can make this work.' That's what was going through her head, but she wasn't able to say it. She's held that against him forever." Chuck says, "I will not take the blame for the decision. The Joni I knew always made her own decisions, and it stands to reason she would have made this one, too."

would come to Toronto, she would often stay, rent-free, at Henry's painting studio on Yonge Street, over Rugantino's restaurant, and sometimes
she'd babysit the Bonlis' daughter Jane. Henry and Elsa were very impressed with Joni's new husband. "We thought Chuck was the better
singer, and that he'd be the star," Elsa Bonli Ziegler says today. During
this particular visit "Chuck and Joni were staying in our studio," Henry
recalls. "We went to see Chuck in concert and everyone thought he was
fantastic." By contrast, "Joni was very vulnerable. She was supposed to
sing at a separate venue, but she couldn't do it; she was too nervous to
sing." This stage fright that Henry recalls is completely at odds with the
audience-entrancing persona that Joni was confidently developing. The
Bonlis didn't know what caused her block and they didn't know that
she'd had a baby, much less recently surrendered it. "She just came and
sat on my lap because she couldn't do it," Henry says. "She just fell
apart."

In Joni's lullaby about her daughter, she sends Kelly Dale off to an
unseen future after telling her, "There'll be icicles and birthday clothes,
and sometimes there'll be sorrow." When she finally recorded the song
(and she didn't until her fourth album, *Blue*), she held its two last syllables—"sor / row"—for a highly extended two measures. Her two grandmothers had endured backbreaking farm work, endless childbirths, and
stormy husbands. But their privileged granddaughter, who was as unfettered and as free to create as they had been overwhelmed and downtrodden, shouldered her own steep emotional debt. And over the years she
paid it.

Soon after her marriage to Chuck, Joni moved from Chess Mate listener
to performer. "Joni came in with her husband and asked Morrie Widenbaum if she could do a set," remembers Tom Rush, who was the featured
performer that week, and who remembers her as winsomely shy, the way
Eric Andersen does (as opposed to the way Chuck does). "Morrie told her
she could. So she stood up and sang her own songs. She was a slip of a
girl: blond, intense. She was probably nervous. The songs blew me

away—their poetry, their visual imagery." One of the songs was "Urge for Going," in which Joni is still hewing to Child Ballad–like expression ("And not another girl in town, my darling's heart could win"). But the lyric is a sophisticated commentary on impulse versus self-control, and she makes those cliché-magnets—climate images—strikingly original: frost "gobbled summer down"; the sun turns "traitor cold"; "bully winds" abound. The Harvard-educated Rush, a leading light in the once-Baez-led Cambridge folk scene, was an almost prettily handsome young man—longish hair grazing good turtlenecks under tweed jackets—somehow possessed of the ruggedly ragged voice of an old rail rider. He wanted to put "Urge for Going" in his repertoire. He struck up a friendship with Joni and Chuck, who invited him to stay at their apartment when he played the Chess Mate. Almost simultaneously Joni learned open tunings from Eric Andersen, who'd also become a friend of hers and Chuck's.* Apart from liking the resonant sound of the open tunings, Joni found that the technique relieved her polio-affected "clumsy" left hand; with open tunings, fretting the chords is considerably easier on that hand. By the fall of 1965, she had a unique playing style and two handsome young male mentors.

Chuck and Joni's Ferry Street apartment had become a way station for folksingers who swung through the Motor City: Eric Andersen and Tom Rush, of course, but also guitarist and MacDougal Street regular Bruce Langhorne, the only black man in Bob Dylan's inner circle ("a wonderful houseguest, who hummed as he made omelettes in the morning," Chuck recalls), and Ramblin' Jack Elliott, who was really Elliot Charles Adnopoz from Brooklyn (and who once took an underage girl home from the club, in those days before such things provoked outrage, or protection, and had a noisy good time with her all night, keeping Joni and Chuck awake). Burly "Mayor of MacDougal" Street Dave

---

* Coincidentally, Eric's soon-to-be wife, Debbie Green—who was Joan Baez's and Betsy Minot Siggins's friend on the Cambridge/Boston folk scene six years earlier (and from whom Joan Baez had actually derived her breakthrough folk style during those evenings at Club 47)—had long ago been a sixth-grade summer crush of Chuck's; their mothers knew each other.

Van Ronk visited but didn't stay over; and so did Gordon Lightfoot, Jesse Colin Young, local legend Loring Janes, and Joni's revered Buffy Sainte-Marie. Through the interplay with these seasoned players, at their apartment and at the club—where Joni and Chuck would crowd into the tiny green room on nights when Rush, Buffy, Lightfoot, or David Blue, or Ian and Sylvia were performing—Joni was listening, learning, and trying out her new songs for the best kind of audience: these colleagues/betters. "Whoever was there, she was on him: 'Listen to this!' She was constantly pitching her songs," Chuck recalls. But what Chuck may have recalled as "what we now call chutzpah," the performers saw as promise. Sainte-Marie and Van Ronk would come away fans. "Buffy [eventually] said, 'You wrote that?!'" about "The Circle Game," Chuck says.

The couple settled on the name Chuck and Joni Mitchell. They would take turns performing alone on the stage and then do some duets. They took their act on the road: driving all over the country in Chuck's 1956 Porsche, performing and then hitting all-night diners, where Joni would order grilled bacon and cheese sandwiches and salad, "slathered," Chuck recalls, "with orange Kraft French dressing." At these far-flung gigs (from Canada to Florida), Joni's feistiness surfaced. "She was not a wilting flower; she had a kind of jackboot feminism and a wonderful sense of righteous indignation," says Chuck. "At a fourth-rate pizza place in Regina she got madder than hell—'You bastards! You fuckers! Listen to me!' when a foursome at one table talked while she was singing." When the two were herded into the police station in Athens, Georgia, after Chuck was ticketed for speeding, Joni was so enraged at the cops, "she's stalking around saying, 'You sons of bitches!' The judge said, 'Young lady, curb your language or I will put this man in jail!' Her attitude was, 'I didn't come all the way from Saskatoon, Saskatchewan, to run into this bullshit!'"

Still, Chuck says, his young wife was largely circumspect. "From her years in those prairie towns where nosy was normal and expected," she had become "careful and compartmentalized. It was a survival mechanism, ingrained. She could be open but careful-open. She'd read a situation, and if it was safe, she'd open up more."

Meanwhile, Joni kept writing. And writing. Chuck may have perceived them as a duo, with her the junior partner, but she was bearing
down on a rich vein of talent that had suddenly materialized, full-blown.
It turns out that she was as natural a songwriter as any who ever walked
the earth and only now was this gift manifesting itself. She completed
the swing-rhythmed, highly syncopated ode to Yorkville, "Night in the
City," to defend the neighborhood that (as she indignantly put it in a
radio interview) "local Torontoans were always slandering—'Dread beatniks walk the streets of Yorkville!' 'Fourteen Yorkville hippies get
busted!' 'A young girl's true confessions of life in Yorkville!'—every week
there's something like that [in the news]." The song's upbeatness puts it
in the minority of her early pieces, many of which, for all her rootedness
in the folk idiom and despite her jazz instincts, are almost Sondheim-
like. "Song to a Seagull," "Marcie," "Michael from Mountains," "I Had a
King," and "Sisotowbell Lane" are all literate, melodic soliloquies that it's
easy to imagine hearing from a spot-lit singer-actor.

Through contacts at the Chess Mate, Joni and Chuck hired Motown
sidemen to write lead sheets for her songs. "They were good solid jazz
players"—not easily impressed, Chuck recalls. The men unenthusiastically
trudged up the four flights to the Mitchells' apartment, but once they got
inside "they listened to Joni and said, 'She's somethin' else!' and they
looked at her hands and said, 'Play that again?'" By now Armand Kunz
was working hard to set Joni and Chuck up as publishers of Joni's own
songs. Chuck had begun seeking (and would within the year obtain)
written permission from Oxford English professor J. R. R. Tolkien to use
the name Gandalf for the publishing company. (After Joni and Chuck divorced, her catalogue of songs moved from Gandalf to her own self-
named publishing company, Siquomb. Chuck's and Armand's efforts
proved very advantageous to Joni; having published her own songs so
early, within her own publishing company, she could not be exploited
the way many songwriters are.)

Joni was "writing songs everywhere," Chuck says. "She had little
pieces of paper and notebooks, filled with her round, girlish hand, with
her proper cursive." She wrote "The Circle Game" during the first year of

the marriage. Joni had started it as a kind of "answer" song to Neil Young's "Sugar Mountain," which Vicky Taylor had played her months earlier. Now she returned to complete it. Chuck remembers their talking about the song-in-progress. "It was a conscious thing she did; she saw the universal nature of the image–'We're captive on the carousel of time'–and played with it; the original toying with it came when we were driving somewhere. I always drove; she'd be sitting there, looking out the window and she'd often write. Even though she was a confessional songwriter, she had a real gift for Tin Pan Alley–the idea of the ponies going round and round: she knew it was commercial." Though Joni was not even twenty-three when she wrote it, the song has an earned-feeling grasp of the finiteness of life; it's darkly sad in the guise of sweet innocence. An answer song to "Sugar Mountain"? A commercial effort? It's hard to believe this is *all* this song is. A *Look* magazine writer in 1970 noticed, on walking through Joni's Laurel Canyon home, that she'd scrawled on a notepad, "Sorrow is so easy to express and yet so hard to tell." Was Joni's secret dilemma, from pregnancy to relinquishment, a "sorrow" that was "so hard to tell" it could only be expressed in a song ostensibly inspired by other, less personal, events?

Or *two* songs? For "Both Sides, Now," which she wrote on the cusp of her estrangement from Chuck, also seems undeniably tied to her turmoil about the baby, despite what she has claimed were the song's roots. She once said that "Both Sides, Now" was inspired by *The Lord of the Rings* (she'd begun to write a children's fantasy based upon it), while Chuck remembers her reading enough of his copy of Saul Bellow's *Henderson the Rain King* to have come upon Henderson musing from his airplane seat: "And I dreamed down at the clouds, and thought that when I was a kid I had dreamed up at them, and having dreamed at the clouds from both sides, as no other generation of men has done, one should be able to accept his death very easily." (Joni has also independently given this version of the song's origin.) But on top of these stated influences, "Both Sides, Now"'s theme of thoughtful indecisiveness and of the shifting, illusory nature of truth suggests it was unconsciously autobiographical. (Fluidity of meaning is "the great thing about songs," Neil Young recently said to interviewer Terry Gross, in describing how a lyric he wrote that was directly inspired by a male friend's phone message was nonetheless correctly interpreted as a love poem to his wife.)

Tom Rush had been singing "Urge for Going" all over Cambridge, and his fans loved it. He was eager for more of Joni's songs. "I remember asking her, 'What else do you have? What else do you have?' So she sent me a reel-to-reel tape. It was a tape of nice songs, and then at the end she says into the mic: 'This is a new song. I've just finished it. It's awful. I don't even know why I'm bothering you with it.' And it's 'The Circle Game.'" Rush phoned her right away. He would not only record the song; he would use the song as the title of his 1968 album.*

Joni's creative fertility and her work discipline were noticed not just by Chuck, who saw in his young wife a penchant to plunge herself into work until it was finished ("whether that work was songwriting or making a pant suit from an old navy blanket"), but by Chuck's friend Armand Kunz. "Joni had incredible focus," Kunz recalls. "If she decided to write, she wrote—it didn't matter what time of day. I remember her being closeted in a little room off their hall, working intensely, working seriously. Joni had a powerful work ethic; I don't recall her ever complaining or saying she was blocked." Kunz had just been made general counsel of the Michigan Bar Association, and his wife Marji had become fashion editor of the *Detroit Free Press*. "Marji's columns were chatty and approachable," Armand recalls, of his late wife. "She wrote about fashion like you were having coffee with her. And, like Joni, she never blocked. 'We need three column inches? I'll get to work on sandals.' Though Joni wasn't writing to space or deadline like Marji, they had that work ethic in common." Foursome dinners were frequent. Both fine cooks, the Kunzes lived in a carriage house in a marginal neighborhood;

---

* *Rolling Stone* credited Rush's *The Circle Game* with ushering in the "singer-songwriter" era. The album also included his versions of Joni's "Urge for Going" and "Tin Angel" and then-barely-known James Taylor's "Something in the Way She Moves" and "Sunshine Sunshine" and then-unknown Jackson Browne's "Shadow Dream Song."

the Mitchells, in their antique-filled "tenement castle" in a student ghetto—totally urban-romantic.

That romanticism became a matter of public record when Marji hired Joni and Chuck to model for the *Free Press*'s fashion page, and then in March 1966, the other Detroit paper got on the bandwagon by running an article about the Mitchells, touting them as connubial tastemakers-about-town. Tucking that news clipping into an envelope, an amused Chuck typed a note to a friend: "The *Detroit News,* treating in rather idyllic fashion the life and digs of a young couple footloose in the big city . . . us'n. We be the new urbanity, it says. How about that?" How about that, indeed? This was the life that a great many twenty-two-year-old American females dreamed of having.

Until right now. Until just this very minute.

For Joni, Chuck was an anachronism. He sang of "wars and wine" to blushing "ladies in gingham," while she, in her "leather and lace," was a fresher breed. Besides, female youth could grow its own wisdom. "Well, something's lost but something's gained, in living every day"—Joni had plucked from the emerging zeitgeist a sister-version of what Carole and Gerry were limning with "Natural Woman," the idea of the young middle-class woman as soulful risk taker. In Joni's freshly minted form, she was a thrift-shop fairy princess, romantically adventurous yet proper and decorous, ensconced in an updated version of a Montparnasse garret.

As Chuck and Joni traveled the country playing together, Chuck couldn't fail to notice how Joni's songs were catching on—and, in a letter to a friend who was the investor in their musical duo, he acknowledged as much, revealing as well a bit of his husbandly gulp at the comeuppance: "Joni is writing beautiful songs," he wrote in April 1966. And in June: "Joni's songs . . . have hit bang: Buffy Sainte-Marie wants some, Joan Baez wants some . . . My skeptical mind reeled at the response. Everyone is scrambling desperately for good material to give to the waiting public. Joni is the only good gal songwriter around." These manual-typewriter-produced missives contradict Joni's complaints (which she gave in interviews long after she became successful) that Chuck wasn't supportive of her songwriting. However—out of naïveté—Chuck was un-realistically optimistic about their performing duo. "We could not have been more enthusiastically received [at the Gaslight, in New York]," he said, in that same June letter, of a joint performance that was, indeed, well received. "We both seem to have that presence on stage which is a valuable and rare commodity." However, despite that strong set, the au-diences were mostly entranced by Joni. She had performed alone at Mar-iposa in August—returning to the seminal Canadian folk festival where, two years earlier, she and Brad MacMath had slept in the field and car-ried equipment—and the crowds had been captivated. (Still, the festival's founder, Estelle Klein, a tough gatekeeper, as well as den mother to Can-ada's folk community, was more measured in her praise. Shortly before her 2004 death, in an interview for this book, she recalled of that perfor-mance, "Joni didn't have that many songs, and she was kind of an airy fairy [though] she did have a poetic sense, and it made her different. I said I really liked her, but if she came back, we would need more mate-rial.")

Then Joni started making solo bookings of her own, over Chuck's protests. ("I was hurt, and I was envious. 'Where am I in all of this?' I wondered.") In the latter half of 1966 she traveled to Cambridge; Tom Rush had arranged for her to open for him during a series of New En-gland engagements. Rush felt proprietary about the "slip of a girl" he'd discovered at the Chess Mate. "I brought her east," is how he recalls it now; adding her to his show was "something I'd campaigned for; I felt like a big brother to her." Joni stayed at Tom's Cambridge apartment, and on their off-night they traveled to his family's home in Connecticut. "She was clearly creating some distance between herself and Chuck, on purpose," he says, adding that although Joni made no "overt" statements about leaving her marriage, "she was in an adventuresome mood."

During this visit, Tom was surprised by his delicate-looking proté-gée's ambition. "She was determined to make it; she was hungry for rec-ognition." It seemed to Tom that Joni was "somebody who just needed more. What you've got doesn't count; it's what you *don't* have that counts." Perhaps defensively—using his folkie idealism to cover his masculine surprise—he was somewhat alarmed by this. "I remember thinking at the time, This is a potentially sad situation. Nothing is going to be satisfying for her. No matter what level of recognition she receives, it won't scratch that itch." (Two years later, when Tom would visit the now-successful Joni in Laurel Canyon, he would note, not happily, that "she was telling me things instead of asking me things." For all its thunderous freedoms and rebellions, the late 1960s would give a woman a very small space to turn around in, even among the most educated, forward-thinking of young men.)

As half of Chuck and Joni Mitchell, Joni previewed her emerging solo persona at various folk club microphones. A November 1966 performance shows her charm. "This is a song about a daydreamer," Joni says (as she fingers her guitar: *strum, strum*), at Philadelphia's Second Fret. Her voice is high, pristine, and polite—as if she's raised her hand and been called on in grade school. She is wearing a minidress, her long wheat-colored hair glinting against its gold lamé. "Do I have time to tell a story?" she asks the stage manager. *Strum, strum, strum.* Permission granted. "One night I walked into a restaurant . . . and there was a couple sitting behind me in a booth . . . and I think it was their first date." She imitates a demure, excited girl: "'Gee! I'm really glad we could go out tonight 'cause I really think you're neat! . . . And I'm really glad we got a chance to go to that movie, 'cause it was a really groovy movie . . . You're really neat. And my friend is going to be furious in school on Monday cause'"—exaggerated abashment—"'she thinks you're swell, too.'" "Gee," "neat," "swell," "golly": this is art-college-faculty-pleasing Joni. Her patter's not witty; it's artless and clunky, playing against the gold lamé, the Nordic beauty. "About that time," she continues, describing the dating couple she's overheard, "he looked up and"—*strum, strum, strum*—"said . . . 'Huh?'" Laughter! "She was completely shattered by . . . a daydreamer! So I figured I should write a song for her." She segues into her (to date unrecorded) composition, "Song to a Daydreamer."

Who is this beautiful—and gabby—young woman? the young men are wondering. The women are thinking that, however—endearingly—corny her example is, she gets it; she's on my side. ("Everybody at the Second

Fret fell in love with Joni, including the owner, Manny Rubin," says Joy
Fibben, who, as Joy Schreiber, was then the club's manager. "They called
her 'The Enchanted Lady' at the Fret," says Gene Shay, then the city's
main jazz and folk radio disc jockey.)

Continuing with that performance: Now Joni's winding up to another
song—*strum, strum, strum*. "This is the song of a young lady who was . . .
pov-er-ty strick-en . . ."—she pronounces those last five syllables with
autobiographical care—"and a young man, who fall in love. She lives
on—oh, let's say Walnut Street, 'cause that's the only street I know in
town. And she has a little apartment in the back of a very nice row
house, and she invites him up to see her apartment one evening. And he
walks in and discovers, by golly, she really *is* poverty stricken, because
in her apartment she has"—now we see and taste brio trumping circumstances—"the following items: she has a rug." Joni plays a couple of bars
of snake-charmer music; the audience laughs. "It's an Indian rug," she
explains. "And, because she's a good hostess, she has a bottle of wine."
Strum, strum. "And over in the corner she has a bea-*u*-ti-ful old bathtub, that kind of sits on its feet. It's an Eastern bathtub. And then off in
the corner is her prized possession—a beautiful, hand-wrought, hand-
fashioned"—*strum! strum! strum! strum!*—"tongue-and-groove-dove-
tailed bed!" The men are amused (all this excitement for *furniture*?), but
the women are hearing code. It's not just furniture; it's the independence
of an elegant young bohemian woman that Joni is bringing alive. ("What
I didn't understand at the time was this business of identification," Chuck
Mitchell says today. "The guys loved Joni because she looked great, but
the girls were identifying with her in droves.")

Now Chuck, who's been on the sidelines, joins her for a duet on the
song that Joni's scene setting has been leading up to. ("He was more serious, more conservative than Joni; they didn't seem to go together,"
Gene Shay recalls.) They sing the new Beatles hit, "Norwegian Wood."
It's about a young woman who's so self-possessed, she leaves for work
while her new lover is still asleep. Waking alone, the man realizes, "I was
alone, this bird had flown." It used to be the man who crisply walked
away after a one-night stand, but John Lennon sensed a change in the

air, wrought in part by the Beatles' own music and the Carnaby Street clothes that went with it. Also, such a "bird" used to be slatternly. Now she's a punctilious, discerning young woman, the kind who'd remark, "Isn't it good? Norwegian wood."

By late 1966 Joni had "flown," at least in terms of duetting with Chuck. As Chuck recalls it, they'd both watched what he calls the "flawless" Jim and Jean (an Ian and Sylvia–type duo) at the Chess Mate one night and she'd said, "We'll never be as good as Jim and Jean, so the duo is over!" Chuck admits, "Maybe she was looking for an excuse" to go solo. Chuck reluctantly conceded, describing the events (and praising his wife's talent) in a letter to the friend-investor: "Joni is an excellent songwriter. I rate her among the best in the business . . . She is ready to go as a songwriter, and this has resulted in further tension . . . Result: the duo has been disbanded . . . Joni simply feels more comfortable performing her songs on her own. Since that is her feeling, and I as a performer know that the critical element of a good performance is comfort . . . I could not disagree, since I could not, in spite of great effort over the past few months, alter her feeling." Beneath this mature exegesis lay ragged feelings. "Everyone wanted her and no one wanted me; did I like it? No!" Chuck says today. Joni recently explained what she thinks was Chuck's reason to continue insisting on the duo: "He made more money with me than he did without me. He held the purse strings completely."

Chuck had begun having what he calls "gut aches" about his young wife outpacing and possibly leaving him. (The idea of the wife's independence threatening a husband was still so counterintuitive that when Joni and Chuck gave a radio interview to announce their decision to perform separately, Philadelphia deejay Murray Burnett, assuming the separation anxiety was *Joni's,* suggested that Joni assuage her loneliness while Chuck was on the road by thinking of a housewife married to a traveling salesman.)

Joni's first solo performance after she announced that the duo was disbanded was a return to the Second Fret, and Chuck insisted that, for her own safety, she stay with a married couple—the club's manager, Joy Schreiber, and her husband, Larry. Joni returned to Philadelphia in late

1966, and the audience at the Fret loved her all over again. Among other songs, she played her secret lullaby to her baby, "Little Green" (without, of course, explaining its significance). "Everyone was saying that there was a magic to her songs," says Gene Shay. "How she'd come up with these marvelous melodies and wonderful words, an artsy way with language." When she wasn't singing, she was drawing. "Pentels were new," Shay recalls, "and she always had them with her, and pads of special tracing paper that gave the feeling of stained glass to her sketches."

Joy Schreiber, Joni's slightly older hostess-chaperone, was also an artist, as well as a worldly bohemian. She had spent 1962 in Tangier, among a crew of artists, writers, and scenemakers that included poets Ted Joans and Gregory Corso. Joni, who had never confided in anyone in Chuck's circle—not even in the seemingly compatible Marji Kunz—now made her first American female friend. Late at night, at the Schreibers' large one-room apartment near Rittenhouse Square—often while the two women took turns on the same rapidograph drawing, with Joy's Siamese cats underfoot—the talk flowed. They realized they'd both been hinterland art students, hungry for adventure. Joni confided to Joy about the baby. "Joni was greatly disturbed; she had many mixed feelings about having to give this child up," Joy recalls. "She told me about the mental and spiritual turmoil she had felt during and after the pregnancy." The two women talked about how illegitimacy was "a dreadful stigma for both the mother and the child"—even in 1966, it was simply a given that you couldn't keep an out-of-wedlock baby.

Despite these troubled evening ruminations, Joy recalls a full-of-life Joni whose talent was literally overflowing. "She never walked in the door without saying, 'I've got to play you my new song!' She'd be playing it before she took off her coat. The lyrics would just pour out of her—she was not self-critical. She was so excited to write something, it never occurred to her how it would be received or what other musicians would say about it. She wrote many songs in my presence; I don't remember her ever changing a lyric." True to the persona she was radiating, Joni was a ladylike, headlong adventuress. "She just wasn't afraid, like the average young woman," Joy says. "She didn't say, 'What happens if I get attacked on the street?' or 'What if I go home with this man and something bad happens?' Or 'Oh, this could be scary' or 'Oh, this could come out badly.' It was all an adventure to her." At the same time, "She knew how to be proper. She had a propriety that was so natural, you didn't notice it. She could completely change clothes in a dressing room full of men without ever going bare; she could put on a whole outfit by putting it on top of the one she was wearing—it was an amazing trick!"

During Joni's time with Joy and Larry, a young musician from Colorado named Michael Durbin was playing in a group at Manny Rubin's other club, the Trauma. "Michael was a very dear man—charismatic, charming, boyish, and very outdoorsy: a breath of fresh air," Joy recalls. Joni and Michael started spending time with each other. They looked "dashing" together, Gene Shay says—Michael with his curly blond hair and his "gypsy-baby, new groovy guy" look; Joni, "gorgeous" in her fairy princess clothes, many of which—lacy, Victorian, seeded-pearled dresses—she now purchased from a Rittenhouse Square antique clothier named Zena. This was new; young women were suddenly strolling around Haight-Ashbury and the East Village, attired as if from Brontë-era trunks and Elizabethan museum displays. For many young people in 1966, the day you first started seeing your peers dressed in clothes from other centuries (had people ever *done* this before?) was the day that Dylan's lyric "Something is happening and you don't know what it is, do you, Mr. Jones?" took on a sharp, delicious significance.

Now Joni wrote the bittersweet "Michael from Mountains," about new lovers ambling through a shut-down city on a rainy Sunday, noticing "oil on the puddles in taffeta patterns that run down the drain" and seeing children in a park as "yellow slickers up on swings, like puppets on strings": uncommonly precise images for a pop song. It is a feminine song, braiding the wet children being scolded by (Myrtle-like) mothers in "wallpapered kitchens" into the story of intimacy on a depressing day; featuring a boy-man who is solicitous, impish, and gallant. The song is traditional—Michael will leave, while she will wait; but its conservatism is the baseline for an ascending series of songs that will break tradition:

Next will be a woman musing about wisdom and freedom ("Both Sides, Now"), then living on her own, risks and all ("Chelsea Morning"), and, finally, achieving the same romantic power as a man ("Cactus Tree"). Before she hit her stride as a writer, songs used to be "what men thought women should sing," Joni has said, "and they carried all the old feminine values, according to the 'master.'" In her own arc of songs, she broke with that ingrained imperative.

At some point after Joni returned to Detroit from Philadelphia, in the early winter of 1966–67, Chuck confronted her. His "gut aches" weren't going away. This wasn't the first time he'd shown his young wife his anger and insecurity. During a summertime trip to New York he'd smoked hash at Eric Andersen's loft in SoHo, and "I got paranoid, and all this garbage was coming out [in my mind] about my trying to control Joni and my resentment" of her success "and my fear" of losing her. During that summer freakout, "Joni had said, 'Charlie, are you okay?'" he recalls, "but when I said, 'I'm scared,' she said, 'You're bringing me down.' I thought: 'Bitch!'" This time, the fight was more heated. "I was pushy," Chuck admits. He repeatedly asked her if she'd had an affair. She challenged his right to ask the question. "She said something like, 'Well, what if I *did*?'" The evening was a stormy one. Joni was so angry at Chuck's possessiveness ("She'd always say, 'Don't be possessive!'") that, Chuck recalls, she picked the brass candlestick off her bedstand "and had it back and clocked for a swing. I had her wrist in one hand and the candlestick in the other."

And then, Chuck recalls: "I turned her over my knee and spanked her."

Soon after that fight, one night when Chuck was out of town, Joni arrived at the apartment with a guy she'd met at a poker game; she had talked him into helping her move exactly half of her and Chuck's antiques down the four flights of stairs. Chuck only later realized that she had moved out within thirty days after she received her green card for residence in the United States. He believes that Joni—partly—used him ("but I didn't mind being used, because we had too much fun"), and to some extent, she probably did. Now she was going off to the inevitable next phase of her life: living alone in New York City. The city would be her base of operations while, acting as her own manager and agent, she booked herself in clubs around the country.

Manhattan was both a magical and a daunting place for a Pentels-and-guitar-case-toting young woman to enter, alone, in the spring of 1967. Downtown had its own ecosystem. The folk scene on MacDougal, to which Joni immediately introduced herself, was centered on the Night Owl (where James Taylor and Danny Kortchmar's Flying Machine had been the house band until James went to London and Danny to Laurel Canyon) and the Cafe Au Go Go (where the Blues Project—"the Jewish Beatles," from Queens and Long Island—held forth), with all the musicians piling into the Dugout around the corner after sets. English rock stars stayed at the Albert Hotel on Fourth Avenue, while beatnik expatriates thrust back on the city holed up at the Chelsea on Twenty-third Street. Uptown couples thronged to the new psychedelic discos, Cheetah, the Electric Circus, the Dom. The center of the hip universe was Max's Kansas City; Wonderland Alices fleeing provincial hometowns could walk into the large Park Avenue South restaurant on a Sunday afternoon and go light-headed from all the dark-garbed, grave-faced Dylan types slouching at the bar. It was a mini-nation of weathered cool, unduplicable in any other city. Owner Mickey Ruskin had his choice of artists, models, and would-be writers as waitstaff—girls eagerly quit straight jobs in publishing to sling plates at Max's. (For 1960s-generation women who'd lived in New York, there was nothing, in ensuing years, more status-conferring or instantly signifying than to have "Max's waitress" on their life résumé.)

Like any great nighttime host, Ruskin turned a congenial mishmash of creators and outcasts into a dazzling elite. His dried-chickpea-munching aristocracy consisted of two-fisted painters and sculptors from places like Nebraska and their symbiotic urban complements (fey poets, cerebral critics); fashion designers and photographers; filmmakers and dancers that no one except *The Village Voice* knew to write about; briny denizens of a secret hard drinkers' bar scene whose unmarked north star was the 55 on Christopher Street; the occasional discreet prostitute, of either gender; everyone from Andy Warhol's Factory; heiresses gone underground; ruined or soon-to-be-ruined bards (Tim Hardin, Tim Buckley); and Park Avenue art collectors in artists'-tab-paying thrall to it all. Party addresses were passed around Max's bar on weekend nights under the twisted-metal John Chamberlain sculpture; the semi-invited took taxis to the empty industrial streets south of Houston and followed Otis Redding's recorded, Stax-backed moans up steep, rickety wooden stairs to lofts (their walls covered with nearly wall-sized paintings) crowded with sexy, brooding hipsters, expensively miniskirted socialites like Warhol Girl of the Year Baby Jane Holzer, Paraphernalia publicist Pam Sakowitz, and fashion photographer Jerry Schatzberg's rapier-cheek-boned hipster actress girlfriend, in months to be shot-out-of-a-cannon famous in *Bonnie and Clyde:* Faye Dunaway. Girls would dance up a fine coat of sweat—to Carole's hit for Aretha, "Natural Woman," among other LP tracks—and collapse behind fabric room dividers on coat-piled beds with cocky would-be Larry Riverses or silky, urbane "spade cats" (a slyly self-embraced term of awe, not insult) who seemed to have tumbled out of a Norman Mailer or James Baldwin novel.

If you got an apartment for, say, $78.50 a month—rent was sometimes calculated to the half-dollar—it often featured "tub in kitchen." Gun-toting landlords could walk in on their single female tenants at will; there was no one to complain to. Joni found a second-floor, street-fronting one-bedroom with high windows (tub, thankfully, not in kitchen and no sadistic landlord) across from a church, off Fifth Avenue, two blocks north of the Village. The apartment, at 41 West Sixteenth Street, had a fireplace and the newly prized exposed brick wall. Today the neighborhood is called Flatiron; it's chic and bustling. Then it was a genteel residential wedge abutting small factories and office buildings. It didn't have a name—the closest neighborhood, Chelsea, lay northwest—but realtors called it Chelsea anyway.

Joni decamped, filling the apartment with her thrift shop antiques, making it homey ("milk and toast and honey, and a bowl of oranges, too"), and she continued what would be her most prolific period. She would write more songs in 1967 than in any other year—upping her output from twenty-five compositions to sixty, and bringing her total of published songs to thirty-eight by the time she turned twenty-four. She walked the city at night—a Whitman, an Arbus with a guitar case: a voyeur to what she would call the "incredible" "street adventures . . . There are a thousand stories in a single block. You see the stories in people's faces. You hear the songs immediately."

As she put it in "Song to a Seagull," she lived self-shipwrecked "like old Crusoe" on that "island of noise in a cobblestoned sea," and she described that vulnerable state with precision: Her character "Marcie" tries to shake off her preoccupation with an absent lover by going uptown to see a Broadway play (a thoroughly New York thing to do), but when she travels back to her apartment via the West Side Highway, "down along the Hudson River, by the shipyards in the cold," we know that the city's touted culture hasn't lifted her out of her pain. Churlish taxi driver "Nathan LaFraneer" ferries an anxious Joni "from confusion to the plane," on which she'll fly to one of those out-of-town club appearances—a jolt of travel that doesn't dispel her life's nagging questions. She's trapped in the back of the angry man's cab, but naïve civility ("we shared a common space") leads her to overtip him (he snarls). These are the songs that would lead *Time* magazine to say of Joni that, among other things, "She is the rural neophyte, waiting in a subway."

She was divorcing Chuck; she was living alone; she was in the big American city with her thrift shop clothes and her hungry heart. She knew she was moving away from Myrtle's approved borders: "My gentle relations have names they must call me . . ." The worry was not gratuitous. During those first weeks in New York Joni was fearful that the existence of her illegitimate baby would be revealed to her parents—and to the public. According to what she told a friend, she worried she'd be blackballed for disbanding the duo and leaving her husband. "I had the impression [that the threat] was insinuated in conversation," says that friend, adding that Joni "was quite concerned about it, as any woman would have been during those years.* I don't remember how the issue was resolved . . . probably [those who threatened the blackballing] simply dropped the idea when she left Chuck, since any other musicians they were handling would have hated them for it." (Chuck Mitchell dismisses such rumors as baseless. He says they "pick up on the 'meddlesome, difficult Chuck' motif" that Joni and her supporters have "put forth for years.")

Like small-town girls turned writers before her, Joni took the measure of the city through windows, which provided both protection and voyeuristic satisfaction. In the same way that, twenty-nine years earlier, Ohioan Ruth McKenney had recorded how she and her sister Eileen had slept so close to open windows in their Greenwich Village basement that men would stick their heads in and say "Hiya, babes!" and "urchins ran sticks across the iron window bars, creating a realistic imitation of machine gun fire"; and in the same way that, eighteen years after *that*, fresh-from-Sacramento Joan Didion, "on a certain kind of winter evening . . . already dark and bitter," peered into East Seventies windows at dinners being made, and imagined candles lit and children bathed; so too, Joni from Saskatoon pressed her nose to her glass pane. "Now the curtain opens on a portrait of today," she announces, in "Chelsea Morning." She's proud—this country girl—to be peering out, from her own perch, at all of this roiling urbanity. "Chelsea Morning"** is a Summer of Love love letter penned by a young woman alone in Manhattan. Here was the fruition of the promise she held out to her female Second Fret audience. Here was the new "Norwegian Wood."

---

* A double standard that is worth pondering. Four years earlier, Bob Dylan—who'd come to New York, letting it be thought he was an exotic vagabond—had been humiliatingly exposed by *Newsweek* as a middle-class Jewish fraternity boy; still, after a brief retreat from the public eye, his glamour was undiminished. Yet Joni now worried that her reputation and her prospects would be hurt by revelation of the baby. Even in rebel-loving 1960s rock, a young man could be forgiven for having a *less* tortured and romantic past than he'd invented for himself, but a young woman had to fear retribution for having a *more* tortured and romantic past than the public knew about.

** The song's ebullient spirit transcended its immediate meaning—inspiring, among other things, a young Yale law student named Hillary Rodham to fall in love with the song as she was falling in love with fellow student Bill Clinton, and to decide, on the spot, to name their future child after the song.

Joni eventually booked herself into the Cafe Au Go Go, where the headliners included her mentor, Eric Andersen, and, on other nights, the cape-wearing, Brooklyn-born black folksinger Richie Havens. One night in late spring, she walked around the corner from the Au Go Go to a new restaurant upstairs from the Dugout called the Tin Angel. Dave Van Ronk was holding forth at the Angel's bar, waxing proud and protective of the girl he'd met as part of Chuck-and-Joni at the Chess Mate. He would soon record "Both Sides, Now," renaming it "Clouds," retrofitting its feminine mulling of "rows and flows of angel hair and ice cream castles in the air" to his sandpaper growl. Joni was suddenly making a name for herself as a songwriter. In January, country-western star George Hamilton IV had an improbable country hit with "Urge for Going"; a month later Ian and Sylvia recorded "The Circle Game," as would Buffy Sainte-Marie, who would also imminently record Joni's newly written "Song to a Seagull." So Van Ronk was showing off Joni to a crowd at the bar that included his former guitar student Steve Katz. The guitarist and vocalist for the Au Go Go's house band, the Blues Project, Katz was a lean young man whose somber-Jewish-boy manner exerted a pull on women. He would later have a passionate affair with Joan Baez's sister Mimi Fariña.

A small group including Van Ronk and Katz ended up at Joni's apartment. "We jammed, and then I asked Joni if she wanted to go back to my place, which we did," Steve Katz recalls. "We spent the night together, and the next day Joni was going off to play a gig or two somewhere in the South. We looked forward to seeing each other when she came back." One of Joni's Southern engagements was at Fort Bragg, North Carolina, an army base where, "hippie" though she was, she entertained the Vietnam-bound soldiers. ("You got a lot of nerve, sister, standing up there and talking about love!" one war-scarred private she referred to as "Killer Kyle"* angrily admonished, at her dressing room door. "So," she would later recall, "I sat down, and he poured his little heart out to me [about] how the war had robbed him of his sensitivity because of the

---

* Twenty-one years later she would write of Killer Kyle in "The Beat of Black Wings."

atrocities he'd experienced. Even the tender act of touching a woman, he felt, was beyond him. So I held him, I hugged him, I felt bad for him.")

Within days of their evening together, Steve Katz was surprised to find in his mailbox "a card from [Joni] which was essentially a love letter." The prematurity and strength of Joni's affection took him aback (and indicate how vulnerable she was at the beginning of this freewheeling time during which she would soon make so many conquests). "At this point in my very chauvinistic young life I did not want to get tied down," he recalls, "and I certainly didn't feel as strongly toward her as that letter might have assumed." He decided, discreetly, to hand her off.

When Joni returned to town, she called Steve, and Steve invited her over, along with his friend Roy Blumenfeld, the Blues Project's drummer. Tall and handsome in a sunny-faced way, Blumenfeld had a girlfriend— a young Frenchwoman named Marie, "who was a very, very fiery Sagittarius," Roy says. Marie was "sexy and European; she had a mockingly combative style and smoked Gauloises." She was back home in Bordeaux for the summer, which turned out to be very convenient.

Roy Blumenfeld remembers entering Steve's living room, "and I see long blond hair draped over the guitar. Joni was playing. She turned toward me, and . . . I was absolutely stunned, knocked off my feet. The high cheekbones, the sculpted face . . . she was the perfect *shiksa*. She was the epitome of the woman I had dreamed of."

Joni and Roy took a walk and talked about their shared love of music and art (Roy had been a student at Pratt Institute). They wound up in Joni's apartment, and, as was her standard gesture, she played Roy her compositions: "Little Green" (she did not disclose the song's meaning) and "Both Sides, Now," as well as the never-to-be-recorded "Go Tell the Drummer Man." "I was listening to a lot of R&B and Motown at the time—'I Heard It Through the Grapevine,' 'Mustang Sally,'" Roy says, "so I was used to macho music; Joni's music was light and melodic and different, but it straddled so many forms. Musically, I was enamored—her music was more original than Dylan's."

Joni and Roy spent most of the summer of 1967 together. To Roy, Joni was "somewhat like a Canadian Dorothy from *The Wizard of Oz—*

pure, clear, surrounded by light, on a mission to get home and that [mission] was her muse and her power source. She was like a . . . *scientist* of love, and I was like other lovers accompanying her on her journey: small dots on [what would be] a great metaphoric line drawing." It was with Roy's help that Joni papered a whole wall of her apartment in aluminum foil,* a flower child touch that gave the room a soft underwater feeling. They danced to the Temptations' "Beauty Is Only Skin Deep" and "I Want a Love I Can See" on the painted floor of Roy's small, $80-a-month East Village loft. They had dinner at Emilio's, an inexpensive Italian restaurant on Sixth Avenue, where, in its tree-swept garden, umbrellaed tables teetered on a pebbled ground, and young couples felt sophisticated. Roy gave Joni musicianly advice: attack the guitar as if it were a drum. They talked astrology—she was a Scorpio, a water sign; he was the opposite, a Taurus—so "we were really connected." They traveled to Philadelphia together and stayed with Joy and Larry Schreiber while Joni played the Second Fret. They frequented the Tin Angel (the sad song she wrote about finding love "in a Bleecker Street café," which she titled "Tin Angel," is likely about Roy). "I was crazy in love with Joan Mitchell," Roy says today. "The way I felt about her . . . it scared me, because I felt I was going to go into this spiral of crazy love." Joni seemed to reciprocate Roy's feelings.

In August, Roy's girlfriend Marie returned from France, found out about Joni, and flew into a rage. Roy did what he thought was the right thing (although he regretted it later). In order to keep peace with Marie—who, after all, had prior claim—he told Joni he had to stop seeing her. Devastated by the news, Joni sat sobbing at the bar at the Tin Angel.

But a very consequential silver lining would emerge that night, by way of one of Roy's best friends.

Consoling Joni at the bar for three hours was Roy and Steve's bandmate Al Kooper, the Blues Project's keyboardist, lead singer, and composer. Kooper was famous in recording circles; two years earlier, his

---

* She might have been influenced by the foil wallpapering of Andy Warhol's Factory, by Billy Linich (a.k.a. Billy Name) three years earlier.

inspired organ-playing on Dylan's "Like a Rolling Stone," which opened the cut in what sounded like a riot of calliopes, had done much to make the song the marvel it was held to be. Al Kooper was crashing at Judy Collins's apartment; the established folksinger was a kind of big sister to young rockers. Joni was still lamenting over Roy at "Last call!" so Al offered to walk Joni home. When Joni invited him up to hear her songs, "she, being sorta pretty, had me bounding up the stairs figuring if the songs were lousy, maybe I could salvage the evening some other way," Kooper recalled in his 1977 autobiography *Backstage Passes,* written with Ben Edmonds. But "in a few minutes, that became the furthest thing from my mind. Her songs were incredible and totally original . . . She would finish one, and I would say: more, more. And she had enough to keep going for hours, most of them brilliant. One song especially killed me, 'Michael from Mountains.' I thought it would be great for Judy." Even though it was the middle of the night, he decided to call Judy Collins and tell her about his discovery.

With almost otherworldly-luminous blue eyes and long light-brown hair, twenty-seven-year-old Judy Collins had, by the summer of 1967, already lived a remarkably full life. Raised in Washington state and Colorado, the daughter of a blind songwriter–radio personality, she'd become a virtuoso classical pianist at thirteen and, like Joni, had weathered polio. She'd fallen in love with folk music in her teens and switched from piano to guitar. At nineteen she married graduate student Peter Taylor and traveled with him from campus to campus as he completed his Ph.D. in English, supporting him with clerical jobs and, with increasing success, by folksinging. She juggled the care for their baby son, Clark, with her blossoming cabaret career, despite disapproval from her mother-in-law and others for being a working—and performing—mother.

In 1963, divorced from Taylor, Collins moved to Greenwich Village with Clark; Taylor sued for custody. In those days, mothers almost automatically received custody of their young children. Judy was that very rare exception. After a highly acrimonious battle waged by her exhusband and his family, Judy lost her son (she believes that being in psychoanalysis led the court to disfavor her), a blow that left her reeling.

Jac Holzman had discovered Judy at the Village Gate one night, and, defying the "she's-just-another-Baez-clone" naysayers, signed her to his Elektra Records. After she recorded her debut *Maid of Constant Sorrow,* Judy was diagnosed with tuberculosis. She had no health insurance; Holzman advanced her against future albums so her hospital bill could be paid. She rebounded and recorded four more albums for Elektra—the latest, *In My Life,* featured her deeply felt version of the Beatles hit of that name, as well as the art song "Suzanne" by her friend, Canadian poet and novelist Leonard Cohen, who was about to release his own *Songs of Leonard Cohen,* offering "Suzanne" and his other poem-songs in his brazenly unmusical drone of a voice.

Collins was a woman who had definitely looked at life "from win and lose"—and, like Joni, she had the WASP choir girl voice and appearance that could render the idea of female worldweariness unthreatening. She was searching for a few last songs for her album-in-progress, *Wildflowers,* which would include two Leonard Cohen songs, "Hey, That's No Way to Say Goodbye" and "Sisters of Mercy." So when Al woke her up, she was receptive. In a few hours Judy would be driving to Newport for the first day of its folk festival, of which she sat on the board of governors. "I asked her to take Joni in her car with her to Newport, listen to Joni sing her songs on the ride, and see if she could find a spot on the bill for her," Kooper says today. Judy agreed to do so.

The next day, an excited Joni—packed and ready—waited, in vain, for Judy Collins to show. "Judy stood me up," Joni has said, "and she was my hero, [so] it was kind of heartbreaking. I waited and waited and waited, and she never came . . . A day went by, and I got a phone call from her, and she sounded kind of sheepish. She said somebody had sung one of my songs in a workshop. It was a terrible rendition, she said, but people went crazy [over the song]. Judy thought I really should be at Newport." She had a car pick Joni up and take her to the festival.

After Joni arrived at the festival grounds, Judy—who had by now fallen in love with "Both Sides, Now" (she has said that the minute she heard it, she "knew it was a classic; I had to sing it"*)—felt deeply com-mitted to getting Joni onstage. An obstruction materialized in the form of Joan Baez and Mimi Fariña's mother, "Big" Joan Baez. Using her con-siderable influence, the matriarch had Joni barred from the schedule, presumably fearing that the comely arriviste would steal the thunder from her daughters.

At this point Judy—who was known as one tough lady—stepped in and pulled weight of her own. Judy told Mrs. Baez, "If Joni doesn't per-form, then *I* won't perform and Leonard [Cohen] won't perform." By dint of Judy's threat, Joni got onstage at Newport. (So did Cohen, who was beset by such stage fright he would only sing with Judy standing next to him, holding his hand.)

Two very important things came of that day for Joni. First, she was riveted by Leonard Cohen. As she would later describe it (in "That Song About the Midway"), in one of her most memorable lines, Cohen "stood out like a ruby in a black man's ear." Her recent fascination with Jewish men—Katz, Blumenfeld—found its ultimate destination in this hound-dog-faced unlikely rock star (whose visage would be uncannily twinned in another handsomely unhandsome young man—*The Graduate* star Dustin Hoffman—who would, within a few months, similarly emerge as an against-type sex symbol). Cohen was a poet in a sea of lyricists. His first volume of verse, *Let Us Compare Mythologies,* had been published while he was a McGill University undergraduate. His lauded second col-lection, *The Spice-Box of Earth,* had earned him acclaim, and his second novel, *Beautiful Losers*—mystical, ecstatic, tortured, and sexual: refract-ing his life with lover Marianne Jensen on the island of Hydra—had moved one critic to liken him to James Joyce.

---

* In her 1987 autobiography *Trust Your Heart,* Judy Collins mistakenly credited Tom Rush, not Al Kooper, with calling her in the middle of the night, with Joni present. Rush says, "It's sweet of Judy to credit me with bringing her the song [but I didn't] . . . I re-member first hearing 'Both Sides, Now' on the radio, done by Judy, and feeling a bit hurt that Joni hadn't offered the song to me. I also recall Joni telling me some years later that when she wrote the song, she thought of me—salt in the wound! None of which is to say that I harbored any illusions that my version of 'Both Sides, Now' would have inevitably achieved the prominence that Judy's did, but I would have liked a shot at it."

Joni embarked upon a love affair with Leonard Cohen. Although their romance was short-lived, its influence was among the most important in her career. In fact, no brief relationship in Joni's life produced as many songs—and so many of her better songs—as did her few-weeks-long romance with Cohen. She seems to have understood that she required a literary writer to ratify her more instinctual (but just as virtuosic) poetics—and that in their polar personifications of the Canadian experience lay a profoundly romantic fit. In "Rainy Night House," she transports herself back to the Sundays in Reverend Logie's North Battleford church, opening her hymnal ("I am from the Sunday school / I sing soprano in the upstairs choir"), standing next to Peter Armstrong while Frankie McKitrick plays the organ: a provincial naïf awed to be approaching intimacy with a counterculture shaman ("You are a holy man, on the FM radio"), whom she addresses as "thee." But that "holy man" is actually fresh out of bourgeois life himself, a life to which he's still tethered: "You called your mother / She was very tan." This is wry sociology and earnest love song in one. The song reflects the times: all over America there were such couplings of opposites, each lover remaking himself or herself away from a conventional, preordained destiny. Joni's image of falling "into a dream" on Cohen's mother's "small white bed," with each of them, in turn, awakening to watch the other sleep, describes the awe of two self-transforming people, each seeking anchor in a lover who is tenderly exotic.

In "The Gallery," which she would sing (on her second album, *Clouds*) in that choir girl's voice, she slyly explains the reason for the brevity of their relationship—Cohen's womanizing—in the consciousness of an impressed innocent who nonetheless knows that only a fool would tolerate such behavior. And it is Leonard Cohen who is reliably believed to be at least half of the inspiration for what may be one of her best songs, "A Case of You," written two years later; its punning title suggesting both "case" as in course of an illness and "case" as in quantity of wine bottles. "I could drink a case of you and still be on my feet": you'd have to ransack the best of country music to find a line as good as that.

"Leonard was a mirror to my work," Joni would later say of the bond that developed in Newport and strengthened at the Mariposa Festival, and then in Montreal and New York, "and, with no verbal instructions, he showed me how to plumb the depths of my own experience." "Leonard," who, being just shy of thirty-three when they met, was roughly nine years older than Joni, "was very much an intellectual—more of a leftover beatnik than a hippie," says Joy Schreiber Fibben. "Joni grew more serious after she met him. She was rarely larking about lyrically after that." During their brief but intense relationship, Joni was also influenced by Cohen's best friend from childhood, Mort Rosengarten, a sculptor, whom she credits with teaching her an exercise that gave her drawing "boldness and energy—he gave me my originality." Rosengarten, for his part, recalls that Joni in early fall 1967 "was driven; she clearly had a path; she was . . . on the trail of her creative truth." As if describing the awe in "Chelsea Morning," Rosengarten says: "Joni was seizing every moment of life that was going by."

But it was Judy Collins's time spent with Joni at the festival that would prove the most significant upshot of the day. Judy would record both "Michael from Mountains" and "Both Sides, Now" for *Wildflowers*. (She would also release "Chelsea Morning" as a single in 1969, the year Joni recorded it on *Clouds*.) Judy opened *Wildflowers* with the first of these songs, perhaps in part because she had her own charming Michael; her boyfriend at the time, tousle-haired, sexily droop-eyed English rock journalist Michael Thomas, told people that the song was about him. But it was the production and recording of "Both Sides, Now," which Judy most loved, that would be key. The arrangement was turned over to twenty-four-year-old Joshua Rifkin, a Juilliard-trained musicologist and Bach scholar whom Jac Holzman knew from Rifkin's work on Holzman's classical label, Nonesuch, and with whom Judy had worked on earlier albums. With Rifkin's celestial harpsichords ringing over, under, around, and through Judy's emotional, reedy contralto, the words sounded as if they were emanating from a cathedral of the collective female soul. When the song was finally released as a single in November 1968 (after almost a year on *Wildflowers*), it sold a million copies. (The record has since been entered into the Grammy Hall of Fame.) "Both Sides, Now" was ultimately recorded by a list of singers that includes Frank Sinatra, Bing Crosby, and Willie Nelson. Indeed, Judy's version of "Both Sides, Now" became to women in their twenties in 1968 what "My Way" would be to males: a kind of personal anthem. In their tiny-mirror-studded, embroidered Moroccan vests over flounce-sleeved, stock-tied blouses tucked into jeans or miniskirts, silk scarves pirate-tied low on their brows—as those "incense owls" (and the roach-clipped billows) spiraled in the air while clay-potted candles threw hypnotic flickers on exposed brick walls—countless young women (some enduring heartbreak over the shadier guys who'd replaced the boring college boys they'd happily jettisoned) heard in Joni's words, through Judy's voice, a shared epiphany about the emotional risks they had chosen.

Another person Joni met at Newport was rock promoter Joe Boyd, a Massachusetts native and Harvard graduate now living in England, who occasioned Joni's first trip abroad by inviting Joni to his adopted country to open for the Incredible String Band at a London club called the Speakeasy. "In her miniskirt and long straight hair, she stole the show completely," Boyd recalls. "She dazzled the crowd of liggers with the power of her voice, the originality of her melodies and lyrics, and her quiet but confident stage presence. Her guitar playing was very strong, and her voice was controlled and powerful in the small room." Boyd found her "gawky, kind of earnest, wholesome, fresh-faced"—in endearing sharp contrast to the "sophisticated, decadent" blond beauties that England was used to: Marianne Faithfull, Pattie Boyd, and Julie Christie. Joni remembers coming home from England during that "Twiggy-Viva era . . . all Carnaby Street, with false eyelashes, sequined belts—flashed out."

By fall, Joni had a manager—and a passionately devoted one; ultimately, they would make each other's careers. His name was Elliot Roberts (né Rabinowitz, from the Bronx), a funny, antic, pot-smoking junior agent at Chartoff-Winkler, and he'd been so knocked out by her talent when he'd caught her act at the Cafe Au Go Go that he'd flown to Detroit to travel with her at his own expense for three weeks before she agreed to his representation. Elliot quit the agency to devote himself to

Joni. Joni had gotten recording contract offers from Vanguard and other small folk labels, but she'd dismissed them all as "slave labor." Roberts resolved to change all that, and Joni seemed to believe him. During the Detroit engagement, Joni stopped in to see Chuck and pick up some items from the apartment. Chuck remembers her sitting against the oak-wainscoted walls "on a rainy fall night, with a moody, golden light coming from the chandelier." Then she stood up, "and I can still see her, standing with her back to me, looking out the window. Joni said, 'It's gonna happen, Charlie. I'm scared, but I'm gonna be a star.'"

Elliot took the tape he'd made of Joni's Michigan performances and made the rounds of the record labels, then almost all still based in New York. He had every confidence he would prevail. "Both Sides, Now," "Chelsea Morning," "That Song About the Midway," "Michael from Mountains": "How could you not hear them and go, 'I'd take a risk on that person'?" he felt. But the A&R men viewed Joni as a singer in the passé folk genre (an art song singer might have been a more apt label); they declined to offer her a contract.

Meanwhile, in late October, Joni had flown to Coconut Grove, Florida, the arty section of Miami Beach, to perform at a club called the Gaslight South. Joni had played the Gaslight—and another club on the South Florida folk circuit, the Flick in Coral Gables—both with Chuck and, in the last year, as a solo. She knew the regular performers, including a seventeen-year-old blues singer named Estrella Berosini, the daughter of a Czech trapeze artist. Tawny-skinned, brown-haired Estrella had grown up touring America with the circus; she could wire-walk and handle elephants. Now she was belting out Bessie Smith and Lightnin' Hopkins at the Gaslight, alternating sets with Joni, who was trilling "I had a king in a tenement castle . . ."—it was a contrast.

Biding his time in the Grove was David Crosby, who'd just been kicked out of the Byrds (by his own design, he told people). Since his eviction from that bellwether group that he'd helped to form, which had established the very genre of folk rock, Crosby had been tooling around

California, landing on various perches of the drug-kissed, rich-hippie set—hanging out with the Grateful Dead in Novato, on the outreaches of San Francisco; and with Jefferson Airplane in their Victorian mansions in the city—acting as a liaison between the still-fractious southern and northern California rock scenes. (The San Francisco groups viewed L.A. as slick, commercial, and even—tainted by images of Johnny Rivers at the Whisky a Go Go—corny. Had it not been for deft persuasion by older local men the psychedelic groups trusted—concert promoter Bill Graham and music columnist and *Rolling Stone* paterfamilias Ralph Gleason—the Dead, the Airplane, and Big Brother would not have taken the stage at Lou Adler and John Phillips's Monterey Pop Festival.) Crosby had recently borrowed $22,500 from his friend Peter Tork* to buy a billowing-sailed schooner, *The Mayan,* and had spent the fall sailing the Caribbean, with Buffalo Springfield's Stephen Stills and the Airplane's Paul Kantner accompanying him part of the way (the three creating the haunting ode to a postapocalyptic dream world, "Wooden Ships," as they sailed).

Crosby knew Estrella from his previous forays, with his brother Ethan, to the Grove. "David would sweep into the clubs with his Byrds cape on," Estrella recalls. His father, Floyd Crosby, was a Hollywood cinematographer who'd won an Academy Award for *High Noon* and then had quit the movie business to sail around the world—and now this was what David was going to do. His plan was to sail—and find and produce singers; the kind of singers who could change the world, he told Estrella. "David was really into changing the world; money didn't matter to him."

Estrella had been catching Joni's set between her own sets, and she was knocked out by the new songs her seven-years-older colleague had written.

---

* Tork—whose membership in the artificially constructed group the Monkees didn't lose him street cred with his "purer" musician friends—owned a house in Studio City, which he termed an "artists' collective." There, beautiful, distinctly non-bimbo women strolled around nude; vegetarian cuisine was whipped up by a chef; and Augustus Owsley Stanley III made personal visits from the Bay Area with his finest fresh batches of acid. Crosby and his girlfriend, Christine Hinton, were frequent guests.

David had not seen Joni sing—he had only seen Estrella and, according to Estrella, he liked what he saw. "David came into my dressing room," Estrella recalls, "literally dropped to his knee, and, in the best imitation of Cyrano de Bergerac, asked to produce me. He said my voice threw him against the wall—words like that." For reasons Estrella isn't sure of now ("I think I knew she was more ready than I was"), she deflected Crosby's overture, then pointed through the diaphanous stage curtain to where Joni was singing a "haunting, lilting melody" she'd written. "Joni was wearing a black dress with gold and blue sparkles, and over her long, straight hair she had an Indian bell necklace—she looked medieval."

According to Estrella, David took a quick look through the curtain, then turned back to Estrella and said, "She's just another blond chick singer." Estrella rebutted, "'No—you're wrong! Listen to her words.' And he's astonished—he's a connected L.A. person in his twenties, and I'm a kid who's just turned down my biggest opportunity, and now he's turning into a dutiful little boy and going to give Joni a listen because *I* said so."

Crosby more than agreed with Estrella Berosini's assessment. By the end of the evening he was not only in love with Joni's singing but with Joni. (Joni soon repaid Estrella by making her—"Estrella, circus girl, comes wrapped in songs and gypsy shawls . . ."—one of the three featured "ladies of the canyon.")

Deleting the Estrella precursor in the account that he wrote (with Carl Gottlieb) in his 1988 autobiography, *Long Time Gone,* Crosby said that, seeing Joni sing, "I thought I'd been hit by a hand grenade. Her voice, those words . . . she nailed me to the back wall with two-inch spikes." As similar as these words were to the ones Estrella recalls him using on her (Crosby was nothing if not passionate), by the time he'd listened to Joni Mitchell, he forgot about the other, younger singer he'd originally been trying to woo.

Crosby had another performer in the club, Bobby Ingram, introduce him to Joni, and he did his best to win her, as a lover and as a protégée. David was pudgy and heart-on-sleeve; not the likeliest lothario—Joni looked at him and thought of Yosemite Sam, the short, hot-blooded

Looney Tunes character. But he'd been a Byrd, which conferred immense prestige. Besides, as Estrella recalls, "David made up for his pudginess with that Cyrano de Bergerac charm—and, with those beautiful cheekbones, he looked like a Cossack." Over the course of the two-week Gaslight engagement, Estrella saw Joni come to reciprocate David's feelings. "They were both smitten; they both had that glow." Joni has said, "David was wonderful company and a great appreciator . . . His eyes were like star sapphires to me. When he laughed they seemed to twinkle like no one else's."

Joni moved onto David's boat. The Gaslight group rented bikes and rode around the Grove, and Estrella and the other girls noticed "that Joni—who looked like a Nordic princess, with her hair in two braids—had jeans that fit perfectly, like a high-fashion model. We wondered, 'How could she get jeans to fit like that?'" Estrella knew about the importance of "costuming" from the circus, "and Joni understood costuming." As she observed Joni over the next weeks and months, she saw that Joni subtly understood other survival skills, too. "You never show fear to an animal—that's a rule in the circus. It's the same in the music industry and with rock 'n' roll men. To get far, a woman must never show fear. And Joni didn't."

One day during the idyll, a love-struck David approached his new kid-confidante, Estrella, and thrust a piece of paper—a poem that Joni had written him—in her face. "He was practically in tears. He said: 'Look at this—it's in perfect iambic pentameter! My career is winding down and hers is taking off! I'm so in love! I'm more in love with her than anyone I ever met before. What am I gonna do?'"

What David Crosby ended up doing was ditching his plan to sail around the world. Instead (as Joni would soon put it, in the moody, internal-rhyme-rich song she wrote about him, "The Dawntreader"), "Leave your streets behind, he said, and come to me." In other words: He would take her to L.A. and produce her first album.

With an introduction to Warner Bros. Records arranged by Crosby, Elliot flew to Los Angeles with Joni's tapes. He secured a contract for her with Warner Bros. (she would be on their Reprise label), which included a rarely granted privilege, especially rare for new artists: creative control.

At the end of 1967 Joni moved out to Los Angeles, her fourth change of city in just over three years. She and Elliot, who was also relocating there, had a plan, which he articulated thusly: "The role model was Bob Dylan, and it wasn't a matter of radio play or hits, it was"—emphasis added—"a matter of *people being guided by your music and using it for the soundtrack of their lives.*" As Joni would later put it, "love and freedom: women in America freeing up their lives" was a main theme in her personal life, and of that soundtrack she was creating. "We had a lot more choice" than her mother's generation, she said, "which was very confusing. There were no guidelines." But with a song—"Cactus Tree"—that she wrote around the time she was leaving New York for Los Angeles, she *did* offer a guideline for that new challenge: women would keep their hearts "full and hollow, like a cactus tree." She invokes sailor David in the first verse of the third-person-narrated song; mountain-climbing Michael Durbin in the second; Chuck in the third; and others throughout (Roy is the "drummer"). Her narrator is not suffering Marcie-like obsession when these men are absent; rather (emphasis added), "She will love them *when she sees them.*" Over the years, frequent quotings of the song's catchy hook—"she's so busy being free"—have tinged its message with disapproval. "Busy being free" seems a self-contradiction and even a petty selfishness. But a woman *did* have to keep psychologically "busy" to match men at romantic free agency in the late 1960s. And the options, comfort, and confidence that young women enjoy today were born of all that busyness—that emotional effort to be revolutionary creatures—of the young women of that era.

As for Joni's "heart" being both "full and hollow"—that tricky duality had been necessary over these last three years. She'd struggled with impoverished pregnancy, a shamed childbirth in a charity ward, the decision to put her baby up for adoption even after she had found a male partner, and divorce and independence, despite the threat of people exposing her secret. Her musical creativity owed to each of those situations and choices, all made in a climate of risk. She'd *had* to have a "hollow"—self-protective—heart to make it this far. But now success seemed in view, so she could afford for her heart to *not* be hollow. And that held its own danger.

carly

1965–1969

After Willie Donaldson broke up with her, Carly was on her own—not least of all, emotionally. Willie's rejection of her "was the first cut in my life," she has said, "and the first cut is the deepest." "She really lost her heart to Willie; it was very, very painful for her," her then newly married best friend Ellen Wise Salvadori (now Questel) remembers.

"There are so many ways that, very narcissistically, I thought of myself through Willie's eyes," Carly says, of their time together; now she had to reconstitute her future. Carly's sister Lucy was married, as were her best friends, Ellen and Jessica, so rooming with any of them was out. Joey, whose mezzo-soprano voice was now in the employ of the New York City Opera Company, had an apartment in midtown, at 400 East Fifty-fifth Street. She deigned to let her recently dumped younger sister move in with her.

Carly took the smaller bedroom, paid Joey rent, and obeyed Joey's many exacting rules. For example, she had to stay inside her bedroom with her door closed whenever Joey entertained men in the living room. And what men Joey entertained! She'd had a long relationship with the urbane, much-older comedian and broadcaster Henry Morgan and had embarked on romances with dashing symphonic con-

ductor Zubin Mehta and with the equally dashing ballet star Edward ·
Villella. (Joanna Simon's penchant for illustrious men would continue
over the decades; in 2006, she would become engaged to Walter
Cronkite.) "Joey was the royalty and Carly was the court," Ellen says.
Leaving college to tour with Lucy, being jealous of Lucy's effect on
Willie (and Sean Connery), taking a backseat to imperious Joey: the
abiding role of her older siblings in her life—the maypole-twirl of their
preening, jostling, scheming, confiding, now-maturing sisterhood—
would lead Carly to write a string of songs ("Older Sister," "Boys in the
Trees," "Two Little Sisters") exploring the relationship so central to her
identity.

Carly was falling into an accomplished young Manhattan crowd.
Through Ellen and Jennifer Salt, Carly befriended Mary Ellen Mark,
who would soon establish herself as a preeminent photojournalist of
her generation, and Mary Ellen's boyfriend, young comic David Steinberg, as well as comedian Robert Klein and his wife, Brenda Boozler.
She had a romance with an Oklahoma-raised Harvard Phi Beta Kappa
and Oxford Rhodes scholar who was just becoming a director, Terrence Malick, and who would soon make a name for himself with *Bad-
lands* and later *Days of Heaven*. She dated comic actor Severn Darden,
who was a friend of Mike Nichols and Elaine May. Later still, Carly
would embark on a romance with the young Czech director Milos
Forman, who would eventually give her a small role in his movie
Taking Off (and whose antic avidity for "groovy" life and klutzy Eastern
European accent supplied the inspiration for Steve Martin and Dan
Aykroyd's "wild and crazy" Slavic guys). In that way New York has of
being several worlds in one small space, the city in the mid- to late
1960s had been a different home for each of the three young women:
Carole had lived, always with family, in the bread-and-butter suburbs
of the bustling Manhattan that was her workplace, not under the tenement rooftops she'd romanticized; Joni had slipped into the musical
demimonde of downtown Manhattan, a solitary emigrée from the hin-
terlands, prolifically documenting the city's tough love. By contrast,
Carly was not the Manhattan outsider; the borough of Gershwin songs

had been hers in childhood, and now, as a young adult, she stretched her lovely, long legs into that milieu's next generation. She didn't have to go looking for the nascent establishment cultural elite (those creative young people who were on the cutting edge but who were too verbal and moored to be "underground")—she had legacy status.

"I did not want a career at all" during this period, Carly has said. In this way, she was typical of young women at the time. "Career" was a fusty, jaunty-spinster kind of word—it called to mind Eve Arden and Joan Crawford at desks with hats and gloves on. "Ambition," Jill Clayburgh once recalled of this time, "wasn't cool or feminine." Not that upper-middle-class young women weren't supposed to make something of their lives, of course. "We *were* expected to achieve," argues Jessica Hoffmann Davis, of their cohort. And, indeed, Jessica, like Ellen, was about to start graduate school. (Jessica would receive an Ed.D., and Ellen, a Ph.D.) But Jessica and Ellen had both resolved their personal lives (and Jessica had a baby), not atypical for a time when the average age of marriage for American women was just under twenty-one. The issue of achievement may never have been absent, but it was only enhanced once the other, pressing priority was settled. For many, even the fulfillment of one's talent came about through other people's notice and suggestion.

Such was the case with Carly. "Somehow I kept getting sucked into [music]," she's recalled. At parties, when she'd take out her guitar and play and sing, "people would pay me a compliment: 'Wow, you have a great voice; you should make a record.'"

Through the Simon Sisters' record producer, John Court, who was the junior partner to Bob Dylan's manager, Albert Grossman, Carly was brought to Grossman's attention. Grossman was a portly man and, despite his stunning wife, Sally (who had just been photographed lounging in a chair in a red dress, cigarette aloft, by an ornate fireplace, with Bob Dylan, for the cover of Dylan's *Bringing It All Back Home*), he wasn't averse to proffering a version of the casting couch to women singers (at a time when the negative notion of sexual harassment didn't exist). As Carly has put it: "Without my dear sister [Lucy]'s protection, I was a sitting duck. [Grossman] offered me his body in exchange for worldly success. Sadly, his body was not the kind you would easily sell yourself for." Carly declined; Grossman apparently didn't hold the rejection against her.

Grossman thought Carly had strong potential, but her background gave him pause. "He didn't like the fact that my parents had been wealthy and that I lived in a big house in Riverdale," she has said. "Albert said to me, 'On a one-to-ten scale as a woman, you're a nine.' I said, 'That's flattering, but where do I miss out?' He said, 'You've had it too easy. You haven't suffered enough. You don't know what working for a living is like.'" Grossman's assessment was in some ways off-point: Dylan himself, for all his talent, had never been the scuffling itinerant he'd pretended to be when he came to New York; he'd been a cosseted middle-class kid. And across the country in Laurel Canyon, no one was rapping the knuckles of handsome young male folk rocker Ned Doheny, whose wealthy family's name was as recognizable in L.A. as the name Simon of Simon & Schuster was in New York, for not "know[ing] what working for a living is like"—he was just part of the stew of handsome Canyon bards, like his best friend Jackson Browne. Maybe it was just easier to exert reverse snobbery on a female. But Grossman's reservations about Carly made a certain measure of sense in this season of in-your-face Janis Joplin and debutante-turned-psychedelic-queen Grace Slick. A witty, polished girl who remained within the verbal junior intelligentsia did not emblemize the cultural moment.

Nonetheless, Grossman wanted to develop Carly as a star. He had the idea of an act called Carly and the Deacon, pairing her with a black male singer.* When the desired "deacon," Richie Havens, declined, that idea was dropped, but Grossman still set out to produce an album for Carly. For one song, he arranged for Carly to collaborate

---

* Grossman had his own, secret logic when it came to image. He had made Noel Stookey change his name to Paul, and he insisted that Mary Travers avoid the sun at all costs, to keep her skin milk white.

loosely with Dylan himself. Carly has recalled, "Albert said, 'You should get Bob to write a song for you. I'll get Bob and you'll go into the studio with his guys.'"

In July 1966 Bob Dylan and Carly Simon met in a cubicle in Grossman's office. There Dylan rewrote, for Carly, some of the words of Eric von Schmidt's "Baby, Let Me Follow You Down," the anthem of the Cambridge folk scene popularized by Dave Van Ronk in the Village coffeehouses. Carly was struck by how "out of it" Dylan was during the session—he was "very, very wasted." (Later that month, in Woodstock, Dylan got on his motorcycle and started to ride it to a repair shop. He crashed, sustaining the serious injuries that would prompt his eighteen-month absence from public view and leave his fan base afire with dire rumors.)

Carly worked daily for weeks on the album—recording the von Schmidt song and others—with a group of tremendous musical talents just coming into their own: Paul Butterfield and, from the group the Hawks—soon to be renamed The Band—Levon Helm, Rick Danko, and Robbie Robertson. With his heavy-lidded eyes, high cheekbones, and air of sophistication, the half-Jewish, half-Mohawk Robertson was profoundly attractive to women (a fact that would emerge—unexpectedly, given the group's backwoods image—in Martin Scorsese's 1978 film *The Last Waltz*). Carly developed a crush on him, and they had a flirtation that culminated with a hot evening at the Chelsea Hotel's Spanish restaurant's bar, "mooning and spooning and June-ing all over each other," she recalls, "but going no further—Robbie and I were shy, a little in awe of each other." When they made a date for the Fourth of July, she looked forward to a romance that would sweep away the pain of her broken engagement. On the appointed night Carly waited and waited. And waited. Robbie stood her up. "I felt this sheer wall of rejection," she says. "Robbie had been my hope of getting over Willie."

The tracks of her album had to be mixed, and that was the job of sound engineer Bob Johnston. But Johnston held off—instead, dangling a quid pro quo: sex for sound-mixing. "If you're nice to me, I'll make you a nice record," he told Carly with casual impunity, since workplace threats were not illegal.* "It was amazing to actually hear it coming out of somebody's mouth," Carly recalls. She took the very circumstance that Grossman and others had held against her—her lack of desperation—and used it as a touché. "I stood, very calm, and said, 'I'm not that hungry.'" Johnston paid her back by refusing to mix the tracks and by bad-mouthing her to Grossman. "Whatever Bob Johnston said to Albert, I was shelved," she has said. "This was the end for me for a very long time. I was frozen."

"This was a very depressing time for me," Carly says. Still living at Joey's, she drew close to her younger brother, Peter; he had felt as wounded by their father's rejection as she did, and he was funneling his feelings into a love of photography. They palled around together during what he's called "that gloomy era" in which Carly "became very down on herself, awfully negative and depressed. . . . It was just a rotten time for her."

Richard Simon had left each of his four children a modest inheritance, and Carly was quickly depleting hers on psychotherapy. So in the fall of 1966, needing cash, Carly took a job at a production company—the kind of entry-level job available to young women: secretary. "I pretended to type and take shorthand, while extending my lunch breaks to drown my sense of failure in more and more puff pastry and puddings," she has written on her Web site.

As the single one among married friends, Carly traced the contrast between her life and Jessica's in sardonically formal letters, which Jessica reciprocated. "Dearest . . . ," they would write, using the same campy, theatrical breathiness with which they'd concocted the *Moll Flanders* essay for Sarah Lawrence. The dozens of letters they ex-

---

* According to Patricia Barry, the attorney who, along with feminist legal scholar Catharine MacKinnon, effectively made sexual harrassment a federal cause of action through the U.S. Supreme Court's unanimous 1986 decision on their appeal of *Meritor Savings Banks v. Vinson:* "Anyone sexually harassed on the job in 1966 would have no remedy because the idea that sexual harassment amounted to sexual discrimination was not raised as a claim of employment discrimination until the late '60s or early '70s. However, even if sexual harassment was actionable in 1966, unless the music engineer was her supervisor, Carly Simon would still not have a claim."

changed during the mid- to late 1960s reflect, Jessica says, "the last vestiges of a time in which girlfriends knew everything about each other and wrote it down so we would never forget." In one letter, Jessica woefully called herself a "Worcester housewife," referring to the Massachusetts town where she and her husband were living. Carly wrote back, "Dearest Jessica, It is with imminent euphoria that I look forward to my brief visit with you in culture-laden Worcester. All the culture is in *your house,* dearest friend."

Carly made some of these trips to see Jessica with her soul mate brother, Peter, who'd gone full-bore hippie-politico: With his hair long and wild, he was student photographer for the Boston University newspaper, of which his friend Raymond Mungo, soon to be a pioneer of the underground press, was editor. Peter was always rushing out to antiwar rallies, and in a couple of years he and Mungo would be knee-deep in Vermont compost, cofounders of the commune Tree Frog Farm. (Mungo called it "Total Loss Farm" in his book of that name.) Tree Frog's rolling meadows were the site of badminton games during which female communards who looked like Kennedy wedding brides-maids, down to the demure smiles and ribboned boaters, wielded their racquets over their bare tits. (Later Peter Simon would become a devotee of spiritual leader Ram Dass, formerly Dr. Richard Alpert, Timothy Leary's fellow LSD professor.)

The kinds of protests in which Peter Simon was enmeshed would grow in number and attendance with the Tet offensive in January 1968, heralding a year in which over half a million American soldiers were in Vietnam, fighting a war the public was now beginning to view as, in Walter Cronkite's words, "a stalemate." Students looked for reasons to foment huge, flashy protests. The occupation of Columbia's buildings in April 1968 was based on a relatively petty complaint: the university's appropriation of Harlem land for a gym. The movement was a brushfire stoked by complementary components—the political people were earnest and tactical; the sex, drugs, and rock 'n' roll people were playful and instinctual—but the two elements burned with the same passion for larger-than-life living. If you tumbled into your adulthood in that magic moment, the players' operatic example of how to live life—in both its serious* and its recreational dimension—became your "normal."

In hindsight, the last three years of the 1960s were like some self-wrought mini–Messianic Age plunked in the middle of the twentieth century. Hubristic prophets spouted melodramatic rhetoric in contemporary versions of Temple squares (the campus, the TV screen, the FM radio, the rock concert, the newspaper headlines); believers found revelations in holy texts (Weather Underground manifestos, acid visions, Dylan or Beatles lyrics); witnesses watched the heavens heave both frogs (dollar bills fluttering from Wall Street balconies; the naming of a pig as a candidate for the Democratic nomination; Jimi Hendrix immolating his guitar) and thunder (the Vietnam War dead, the political assassinations). The original proclamations upon which much of this change had been built had featured a Sermon-on-the-Mount-like grace; SNCC's founders had declared, "Love is the central motif of nonviolence"; SDS's (male-pronounced) Port Huron Statement had declared that "human relationships should involve fraternity and honesty . . . human brotherhood must be willed." But they'd devolved into tableaux both satirically grandiose and improbable: the (revolutionary) daughter of a wealthy advertising executive and the (revolutionary) daughter of a wealthy leftist lawyer blithely preparing to take a sauna in a luxurious town house, while in the basement their friends were making fatal nail bombs; bereted, rifle-wielding Black Panthers posing for photos in wicker chair thrones, then nibbling canapés at

---

* Sociology professor Todd Gitlin, former SDS president and memoirist-historian of the political side of the era, describes, in his authoritative *The Sixties: Years of Hope, Days of Rage,* the passion and melodrama that radical politics had attained: "[The movement] did not merely want you to support a position, it wanted you to dive in, and the more total the immersion the better. The link between feeling and action was a short fuse. Actions were taken . . . to 'dramatize convictions.' . . . [T]he movement's rites became epiphanies. Confrontations were moments of truth, branded into memory, bisecting life into Time Before and Time After. We collected these ritual punctuations as moments when the shroud that normally covers everyday life was torn away and we stood face to face with the true significance of things. Each round was an approximation of the apocalyps[e.]"

Leonard Bernstein's cocktail party. Life *had* to be grand-gestured and cosmically mischievous, or you were missing something. But under the mischief lay a hoary earnestness. Highly educated young culture warriors, whether of the political or sex-drugs-and-rock-'n'-roll stripe, believed as straightfacedly that the Revolution was coming as evangelicals today believe in the Rapture.

This was not the moment to be a secretary. Carly found a job as backstage handler-hostess for the talent on a new TV show, *Live from the Bitter End*. The show was televised from the Bleecker Street rock club that was right next door to the Dugout and the Tin Angel, where Joni would soon be hanging out with Dave Van Ronk and the Blues Project. Carly dropped the role of budding songwriter. "I didn't try to sell my songs. I took care of Marvin Gaye and the Staple Singers and Redd Foxx and the Chad Mitchell Trio and Peter, Paul and Mary. I brought them tea and honey and cough drops." One night, when Carly asked Marvin Gaye if he wanted anything to drink, he told her to stick her tongue out. She obeyed and found herself in the midst of a soul kiss. "I couldn't release my tongue for a little while, let's just say that," she's recalled. (Forty years later she'd rate Gaye's *Sexual Healing* as one of her ten favorite albums.)

Carly's next low-level job—attained with the help of Jeanie Seligmann, who was a "researcher" (that is, a reporter who didn't have a penis) at *Newsweek*—was in that magazine's lowly Letters department; she was hired to read, forward on to editors, and respond to reader mail. Already a bit chubby, Carly gained even more weight by being one of many Manhattan women to fall for a diet scam of locally sold "low-cal" milk shakes; the supposedly ninety-calorie shakes were later exposed as having ten times that calorie load, so everyone who "dieted" on them got fat.

By spring of 1967 Carly had taken stock of the year and a half: being dumped by Willie Donaldson; being subject to house rules by Joey; the what-would-now-be-called sexual harassment from Bob Johnston; Grossman's scuttling her record and freezing her out; the rejection by Robbie Robertson; the depressing secretarial job; her lunchtime gorging and weight gain; the boring *Newsweek* job and *more* weight gain. It was time to get out of Dodge, at least for the summer. In July Jessica opened a letter, postmarked Stockbridge, Massachusetts. Carly had taken a job as—of all outgrown things—a camp counselor.

The camp, nestled among the stately Colonial homes in Norman Rockwell's late-adopted hometown in the Berkshires, was called Indian Hill. Housed on the grounds of a stone mansion just around the corner from the psychiatric hospital Austen Riggs,* it offered an elite arts program that drew culture-loving upper-middle-class kids. (In 1967, director Julie Taymor, who, forty years later, would evoke the era in her magical movie *Across the Universe,* was a camper, and *New York Times* theater critic and cultural/political columnist Frank Rich was a recent alumnus.) It was a milieu Carly knew *so* well, it might have seemed that—as she arrived there, guitar in tow, from a city in the sexy clutch of the Summer of Love—she was regressing to her childhood. Yet it would be here that she'd meet someone who would help her realize her future.

Carly was a music counselor, and one of the first things she did was start a rock group. She was its lead singer and lead guitarist, and she gathered up four male campers—a pianist, bass guitarist, two drummers—who started rehearsing in the barn, providing, as the camp yearbook would note, "a swinging life for the boys." She named the group Lust for Five and she wrote a song, "Secret Saucy Thoughts (of Suzy)," for them. Lust for Five held forth in the camp's improvised discotheque, Carly stimulating fantasies in more than a few male campers. In at least one case she returned the favor, harboring a crush on a seventeen-year-old trumpet player, and (shades of Andrea) wondering, could she get away with having a relationship with the kid?

Rippling through the pines during that first week of camp was an-

---

* Unguessable from his *Saturday Evening Post* covers of orderly, apple pie–innocent small-town American life, Rockwell had moved to Stockbridge because his mentally ill wife was undergoing shock treatments at Riggs. In a year's time James Taylor would enter Riggs to (temporarily) detox from his heroin addiction.

ticipation for the delayed arrival of head counselor Jacob Brackman. Popular with the campers from years past, Jake was a tall, handsome twenty-four-year-old Harvard-educated writer who was suddenly a little famous: his just-published *New Yorker* essay, "The Put-On"—in which he analyzed the new hip form of humor, with examples from Warhol, Dylan, and the Beatles—was the talk of New York's young intelligentsia, drawing comparisons to Susan Sontag's "Notes on Camp," which had been published in *The Partisan Review* three years earlier.*

Carly and Jake met at the campfire hootenanny. "She seemed like Daisy Mae, in a little denim miniskirt and a halter top and a straw hayride hat—lots of bare arms and legs, very Al Capp-y," Jake recalls. Something clicked between them, and fortunately it wasn't a sexual click (though over the course of their friendship, they may have made half-hearted attempts to enter that more predictable precinct), because that might have deprived them of a rich and useful lifelong friendship through which many of the most important breaks and relationships in Carly's life would materialize.

While dodging mosquitoes in the pines, and during the bumpy bus rides to Tanglewood (summer home of the Boston Symphony Orchestra) and Jacob's Pillow (outdoor stage to avant-garde dance troupes), Jake became Carly's confidant. She told him about her crush on the high school student trumpet player—"I was listening to her strategize about whether or not she could put a move on this seventeen-year-old," he says.

The last couple of years bumping around had taken their toll on Jake's new friend. "Carly didn't have the confidence she would have a year or so later," Jake says. "She didn't trust herself in a social situation to say something that just came out of her mind that may be quite funny." Jake took advantage of her vulnerability. "I was cruel to Carly. I would encourage her to eat fattening things and then make her

---

* Brackman never wrote another essay with that cachet, but he did become *Esquire's* film critic and soon after a screenwriter for the Bob Rafelson–directed *The King of Marvin Gardens* and executive producer of director Terrence Malick's *Days of Heaven*.

feel bad for the weight she was gaining." Later Jake would see that whole sweep of time for Carly this way: "She was in a down period; she had grown up" in a glamorous, accomplished world "and she had lost her rightful place in it. The only way out for her was to become a star."

Carly and Jake and the other counselors guided the campers through an ambitious arts gauntlet: stagings of plays by Arthur Miller, Samuel Beckett, and Euripides; readings of Joyce, Sandburg, Shakespeare, Brecht, and Dylan Thomas; dances to Varèse and Schoenberg; recitals of Haydn, Handel, and Mozart. The campers hoisted posters of Yippified Allen Ginsberg in his American flag top hat, drew sketches of John Lennon, wrote poems and essays with the names of Stockbridge favorite son Arlo Guthrie* and Ravi Shankar and Miriam Makeba sprinkled through them, and they "voted" for the legalization of both marijuana and (this was over five years before *Roe v. Wade*) abortion.

After Carly hugged her sunburned campers good-bye, she moved back to her bedroom in Joey's apartment on East Fifty-fifth Street; and Jake, to his borrowed house in Vermont.

Carly's crowd, like everyone's crowd, was living the stoned life now. "Those were crazy, heady, exciting times—no rules and no consequences," recalls Ellen. Carly was intermittently trying to place her songs (she tried in vain to interest the group Every Mother's Son in "Secret Saucy Thoughts"), as well as looking for jingle-writing gigs. Ellen's brother Stephen (brilliant and unstable, he would eventually fall to his death from the rafters of a converted church) came up with a chicken nuggets idea, a precursor to the McDonald's gold mine, which he wanted to market to dope smokers; Carly wrote a jingle with the hook "Long-term physical effects are not yet known," implying that the nuggets were psychedelic. Neither nuggets nor jingle got off the

---

*   Woody Guthrie's performer son lived in the area and, through his satirical antiwar song, "Alice's Restaurant," about his Stockbridge friend, funky restaurateur Alice Brock, he had made Stockbridge counterculturally iconic in colleges all over the country.

ground. (Carly did, however, eventually, get an assignment to write and record a jingle for a Massachusetts bank.)

At some point in 1968, Carly contributed a song she had written, based on a Brahms melody, to a project sponsored by the New York Symphony Association, through which rock groups would collaborate on classical music. A pop-rock group called Elephant's Memory was chosen to play her song at Carnegie Hall. The band needed a female singer; Carly was signed without even an audition. It was a match *not* made in heaven.

The jazz-flavored group, which consisted of what Carly has recalled as "very New York street-smart jazz hip people" (they would later back up John Lennon and Yoko Ono), took an instant dislike to Carly. Though they liked her singing and her animated stage presence fine, and they approved of the songs she'd written enough to continue to play them (one, "Summer Is a Wishing Well," in particular) even after she left the group on bad terms, they were *not* going to cut the uptown girl a break. They had the same antipathy for her background that Albert Grossman had, except they expressed it more baldly. "They pretty much said, 'Get off your fat ass and help us carry our speakers,'" Carly has recalled, adding, "I *did* have a fat ass at that point, by the way."* Speaking for himself, Myron Yules, who was the group's trombonist, admits he resented Carly's air of privilege: "I thought she was a spoiled brat; she didn't want to rehearse much, she didn't think I was up to par musically, so I resented that, and I personally didn't like women standing around and not carrying the mic stand." One night, when the group was rehearsing at a club named Wheels, a dispute occurred (its source forgotten) and all seven musicians verbally ganged up on the fat-assed rich girl. In return, she boycotted the show that night, which only increased their resentment. In late-1960s rock, it hurt to emanate a certain upbringing. You could only get past your de-

* Carly's short, mostly unpleasant period with Elephant's Memory had an even more unpleasant afterlife. Although she'd signed a contract with them to be only a singer, not a writer, once she became famous, they sued her—unsuccessfully—for rights to the hits she had written.

spised caste by turning it into a goof, like cool, sarcastic Grace Slick (who several years but another lifetime ago had walked down the aisle in a white wedding gown in a San Francisco cathedral) did, by bringing Abbie Hoffman to her Finch College reunion to prank-out fellow alum Tricia Nixon. Carly "hated the gigs" with Elephant's Memory, she has said. But one providential chance encounter grew out of the experience.

Among the clubs Elephant's Memory played was the Scene, with a house band led by a longish-light-brown-haired, mustachioed young guitarist named Danny Armstrong. Danny thought Carly was "a good singer, very musical, and she had all kinds of sex appeal." But Danny was too cool—and too married—to let on that he'd noticed her. Danny Armstrong's middle-class, Midwestern background and his child-barnacled present made him vastly different from Carly's more compatible previous beaux, the wealthy, cultured, and unencumbered Delbanco and Donaldson. Danny was an engineer's son from Cleveland who'd started playing guitar on Ohio's weddings-and-polka-band circuit and had moved to New York to be a jazz guitarist, working with Kai Winding. Between children he had with his wife and those from a teenage relationship, he had four sons and a daughter.

Electric guitars were Danny Armstrong's life. He was gifted not only at playing electric guitars but at designing, constructing, and repairing the instrument that was now the focal point of all rockdom. In fact, playing at the Scene had been a parting-shot gig—he'd become a guitar entrepreneur. The previous year he had opened Dan Armstrong Guitars, on West Forty-eighth Street, and his timing had been dead-on—he had captured an exploding market. As he immodestly put it, in one of a number of interviews conducted for this book before his death from emphysema in 2004, "I was the first and [at the time] only electric guitar specialist in the world, and I knew every big-time guitar player in the world—I just plain *owned* New York at the time." When Cream came to town to play concerts featuring their haunting underground hit "White Room," Eric Clapton and Jack Bruce would sit with Danny in the back of the store, the three playing blues riffs—and, according to Armstrong, "Clapton only knew *one* way of playing blues riffs and I knew *twenty*."

All the British and American rockers and jazz and blues musicians sauntered into Dan Armstrong Guitars (the only one who excited Armstrong was his idol, Wes Montgomery), but only for freshly anointed Zeus-of-the-instrument Jimi Hendrix did he—begrudgingly—keep the store open after hours. The women on his staff were amazed that, for all his trademark pyrotechnics and sexual gestures, the slightly built Hendrix would lope into the store in a shy, pigeon-toed way, as plaintive as when he used to ply sustenance as an impoverished child in Seattle: an otherworldly gypsy—silver-ring-banded Borsalino floating atop his black-cotton-candy hair; Elizabethan blouse billowing out from under an antique embroidered vest; velvet pants tight across his uncommonly thin hips. As he padded around, the women saw what made him so captivating: Hendrix's charisma derived from his *fragility*. Accompanied by Experience mates Noel Redding and Mitch Mitchell or his friend, drummer Buddy Miles, Jimi would pick up, plug in, and *go at* any custom rarity that caught his fancy—and his keening, twanging, psychedelic talking blues would practically bounce sparks off the glass counters. Then, back down on the sidewalk, Hendrix would make a big shouting scene as he tore up the ticket he'd gotten for parking his Corvette at a hydrant—and zoom away, tires screeching. Danny Armstrong always had to be the king of his store; he pronounced Jimi Hendrix "an asshole."

One day in 1968 Danny looked up from his desk "and in she strolls, a nice-looking lady in an orange, pink, and yellow print dress. Certainly vivacious. Lots of charm. *Big* smile. Carrying a guitar that needed work." He recognized her as the Elephant's Memory singer. "She introduced herself. I said, 'Where'd you get a name like Carly?' and she said, from her aunt. She said she was a singer-musician going to music school"— Carly was taking a notating course at Juilliard. Carly recalls, "Oh, Lord, Danny! What a comely guy, when I first met him in his guitar shop. His face . . . like Rhett Butler! He had arms that were too short for his body, but I guess that's the price you pay for being so handsome."

The sexy, charming, "midtown-cool" (as Danny pegged her) girl with the strange first name came back with her guitar a couple more times; she always put a smile on his face. But Armstrong kept his interest low-watt—"I was just being me, not coming on too hard."

Eventually Armstrong and his wife broke up and he moved his store to a new location, on the newly renamed La Guardia Place (formerly West Broadway) near Washington Square Park. When Carly sailed into his new store one day, he ended up going back to her and Joey's apartment to play guitar while Carly played piano. He sensed she saw her efforts stymied by her privilege (and her race). "To her, and to me, Bessie Smith and Billie Holiday, and Odetta, for her, were the only singers that counted. She said she wished that she could sing like that, but she knew she never could." Still, he noticed, as Nick had: "Carly always wanted to be a celebrity."

Their first "real date," as Danny recalled it (even though "dating" was now a thing of the straight-world past), was a trip, in car-crazy Danny's red 1965 Karmann Ghia convertible, to the Lincoln Continental Dealers Convention in Harrisburg, Pennsylvania. Thus would commence an almost two-year-long relationship.

"We were just trotting along together, holding hands; we were just little bells, little playmates—Carly made up a nickname for me, Porcus Pinky. I called her Carl," Danny said of those first months. "Most things between us were shrouded in a cloud of pot smoke," says Carly. Carly's neuroses were out of view. "If she was insecure and phobic and all that, she sure hid it from me," Danny said. "She never hated anything. She never complained about anything. She was a calm, comfortable little playmate. I asked her brother, Peter, one time, 'Is she always so cheery?' and he said, 'Yes, but sometimes she's a little sad.' Carly was someone I *never* saw cry. And we never fought." ("Danny and I did have a fight once," Carly amends. "He hit me in the face with an open avocado.")

"We definitely fell in love," Danny said, and Carly agrees: "I really loved him." One day when they were driving, Danny turned to Carly and said, "You're all I need to make me happy." She picked up her guitar and started to turn it into a song.

Carly was so available for Danny that even though she was always writing songs, years after the fact, Danny couldn't remember her doing so. But it was he, she says, who suggested she put her Juilliard notating course to use by writing lead sheets of her songs and sending them to artists who might want to record them. She did so—sending her songs, in vain, to Judy Collins, Burt Bacharach, and again to Dionne Warwick.

Danny moved to an apartment over his store, thick in the middle of the action: around the corner from the Dugout, the Tin Angel, and the Bitter End; two blocks from the MacDougal Street folk clubs; and close by the offices of *Eye*,* a young, counterculture version of *Life*, staffed, at Hearst Magazines' expense, largely by genuine artists and near-hippies, and for which Gerry Goffin wrote a long piece on Aretha, and Steve Katz wrote reviews (as did soon-to-be Warner Bros. executive Andy Wickham).

Carly recalls Danny's apartment as "fairly squalid." "She'd always say to me, 'The trouble with you is, you have no taste!'" he recalled, "but I

---

*   The tragedies and notoriety of the staff of and contributors of the briefly flourishing *Eye* are a thin-slicing of the era's melodrama. *Eye*'s rock scene den mother, the charismatic Lillian Roxon (who inspired Helen Reddy's "I Am Woman"), died too young of an asthma attack. Its art director—beautiful, Pocahontas-braided Judy Parker—and chief photographer, her pint-sized British boyfriend, Michael Soldan, took acid after their boss, *Cosmopolitan* editor Helen Gurley Brown, scolded them for their hallucinogenic colors; then got in their boat on the Long Island Sound in a storm and drowned. Judy Collins's boyfriend Michael Thomas wrote for *Eye*; so did Jac Holzman's girlfriend Ellen Sander (who'd stroll around their home nude amid company). Susan and Michael Lydon (the Joan Didion and John Gregory Dunne of the counterculture) filed dispatches from swinging London, the Haight, and Berkeley; then Susan split from Michael and became, in this order: Janis Joplin's guitarist's girlfriend, a member of one of the first consciousness-raising groups, an essayist on the politics of orgasm, a leader of the self-fufillment cult Arica, in near-middle-age a street-dwelling crack addict, and, finally, before her death from breast cancer in 2005, an authority on knitting (and, one might add, on survival). The photographer in the crowd was a long-legged young woman who'd grown up on a leafy estate just north of Manhattan, had been married to a professor, wore tailored skirts and blouses, and was the receptionist at *Town and Country*. Her blasé preppy-debutante airs made her fascinating to rock stars. Her name was Linda Eastman. She promptly went to England and married Paul McCartney.

hated the wallpaper she picked out for the bedroom." Also troublesome were Danny's kids, who regarded Carly with the skepticism that children of divorce often train on their father's new girlfriend. But she got past the taste and the kids; she thought Danny immensely talented as a bass guitarist and was in thrall to him. "Carly was in Danny's store all the time, swooning over him," says Matt Umanov, Danny's mentee, who opened his own guitar store on Bleecker Street. "Danny, oh my God! Danny was another example," after Nick, "of the man carrying the creativity and the skill [in the relationship] for Carly; it was *always* about Danny's guitar playing," says Ellen Questel. Ellen understood Carly's impulse to minimize herself for Danny, because she was doing the same; now that her husband, Vieri Salvadori, was teaching art history, Ellen put aside her own graduate psychology studies to sort index cards for his lectures.

Carly introduced her onetime-polka-guitarist beau to the world of casual wealth and celebrity. Danny spent time at the Riverdale house, looking at its walls covered in pictures of illustrious authors who'd been friends of the family. He kept his middle-class defenses up; he resented her "rich college girl" polish. Curiously, of the young woman perceived by her friends as so vulnerably emotional, "I felt like she was following the directions on life's box. She never cried, or raged, or laughed from down inside."

Lucy Simon Levine was pregnant. Danny, who definitely did not want a sixth child, felt disapproval from Carly's older sister. "Lucy looked at me as the person who was keeping Carly from an orderly life," he said. "Lucy's life was orderly and conventional. She was married to a psychiatrist. She was having a baby. Carly's life *wasn't* orderly—she wasn't married, she didn't have a baby. Carly sort of envied Lucy's ability to have her life in order, and I thought that there was pressure on Carly to live like Lucy."

But far more than even the conflict between orderliness and spontaneity; far more than his girlfriend's good taste, her vivaciousness, or the fact that she could marshal an infinite amount of time to be with him, what struck Danny most about Carly was her intense sexuality. "To put it in one sentence, as bluntly and smoothly as possible: Carly loved sex," he said. "She *needed* it. I've never known many women who loved sex like that."

Carly also possessed a kind of mischief Danny had never encountered before. In winter Carly knitted Danny a ball warmer. But making the novel item was only half the gift; the presentation was the other half: Carly had Joey's beau Edward Villella jeté through Joey's living room, naked except for the tiny pink and purple garment. It was the era of scampish young women; whether outlawlike (Faye Dunaway in *Bonnie and Clyde*) or playful (Genevieve Waite in *Joanna*), cheekiness was in order. Still, who but Carly Simon would knit a *ball warmer* and then have a member of the New York City Ballet nude-model it?

"Carly was game; she would do things on a dare. Being cool mattered to her," Danny said. Danny parked a kilo—$5,000 worth—of grass in her bedroom closet at Joey's, and he sold the lid, brick by brick, to musicians for a happy profit. Once, when Danny and Carly got into a taxi, he dared her to have sex with him, right then and there, as they hurtled along the avenue, in earshot of their cabbie and in possible view of the other riders and drivers. Carly's reaction? Danny recalled: "'No problem.'" Another time, "I said, 'I bet you wouldn't fuck me under one of those pedestrian bridges in Central Park.' And she did, of course." Her security with her innate respectability; her parents' seamless meld of unconventional paramours with high intellectual standards, worthy causes, and impeccable social standing: all of this made sexuality for Carly Simon *not* what it might be for other girls—not a barricade to be stormed, not a potential retractor of virtue (there were no "gentle relations with names they must call me," as there were for Joni, or, as Carole had feared, children who might do the math on their parents' months of marriage at the time of their birth), not even anything *earnest*. Danny put it this way: "Carly wasn't bohemian, and she wasn't rebellious." After a pause: "She *didn't have* to be."

In early 1969, the focus shifted, from Carly and Danny to Carly and Jake—from Carly the available girlfriend to Carly the songwriter and potential performer.

Jake had moved into an apartment in Murray Hill. Soon after, Carly moved out of Joey's place and signed a lease for a one-bedroom apartment just around the corner from Jake, on Thirty-fifth Street, between Park and Lexington avenues.

Danny and Carly were more or less engaged now—*he* thought. According to Danny, they'd planned to have a wedding "in a pine forest somewhere." They were looking at houses; "we even found one in Silvermine, Connecticut." Lucy had her baby—a daughter, Julie—"and that put more pressure on Carly," Danny observed. "Women are programmed to fall apart over babies, and Carly was falling apart over this baby."

At the same time, however, Danny could feel Carly's priorities shifting. "When she moved into the new apartment, I suspected she had intentions of forming a new sort of base of operations," he said. During this period "Jake and I became inseparable," Carly has said. Carly had had years of talking to therapists about her childhood. Now she shared the stories with Jake, and to his fresh ear the "rich girl's problems" that had been deemed meritless by the reverse-snobbish times achieved a universal poignance. An image stayed with Jake: Richard Simon, in failing health, silent in the dark; Carly yearning for his attention.

One day Carly handed Jake a notated melody she had written months earlier but for which she couldn't come up with lyrics. The melody's opening bars, shifting back and forth between two minor-mode sequences with close dissonances, were so tensely poignant that *Village Voice* rock critic Robert Christgau would later, upon hearing them on the car radio, be "grabbed" by their "calculated drama." She had composed the melody as the soundtrack for a proposed TV documentary called "Who Killed Lake Erie?"—one of her freelance jobs—but nothing had come of it, "and I was stuck," she remembers; in writing songs by herself, it was easiest for her to start with the lyric, not the melody. "So I had that melody for so long that I was blocked." When Jake came over, "She gave it to me with *la-la-las*," Jake recalls.

Thinking of what Carly had told him about her father, Jake wrote: "My father sits at night with no lights on / His cigarette glows in the dark."

Jake used that childhood view of the sadness of marriage as a bridge to skepticism about friends from college being married. "They have their houses and their lawns." Jessica, Ellen, and Lucy were happily married, but the larger point was that young women had suddenly stopped seeing marriage as the ultimate event of their early twenties. Two souls huddled against the world—the romantic image that had prevailed when Carole and Gerry had gotten married—was an archaic position. There was too much *in* this new world; romance, belonging, and ecstasy literally flooded the senses. Sometimes it seemed to require a lack of imagination for a couple to stay together.

Danny initially worried that Jake was "putting moves on" his girlfriend, but he quickly saw that their intimacy was not physical. They were partners. "I wrote lyrics for Carly," says Jake, "like a playwright writing for an actress." It would take the first step of this partnership to boost Carly to a point where she'd start writing a stream of her own songs, increasingly prolific, well crafted, and era-defining—all of this so near but far from the scene Danny saw, of Carly and Jake, "sitting on the couch, talking over phrases, talking them into lyrics," he recalled. "She'd say, 'This isn't quite what I wanted to say here . . .' She brought him the melodies, and a lot of the ideas for the songs were hers. Jake would be like a blacksmith and hammer the songs together, and she'd steer him; she'd turn the songs in her rich-college-girl direction."

One night Carly went to the Village Gate to see David Steinberg's comedy routine. A friend of David's, a young woman named Arlyne Rothberg, who was starting out as a manager, came backstage to say hello to David and his girlfriend, Mary Ellen Mark. "It was a long, narrow club, and the dressing room was in the back," Arlyne Rothberg recalls, "so I'm walking toward a sofa in the dressing room . . . and I see a pair of legs hanging out. And as I'm getting closer, I see more and more of the legs. It was mesmerizing—she has these unbelievable legs. And she's seated, and we're introduced. She was heavier in those days," but, Arlyne thought, here was a woman who couldn't "do anything that isn't sultry and seductive while she's smiling and laughing."

Carly and Danny were spending less time together—"We weren't firing on all cylinders," he said. He could tell their romance was "thin-ning out," but the man who thought himself a more accomplished electric guitarist than Eric Clapton couldn't quite accept that he might not be the one to end it. Still, one day, at a recording session with Carly, he couldn't escape the conclusion that his sexy rich dilettante lover had a striking talent. For an album that Lucy and Carly were making, *The Simon Sisters Sing the Lobster Quadrille and Other Songs for Children,* Lucy had set classic poems—by Edward Lear, Lewis Carroll, Robert Louis Stevenson, and others—to music, among which was Robert Burns's "A Red, Red Rose." When Carly took the micro-phone in the studio and sang, "My love is like a red, red rose that's newly sprung in June . . . ," Danny thought, She sounds like an angel. (So moved was he by what critics have called her "low, earthy, and subtle" voice on that song that for decades he "heard" her singing it.)

One night Carly came down hard on Danny for smoking. His two-pack-a-day habit had always annoyed her, but that night "she lost pa-tience," he recalled. Danny Armstrong wanted to think that the breakup with Carly was about her hating his smoking. It was easier for him to think *that* than that his girlfriend was moving on. But one day soon after, Danny dropped by Carly's apartment, knocked on the door—and "a youngish guy answered and said Carly wasn't home." That bird had flown.

Danny Armstrong had underestimated his uptown-cool girlfriend. He thought she was a dilettante, but she was turning out to be ambi-tious. He thought she was a happy little rich girl, but she'd had her share of desultory jobs, rejections, insults, and depression. He thought that *he,* who didn't want any more children, would decide when it was over between them, and that she craved the stability of Lucy's life—women *wanted* that. Didn't they? And he thought the "preppy girl" song she and Jake were writing was inconsequential. That, too, would turn out to be a misperception.

PART FOUR

"i feel the earth move
under my feet"

joni
late 1967 – mid – 1970

The word of mouth that Joni Anderson Mitchell had earned for herself in New York accompanied her to Los Angeles. She arrived around Christmastime with her new, devoted manager, Elliot Roberts, and her boyfriend and chief champion, David Crosby. Having as strong-minded and talented a woman as Joni for a girlfriend was new for David, who had dominated his previous girlfriend, Christine Hinton (he'd broken up with Christine when he'd fallen in love with Joni, but they would later reunite). All he'd had to do was shout, "Christine! Joint!" and she was rolling and handing him a slender reefer. "Christine was always anxious, always ready to please," remembers Hinton's then-close friend Salli Sachse, who lived at Peter Tork's artistic collective. "David treated women badly, but then, so many guys did."

By contrast, Joni would never be servile, and according to Salli, David "respected her as a peer." She was also emotionally "turbulent"—David's word—and so, in those first weeks in L.A., it was often left to Estrella Berosini, who'd moved from Florida to L.A. at the same time, to play the little sister buffer and mediate between the two headstrong singers. One night, when they were all driving up to Stephen Stills's house (and David and Joni had unaccountably broken out into a chorus

of "Abba dabba dabba dabba dabba dabba dabba, goes the monkey to
the chimp"), David came down hard on Joni for her expensive purse.
While they were still in Florida, he had gotten her to scrub off her Carnaby Street eye makeup in favor of the natural look; now he wanted her
clothes to be more hip and funky, less discotheque-y. "*That's* the right
purse!" he'd said, pointing to Estrella's raggy fabric pouch (while Estrella
longed for Joni's handbag, "which she probably bought on Madison
Avenue"). "You know, Estrella," Joni said to her young friend, one day
during those early weeks in L.A., "I really do love David, but when we
get together, we just don't get along."

Still, there existed no more heartful trumpeter for Joni's arrival in
L.A. than David. He presented Joni like a showman. One night, for example, he lured members of the San Francisco–based theater group the
Committee up to a house in the Canyon, where, as he and memoir coau-
thor Carl Gottlieb described it, "a half dozen stoned and lucky actors
heard a never-before-recorded Joni Mitchell sing half her new album in
the predawn light. The company was stunned." One of them apparently
said: "We thought we hallucinated her." David's account sounds exaggerated, but Leah Cohen Kunkel, the sister of Cass Elliot and, at the time,
the new wife of a young drummer up from Long Beach, Russ Kunkel,
says it isn't. "When Joni would sing over that guitar, men were riveted—
they stopped what they were doing, they were absolutely enamored.
Before that it was always women [in the Canyon] riveted by the male
guitarist—this was the first time it changed. Joni got introduced to the
cream of the pop rock world, and she was accepted right away."

Russ recalls the new-to-the-Canyon Joni this way: "Most of the
women there were pretty magical then 'cause there was this incredible
feeling of freedom that was enhanced by various things, including drugs,
but Joni was *drop-dead beautiful.* And she had this amazing voice: her
voice register and her guitar tunings, which no one had heard."

Joni recorded her first album, *Joni Mitchell,* which, in subsequent
pressings, came to be known as *Song to a Seagull,* in the first weeks of
1968. David had himself named producer of the album; Joni termed him
its "conservationist" because he held the line against those who might

complain that as she put it, she'd "had a whole paintbox and use[d] only brown." In reality Joni was in control of her product, an unusually nervy move for a newbie on her maiden voyage with a major record label. She kept the album acoustic and intimate: just Joni and her guitar and piano. The album may have suffered from the spareness, for it had an astringent forlornness and never got past #189 on the *Billboard* chart.

The album cover was a painting by Joni. Her psychedelic mélange of voluptuous flowers in orange, green, and yellow enclosed a fish-eye-lens photograph of her standing on a dark, trash-can-strewn New York street, dressed for winter, carrying her belongings, hoisting an umbrella over her head. Her sketch of Crosby's boat was off to the right, under the words "Song to a Seagull," etched brokenly by a flock of gulls. Amid the painted flowers—petals opening from stamen—were two almost anthropomorphic cacti, for her alter ego, the cactus tree. Joni dedicated the album to Arthur Kratzmann, the seventh-grade teacher who had mercilessly scrawled "Cliché! Cliché!" all over her essays until she finally learned to write with originality.

The songs introduced listeners to veiled snippets of this still very unknown singer's life. In "Part One [A side]: I Came to the City" there unfolded, in this order, her marriage-gone-wrong to Chuck in "I Had a King"; her affair with Michael Durbin in "Michael from Mountains"; the joyous "Night in the City," her touché to the small-minded moralists who'd looked on the Yorkville folksingers (including that poor, pregnant one) as degenerate hippies; and, finally, with "Marcie" and "Nathan LaFraneer," her testimony to the trials of a young woman alone in Manhattan. She named the B side "Part Two: Out of the City and Down to the Seaside," making her meeting of David in Florida into a kind of deliverance—which, in career terms, it was. "Cactus Tree" is the stem winder on that side. Joni's atypically rousing guitar intro, a change of pace after the more melancholy fare, creates the impression that she's bounding out from behind a curtain, ready to present this female-triumphal anthem as an encore to a worked-up audience. At least that's how it sounds now, with almost forty years' hindsight.

The reviewer for *Rolling Stone* was breezy—"Here is Joni Mitchell. A penny yellow blonde with a vanilla voice . . . a lyrical kitchen poet"—but ultimately respectful. He duly noted her reputation among folk music followers and her excellently recorded songbook, but he couldn't quite get excited. "The . . . album, despite a few momentary weaknesses, is a good debut," he concluded.

The album had been initially put at risk by a tape hiss that was audible only after all the tracks were laid down. A worried David Crosby had driven the tapes to the Laurel Canyon house of Elektra sound engineer John Haeny. "The tapes were a mess," Haeny has said. Slipping into the studio, he remixed Joni's album, rescuing it.

Around this same time, Haeny awakened in his Ridpath Lane house one morning to "some chaos" and found Judy Collins, nude, amid a tangle of yellow flowers at the wooden fence in his yard. Judy was a friend, and she was having herself photographed for the cover of the Joni-song-filled album *Wildflowers*. Judy had recently broken up with rock writer Michael Thomas, so Haeny introduced her to his friend Stephen Stills, who proved a good match for the tempestuous Collins. Educated in military school and raised in Florida and Louisiana, Stills was conceited and combative; some used the word "obnoxious." With his sleepy-lidded blue eyes in a wide, high-foreheaded face framed by muttonchop sideburns and wispy blond hair (and despite—or maybe with the help of—his terrible teeth), Stills was very sexy in a young Steve McQueen kind of way. (Had many people known that he'd auditioned to be part of the Monkees, some of his edgy charisma might have evaporated.) Just before the Collins-Stills match was made, another interlocking connection was struck during Joni's recording sessions. In the adjacent studio, Stills and the Buffalo Springfield were recording; one of Stills's group mates was Vicky Taylor's good friend from Toronto, Neil Young. Stills, who was (of course—wasn't everyone?) a friend of Crosby's, ended up playing bass guitar on "Night in the City," the only outside musician (except the banshee player) to intrude on Joni's solo performance. Joni introduced Neil Young to Elliot Roberts, thinking their humor made them kindred spirits, and Roberts became Young's manager, too.

Completing this new musical circle was a gentle English rocker who would become one of the great loves of Joni's life.

Graham Nash was, as he says, "a poor man's son," from Blackpool, England. When he was fourteen, he'd wanted nothing more than to use his voice and guitar to make others feel like *he* felt when he listened to the Everly Brothers. He and his friend Allan Clarke had formed the Hollies and, with the group, were part of the British Invasion. "Bus Stop" and "Carrie-Anne" were more-than-likable hits—the former, dark; the latter, fetching—in 1966 and 1967, the twilight of formula English pop. Nash, who was one year older than Joni, had married young and was divorced. He was a tall, thin, approachably handsome man with intense, closely set eyes in a narrow face framed by a rich mass of shaggy dark hair, and his manner was both gracious and intimate. In his travels to Laurel Canyon, he'd struck up a close friendship with Cass Elliot, to whom he found it comfortable to pour out his heart. He was a romantic and an appreciator. To him, Laurel Canyon was like "Vienna at the turn of the century or Paris in the 1930s." But he was edgy, too (what rock star wasn't?), and he dressed with neo-Edwardian panache. When Joni ran into him at a radio station's party for the Hollies at a hotel in Ottawa (where they were appearing in a concert hall and she in a coffeehouse) shortly after she finished recording her album, "he was very British mod," Joni has said. He was wearing one of "these ankle-length black velvet coats and yards and yards of pink chiffon, almost foppish, like the way Jagger and a lot of the British bands dressed at the time."

Knowing they'd be in the same city, David Crosby had given Graham (they'd met through Cass) advance word on Joni. "He'd said, 'Watch out for this woman'—in a good way, that she was very special and very beautiful," Graham recalls. But Nash had all but forgotten those words when "through the usual lineup of beers and juices, I saw this woman sitting by herself with what looked like a Bible on her lap. [It was actually an antique photo album encasing a music box.] She was something to behold."

Meanwhile, Hollies manager Robin Britten had grabbed Nash's ear. "He kept talking to me about business," or so it seemed, "but I just wasn't there," Graham says. "My attention—my essence—was over in the corner, with that girl. Then Robin said, 'Shut up for a moment! There's a woman I'm trying to tell you about and you haven't heard a word!' I said, 'That's because I'm looking at *this* woman.' He replied, '*That's* the woman *I'm* talking about.'

"So I walked over to Joan and introduced myself, and she invited me to her room in the hotel, and I ended up spending the night with her, and"—he admits, thirty-five years later (and in the midst of a long, happy marriage to another woman)—"I haven't been the same since." In the dim light of her room at the Hotel Château Laurier, which gave off on a romantic view of rooftop turrets and the adjacent Parliament building, Joni took out her guitar. "But I loved her before she played a note," Graham says, "just from looking at her and talking to her and realizing what her spirit was." For her part, Joni thought Graham "very gentle, soft-spoken, and kind, with a certain degree of rock 'n' roll arrogance mixed in."

Joni wooed the already smitten Graham as she had Roy Blumenfeld, Leonard Cohen, and David Crosby—with her songs. Despite her femininity, like a man, she displayed her *work* to her would-be lovers. "She played fifteen songs, almost her entire first record, and a couple of different ones, too," Graham says. "By the time she got through 'Michael from Mountains' and 'I Had a King,' I was gone. I had never heard music like that."

Graham returned to England, but on the basis of transatlantic counsel from Mama Cass, he began thinking of quitting the Hollies, moving to L.A., and trying to launch himself as a solo act. He had already written the bouncy, quite wonderful "Marrakesh Express" about the trend that the rich English hippies had started—and American counterparts would soon pick up—of traveling to that fabled souk-laced city in Morocco and paying a court visit to Ahmed, the wacky, notorious "King Hash," in his rug-smothered lair.

Meanwhile, Joni continued her Canadian tour and struck up a platonic friendship with Jimi Hendrix, for whom she opened at a subsequent engagement in Ottawa. Like many women coming upon Jimi in private, Joni found him to be the startling opposite of his reputation. He was "sensitive, shy, sweet," she'd recall—and obsessed with getting away from what she called the "phallic" aspects of his performance. (Writing in his diary, Jimi called Joni a "fantastic girl with heaven words.") After the evening's show, Joni, Jimi, and his drummer, Mitch Mitchell, stayed up late, talking and playing in one of their rooms. It was all "so innocent, but the management—all they saw was three hippies," she later railed, angrily. "A black hippie! Two men and a woman in the same room!"

After her tour, in the spring of 1968, Joni bought a house in the Canyon, a romantic aerie with wide plank floors, broad-paned leaded windows, and wood-beamed ceilings at 8217 Lookout Mountain. It was close by Carole's house, but the two women did not know one another. The house was built in the 1920s, right into the side of the mountain, "so when the trees spread out," Joni has said, "the branches were right at the window; birds flew in and nested." Joni filled the house with antiques, quilts, and flowers, and she set her guitars on her Priestly piano. A Tiffany lamp and the stained-glass window panels caught the Canyon sunlight, which of course poured in like butterscotch.

In July, Graham moved to L.A. and moved in with Joni. "We were both pretty terrified of a deep relationship," Graham says, but they slipped into one anyway. "I'd been divorced—both of us had—and I knew she was a little skittish about [commitment]." Joni's family history was not far from her mind. "She didn't want to be like her grandmothers," Graham says. "They had given up artistic careers to take care of husbands." That lesson was "always an unspoken thing between Joan and me."

One night, shortly after Graham moved in, David and Stephen came over to Joni's. The ex-Byrd and the Springfield member had been spending days writing and singing together. For all his rock-bad-boy panache, David was a folkie at heart; he'd originally had trouble playing his guitar while standing rock-style, rather than sitting, and his bottom tenor was luminous. As for Stills, it was his scratchy, bluesy voice that had made the Springfield's "For What It's Worth" a radical political battle cry.

Stephen had penned a song, "You Don't Have to Cry," for Judy Collins, whose high-powered career was pulling his macho nose out of joint. "In the morning, when you rise," the song asked. "Are you thinkin' of telephones / And managers and where you got to be at noon?" (Stills's "Suite: Judy Blue Eyes" would be his swan song to her.) Both Crosby and Stills had heard kudos for Nash's high harmony from everyone from Cass Elliot to the Lovin' Spoonful's John Sebastian, but they'd never tried to sing with him. Sitting around Joni's living room, getting high, Stills and Crosby sang the first bar of the new song: Crosby the tenor, Stills the alto. Nash asked, "Would you sing that again?" Stills and Crosby repeated the bar. Nash listened intently and again asked them to sing the line. When they did, he queried a third time. This time when they reprised the bar, Graham chimed in, producing a straining, poignant, slightly sour top note that lifted the song to an ecstatic new dimension. "All four of us—the three of us fellows and Joan—*knew*! It was a truly amazing moment," Graham recalls.

Crosby, Stills and Nash would become a phenomenon—three stars of three different groups, each contributing beautiful songs (Stills's two for Judy Collins; David's rich-hippie dreamscape "Wooden Ships" and his elegy for Bobby Kennedy's murder, "Long Time Gone"; Graham's "Marrakesh Express" and his ode to his domesticity with Joni, "Our House") to their eponymous album, sung in their piercing harmony. But it would be a song of Joni's—one of her finest and most sociopolitical—that would fully introduce Crosby, Stills and Nash to the nation and would give them their signature hit: a hymn to the capstone cultural event of their generation's decade. That would come a year later.

Graham adored Joni, and he made no secret of his awe of her. "There was always this edge of me looking at Joan and thanking my lucky stars," Graham admits today. "I felt a little like, 'What the fuck am I doing here, with this woman? This woman loves me? This is insane!' I looked at Joan as a goddess, and she was." He called her Joan (her subsequent boyfriends would, as well); she called him Willy, the diminutive of his middle name. Did Joni recognize her power over men? "I don't think you can have that power and not recognize it. Did

she utilize it or abuse it? Absolutely not. But you can't be that beautiful and talented and not know that guys are falling for you, right, left,
and center."

Joni and Graham would race each other to the piano after morning
breakfasts at Art's Deli in Studio City. "It was an intense time," Graham
has said. "Who's going to fill up the space with their music first? We
[were] two very creative writers living in the same space, and it was an
interesting clash: 'I want to get as close to you as possible.' 'Let me alone
to create!'" Those songs of Joni's that are clearly or presumably about
life with Graham reflect that push-pull of intimacy, in lyric styles rang-
ing from biblical reverence ("He would read to her / Roll her in his arms
/ And give his seed to her," in the achingly lovely "Blue Boy"), to Nash-
ville-worthy wit ("But when he's gone, me and them lonesome blues col-
lide / The bed's too big, the frying pan's too wide," in "My Old Man").

"We'd make love, often, in her tree house," Graham volunteers. "We'd
do crazy stuff. Once, we went to New York, and we saw these kids who
had opened a fire hydrant. We got out of the limousine and into the
spray of the hydrant, and then we got back into the limousine, completely soaked." During this or another trip to the city, they ran into
Gene Shay, the Philadelphia deejay, at a drugstore in Sheridan Square,
and Shay was touched by how Graham "gallantly" kept guard in the
aisle so that no one would see Joni purchasing sanitary napkins. Graham's decorousness is reflected in the opening line of his "Our House"—
"I'll light the fire, you place the flowers in the vase that you bought
today." Respectively Canadian and English, both from Queen-loyal, tea-
sipping, lower-middle-class Protestant homes, they were to each other
known quantities within a swirling rock-world ethnic melting pot. For
Joni, Graham was a natural mate and a resting point. His talent was
overmatched by hers, but he knew it and his humility made him charming. He saw her turmoil: "She was vulnerable, lonely inside, and angry,
even though she was surrounded by people who loved her," he says—and
it echoed his own vulnerability. "I had never been so much in love. I had
never been so unsure of myself. I had never been so fragile." Yet, "people
would say we would light up a room when we walked in," he says today.

Perhaps it was the fragility shining through their confidence and glamour that made them evanescent.

Joni did not tell Graham about her baby right away. "When you're wooing a new lover, you don't say, 'By the way, I've got this kid I gave up for adoption.'" But when she did broach the subject, she spoke of the pain of the "shame and guilt and wanting a life" and of the "rejection" she knew she would have faced from her parents had they known about the birth. She recalled her ordeal, describing it all with still-fresh emotion and blaming Chuck—a version of events she had now settled into. Graham felt the surrender of the baby "was devastating for her. It had a tremendous effect on her emotional growth."

Joni began to spot her daughter at music festivals. "At concerts, she would see a little girl's face, and she would wonder," says a friend from those years, Ronee Blakley.

The first Kelly sighting was at the Big Sur Folk Festival that summer.* "We thought we saw her daughter," says Graham, for he, too, having absorbed her emotions, believed it. "There was a sound check before a communal early dinner. We lined up to get our food. And I remember this young—eight- or nine-year-old—blond girl in line, waiting to go to dinner. The little girl said, 'Who are you?' Joni said, 'I'm Joni Mitchell.' And the little girl said, 'No, you're not; *I'm* Joni Mitchell.' And then Joan looked at me—it was one of those strange, *Twilight Zone* things—and then the little girl disappeared." Of course, in 1968 Joni's daughter would have been three, not eight or nine. But the incident reveals how fixated

---

* Joni's attendance at the festival was significant for another reason. Though she didn't perform that year (organizer Nancy Carlin, a close friend of Joan Baez's and Mimi Fariña's, says, "We didn't even know who she was at the time; we didn't have accommodations for her because we weren't expecting her; she offered to sleep in the station wagon"), Joni met Joellen Lapidus, a hand-carver and crafter of the Appalachian dulcimer. The dulcimer, which lies flat across the lap, may be the only musical instrument indigenous to America. Joni once described its myth-shrouded origin as the result of either the "Scots coming to Appalachia and longing for their bagpipes [or] . . . the Swedes coming and longing for their zither, [though] other people say that one day they just took a fiddle and stretched it out and put it on their lap." It makes a vibrant, plucked sound. Lapidus made Joni a beautiful dulcimer, which would become a staple of her composing and singing, and her accompaniment on much of *Blue*.

Joni was on the loss. Graham believes: "Joni's daughter has haunted Joan since the moment she gave her up."

Shortly after Big Sur, Joni flew 3,000 miles northeast and attended the Mariposa Festival. There, she had another encounter with a little girl, closer to Kelly Dale's real age and closer to her likely home now. As Joni later recalled, she and the other performers were corralled behind a fence, but a festival representative came to fetch her—there were some people who wanted to have a word with her. Approaching the fence, Joni saw a young couple. The man had a little boy on his shoulders; there was a little girl (whom Joni judged to be about three) beside them— "a small, curly-haired blond girl—my child had thick, thick curly hair," Joni noted (apparently referring to her memory of the several-months-old Kelly Dale in the foster home). The child's fingers clutched the fence's chain links. "I looked at [the family]. Nobody spoke. Nobody spoke until the child spoke. And she said to me, 'Hello, Kelly.' And I said, 'My name's not Kelly. My name's Joni.' And she said, 'Nooo . . . no, you're Kelly.'" The mother warmly intervened, explaining that the little girl's name was Kelly. But the child herself continued insisting that Joni was named Kelly. Joni believed the child was trying to tell her: *I am your Kelly— your Kelly Dale—and you are my mother.*

Joni asked the parents: "Do you have anything to say?" They didn't, and they walked off. Did the encounter really happen that way? Or did Joni part-imagine it? For twenty-five years Joni "always suspected" that that curly-headed girl at Mariposa was her daughter.

In fact, Joni's daughter went nowhere near a folk or rock concert during those first three years of her life (although she did live near the Mariposa site, in a Toronto suburb called Don Mills, and she did have a brother). Her adoptive parents, schoolteachers David and Ida Gibb, were bookish, earnest, and introverted—the last people one would expect to find at a pop or even folk concert, says one who knows them. David had been born in Scotland and migrated to Canada with his parents as a boy; Ida was of Ukrainian descent and grew up in Winnipeg. The Gibbs' biological son, David Jr., was four on the September 1965 day that Joni's seven-month-old baby, Kelly Dale, was officially named Kilauren Gibb.

(The similarity between the names "Kelly" and "Kilauren"—the latter, chosen to honor David Gibb's Scottish heritage—is coincidental.) David Jr. was blond, like his adopted little sister; they looked enough alike to be natural siblings through early childhood. Still, by summer 1968, when Joni was experiencing these cryptic encounters with little girls, members of the Gibbs' Donalda Country Club were beginning to wonder how the beautiful little spitfire could have been born of two cautious, not-very-attractive parents. Every passing year, a few more people in Don Mills would speculate if Kilauren Gibb was adopted.

Joni began work on her second album, *Clouds,* in early 1969. A sound engineer with an interest in Buddhism, Henry Lewy, played producer on the effort, in the same "beard" role that David Crosby had, on her first album. Again, Joni was in control. This time she used guitar accompaniment only (on *Joni Mitchell,* she had also played piano). For album cover art, she painted a super-realistic portrait of her face: hair streaming over a black turtleneck, she is holding up a bright red, too widely open flower, pointing it at the viewer, at whom she is staring. The exaggerated tips on the petals match the exaggerated tips on her tightly closed lips. The message is one of great self-exposure *and* great rectitude, all wrapped up in feminine symbols. Behind Joni was the Saskatchewan River—yellow clouds broodingly descending into the dark water—with the medieval turrets of the Bessborough Hotel on the far shore. She dedicated the album to her grandmother Sadie McKee, whose legacy of frustrated creativity she was expressing. The confrontational self-possession was almost groundbreaking, "almost" because, by now, Laura Nyro had raised the bar for female confessional songwriting, a genre she had virtually invented. (Joni would meet Laura in a few months, by way of their mutual manager, David Geffen. They would admire each other's music.)

But Laura Nyro's songs were now almost hysterically vulnerable and esoteric. Her *Eli and the Thirteenth Confession* and imminent *New York Tendaberry* were tender, frantic operas, full of leaps and hints and dream shards. A listener either *got* Laura's plotline of a female naïf baptized by the sanctifying rough-play of soulful life, or was so overwhelmed by the passion that she took it on faith. Joni's songs were more conventionally melodic and satisfyingly narrative.

Two of Joni's songs on *Clouds* were for Leonard Cohen—"That Song About the Midway" and "The Gallery." There was also "Tin Angel," in which a woman is surrounded by the accessories one would imagine in the antique-bed boudoir that she had described at the Second Fret: measuring her soothing mementos against the insecure love of a "sorrow"-eyed man. She added her most iconic songs—"Chelsea Morning" and as last track "Both Sides, Now," which she'd finally stopped hiding behind—Judy Collins's lusher, accessible covers of which declared that Joni was, first of all, a writer. Her mournful "Songs for Aging Children" would soon be included in the Arthur Penn–directed antiwar film version of Arlo Guthrie's song *Alice's Restaurant.* "I Don't Know Where I Stand" gave listeners the cactus tree, despiked and humbled, feeling her way through an infatuation so fresh that "even the sound of your voice is still new," with all its self-consciousness and bet hedging. "I Think I Understand"—full of Child Ballad hoariness—paid homage, like "Urge for Going" had, to the form her own songs had supplanted.

A Carnegie Hall concert on February 1, 1969, announced Joni as a celebrity. Her parents flew down from Saskatoon and stayed at the Plaza. Backstage, Joni stood with Graham (who looked suitably rock-star foppish) in her thrift-store felt skirt with sequins in the front and giant artichoke and American flag appliqués. Myrtle, aghast, said: "You're not going onstage at Carnegie Hall wearing that, are you?" Bill Anderson placated his wife. "Oh, hush, Myrtle, she looks like a queen in those rags," he said, as their daughter took the stage for the performance that would earn her a standing ovation.

At her next concert, in Cambridge a month later, a lanky, handsome unknown with deep-set eyes, long brown hair, and a thin mustache opened for her. He played a song he'd written, "Something in the Way She Moves," and when he got to the words "my troubled mind," his nasal-voiced melancholy hinted at a *real* troubled mind, though his well-bred manner belied all his brooding and slumping. His name was James

Taylor, and he was back in America, after making his first Apple album, dividing his time between his family's Martha's Vineyard home and L.A., where he would soon start recording his second album, *Sweet Baby James*. He was hanging out with Kootch's crowd. James came back to Joni's dressing room and said hello. But she was involved with Graham Nash, and he with Margaret Corey.

Meanwhile, the fan base Joni had first found in her post–Chuck and Joni concerts was gathering number. *Clouds* would better *Joni Mitchell*'s *Billboard* standing by half (it charted at #93). Joni's face—framed by her waxy blond hair; sporting a wary, sideways expression, her long, manicure-nailed hands forming a little teepee in front of her lips—filled a *Rolling Stone* cover in May, accompanying an article that began: "Folk music, which pushed rock and roll into the arena of the serious with protest lyrics and blendings of Dylan and the Byrds back in 1964, has reentered the pop music cycle." The review ended with, "Joni Mitchell has arrived in America."

Significantly, the article mentioned that Joni "shares a newly purchased house with Graham Nash." This, of course, was *Rolling Stone*—not a "straight" magazine like *Life*. Still, in mid-1969, a tossed-off reference to "living together" announced an avant-garde state. Choosing to cohabit out of wedlock with such thoughtful, romantic gentility as Joni and Graham were applying to their lives (the article took note of Joni's "antique pieces crowd[ing] tables, mantels, and shelves, . . . [her] antique handbags . . . on a bathroom wall, a hand-carved hat rack at the door . . . castle-style doors . . . a grandfather clock," and mentioned that during the interview, Nash was "perched on an English church chair" while Joni was "in the kitchen, using the only electric lights on in the house . . . making the crust for a rhubarb pie") elevated the seedy state of cohabitation to elegance and proved you could get the piety of the wedding-in-the-woods *without* the wedding. Increasingly, young middle-class-turned-hip women were choosing to "live with" their boyfriends, not marry them. You had to have a name for your living-withee, so, to cut against the elite sweetness of the lifestyle, gruff working-class terminology was appropriated: "my old man," "my old lady." Joni wrote "My Old Man" to legitimize this phenomenon and to locate herself and Graham within it; Graham's "Our House" seconded the motion.

Being someone's old lady was a proud sign of emotional security (a young woman didn't *need* marriage to feel that she was *not* being taken advantage of by her boyfriend), and it was the expression of a new—negative—way of viewing the institution of marriage. It wasn't just the guy who liked things fine the way they were, who (as the crass saying went) wouldn't buy the cow now that he'd started getting the milk for free, while the girlfriend longed, and lobbied, for commitment. Rather, it was the *girl* who now disparaged marriage in her own right, out of idealism and anti-authoritarianism. Joni presented the argument, in folky dialect: "We don't need no piece of paper from the city hall, keeping us tied and true." ("And we *did* feel that way," Graham says. "We *didn't* need to get married to feel that way.") Living with a man without a wedding license had always been considered low-class ("common-law" marriages were for common people), desperate, or morally shady—or all three. Now, the choice to live in a situation that included sex but not a wedding license was a mark of enlightenment for a young woman.

Crosby, Stills and Nash had cut their album, and the atmosphere in the studio had been giddy. "It was scary; once we knew what we had, you could not pry us apart with a crowbar; we knew we'd lucked into something so special, man," Crosby has said, of their aural combination. And Joni said, "The feeling between them was very high, almost amorous. There was a tremendous amount of affection and enthusiasm. . . . Part of the thrill for me being around them was seeing how they were exciting themselves mutually. They'd hit a chord and go, 'Whoooaa!,' then fall together, laughing."

"Joni was one of the boys," Graham says. "She would have picked up a basketball and shot hoops. It wasn't that we were in a club that she needed inviting to. It all came naturally." She accompanied them to rustic Big Bear to shoot the inside photographs of *Crosby, Stills and Nash*. In pictures from the day, she's in the back of the limo between dapper, mustachioed David and handsome, scruffy Graham: demure in a cap-sleeved sweater, a cross dangling on a chain around her neck; straight hair streaming, topped by a knit cap. She kisses a delighted-looking Graham's hand as she pens a lyric for a song about him, "Willy," on a notepad: "Willy is my child, he is my father / I would be his lady all my life."

In mid-August, Joni and Crosby, Stills and Nash (now with Neil Young, with whom they would record their next album, *Déjà Vu*) flew to New York to appear at the Woodstock Music and Art Fair, and for her booking on the prestigious *Dick Cavett Show* the night after the festival. By now she had opened for her boys at several packed concerts, and the huge fan reaction had proved that three (now four) male rock stars were exponentially more charismatic than one female folksinger.

Woodstock, "Three Days of Peace and Music," was a festival planned for August 15, 16, and 17 in Bethel, New York, at $18 to $24 for the entire three days. Two promoters in their early twenties, Artie Kornfeld and Michael Lang, backed by a twenty-six-year-old financier named John Roberts, wanted it to be the biggest rock festival ever. They had duly emptied their pockets, doubling Jefferson Airplane's going $6,000 fee to $12,000, and paying Jimi Hendrix, now the biggest rock star in the country, $32,000 (his manager had asked for $150,000 but settled on the smaller figure on the condition that no act follow Jimi). Woodstock would feature the most glamorous, top acts: Janis Joplin, Jefferson Airplane, and Richie Havens (who would open the show); Jimi Hendrix, who would close it, providing, from the depths of a soul torn between erotic showmanship and an embrace of aboriginal New Music, the most dramatic "Star-Spangled Banner" in recent history; the Grateful Dead, the Who, Joan Baez, Country Joe and the Fish, Tim Hardin, The Band (becoming *the* group, by way of their quirky Canadian-cum-Deep-South roots, fresh-from-the-Civil War sound, and adoption by Bob Dylan), Ravi Shankar, Blood, Sweat and Tears (which included Joni's Blues Project friend Steve Katz and had been founded by Al Kooper, who was no longer in the group), and tomorrow's stars: Sly and the Family Stone, Santana, and Creedence Clearwater Revival.

Throughout Kornfeld and Lang's negotiations with the town of

Wallkill, New York, they continued to insist that a crowd of, at *most*, 50,000 would be attending. But, given the aggressive promotion the festival was receiving in *Rolling Stone, The Village Voice, The New York Times,* and on the radio, the townspeople doubted the numbers would stay that low. A month before the festival, the town of Wallkill abruptly rescinded its offer.

The promoters looked for a savior, and they found one in Max Yasgur, the biggest dairy farmer in the valley and the holder of an NYU law degree. Yasgur offered his 600-acre farm for $75,000, even though, with the crowd count now whispered to be an astonishing 200,000, extensive trampling seemed likely. The promoters enlisted the Hog Farm, the country's most famous commune, led by ex-Cambridge folkie Hugh Romney (an old friend of Joan Baez and Betsy Siggins), who now called himself Wavy Gravy, to bestow back-to-the-land authenticity and to provide infrastructure: security, food stands, shelter, a "free school" for kids. Wavy Gravy called his cross-country counterpart, Ken Kesey, at his commune in Oregon, and dozens of overalls-clad, acid-tab-bearing Merry Pranksters were promptly dispatched east in psychedelic school buses.

The divide between young/hip and old/straight had been around since 1966's Human Be-In in Haight-Ashbury, and it had been celebrated with every smoked joint, every dunking of a knotted cotton T-shirt into a tub of Rit dye, every raised two-finger peace sign. It had taken three years for the lifestyle's tentacles to stretch to the vast domain of American middle-class youth, and now that it had, a haj to a mecca seemed in order. Where Monterey Pop had been the hip elite—a jazz concert's savvy crowd of fans close to the age, taste, and coolness level of the performers—Woodstock would be hip democracy: wildly enthusiastic college kids, working- and middle-class hippies, and drug-brined riffraff. Where Monterey Pop had been a bellwether boutique, Woodstock would be Wal-Mart. As Arnold Skolnick, the artist who designed the festival's catbird-on-guitar logo, put it, "Something was tapped—a nerve—in this country. And everybody just came."

As Joni, Graham, David, Stephen, and Neil were preparing to fly to New York, the Bethel town elders and Yasgur's neighbors were angrily hectoring Yasgur to give back the money and keep the hippies from over-running their orderly town. But Yasgur held firm to his agreement, even as reports shot through the news that 800,000 people—sixteen times the original maximum estimate—were on their way there.

Joni wanted to perform, but Elliot and David Geffen were fearful for her safety. Besides, even if she got to the festival safely, would she get back in time for the Cavett show, the next night?* The festival had already started; the round-the-clock performances were a half day or more behind schedule; traffic was blocked for twenty miles; many festival-goers had left their cars on the highway or sides of the streets and, truly like pilgrims now, were walking. The stars were being airdropped in by army helicopter.

The boys hired a small plane to fly them into the festival; Joni went to Geffen's apartment and, from the point of view of "the girl who couldn't go to the party," watched it on TV. "The deprivation of not being able to go," she has said, "provided me with an intense angle on Woodstock." That longing showed up in the song she wrote.

Ultimately, some 450,000 exuberant souls came to the festival, to withstand the rain and mud and the inadequacy of facilities (there were only 620 portable toilets) with joyful brio. Street signs sprouted up: Groovy Path, Gentle Way, High Way. People made love and shared food, tents, acid, dope, Band-Aids, water, blankets. A couple of babies

---

* When Joni and Jefferson Airplane appeared on *The Dick Cavett Show,* David and Stephen bounded in, mid-segment, fresh from Bethel. In her long, low-cut, loden green crushed velvet dress, Joni exuded a blushing but steely, farm-girl dignity, next to tanned, lean, tartly sophisticated Grace Slick in tie-dye. Slick, still the reigning Acid Queen, got the lion's share of attention, sparring with Cavett (when she dismissively referred to him as "Sam," he shot back, "Stop calling me the wrong name, Miss *Joplin!*") as if they were some odd-couple comedy team, but Joni's "Chelsea Morning" drew an almost awed ovation. Word of the transition from tough psychedelic hard rock to thoughtful, sincere music—soon to be advanced by James Taylor, and then, most fulsomely, by Carole on *Tapestry*—would be flowing from music critics' pens in a year and a half's time. The contrast, during this show, between Grace and Joni was the early, female version of that baton-passing.

were born. Three people died, and four hundred bad acid trips required medical attention, but no violence broke out. Swami Satchidananda wafted in and gave the crowd his blessing. Max Yasgur (suddenly the biggest rock star of all) intoned to the mic, "This is the largest group of people ever assembled in one place, and I think you people have proven something to the world: that a half a million kids can get together and have three days of fun and music and have nothing but fun and music, and God bless you for it!" Joni, who had been feeling religious of late, felt that what she was watching on TV was "a modern miracle, a modern loaves-and-fishes story. For a herd of people that large to cooperate so well, it was pretty remarkable—there was tremendous optimism." She also viewed the spectacle through the eyes of a girl from a long line of farmers; Yasgur (she would cite his name early in her song) had done all farming folk proud, including her grandparents.

Joni wrote her song about the raucous weekend in counterintuitive minor mode; it had a primordial, Nordic winter-forest sound, with biblical echoes that started with the first line's mention of the "child of God." The mirage of "the bombers riding shotgun in the sky"—she conflated the peaceful helicopters soaring into the meadow with the military craft of the Vietnam War—"turning into butterflies across our nation" mirrored the naïve hope that had fueled the day. But it was the first line of the chorus—"We are stardust, we are golden"—set to those spectral, pessimistic chords—that made the song so hauntingly elegiac and conveyed the impression of hundreds of thousands of people speaking as one. Years later, cultural critic Camille Paglia, in her book *Break, Blow, Burn*, would feistily place the lyrics to "Woodstock" along with works by Robert Lowell, Sylvia Plath, Emily Dickinson—and Shakespeare—on her list of the forty-three best poems produced in the English language.

By the time the boys got back—talking of how they'd commandeered a pickup truck with Jimi Hendrix to get from the airfield to the festival tent and how they hadn't performed until four in the morning—Joni had completed the song. She'd intuited the significance of Woodstock from her armchair. "[Joni] contributed more towards people's understanding of that day than anybody that was there," Crosby has said, of the song that, in rock version, he, Nash, Stills and, technically, Young (whose voice is not heard on the cut) would make into their defining hit.

Days later, back in L.A., Joni opened for her boys at the Greek Theatre. If there had been doubt as to where she was now positioned in relation to this male group she'd helped ignite, it was banished by *Los Angeles Times* critic Robert Hilburn, who called Crosby, Stills, Nash and Young's performance "a triumph of the first order" and said that Joni's performance had been "overwhelmed" by theirs. She may have been beginning to wonder: What was the price of being someone's old lady?

On the one hand, being an old lady, or a "lady"—the kind of arty, sensual, esoterically spiritual chick for whom the coolest men had lust and awe—well, you couldn't beat that. All over the country, young women were trying to shoehorn their personalities into that fashionable archetype: talkative girls got stoned and talked slower; unaesthetic girls took to wearing dangly jewelry; pragmatic girls started reading their horoscopes. Verbal, argumentative girls pretended to be anti-intellectual and serene. But many young women (especially, it seemed, in Laurel Canyon) didn't have to try; they naturally personified this glamorous new femininity. For example, there was Annie Burden, the wife of architect-turned-album-designer Gary Burden (he'd designed *Crosby, Stills and Nash*), standing at the door of her house near San Vicente, proffering delicious organic treats with a baby on her hip. Then there was David's pal Trina Robbins, the comic-book artist and designer who made clothes for Cass Elliot, and Donovan, and Jim Morrison's girlfriend Pam Courson; Trina's lace-trimmed velvet miniskirts had been all the rage in the Canyon two years before, and, with her long blond hair streaming over her wide-shouldered thrift-store skunk coat, she was a hippie version of a 1940s movie star. And let's not forget Joni's kid-sister-like Estrella—she of the blues riffs and the savvy with elephants, who was often "sailing ships and climbing banyans": there was adventure in that circus girl's bones!

Joni turned the three into her "Ladies of the Canyon,"* according a verse to each. The antiquated-sounding term that Joni coined gave a just-right handle to the now-flourishing style that she had helped establish.

On the other hand, medieval courtliness had its blowback: When you were someone's old lady, a piece of you belonged to your old man—and he was always coming out ahead, because he *was* a man. David was madly in love with Christine Hinton again; he elegized her as "Guinnevere" (though one chorus of the song had been written for Joni), and they'd stroll the beaches hand in hand, both of them as long-haired and nude as Lady Godiva. Still, he dominated her. And while there was no dominating Joni, there was this annoying fact: she had written all her songs and had produced her two (soon, three) albums, yet the *guys* were the headliners. Before long, she would muse aloud to a confidant: was she an artist—or a Crosby, Stills and Nash groupie?

As their live-in relationship went into its second year, Graham says, "Joni was very cognizant of the power of men on her life, and its trials and tribulations. Only in talking to communal friends, when we should have been talking to each other, did I find out that Joni thought I was going to demand of her what her grandmother's husband demanded of her grandmother." Almost plaintively Graham insists: "There was no way I was going to ask Joni Mitchell to stop writing and just be a wife!"

However, looking back on that time, Joni has said, "Graham was a sweetheart" but he "needed a more traditional female. He loved me dearly . . . but he wanted a stay-at-home wife to raise his children." (In support of Joni's concerns back then, Debbie Green, with whom Joni has been close for decades, makes the point that after Joni, "Graham was never with another creative woman.") But, in all this after-the-fact cate-

---

* Apparently struck right away by the unique geography and female sociology of the place and scene she'd just moved into, Joni actually wrote the first version of the song in early 1968, when she was recording *Joni Mitchell*. Announcing, "I have a surprise for you," Joni sang the Trina verse for Trina at the recording session; in gratitude, Trina promptly made Joni a black minidress with an antique lace pocket.

gorization, a question is lost: Did Joni sense that Graham wanted her to give up her writing, recording, and performing? Or did she perceive the comfortable domesticity with Graham, in and of itself, as a threat to the edge and the hunger she needed to do her best work? That is more likely. "Women of Joan's generation raised the bar of how men should treat women and how women should treat themselves; they were the first to say, 'I'm not wearin' this bra!' and 'Go fetch your own tea!'" Graham concludes today, implying that their relationship may have been a casualty of that process.

In the early stages of Joni's grappling with this old lady vs. independent woman dilemma—in fact, at the peak of her boys' fame, September 30, 1969, the day that *Crosby, Stills and Nash* went gold—tragedy struck their circle. Christine Hinton got behind the wheel of David's VW bus to take her two cats to the veterinarian. As she manuevered onto the highway, one of the cats escaped the arms of her friend Barbara Langer, who was sitting in the passenger seat. The cat pounced on Christine, sending her into a collision with a school bus; Christine was killed. "David was completely crushed, and for days he could barely look at Barbara without seething. Christine's parents were there, but they had to wait on David to see how she would be buried," says a friend.

"Want to go sailing?" David asked Graham. Christine had been cremated, and David wanted to toss her ashes into the ocean from the deck of the *Mayan*. "I had never been sailing in my life," says Graham, "but I knew David was fragile and decided to stick close by him." When David proposed flying to his boat in Fort Lauderdale and sailing to L.A., Graham stammered: "Hey, wait a second. Isn't that on the other side of this . . . *large* country?" Indeed, it was; a nine-week sail—through the Gulf of Mexico and the Caribbean, across the Panama Canal, and up the Pacific—was hatched. Joni boarded in Jamaica; she watched 1969 turn to 1970—everyone's first new decade as an adult—on the deck of the schooner. It was on this voyage that Joni first talked to Graham about breaking up, a decision put on hold while they were on the high seas but wrestled with for weeks thereafter.

Also aboard was Florida-based folksinger Bobby Ingram (who'd introduced David to Joni) and his wife—and a young unknown singer named Ronee Blakley. Ronee was a girl from Idaho who, on the strength of hearing Joan Baez's "Barbara Allen," had bolted for a creative life in northern California. Ronee attended Mills College, then Stanford, became a political activist, had a romance with the university's radical student body president David Harris (who later married Ronee's hero Baez and was currently in jail for draft resistance), moved to New York, and was now relocating to L.A. As the *Mayan* cut through the volatile ocean and David searched for the right place to toss Christine's ashes, "Joan and I would ride on this little seat off the aft—it was like being on a roller coaster through a canyon of waves," Ronee recalls. "The waves could be extraordinarily high; sometimes they would break on top of us, and we were all greased up with Bain de Soleil, so we'd slip and slide and have to hang on to the cables not to go overboard."

The trip was like the group's song "Wooden Ships" come to life— hippie superstars huddled together, alone on the vast sea with their dreams and their body heat. A hired cook made what Ronee recalls as "grand feasts" as joints were passed, guitars were strummed, and the music that, many hundreds of miles away, was wallpapering U.S. FM radio tinkled, a cappella, over the inky swells beneath the starry heavens. "David was a great sailor, and Graham did the celestial navigation," Ronee recalls. "The men took four-hour turns keeping watch all night, and they manned the sails; the women took care of the galley." At one Caribbean dock the ship was impounded and searched stem to stern. But once it passed muster, peace was made, and David sang "Mr. Tambourine Man" to the island's suspicious-constables-turned-excited-autograph seekers.

Ronee got on David's nerves. The sound of her typing her memoirs so irritated him, he tossed her typewriter overboard; then she lost her copy of *Crime and Punishment* and it was found in the bilge, blocking the pipes. But it was that very urgently expressed literary streak in Ronee that would form the basis of her friendship with Joni, which was consolidated after they docked in L.A. "Joni's core was that of an artist, and I was trying to be an artist," Ronee says. "I carried my weight in the friendship, but she was certainly way ahead of me. Whether we were meeting for dinner at Dan Tana's or running down to Palm Springs, or calling each other on the phone to play our songs, she was an artist, a pure artist: searching and open-minded and sensitive and vulnerable and tough and disciplined. Anything she did or felt went into her work."

Ronee and Joni listened to Edith Piaf and Billie Holiday records together. They both found Nietzsche inspiring and would comb through *Thus Spake Zarathustra* for signifying phrases: Joni was struck by "Anything worth writing is worth writing in blood," which had been her writing teacher Arthur Kratzmann's motto, and she was jolted by the passage where Nietzsche was "scathing," as she'd put it, toward poets— calling them vain—but then talked about "a new breed of poet, the penitent of the spirit," which was what Joni wanted to be. Joni taught Ronee how to draw, and Ronee, knowing Joni admired Van Gogh, bought her *Dear Theo,* Van Gogh's letters to his brother. Many of the lines the Dutch master had scribbled to his sibling had resonance for Joni. "Where there is convention there is mistrust": that was the small-minded Canada she'd fled. "I want to go through the joys and sorrow of domestic life, in order to paint it from my own experience": this validated her confessionalism. And "It sometimes happens that one becomes involuntarily depressed": this was happening to her, and Graham was noticing it. Finally, "Parents and children must remain one": she had violated this maxim.

Ladies of the Canyon was released in March 1970 (just as *Clouds* was winning the Grammy for Best Folk Performance), and it was shot through with idealism and idealization: idealized long-skirted ladies, the pitfalls of worshipful love, the chafing between idealistic women and "straight" moneyed men (whose offices bear their "name on the door on the thirty-third floor"), the inequity between a rock star's wealth and a street musician's poverty, the misguided destruction of "paradise" for the sake of money. Henry Lewy again engineered the spare album (with Joni actually in charge), which contained the title cut, and her two odes to

Graham–"Willy" (but with the roles reversed: in the song, the woman is the needier partner) and the haunting "Blue Boy." "Conversation" and "The Arrangement"–as literate as Sondheim, as so many of her songs seemed to be–both describe a sensitive girl's affair with a prosperous man who has a superficial wife. "For Free" puts a halo on the shabby "one-man band by the quick lunch stand" while Joni guiltily notes her musical fame. Joni's big hit from this album (only one of four Top 40 hits in her career), "Big Yellow Taxi," was written during her and Graham's trip to Hawaii. "They paved paradise, put up a parking lot" was Joni at her Tin Pan Alley best. "Woodstock," her lovely "Rainy Night House" for Leonard, and her tuneful "Morning Morgantown"–quaint Canada Joni–round out the album. The last cut is "The Circle Game," finally recorded in her own voice.

But still she withheld "Little Green," the song about her baby.

With this album, Warner Bros. finally understood young women's identification with Joni. They created a full-page *Rolling Stone* ad, in the form of a story–"Joni Mitchell's New Album Will Mean More to Some Than to Others"–about a hypothetical young woman, one "Amy Foster, twenty-three years old and quietly beautiful," whose old man just took off with another chick. Amy is blue, and she's thinking of getting in her van and splitting. Listening to *Ladies of the Canyon,* Amy is consoled knowing "there was someone else, even another Canyon lady, who really knew" how she was feeling.

That *Rolling Stone* ad–with "Amy Foster" planning to drive to Oregon, alone–captured another new reality about young women: they were going on the road, *splitting,* taking off on (as the paperback jacket copy of Kerouac's *On the Road* put it six years earlier) "mind-expanding trips into emotion and sensation . . . [while] passionately searching . . . for themselves." As Joni would soon sing, in "All I Want": "I am on a lonely road and I am traveling, traveling, *traveling, TRAVELING* / Looking for some-*thing,* what can it be?" The Marrakesh Express, which Graham had made famous, and the circuit of glamorously primitive rich-hippie enclaves–Ibiza, the middle-sized of the three Balearic Islands off the coast of Barcelona; Matala, Crete, the ancient port on Greece's Mes-

sara Bay; and tropical Goa, on India's western Konkan coastal belt—
brimmed with long-skirted young Americans, traveling with girlfriends,
with boyfriends, or alone. In this new form of travel, everyone went
native because they already—naïvely—*felt* native.

For females, this meant getting lost in packed, mazelike souks, with
angry rug merchants running after you because you'd accidentally bar-
gained *too* successfully; watching (on acid) someone you'd just made
love to break his neck jumping off the Formentera cliff during full moon;
being the only English speaker, and in the minority of two-legged creatures, on a steamer on some body of water in the middle of nowhere;
barricading the inside of your door in a hotel in Mauritania because the
desk clerk, who was banging on it, assumed any solitary Western woman
guest was a prostitute. None of this suddenly-typical fare was covered in
Arthur Frommer's guidebook.

The ultimate adventure—nothing could make a girl feel more like
Bonnie of *Bonnie and Clyde*—was to smuggle hash out of Afghanistan
or Morocco, often by packing it in girdles and feigning pregnancy.
Rolling Stone regularly devoted a two-page section, "The Dope Pages,"
to such applauded hijinx, including the story of a young female graduate of UC Berkeley (initials: L.C.) who spent a full year muling hash all
over the world as a "pregnant" traveler: flying from Pakistan to New
York via wildly zigzagging routes that took her to Alaska, Denmark,
Brazil, Portugal, and Luxembourg. Today she heads a division of one of
the largest insurance companies in the country. She reflects on her
youth: "The first thing I'd say is, I should have stayed away from that
married junkie musician who used my innocence to make money. But
after that, I'd have to admit that the adventure taught me skills—about
functioning under stress, making split-second decisions, reading behavior, assessing risk, suppressing fear, and thinking outside the box—
that have helped me in business and even helped me overcome two
serious health crises. Plus, I got to star in my own movie (and, believe
me, it *was* one)."

* * *

True to her cohort, in early spring 1970, at just about the time of *Ladies of the Canyon*'s release, Joni split for the Mediterranean with a Canadian poet friend named Penelope. "I had difficulty . . . accepting my affluence and my success," Joni later said, of this period. "Even the expression of it seemed distasteful."

In Crete Joni and Penelope drove a mountain road through citrus orchards to a harbor enclosed like a half-curled hand by sandstone cliffs that dropped down to the azure sea. The cliffs housed 1,200-year-old tombs turned caves, originally the homes of the ancient Minoans. People still lived in them. This was Matala.

The two women rented an apartment in town. One night they went for ouzo at Dephini's, a beachside taverna, where a wild-eyed, twenty-four-year-old North Carolinian held forth. His name was Cary Raditz. Cary had been an ad copywriter in Winston-Salem and had worked at an art gallery in Chapel Hill in his two postcollege years, but after running off to Matala, he had morphed into a larger-than-life character with long, curly red hair and a devilish beard. One night he dressed like an Afghan horseman—in Pakol cap, loose pants, tunic, and sandals; the next, like a Greek shepherd in blouselike shirt, flared pants, short jacket, and knee-high fisherman's jackboots, with embroidered *caskol* tied around his brow. A crooked walking stick completed the conceit. In his one year in Matala, Cary had commandeered a cave to live in, had opened a leather shop and begun making what he boasts were "the best sandals in southern Europe," and had taken several murky trips to Afghanistan, barely evading arrest, which heightened his prestige among the hip and druggy expats. "I was an outlaw," he recalls now, "and a self-created sonuvabitch."

Cary *was* Dephini's—he was cook, bartender, dishwasher, waiter, and bouncer. He also marketed his sandals there. Diners would take their shoes off and Cary would trace their feet on parchment for his partners at his shop, while he danced around, Zorba-style, simultaneously manning the oven, the bar, and the cash register.

"All these other men were putting Joni on a pedestal, and she didn't like that," notes Estrella. "Cary didn't have the misfortune of seeing her perform—he met her in neutral territory; that's why she went [to Crete]. She needed life to be harder."

Actually, Cary Raditz *had* heard "Both Sides, Now." But he wanted to bust Joni a bit. "I had heard that Joni Mitchell was in town, and I saw her with my friends, and they'd get weird—giddy and silly and kind of obsequious," says Cary. He figured he could cut her down to—maybe even seducible—size by the oldest male trick in the book: being mean to her.

The night that he saw Joni in the taverna, "I was short with her, I was dismissive of her." During the wild dancing, everyone in the taverna broke their plates. Witnessing the ear-splitting crash of china to floor, Joni—Myrtle Anderson's daughter, after all—instinctively took a broom and swept up the crockery shards created by the people in her party. "Joan sweeps the stuff up from the floor—the plates, the mess—and brings it to me, helpfully," Cary recalls. "'Here,' she says. 'Thanks,' I say, looking her in the eye. And then I throw it all back on the floor."

A few more days of this back-and-forth ensued, with Cary playing the intriguing bastard, ignoring Joni's fame and charm. It worked. He says, "One evening Joni came over to my cave." Carrying her Joellen Lapidus dulcimer, she trooped up the sandstone cliff, and, walking through the natural proscenium arch, beheld the gleaming sea. "I was sitting there, watching the sunset" when she turned up, Cary recalls. He showed her around his lair, which was lined with tapestries from his travels but had no indoor plumbing. His bed was placed over an ancient burial crypt. Sometimes he dug into the sediment and unearthed human bones; he'd stuff them with herbs, thyme, and rosemary, dry them out, and make them into chillums to smoke hash in, like he was doing now. It was perilous to descend the cliff at night. So they didn't descend the cliff that night. Joni stayed with him.

"Joni and I got to know each other. We were drunk. We talked about a lot of things. Her music. How she had become a qualified studio technician over the course of her three albums, and she was proud of that. She was concerned with her life. It was shifting. We talked about the importance to her of being an artist and relationships." Joni had left the

Even in first grade in North Battleford, Joan Anderson (far left) was thinking outside the box. On Halloween, she dressed in her father's tie and held bunny ears. *(Courtesy of Sandra Stewart Backus)*

Joni evinced the poise of a model and the thoughtfulness of an artist in thi circa 1958 photograph with close friend Anne Logie. The budding photographer and the painter and budding folksinger often rhetorically asked each other, "Why do we have such square parents?" and answered "To have something to rebel against. *(Courtesy of* Elm Street *magazine)*

Joni ran for queen of the Southern Alberta Institute of Technology in 1964 and came in second, a verdict over which she appears less than delighted. The other runner-up did not share Joni's imminent fate of becoming a charismatic performer. *(© SAIT Polytechnic, used by permission)*

Joni was already outpacing her husband and musical partner, Chuck Mitchell, when they sang Gordon Lightfoot's "When Spring Was O'er the Land" into their tape recorder in 1966. She had written "The Circle Game" and would soon write "Both Sides, Now." (*The Detroit News*)

Graham Nash and Joni Mitchell were Laurel Canyon's most romantic couple at the dawn of 1970. For about two years, they lived in her cottage, writing songs that were sometimes about each other. Here, they ride to the photo shoot for Crosby, Stills, and Nash's mega-hit album. *(Henry Diltz)*

After leaving Graham, Joni embarked on a hippie ramble through Europe. She *did* meet a redneck on a Grecian isle and she *is* smiling. His name was Cary Raditz, and she memorialized him in two of her songs on *Blue*. *(Courtesy of Cary Raditz)*

By late summer of 1970, Joni and James Taylor were in love, and their fans could tell. When they performed together, he deferred to her as the more accomplished writer, and they giggled between her "California" and his "You Can Close Your Eyes." *(© Sherry Rayn Barnett)*

Joni fell in love with jazz drummer John Guerin (she has her arm around him here, with members of his band, the L.A. Express) in late 1973. From *Court and Spark* through *Hejira*, he "mirrored [her] back, simplified" and would be one of the most important men in her life. *(Henry Diltz)*

Once a penniless rooming-house girl in Toronto and then a long-skirted lady of the Canyon, by the late 1970s Joni was living in Bel Air and socializing with friends like Jack Nicholson. But she never lost her artist's soul. *(© Sherry Rayn Barnett)*

Joni's marriage, in the early '80s, to musician and record producer Larry Klein, brought her
peace—though not, perhaps, her best records. *(Henry Diltz)*

In the mid-1990s, Joni reunited with her relinquished daughter, Kilauren Gibb, and with Kilauren's father, her old art school boyfriend, photographer Brad MacMath. Life was, indeed, a circle game.

world of fame and touring, she told Cary, because "she did not like getting patronized, cheated, and screwed over by the music industry. She
understood the trap of catering to the demands of the audience such that
you become a branded product. She was always moving, perhaps to
escape becoming a thing." In this and later talks, the subject of "Little
Green" came up, as it now did with all her confidants. She told Cary
about the Mariposa sighting. "She said that she regretted giving the baby
up for adoption, but what was she going to do?"

A few days later, Graham Nash was laying a new kitchen floor in the
Lookout Mountain house when the doorbell rang. It was Western Union.
Joni's old man took the telegram from Greece, tore it open, unfolded the
piece of paper with its pasted strips of jagged type, and beheld a single
sentence: "If you hold sand too tightly, it will run through your fingers."
Graham's heart sank. "I knew right away—it was over."

That night, Graham sat down at Joni's piano and wrote "Simple
Man," with straightforward lyrics: "I have never been so much in love
and never hurt so bad at the same time."* In answer to the worry (and
accusation) that Joni had voiced, he said: "I just want to hold you, I
don't want to hold you down." But perhaps at this time in her life Joni
was simply unholdable. And that was a new thing for a young woman
to be.

Joni moved into Cary's cave and stayed for five weeks, gaining
weight on his "good om-e-*lettes* and stews" and feeling the addictive infatuation with the primitive hippie expat life. "To me it was a lovely life,
far better than being middle-class in America," she would later tell an
interviewer. One time she cooked him oatmeal on his small cave stove
and accidentally used kerosene instead of water. "Worst oatmeal I've *ever*
had," Cary recalls, "and I'm grateful she didn't set herself on fire." Of her
enthrallment with him, he says, "You'll have to ask her why she was attracted to outlaws." She cheerfully acknowledged (in "Carey" and "Cali-

---

* Although the official lyrics are "Never been . . . ," Nash, musing about that moment in
time, spoke them to this author as "I have never been . . ."

fornia") that he was "a mean old daddy," a "red red rogue,"* and "the bright red devil who [kept her] in [that] tourist town."

Joni's idyll with Cary was not untypical. Guys like Cary Raditz were dotted around the reliable outposts in those dope running and vagabonding years, and young women prone to sweeping up crockery shards found vicarious rebellion through the jolt of their outrageousness. It was cathartic to laugh one's blues and uptightness away, even at the risk of being ripped off in the process. (In "California" Joni grumblingly concedes that while Cary "gave me back my smile," he also took—and sold—her camera. "Yes, I probably did say to Joni, in my ungracious way, 'I can probably sell it,' when she left me her camera," Cary admits today. "I was an asshole. *I* wouldn't have wanted to be with me.")

Joni left Cary in Matala and traveled to Ibiza, which in 1970 was the international capital of rich hippie swagger. The chalky white Old City rose from the port in fairy-tale Moorish cliffs, its narrow streets peopled with beautiful young expatriates—sexy, decadent, a few of them wild-eyed—who seemed to have congregated through some secret whispered game of Telephone. They all carried, hanging on long straw strings from their shoulders, big trapezoidal straw baskets, stuffed with *pan* and *queso,* as they made the daily rounds: *café con leche* at Café Montesol or Alhambra, on opposite corners of the dusty main drag; later, dinner at the vegetarian Double Duck, whose owner knew Mick Jagger and the young Aga Khan's new bride. At night they carefully segregated themselves from the hoi polloi—fresh-off-the-ferry backpackers—at Brooklyn Arlene's harbor-front La Tierra, where they downed shots of the anise liqueur *yerbis,* then headed home to their rented four-hundred-year-old stone *finca*s in the paradisiacal Santa Eulalia Valley, to mescaline trip or snort (and sometimes mainline) cocaine to the strains of Van Morrison's highly compatible *Astral Weeks* on battery-run record players.

Joni was the guest of some of these "pretty people," and, with them,

---

* After a bit more international roving—in Nepal, among other sites—and time in Marin County and New York City, the "red red rogue" became a yoga teacher and investment adviser who today shuttles between the D.C. area and Nairobi, where his wife is an executive of an AIDS-related humanitarian organization.

she "went to a party down a red dirt road," where, even in their rusti-
cated otherworldliness, they were, as she noted in "California," reading
Rolling Stone and *Vogue* to stay connected to their publicity. But it was
through sheer serendipity that she stumbled upon Taj Mahal (whose
"Corinna" was the second most played song on the island that season).
Hearing what she thought was Taj Mahal's record wafting from inside a
stone *finca,* she knocked on the door—and there he was, in the flesh.
They jammed together, and she would pay him homage in "A Bird That
Whistles" on her 1988 *Chalk Mark in a Rainstorm.* Joni the Celebrity
Road Chick came, and saw, and conquered Ibiza. But Joni the Sensible
Canadian Girl quickly left that neverland; stopped in Paris—so "old and
cold and settled in its ways"—and, like a homesick, guilty lover ("Will
you *take* me as I *am?*"), returned to what, after five years of city-hop-
ping, was finally home: California.

One night, shortly after she returned to Laurel Canyon (and Cary had
joined her there, courtesy of the first-class Athens-to-L.A. ticket she'd
sent him), a spontaneous burst of women's music bloomed at Joni's
house. Estrella and Joni had been speaking to each other in "prose
poetry"—falling into "our creative processes, not interrupting the right-
brain hemisphere function, to a point where we spoke in free-form song
lyrics," Estrella says. Friends of Joni's—other Canyon-lady musicians and
singers—came over, one by one, Estrella remembers. "There were, like,
twenty-five women in the house; it was this magnetic female jam session. Cary was the only man, practically *levitating* from all the estrogen." Joni had already begun writing the songs that would be collected
in *Blue*—"California," "Carey," and "My Old Man." She was falling into
what she would later call her "emotional descent . . . when you're depressed, everything is up for question." And she was listening with care
and interest to Laura Nyro, whose confessionalism was piercing.

Among those at the female jam session was another Laura, a northern California singer and songwriter named Laura Allan, whom Joni had
met through David Crosby. Barely out of her teens, the daughter of a
jazz trumpeter father and psychologist mother, Laura was part of the Bay
Area art and music scene. She and her boyfriend, artist Dickens Bascom,

were in a clique of "glue artists" who would Bondo found objects to car-ousel horses, cars (one of which they drove), and toilet seats; she per-formed at the Renaissance Faire, and she would eventually write a rocking paean to the area's generational ground zero: Berkeley's Tele-graph Avenue. Like Joni, Laura played the dulcimer; she was a friend of Joellen Lapidus, who'd made Joni's instrument, and who was also at Joni's house that day.

According to Estrella Berosini, the recitative phrasing (a departure from Joni's earlier style) with which Joni would eventually record the songs of *Blue* sounded much like Laura Allan's phrasing. "Take the first four bars of 'California': 'Sittin' in a park in Paris, France' to 'That was just a dream some of us had.' The vocal phrasing over the strum on the dulcimer, the almost-talking style of lyric, the run-on sentences, the childlike detachment: they all couldn't sound more like Laura. The lyric content is all Joni, but it was entirely Joni's version of Laura, and a stunning version. Joni's special brand of magic was so consummate that she could put on someone else's style as if it were a beautiful second-hand dress, and it looked like it had been made just for her."

In late July, Joni returned to Mariposa. The festival's steely director Es-telle Klein had also managed to lure James Taylor to the event. James was now a star, on the basis of his second album, *Sweet Baby James,* and its hit single, "Fire and Rain." His manager, Peter Asher, had asked for $20,000, Taylor's going fee. But Klein had crisply retorted: "$78 a day is what we're paying." Asher and Taylor had agreed to the token payment.

Joni had met James briefly the year before, in Cambridge, but now at Mariposa they began a romance. Peter Asher, who was there with James, thought the pairing inevitable, and so did others. "I think they saw a lot of themselves in each other" is how drummer Russ Kunkel puts it. "Both singer-songwriters, tall, handsome/beautiful, soulful, and talented." "It was no surprise" that they became involved, says Danny Kortchmar, noting that when Joni and James were together "they were both pain-fully quiet, sensitive, encircling each other."

James's infatuation with Joni would end two other romances he'd been having with women within his own circle. Also in that circle was another Canyon woman, his friend, who was now expressing from a different angle and in more populist terms the same changed world that Joni was singing about. As James would later write, in bemused amazement: "Who can explain it? This girl from Brooklyn, unannounced, on the scene . . . a tunesmith, a Brill Building pro, inventing popular music, hammering out songs for any occasion . . . [now writing] very accessible, very personal statements, built from the ground up with a simple, elegant architecture." Who could explain it, indeed?

It was finally Carole's moment.

carole 1969–1970

joni 1970

carole and joni

early 1971–1972

As she entered the last year of the decade that had started with the soaring success of her semiautobiographical "Will You Love Me To-morrow," Carole learned to live with the ambiguity of her on/off relationship with Charlie Larkey. While she might not always be in control of her relationships with men, *work* was something over which she always had mastery. "Here she shined, she excelled," says Stephanie Magrino Fischbach. "She made it look easy to her peers. Whenever you'd come over to Carole's house, she was sitting at the piano, writing, between the kids' dentist appointments and picking them up from school."

Carole continued to write with Gerry, as long as his mental state was relatively stable, since it would financially benefit her daughters, Louise and Sherry. Gerry now had his own studio, Larrabee Sound, on Beverly Glen, but mostly, after discussing the tone and spirit of their envisioned song, Carole would take Gerry's lyrics and write the melody at home. It was the same way she'd begun to work with Toni Stern. Toni, who didn't know anybody else who had young children, was in awe of Carole's efficiency. "One time she was playing the piano with one hand and helping one of her daughters get dressed with the other. I was slack-jawed."

The idea of casting herself as a "singer-songwriter" may have been sparked in earnest a year earlier, in the summer of 1968, when Carole first met with Lou Adler before she, Danny Kortchmar, and Charlie recorded *Now That Everything's Been Said.* Lou had remembered how, in the early 1960s, people in the industry loved Carole's demos so much, "I'd loan them out—and never get them back," he says. "One of the first things Lou did was give us a copy of Laura Nyro's first album, *More Than a New Discovery,* which was not well known outside the industry," says Charlie, "and we took it home and listened to it a lot." Like Carole, Nyro was a young outer-borough woman writing her own Broadway- and pop-soul-influenced songs and singing them, accompanying herself on the piano rather than on the now-fashionable guitar. As a teenager, Nyro's a cappella group had sung the hits of the (local-hero) Chantels—and the Shirelles, including "Will You Love Me Tomorrow," which she would eventually cover; and songs on Nyro's first album, like "Wedding Bell Blues," and on her virtuosic *Eli and the Thirteenth Confession* ("Sweet Blindness") hint at Carole's influence on her. Laura (her unfortunate bombing at Monterey Pop notwithstanding) was a solo act; why not Carole?

Still, for Carole in the middle of 1969, the comfort of collaboration beckoned. Charlie, who was now playing bass at the Troubadour, proposed a jam session with Danny and Abigail Haness and Ralph Schuckett, "and I asked Carole to join in." They all went to Abigail's boyfriend, drummer Michael Ney's house. After a couple of sessions Michael was replaced by Joel O'Brien, who was now living nearby with wife Connie. The friends came up with the name Baby Toshiba and the Delrays (someone had a Toshiba TV) and landed a gig at a Beverly Hills club called the Factory, a favorite of Sinatra's Rat Pack. By now Carole had bowed out of the group.

Baby Toshiba changed its name to Jo Mama, as in the street-corner "dozens" game ("Yo mama . . . !"). Abigail was lead singer, her long, lustrous auburn hair whipping around as she belted out bluesy numbers, many written by Danny. Danny, Charlie, Abigail, Joel: here was the New York-to-L.A. crowd (plus Ralph). The only ones missing were Carole, Stephanie, John Fischbach, and James Taylor. Within months, they would all coalesce.

In the middle of that coalescence, Carole had herself an adventure.

Like many other young women of the time—like Joni, soon off to Crete—Carole wanted to get as far away from her known world as possible. In December she flew to Bangkok, met up with her neighbor Michael Schwartz, who was in the midst of a hippie trek, and the two of them flew to Calcutta and then vagabonded around India. Carole had a mission: Bob Dylan's manager, Albert Grossman, had given her a copy of *John Wesley Harding* to deliver to one of the two Calcutta men who were photographed with Dylan on the cover. But mainly Carole and Michael let themselves groove on the sheer wonder of the subcontinent. They stayed in cheap hotels, sleeping on rope beds and sharing primitive bathrooms with others; as with Joni in the toiletless cave, privation was part of the experience. They walked the teeming streets amid beggars, oxen, and the supine bodies of what they'd assumed were sleeping men *until* they saw those bodies being tossed into funeral carts. "It was an extremely intense experience—a girl from Brooklyn, a boy from San Diego—we'd never seen anything like it," says Michael. They were in Bodh Gaya on New Year's Eve and watched the 1960s turn to the 1970s at the site where Buddha had sat under the Bodhi tree. They took a train to the holy city of Benares. When they parted, Carole continued traveling on her own—it was a declaration of independence for the dawn of a new decade. Carole had gone from living with her parents to living with her husband to moving to L.A. with her daughters; now she was alone in the Third World, among strangers speaking an indecipherable language.

Even before Carole flew back to California, the news in her crew was that Kootch's friend James Taylor had arrived to record his second

album, *Sweet Baby James*. Most of James's year back in the States had
been bumpy. After methadone treatment in England and rehab at
Austen Riggs (during which his girlfriend Margaret Corey took to referring to him as "my boyfriend who's in the loony bin"), over the summer
he had injured both his arms and both his feet in a motorcycle accident—to make matters worse: on a motorcycle he'd "borrowed" from
the local Vineyard police chief. Peter Asher was by now baptized into
the angst and confusion of managing an addict: "There were bizarre
moments, like scouring Chicago with some doctor friend to find methadone so James could finish his last show, with the attitude, Let's just get
him through these shows and *then* figure out what the hell to do."

Peter asked Carole if she would play piano on James's new album,
since James had loved the great Carole-and-Gerry hits. Carole hardly
had to be persuaded; she'd heard James's Apple album and she was a
"huge James fan," says Peter. Carole came to the Ashers' rented house
on Olympic and Longview, on the fringes of then-dowdy Hancock
Park, for three rehearsals, and she and James formed, as Charlie puts it,
a "musical mutual admiration society." Also at the rehearsals was tall,
lanky Russ Kunkel, a new drummer from Long Beach by way of Pittsburgh. His wife, Leah, Cass Elliot's younger sister, had paid to get his
missing front teeth replaced; he'd done some playing with David
Crosby, but other than that was unknown. "Russ had never done a session before; he brought his own drums and arrived early," says Peter.
But his drumming turned out to be inspired, highlighting the plaintiveness of Taylor's singing, and helped make the record a zeitgeist-turning
hit. Kunkel would soon become *the* session drummer in the new soft
rock, an important component of Joni's *Blue,* and James's best friend.
(Later on, in the 1980s, by way of Carly, things would get more complicated between the two men.) Russ's first impression of James: he was
"tall—even taller than me—quiet, handsome, and soulful."

James didn't just want Carole to play on his album, which she did;
he wanted her to tour with him. "Carole had terrible stage fright; she
was very insecure onstage," says Danny. She would have said no to
others, but she couldn't refuse *James*. "James had a powerful allure,"

says Peter. "If you made a list of women from that time who were secretly in love with James, it would be fairly long, and I don't think Carole would deny being on it." (Betsy Asher echoes, "You could tell Carole had a crush on James.")

Two others who were on the James "list" were Stephanie Magrino and Toni Stern. Toni met James at the *Sweet Baby James* sessions through Danny's wife, Joyce, and "James and I became boyfriend and girlfriend," Toni says. He spent a lot of time at Toni's Kirkwood cottage, he called her "Mama," and when he was cast in the movie *Two-Lane Blacktop,* he moaned, "Mama, they're making me shave off my mustache!" "James was beautiful," Toni says; they were "two souls who had some depth and were looking for love but didn't have a clue about it, moving toward each other." James was also romancing Stephanie, whenever she and John Fischbach were in an "off" mode. "She was my honey before she was your honey!" James once heatedly informed John over too many rounds of sake. Stephanie would eventually leave James in a Toronto hotel room after John called her and told her he loved her and to come back home to L.A. All this bed hopping was to be expected, of course. "It was a magical time," says John. "We were in love with each other, and with life. *I* loved everybody! We were in our early twenties, with raging hormones, a little bit of dough, and, eventually, a little bit of fame—that'll take you a long way." Even though Margaret Corey was still James's official girlfriend, they were not meant to last. "James broke up with Margaret" toward the end of 1970, "because his life was too frenetic," says a woman in their inner circle.*

Carole got a taste of performing on the road with James. She played piano for him, an anonymous band member. "Then James would bring her onstage and introduce her as the 'legend' who wrote 'Loco-Motion'

---

* Margaret went on to marry and have a son with a ballet dancer who then came out as gay. After they divorced, she married a man who was Hasidic; she became Hasidic, cutting off her long hair and covering her head with a wig. She spent her days washing the bodies of the dead, according to Jewish burial rites. In 1997 Margaret Corey died of an asthma attack.

and 'Natural Woman,'" says Danny, "and you could see his fans going: '*She* wrote *that?* No way!'" The skepticism-turned-excitement spurred her on. "'Yeah, they're my songs!' She had no problem after that."

Actually, it was a little more complicated. Carole said, at the time, that "if I think of it as 'I'm getting up there to sing these songs' and sing, with the emphasis on *sing,* I get really spooked. But when I think of it as 'I'm getting up there to bring the songs to the people . . .' with the emphasis heavy on the *songs,* then it's easy, because the songs carry themselves." When she'd play "Natural Woman," "I'd say something about Aretha being a very hard lady to follow. And she *is.* Then I'd ask the audience to make believe that they're hearing the demo before [Aretha] got it, and that kind of makes me relax."

But sometimes those performances became a humiliating trial by fire. As spring 1970 turned to summer and James became more of a phenomenon and a heartthrob ("Fire and Rain" would reach #3 in August), his fans were not in the mood to put up with any interloper. "They'd boo Carole; they wanted to hear James," says writer Susan Braudy, who was along for many of the concerts. "But Carole would sing and play—'Up on the Roof' and 'Natural Woman'—over the booing." As Joni had found with Crosby, Stills and Nash, it was hard—so far, at least—to beat the power of a *male* superstar.

And a superstar James Taylor *was* becoming. Touted a "new troubadour," he was a hauntingly romantic figure with stringy, uncombed hair, penetrating eyes under thick, straight brows, and handsome, patrician features—the whole look calling more to mind an anguished Civil War deserter than a contemporary rocker. The effect was compounded by his brooding, tender, somehow classically American songs (his inclusion of "Oh, Susanna" on *Sweet Baby James* seemed natural, as if it extended a lineage), some of which—"Rainy Day Man," "Sweet Baby James"; eventually "You Can Close Your Eyes"; later, "Walking Man," "Shed a Little Light," and "Shower the People"—contained a piercing, life-affirming sweetness. For all his shambling disaffection, there was a rock-ribbed dignity to him—a whiff of the modern-day Gary Cooper—

that caused men to pleasingly identify. "He lopes into the spotlight, a tall, spare figure in jeans and a green T-shirt, lank, dark hair falling across his gaunt, sensitive face," writer Ernest Dunbar would soon elegize in *Look*.

Even more moved were the female scribes. "James Taylor . . . hunches his broad shoulders and wipes his sweating palms on his worn dungarees" as 4,000 fans wait for him in an Ohio auditorium, Susan Braudy wrote in a *New York Times Magazine* profile. "He pushes a hank of his long hair behind his ear and stares at the floor, oblivious to stagehands," one of whom opines, "'You sure ain't no Liberace when it comes to dressing,'" to which "James looks up for the second time in 10 minutes, grins . . . closes his eyes and monologues quietly in his gentle North Carolina cadence, 'Well, doctor, it's like this, man. I keep havin' the same outasight dream . . . there are 4,000 people waitin' for me to sing, but I can't figure what they really want from me.'" Though James's natural speaking voice was not Southern, he knew how to punch up the alienation, folksiness, and self-deprecation—and how to casually refer, as he did in the interview with Braudy, to his heroin addiction (which he put in the past tense, even though it was not) and his time spent in institutions. "Cynics may wonder if James's myth-making mental anguishes have been packaged-for-sale by the businesspeople around him," Braudy wrote, but "James seems to have made the decision to speak freely and honestly about himself."

"I think I fell in love with James while writing that piece," says Braudy, who at the time—serious, long-legged, and quite beautiful—was a prized girlfriend to New York's male media elite. Soon to be one of the original *Ms.* editors, she was just separating from her Yale-educated Columbia University professor husband—today, esteemed social critic Leo Braudy—and would eventually date Brian De Palma and Warren Beatty, with Woody Allen basing the Diane Keaton character in *Manhattan* on her. In between her travels to James's concerts, Braudy was always set upon by people at Columbia professors' parties who wanted to know what James was *really* like. Whereas Mick Jagger and Jim Morrison implied slumming for culturally snobbish women, James Taylor was a gorgeous junkie rock star who seemed to be one of their own. "James was one of the most complicated men I'd ever met," Braudy says. "He was a bird with two broken wings . . . like a genie, with those beautiful tunes, and yet his nose ran, he was doing drugs, and when he took off his shoes, his socks smelled terrible," all of which added to his "passive-aggressive charisma. He would walk into a room dejected, and he catalyzed the room." Much of the angst was real; his new fame "was tremendously stressful; he was very shy, and it happened so quickly," says Danny. "James," says John Fischbach, "was a really, really funny guy, but also a somber guy; he had his demons," which he knew how to parlay. "No one gets on the cover of *Time* magazine"–as James would in March 1971–"by accident," remarks Peter Asher wryly.

When, in the last week of July, James took a break from the tour to attend Mariposa, Joni was there, too, and his charisma and pain found its mate in hers.

Shortly after Mariposa, in August, Joni flew to Tucumcari, New Mexico, where James was filming *Two-Lane Blacktop*. He'd been calling Toni Stern "Mama" when he'd gotten the role; now Joni was his old lady. On the set Joni knitted him a sweater vest, which he took to wearing constantly. He clearly seemed in love with Joni, Susan Braudy says, but later Joni would tell three confidantes that, as one puts it, "he was always judging her harshly; it was almost intimidating." And, as another says, "James could be cruel; he had a dark side–he could go from Mr. Hyde to Dr. Jekyll." At a nearby Hopi reservation, Joni bought a skirt made by tribal women. James called it ugly. "It was James acting like her mother: 'How could you wear that?!'" this second friend says. "Joni said he was very critical of her *all the time*–and she couldn't take it." "Today," the third friend says, "what she remembers is all the times James chastised her." But "James *really* loved Joni," Peter Asher recalls of this period.

Joni seems to have written "This Flight Tonight" about that time in New Mexico. Her "gentle and sweet" lover hurts her with "that look, so critical," but she regrets leaving almost as soon as the plane takes off.

She replays a tender moment of their watching a star in the sky between the movie set trailers and wants the pilot to "turn this crazy bird around" so she can return to him. Her confusion and vulnerability suggest depression, and now she understands its source: the relinquishment of the baby. As she later put it, "Soon after I'd given up my daughter for adoption, I had a house and a car and I had the means, and I'd become a public figure; the combination of those situations did not sit well. So . . . I began to go inside, and question who I was. And out of that [the songs of] *Blue* evolved."

Joni joined James for a couple of months in England at the end of the summer. Peter Asher lived with them in a London flat. "I have a distinct memory," Peter says, "of listening to Joni play 'Blue,' which she'd just composed, on the piano." Asher thought the song (which *Rolling Stone*'s Timothy Crouse would call "beautiful[ly] mysterious and unresolved") was extraordinary. (Its references to a drug addict's "needles" and Joni's proffering a seashell to her lover—John Fischbach remembers Joni giving a seashell to James one evening in L.A.—make it fairly clear that "Blue" is about James.) Joni also played her newly composed "A Case of You"* on the dulcimer—"I thought it was just a masterpiece," Peter Asher says.

While in England, during which Joni performed at the raucous Isle of Wight festival (and skillfully calmed the obstreperous crowd), Joni wrote a letter to Cary Raditz, who was still in California, asking him to join her and James. "She said, 'I hope you're not offended, but I'm with James and I wanted you to be here and meet him,'" Cary recalls. Cary already understood that their Matala romance had been downgraded by Joni to "some sort of friendship relationship" . . . so "I wasn't jealous." The "red red rogue," about whom Joni had already written two songs, good-naturedly adjusted from lover to, as he puts it, "sidekick and third

---

* "A Case of You" may be one of the rare Joni songs that was written about two men. Although she told a confidante in the mid-1990s that it was about Leonard Cohen, she told Estrella Berosini that the song's signature line referred—literally—to intimate moments with James (who, in a 2004 magazine interview, Joni said was the best lover she'd ever had).

wheel." Cary flew to England; he, James, and Joni went "to music industry parties, eating, drinking well, riding in limousines."

Joni and James's mutual infatuation was evanescent when they performed at London's Royal Albert Hall on October 28. James introduced Joni's songs like a prep school boy awed by his slightly older, more accomplished girlfriend. He dutifully listed the places ("partially in Paris and partially in Ibiza") where she'd written "California." Joni giggled and interrupted James's patter with private-joke puns on his song titles and past venues ("I'm a night owl, baby . . ."). She also proudly talked of her weeks among fellow "freaks" on Matala and referred affectionately to Cary, who was standing backstage, as "my friend from Matala, from London, and Los Angeles—and North Carolina." As Joni and James tuned their guitars, their talk seemed coyly double-entendred ("Ready when you are, James," she said; "I *know* . . . ," he answered, to laughter from the audience). And when he thanked the cheering audience by saying, "You're too kind," he drove home the source of his appeal: those upper-crust manners juxtaposed with the brooding-junkie pathos. They performed a heavenly duet on "You Can Close Your Eyes," which James was said to have written for Joni.

Joni, James, and Cary flew back to the States in November and lived together at New York's funky Albert Hotel and the glitzy Plaza Hotel. On Joni's twenty-seventh birthday—November 7—James was playing a concert in Princeton, New Jersey, when he suddenly laid his guitar on his lap and started to sing, "Happy birthday, dear Joni . . ." "Is it her *birth-day*?" several girls screamed. After James smiled, the audience called out: "Bring out Joni!" Joni came onstage, to the crowd's wild applause. According to Susan Braudy's *New York Times Magazine* article, "The crowd's shouts and applause have reached a manic pitch. As [Joni] sits down . . . James breaks out into . . . 'You Can Close Your Eyes'" and "a few voices from the audience interrupt him . . . and the whole audience is singing 'Happy Birthday' to Joni Mitchell. After it's over, both James and Joni are nodding their heads in the same polite, distant way, and someone in the crowd loses her control completely, screaming, 'Oh, God, I just love you two together! You're beautiful!'"

* * *

By now Carole had cut a solo album. John Fischbach and his friend Andrew Berliner had built their studio, Crystal Sound, and, says John, "I said to Carole: Why don't you be a singer-songwriter like James?" John's suggestion, of course, was something Carole had already been discussing with Lou Adler; it was inevitable that there would be a Carole King album. Carole wanted to record it at John's studio and give John his first record producer credit (he went on to produce Stevie Wonder) because she felt so close to him and Stephanie. They were there for her when she got emotional over Charlie–John, like others, saw how confident Carole was about her talent yet how vulnerable she was about men. More, John had recently taken to rushing to Carole's house to protect her against Gerry.

Gerry had started appearing at Carole's doorstep, literally "frothing at the mouth," says John. "He wanted his family back. It scared the hell out of everybody, especially his kids. Everyone was afraid of Gerry. Not that he was doing it on purpose–he could be the sweetest guy in the world when he was on his medication, but when he was off it, it was another story." One of Gerry's doorstep visits occurred when Carole was on the phone with Jerry Wexler. Wexler heard, through the wire, Carole trying to placate the emotional Gerry.

Gerry's acting out seemed a desperate attempt to reverse what, even over two years in, he'd had trouble grasping: that the woman he'd always taken for granted had moved on. Jack Keller had predicted as much. "Gerry didn't treasure Carole and over the years he lost her" is how Keller put it. "When you lose somebody who was madly in love with you, you're screwed. Gerry was totally destroyed when Carole left him."

The sessions at Crystal Sound in March and April 1970 were a family affair. Carole did the arrangements, vocals, and piano; James was on acoustic guitar and singing backup; Danny on electric and acoustic guitar; Charlie on Fender bass; Joel on drums, percussion, and vibes; Ralph on organ; Abigail singing backup vocals; and John on

Moog synthesizer. Gerry did the sound mixing. Carole forthrightly named the album *Writer*. On the cover she is standing against bare winter trees, with her long hair straightened. She's wearing a form-fitting, bold-patterned granny dress (which Stephanie had made). Un-smiling, she looks uncomfortable; she hasn't yet brought out that piece of herself the public will take to its heart.

Most of the songs were Carole-Gerry compositions, and their eclec-ticism shows the now-divorced couple continuing trying to retool their Brill Building magic for an FM-playlist age. There are outright rockers like "I Can't Hear You No More" and the album-opening "Spaceship Races." Critics would later note that Carole sounds like Grace Slick in this song, and the aria-rocker melody does recall the Airplane's "Volun-teers," but Gerry's opening lyrics are—rare for him—tired and strained. By contrast, the beautiful "No Easy Way Down" is an example of the best of classic-Carole-and-Gerry meeting the new era: the song is gospel-driven—*Rolling Stone*'s Jon Landau would call it a "masterpiece of a pop ballad with almost symphonic crescendos"—and its message about the inability to ease emotional collapse seems to reflect Gerry's own breakdown. "Goin' Back," with its Byrds-friendly bridge, essen-tially describes, through her ex-husband's words, Carole's last three years, morphing from a mah-jongg-playing, tract-house-dwelling Cadil-lac driver to a jam-session-ing, India-trekking Canyon chick. "Eventu-ally" is Carole and Gerry's hymn for Martin Luther King and Bobby Kennedy. The album closes with Carole singing "Up on the Roof." While the other tracks have a garage band feel, in this one alone Carole and her resounding, confident piano stand at the center of the universe, pointing to the approach she will next take.

Writer was almost as much of a failure as *Now That Everything's Been Said* had been.

Around the middle of the summer of 1970, during an "off" time with Charlie, Carole embarked upon a new romance with a young man named Tom Neuwirth. Neuwirth was a film buff and eventually became a cinematographer on TV shows and feature films. "He was sexy, handsome, serious but fun," says a friend. "If they had stayed together, Tom would have married her." The romance may have been the shot of competition Charlie Larkey needed to realize that if he didn't act quickly he could lose the woman who was in love with him.

Charlie asked Carole to be his wife. She happily accepted.

Carole married Charlie on a hot September day in a simple, homey ceremony in her Wonderland backyard. Charlie's parents, sister, and brother flew out, as did Sidney and the remarried Genie. A rabbi offici- ated; Louise and Sherry were the flower girls; Connie O'Brien brought food she had cooked. Carole wore the simple, white empire-line dress that Stephanie sewed for her; Carole put in the zipper. "The wedding was hippie-dippy, just like we were," says Abigail, who came with Danny— broken up from Michael and Joyce respectively, they were now a couple. To friends of Carole, the day was a triumph. As one puts it, "Carole loved Charlie deeply, and in time he came to love her deeply, too."

A few months after getting married, Carole and Charlie moved up the road, to a larger house with story-book turrets on Appian Way. She placed her grand piano in its large white living room. Charlie made a decision that wisely gave his career independence from Carole's, at least for a while. He decided "if bass playing was going to be my career, I better know more about it." On the Fender bass, he was, as his band mates noted, an insecure player; "he'd play his parts but he never really *owned* them," one says. (James once introduced him onstage as "the Electric Elephant.") He wanted to learn the upright bass, so he ar- ranged for private lessons in classical bass with Milton Kestenbaum, who played with the L.A. Chamber Orchestra.

The James Taylor, Carole King, and Jo Mama tour resumed. "Carole and Charlie cuddled a lot, which was sweet," remembers Ralph. "I think every time Carole nuzzled up to Charlie and every time she deferred to Charlie," Abigail says, "she felt a little less in charge and a little more womanly, as if she hadn't lost her youth, running her little Carole King empire." On the bus and on the road the group was a bou- quet of personalities. Charlie was low-key, guarded, and serious. Joel, nicknamed Bishop, was everyone's bebop older brother: charismatic, cool, a brilliant fount of music and film trivia—and self-destructive. Joel would remain on heroin even when James swore off. Connie was warm and compassionate; the women felt sorry for her, being married to an addict. As for Kootch: "Danny was probably the most outspoken person in that crew—a born leader and almost as much a driving force as Carole and James," says Ralph. "Danny was always a little sharper than the rest of us; I looked up to him," says Charlie. Abigail was a good match for Danny.* "She had a big personality, too," says Ralph. "The two of them were tough, savvy, volatile, highly opinionated New Yorkers. Danny, Joel, James, and Abigail were very witty. Sometimes the repartee was hysterical." Ralph hung back, playing cool to hide his insecurities. Stephanie, with her art-school chops and cooking and sewing skill, was the resident hippie Martha Stewart.

As for James—"James was *magical*," says Abigail. "Stephanie and Abigail formed a picket fence around James; I think Joni was very intimidated by all these women circling around him," says Betsy Asher, who had stopped regarding her husband's find as a freeloading younger brother and now understood James's "romantic and mysterious and unavailable, deep, brooding" charisma.

At Carole's house—where Willa Mae ran the show and was deferred to and loved by one and all—Carole, Stephanie, and Abigail had a chicks' sewing circle and made Nehru shirts for Charlie, John, and Danny. On the road, Carole and Abigail whiled away their time with needlepoint. When any of the guys was giving any of the girls a hard time, they'd have feminist bitch sessions. "We'd make sure Sherry and Louise were asleep and couldn't hear us and then we'd be: 'Fuck *this* shit . . . !'" says Stephanie. There were no secrets. "You couldn't beat the closeness that comes from being on the road together—we were a reinvented family," says Abigail.

It was a family based on equality. Despite James's sudden success, "he was just our friend and we were glad he was making it," says John. Abigail says, "I never had an inkling Carole was a wealthy woman. She

---

* Danny and Abigail eventually married, as did Stephanie and John. Both couples are now divorced.

must have had money from her years of success with Gerry, but she didn't live any differently than we did. If there was a pecking order, I didn't sense it." "We were just a bunch of hippies, for God's sake," John says. "Just hippies who happened to have money and live in bigger houses, but we were like everyone else at the time." The guys imitated the cool of the bebop greats and the Southern rockers (Leon Russell, Dr. John, Levon Helm) they idolized; the girls were part of the "no-bra, hairy-underarm" ethic, says John. "Every one was an earth mother."

But while all were earthy, Carole was a little more motherly. She was the only real mother of the crew, and she'd been the first single mother many of them had ever known. When most of Laurel Canyon was "still sleeping off drug hangovers," says Betsy Asher, "you'd go to Carole's house and she was already making stuffed peppers for dinner . . . at *eleven a.m.*" Carole kept lists and schedules. Carole had everyone over for Passover seder. Carole—despite her yoga and vegetarianism—smoked cigarettes, shopped at Ralph's Market, and didn't hide her Brooklyn accent. And she was always shoring up that ex-husband of hers; when Gerry's romance with Sue Palmer ended and Stephanie fixed Gerry up with her friend Barbara Behling, a tall, blond ex–New Yorker who had a boutique on Sunset, Carole had them over to support the new relationship. "Carole was *haimische,*" says Ralph. "A sincere, homey person who does the right thing, who you felt you'd known all your life." But if she reminded the others of a real world beyond their hip, new world, the influence went the other way, too. "I think Carole was comforted and inspired by the freedom and the closeness she found with us," says Stephanie. "She blossomed."

All around the country, there were "families of friends" like the one Carole was now a part of. Many young Americans were forming communes, transforming homes to group-living spaces, from suburban Long Island to Berkeley (where Tom Hayden's Red Family was established on Hillegas Avenue, complete with a day care center, Blue Fairyland). Even when they weren't in actual communes, a funky, loyal communitarian spirit prevailed. The young writer Ann Beattie would soon be publishing, in *The New Yorker,* her keen-eared short stories about, as one writer-critic described them, young "characters [who] have come for weekends, broken up relationships, fixed themselves scrambled eggs, rolled joints, flipped coins to determine where they should go next" and where there were "lots of extra mattresses or sleeping bags lying around these houses, and a constantly shifting number of occupants." (The reason the 1983 movie *The Big Chill* was so magnetically nostalgic is that so many people really had lived that way.) Within such circles there was often a Carole: the salt-of-the-earth woman who had the slightly wider, wiser view.

And increasingly, such salt-of-the-earthiness and such a wider view were valued. The assassinations of Martin Luther King and Bobby Kennedy and the Democratic convention riots had not, it turned out, been the crowning violence of the late 1960s. In November 1969 it was revealed that U.S. troops had slaughtered hundreds of unarmed Vietnamese, mainly women and children, in the village of My Lai; and in May 1970 four students at Kent State University in Ohio were killed and nine others injured by National Guardsmen trying to stop an antiwar protest.

Violence was coloring the world of music, as well. Dashing Woodstock's dream a mere four months in, in December 1969 a man was killed during a Rolling Stones concert in Altamont, California, by rampaging Hells Angels; three-quarters of a year later both Jimi Hendrix and Janis Joplin died of drug overdoses. Jim Morrison's drug-induced fatal heart attack would follow in July 1971; all three were twenty-seven. The triumphalist chaos of late '60s rock, the radicals' political opera, the psychedelic madness: it all seemed to have backfired. There was a longing for decency and earnestness. Bobby Kennedy had said, "We're here to make gentle the life of this world." *This* seemed the time to try to do it.

Older intellectuals in thrall to youth culture evinced (despite their awe at the ecstatic euphoria that had dominated for the last several years) such earnestness. In his book *The Making of a Counter Culture,* which coined the term that has become the widely accepted description of the amalgam of political and cultural changes that marked the times,

California State history professor Theodore Roszak, in 1970, pleaded that the question facing the country was not "How shall we know?"* but "How shall we live?" An even more sincere and impassioned tome, published that same year by Yale University law professor Charles Reich, decreed that the country was on the brink of a youth-led non-violent revolution to yield a life "more liberated and more beautiful than any man has known, if man has the courage and the imagination to seize that life." Reich's *The Greening of America* started out as a *New Yorker* essay that drew almost half a million letters to the editor and became a #1 *New York Times* best seller. People *wanted* to believe in a "greening"—a sweet new consciousness—in America. That same year Earth Day became a national holiday, *The Whole Earth Catalog* reached its apex of readership, and at Esalen Institute clones thousands of people were being taught to relate to one another without "game playing." There was a welcoming of sincerity and (as Ralph had described Carole) of *haimisch*ness.

At some point in the summer and fall, Carole began doing something new: writing whole songs—melody *and* lyrics. She was becoming spiritual; her classes at Swami Satchidananda's Integral Yoga Institute, coupled with her trip to India, had led her to meditation. (She would eventually take the disciple name Karuna.) Meditation may have helped the pragmatic young woman tap a deeper vein of expression, for, as prolifically as Carole was writing these new songs, Danny noticed that "they didn't sound like they came from a journeyman or a mere craftsman. They sounded like they came from somebody who was deeply feeling what she was writing." The songs trace the course of this once conventional young woman's adjustment—with anguish, awe,

---

* In the same way that the otherwise great minds at the 1964 World's Fair missed the mark by thinking that "revolution" for U.S. women would be exotically supercharged house-cleaning equipment, Roszak thought U.S. youth's loathed enemy was technology.

and finally joy—to the new life she has made, and they celebrate the integrity of improvised "families."

In "Tapestry"—melodically, a Broadway-tinged story song—the narrator is a young woman looking back on an eventful past ("a tapestry of rich and royal hue"), marveling at ephemeral new sensations ("a wondrous, woven magic . . . impossible to hold"). She enters the rustic tableau she is needlepointing and comes upon "a man of fortune, a drifter passing by" in a "torn and tattered cloth." Is he a Calcutta beggar? A Satchidananda-like guru? A capped and knickered figure with crooked staff, from one of those sew-by-numbers tapestries that adorned many a Brooklyn living room? Whoever he is, he's warning her that rewards from this bucolic new world can be chimerical, but she knows that already; too much freedom has never been her style. "A figure gray and ghostly" comes to take her "back" to responsible life.

"So Far Away" is the first of three songs that puzzle out a new idea of "home." She has moved clear across the country as if it were no big deal, but in 1970 people are really just two generations away from travel by animal cart. If you ask the song's question ("Doesn't anybody stay in one place anymore?") at face value, it sounds like the kind of quip uttered by common-sense housewives in Carole's childhood neighborhood. *Rolling Stone*'s Jon Landau would cite the song's melancholic opening to say that Carole was now "her own best lyricist."

"Home Again" makes the same point, but more worriedly, yet "Way Over Yonder," set to a deep gospel melody, the final song in the "home" trilogy, seems to say: yes, a crew of renegades from dysfunctional traditional homes *can* create its own nurturing community. "You've Got a Friend" is a vow of loyalty, leaving no question as to the salience of posttraditional ties. The arrangement Carole wrote for it opens it with the solemnity befitting a congregation's favorite hymn. Stephanie says, "I think Carole wrote 'You've Got a Friend' for all of us."

When Carole tried out "You've Got a Friend" on Toni Stern, Toni thought it was "too obvious," and when she tried it out on Cynthia Weil, Cynthia thought it was "too long." But Cynthia's overwhelming feeling—while watching Carole, who was in New York on the James tour, sitting at the piano at the Mann-Weil apartment, playing the new songs she'd composed—was great surprise. "I had no idea that Carole could ever write lyrics or was ever interested in writing lyrics; it was a complete shock, because Gerry had been so powerful." Cynthia believes that having a different kind of marriage helped make the leap possible: "Charlie was a supportive husband, instead of the one who was leading the way. Carole was able to be her own lyricist and express herself. She'd come into her own."

Although Toni and Cynthia weren't crazy about "You've Got a Friend," it did have one big fan, who accurately took the measure of its appeal, and for good reason: his own meaningful friendship with the writer. When James heard the song (which *Rolling Stone*'s Landau would later deem "perfection"), he loved it so much that he said, "Damn! Why didn't *I* write that?" (He would end up recording it; it would be his only #1 hit.)

Writer had been almost all Gerry-Carole songs, but in this new album, Carole included only one Gerry coauthorship—"Smackwater Jack," a rocking yarn about a colorful western outlaw. She would include two songs she cowrote with Toni, both bearing the productive tension between the sometimes-sentimental pro songwriter and the cool bohemian. Carole had written most of the lyric of "Where You Lead" as well as the music, but then she got stuck. She handed the incomplete song to Toni and said: "I can't write the bridge to this; if you can figure out the bridge, you can get credit for the song." Toni looked over the lyrics—it was another full-throttled loyalty song but over-simply conceived*—and thought, "*I* would *never* write a lyric about a woman *following* a man!" If the girl was going to follow the guy, it would damn well be on *her* terms. Toni lay down on her couch and the words fell out: "I always wanted a real home, with flowers on the windowsill. But if you

---

* A portion of the song's lyrics would, years later, be criticized as antifeminist—"Where you lead / I will follow" did sound servile. When the song became the theme song for *Gilmore Girls* in 2001, Carole and Toni took out the male-female references and rewrote the song to reflect the idea of loyalty, not slavish devotion.

want to live in fucking New York City, honey, you know I will." Carole cut the "fucking," asked Lou if the "New York City" was okay (he said yes), and the song was a go.

As for the song that would be the album's monster hit: though Toni often agonized over lyrics (as Gerry had), "I wrote 'It's Too Late' very fast, in a day," she says. Toni pointedly says that she wrote the heartfelt lyric *after* her love affair with James Taylor was over (he'd gone on to Joni), but then she carefully adds, "I won't say who 'It's Too Late' is about—I don't kiss and tell." Whoever inspired it, the lyric expresses a blithe woman's depressed, *embarrassed* realization that a romance she'd secretly banked on is over. On the surface she's shrugging and cool—the two of them "really did try to make it"—but the insistent internal rhymes ("inside," "died," "hide") trumpet her hidden emotion.

Tapestry was recorded in January 1971, when everybody had just come off a leg of the James–Carole–Jo Mama tour. "We were loose, because we'd been playing a lot, and we were looking forward to recording," says Charlie. Carole, Charlie, Danny, Joel, Ralph, and James piled into snug Studio B at A&M Studios on Sunset and La Brea; Lou Adler had expert sound engineer Hank Cicalo on hand to crisply separate the sound of every instrument. "Lou and Hank knew just how to mic Carole," says Toni, who arrived with her dog and watched everyone across the control booth glass for the first of the three-hour sessions. Carole handed out the charts while tending to Louise and Sherry. Ralph, for whom "little kids were like aliens from another universe," was "impressed that she could lead a recording session and fully relate to her kids like a hands-on mom, and she didn't take shit from them, either." Hank Cicalo found Carole an exception to the difficult rock stars he was used to. "She knows just what she wants on a record," he said, and when something went wrong with the equipment, "Carole [had] enough of a head on her shoulders to wait until the problem [was] corrected—she's very professional. Best of all, she makes everyone feel at home. There's no tension when she's around." "The credit for the smoothness of the *Tapestry* sessions goes to Carole," says Toni. "She was singer, writer, arranger; she set the mood."

"It's Too Late," "You've Got a Friend," and "I Feel the Earth Move" were nailed in that first session. "Carole would suggest a couple of overdubs and she would overdub a few harmony parts," says Danny. "'Done!' 'Done!' 'Done!' *Snap! Snap! Snap!*—three, four, times a day." The entire album, Carole's later overdubs and all, was completed in under two weeks. The sessions yielded what John Rockwell of *The New York Times* would call Carole's "signature" sound of "consoling chords, full of homey fifths and octaves; [a] relaxed, softly rocking blend of folk music and gentle soul funk." Her voice (which Jerry Wexler and Mike Stoller had always loved) had attained a confidence. It was strong and theatrically enunciated yet also earnest and breaking: a trusted friend, cajoling you to listen to a mulled-over insight—or a yelp of fun—in a quiet bedroom. Her inclusion of a sombered "Natural Woman" and "Will You Love Me Tomorrow," on which Joni sang background*—like "Up on the Roof" on *Writer*—told "serious rock" fans not only that she could join the club but that she'd always belonged there.

Just as with *Writer*, "we didn't have any expectations here, either; we just wanted to play as good as we could," says Charlie. Lou Adler alone seemed to know that this was no ordinary album, despite his trademark übercool at the session. When Danny asked Lou if he thought "It's Too Late," which featured his solo electric guitar vamp, came off okay, Lou allowed, "Yeah, man, it's gonna be huge."

This time the cover was just right: There is Carole in a nubby gray sweater and roomy blue jeans, splay-foot barefoot on her Wonderland window-seat in her unlit living room, working on her needlepoint, with her about-to-pounce cat, Telemecat, comically hogging the camera. Light pours in through the transparent Indian-fabric curtains (which she'd sewn herself), illuminating half of her unsmiling face;

---

* Joni and James did their background parts a week later; they are credited as "the Mitchell/Taylor Boy-and-Girl Choir."

glinting off her rippling, frothy hair. Carole looks like the earth mother next door.

Tapestry was released in early February and started to work its way onto the radio. The first two reviews unsettled—even frightened—Lou Adler, who had silently predicted that the album would be to music what *Love Story* was to movies: *The Long Beach Independent* and another small paper had dismissed it and had complained of Carole's "squeaky" voice. (Could Adler have been so off?) But then came Jon Landau's long review in April in *Rolling Stone.*

Landau introduced Carole to the serious rock crowd. He recapped her Brill Building career, her switch to singer-songwriter, and then he puzzled out the subtle punch of her new album. There is an "area of feeling on this record that is hard to get at," he says. "This music is not the product of someone adopting styles and then discarding them . . . It is an album that takes a stand." *Tapestry,* he realizes as he writes, "is an album of surpassing personal intimacy and musical accomplishment . . . The simplicity of the singing, composition and ultimate feeling achieved the kind of eloquence and beauty that I had forgotten rock is capable of." The closeness of the musicians registered with Landau: "Every note reminds you that [it] is not the work of pop star hacks diddling around in the studio to relieve their boredom." He concluded: "Conviction and commitment are the lifeblood of *Tapestry* and are precisely what makes it so fine . . . Carole King reaches out towards us and gives everything she has. And this generosity is so extraordinary that perhaps we can give it another name: passion."

By June *Tapestry* had sold a million copies, and the single released from it—"It's Too Late," backed with "I Feel the Earth Move"—hit the #1 mark, staying there for five weeks. "There was hardly an under-thirty soul in the Western hemisphere four years ago who couldn't hum at least a few bars of 'It's Too Late,'" *The Washington Post*'s Alex Ward would write in 1976. ("How the *fuck* did *you* know, man?" Danny asked Lou Adler. In response, "Lou smiled and lit a joint—he just *knew,*" Danny says.) "Earth Move" got almost equal airplay; both sides were hits. In July "It's Too Late" went gold, and James Taylor's version of "You've

Got a Friend" hit #1. By now *Tapestry* had become the #1 album in America; it would stay in that position for fifteen weeks. "So Far Away," backed with "Smackwater Jack," was released as a single and peaked at #14 in October. By the end of 1971 *Tapestry* had sold 3 million copies and was still selling 150,000 copies a week. It would be named, by the National Association of Recording Merchandisers, the best-selling album of 1971. Cynthia Weil puts it this way: "Carole spoke from her heart, and she happened to be in tune with the mass psyche. People were looking for a message, and she came to them with a message that was exactly what they were looking for, were *aching* for."

There was a uniting quality to the album; it was hummed along to by working-class young marrieds pushing strollers *and* Ph.D.-laden back-to-the-landers, listened to by teenage girls *and* their mothers. Ironically, though it was the most clearly "white"-niched and non-urban music Carole had ever written, it was only through it that she got credit for how unself-aggrandizingly *non*-white her more commercial music had always been. Timothy Crouse made the point in *Rolling Stone* that "Carole King is the most [emphasis added] *naturally, unaffectedly* black of our white pop stars—black in her phrasing, in the feeling of the songs she composes, and in her deep love of rhythm and blues." The crossover of the gospel-soul hitmaker to soft rock singer-songwriter was picked up on by young soul performers trying to go mainstream themselves. Of *Tapestry*'s impact on him as he was starting out with the Commodores, Lionel Richie recently said: "Oh, my God, please! That record was just crazy to me! It was a greatest-hits package in itself."

Not only did it cross social class, generational, and in some ways racial lines; *Tapestry* became that rare thing in pop music: a perennial. It would stay in *Billboard*'s Hot 100 for *six years* and go on to sell 24 million copies worldwide.

Recorded in March 1971, when Joni was at her most vulnerable, *Blue* was the album to which, appropriately, she entrusted the song she had withheld for so long, "Little Green." The song is so deftly coded, its love and relinquishment are crystal clear even while the subject is inscrutable. (*Rolling Stone*'s Crouse annoyedly declared its references so esoteric, they "passeth all understanding.") Critics guessed, from its more conventional meters, that it had been written earlier than her breathless, stream-of-consciousness new offerings, like "All I Want," "Carey," "Blue," "California," "This Flight Tonight"—but they couldn't know why she'd waited until right now, or why a song with a wistful adieu ("Little Green, be a gypsy dancer . . .") bestowed on a mysterious person "call[ed] . . . Green, and the winters cannot fade her . . ." belonged in *this* album. But, of course, the long shadow of Little Green entirely underscored *Blue*.

Joni was in such a state of fragility when she recorded *Blue*, "not only did I have no defenses, but other people's defenses were alternately transparent, which made me very sad." Joni has described this feeling as akin to being "clairvoyant"—". . . or people really tend to aggress on you when you're weak." Perhaps thinking of her high school poem "The Fishbowl," she said, "It was like being in an aquarium, with big fish coming at you . . . It was like the scene in *All That Jazz* [in which Bob Fosse 'dies'], when suddenly the heartbeat becomes dominant." She was also suffering from a physical infection, the result of an ill-considered alliance, a rebound relationship after James. Still, says Leah Kunkel, who was present for many of the *Blue* rehearsals, "my impression was that Joni was raw, but she wasn't weak. I didn't ever think of her as a shrinking violet."

Joni's *Blue* was in every way the counterpoint to Carole's *Tapestry*. Whereas *Tapestry* was created in a sense of communality, *Blue* was recorded in almost utter privacy—so "transparent" was Joni now that "if you looked at me, I would weep; we had to lock the doors to make that album. Nobody was allowed in" except the backup musicians, who included Russ Kunkel (on drums and hand percussion on "California," "Carey," and "A Case of You"), Stephen Stills (on "Carey"), and James (on "California," "All I Want," and "A Case of You"). While *Tapestry* was an enormous commercial success, one whose own musicians, while they enjoyed playing on it, didn't think it was such a big deal ("What did I know?" says Danny Kortchmar. "I loved the Isley Brothers"), *Blue* was a more moderate success (it peaked in the Top 20 in September) that accorded Joni legend status in the rarefied world of her musician peers. After hearing that album "people were throwing themselves at Joni's feet; nobody didn't think she was fucking brilliant," says Leah Kunkel.

Indeed, Kris Kristofferson, who had just given Janis Joplin her posthumous #1 hit "Me and Bobby McGee," says, "I was in awe of Joni from the moment I met her [at the Isle of Wight concert]; I thought at one point she was Shakespeare reincarnated." Kris was so struck by the vulnerability of the songs of *Blue,* he urged Joni: "Please! Leave something of yourself." Danny says, "People used to burst into tears when they'd hear it; they couldn't get through it." And Russ Kunkel says that he and others had come to believe, on the basis of that album, that "Joni was as distinct a woman performer as Jimi Hendrix was a male performer, and her effect on the music scene was as bold. When I heard the songs of *Blue,* while playing on the album, it was the same as hearing 'Hey Joe' or 'Purple Haze.'" During the *Blue* sessions, "She was harder on herself than she was on anybody else; she was always trying to perfect her performance," says Russ.

The cover of *Blue* (designed by Gary Burden, the husband of "lady of the Canyon" Annie Burden) was a departure from Joni's previous albums. No Joni paintings, no esoteric feminine symbols. Rather, the cover was that of a *jazz* singer's album: a blue-tinted Tim Considine* performance head shot of a passionate Joni, as if mid–torch song. Like the cover of a Billie Holiday or an Ella Fitzgerald album, it was forthright.

Tapestry and *Blue* provided two different views of the new freedom women were creating for themselves. While Carole had found (or remade) a "home," restless Joni was still "traveling, traveling, *traveling."* While *Tapestry* sprang from the life experience of a young woman who had adapted the options of a changed culture to her own life and ultimately found loyalty and creativity (and while the example of its enormous success created opportunities for other women in music), the freedom and creativity that *Blue*'s narrator has staked her life upon were obtained by

---

* The child actor from television's *My Three Sons* had become a photographer.

a decision that was *supposed* to have been liberating but has haunted and dogged her, exacting its price. Furthermore, love—for this woman, Joni, who (male) critics duly noted was "no longer the innocent of her earlier days" (Don Heckman, of *The New York Times*) and who was "a freelance romantic, searching for permanent love" (*Rolling Stone*'s Crouse)—was not the adventure it had been a few years ago. She now knows how love subtracts from autonomy ("I love you when I forget about me," in "All I Want"); she can recite all her faults ("Oh, I'm so hard to handle, I'm selfish and I'm sad," in "River"); she sees through men's bullshit ("Constantly in the darkness? Where's *that* at?" in "A Case of You"); and she rues the destructiveness that's come with her choices ("I've gone and lost the best baby that I ever had"); yet she *so* cannot escape the crazy integrity that's behind them, her responsibility feels unbearable: "I wish I had a river, I could skate away on."

One critic negatively prognosticated the risk in *Blue*'s rawness—Heckman "suspect[ed] this will be the most disliked of Miss Mitchell's recordings, despite the fact that it attempts more and makes greater demands on her talent than any of the others"—but women who, like Joni, had reached their late twenties eschewing commitment despite its risks found the album tremendously consoling and affirming. Decades after its release, two women fans told Joni, speaking of *Blue*, "*You* were our Prozac." Younger women writers, in all media, would take from it a bracing lesson; the novelist-essayist Meghan Daum recently said: "If there's anything I've learned from listening to [Joni] over the years, it's that if you don't write from a place of excruciating candor, you've written nothing." *Rolling Stone*'s Crouse got it; he saw this "very powerful" album as a gamble, and one well taken: "In portraying herself so starkly, she has risked the ridiculous to achieve the sublime."

Joni—who by now had the audacity to think of herself as a sacrificing artist, like her adored Van Gogh, who'd cut off his ear for truth (while Carole thought of herself as, as her then-publicist reductively put it, "a housewife")—viewed her nervous breakdown as the price of *Blue*. With her trademark immodesty, she has likened *Blue* to a Charlie Parker "pure opera of the soul" and has called it "probably the purest emotional record that I will ever make in my life . . . [T]here is not one false note in that album. I love that record more than any of them, and I'll never be that pure again."

Since personal breakthroughs can reflect a shared mood, and since a feeling "in the air" can ballast individual psyches, it was probably not an accident that Joni was writing the songs for *Blue* and Carole was writing the songs for *Tapestry* while a demo tape of songs written and sung by Carly Simon was finally being heard by a record executive. He would take her out of the shadows and catapult her toward musical stardom at the very same moment, the summer of 1970, that the new movement, feminism or women's liberation, was being lobbed into the public sphere. "We were already feeling like pioneers—with birth control, with psyche-delics; we were already feeling empowered," says Leah Kunkel, of women her age on the music scene.

Almost every national magazine had published an article on femi-nism by the summer of 1970. The women of *Newsweek* had successfully sued the magazine for job discrimination; *Ladies' Home Journal* (follow-ing a women's sit-in in the offices of its male editor) had an eight-page supplement on the movement; and feminist academic Kate Millett was on the cover of *Time*. Then, on August 26, on the fiftieth anniversary of women's suffrage in the United States, tens of thousands of marchers—many, long-haired young women in blue jeans and T-shirts—thronged Fifth Avenue with banners, and at a city hall rally Gloria Steinem—a political writer for *New York* magazine in her midthirties who had em-braced the civil rights and farm workers' movements and was now find-ing her cause in feminism and would soon become its enduring national figurehead—was speaking out on behalf of community-controlled child care, job and education equality, and abortion on demand. (Steinem's zeal on that last issue was fired by the fact that, at recent New York state legislative hearings, fourteen out of fifteen "experts" on women and abortion had been male.) The movement—like all those earlier cultural whipsaws: the birth of rock 'n' roll, John Kennedy's election, psychedelia and the counterculture—was overnight *and* overdue: certainly the latter in an era when married teachers were routinely fired when they were pregnant (and so many working married women *were* teachers), when some women had to actually show banks doctors' certifications of sterilization to obtain their own mortgages, when Radcliffe magna cum laudes could only be researchers while male state college grads were reporters, when female assistant district attorneys had to give permission notes from their husbands to work on homicide cases.

The movement had germinated in 1964, when Casey Hayden, Tom Hayden's estranged wife and fellow SDS-er, and minister's daughter and SNCC volunteer Mary King asked (in the tentatively named document "A Kind of Memo") why, if women were so active in the civil rights and anti-war movements, they were being treated as second-class *within* those movements. As it mushroomed underground, especially after 1967, the cause was advanced by a new vocabulary: NOW member Jo Ann Evans-Gardner pushed for the resuscitation of the fourteenth-century English term "Ms." to replace "Mrs."/"Miss," so the first thing you always knew about a woman (though not a man) was *no longer* whether she was married; and kindergarten teacher Anne Forer named the process of women's-experience-sharing "conciousness raising." Either Iowan Carol Hanisch or former child actress Robin Morgan (accounts vary) came up with "The personal is political"; *New Yorker* rock critic Ellen Willis injected "sexist" and "sexism" into the national conversation; activist Kathie Amatniek bestowed "male chauvinism" on a public that had never even heard of the French-origined noun, and also coined the anthem "Sisterhood is powerful!"

The movement was the biggest achievement of the women of Carole's, Joni's, and Carly's generation, and all the heady new freedoms for women that had nourished and preceded it now suddenly seemed to have been leading, inevitably, *to* it: both as epitome *and* corrective.

A year earlier, Joni had traveled to Canada with Ronee Blakley, looking for land to build a house on, but she had deferred the decision. Now was the right time. Joni bought acreage in British Columbia, north of Vancouver, and helped build a stone house in the woods, overlooking Half Moon Bay. It was here that she would write the songs for her next album, *For the Roses*. Five of the songs were about James. "For the Roses" takes musing account of his celebrity: she remembers how it was at the beginning; he'd slump in that way he had that, Kootch had said, made *every* woman fall in love with him. In "See You Sometime" she describes James as famous and in demand, but reminds him that *she* had fame first ("I tasted mine"); *he* had been awed by *her*. Now, in the Canadian woods, she was "spring[ing] from the boulders like a mama lion"; still—damn it!—despite all that flamboyantly exercised strength and independence, his rejection could still get to her. These two songs walk the fine line between the slightly bitter gloat (at having chosen the purer path: solitude) and the regret despite one's better judgment of someone who parted with a difficult lover whom the world is *now* informing her she'd undervalued.

But there *was* a reason that being with James was uncomfortable, and "Lesson in Survival" explains it. In the song she complains about how James's "friends* protect you [and] scrutinize me" as she sank into the "damn timid" pose that was "not at all the spirit that's inside of me." "Blonde in the Bleachers" gives his fame the same who-wants-it? treatment that "Cold Blue Steel and Sweet Fire" darkly gives his addiction. With these five songs, protesting too much was Joni's best revenge; she was getting James out of her system by using him in her art—a defense she favored and urged upon others. (When, one day, Leah Kunkel told Joni that things were "not good" with her and Russ—he was philandering—Joni immediately replied, "At least you can use it for material.")

"Let the Wind Carry Me" describes her ongoing struggle with her judgmental mother for permission for the freedom of "the road" and "the wind" that she craves. "Mama let go now" she pleads. In "Woman of Heart and Mind," she uses herself (and her secret relinquishment of the baby) to issue feminism's essential statement, *a woman is whole by her-*

---

* Although James's women friends had, as Betsy Asher noted, formed a "fence" around him, Joni's confidantes recall that it was his family, not his friends, who intimidated her.

self. It's the next in a row of archetypes we'd seen evolve from the traditional ("Michael from Mountains") to the self-liberated ("Cactus Tree" and "Chelsea Morning") to the communal countercultural ("Ladies of the Canyon," "Woodstock," "My Old Man"). Now, nearing thirty, Joni feels whole. The lovers who've come and gone: they *matter less.*

For now, at least.

Carole and Gerry's relationship had always been a symbiotic melodrama, and *Tapestry* gave that saga one more–sad–chapter. That Carole was writing her own lyrics now was surprise enough to her ex-husband–"she never wrote a lyric before!" he says–but the *merit* of those lyrics was the real blow: "I thought [her *Tapestry* lyrics] were better lyrics than I would have written." Consequently, "she didn't need me anymore. It was really crushing"–so crushing that Gerry decided "I was going to quit music." Turning the clock back eleven years, to his last day at work at Argus Labs before the Shirelles recorded "Will You Love Me Tomorrow," he says, "I went back to school to study to be a chemist." He and Barbara Behling, who was now his wife, moved back east; he enrolled at New Jersey's Fairleigh Dickinson University to pick up where he'd left off at Queens College. Spending about a year there, he "almost got a degree" before going back to songwriting, with some quixotic/heroic intermissions.*

The massive success of *Tapestry* was "a double-edged sword for Carole," a friend says. On the one hand, her leap from songwriter to artist was tremendously gratifying–she was now looked up to by peers who'd once dismissed her. She was also happy for the financial security. Unlike so many other young pop music stars, she'd been a breadwinning mother (with an unstable ex-husband) for twelve years. But the loss of an anonymous personal life was hard on her, and she virtually barricaded herself from her fame. "We just never went out," Charlie

---

* In 1974, Gerry went to Boston on a self-appointed errand to intervene against the anti-integration school busing rioters; he returned home, Barbara says, "all bloody" from the confrontation. The next year he flew to Israel and tried to enlist in the Israeli army.

says, adding, "We just kept living our lives; things didn't change that much at all. We went to movies, and out for Japanese food with John and Stephanie a few nights a week, but that was it." But his decades-later picture of those times' breezy ease contrasts with what a friend of Carole's says: it was hard to be a sudden superstar; the attention was unwanted. During this time when "you literally couldn't turn on the radio without hearing [*Tapestry*]," Charlie matriculated from his private classical bass lessons; he auditioned for Daniel Lewis, the director of the USC orchestra, and was accepted. As a bass player in a symphony orchestra, he now had his own musical life, apart from his now extraordinarily successful and famous wife.

In June, Carole flew to her hometown, New York City, and filled Carnegie Hall to capacity for two performances, finding what *The New York Times* called a "highly responsive audience" eager to cheer on the local heroine. She introduced Charlie and Danny; through the performance, her patter was diffident and she sounded vulnerable. When she told the audience that she was a proud daughter of Brooklyn, they cheered, but that cheering grew downright ecstatic when James Taylor walked out (Carole impishly acknowledged his entrance with a "Well, well, well . . .") and duetted with her on "You've Got a Friend." Though they were now considered coequal pioneers of the new soft rock, they had different roles: James was the male idol and Carole—well, Carole was something that pop culture hadn't seen before: an embodiment of youthful female *substance*. The next month the *Los Angeles Times*'s Robert Hilburn led off his review of Carole's concert at the Greek Theatre with this mash note to her character: "I love Carole King. I really do. Not just for her music—though that is certainly reason enough—but for the uncompromising way she refuses to assume any false airs or to surround herself with any show business pretentiousness."

Carole was pregnant during the Greek Theatre concert.* She'd

---

* Late in her pregnancy, Carole had occasion to run into Warren Beatty, who (recalls Abigail, who witnessed the scene) begged Carole to have sex with him, saying he'd never had sex with a very pregnant woman and wanted to know how it felt. Carole declined.

given birth to Louise under anesthesia in a Brooklyn hospital with Gerry smoking in the waiting room, his terror about fatherhood met with commiseration by Jack Keller. She'd had Sherry with added angst from the fact that Gerry was enthralled with Jeanie Reavis. Mothers didn't breast-feed in those days, and, in any case, subwaying with infant Louise to 1650 Broadway, and plopping her in the playpen while she hammered out songs, afforded her little opportunity. This time, things would be different, not just because Carole had changed, but because the entire approach to child rearing had. On a December day, with Charlie attending, Stephanie as birthing coach, and John holding the mirror so Carole could see the baby crown, Carole's third daughter was born, by natural childbirth*—at *home,* which was newly hippie-fashionable but not yet embraced by middle-class culture. Carole and Charlie wanted an old-fashioned name; they'd debated Molly and Nora. They chose Molly. Carole was thrilled to have Charlie's baby. For Charlie, beholding his daughter was "an amazing, life-changing moment."

Shortly before Molly's birth, Carole recorded her third album, *Music,* with Charlie, Danny, Joel, Abigail, Ralph, and James joining in again. On the cover, she's photographed smiling (her face, pregnancy-plump), granny-dressed, and shoeless at her grand piano in her Appian Way living room. *Music* was released at the end of 1971 and immediately rose to the top of the charts, reaching #1 on New Year's Day 1972; its buoyant "Sweet Seasons," written with Toni, became a Top 10 hit. Another tough-Toni/sentimental-Carole collaboration, "It's Going to Take Some Time," portrays a woman who knows she's messed up a relationship, has to learn to master the art of compro-

---

* When Stephanie and John's son Noah was born two years later, it would be prac-ticed mom Carole who held the jaundiced newborn while the doctor gave his heel a needle prick. And when Carole and Stephanie were at a Connecticut Howard John-son's in 1974 and the manager told Stephanie to cover herself with a blanket because the other diners were disturbed by her breast-feeding, Carole pointed to the one-year-old and coolly retorted, "Well, *he* seems to be happy." "We were crusading hippie moms," says Stephanie.

mise, and is on to the next. The album's full of homage-paying—
"Carry Your Load" channels Laura Nyro; "Brother, Brother," Marvin
Gaye (Carole's soft "oh, brother *of mine*," suggests she's thinking of
her real brother, Richard). In "Surely" Carole attempts blues; she
scats in her remake of her and Gerry's "Some Kind of Wonderful"
(and, in a whipsaw from the Drifters' original, insets a deliciously
melodramatic girl-group refrain by Abigail); she morphs into a piano-
bar busker on "Music" (and then turns the floor over to Curtis Amy's
bleating, Pharoah Sanders–like tenor sax). The most evocative cut is
"Song of Long Ago," which—with its reverence for human community
("Here is a lamp I've left unlighted / Aren't you someone I should
know?"), its yearning, James-inspired melody, and James's *la-la-
laaaa*s—sounds like it belongs on *Tapestry*. Such comparisons would
become her nemesis.

That same month, Carole was chosen as one of the *Los Angeles
Times*'s ten Women of the Year. In his profile for that occasion, Robert
Hilburn articulated her significance:

> Slowly but surely, the creative/influential center of contempo-
> rary pop music has shifted during recent months from the
> loud desperation and exaggeration of such performers as Janis
> Joplin and Jimi Hendrix to a more reflective, more reassuring
> gentleness. One of the main reasons is Carole King . . .
>
> For a generation that has been trying to recover some of
> the balance shattered during the troubled, riot-torn, confron-
> tation-bent late 1960s, such performers as Miss King and
> James Taylor have provided direction. They've tried to refo-
> cus attention on such simple, classical values as friendship,
> loved ones and the home . . .
>
> Just as their music is different from much of the music of
> the late 1960s, the lifestyles of Miss King and Taylor (who
> are as close personally as their music is close in style and
> outlook) are also different from the stereotypes of rock musi-
> cians that have been built up in recent years. Miss King and

Taylor neither wear flamboyant clothes nor take pride in outrageous, shocking behavior. They are, in addition, almost reluctant heroes, valuing their privacy almost as much as their artistic success.

"I don't want to be a star with a capital S," Miss King said.

Nothing proved Carole's aversion to stardom more than her nonattendance at the Grammys, which were held in New York in mid-March 1972. Citing her desire to stay home with three-month-old Molly, Carole was a no-show at the most victorious moment in her entire career (and a rare triumph in *any* recording artist's career): a sweep of the three most important awards of 1971. Lou accepted the gramophone statuettes when "It's Too Late" won Record of the Year (Carole's main competitors were George Harrison's "My Sweet Lord" and her own "You've Got a Friend," sung by James), *Tapestry* won Album of the Year, and "You've Got a Friend" won Song of the Year. Carole also won Best Female Pop Vocal Performance for "Tapestry" and James won Best Male Pop Vocal Performance for "You've Got a Friend." All told, Carole King had dominated all five top categories. Watching the show on TV, Carole felt "joy, happiness, and pride . . . for her *work*," says Stephanie, who was with her. "But she always separated her *life* (her children, Charlie, our circle), which was more important, *from* her work."

With the Grammy sweep for *Tapestry*, Carole had now created for herself an almost unmatchable gold standard. Some critics were sympathetic—"After the mind-boggling success of *Tapestry*, there was no way Carole King could have produced a more successful follow-up, and there's no reason why she should," prefaced *The New York Times*'s Don Heckman before saying, "*Music* doesn't quite match *Tapestry*." Others were blunter. *Rolling Stone*'s Crouse declared that "the songs on . . . *Music* are not as immediately likeable and the new album doesn't have its predecessor's sure, unified sense of style." The clock to produce another *Tapestry* had just been set and was ticking.

carly

mid-1970-early 1973

The same year that Carole swept the Grammys and that Joni's *Blue* was released to the awe of her peers, Carly won the Grammy for Best New Artist for her first album, *Carly Simon*. Her career had taken off later than theirs, not only because of her ambivalence about having a career but also because of the zeitgeist. When everyone wanted to be radical and funky, she'd been dismissed as too wealthy and too polished and entrenched in too "straight" and elitely educated a social context (although, as one of her Sarah Lawrence friends puts it, "Carly was always a visceral among cerebrals"). While the focus was on Laurel Canyon—and, before that, San Francisco—Carly was a stone Manhattan chick, not just in geography but in sensibility.

But suddenly the idea of "privilege" was being turned on its head, and "the struggle" (as the steady rotation of political movements had come to be called) was changing from poor vs. rich and hip vs. straight and shaggy vs. slick to something no one had anticipated: female vs. male. In *this* revolution, it was cerebral, psychotherapy-partaking, sister-ensconced New Yorkers from top women's colleges who were leading the way.

It was a season where the gaze shifted from the bucolic neorural—

rich-hippie and *Big Chill* communal—to the urban; where the medium was not feelings but ideas; where, even if "upper-middle-class" remained a never-uttered dirty word, it was no longer an unuseful skill set. One began to see a lot of sleek Seven Sisters alumnae—Ali MacGraw (Wellesley), Jane Fonda (Vassar), Erica Jong (Barnard), and, of course, Gloria Steinem (Smith)—sexy in stovepipe pants and ponchos, raising fists at political rallies, tossing off a sarcastic remark, or performing a muckrake onscreen (or off-), debating literary lions now viewed as troglodytes, penning theoretical tracts and erotic novels. Carly Simon had the right look, alumna status, and attitude to match the spirit of the times, as well as an air of mischief—a nice, acidic antidote to the slightly-too-satirizable earnestness of this new idea. She had something else: a sense of sensual entitlement unmediated by any history of guilt. She could radiate something young women knew but which hadn't yet been driven home to a double-standard culture: that a female could be respectable, sensitive, serious, thoughtful—in our supposedly classless society, "classy"—and, at the same time, have a wholly liberated sex life.

Carly's transformation began in the spring of 1970, when Jake Brackman had an idea: he would find Carly a manager.

Ellen's friend Jennifer Salt had a best friend, fellow actress Janet Margolin, who was married to a mover-shaker nightlife entrepreneur named Jerry Brandt. Brandt owned the discotheque the Electric Circus and was managing and producing the debut record of a troupe of twenty black teenagers, the Voices of East Harlem. Brandt was an aggressive guy and was open to managing new artists. So Jake, with his British girlfriend, Ricky, invited Janet and Jerry over to his apartment—"which was very 1960s Marrakesh Express: Indian fabric on the ceiling, casbah-style, with lots of sequined, mirrored pillows," as Ellen Wise Questel remembers it—for dinner. After dinner Carly just happened to drop by—this was planned by Jake, of course. She had lost weight; a good twenty pounds were gone since he'd teased her for being chubby at Indian Hill Camp. She looked great, and she sang a few songs. No one could tell by Jerry Brandt's face what kind of an impression Carly was making on him; after he and Janet left, Jake turned to Ricky and wondered aloud, "Did this land or didn't it?" Happily, it *had* landed. Brandt called Carly a day or two later and said, "I'd love to manage you and I'd love to put up money for you to do a demo." Carly accepted on the spot.

Brandt had folk guitarist David Bromberg produce Carly's demo, which consisted of five songs, the featured one of which was a Carly composition: "Please Take Me Home (to Bed) with You." Brandt brought the record to Clive Davis, who—having signed Janis Joplin to Columbia, and having presided over Columbia when the Byrds were on the label—was considered, as one A&R man puts it, "the ears of all time." Davis listened briefly and thought he was hearing a Barbra Streisand type. "Clive practically threw it across the room and told Jerry, 'What do I want with another Jewish New York girl!?'" Carly says Jerry told her. Brandt brought the demo to Jac Holzman, founder and president of Elektra Records. Jac had discovered Judy Collins and overseen Collins's version of Joni's "Both Sides, Now"; he'd signed the Doors, lighting the fire of Morrison's megalomaniacal grandeur. Holzman recalls, "Jerry said, 'Look, I think this girl is rather unusual. Her name is Carly Simon. I asked, 'Is she one of the Simon Sisters?' One of my favorite songs was a little lullaby called 'Wynken, Blynken and Nod.'"

Still, Holzman was preoccupied with his imminent trip to Expo '70 in Japan. "Almost as an afterthought," he recalls, he dropped the tape in his suitcase. Sleepless in a hotel outside of Osaka at four a.m., he dug out the tape and popped it into his cassette player. The tart strains of Carly singing "Please Take Me Home (to Bed) with You" made him sit up straight. He thought: She's wonderful. Her voice had "a toughness and sinewyness." When he got to Tokyo, he called Jerry Brandt and told him he wanted to work with Carly.

Back in New York, Holzman played the tape for his employees. "Nobody was very impressed," he recalls, "but it was my record company, so I didn't pay any attention."

One day at the end of summer 1970 Carly took the elevator to the top of the new Gulf + Western building on Columbus Circle and tried not to get phobic when she realized that the building was swaying (as intended by design). Holzman, who had grown up on Madison Avenue and whose family had attended the Park Avenue Synagogue, recognized that he and the singer "were from similar backgrounds—haute Jewish New York," as he puts it—which made it easier to relate, "although she was certainly more Brahmin. Those people can be pretty snooty, but Carly wasn't." Thus, the social-class issue that had been a minus to Albert Grossman, the members of Elephant's Memory, and even to Danny Armstrong was a plus to Holzman. There had always been a niche for the sophisticated, urbane—almost "society"—girl in the world of popular music. Kay Swift, the classically trained musician who wrote "Can't We Be Friends?" and the score of Broadway's *Fine and Dandy,* who'd married a Warburg and had a love affair with George Gershwin, had filled it in the Depression era; Helen Forrest, the impeccable interpreter of Big Band lyrics, who sang with Artie Shaw, Benny Goodman, and Harry James, had filled it in the late 1930s and 1940s.

Holzman wanted Carly to record the songs of Tim Buckley, Tim Hardin, and Donovan. He didn't see her as a writer. Carly set out to prove Holzman wrong. "I wanted to be a writer more than anything else." By now she was "already in love with James Taylor from a distance—that whole sound," she's said. James's drummer on *Sweet Baby James,* Russ Kunkel, was "a kind of demigod to me," and "in my mind I fashioned myself like a Carole King. [So] I just went about my business, writing my own songs," ultimately convincing Holzman that they were worth recording.

The songs she was writing reflected her playfulness, vulnerability, and romanticism. In "Alone"—whose jaunty melody suggests those living room musicales with her show-biz uncles—she's reassuring a lover, "It's not to leave you that I'm goin'"; rather, she wants to revel in the "ache" of solitude and memory, an odd need that her sensual voice makes believable, with asymmetrical phrasing and unexpected harmony. "Reunions," with its stately Broadway-revue-like melody, is one of the most undiluted of those upper-middle-class slices of life that would become her trademark, which some listeners would gratefully relate to ("To be sad in your beautiful house, with your mother reading *The New York Times* and your father coming home late—Carly made that an okay story to tell; it was okay to be smart, to be witty," says her friend Jessica Hoffman Davis) but which many critics would forever resent and mock her for. Her elegant lyrics about the tension between a group of old friends—"wind blows through thin smiles / Someone made a wrong turn / missed a joke by miles"—redeems it for even the staunchest reverse-snobs. Another wistful art song, "The Best Thing," regretfully mulls the loss of a man of a different background: "I was his foreigner and he was mine."

But of those songs Carly brought to Jac, the one he was most riveted by was "That's the Way I've Always Heard It Should Be," which she'd written with Jake. "All the other songs had some aspect of conventionality, which you expect in a song," Jac says, "but this was different." Jac's staff said the title was too wordy and the song too stuffed with emotional activity—the parents' bad marriage; the friends' unhappy lives; the boyfriend's enthusiasm for marriage but controlling nature; the woman's initial resistance and ultimate capitulation—to be released as a hit single. "Everyone [at Elektra] argued that it was too complex, blah blah blah—'it's not going to be played on Top 40 radio,' and all that was true at the time," Holzman says. "Still, that didn't mean it couldn't be a first."

Jac knew *this* was the single; it was a "signature song; it conveyed who Carly was." "That song was so much *me*," Carly has said. Not only did it draw on her childhood, it described her last few years: she had moved on from three men she might have married—choosing to break off a pre-engagement with Nick Delbanco and a tacit engagement to Danny Armstrong, and suffering Willie Donaldson's severance of their engagement—while her sister and best friends had married and were having children. She was never dishonest about her sexuality (when she moved into her own apartment, "I still had a hard time sleeping alone," she has said, "so I never did, and since it was 1969, there was no reason to") and her datebook was full. Through Jake, she'd met and had a fling with Jack Nicholson and then with Bob Rafelson (the star and director, respectively, of *The King of Marvin Gardens,* which Jake had written) and was now dating Rafelson's brother Don, while still carrying a torch for Danny Armstrong. (Having many lovers didn't harden Carly's heart, her friends would note; it only multiplied the times it could break.)

And all of this was representative. In a brand-new poll of college women, 10 percent more respondents called marriage "obsolete" than had described it that way the year before. Such skepticism had started as idealistic nose thumbing at what the *state* demanded two lovers do, an idea Joni had expressed in "My Old Man." But now feminism had added a new component: it was no longer that two lovers didn't need a "piece of paper from the city hall"; more than "city hall" being suspect, your old man was. *He,* not "the state," was going to "cage [you] on [his] shelf." Men had long quipped that marriage overdomesticated them; now *women* did. "*I* want a 'wife'!" Judy Syfers had just written, in a common-sensically funny, much-talked-about essay in the premiere issue of *Ms.*

Carly and Jake's critique of marriage was a musical version of what women in their circle were doing in prose—and in life. Sally Kempton, Carly's Sarah Lawrence classmate, had just published a long buzz-magnet of an autobiographical essay, "Cutting Loose," in *Esquire,* where Jake's film criticism appeared; it eventually led to her divorce from her producer husband. Jonathan Schwartz's wife, Sara Davidson, had covered the women's movement for *Life* magazine; she'd describe her marriage's dissolution in *Loose Change.* Susan Braudy, a *Newsweek* deskmate of Carly's cousin Jeanie Seligmann (and the author of the James Taylor profile in *The New York Times Magazine*) was document-ing her separation from her husband in *Between Marriage and Divorce.*

The average age of first marriage for U.S. women had been going up a little every year since 1965—the year that Joni had delivered her

Second Fret stage patter about women living alone in tasteful lairs—and the increase would proceed unabated.*

Still, for all Carly's enthusiastically exercised freedom, she'd absorbed lessons from her shrewd coquette mother on how important it was to hold a man's attention. Danny had felt she was "pressured" to have an "orderly" married life like Lucy's, and she had always felt that pressure herself. As she put it while promoting her record, "We were all brought up playing with bride dolls and taught to believe that having children was *it*." More, she had valued both Danny's and Nick's careers over her own, as they had *expected* her to.

The tension in Carly's song (the narrator has fears that won't go away but are too threatening to act on) seemed to match the New York–locused, early-mainstream feminist moment.** Writer and film critic Karen Durbin recalls how she felt, in 1968, when her *New Yorker* colleague, Redstockings cofounder Ellen Willis, started talking about women's liberation." It was "a subject I found so seismic that I kept my hands under the desk so she wouldn't see them shaking while I casually protested that it really wasn't my thing." By early 1971, that sense of being threatened but compelled was widespread: any woman who picked up Susan Sontag's essay on feminism in *The Paris Review* or Vivian Gornick's in *The Village Voice* feared that once she read it she could never turn back. (In "Click! The Housewife's Moment of Truth" in the preview issue of *Ms.*, Jane O'Reilly coined a word for that moment of can't-turn-back epiphany—the feminist "click!") But read on she would. Shoving doubts under the rug (as Carly's song's narrator

---

* By 2005, the average age of first marriage for a U.S. woman was just under twenty-six years old—a highly significant 5.5 years older than it had been in 1955, when the typical American bride was just over twenty. (The very fact that the term "average age of first marriage" sounds stodgy and even prejudiced today shows what this generation of women, its bards, and feminism did: they made marriage optional. Just about every educated urban woman who was born in the mid-1940s can count friends who have never been married or never had children yet have led exciting, distinctly unpitied lives. This was never the case before.)

** Helen Reddy's jingoistic "I Am Woman" became a hit a year and a half after Carly's, in September 1972.

does) was like keeping shaking hands under a desk: a stopgap measure that *both* women knew would merely delay a life-changing confrontation.

Carly's persona—sexy *and* uptown hip—also matched the moment. Between the fiercely anti–"sex object" early feminism and the so-called padded-shoulder "power suit" feminism of later years lay that glamorous little wedge of early 1970s when feminism had an in-your-face sex-focus and a Manhattan-cocktail-party panache.

First, the sex part: Ingrid Bengis's *Combat in the Erogenous Zone*; Erica Jong's erotic *Fruits & Vegetables* and ribald super–best seller *Fear of Flying* (with its famous "zipless fuck"); "The Myth of the Vaginal Orgasm" by Anne Koedt; "The Politics of Orgasm" by Susan Lydon; Ellen Frankfort's *Village Voice* columns-turned-book, *Vaginal Politics*; Shulamith Firestone's *The Dialectic of Sex*; Kate Millett's *Sexual Politics*; the swaggering lustiness of Amazonian Germaine Greer (despite her book's title *The Female Eunuch*); lines like "My sexual rage was the most powerful single emotion in my life" in Kempton's *Esquire* essay— sex-forwardness *sold* the women's movement in those years, when the shedding of "hang-ups" was a political mission, "promiscuous" was as reviled a word as "nigger," and monogamy was something good people didn't "believe" in. (Carly makes the *sotto voce* quip women her age often share in these long-AIDS-sombered times during which the word "slut" has slipped back into usage, "*Young* women have no idea what it was like in those days . . ." And, in Lesley Dormen's novel, *The Best Place to Be,* late-fiftysomething narrator Grace Hanford says, of the very early 1970s, "Those were the days when you slept with every man who so much as caught your eye across a party.") That lack of apology about sexuality gave the movement its boldest victory: January 1973's U.S. Supreme Court decision in *Roe v. Wade,* which made abortion on demand legal.

Then there was the chic. The almost–50 percent Seven Sisters alumna-staffed *Ms.* magazine—which included many extremely *un*dowdy editors (*Vogue*-stylish Ingeborg Day, who also wrote dark erotica, and edgy fashion editor Mary Peacock are just two) and famous

editors (Gloria Steinem)* and editors on the cusp of fame (Alice
Walker edited there just before she catapulted to renown via *The
Color Purple*)—had so much glamour that Robert Redford actually
kept a secret office within *Ms.*'s suite. Feminist editors of that era
might have expressed a preference for, say, Billie Holiday over the
music of a white publisher's daughter, but it was the publisher's daughter whose life and issues more closely matched most of their own. And
beyond the reverse snobbery of liberal-political Manhattan, Carly's example was less ambivalently welcomed. "Women adored her," says
Arlyne Rothberg, who quickly took over as her manager from Jerry
Brandt, and who would notice, over the years, that when a newborn
girl was given the name Carly—virtually unheard of before 1971—"it
was usually the mother who had chosen it." "Women looked at her and
said: 'Oh, you can be gorgeous and smart and educated . . . *and* be a
rock star?'"

Lucy Simon had sensed, when they were retiring their duo in 1966,
that Carly's lower-register voice would be commercial—and by late
1970 that voice had ripened to a confounding richness (it could bleat
and purr at the same time) that mirrored Carly's fluid looks. (When
Holzman's A&R man Steve Harris first met Carly, "there was something
about her [face] I couldn't put my finger on," he's said.) The voice Holzman thought "tough and sinewy" was called by one reviewer "poised
and dusky," and "lightly cutting" and "almost harsh" by *The New York
Times*'s Mike Jahn, who added that it brought "a breathtaking note of
anguish" to her "pastel" scenarios and "combines" with her pronounced
femininity "to cause in the listener a wonderful fascination and curios-

* The original interface of glamour and feminine charisma with effective, mainstream,
sell-it-to-America feminism can be seen in reading an early 1970s profile of Gloria
Steinem by Leonard Levitt in *Esquire*. The intoxicating charm of Steinem to the many
men with whom she (like Joni and Carly) was involved, and her just-prefeminist ability,
through the 1960s, to become (as a song Carly would write with Jake puts it) "the girl . . .
you want [me] to be" to the string of Kennedy-associated political figures and Manhattan journalists, editors, and publishers who were her captivated beaux was—not unad-
miringly—described by Steinem's *friends*. The article was excoriated as an antifeminist
hit job.

ity. She strikes several emotions at once and makes them feel glad to be struck." Stephen Holden, writing in *Rolling Stone* (he would later move to *The New York Times*), praised her "radiant vocal personality," adding, with faint-praise-turned-full: "She has the whitest of white voices and uses it well, singing full throat with her faultless enunciation. Her almost literal note-for-note phrasing of songs is uniquely ingenuous." *People's* Jim Jerome would sum it up by calling Carly's "one of the most powerfully affecting voices in pop rock."

Holzman decided that Jimi Hendrix's record producer, Eddie Kramer, was the tough producer Carly's tough voice required. "Eddie was skilled at creating a rich, fat sound, each instrument or voice being heard with its proper weight," and that's what he wanted for Carly's debut. They began recording in late fall. Carly and Kramer fought over the arrangements of the album; Holzman stayed away for a while—"Let them duke it out" was his philosophy. "I don't mind if the producer and singer don't get along; typically, the fighting brings out some very good stuff; that's why I like to hide," he says. Holzman entered the studio only when he had to, to make sure the production was "full and clean; you had to hear all the nuances. With Carly, that was the critical part." The album added three non-Carly-written songs: "Dan, My Fling," a Jake Brackman–Fred Gardner collaboration (based on Gardner's civil rights song, "Ruth My Truth"), which Carly used as a vessel for her aching regret over breaking up with Danny Armstrong; Mark Klingman's "Just a Sinner," which presented Carly at peak belting form; and Buzzy Linhart's "The Love's Still Growing," whose plaintive toughness matched her voice. Jac Holzman was "buoyed" by the finished product. "The songs were sophisticated and openhearted, which is a rare combination. Some of the lyrics reminded me of Stephen Sondheim, with their keen sense of the crosscurrents of life and the human condition. Though Carly sang with a rock backing, her polished, well-bred voice was of a kind rarely heard in that context."

Holzman had designer Bill Harvey give the album cover "a soft, matte finish, a mark of substance and quality." The photo showed Carly in a tight-bodiced, antique lace dress with lace curtains behind her—her head, to use her own later words, "strategically dipped" on one palm; her legs, as Holzman pointedly put it, "gloriously akimbo," the skirt tent-taut over the heels-together knees-out underneath. The implication of wide-open thighs under a decorous dress was the first of a sex-teasing leitmotif in every one of Carly's early albums. Carly's face, Holzman has said, bore "a challenging look, as if she was waiting for the world to finally notice her."

Carly Simon and its single "That's the Way I've Always Heard It Should Be" were released in February, and Jonathan Schwartz did his longtime friend the favor of giving the single heavy play on his radio show. Along with Carly's sisters, he would soon be shocked at her sudden astounding fame. (Carly's reaction to Joey's and Lucy's stunned understanding that she had upturned the sisters' expected order of things? "Yes, there was guilt," says her second husband, Jim Hart. "But let's get this straight: *First,* there was *glee—then* there was guilt.") Jac's plan was to get the song to female ears. "I knew that once women heard it, we had a shot." So he sent extra copies to the secretaries and receptionists at the radio stations. Holzman believes the record's national buzz came from them, their consciousness piqued by the new feminist spirit. By the time Carly came back from her brief vacation to Jamaica with Don Rafelson, "That's the Way I've Always Heard It Should Be" was #35.

The single and album could not languish; both had to be promoted. Jac insisted that Carly commit to a performance engagement. This prospect terrified her. She'd wanted to be a songwriter more than a singer so she *wouldn't have* to perform.

Now Holzman's A&R man, Steve Harris, took over. Steve had seen Carly's face take on "a beauty [that] was completely transforming" when she'd picked up her guitar and sang, when they'd first met, through mutual friend David Steinberg. He *had* to get her onstage. Harris called Doug Weston, the owner of L.A.'s Troubadour, and got her booked for three nights, starting April 6, opening for Cat Stevens.

With a tremulous voice that few but Neil Young could equal, twenty-two-year-old Stevens (real name: Steven Demetri Georgiou) was the British-raised son of a Greek Cypriot father and a Swedish mother. Dark, hirsute, and handsome, he had become an adulated star (he was an "exceptional singer . . . without question a serious, original artist," raved the *L.A. Times*'s Robert Hilburn) by way of the catchy but patronizing (a young man is telling his ex-girlfriend to be careful) "Wide World," from his *Tea for the Tillerman*. He would eventually have a second hit in the exquisite "Morning Has Broken."

After nailing the deal ("I don't remember the details, but Weston probably wanted custody of Carly's firstborn child—that's what he was like in those days"), Steve called Carly and said, "We're going to the Troubadour, on April 6!" The single was now at #25.

"I was completely flustered," Carly remembers. "It had never occurred to me that the record was going to take off." Steve went over to Carly's apartment and tried to soothe her over the obstacles: one, her fear of flying. Steve said he, too, was afraid (this was true)—they'd attack it with Valium and cocktails. Next, Carly's lack of a drummer she liked. In a sheepish effort to nix the date, Carly said she wanted a drummer who sounded "exactly" like Russ Kunkel—she knew, because she'd been "following James's career with a fine-toothed comb," as she puts it, that Kunkel was off touring with Taylor (with Carole and Jo Mama) and wouldn't be available.

Steve outwitted her. He called Kunkel and booked him on April 6 for $500.

After a long pause, Carly whispered, "Now I guess I have to do it."

In March, the L.A. pop music community received enthusiastic advance word of Carly by way of an article, headlined "Carly Simon Has Impressive Album," by Robert Hilburn. "Ever so rarely an album by a new or virtually unknown artist arrives with little or no fanfare that turns out to be one of the classics of the year," Hilburn opened, in the *L.A. Times*. "In 1971, it may well be Carly Simon." He grouped her as "one of those individualistic singer-writers that one almost instinctively associates with such artists as . . . [Randy] Newman, Laura Nyro, and Joni

Mitchell." He was struck by her "strong, always vigorous point of view," and he analyzed her single: "Miss Simon (and cowriter Jacob Brackman) gives a rather stinging picture of the whole courtship/marriage attitude. She opens the song by painting a rather somber, tragic forecast for the marriage potential . . . then . . . concludes [the song with] the almost inevitable resolution, based on family expectation and emotional fatigue, to proceed [with the marriage] anyway."

Russ Kunkel told his new friend James Taylor about the gig; Taylor, who may have remembered Carly and Lucy from the Mooncusser in the Vineyard, said he'd catch it.

Carly and Steve flew out to L.A. several days early, alighting amid the palm trees. The young woman who'd lived in France and traveled to England was amazed at how "provincial" she was—how "backward in terms of my expansion into the world; this was a whole new world for me—how could I have lived that long and gone nowhere?"

By now, the fever of having a hit record and an engagement at the top rock club in L.A. was hitting her. At a dinner party she met towering Michael Crichton, a.k.a. "Big Boy." "She went out with him a couple of times before the gig," Steve says, "so we were having a great time and the idea of performing was somewhere in the back of her mind." She fell in love with her future at the Troubadour rehearsal, fell in love with the idea of having her own band: bass guitarist Jimmy Ryan, pianist Paul Glanz, and drummer Andy Newmark would stay with her. Rehearsing with Russ Kunkel in the darkness of the Troub, "I was in awe of him," she's said. (Leah Kunkel arrived and saw Carly sitting on her husband's lap. Leah recalls reaching out to shake Carly's hand "and say[ing]: 'I'm Leah—Russ's *wife*,' and off his lap Carly came.")

The Cat Stevens–Carly Simon shows were sold out; "all of rock aristocracy was coming," Steve Harris learned from Doug Weston. All day, Arlyne Rothberg and Steve were enmeshed in "high drama," Arlyne recalls. Was the stage-terrorized Carly "going to make it" onto the stage? "Steve was calling every few minutes" with updates on how he was staving off her meltdown. Carly trembled and stuttered through the day, but sailed through the performance, and then met James Taylor backstage.

When Danny Kortchmar learned that Carly Simon was a rising star, he thought: *Of course* she and James will end up together; it wasn't a matter of *if* but of "What took you so long?" But tonight was not yet their time.

The next morning Robert Hilburn gave Carly shared billing with headliner Stevens in his glowing review in the *L.A. Times,* calling them equally "extraordinarily gifted," predicting that Carly was "destined" to be "acclaimed" and that "[a]s a singer and writer, she has exceptional skills. She's not just a newcomer who is promising; she is, after just one engagement, a new artist who has arrived." In his *Rolling Stone* review of her album, published almost immediately after the Troubadour engagement, Tim Crouse defended Carly against class-bashing critics like Robert Christgau of *The Village Voice.* Christgau had been pleasingly riveted by the anti-marriage radicalism in "That's the Way I've Always Heard It Should Be" until he learned of Carly's background; then he deemed her voice "pure ruling-class honk." The "Updike or Salinger short story"–like songs "strike close to a lot of middle-class homes," Crouse said, and are essentially "dedicated to the proposition that the rich, the well-known, and the college-educated often find themselves in the highest dues-paying bracket." More, her own feeling that her true self could best come through her own songs was justified; Crouse correctly perceived that Carly was "passionately romantic and cynically realistic" at once.

The Troubadour shows helped catapult "That's the Way I've Always Heard It Should Be" into the Top 10; it would stay in the Top 40 ten weeks. *Carly Simon* would end up selling 400,000 copies.

When Carly flew back to New York, Cat Stevens did too, and he asked Carly out. On the appointed night, she waited and waited, as she had for Robbie Robertson. Cat, who had recently been involved with Andy Warhol actress Patti D'Arbanville, was late. When he did finally arrive, "I was sitting on my bed and really nervous, because we hadn't officially had a date yet. And I picked up my guitar and I tuned the low E string down a whole step to D, and I wrote a song for him, because I was so excited and nervous to see him, and I'd been wasting so much time" *on* those feelings. Echoing the rhythms of Cat's own songs, she wrote "An-ti-ci-pa-tion / An-ti-*ci*-pa-*a*-tion / is making me late / is keeping me wai-ai-*ai*-ai-ting." "I wrote the whole song in fifteen minutes," she says.

Cat Stevens reminded Carly of William Blake—"he was extremely airy in that Blake way, and spiritual.* And he would look at me and it would be dazzling, the reflection of all things miraculous. He was amazing; sometimes we would sit on his bed for hours; he'd be watching TV and playing the guitar and looking at me at the same time—he could multitask." A person close to Carly at the time adds that Cat was "confusing to Carly—there were girls and boys" in his world. He remembers wondering: Was Cat *gay*? ("But isn't everyone just a *little* bit gay?" Carly says today, remembering his sweetness.)

Meanwhile, people had been talking about Carly's physical resemblance to Mick Jagger, so she thought it would be fun to interview him. Seymour Peck, the editor of *The New York Times*'s Arts & Leisure section, encouraged the idea. Carly called Jagger in the south of France, just before his May 12 marriage to his pregnant fiancée, Nicaraguan beauty, Sorbonne student, and recent girlfriend of Michael Caine, Bianca Pérez-Mora Macías. Carly recalls that she and Mick casually flirted through the interview, each saying they'd "really love to meet" the other. The Stones' *Sticky Fingers* had just shot to #1 in *Billboard,* and here was Mick Jagger, the sexiest rock star in the world, ingratiating himself to her. It was a little heady. "Carly was trying to figure out her place in all this," says Jake Brackman. "Was she in this celebrity world? It wasn't so long ago that she was in the Letters department of *Newsweek*." (In fact, while Carly's first album and performances were being positively reviewed, residents of central Massachusetts could also hear her, on local radio, singing the jingle she'd written for Worcester Savings Bank.)

The headiness continued. On May 21 Carly opened for Kris Kris-

* Stevens, it would turn out, *was* spiritual. After a near-drowning in Malibu in 1975, Stevens vowed to pay God back for saving his life; he converted to Islam in 1977 and has lived, taught his religion, and (until recently without the religiously forbidden musical accompaniment) sung under the name Yusuf Islam ever since.

tofferson at New York's Bitter End. "And this was when Kris was *the* most beautiful man," says Ellen Questel, who was in the audience, "with that curly hair, and wearing that deep-V-necked semisheer white Indian shirt." Kristofferson was smitten by Carly when he glimpsed her as they'd both exited their adjacent dressing rooms. "So I went out front to watch her, and I was just knocked out," Kristofferson says. "She was beautiful. She had this off-the-shoulder kind of peasant blouse on, and she was playin' the guitar and singing her heart out. Her songs were great, and she seemed totally confident. She was pretty hard to resist." Jake, who was standing next to Kristofferson at the time, heard him mutter a remark about his lust for Carly "which," Jake says, "is definitely *not* for publication."

Kristofferson, thirty-five—Rhodes scholar, ex-army pilot—had been hailed ten months earlier by *The New York Times* as "the hottest thing in Nashville" and the voice of "the new Nashville." He had been having, as he puts it, a "roller coaster" of a year. "It was heaven in one sense, because after struggling for five years, I got my foot in the door." After haunting the Village clubs with buddies Shel Silverstein and Bobby Neuwirth, he had finally become a sensation, giving his mentor Johnny Cash a hit with his "Sunday Morning Coming Down," Sammy Smith a hit with "Help Me Make It Through the Night," and his close friend Janis Joplin a #1 hit with "Me and Bobby McGee," among others. But the overdose deaths of Joplin (who'd been enamored of him; they'd traveled together much of the last year of her life) and his new friend Jimi Hendrix had emotionally thrown him. During the subsequent months, "I worked solidly either in film"—Dennis Hopper's (disastrous) *The Last Movie* et al.—"or on the road," he says, trying to avoid his grief, anger, fear, and exhaustion. When he appeared as a headliner at the Bitter End, he was only sober when he had to be, which meant, not a whole lot of the time.

After Carly's set—in which she sang the new song she'd written for Cat Stevens without acknowledging its inspiration (it was then called "These Are the Good Old Days")—Kris brought Carly out to sing duets with him. Everyone in the audience witnessed their chemistry. "It was a full-blown version of seeing her onstage with Timmy Ratner in *Girl Crazy*," says Ellen. Arlyne recalls, "It was just romantic as hell. He was gorgeous. He was a vision. I remember"—later on—"seeing him coming up Carly's stairs, all in chamois, with the guitar, and I was: Oh my God, I've never seen anything like that! With all that charm!"

After they took their bows, Kris and Carly went back to his suite at the Gramercy Park Hotel. He began writing a growling, lusty song for her, "I've Got to Have You," and they embarked on what would be a summer-long love affair. So recently an office worker, camp counselor, and jingle writer, Carly would marvel, "'Kris Kristofferson *likes* me!'" Steve recalls. "She loved it that he knew Dylan; that, through him, she met musicians and was treated like a fellow artist. We'd walk down the street and she'd say, 'People are saying hello as if they *recognize* me' and I'd say: 'They *do* recognize you, Carly.'"

The next week Carly opened for Cat Stevens at Boston's Symphony Hall. Kris sent her roses before the show (though it was Cat with whom she'd rendezvous afterward). Carly would fall hard for Kristofferson, but the relationship would prove challenging. "Kris was an alcoholic at the time," Arlyne says, "but Carly, with her sense of humor, could see the ludicrousness in her situation," attempting emotional intimacy with him. As Kris got drunker and drunker, Carly would file phone dispatches with Arlyne. "She'd call me and say, 'Just as I was telling him about my life and my problems, he *fell asleep!*'" And Kristofferson could be gruff. Flying back to New York from a performance in Delaware, "Carly was scared to death on the airplane," Kris recalls. "Oh, man, she almost got sick from it. I don't think I was a help in any way—I said, 'Buck up! Get tough.'" Looking back on the romance, Kris says, "I was pretty self-absorbed in those days. Carly was funny and really smart—she had more brains than I did. I have a hard time now believing she tolerated my company."

Still, he dropped her. After that bumpy flight back from Delaware, "Kris didn't want to see me for a while," remembers Carly. Jake says, "The romance was a bigger deal for her than it was for him." In subsequent months, Kris became involved with his next co-performer, Rita

Coolidge, and when he brought Rita out to do closing duets, Carly was hurt "that she slipped into my shoes so easily. I thought, 'Oh, God, we're completely interchangeable here.'" (Kristofferson and Coolidge were married in 1973.) Ellen Questel says: "I can't tell you how very often I've seen it that the expectation Carly has had about somebody has not been reciprocated. I've seen this over and over and over. She's not without humor and wit about these things. I don't want to portray her as a defenseless babe, because she's not, but I wish I'd seen it less."

Throughout the romantic whirlwind, Carly continued to write new songs—not just "Anticipation" about Cat but "Three Days" about Kris. The intensity of her feeling for him is reflected in the first lines, "If I have known you only three days, then how will I remember you in ten?" and in the image of two shining stars crisscrossing the heavens on their way to opposite bookings—one to L.A., the other to London.

Meanwhile, Carly was off to London to record her second album, *Anticipation*. Jac Holzman chose Cat's own producer, Paul Samwell-Smith, to produce it with a "softer but solid" sound. "Carly is one of those artists whose incandescence burns brightest with a new producer for each album," Holzman has said. "After they have squeezed the juice out of each other, it's on to the next, rather like a holiday romance, which in some cases I'm sure it was." It was, with Samwell-Smith; he and Carly became lovers.

Along with her songs to Cat and Kris, Carly interpreted Kris's song to her, "I've Got to Have You," to end the album; *Rolling Stone*'s Stephen Davis opined, "When Carly moans, 'I can't help it . . . I've got to have you,' we're being shown something so primal and so private that it takes your breath away." The album, which Carly dedicated to Steve Harris, was spare—just Carly and her band: Glanz, Newmark, and Ryan, with Cat helping out on some vocals. Today Carly says she loved recording it, though, during the course of recording, Steve remembers that there was angst between Carly and her lover-producer. Still, *Anticipation* was a more confident effort than *Carly Simon*. In it are the beginnings of what would be trademark Carly touches—her lusty belting on "Anticipation" (its reviewer-dubbed "dazzling, can't-put-down refrain" has an all-out,

drum-heavy rock arrangement, with suspended time between drum-
beats that perfectly mirror the suspended time she was singing about);
her sarcastic takedown of an arrogant man in the bongo-syncopated
"Legend in Your Own Time"; her tremulous vulnerability in "Our First
Day Together," which featured what *The New York Times*'s Don Heckman would call "a remarkably sophisticated melodic structure"; and the
operatic emotion in "Share the End," with a moving, anthemlike quality
that would be most fully realized, years later, in her Academy Award–
winning "Let the River Run." "Summer's Coming Around Again" paid
homage to Antonio Carlos Jobim's "The Girl from Ipanema."

The blue-tinted cover of *Anticipation* shows Carly in a sheer, butterfly-winged top over a shimmery skirt, holding open both sides of a
formal, wrought-iron gate. Her long legs are wide apart, and, all the
way from hips to boots, they're visible beneath the fabric.

Anticipation was released in November 1971. The title song remained in the Top 40 three months; the album sold 400,000 copies in
the first four months, stayed in *Billboard*'s Hot 100 for thirty-one weeks,
eventually selling over half a million copies. Carly headlined at the Bitter
End on December 18. Don Heckman had, three months earlier, written
an impressed review of Carly's originality: "In Carly Simon's music one
hears . . . the folk experience . . . synthesized through the consciousness
of an enormously eclectic musical point of view, and shaped and molded
by an esthetic that recognizes none of the traditional boundaries between pop styles." Now he raved about the "explosive" new singer-songwriter's performance:

> In the eight months or so since the release of her first re-
> cording, Miss Simon's brightness has been dramatically in-
> creasing in magnitude. After hearing her Thursday night I'd
> say, good as she is already, her talent . . . is still growing.
>
> Miss Simon does everything superbly. Her voice is rich
> and full and versatile enough to go from high, pure, vibrato-
> less head tones to deep, tigerish growls. She plays guitar so
> unobtrusively that it would be easy to overlook her unusual

dexterity on the instrument. And tying her many gifts together is the electric presence of a born performer—the
almost unconscious command of a stage that comes as naturally to her as walking.

Her older songs—"That's the Way I've Always Heard It
Should Be," "Anticipation" . . . —are familiar enough, but
the new ones suggest an admirable broadening . . . She's
flying high now. High and far.

She was flying high romantically, too. On November 9 she'd attended James Taylor's concert at Carnegie Hall. Jo Mama was opening
for him (Carole was home, awaiting the December birth of Molly).
Joni and James were no longer a couple, and James's lawyer, Nat
Weiss, offered to take Carly backstage to say hello to James. Danny
Kortchmar and James's bass player, Leland Sklar, saw Carly wielding
her charm. "They pegged it," says Abigail Haness. "Danny and Lee
looked at each other and said, in unison: 'Mrs. Taylor.'" Aside from
being some few years older than James, "Carly is so much more sophisticated than James," Abigail continues. "She knows how to work a
room, while James lifts his shoulders and puts his hands out in that 'I
don't know, life just *happened* to me . . .' wingspread. Carly certainly
didn't try to dupe him, but she knew what she wanted."*

Actually, they both did. "If you ever want a home-cooked meal—"
Carly offered.

James replied, "Tonight."

(That may be the cleaned-up version. Carly described their meeting to *Rolling Stone* this way: "James came up and embraced me . . .
and then we went in the bathroom and fucked.")

---

* Abigail adds, "I think Carly's graciousness and generosity might have been mistaken
for conceit by some people at the beginning—'She has so much; why does she flaunt it?'
That kind of thing. Maybe some of the guys were a little suspicious of her." But a few years
later, "when Danny and I were in some turmoil, Carly invited me to stay with her and James
at the Vineyard. She was wonderful." "Carly worked double-time to win over James's
crowd," Betsy Asher says. "But there was real caring underneath her social effectiveness."

"From that night on, we never spent a night apart from each other," Carly says—at least when they were in the same geographical location, which now was most of the time. "All that" romantic activity of Carly's "kind of stopped on a dime, with James," says Jake, "with a little bit of overlap."

As for that first bit of "overlap": a week later, on November 18, Carly and Steve and Jake flew back out to L.A., where she performed again at the Troubadour. She was the main attraction; Don McLean, the opener.

After the show came a knock on Carly's dressing room door. She now had a roadie, named Wuzzy. Just as Wuzzy was saying to the uninvited visitor, "Miss Simon can't see anyone right now," Steve, recognizing the man at the door, said, "Wuzzy! Yes, she *can*." And into the dressing room walked Warren Beatty. Beatty was involved with Julie Christie, but that hadn't deterred him before and wouldn't now. As Arlyne—who soon also managed Diane Keaton, who eventually had a long romance with Beatty during the '70s—remarks: "If you win an Academy Award," or the equivalent, "he's right behind you."

Later that night Carly and Jake were in her room at the Chateau Marmont when Beatty knocked on the door and came in again. Steve Harris cryptically relays Carly's description of her private time with Warren: "He was very persuasive. Very, *very* persuasive."

After the Troubadour engagement, Carly returned east and traveled to Martha's Vineyard to be with James. When they were together in the house he'd just built, things turned very serious very quickly. He had been the Man for three years now, and she was the glittery new girl in town. They were rock-star prom king and queen, and the fatedness of their coupling (which Danny Kortchmar and Leland Sklar had predicted) was intensified by their puzzle-piece-fitting backgrounds. "We felt like we'd known each other all our lives," Carly has said.

They talked about the meaning that performing and success held for them. James said that when his father had gone off to Antarctica with the navy when he was six, he'd bonded so intensely with his mother that it felt Oedipal. Succeeding always carried, he said, a sense of "inherent and impending retribution"—if he succeeded, he'd go from being the vulnerable child to the father-killing man. Carly could relate; performing was, in a different but seemingly parallel way, about love for her, too—about her father's love.

Betsy Asher thinks Carly's outgoing, solicitous nature was compelling to James. "He and Joni had spent a lot of time trying to work it out, so when Carly showed up, she was so sociable and sunny and took up all the slough that it sort of completed him to have all that social" energy. Others have noted that Carly had facial features—the low-bridged nose and full mouth—similar to Margaret Corey and Susie Schnerr. "Every man has a certain physical type," says a woman who knew James well during those years and who, over time, saw Carly as "the love of James's life." Whatever the essence of the immediate depth of attraction was, within days of their union in the Vineyard, they were, with lovers' hearts and psychics' power, envisioning a family. "We were talking dreamily," Carly recalls, "and James said, 'We'll have children and give them names like Ben and Sally.'" The quiet, elusive man had fallen hard. "My love for Carly is a very religious thing," he would eventually say. "I just exchange with her so completely, I don't know where I end off and she begins."

Carly had a November 28 concert booked at the Shady Grove Music Fair in Rockville, Maryland, but she canceled it and stayed with James. The problems—starting with the fact that James was a heroin addict—would intrude soon enough, as would the stinging fact that James dismissed Carly's music. (After they'd become a couple, he came upon her first album at a friend's house and said, of the cover, "That's a fine-looking woman . . ." His friend said: "That's *your* girl—that's *Carly*," and James realized, "Oh, so it is.") But for now there was new love, and with a man of decency and honor. Carly recalls an incident that illuminated the best of James's character: His younger sister Kate had been treated badly by the man she was seeing, "a guy," Carly says "who was about six foot eight and was a black belt in karate and had almost died three times in Vietnam. James had just asked the guy to get out of the house, and the guy had swung his fist at James, and James was very tall but not tough physically"; still, James took him on. Carly was powerfully moved by James's loyalty to and defense of his sister and his willingness to go mano a mano with the bruiser. In Jake's view, Carly had always wanted her father to rise up out of his passive silence in his study chair, especially during Andrea's affair with Ronnie Klinzing, and say, "This is my house! I'm taking control!" But he never did. Later that night, "James got very drunk," Carly remembers, "and then he went out to the back of the house and started chopping wood in the moonlight. And as he chopped, he called out, 'Carly! Carly! I *love* you! I love you!'—the beautiful voice of this brave, beautiful man, bellowing forth through the cold, sharp night.

"And that," Carly says, "is when I fell *cementedly* in love with James Taylor."

The drama of the evening aside, she saw correctly into her new boy-friend's old-fashioned sense of honor. Years later, when James's Warner Bros. records were not selling very well (while Carly's albums *were*), Walter Yetnikoff, the aggressive new head of CBS Records, wanted to steal James away, to produce and promote him better. Even on the night of the signing of the CBS deal that eventually revived his career, Taylor was troubled over leaving the label that had launched him. "I have feel-ings about this; I want my integrity intact," Taylor told Yetnikoff; he said he needed to take a walk to think things over. As he stood to leave, he *bowed* to Yetnikoff. "The gesture was neither gratuitous nor sarcastic; it was the gesture of a gentleman," Yetnikoff has said. After the walk, James returned to sign the career-charging contract, but still with evi-dent ambivalence over what he feared was his disloyalty.

Younger than Carly (as he'd been younger than Joni), James had an endearing boyishness. During another trip Carly made to L.A., in early 1972, James accidentally left her apartment without turning off what he thought was a nonworking shower spigot; he returned to find her apartment flooded. When he walked to a phone booth (the water had damaged the phone line) to call her with the bad news, he was so uptight, she recalls, "he said, 'Hello, Carly, this is James Taylor' . . . his full name, like he didn't know me! It was adorable."

But related to that charming diffidence, there was another quality that Carly saw in those first months which, even though it had bene- fited her, heralded a future danger sign: James's flashes of coldness; his extreme eschewal of confrontation ("He will walk twenty blocks around a confrontation if he can do it," says Russ Kunkel) and abrupt—even cruel—termination of contact when he was "finished" with someone, especially a woman. After they started living together, James got calls at the Vineyard house from both Margaret and Joni. He was "rude and impersonal" to them, Carly recalls (Joni described his telephone brush-off of her—"it hurts!"—in "See You Sometime"), telling them not to call him anymore, and Carly remembers feeling that "if it were me, I would have been deeply hurt." Carly interpreted James's attitude toward Joni as: "I was his new queen and she was Anne Boleyn on her way to the Tower. I saw how determinedly she was banished. I was wounded for her, empathic for her—presciently, as it turned out." (In the years since their divorce, Carly has found James's "dismissal" of her "as confounding as I could ever imagine any- thing would be. It has beaten me back, self-esteem-wise, too many times and I'm ashamed of my weakness.")*

As for Margaret Corey: One day, early in her relationship with James, Carly ran into her at Capezio; they recognized each other by the names on their credit cards. According to Carly, Margaret may have

---

* Shortly after Carly and James married, in 1972, Arlyne Rothberg arranged a lunch, at Mr. Chow's in L.A., between Carly and Joni, at Carly's request. Arlyne invited Linda Ronstadt along to dilute tension. Carly and Joni were so wary of each other that they barely lifted their forks and mediator Arlyne didn't either, out of anxiety about the situa- tion. *"Linda,"* Arlyne says, "was the only one of us who ate. She ate everybody's lunch!"

In 1996, Joni and Carly had dinner together. Afterward Joni told a friend, "I had no idea what a great person she was." They talked about James, and when Joni realized that Carly had essentially never gotten over him—the man Joni had come to view as cruel (and may not have entirely gotten over herself)—Joni was very moved. Ultimately, says a friend, the two women ended up "laughing about him." In subsequent meetings—one with Betsy Asher—they talked about themselves (with notoriously voluble Joni doing most of the talking), instead of about the man they had shared so long ago.

asked her how she was dealing with Trudy Taylor's WASP propriety. According to what Richard Corey says Margaret told him, Carly thanked Margaret for paving the way to James's mother's acceptance of a half-Jewish girlfriend for her son. (Perhaps to cater to her new mother-in-law, in 1975 Carly told *Rolling Stone*'s Ben Fong-Torres, "I'm only one-quarter Jewish; the rest is German and Spanish.")

Rolling Stone's Timothy White would call Carly and James "two lanky aristocrats" who would come to embody the "intelligent, self-conscious style and sex appeal that characterized soft-rock stardom in the Seventies." "But they were different," adds Tamara Weiss, who's known them both for decades. "Carly is passionate, funny, wacky, loving, wild; James was more contained, quieter, withdrawn—and he was stoned a lot of the time, back then." "Carly is vivacious—vastly more social; James is more taciturn, more reticent," says Danny Kortchmar. "It became a big source of conflict for him, all the attention they ended up getting as a couple, which outweighed the attention they got individually, which was already huge."

The personality difference would also fit into their dance with the third partner in their relationship: James's addiction. James's drug habit was "harrowing" to Carly. She hadn't understood when she fell in love with him how deeply he was hooked. The wall the addiction set up between them—the "remoteness" from James—was confusing and painful to her. For the sake of their relationship, James tried to quit three times in their first six months, throwing out his "works," his strap and syringes. "I needed her very much," he's said of that time. For a poignantly addicted man to try to quit drugs, three times, for love of you: in Hip America, there was no more moving—or flattering—soap opera.

Carly was now writing songs for her third album, *No Secrets*. The title song, "We Have No Secrets," was both personally—echoing Carly's boundary-less but betrayal-laced childhood family life—and culturally resonant. The book *Open Marriage* had just been published (essentially for slightly older couples who thought they'd missed out on

hippie hedonism and wanted a bit of it for themselves), and its anthropologist authors' endorsement of nonmonogamous marriage was one of
the first planks in the house that Tom Wolfe would call the Me
Decade. Carly's pithy line, "You always answer my questions / But they
don't always answer my prayers," nails the tension between this supposedly wholesome straying and the realities of human nature. (By the
end of Carly and James's marriage, the price of secrets would be all
too clear to both of them.) "The Right Thing to Do," with its fetching
melody, is also explicitly about James. In it Carly is both the romantic,
stubbornly looking past her man's serious problem, *and* the realist,
shrewdly assessing her fading value in the sex-and-love marketplace:
"And it used to be for a while / That the river flowed right to my door /
Making me just a little too free / But now the river doesn't seem to
stop here anymore." *"Making me just a little too free"*: the sly acknowledgment of her sex-forwardness *and* her opportunism was, to her identifying female listeners, flattering in its sophistication.

However, the river *did* still stop at Carly's door. In June of 1972, at
Ahmet Ertegun's party for the Rolling Stones, Carly connected with
Mick Jagger. James had recently gone back to heroin again, "so there
was room for a little Mick feeling; there was an opening," Carly says.
She asserts that she did remain faithful to James, which Jake qualifies:
"in a kind of Bill Clinton definition of faithful."

Jac arranged for Carly's third album to be produced by Richard
Perry, a Brooklyn-born University of Michigan graduate who'd discovered Tiny Tim and had most recently produced Harry Nilsson. Perry
had wanted to work with Carly from the day he heard, and saw, her
first album. ("That *sound!* That striking-looking woman!") By the time
Anticipation came out, Perry was "already imagining what our album
would sound like." He was thrilled to get the assignment, although, he
recalls, "with her first two albums, she'd had affairs with her record
producers, so when we were getting ready to meet, Arlyne Rothberg
made her sign a blood oath that under no circumstances would she
have an affair with me." This would become a running joke between
Richard and Carly, since, says the very tall man with the strong-

featured face and dark hair, "if *any* two people should have had an affair, it would be *us;* we looked like sister and brother."

Carly came to see Richard at his Laurel Canyon house in May 1972, bearing a song she had just written, the gentle, somewhat folkie "Ballad of a Vain Man" (she'd loved Dylan's "Ballad of a Thin Man"). The song had come together in four separate parts. First, about a year earlier, she'd sketched out in her journal the beginning of a song called "Bless You, Ben." Then, on a flight from L.A. to Palm Springs for the Elektra Records convention, she'd added another, totally unrelated line to her journal when her seat mate, musician Billy Mernit, looked into the cup on his tray and said, "Doesn't that shape look like clouds in my coffee?" Thirdly, at one point when she was feeling vengeful about the men who'd emotionally laid her low, she'd scribbled another, tauntlike, line into her journal. The line was waiting for context and meaning, but she knew it was good: "You're so vain, I bet you think this song is about you." Finally, everything came together at a party in L.A. A man she knew walked in, with a certain attitude, "and I said to myself, This is *exactly* the person that 'You're so vain, I bet you think this song is about you' is about!" Carly says today. "I envisioned him looking in the mirror and the scarf twirling, and the imaginary gavotte, and all the women wanting to be his partner." After the party Carly realized that drippy "Bless You, Ben" was going nowhere, so, elongating its melody by three beats, and syncopating it, she substituted: "You *walked into* the party / Like you were *walk*ing onto a yacht"—she thought "walked into" had a "nice flicker" to it—and kept going.

The song reflected her belle-of-the-ball year and a half, which had negatively affected her self-esteem more than it seemed on the surface. Carly had belt-notched all those coveted hotties—Cat Stevens, Kris Kristofferson, Warren Beatty, Jack Nicholson, Mick Jagger, not to mention the unfamous ones (and her truly loved James)—and with her "extreme intelligence and worldly wit," Ellen observed, she had enjoyed the party. Yet, Ellen adds, "I don't think she knew how to do it in her heart." Jake agrees. "Those were all wrenching emotional affairs for her." Sexual revolution or not, she'd felt used. "And this thing that Nicholson and

Beatty* had, where they find a new girl and then they want to share her as a male bonding thing, that passed-on feeling [translated to]: 'You gave away the things you loved, and one of them was me . . .'"

As Carly sat down at the piano and started playing "Ballad of a Vain Man," Richard Perry grabbed his bongos and started "banging them up to a thunderous crescendo," he recalls. Sure enough, inside the gentle folk song was a full-blast rocker. "Just listening to that song for the first time, I thought, Oh, my God—*what a hit this is!*" he says.

Carly flew to London in the middle of the summer to record *No Secrets*. James joined her when he finished a lengthy round of political fund-raisers with Carole for George McGovern's presidential bid. James and Carole were the first rock stars ever to stump for a presidential candidate; Warren Beatty organized the concerts and James's participation came as a favor from Carly to Warren. By now, "Ballad of a Vain Man" had turned into "You're So Vain"—the anthem of a woman exerting power over the boyfriend who did her wrong. The narrator's bitchy playfulness lights up the song. ("I bet you think this song is about you, don't you?" is Carly's adult version of her waving Ronnie Klinzing's jockstrap aloft.) The clunky-as-a-yearbook-autograph rhyme—"yacht," "apricot," "gavotte"—signals that this rock song is boldly uncool. It's a chick song. Happily using these ill-fitting words, the narrator is observing the employment of clothes, status symbols, and gestures of narcissism and insecurity in the war for self-esteem. But rather than using these things to shore herself up (or to put another woman down), she's using them to

---

* The "man" at the party who inspired that line was almost certainly Warren Beatty. "Oh, let's be honest, that song is about me; it's not about Mick Jagger; it's about *me,*" Beatty proudly told an interviewer in 1999. However, in one of Carly's very earliest comments about the song (in November 1972—before it was released, much less gossiped about), she let slip that "I had about two or three people in mind" when she wrote the song. Jake's rightful packaging of best friends Beatty *and* Nicholson—both lovers of Carly's in that last year (as were their friends Bob Rafelson and Rafelson's brother Don) whose "passing on" of her from one to the other to the other to the other felt hurtful and ultimately offensive to her—leads to the likelihood that the "vain man" was really the "vain *men*": that whole clique of cocky, hip, filmmaking—and girl trading—bachelors who often "walked into" Hollywood parties, together or separately, with yacht-boarding entitlement and aplomb.

mock a powerful man. This is what makes people view the song as feminist—real-life feminist, not academic feminist. "Carly understands
middle-class women," Arlyne Rothberg says.

Over the course of their week working on the track, Richard Perry says,
"anyone who heard that record would giggle, because you knew it would be
a massive hit, and it kind of tickled you to have that feeling. Normally, no
matter what something sounds like, you still hold a little quotient [of hope]
in reserve. But with this record, *everyone* knew." "Take it to the bank!" Steve
Harris laughed, when he heard it. "Bet the house on it!"

Of the several providential touches that made people feel that way,
the first was Jagger's walking into the studio one day, at Carly's behest, to
sing vocals on the chorus. Perry was delighted and stunned. "It was the
peak of the Rolling Stones' success and Jagger *never* did anything like
that"—but there he was, adding his unmistakable cracking voice to Carly's sarcastic "*Don't* you, *don't* you, *don't* you?"s. "I honestly credit Mick
with making my entire career," Carly says, "because his voice was so important on 'You're So Vain'—the sound, the mystery of who the song was
about: it had a lot to do with Mick." James, however, may have felt more
unbalanced about Mick's participation—and about other men in Carly's
past and present in general, at least according to one observer: Danny
Armstrong. Danny happened to be in London, so Carly invited him to a
session. "James was standing in the control room—I saw him as a very
nervous, upset-but-keep-it-cool-on-the-outside person," Danny said,
when interviewed for this book. "He kept looking at me—he was interested in what the heck I was about, and it went both ways."

The next key moment in the making of the record was Perry's happening upon bassist Klaus Voormann, warming up his fingers by doing
a fast brush of the strings—Perry seized on that ominous-sounding,
minor-mode accidental lick and had Voormann repeat it for the song's
introduction, over which Carly whispers, "Son of a gun." Finally, when
everyone thought they had the track nailed, Perry still felt "it wasn't
100 percent"; the drumming was good, but not good enough. Jim
Gordon (who'd played on Carole's album with The City, *Now That
Everything's Been Said*) came in at the last minute and did a run-

through—and Perry knew: *this* was the drummer.* When Carly arrived at the studio the next day and Perry asked her to do the track yet again, she was beside herself. "I thought we *had* it!" she said, and burst into tears. "Look, you gotta trust me," Perry pleaded. *"This* is the *one.* This is the record we've been *dreaming* about."

The cover of *No Secrets* shows Carly, as Arlyne puts it, as "the epitome of the 1970s educated woman." Long, layered hair streaming out of the bottom of her wide-brimmed, high-topped hat, she is in errand-doing, lunch-date-going motion in velour jeans, tote bag swinging. Under her long-sleeved tight jersey, her nipples are discreetly visible.

After recording *No Secrets,* Carly returned to New York with James. "Mick and I had spent time together" in London, she says (while denying there was an affair between them), "but I really didn't want to be with anybody but James." Steve Harris could tell "it had become more serious—there was a we're-going-to-get-married kind of feeling. Carly wanted it to be permanent."

On November 1, the phone rang in Carly's apartment. It was Bianca Jagger "and she said to James, 'You know my husband and your fiancée are having an affair,'" Carly recalls, "and James said, 'That's not true'; he defended my integrity so beautifully."** (Confirming that she made that call, Bianca Jagger says that she suspected an affair because her husband sang chorus on Carly's song, and she says she found "a letter from Carly to Mick and a letter for Mick to send to Carly.")

---

* Jim Gordon's intensity with the drumsticks unfortunately portended future dysfunction; he later became a schizophrenic and is currently in prison for murdering his mother.

** Some close to James Taylor believe that he never got over his sense of competing with Mick Jagger, and that he may have felt that a flirtation, or more, between Carly and Jagger had re-upped toward the end of their marriage (during the same period that James had a lover). "It burns him to this day," says one insider. During one Australian concert, when James was already divorced from his second wife, Kathryn Walker, James discovered that the Rolling Stones were staying in the same hotel as he was, and were playing a bigger stadium. He was "furious at this," says someone who spoke to him during this time—"and you don't carry that around for thirty years unless you really have a problem with Mick."

Carly says that she and James had, some days before the phone call, planned to marry quickly, but she also says, "There's nothing that gets men so crazy as other men pursuing their women. Boy, did we decide fast!"

Two days after Bianca Jagger's phone call—on November 3, hours before James was to appear at Radio City Music Hall*—an extremely minimalist wedding ceremony was held in Carly's apartment. Arrangements were so rushed that "certain tests were waived," Carly says. The only guests were Andrea Simon and Trudy Taylor—the two opinionated matriarchs eyeing each other warily—and Jake Brackman, who served as best man to bride *and* groom. Just before the judge arrived, Carly called Jessica and Ellen with the happy news so they wouldn't have to learn it from the media. While Peter Asher was denying to reporters the rumors that a marriage was taking place—because he didn't know it was happening—James and Carly became man and wife. (However, the Ashers certainly knew the seriousness of the relationship and that a marriage was pending. Betsy—whom Joni had been calling during her months in Canada, playing her her new James-based songs for *For the Roses*—"was," she says, "designated to tell Joni that James and Carly were going to get married." Joni's reaction, Betsy says, was "'Oh, okay.'" She concentrated on what she hadn't liked about James. "James's Martha's Vineyard scene was not for her. James had employed the whole island and all his brothers to build his little cottage. They were smoking dope on the roof. She'd passed on that." Another friend of Joni's says that by that time it was definitively over with James. "She was ready to let him go.")

Later that night, James told his Radio City Music Hall audience that he had just married Carly Simon. Cheers went up. A midnight party followed. Radio deejays announced the marriage—the first between two rock stars—as if it were a union of royalty.

---

* Peter Asher had used his erudite British accent to beg Laurance Rockefeller, the chairman of the board of his family's Rockefeller Center, in which Radio City is housed, to allow, for the first time ever, a *rock* concert to be held on that wholesomely tourist-friendly stage.

Two months after their marriage, Carly and James were the subject of a ten-page *Rolling Stone* interview, in its January 4, 1973, issue. Writer Stu Werbin referred to them in the article as Mr. and Ms. Simon-Taylor. They were posed, honeymoon style, lei-bedecked, by a boat rail—he in a white suit, she in a bikini bottom and a macramé-backed lei. The elusive, head-in-his-sound-hole James Taylor was remarkably open, declaring, "Carly and I are in love with each other." (Perhaps fearing he'd gotten too earnest, he also played the tough rocker, adding, "She's a piece of ass; it bothers me—if she looks at another man, I'll kill her.") He revealed that they'd already named what he called their "hypothetical children" Sarah and Ben. (That the naming of his future children had not only been *done* by the inscrutable, hard-drugging James Taylor but volunteered *by* him to *Rolling Stone* was startling. Male rock stars weren't supposed to be romantic and domestic; this was *girl* stuff. This interview would lead to Carly and James being called everything from—in *The Washington Post*— "the Rainier and Grace of Rock" to, negatively, in hard rock circles, "the Ozzie and Harriet of Rock.") James talked very honestly about his addiction, and, in a remark that would prove more truthful than she imagined, Carly said she was "addicted to James."

Then Carly turned the conversation to gender politics, using her marriage as a vehicle.

Carly voiced concern at the fact that, until *No Secrets,* James had never listened to her music. He replied that he didn't *ever* listen to records, not even his own, but that answer didn't cut it with her. (She didn't tell *Rolling Stone,* but early on he'd told her he didn't *like* her songs—and this deeply hurt her). She used the interview to ponder aloud a disturbing realization that she and many other women were having, now that they were analyzing their romantic history through this new lens: "Any male that I've been involved with in the past," she said (silently conjuring Delbanco and Armstrong), "has not liked my success, has not wanted me to be successful, has been threatened by that fact."

James came through—sort of. "I'm very much interested in not

seeing Carly behind the kitchen stove, because I see females live totally vicariously through their husbands and it drives them crazy and it
drives the husband crazy, too." Still, he was speaking to one easy issue
(a woman giving up her career), when she was expressing anxiety
about a more challenging one: What if she *surpassed* him? The much-
buzzed-about *No Secrets* and the meteoric "You're So Vain" were about
to be released. So were James's less promising *One Man Dog* and its
single "Don't Let Me Be Lonely Tonight."

Carly had made feminist points before, telling the *Chicago Tribune*'s music critic Lynn Van Matre that, as Van Matre put it, "she'd
never liked the term female singer-songwriter, with its implications
that there is something unusual or somehow distinct about a woman
who writes her own material as opposed to a man who does." But in
the *Rolling Stone* interview she became most fully what her female
fans had approvingly suspected she was: a thoughtful, college-paper-
word-using woman, laboring to turn the big ship of man-woman relations right along there with them. She said children should be raised
to learn that gender differences don't mean male "dominance" and
female "subservience," and that "men can be emotional and women
can be breadwinners," that gossip columnists' interest in her love life
rather than her work was "an extension of male chauvinistic pigism."
And she knew what she had to overcome: "My own conditioning is
that one voice says to me, 'Carly, you mustn't try to dominate the situation . . . [and] you mustn't expect James to do the dishes.'" But the
other, *new* voice was saying, "'I want my musicians to play in a slower
tempo and it's James's turn to do the dishes tonight.'"

Carly said that James's indifference to her work "worried" her
"terribly"—it seemed to strike a too-familiar nerve. Looking back
today on her sister's marriage, Lucy Simon thinks she knows why:
"James was so similar to our father in terms of looks and brilliance
that I think Carly transferred *to James* the need she felt to prove her
worth to our father, who died before she could know he loved her.
And," over the course of the marriage, "she *kept* on trying to prove
something to him." Jake makes a similar assessment: "James was not

at all delighted with Carly's creativity. But her dad wasn't, either. In some way she was *looking* for that; that was what she knew. A withholding man was familiar."

"You're So Vain" struck like a brick through a window. The star power that early listeners had heard in the song came through to critics and fans alike. Even Ellen Willis, who was to rock criticism what Renata Adler was to film (and whose lower-middle-class background and radical politics had made her resent and distrust Carly's perspective on previous songs), had to admit, in *The New Yorker*, that this was "a great rock 'n' roll song." Willis likened the lyrics' "inspired sloppiness" to Dylan's, and she loved the "good-natured nastiness" of Carly's delivery. The song's humor made its feminism an easily swallowed pill, but in the long run it was that aspect of the song that would endure: fifteen years later Stephen Holden would credit the "magnificently vulgar pop masterpiece" with "asserting a new balance of power in male-female relationships."

"You're So Vain" hit #1 as soon after its release as a single could. ("The Right Thing to Do" and "We Have No Secrets" also became hits.) *No Secrets* also hit #1, a rare double jackpot. Carly now had the success that no one would have predicted for her three years earlier. Now, as she neared thirty, it was time to have that little Ben or Sarah. Carly and Arlyne both became pregnant in spring 1973, "when no one else was," Arlyne says, only slightly exaggerating. In feminist ground zero New York, marriage and motherhood were now considered retro and suspect and, by Me Decade values, the package was unappealingly self-limiting. Carly and Arlyne combed the unpromising maternity clothes racks together, two plumped-up women in a sea of svelte self-actualizers. Carly wrote "Think I'm Gonna Have a Baby" about how *not*-the-thing-to-do it was to be knocked up in I Am Woman 1973. The song would be the centerpiece of her next album, *Hotcakes*, which would show a glowingly pregnant Carly, in a gauzy caftan, sitting by a kitchen window in the town house she and James had bought on East Sixty-second Street.

And as she, who'd been "just a little too free" for so long, settled into domesticity, across the country a woman who'd been just a little too *sensible* for so long was poised for a leap. The estimable Ellen Willis once wrote that the coming-toward-middle-age members of the 1960s generation had trouble eventually grasping 1980s "identity politics" because identity politics glamorized that which you were born as, which was exactly counter to the '60s dream of becoming the *opposite* of what you had been born as. Sometimes this transformation happened by bonding with the Other so deeply you became a "new" person in attitude, passion, geography. The 1960s were over and that romance was fading; still, such a transformation would come—late but very hard—to the woman who everyone thought was the steadiest: Carole.

PART FIVE

*"we just come from
such different sets
of circumstance"*

CHAPTER THIRTEEN

carole

1972 – 1984

On a damp twilight in late May 1973, Carole—in a blue and white tunic over jeans, her hair newly short—strode onto the stage in Central Park's Great Lawn and even before she hugged Mayor John Lindsay (who'd proudly introduced her), the more than 70,000 assembled fans let out wild, grateful cheers. "We *love* you, Carole!" "Sing 'Natural Woman'!" "You've got a friend, Carole!" they shouted. Carole surveyed the small city of euphoric faces and reminded them: "It was supposed to . . ."—spelling the word, so as not to tempt fate— "R-A-I-N." Laughter and *more* cheers—yes, despite the forecast, they'd camped out on the moist grass for hours. In the VIP section sat Jack Nicholson—and Joni: living in Bel Air now (and feeling "really *uncomfortable*" wearing Yves St. Laurent pants at a rock concert) and having recently had a brief fling with the ubiquitous Warren Beatty, Joni had been absorbed into young A-list Hollywood, though she still retained her artistic bohemian heart. "This and the Ellsberg trial* are the only

---

* The public gallery in the L.A. courtroom in which Daniel Ellsberg, former RAND Corporation military analyst, stood trial for leaking the Pentagon Papers (secret government documents pertaining to the Vietnam War) to *The New York Times* was star-studded—Barbra Streisand and Joan Didion attended daily. And when Ellsberg turned forty-two, a month before Carole's Central Park concert, all four Beatles attended his birthday party.

375

two events it's proper to be seen at in public," Nicholson told reporters at the concert.

As Carole sat down at the grand piano (which Genie had fretted might not have been properly tuned) and curled her hands over the keys, the noise receded to cricket-hearing silence. Two years after its release, *Tapestry* officially stood as the biggest-selling rock album in history and was still as well loved now as when it had freshly hit the airwaves, and this was Carole's first hometown performance since the scope of her triumph had seeped into the city's jaded consciousness. As she pounded out the opening chords of "Beautiful," the audience went crazy—applause and whoops rippling like a great aural wave from the penthouse tops of Fifth Avenue to the penthouse tops of Central Park West. During this and her next nine songs—amplified by a five-piece band (with Charlie on upright bass) and six-man horn section—the fans tossed bouquets, pushed at the stage fencing, and had to be chased down from some of the 200-odd scaffolding frames that held the speakers aloft. Unlike every other concert on this twelve-city tour, tonight's was free, Carole's "small way of giving something back" to the city, she said. It rated reporting ("Carole King Draws 70,000 to Central Park") on page one of *The New York Times* the next day, side by side with the lead story about hazards for the astronauts on America's first space station and major news in the Watergate scandal: "Prosecution Is Said to Link Haldeman and Ehrlichman to Ellsberg Case Break-In."

Carole hadn't toured since giving birth to Molly. She'd turned down almost every publication, even declining the cover of *Life* magazine—and her stiff refusal to give interviews during this current tour seemed too curious for the press to miss. *The Washington Post*'s Tom Zito noted: "Carole King, who has sold more than 15 million albums in the past three years, would rather not talk about it. 'Carole is basically a woman with two children and a new baby and she's got a home life,' says . . . her manager's publicity man. 'She just feels it's a lot easier if her life isn't reviewed every time she performs,' says manager Lou Adler. 'She has her private life and she wants to keep it that way.'"

The reason for the diffidence? She loved Charlie deeply, and her fame "was a tremendous burden and challenge for them," says a close observer. "It was a terrible struggle for her," trying to uphold the equilibrium of her marriage through the stress of maintaining the level of success to which she had skyrocketed. Carole's getting all the attention unintentionally became "like a smack in the face to Charlie; if she introduced him" during a concert or event "he would thank her for acknowledging him; he would feel she was only doing so to [make him feel important], that her fans didn't care about him." When people noticed Carole in public "sometimes the timing was all wrong," the observer continues, "and it was very upsetting to her, especially when Charlie was there."

It's not that Charlie was temperamental or demanding. He was supportive, but that was the problem. Says John Fischbach, "There was nothing wrong with Charlie Larkey; he was a normal guy. It just would have been very difficult for any man in that situation to be 'Mr. King'; you pay for that.'" Especially if you're an unproven musician. "Being married to Carole wasn't good for Charlie's career," says Danny Kortchmar. "He hadn't made his bones"—established respect as a musician—before becoming involved with her. "People thought he was just getting hired because he was married to Carole. And he was overshadowed—Carole was a very strong and determined woman."

Carole had made two albums since *Music*. *Rhymes & Reasons* was released at the end of 1972, quickly shot to #2 on the *Billboard* chart, and stayed there for five weeks. Her significance to the culture was expressed through its large, grainy, close-up cover shot: Carole in profile, almost expressionless: her frizzily curly hair and prominent nose filling the cardboard square. She'd become America's sweetheart despite physical attributes she'd once despaired of but which she (along with an evolved public) now embraced.

Like much of *Music, Rhymes & Reasons* has a noncommercial, almost piano-bar feel, and Carole's voice has an undertone of vulnerability, even weariness. Four of the album's songs were cowritten by Toni, and in these Carole, who had *never* lived alone, gains an alter ego in Toni, who, as an adult, had lived *only* that way. From a distance of over three decades, these then somewhat overlooked songs (critics tended to lump them in with Carole's solo compositions as being optimistic friendship songs—they were actually more sophisticated) seem like time capsules of how it felt to be a single woman holding her own in a time and town where sensitivity was valued in the political and spiritual abstract but not practiced in the male-to-female interpersonal. "Come Down Easy" is the breezy plaint of a post-1960s woman for whom "enough space . . . enough time . . . pieces of fruit and glasses of wine" are happy compensation for being alone. The heroine of the dolorous waltz "My My She Cries" disappears—what effort it takes to stay balanced, confident, and visible in the brand-new normal of extended female independence. "Peace in the Valley"'s narrator duns herself for gossip (indulging in "talk that kills for fun") and self-absorption ("I know that man's my brother / and that I'm the selfish one"), indirectly revealing that altruism is the luxury of the securely situated. The infectious "Feeling Sad Tonight" (which Carole set to a counterintuitive, thumping stridence) features an everywoman on a barstool, "always feeling half right and half safe." "Half right and half safe": it was that so-well-put sense of marginalization and risk that the innately conventional, always domestically occupied Carole had avoided all her life. "The First Day In August" is a love song Charlie and Carole wrote together—he, the words; she, the melody. "And nothing will come between us," they vow, against substantial odds.

Carole wrote six of the songs wholly herself, and these are strikingly, if casually, confessional. In the scatting "Bitter With the Sweet," she grumbles about the invasion on her time and privacy; in "Goodbye Don't Mean I'm Gone" (with twangy country interlude) she unapologetically tells old friends that her inaccessibility isn't swelled-headedness;*

---

* Carole lost touch with both Camille and Barbara, her closest childhood friends. Especially hard for Camille was one occasion, in 1976, when she and her mother, Mary (bearing a hand-crocheted pillow with *"Will You Love Me Tomorrow"* embroidered on it), tried to visit Carole backstage at the Beacon Theatre (Carole's performance had featured special guest Bruce Springsteen, who duetted with her on "The Loco-Motion") and were turned away, very likely without Carole knowing they had come. They left her a note and never heard back. Shortly after that, Camille and Barbara tried to contact Carole about their Madison High reunion. They got a form-letter refusal back from Carole's publicist.

rather, "It's all I can do to be a mother." "I Think I Can Hear You" expresses her belief in a deity, likely reflecting her devotion to Swami Satchidananda;* "Stand Behind Me" describes her resistance to the "blind[ing]" "dazzlement" of her shocking fame, and her reliance on her loved ones. But it was the more polished "Been to Canaan" (named for both the biblical land and the Connecticut town in which she and Charlie had just bought a farm in order to have a base near their families, which they rarely used), featuring its bounce-as-you're-driving hook "been *so* long . . ."–that became the album's Top 10 hit. Still, Charlie remembers something about its recording that underscored their no-win situation. Long after the track was cut, "she and I were talking and she said she had been a little disappointed in my bass playing on it but she hadn't said anything [during the session], and [when we talked about it later] I thought: That was the best I could do. I thought it was a good track at the time. I hadn't realized she wasn't completely satisfied with it." Carole was not only the star and the breadwinner but also her husband's boss–the highly seasoned arranger, pressured to prove that *Tapestry* wasn't a fluke. Choice: Lean on your bass player (dominate your husband) to get the most out of the money track? Or don't push him, don't humiliate him, and risk less of a hit? Men in Carole's position didn't have that problem.

After *Rhymes & Reasons,* Carole tacked from the ruminatively personal to the sociopolitical. *Fantasy* is a pop opera explicitly remining those issues (race, poverty, longing) that she and Gerry had had to tiptoe around ten years earlier. Carole wrote all the songs herself and sings in the personae of society's underdogs: a black man struggling for pride, a welfare mother fighting for dignity, a deflated white housewife, a young pregnant woman whose man has fled, a barrio Hispanic, and so on. *Fantasy* was a "concept" album, the tracks bleeding into one another much in the manner of Marvin Gaye's brilliant *What's Going On,* of two years earlier, and with a sound that echoed

---

* She would soon purchase hundreds of acres of land in Connecticut for the guru, the sale of which eventually helped fund Yogaville, the guru's town in Virginia.

(the insuperably humane) Curtis Mayfield's recent *Superfly* soundtrack. The fluid-track sound would also prefigure the looming pop music trend: disco.*

The album, with its one hit, the peppery Spanish-language "Corazón," was released in June 1973 and promptly went gold. But artistically it didn't touch the *Tapestry* bar, and her once greatest champion seemed the most keenly disappointed: the *L.A. Times*'s Robert Hilburn would eventually write that her two post-*Tapestry* albums, "while . . . polished and nicely crafted, sounded so much alike to most critics and fans they could barely suppress the yawns when talking about them." *The New York Times*'s Lorraine Alterman called Carole's attempts to highlight the plight of disadvantaged women laudably feminist but warned of the dangers of inflated expectation (*Fantasy* had been pre-touted as a "masterpiece"). "Though her more ardent followers think of her as a genius," Alterman wrote, "King is really a skilled writer of popular songs, but"— unlike Joni, Alterman made clear—"she doesn't possess that bold leap of the imagination that transforms craft into art." The *Chicago Tribune*'s Lynn Van Matre's irritated reaction to *Fantasy* seemed to bear out Alterman's warning about the dangers of oversell: Carole's voice, Van Matre griped, was "slightly appealing rather than good," "thin," "occasionally even whiny," and her lyrics were "often cliché."

Turning her thoughts to a next album in 1974, Carole came to terms with her stretched limits: she had written all of *Fantasy* by herself,

---

* Though disco music (which enveloped the country from 1974 to 1977 and whose female queens were Gloria Gaynor, Bette Midler, and Donna Summer) is generally dismissed as trivial, it was not without significance. It legitimized gays as a force in the social and popular cultural fabric of America. Although the Stonewall riots that triggered the gay rights movement occurred in 1969, as late as November 1973 it was not eyebrow-raising for Jackson Browne to toss off the words "faggots" and "fag" in an interview with Cameron Crowe in *Rolling Stone*. That publication, from its 1967 inception, stood for a rock world that was every bit as macho as sports and the military—as was its publisher, Jann Wenner. It is a measure of how things have changed that today Jann Wenner (still firmly in control of and identified with his *Rolling Stone*) is "married" to a man and they are the parents of a child, conceived by a surrogate. Wenner and his partner, Matt Nye, even gave themselves a baby shower. Imagine traveling back to 1971 and telling the magazine's readers and subjects that such a thing would happen.

had just finished an exhausting tour, and she and Charlie just found out they were going to be parents again. She needed a cowriter to relieve some of the pressure. She turned to ex–Myddle Class member Dave Palmer, whose ex-wife Sue had been her best friend in New Jersey and then Gerry's girlfriend in California. Dave had been the vocalist for a new band led by two edgy ex-Bard students, Donald Fagen and Walter Becker, who named their group for the dildo in William Burroughs's *Naked Lunch:* Steely Dan. Dave sent Carole and Charlie a prerelease copy of the Dan's *Can't Buy a Thrill,* and Carole knew it would be huge.

When Dave lost his job with the Dan (it was decided that Fagen's own angst-filled voice best expressed his and Becker's compositions), Carole contacted Dave about collaborating. One of the first lyrics he sent her was a smartly internally rhymed piece about a person coaxing a saxophonist, "Jazzman, take my blues away," which Carole set to an urgent, rocking melody. "Jazzman" would hit #1 and become the second-biggest single she ever recorded ("It's Too Late" being the first). Dave and Carole ended up writing the whole album, which would be titled *Wrap Around Joy,* together. Midway through, Carole paused to have her baby—a boy!—joyfully welcomed by Charlie and her family of daughters. They named him Levi for Charlie's great-uncle (though the Four Tops' lead singer, Levi Stubbs, constituted additional inspiration for selecting the name).

In addition to the hugely successful "Jazzman" (which earned Carole another Grammy nomination), *Wrap Around Joy* yielded a second hit in "Nightingale," on which Carole's daughters Louise and Sherry sang backup. But the fact that none of these songs were wholly written by Carole (or with a collaborator—Gerry or Toni—with whom she'd had a deep, prior fit) put it somewhat at a remove from the soul-baring arc of *Tapestry* and its two offshoots. (The exception: "Change in Mind, Change of Heart," featuring graceful, contemplative lyrics and Carole's wistful delivery and gospel piano chords.) Carole seemed to have been consciously trying to create a crowd pleaser, and by some accounts she succeeded. "I know you're going to be skeptical," Robert Hilburn backhand-complimented, "but Carole King really does finally have another album you're going to like . . . her most fully satisfying work since *Tapestry*." But *Rolling Stone*'s Jon Landau, whose startled enthrallment with *Tapestry* had started it all, ended his trying-to-love-it review by putting his finger on Carole's gathering dilemma: "King . . . [is] forced to live in [*Tapestry*'s] oppressive shadow."

Stepping off the outdo-or-at-least-equal-*Tapestry* treadmill, Carole collaborated with seventy-year-old Brooklynite Maurice Sendak on his animated children's TV special, *Really Rosie*. Sendak, whose sweet, fanciful (and genially perverted) children's books, such as *In the Night Kitchen*, were beloved by progressive parents, had created a nostalgic cartoon opera about the spunky girl he'd glimpsed through his Sheepshead Bay window as a young man. Plunging herself back into her girlhood world, Carole delivered a soundtrack full of *bulabasta* brio, ethnic shtick (including a chorus of "oy vey!"s), and piano pounding on songs with names like "Chicken Soup with Rice," "The Ballad of Chicken Soup," and "Avenue P." *The New York Times*'s John Rockwell, having joined the chorus in feeling that her post-*Tapestry* albums had been "something of a letdown," seemed relieved to be able to rave again: *Really Rosie* was "absolutely delightful."

In 1975 Gerry and Carole once more sat down to write together. Gerry says that Carole wasn't emotional when they were married, "but later she was—later we would get together and talk about old times and she was *very* emotional." Judging from the poignance of the songs they produced now—especially the wistful, elegiac "High Out of Time," which stands as one of their best songs ever—this might well have been the period he was referring to. Carole had reason to be emotional; her marriage to Charlie was crumbling. They had rented a summer house in Malibu, but she ended up living there alone with the girls while he quietly rethought his future. (Charlie left music briefly to try his hand at acting, then to work for an aerobatic airplane dealer—and, in short order, as an aerobatic pilot and flight instructor.) The dissolution of her second marriage led Carole to the tender and unusually personal "Only Love Is Real," in which she invoked "my son and daughters" and expressed regret that she hadn't had the wisdom to have "spared" someone, presumably Charlie, from "giving your youth to me."

Recorded at the end of 1975, and graced by collaborations with Gerry, *Thoroughbred* would be the first solo album she made without Charlie, and her pressing, questing voice seems to be searching the room for that missing comfort. It's as if the tracks (with background help from James Taylor, plus David Crosby and Graham Nash, rendering "High Out of Time" celestial) are saying, Here I am, single again, with four children, adjusting the things that matter to this behemoth: fame; *what is next for me?* Aptly, *Rolling Stone*'s Stephen Holden, hearing the emotion packed into every chord and syllable, called *Thoroughbred*, which was released as the year turned, Carole's "finest album since *Tapestry*"—which was then in its *fifth* year in the Top 200. (Other critics, however, angrily accused her of coasting. *The Washington Post*'s Alex Ward thundered: "For King to wait two years and then come out with more of what we've heard before . . . strikes me as not only unimaginative but also a bit smug.")

Carole closed *Thoroughbred* with an optimistic rouser, "It's Gonna Work Out Fine," which she wrote alone. The song's attitude essentially predicted her first six months of 1976. She had a romance with a lothario of the Canyon and prince of the Troubadour's bar, singer-songwriter J. D. Souther (who'd also had a brief romance with Joni and a long relationship with Linda Ronstadt). She and Stephanie Magrino Fischbach (who was now separated from John) spent the summer of 1976 on the beach with their kids. One day they ran into Bob Dylan's wife, Sara. When Sara heard that Carole was getting a divorce, she wailed: "*I* want a divorce, too! I have five kids with this man!* How do you get one!?" (The Dylans divorced a year later.)

But the lighthearted ease of the summer was not to last.

---

* One child of the five was hers from a previous marriage, whom Dylan adopted.

* * *

"Hey, you smoke cigarettes?" the twenty-year-old "trusty" (that was the prisoner whom the wardens at Idaho's Bonneville County Jail* trusted to take dinners to fellow inmates) asked the new teenage inmate, one day in 1967. "Sure," the inmate, fifteen-year-old Randy Stone, answered. Stone had been arrested for breaking into a train and stealing 150 cases of beer, sentenced to probation, and had broken probation. That's why he was locked up. The "trusty" was Richard Edward Morrison Evers,** a handsome, blond twenty-year-old who'd pleaded guilty to forgery a year earlier and had been sentenced to four years. Even though Evers was risking extra jail time by distributing contraband to a minor, he pushed seven smuggled cigarettes under Stone's cell door. He was proud to be a troublemaker. As his future wife would put it, it was Rick Evers's style to refuse to "blindly accept" the "choices" that authorities doled out to him "as his *only* choices."

Even by local standards, Rick Evers was a "scrapper," his friend, professional cow herder Bruce Stanger, recalls. "He scrapped over girls; he scrapped over cars; he scrapped over horses. Guys in Idaho scrapped, but Rick scrapped *a lot*." He'd grown up "rough and poor," Stanger says. "I don't think his dad was in the picture much. His mom was a waitress for a while." He was a high school dropout who'd spent some of his teen years in St. Anthony's Reform School, a juvenile detention facility in his native Idaho Falls. When he was arrested for the forgery, he'd listed his profession as "radio announcer"; he had a gig at a local station.

Rick was released from jail in late 1967 (and granted final discharge in March 1969); Randy Stone was out, too. A year after Rick cleared his sentence, he went to work for Randy at a Boise head shop Randy

---

* Even though the facility was a jail and not a prison, convicted men sentenced to several-year sentences were incarcerated there.

** On some legal documents "Edward" is given as Evers's middle name; on others, "Morrison" (his mother's maiden name) is.

had opened called Head Quarters. By now Rick—his hair shoulder length, and customarily dressed in bellbottom pants and buckskin shirt—had become the devotee of a hippie spiritual group heavily sprinkled with Native American lore, led by a Denver lay preacher. Like many locals, the religionists—not without reason—believed not only that the nearby desert town of Arco was radioactive (there had been a fatal nuclear accident at the Arco-based Idaho National Engineering and Environmental Laboratory, INEEL, in early 1961) but also that dangerous nuclear experiments were *still* going on there and, most exotically, that INEEL workers had tapped into a secret network of ancient subterranean Indian lagoons that could transport a south Idahoan, *underground,* from Idaho Falls up through Washington and out into the Pacific Ocean.

With its spectral deserts (with such names as Craters of the Moon), majestic mountains, real and imagined underground lagoons, and nuclear myths and perfidy, southern Idaho was a mystique-laden place, and Rick took on his own aura of vague mysticism. But becoming a hippie hadn't calmed the explosive frustration he'd had throughout his young life. Postjail "Rick was a tough guy," Randy Stone, today a house builder and a gemsmith, says, "He was known for breaking a few jaws. He had a part there where he could snap. In fact, I got popped in the mouth by him once. We got into an argument about something stupid and he popped me so hard, all's I saw was black. It was a pretty tough punch. Right after that he split."

In the way that some young Idaho women taxonomized their males—dividing them between "cowboys" and "mountain men"—Evers was the latter. As one native Idahoan, "Cassie" (not her real name), who knew Rick well, puts it, "Cowboys are more 'yes-ma'am': eager-to-please and charming to women, but in a strong way. Mountain men treat their women like squaws: 'Help me pack my gear! Haul some more wood in the house 'cause I'm busy hunting elk.' Not that they aren't charming and wonderful in their own way, but" mountain men like Rick are more difficult, Cassie says.

In the early 1970s Rick Evers was at the center of a small group of

Idaho hippies, young people who didn't have to go *"back"* to any land. They'd grown up amid the state's eighty majestic Ponderosa pine–filled mountain ranges dotted by hidden hot springs and creeks that meandered into rainbow-hued sage-and-alfalfa beds. "Rick was our leader," Cassie says, of the small group of friends gathered into a commune. "He had a stubborn streak and an anger—you didn't want him to get mad—but he was *very* handsome and he was intuitive and he was brilliant and he was wise and he had charisma. He was a sort of guru—he could go right to the core of a situation and be instrumental in making sure that people were happy and that their needs were met." Cassie pauses, then she adds, as if the point was missed: "Rick was our king." Says Roy Reynolds, a cow herder and artist and friend of Rick's, "He was a hippie—unlike a lot of cowboys, I had hippie friends. He had been in trouble all his life; he had some trouble with dope, but when he was straight he was one of the sweetest people I knew—an absolute angel. And he looked like an angel. And," Reynolds adds, "Rick needed love."

By the mid-1970s Evers had gotten his girlfriend pregnant; she left him and moved with their young son to Hawaii. He started hand-tooling leather goods and fringed buckskin jackets, and he fancied himself a guitarist and songwriter. "He did have capabilities and talents," says Bruce Stanger's brother Mike, a musician and artist. "He could make leather goods and he was into music; he was a hummer and a strummer. But Rick's best talent lay in quiet, timely self-promotion—he was the ultimate wannabe."

Around the summer of 1976, Rick spent six weeks on a spiritual retreat in the mountains outside Boise. "He went there alone, with nothing but the clothes on his back—wandering around, adventuring," Cassie recalls. Shortly after that rite, he packed up his leather goods and guitar and took off for L.A. to seek his fortune.

Serendipity struck. "Rick was stranded on the sidewalk of Wilshire Boulevard," Roy Reynolds says, "and he was wearing a beautiful coat he had made and carrying a load of leather and furs. The Eagles happened to be driving down Wilshire and they spotted him." Led by Michigan boy Glenn Frey and Texan Don Henley, the Eagles were not an organic but rather an evolved-in-L.A. group of talented, connected country rock musicians from different disbanded groups whose focal point for years had been the Troubadour's bar. Their at-home-in-Death-Valley image (and bleating-lost-boy-in-expensive-boots sound on "Hotel California," and "Take It Easy") had become era-definingly successful. "They liked Rick's coat," Roy Reynolds continues, "and so they picked him up and took him to a Hollywood party." Maybe Evers seemed like a real cowboy to these pseudo-cowboy millionaires.

Carole had come to know the Eagles through her romance with their close friend J. D. Souther; she was at the same party to which Rick Evers had found himself invited. The superstar and the hitchhiker were immediately attracted to one another. He was undeniably handsome, with his shoulder-length flaxen hair and strong, even features. According to the account Rick gave to a friend, as he and Carole started talking, they both confided that they'd been celibate for a while; then Rick suggested they go back to her house "and be celibate together."

And so it began. "Carole and Rick fell madly in love with each other," says Roy Reynolds, who became one of the closest witnesses to the relationship. "They both had been lonely, and they just . . . found each other."

During their first enraptured weeks together, in what Carole later called "a celebration of our heart-space," they cowrote a song called "Wings of Love," a solemn, over-the-top-romantic ballad about being filled up with a love so deep its "truth" "makes the kingdoms ring." In the song's excruciating earnestness and heightened emotion are hints of a woman losing a grip on judgment and of a man, perhaps, whose intense romanticism so contrasts with his rough-hewn machismo that, in the right eyes, he is spellbinding. In a nod to their overcoming the vast difference of their backgrounds, the song invokes "rainbow people" who "build bridges of life that blend our hearts."

Rick moved in with Carole and the children, and both her puzzled friends and his tried to analyze the heated situation. "He was a dia-

mond in the rough, and I don't know a woman who can resist a diamond in the rough, somebody who's 'worth saving'" is how Roy
Reynolds saw it. "Rick Evers was sure different from those nice Jewish
boys from New Jersey," Danny Kortchmar muses. "It was a big stretch—
this guy from the Rocky Mountains who'd had a rough life." Mike
Stanger agrees: "I'm sure Rick was a romantic creature to Carole. Was
he using her? Well, it was probably mutual. They weren't really using
each other, they were just filling each other's needs. Rick was [eventu-
ally] getting a lot of money"—Randy Stone remembers that he started
driving around in an Excalibur—"and Carole was getting a new life."
Indeed, they began traveling to Idaho, whose wild magnificence Carole
was falling in love with along with the man who was introducing her to
it. People in L.A. saw Carole becoming besotted with Rick. "You would
see her perform," recalls one man on the scene who watched her with
David Crosby and Graham Nash, "and he would always be right offstage in a place where she could see him." There was "an almost Ras-
putinesque, unhealthy magnetism where . . . you'd feel, Carole, are you
sure you know what you're doing here?" ("He just got ahold of me" is
how she would describe her infatuation much later to the wife of a
close bandmate.)

Others were less charmed. The Eagles (for whom Rick made some
garments) viewed him as a hothead. As for Lou Adler, he tersely allowed, "Rick Evers doesn't have one redeeming quality." Carole's
friends couldn't stand him. Rick would get angry for no reason—when,
say, he didn't get "respect" from someone at a party who was talking
to Carole, making him feel excluded. Because Rick's temper was so
hair-trigger, "he would make Carole seem stupid by her having to constantly defuse those situations he was creating," a friend says. "His
attitude was: she's just my bitch. The relationship seemed to go against
everything you knew about her. In social situations, they'd often leave
early to avoid further discord"—and so that Carole could avoid feeling
that he (or she, or their relationship) was being judged by the people
who'd long known her. But from Rick's point of view, "it was hard
for him," Cassie says, "to be such a leader in his world and try to fit

into Carole's world. He only got mad at someone if they attacked his honor." When he talked about Indian spirituality, the people in Carole's circle were unimpressed, even condescending. "He would try to get that stuff to fly, but as soon as he opened his mouth, his foot would get in his tongue's way," one says.

It was obviously awkward for Carole's colleagues and friends to so strongly dislike someone she was clearly madly in love with, and her need to be out of their view may have led to what, in December 1976, the *Los Angeles Times* called a "surprise move": Carole left Lou Adler's Ode label and signed with Capitol Records. *Tapestry* now stood at 13.5 million units sold worldwide (combined sales of all her eight solo albums was a global 20 million) and was no longer just the best-selling *rock* album in history but was now, as the *Times* noted, "the biggest selling album" of *any* genre "in the history of the industry." "We are most honored to welcome Carole King to our organization," said Bhaskar Menon, the president and CEO of Capitol, never imagining that all Carole had spent her life achieving might dissipate by way of one personal decision: Carole would make her albums with Rick now; they would cowrite songs, he would play guitar on her records, and more. Indeed, on the double-fold interior of her next album, *Simple Things* (recorded in spring 1977), the higher photo was not of Carole but of *Rick*, gazing beatifically skyward amid an illustration of galloping horses, as if this hagiographed man is a glorious stallion himself. Lower down and larger, as if she is the dreamer beneath the dream, is a very unflattering photograph of Carole, who looks as homely as he looks beautiful. Yet she's smiling proudly. The effect is discomfiting: an ethnic girl mooning over, as one observer thought of Rick, "the quintessential Hollywood-pretty, blond mountain boy" she has landed.

Rick cowrote the title song, "Simple Things" (which the *L.A. Times*'s Robert Hilburn found "engaging, lilting, and warmly innocent"): a bells-laden, rousingly produced paean to childlike naturalness. But much of the album reflects a woman who feels fully let loose from her past; her newly edgy, deeply felt personal life is finally filling the boots of those dark, bluesy, careworn gospel chords she wrote for Aretha.

The album's loveliest cut, "In the Name of Love" (written wholly by Carole) is dedicated to Willa Mae Phillips, who had recently died and "whose loving energy throughout the years," Carole wrote in the liner notes, "allowed space through which the music could flow." Carole's ex-husband Charlie and John Fischbach had been pallbearers at Willa Mae's funeral. Had Willa Mae been alive when Carole met Rick Evers, it's easy to imagine the kind of talking-to this maternal figure would have forced on Carole.

Early in the summer of 1977 Carole moved with Rick to Idaho. She trundled three-year-old Levi, five-year-old Molly, and a reluctant Sherry, fourteen (who would be enrolled in Boise High School in the fall). Louise, almost seventeen and a half, stayed behind in the Canyon house. She had a boyfriend across the street; she was already beginning to carve out her life as a young adult, as early as her mother had carved out her own adulthood.*

They—that is, Carole—bought a small ranch on a spread of land in an idyllic valley by a stream called Robie Creek. Carole got an Appaloosa named Whiskey so she could ride with Rick every day; and some of the people Cassie had referred to as Rick's followers (Cassie and her boyfriend included) moved into buildings on the property, where Carole and Rick were having a triple-decker dream house built. (It turned out to be a kind of hippie-dippy abode, with little insulation, with astrological signs carved into the wooden door frames, and with egg crates apparently providing primitive soundproofing for the basement music room, but it had a stairway built by a master craftsman.) Financed by Carole and led by Rick, the ranch was a kind of commune. There were meetings around the campfire, fishing in the rivers,

* That life would soon take a somewhat startling turn. Danny Kortchmar, now divorced from Abigail, would, as he puts it, "fall madly in love with Louise" the next year, 1978. They would live together and he would produce her first, self-named album. Abigail was appalled by her ex-husband's romance with a barely of-age girl they'd known since she was nine. Abigail asked Carole: "How could you let this happen?" According to Abigail, Carole replied, "I like Danny." The two women didn't talk for a while.

and many hours spent soaking in the natural hot-spring pools—Levi and Molly anchored between Carole and Rick.

As in the many communes that had proliferated in the West, gender traditionalism reigned. The women (Carole included) baked bread from scratch and canned fruit for winter. Carole had been a city earth mother in Laurel Canyon, so this grittier version was a logical next step. Especially in the early 1970s (Carole was a kind of late entrant to all of this), traveling deeper and deeper into the vortex of authenticity was the thing to do; whether in matters of spirituality, rustic living, or fealty to gurus, the race went to the most untimidly devoted.

Carole acted as birthing coach to some of the women in the commune, and during one complicated birth, a registered nurse named Joy James* was called in to assist; she ended up staying a while. Over weeks of tending the communal garden with Carole, Joy waxed lyrical about a community of cabins she managed farther north, in Burgdorf Hot Springs. Especially in winter Burgdorf was a magical place—snowbound, thirty-five miles from the nearest road—where the cabin renters lived in a primitive simplicity (no electricity, no plumbing) that cleansed their souls. Joy invited Carole to visit.

In August, Carole, her band Navarro, and Rick went on tour. Robert Hilburn attended her Greek Theatre concert, just as he'd attended her first Greek Theatre concert in 1971. But in contrast to his previous rave, his review, headlined "King's 'Tapestry' Wearing Thin," was harshly critical. Carole's fans "did their best to make her return . . . as memorable as her debut there," he wrote, "[b]ut none of the [fans'] enthusiasm hid the fact that this King performance . . . was far less regal than the first." While Hilburn had compliments for some of the tracks from *Simple Things,* he ratified the complaint that other critics had been making over the last several of Carole's albums: "Though each [post-*Tapestry* album] contains some rewards, none has the . . . artistic thrust to stamp it as the work of a major—as opposed to capable—pop

---

* At the time she was known as Joyce, her given name. She later shortened it to Joy, the name she goes by today.

figure." Having heard this so often now, Carole began "to protect my sanity" by thinking of "Carole King" as an outsider. "I would perform . . . and critics would say, 'It was a terrible concert' and I would say, 'He's talking about Carole King, not about *me*.'"

By now she was no longer Carole King, or even Carole Klein/King Goffin Larkey.

Rick had summoned hippie preacher Larry Norton to a clearing in the Boise mountains, where Carole had happily become Carole Evers. When the newlyweds returned to Robie Creek, a sign Sherry painted was draped from the main house's roof: "Welcome Home!" From that point on, the homestead was called Welcome Home Ranch.

And it *did* feel like home to Carole. One day, when the women were canning and gardening and the men were hammering the planks and watering the horses, Carole was seized with the beauty of the commune. "The sight of everyone working together, building things and feeling good—just being friends in the sunshine—was too much for me." She ran to her piano and composed a joyous song, "Everybody's Got the Spirit." Another time Rick wrote a poem about a "sunbird" whose innocent, perfect freedom he—a former jailbird—was emulating. Carole was greatly moved by the words that expressed her husband's striving and she set them to music. The bird was "enough just *be-ing* / fulfilled in its own existence." The two songs would be among those collected in her next album, *Welcome Home*. Its hosanna-chorused title song, about the profound transformation her life has taken with Rick, is one of her most vulnerable, earnest statements, and, largely but not solely for that reason, this almost completely overlooked song is one of her most beautiful. "Welcome Home" is a marker of her emotional and geographical journey in 1978: adventurous, open-hearted—and dangerously naïve.

In January 1978, she and Rick went to L.A. to record *Welcome Home*. The moment was fraught: *Rolling Stone* had just named *Simple Things* "The Worst Album of 1977." To save her plummeting career, Carole had to do the one thing she'd always done so well but which was anathema to Rick: take control of the recording session. L.A. was flush with cocaine, and Rick was flush with Carole's money, with bombast, and with anger. "He was jealous of Carole—*he* wanted to be a star—and he was controlling," says Roy Reynolds, who was with them for much of the trip, serving unofficially as Rick's minder and Carole's protector.

This time, it wasn't good enough for Rick that his image be inside the album jacket, as it had been on *Simple Things*. It had to be on the *cover*. Roy, who already thought that Rick's preachy lyrics were ruining Carole's music, tried to explain to his friend that this was *Carole*'s album, but Rick dug in his heels, and Carole appeased him. As a result, two-thirds of the cover of *Welcome Home* depicts a dashingly handsome, expensively attired hippie cowboy (Rick), commandingly holding the reins of his Appaloosa. Carole's head is way down in the lower right corner: under Rick, under the horse's belly, she's ducking beneath a wooden fence rail.

From January to mid-March, when Rick and Carole were commuting from L.A. to the ranch and back (the dream house was finished in February, and the builder etched a note into the wood, near the astrological signs, declaring that he'd built the house "for Carole Evers"), even Rick's acolytes were worried by his drug-fueled temper. "Rick had an addictive personality and we could see it get out of hand," says Cassie. "He was *powerfully angry*. We were all concerned; we were talking. But Rick wasn't the kind of person where you could say, 'Hey, knock it off, dude.' He was definitely steering his own ship. He had a stubborn streak. And he was our leader."

Powerless to force her to leave Rick, Carole's friends eased their tremendous worry about her safety by making dark jokes about chipping in and hiring a hit man to get rid of him.

By March Rick was snorting and shooting every drug he could get his hands on, and "he was *begging* me to stop him," Roy says. "I was doing everything I could to get him off the stuff," including rounding up and hauling off all the drugs and syringes "in a big sack" and dumping them in a Laurel Canyon Boulevard garbage bin. But the intervention proved futile. "Rick was shooting up between his toes because that was the only part of his body left." Carole had known benign, gentlemanly drug addicts—James Taylor and Joel O'Brien—but the ravages that Rick was going through were horribly new to her. (Some of Rick's Idaho friends were sadly unsurprised by his unraveling. Given Rick's emotional set and grandiosity, "he was in way over his head" with a famous wife. "He didn't have a chance" of coping less chaotically with the stressors and temptations, says Bruce Stanger.)

On March 19, Roy interceded, alarmed by a drugged-up, stormingly jealous and angry Rick. "I took Carole and put her on a plane, the next day, to Hawaii," Roy says. Carole's friends were greatly relieved. The day after she flew to the islands—on March 21, 1978—Rick went to a Beverly Hills apartment (perhaps a dealer's or a drug buddy's) and shot himself up. Speed, coke, heroin: "Everything you could possibly think of was found in his blood," says Roy, who was called by the police to identify the body. It was never determined if the death was a suicide (there was no note), an accidental overdose (this is Roy's belief), or if some angry dealer "popped him—gave him bad dope or too much dope because Rick owed the guy money." Roy had Rick cremated, in accordance with his wishes, and he sprinkled his ashes at Robie Creek.

Released in May, *Welcome Home* was a memorial to Rick Evers. Family-album-style photos of Carole and Rick, with Molly and Levi, filled a four-page inset, and Carole wrote a eulogy in the liner notes. Rick, she wrote, "often stretched beyond what some of us could understand. He didn't always do 'sensible' things. He often got angry and frustrated about things that many of us couldn't see." But, she made clear, there was another facet. "He had more love to give than anyone I've ever known." This side of Carole's troubled man was one her friends did not see, but then, love is as much a locked box of esoteric intimacy that dissolves when it meets air as listening to a song is.

Carole's friends assumed that this would be the end of the Idaho mountain men in her life. They were dead wrong.

Carole returned to Robie Creek, but amid the painful memories (and Rick's ashes), she knew she couldn't stay there. So she took Joy James up on her offer to see the former gold mining ghost town at Burgdorf Hot Springs. She, Molly, and Levi stayed in one of the tiny

nineteenth-century log cabins near the large hot springs pool, surrounded by a meadow full of calving elks ringed by the tall pines of a
national forest. "Carole had an epiphany there," says Joy James. She
wanted to "winter in": to be snowbound in acerbic simplicity. This rite
would be boot camp, meditation lodge, escape from her now-loathed
L.A.–and, perhaps, since she may have felt her fame had exacerbated
Rick's volatile frustration, penance. A barter was arranged: Carole
could have a cabin in return for agreeing to watch the place when Joy
was out–to check on guests and order helicopter rescue from the forest
service in life-threatening situations. "Molly and Levi were so excited
when Carole told them," Joy recalls. "They said, 'You mean we get to
spend the whole winter making snowmen?!'"

A man Joy knew was crashing on her cabin floor during Carole's
summer stay. His name was Rick Sorensen, but everyone called him
Teepee Rick because he was a kind of survivalist. Teepee Rick was a
big, strapping, rough-hewn thirty-two-year-old whose face and stringy
long hair made people think he looked like Jesus. He was originally
from the Chicago area and had taught school in Hailey (near Sun
Valley), but his civilized ways were long gone. For seven years, he'd
been living in a teepee in the mountains, surviving by what he killed. A
bear he'd shot between the eyes became his tent rug; the buffalo he
killed provided the meals he cooked over fire kindled in wood he
chopped; even the elk hide of his fringed buckskins was procured
through his old-fashioned muzzle loader. Teepee Rick hated the federal
government and he hated the forest service. "He was an alpha male, a
warrior, quite a dominating man," says Joy–so much so, that she didn't
like having sustained time with him (it always led to confrontation), but
she'd let him crash on her cabin floor for these few days and hunt in
the adjacent woods.

When Carole saw Teepee Rick outside Joy's window, she excitedly
asked to meet him. Joy made the introductions, and, as she recalls: "It
was just like a lightning bolt. Everyone else [in the cabin] wanted to
stand back because it was so profound–it was electric." Though no last
names were exchanged, Teepee Rick may have known who she was–

"Gossip travels in the backcountry air faster than by telephone," Joy says, "but, trust me, he didn't care [that a famous woman was in the area] because he had a beautiful lady, named Chris, who he was living with. But there was just *such chemistry* between [him and Carole]."

A few hours later, everyone was in the hot pool and one by one they left to go back to their cabins. According to what Carole told Joy, as Carole stood to leave, Teepee Rick grabbed her ankle and–me-Tarzan-you-Jane-style–demanded, "Where are *you* going?"

And that was the beginning of what would be Carole's time with the man her friends would call Rick Two (Rick Evers being Rick One)–and her half-dozen years of seriously Going Native in the wilds of Idaho.

Welcome Home was the first Carole King album that was not a chart hit–a huge comedown for her and the beginning of what some music historians would call her "lost years." After spending much of the summer at Burgdorf, she embarked on a small East Coast concert tour, concentrating on her classic, loved hits–"Will You Love Me Tomorrow," "I Feel the Earth Move"–a reliable formula she would now come to favor. She seemed to be looking for support ("Miss King's gushing love for her fans–and their return of it–cloyed at times," said *The New York Times*) and for buoyance ("and so did her consistently upbeat renditions of songs whose original recorded versions expressed . . . considerable sorrow," the *Times* continued) to offset what a confidante during those years calls the "deep, deep depression" she was sinking into and would remain gripped by for several years.

Despite or between these East Coast concert dates, she had had a winter's supply of food and clothes moved up to Burgdorf; then, before the roads became impassible, she and the children settled into their cabin. Joy was surprised to see that Rick Sorensen had become, as she puts it, "part of the family." If she'd known this combative man had been part of Carole's package, she might have thought twice about making the arrangement with Carole. As it turned out, Sorensen had broken up with his girlfriend Chris, who "took it very hard," Joy says, "just crying and crying, riding through the meadow." Joy adds: "Rick Sorensen is very hard on his women."

With the (admittedly considerable) exception of her full-length mink coat, Carole wintered in at Burgdorf like all the more modest cabin dwellers. She used the outhouse. She bought two goats to eat her family's garbage, tying them to the common outdoor stanchion. "And she'd be down there milking the goats in thirty-degrees-below-zero weather at five in the morning," says Joy, adding that "it got so cold that winter, your hair would freeze between getting out of the hot pool and walking back into your cabin." A fire was all that kept Carole and the children warm inside, and a kerosene lamp lit the small room where Carole homeschooled Molly and Levi. She washed her dishes outside, from the hot water spout under the hot pool. Rick killed buffalo, of course, and Carole broke her vegetarian regimen by making buffalo stew (she also made "delicious" goat milk yogurt, says Joy). Sometimes, when four feet of snow fell overnight, people skied off their cabin roofs. In one letter that Cynthia Weil received, Carole apologized for her delayed reply: "It took me a while to write back because we were snowed in and I had to walk three miles in snow shoes to mail this to you." In the same way that Joni Anderson's secret pregnant-and-penniless travails were more dramatic than Bobby Zimmerman's weeks reading old newspapers in the New York Public Library, Carole King's quiet embrace of the rugged West was more authentic than, say, the Hollywood Hills–dwelling Eagles' photo shoots amid parched coyote skulls.

Joy had problems with Teepee Rick. He sawed through the historic cabin wall so he could visually track the elk herd; he barked at the snowboarders. The worst confrontation was when he stormed over to the hot pool, brandishing a gun, angry that nonresidents (a group of *elderly* folks Joy had invited in) were enjoying the waters. ("But he had the good sense to apologize," Joy says.) Carole, Joy could see, was growing "very in love with Rick," but toward winter's end Joy was annoyed at this man who, as she viewed him, was "a warrior and he always needs to have a war." She angrily skied out of Burgdorf, leaving the cabins for Carole to manage.

After the roads had thawed out enough, Cynthia Weil, Barry Mann, and Brooks and Marilyn Arthur arrived for a visit. The reunion was like a sitcom, with the New York–to–L.A. former Brill Building–ites sti- fling gulps at Carole's new life. (They had missed the Rick One chapter so they weren't prepared.) "The outhouse!" exclaims Cynthia. "Rick didn't like us. He was not happy that we were there; he was not very friendly; he really wanted to cut her off from some of her old friends." Brooks had brought $200 worth of nuts and dried fruit, but in no time his stash was gone; the others kept dipping into it. There was some-thing about the fresh-killed buffalo meat Carole made for dinner that was less than irresistible. Reboarding the plane for L.A., the group thought: Now, *that* was an adventure . . .

Carole released three albums in the next two years—*Touch the Sky* in 1979 and *Pearls* in 1980, both on Capitol, and *One to One* in 1981, on At-lantic. By this time, Capitol had dropped her. Only *Pearls,* which was comprised of her and Gerry's classics, gained any traction; Carole's rendition of "One Fine Day" was a hit single. But between the album-making forays to big or medium-sized cities, Carole's life was mostly enmeshed with Rick in the deep forest. In 1981 she purchased a former dude ranch and mining camp, the Robinson Bar Ranch, on 118 acres of forest in Custer County, Idaho. Sixteen miles from the tiny town of Stanley, it afforded the kind of solitude Rick liked. Carole milked her cows and Rick went out shooting, and his pugnacious distrust of the government and outsiders eventually led them both—she as much as he—into a protracted, volatile legal battle with the county and the U.S. Forest Service, as well as the locals, over their locking the gate to a road, long taken for public, that ran through their property.

This was a new Carole: one who accused a forest service officer of shoving her twice and purposely turning off the electricity when she and Rick were searching for land deeds in the government office files, and one who threatened to send the forest service (when they denied the use of her land for grazing) cow dung to prove that she and Rick were running a livestock operation. Joy had said that Teepee Rick was a warrior always looking for a war. Well, he had found one, and Carole joined him in it, applying the same determination she'd used to get the cellos onto the Shirelles track to fighting for her property and privacy rights. A forest service officer remarked, during the long battle: "With Carole it's all or nothing . . . She can't take no for an answer. She's a strong-willed person and will push and shove for her beliefs, come hell or high water." Danny Kortchmar (now his friend's de facto son-in-law through his relationship with Louise) was confused. *Why* was Carole packing a .44 automatic? *Why* was she so up in arms about some road? Obliquely referring to this new attitude, Lou Adler has said, "Carole has gone through a lot of changes, a lot of it depending on who the man in her life was." Carole wrote a song called "Golden Man" for Rick Sorensen, praising him for teaching her the "pain" of the earth. In its emotional, torch-singer-like long cadences, she calls him "*son,* lover, brother, father, and friend." The lyrics are as exceedingly romantic as her songs for Rick Evers had been. Toward the end of the summer in 1982, in a sunrise ceremony in their mountains, Carole King made Rick Sorensen her fourth husband. He was identified in the local papers as the "foreman" on her ranch. (Later, in rare articles, he was re-ferred to as "her husband, rancher Richard Sorensen," the big-city media seemingly assuming that Carole had become the trophy wife of some wealthy landowner.)

Carole called a local radio station to announce her marriage to Rick while they were at a government office, filing papers in their battle with the county. The statement she gave was not what you'd expect from a woman announcing a marriage. It was wounded and defensive, reflect-ing the rancor building up against her in the community—and perhaps locals' whispers about whether Rick Evers's death had been an acci-dent, a suicide, or foul play: "My music and my life shine like a beacon in the forest of lies and the sea of rumors." In this new strand of her life tapestry, Carole—angrily hiding from the overwhelming and unsought fame for which the critics seemed to have punished her, and feeling, Roy Reynolds says, "deep hurt"—stripped her life down until it was as dark and pure as the woods. She now answered to "Carole Sorensen," and she would soon express, to the rare interviewer who found her, both the triumph and wound-licking comfort that this new land and identity was giving her: "When I first moved here I used to be afraid of getting away from my house and going up into the woods, where all the boogie creatures were going to get me. Now I realize the boogie creatures are in civilization, and you're perfectly safe in the woods."

"We love you, Carole!" "Sing 'Up on the Roof!'" "You've got a friend, Carole!" those 70,000 fans had screamed at Central Park in 1973. When she returned home in 1984, the bemused headline of Stephen Holden's *New York Times* review relayed the irony: "Back for a Night at Town Hall: Carole King of Idaho."

CHAPTER FOURTEEN

joni

1972 – 1982

Joni has said that her post-*Blue* months alone in her house in British Columbia, where she repaired to write the songs for *For the Roses*, were a retreat from "severe depression" and, as her second husband, Larry Klein, puts it, "her existential grief" about the baby. She armed herself with her bible *Thus Spake Zarathustra*, and more. "Before leaving L.A.," she has said, "I bought out all the psychology and philosophy departments of two major bookstores. But, ultimately, those books didn't help. I sat there in the bush, throwing those books at the wall, saying, 'Bullshit! Bullshit!'" Then the cure came magically, naturally, and spontaneously:

> I jumped off a rock into this dark emerald green water with yellow kelp in it and purple starfish at the bottom. It was very beautiful, and as I broke up to the surface of the water, which was black and reflective, I started laughing. Joy had just suddenly come over me, you know? And I remember that as a turning point. First feeling like a loony because I was out there laughing all by myself in this beautiful environment. And then, right on top of that was the realization that what-

401

ever my social burdens were, my inner happiness was still
intact.

That sure makes a great story. If only it were so simple.

At the very beginning of 1972 Joni left Canada to embark on a concert tour, making a triumphant return to Carnegie Hall, playing the Midwest, England, and returning to L.A. to record *For the Roses,* as well as
to perform at McGovern rallies. *For the Roses* would be her first album
on her friend (and her manager Elliot Roberts's business partner) David
Geffen's new label, Asylum. Geffen, who'd started out as a mailroom boy
like Elliot had, was now a wealthy young man. He bought Julie Andrews's house on Copley Drive, a manicured wedge of Beverly Hills near
Bel Air, and asked Joni (who'd been subletting her Lookout Mountain
house for a pittance to friend Ron Stone) to be his roommate.

Joni consented. Yes, she and David had had their art-vs.-commerce
differences. She'd written what she called her only "blatantly commercial" song, "You Turn Me On, I'm a Radio," to placate David's desire for
her to have a hit on *For the Roses.* (Her instincts, and his implicit goad-
ing, proved correct: with it, she reached #25 on *Billboard.*) But moving
in with him didn't mean she'd have to stop playing the superior, ag-
grieved creator to his commercial kingpin. Beneath their differences, she
liked David. She wrote a song, "Free Man in Paris," in his honor. In it, a
pressured executive who'd been "stoking the star-maker machinery" goes
to Paris to feel—that unlikely first adjective had an elegant flightiness—
"unfettered and alive."

On her early-1972 tour, Joni's opening act was someone whose debut
album David was about to release: Jackson Browne.

The son of a journalist father and teacher mother, Jackson (who'd
dispensed with his first name, Clyde, just as Joni had ditched Roberta)
had run in the same circles as Joni in California. But originally there'd
been a glamour and status disparity. When she was the girl among the
boys—leaving David Crosby for Graham Nash—teenage Jackson and his
friend Ned Doheny were essentially "Crosby, Stills and Nash *groupies,*"
says a woman on the scene. Jackson was disconcertingly fair-faced,

teen-actor handsome, with chiseled features and a credulous, androgynous prettiness. But despite his time in the Nitty Gritty Dirt Band, he'd been less a performer than a writer—and a good one. David Crosby loved his songs. Jac Holzman had given him a publishing contract, and, of course, Tom Rush had recorded a song of his on his *Circle Game*. Most recently, from a rented house in rundown Silver Lake, Jackson had worked hard to craft a body of signature pieces with which to launch himself as an artist. Sending a glossy headshot (along with an almost obsequious letter) to Geffen, who was not yet "out" but *was* gay, hadn't hurt. Jackson Browne was almost too pretty to be a rock star, but now, even at a mere twenty-three, he was, by the day's standards, a seasoned songwriter, and that prettiness helped rather than hurt.

Jackson was a romantic; "I got my heart crushed about eight times in a row. It would happen every two years or so," he said in the early 1970s. As a barely-eighteen-year-old, he'd fallen for Nico, the stunning, decadent queen of the Max's Kansas City night, who, he would complain, seven years later, "*used* me, man; she fucked me around!" He'd had a romance with a very opposite kind of woman, Laura Nyro—musically brilliant, but zaftig, reclusive, socially insecure, and easily wounded. Most recently, he'd been in love with Salli Sachse, the San Diego–raised beach movie actress who'd been part of Peter Tork's "artistic collective" and a close friend of David Crosby's lady, Christine Hinton. Beautiful, long-haired Salli exuded an air of sorrow; she'd weathered not just Christine's sudden death, but earlier that of her husband, Peter Sachse, who had perished in a stunt-plane crash. As Browne wrote of her, in his song "Something Fine," Salli "took good care" of him during their love affair in London before she hit the road, as girls, of course, were wont to do, for Morocco.

Jackson Browne was released in early 1972. The album's cover showed the artist in a faux-antique tinted picture, his name semicircling the photo in Old West typeface. Like James Taylor on his debut album, Browne evoked an earlier era with his piercing-eyed, Civil War poster-worthy countenance. "Jackson was a West Coast version of James; James is an East Coast version of Jackson" is how Russ Kunkel characterizes them. Indeed, if James's songs exuded Carolina and the snowy turnpike from Stockbridge to Boston, it was the car culture anomie of his native Orange County that surged through Browne's songs, which nonetheless attained a stirring eloquence that was hinted at in their beseeching, quasi-biblical titles ("Doctor My Eyes," "Rock Me on the Water"). His huge, Springsteen-like hit "Running on Empty" and his coauthorship, with Glenn Frey, of the Eagles' megahit "Take It Easy," which emblemized the male mid-1970s, were more literal evocations of Browne's provenance. In early 1972 Bud Scoppa in *Rolling Stone* called *Jackson Browne* that "rare album sufficient to place a new performer among the first rank of . . . artists."

Still, during the very first dates of Joni's tour, the local reviewers, who didn't know of Jackson's album, dismissed him. (The *Detroit News,* while generally praising Joni, called Jackson's performance "inexcusable.") By the time they got to England, Joni was still the "high priestess," as one British critic put it, but Jackson was now viewed as the intriguing comer, since his infectiously rocking "Doctor My Eyes" had become a major U.S. hit. When Jackson and Joni duetted on "The Circle Game," fans saw a chemistry between them. By the end of the tour, Jackson was a full-fledged headliner and "Joni and Jackson were together," Danny Kortchmar recalls. (That fact probably made it easier for her to be in James's company, now that James was virtually engaged to Carly.) "Jackson and I are in love" is how Joni put it to her old flame Roy Blumenfeld when he visited L.A.

Jackson had the same twinness with Joni that James Taylor had exuded two years earlier. Both were beautiful, high-cheekboned WASPs who wrote angst-laden songs. They had bits of background in common: both their mothers had been teachers, and Jackson's maternal grandparents, like Joni's paternal ones, were Norwegian immigrants to midwestern North America. Ultimately, though, none of this mattered. "She just fell for him," says a confidante.

* * *

For the Roses was released in the fall of 1972, and the reviews were ecstatic. Of the album whose chord progressions would be called "mind-
boggling," *The New York Times* raved, "Each of Mitchell's songs . . . is a
gem glistening with her elegant way with language, her pointed
splashes of irony and her perfect shaping of images." The *Times* articulated what her fans had come to realize [emphasis added]: "*Never does
Mitchell voice a thought or feeling commonly.* She's a songwriter of
genius who can't help but make us feel we are not alone." Stephen
Davis of *Rolling Stone* operatically wrote, "Love's tension is Joni Mitchell's medium—she molds and casts it like a sculptress, lubricating this
tense clay with powerful emotive imagery and swaying hypnotic music
that sets her listener up for another of her great strengths, a bitter facility with irony and incongruity"; he went on to praise her "gorgeous
piano lin[es]" and, respectfully using the new feminist-speak, her "large
dose of Woman Truth." Less obsequiously (Ellen Willis was his girlfriend; he must have felt politically secure), *The Village Voice*'s Robert
Christgau noted, "Sometimes her complaints about the men who have
failed her sound petulant, but the appearance of petulance is one of the
prices of liberation."

Though she was mainly living at Geffen's, by the end of 1972 Joni
also rented an apartment in West Hollywood, on one of those sharply
hilly streets between Santa Monica and Sunset that shoot into the Hollywood Hills. Things were not going well between her and Jackson. "It was
a high-strung relationship," says a confidante. Nevertheless, Joni remained in love with Jackson. Newly lionized, handsomer now that time
had slightly lined his baby face, well placed in the Troubadour-Canyon
elite ("*Everybody* loved him," Joni's friend remembers her feeling), six
years younger than she: the power was shifting, and all her worshipful
reviews wouldn't change that. When she first came to the Canyon, she'd
been the awe-inspiring queen. Now, the gravity of sexism (or reality) had
pulled her down a notch. *He* had the advantage.

One night at the Troubadour bar Jackson Browne saw a beautiful
young blonde being screamed at by her boyfriend. Browne interceded in
her defense ("I was doing my very best Bogart" is how he put it, in his

"Ready or Not"), and the boyfriend threw a punch at Browne. Browne's gallantry was rewarded; he went home with the damsel in distress, a Southern California girl who, with her mother's booking and chaperoning assistance, had recently been a successful model in Europe. Her name was Phyllis Major.

Jackson's attention to Phyllis Major felt, to Joni, like "a great loss and a great mind-fuck," says her confidante. One night Joni was at her apartment on that hilly street, expecting Jackson to come over. He didn't show up.

After that, Joni got a recommendation from David Geffen. "She went to a 'think tank' for therapists" in a residential setting, the confidante says, "and the head guy said to pick the [therapist] you want to work with." Joni wrote "Trouble Child" about this experience. In the song, whose airy, hazy melody and long pull on every fourteenth beat mimic the effect of sedation, she writes of being "up in a sterilized room," rendered "weak" and "spacey." She refers to her dogged depression, which has kept her in torpor and which rules out her ability to "give love," even though she knows she "need[s] it." The indignity of psychiatric intervention, for a strong, proud person like Joni, snaps through the lyrics; no wonder she's called these songs of *Blue, For the Roses,* and *Court and Spark,* her next album, "scrapings of my soul." (Still, many critics didn't know how autobiographically she was speaking. *Rolling Stone*'s Jon Landau, for example, would catch the "tragic" story being told in "Trouble Child," but he assumed its "infinite compassion" was trained on someone else.)

During this same postbreakdown moment, she wrote "People's Parties"—complex, its lyrics "through-composed," like many of *Blue*'s songs—to describe the acute self-consciousness she had still not overcome. Now the parties weren't hang-loose Canyon gatherings but Hollywood bashes that she attended with the likes of Beatty, whom she'd unwittingly shared with Carly. Some of her gaffes at these parties were funny, at least in retrospect. Joni went with Beatty to Hugh Hefner's one night and slipped off her clothes to skinny-dip in a pool on what *seemed* to be a totally deserted part of the estate, only to find herself stuck, in the water, *nude*, while the entire party moved poolside. In her telling, she bolted from the water, dressed, got in her car to drive off, only to run out of gas. The experience left her mortified. But more often she was the deft observer at such fetes. As she'd limned the Ibiza party on the red-dirt road, she dissected the stylish people with "passport smiles . . . giving to get something."

Her near-simultaneously written "The Same Situation" is thought by at least one of her subsequent boyfriends, Dave Naylor, to be Joni's Warren Beatty song, just as "You're So Vain" was Carly's. Tucked inside this sensitive song about her unceasing "search for love" lies a Me Decade celebrity-romance chess game. A bored playboy who's gone through an infinite number of desirable women now fixes his "gaze" on her. *She's* blasé as well, having been, "for so many years" now, in that "same situation" of being desired and narcissistically pampered (those ringing phones, those proffered mirrors), and she assumes they're equal. The man is an earnest, cerebral, let's-really-communicate sort. With Joni, brutal candor is best withheld for her songs, where she keeps all the power, so his pseudo-caring entreaty that they be "truthful" is as threatening as if it had come from "the church . . . a cop . . . [or] a mother." When she obligingly lets down her guard, he turns around and uses her candor as a "weapon" against her. By now, she's snared; she craves his "approval." Game over.

Meanwhile, as Joni was recovering from her breakdown in the sophisticated, hip Hollywood fishbowl, Jackson was making a life with Phyllis Major. Phyllis had quickly become pregnant, and their baby boy, Ethan, was born in early November 1973.

Joni remained deeply angry at Jackson for years. Said percussionist Don Alias, who became her serious boyfriend for several years in the late 1970s, "She really had this hatred of Jackson Browne; the whole Jackson Browne thing was really heavy for her." A woman very close to Joni was left with the belief that "you may have to be very strong to take on Jackson—from what I've heard he's a classic example of someone who has a Madonna-and-whore complex." (However, Jackson's pre-Joni girlfriend Salli Sachse experienced nothing negative in their relationship.)

The Jackson Browne story had a tragic dimension that kept it smoldering for Joni. Shortly before or after she married Jackson (in December 1975, two years after their son was born), Phyllis Major attempted suicide. People in their immediate circle knew about the attempt; among other things, she'd discreetly stolen drugs from them for that purpose. "Phyllis went around and gathered up everything," says one woman who was a close friend. "I had some chloral hydrate"—a sedative—"and a little vial of opium, and she just scooped up everything. She left notes for everybody—to me, to Jackson—saying 'I'm sorry' and words to the effect of, 'I can't stand the pain.'" Phyllis was revived in time. But then, on March 25, 1976, with two-and-a-half-year-old Ethan and the nanny in an adjacent room, Phyllis succeeded in taking enough drugs to kill herself. "It was terrible, just terrible," says the friend. The tragedy was a brushfire through their circle, which Joni memorialized in a coded reference in her 1976 "Song for Sharon" on *Hejira*. Their friend had "drowned" herself—perhaps, Joni noted with an esoteric pointedness, to "*punis[h]* somebody."*

Joni attended Phyllis Major Browne's funeral in Santa Barbara (Jackson was angry that she'd come), and the parallel struck her deeply and bitterly. *She* had made a suicide attempt over Jackson; Phyllis had tried and failed. And now Phyllis had succeeded.

Years after that, in September 1992, Jackson Browne's longtime girlfriend, actress Daryl Hannah, accused him of beating her up. The widely reported alleged incident (its notoriety had spiked when Daryl's ex- and future boyfriend John Kennedy Jr. came to her rescue and flew her back

---

* "Song for Sharon" is a mélange of many references. Named for a childhood friend, Sharon Bell, who shared young Joni's enamorment with weddings, it is, like three other songs on *Hejira,* about recovering from, mourning, and coming to terms with her breakup from subsequent boyfriend John Guerin (with whom she *did* have a noisy blowup "at"—or at least near—"the North Dakota junction"). It describes her search for a mandolin in Staten Island with her friend Joel Bernstein; it presents a chorus of real-life close females—her housekeeper, Dora, her best friend, Betsy Asher, and her mother—advising her on how to use her ample free time as an unattached single woman, while, she admits, all she really wants to do is "find another lover." *And* it tells, namelessly, of Phyllis Major Browne's suicide.

to New York) remained murky for months after, with no charges ever pressed by Hannah, with Browne and his friends denying he'd struck her (the incident was "grievously misreported," says a Browne fan site), and with a flurry of contradictory accounts by after-the-fact witnesses and authorities.* It was after this scandal that Joni went public with her anger at Jackson Browne by way of "Not to Blame," her song about domestic violence on *Turbulent Indigo*. It mentions his recent news-making fight with Hannah, his denial of beating her, and his friends' support of him. *Obviously*—Joni sings, with hurt and anger—he was "not to blame"; surely, the woman brought it on herself. The song is unusually biting. (In a questionable move, Joni describes a child seemingly meant to be three-year-old Ethan Browne in a gratuitously negative light.) It then moves from (the unnamed) Daryl to (the unnamed) Phyllis, and recalls a scene at Phyllis's "lonely little grave," where the funeral guests didn't shed tears for their friend and didn't blame Jackson for her death.**

Joni went back to living with Geffen, and she planned her next album, *Court and Spark,* which would include the three veiled songs about the Jackson-centered breakdown, as well as the baleful "The Same Situation." The album's title song opened with some of the most arresting

---

*   Daryl Hannah's uncle, cinematographer Haskell Wexler, claimed to have seen Daryl in the hospital after the incident with "ugly black bruises on her eye and chin and on her ribs" and asserted, in a letter to *Us* magazine, that "Jackson beat Daryl." Browne responded to Wexler, in part: "I did not beat [Daryl]" and offered to "describe Daryl's actions to you and then judge for yourself as to how these injuries may have occurred." A November 1992 statement by the Santa Monica Police Department said: "We went to the house where Jackson Browne lives regarding a possible disturbance. We resolved the situation in about five minutes. There was never any assault. There are no charges pending and no prosecution sought by or intended by the District Attorney."

**   Shortly after the song's release in 1994, Jackson Browne gave a radio interview in response to the song. He said that Joni was a troubled person; he added that she had "never gotten over" him. Though the first statement is understandably defensive, the *second* statement (coming from a mature musical icon and social activist) sounded tackily boastful—unless, of course, one understood what was there but *unsaid,* that she had never gotten over how she'd put herself at risk because of her feelings for him.

images she'd ever conceived, describing love as showing up like a scavenger on a porch, "with a sleeping roll and a madman's soul."

Joni started doing demo recordings of the songs of *Court and Spark,* with Henry Lewy assisting as usual, in the summer of 1973. Russ Kunkel was signed on as drummer, but, with these new songs, something wasn't working. "I was trying to lead [Russ] through this piece of music, and there were grace notes and subtleties and things that I thought were getting kind of buried because Russell has a great, strong kind of rock style," Joni has said. "Russ said, 'Joni, I can't play to this music. I think you should get yourself a jazz drummer.'" So Joni went around to jazz clubs with Lewy, and at a club called the Hot Potato she listened to the jazz-rock fusion group L.A. Express, led by saxophonist Tom Scott (who'd played on *For the Roses*). Scott's group was brought in to work on *Court and Spark* (they were finishing up an album of their own in the adjacent studio); its drummer—Kunkel's replacement as the album's heartbeat—happened to be one of the best young jazz drummers in L.A., John Guerin.

Guerin, thirty-three, had grown up in San Diego after spending the first three years of his life in Hawaii, the son of a navy man. (Having been a toddler during the Japanese strike at Pearl Harbor, he recalled that for years after "whenever I heard a siren, I'd go looking for a tree to run under.") Guerin played only jazz; he listened only to jazz; he was a "jazz snob" who had worked with most of the greats—Ella Fitzgerald, Sarah Vaughan, Frank Sinatra, Carmen McRae. "The only one I missed"—she'd died a year before he'd turned pro—"was Billie Holiday," Guerin said (speaking, here and throughout, in an interview that he gave for this book four months before his January 2004 death). When Scott proposed they work with Joni, Guerin thought: What am I doing backing a *folk*singer?

But when he listened to her songs, he was awestruck. "She was the whole orchestra in one guitar!"

As they sat directly across from one another during the weeks of sessions—Joni in her glass half-isolation booth—an intense connection developed. John was a sexy guy with a wide, pug nose, toothy devilish grin (telegraphing his wild ways), and a mop of thick dark hair, like Warren Beatty would soon sport in *Shampoo,* only messier. He and Joni played to each other, voice to beat, eye to eye—a *click!* that, in Guerin's experience, was often struck between two bell-jarred session musicians, regardless of gender, who found themselves really cooking. Joni, he realized, was *no* folksinger—or *any* kind of conventional singer or composer. "You didn't go whistling Joni's tunes. They were much more complicated; not A-A-B-A form, not Gershwin. Joni's songs didn't have the usual hook; she would form the music to her lyrical thought and sometimes go across bars and in different time signatures—she didn't care." Guerin and the others in the Express went along with her plan, puzzled at first. "But then it *all* made sense. It really did."

"Court and Spark"—the stark a cappella opening lines of the poem (delivered in Joni's chain-smoking-lowered voice) unexpectedly opening up into a kick-ass, wailing-sax, full-band blow-out—announces right away that this is no typical Joni Mitchell album. For "Help Me" and "Free Man in Paris" she marries her signature vocal bends to a jazzy, commercial feel. "Raised on Robbery" is a boogie-woogie-bugle-boy-tinged rocker. "Car on a Hill" has movie sound effects; "Make it sound like cars and traffic!" Joni had ordered Tom Scott and slide guitarist Wayne Perkins—and they *did.* The juxtaposition of dark, crashing "car" horns with sugary, girl-group backup on the "*climb*-ing"s gives the song a mysterious, ironic, likable energy. One reviewer called it "wrenching." Her three vulnerability songs ("The Same Situation," "Trouble Child," and "People's Parties") are joined in pensiveness by "Down to You" and leavened by the balmy, bemused "Just Like This Train" (with its witty locomotive metaphor for her history of being emotionally high-maintenance—"shaking into town / with the brakes complaining") and her Carly-esque fantasy of "dreaming of the pleasure" of taking a vain man down a peg. She closes by channeling her teenage role model, Annie Ross, in "Twisted"; she uses Cheech and Chong (*"No driver on the top?!"*) to have some bebop-chorus fun with it. Joni had needed a band of guys to shake her out of her blues (today, she has a group of pool-playing buddies she's dubbed the Sunday Boys, for this same reason), and the jazz-rock listener-friendliness (sometimes just barely skirting TV-soundtrack slickness) of this album lofted Joni to a new commercial dimension and buoyed her to emotional health. *This* was her plunge into the Canadian waters.

Guerin, who was divorced, had dated lots of singers, but they'd merely interpreted material. "Joan was a different kind of animal," he said. She *created*. "A lot of" what he fell in love with "had to do with her out-and-out talent. I was amazed at her talent for most of our relationship. She didn't have patience for repetition or rules. I never paid attention to lyrics before; I listened to a singer's timbre or phrasing or the quality of her voice. Boy, she changed that for me! She opened up my ears to *words*. For Chrissakes, she turned me on to *James Taylor*"—whom he'd never listened to, on jazz-snob principle—"who I love!

"And I taught her things, in exchange. She learned what the rhythm section does—she'd never paid any attention to that, or to jazz, for that matter." John played her a steady diet of Horace Silver and Miles Davis and "definitely Coltrane. She just drank it in—which she does; she's self-taught, like I am. It was a wonderful trade."

But the key to the trade was their personalities. Joni was only half out of her depression when they met, and John's down-to-earth (and hell-raising) quality seemed to pull her the rest of the way out. As she later put it in "Refuge of the Roads" (one of her favorite of her own songs), he was the "friend of spirit" who "mirrored me back, simplified." He, too, saw their fit that way; "Joan's a very complicated person and I'm a pretty straightahead guy. I think she lightened up a lot with me"—even though, as she put it in the song, their "perfection would always be denied." Says a close friend, "It was a very turbulent, highly sexually charged relationship; they broke up six or seven times" over five years. John Guerin would be one of the great loves of her life. And, for increasingly grudge-holding Joni ("If you're in Joan's life, you're gonna get blamed," says subsequent beau Dave Naylor; "Joan rewrites history really well, and once she tells a story once or twice in her head, it becomes true to her—I call it her 'iron whim'"), Guerin was that rare lover "who she never said anything bad about," says another friend. "She was *crazy* about John Guerin."

One of their first breakups occurred just after *Court and Spark* was finished. John was unfaithful, which she would document in *Hejira*'s "Blue Motel Room." She paid him back by having a six-week liaison with session guitarist (and sometime Leon Russell bandmate) Wayne Perkins, a handsome half-Cherokee Alabaman. Perkins was just twenty-two, but having grown up in a big country-and-church-music-playing family, he had good music sense. He'd helped talk Joni into putting "Free Man in Paris" on the album, and he played her vintage discs of regional legends Lord Buckley, the Alabama State Troopers, and Furry Lewis, a seminal blues guitarist who started out as a protégé of W. C. Handy. Joni was very taken by Furry, who was still alive (though in decrepitude) in Memphis.

Joni's house-sharing with Geffen had a wacky eye-of-the-needle glamour, like an early-1970s elite Hollywood version of the TV show *Friends*. One night Joni and Wayne were on their way downstairs for a midnight swim in Geffen's pool when, on the stairs, they bumped into Geffen and his then-squeeze Cher—"bouncing off the walls, laughing like crazy," Wayne remembers. "They couldn't get upstairs [to his bedroom] fast enough," which only put Joni and Wayne in a hotter mood for skinny-dipping and its aftermath. (Geffen came out as a gay man after the Cher romance.) Another time, Wayne woke up to Joni's proffering of "this huge stein of tea, with milk and sugar, the way the English and Canadians serve it," and went downstairs to find Bob Dylan on a bar stool reading *The New York Times* and talking with Geffen about their just-released *Planet Waves,* along with Joni's dulcimer maker, Joellen Lapidus. Joni made omelettes, and the morning turned into an all-star guitar-dulcimer-tambourine jam session.

Joni and John Guerin reunited shortly afterward.

Court and Spark was released in January 1974, and the pleading, scatty "Help Me" was released in March, becoming Joni's first—and only—Top 10 single. The critics were even more ecstatic than they'd been with *For the Roses*. Robert Hilburn called it "a virtually flawless album that may well contain the most finely honed collection of songs and most fully realized arrangements in the singer-songwriter's distinguished career." Robert Christgau of *The Village Voice* decreed Joni "the best singer-songwriter there is right now." *Rolling Stone*'s Jon Landau called the album "the first truly great album of 1974" (granted, 1974 was only two months old when he wrote that). The *Chicago Tribune*'s Lynn Van Matre, who always lent a bit of feminism to her reviews (and who paired her review of Joni's sixth album to Carly's near-simultaneously released fourth one, *Hotcakes*—giving Joni points for depth and Carly points for humor, and having the good sense to *not* mention James Taylor), agreed. *Court and Spark,* Van Matre said, was "pure Mitchell," but with "clearer lyrics" than before, Joni "connec[ting]" to the listeners "beautifully." At this point, though, reviewers were painstakingly trying to figure out what Joni's songs *meant,* other than the eternal balance between love and freedom. Landau says, "The lyrics lead us through concentric circles that define an almost Zen-like dilemma: The freer the writer becomes, the more unhappy she finds herself." And: "No thought or emotion is expressed without some equally forceful statement of its negation." His effort and tolerance reveal what would be a problem: you can't keep writing endlessly about the ups and downs of love; freedom has its limits as a subject. Joni would have (after *Court and Spark*) one masterful exploration of that theme left in her—*Hejira*—and then, like Carole after *Tapestry,* where she would choose to go and where her fans *wanted* her to go would, painfully, diverge.

Court and Spark was Joni's first smash hit. It charted at #2 and stayed there for four weeks, then went platinum, with over a million copies sold. It received Grammy nominations for Album of the Year and Record of the Year ("Help Me"), and Joni for Best Pop Female Vocalist. (When Olivia Newton-John won instead, there was audible dismay from the audience.) Joni and her boys went on a fifty-city tour, from which was produced a live album, *Miles of Aisles,* which, in November, *also* reached #2. This rush of mainstream success was new for Joni, and road life had been grinding. She let her friend Ron Stone remain at her Lookout Mountain house, and, by the end of 1974, she bought an elegant Spanish home built in 1929 atop a private Bel Air road. Its intricate wrought-iron gates opened into a fountained courtyard, and there was a pool, of course. John Guerin packed up his drums and jazz records and moved in with her.

Over the next year and a half, working with a decorator, Joni would turn the home into a Mediterranean palazzo of warmth and glamour. She hired a live-in South American maid, Dora, who would become her life manager and who enjoyed Joni's largesse—driving around town in a little red sports car, taking Club Med vacations—while putting up with her boss's temper. (In the middle of one argument, Joni struck Dora.)

Despite the luxury, Joni continued to think of herself as "a 'seeker,'" John said. "She had this image of herself as being an artist who'd go up to Canada and be a hermit and starve herself—and *that* I *wouldn't* let her do. She was driven; she'd get tunnel-visioned: She'd be up all night honing lyrics, and she'd hone them again and again. I'd say, 'Joan, that's beautiful!' The next night she'd rehone it. I'd say, 'Damn, Joan, I love it!' Tomorrow it's a little different, and I usually loved it more."

John helped her have fun—they went to Rio and Bahia during Carnival and had wild nights dancing the samba. They were crazy in their different ways. "He was this wild man who would give big bashes; one time Sarah Vaughan came, and the party went on for days," a friend says, while Joni was the pushy adventurer ("She just put herself out there, got herself in there . . . ," John said, bemused): dragging him along on explorations that often led to her being bawled out or run out of town. They were screamed away from the doorstep of an Indian turquoise craftsman she'd insisted on visiting in the middle of the night; the next day she was angrily stared down by Hopi kids whose pictures she tried to take. Another time, Joni was snapping pictures of the old people "who didn't know who she was" in rural Canadian luncheonettes. John expected one of them to take her camera and smash it. And, through a Beale Street pawnbroker, Joni sleuthed out the great Furry Lewis and arrived at his house bearing gifts: a fifth of Jack Daniel's and a carton of Pall Malls. But while he was sitting there ("propped up in his bed, with his dentures and his leg removed"), something popped out of Joni's mouth that made the cranky old bluesman turn nasty. He loudly snarled to another person present, "I don't like her." (Joni used the line in "Furry Sings the Blues," on *Hejira* and—in certain cases, she could get as well as she could give—Furry claimed she owed him royalties.)

Joni's next album, *The Hissing of Summer Lawns,* was released in November 1975, and it embodied the duality between the wealthy mansion dweller and the gleefully nosy provocateur. The awkward title (named for the sound of Bel Air sprinklers in the title song about a trophy wife) shouted "upper middle class." But like a conceptual artist, Joni *played* with this fact. The album's internal photo showed her submerged in her Bel Air pool, and the Joni-painted cover—a miragelike downtown L.A. in the backdrop of a surreal pea-soup-green megalawn on which African tribesmen are carrying a long, snakelike communal drum (illustrating the album's most innovative—and strange—cut, "The Jungle Line," featuring drummers from the African nation of Burundi)—announced that she was mocking her own affluence with intentionally controversial symbols.

Joni was leaving behind the confessionalism that had intensely defined *Blue, For the Roses,* and *Court and Spark.* This new album, as Stephen Holden put it, was Joni doing "social philosophy. All the characters are American stereotypes who act out socially determined rituals of power and submission in exquisitely described settings. Mitchell's eye for detail is . . . precise and . . . panoramic." The intellectual substance Holden saw in *Hissing* (for which Guerin played drums) was small comfort to her bewildered fans, who had come to Joni to *feel.* There are hum-along-with cuts—the lovely "Shades of Scarlett Conquering," which presents (a disguised) Ronee Blakley, who had just had a star turn in Robert Altman's *Nashville,* as a diva coquette; and the bubbly, sexy "In France They Kiss on Main Street," which evokes her teen years at the Y dances and Commodore Cafe, and which became a moderate hit. But others—"The Boho Dance," about starving-artist hypocrisy; the pretentious, semiliturgical "Shadows and Light"; and "Harry's House," about a wealthy man and woman separating—seem preachy or (odd for Joni) *wordy,* though a Lambert, Hendricks and Ross song inset on that latter song is wittily sublime. Joni had recently been the subject of a major *Time* profile, in which she said, apparently unfacetiously, that her "lover was a man named Art." Despite the fact that her real lover was meat-and-potatoes-and-*Monday-Night-Football* Guerin, with whom she talked shop (they had endless arguments about "the root of the chord"), that self-seriousness on *Hissing* was undisguised. Although *Hissing* shot to #4—*Court and Spark*'s wake was strong—the negative reviews (the *Detroit News,* for example, called it "sometimes so smug that it is downright irritating") upset her.

"Joni was very self-involved and thin-skinned," John recalled. "Elliot would keep the bad reviews away from her, which I thought was really dumb—I thought it was abnormal; she should have been way past that. But Joan remembers everything any critic said about her." Joni was vulnerable in general. "There were days where she'd lose her self-confidence—and days when she didn't feel like the prettiest girl on the block."

At some point in 1975, Joni and John became quietly engaged. "We had wedding rings made," he said. "Joan designed them—gold, with a kind of hieroglyphic that meant 'lasting relationship' in some Eastern language." (John, who was married twice after his breakup from Joni, kept his ring until he died.) "We had dinner with her folks and discussed where the wedding was going to be." A baby was not in the picture, John said. As for the baby she'd already had—"there were times she would feel maternal, but she didn't dwell on it. It was gone. Who knows what kind of guilt she really felt, but she had set up a defense mechanism a long time ago and that's the way she handled it."

At the same time that *Hissing* was released, in November 1975, Joni flew to the East Coast to join Bob Dylan's Rolling Thunder Revue, an intentionally nostalgic coast-to-coast rock tour that doubled as a fund-raiser for imprisoned prizefighter Rubin "Hurricane" Carter, who was seeking a retrial after having been convicted of murder. The tour, which featured Dylan and Baez singing "Blowin' in the Wind" as if it were 1963 all over again, was tinged with historical symbolism (it kicked off near Plymouth Rock, for one thing). It was also, behind the scenes, full of drugs, angst, and misunderstandings—as Joni would put it, in song, the participants were indulging in "pills and powders to get them through this passion play." (It was during the tour that Joni's friendship with Ronee Blakley was severed.) Along on the tour—he would cowrite, with Dylan, the movie *Renaldo and Clara* that essentially came out of it—was Sam Shepard.

Shepard was one of the most award-winning of Off-Broadway play-wrights (he later won a Pulitzer), a sometime musician, film actor, former downtown Manhattan scene-maker, self-styled cowboy—and a devastatingly attractive man. Shepard and Joni were exactly two days apart in age; they both turned thirty-two during their time on the tour. He was a physical type she had cottoned to before; like Eric Andersen, Tom Rush, James Taylor, and Jackson Browne, he was, under his long hair and scowly sensitivity, as neatly WASP-handsome as any debutante-escorting Wall Street scion out of F. Scott Fitzgerald.

Joni had planned to follow the tour for only three cities, and, at that, as an observer. But, for what she has called "mystical reasons of my own," she stayed on for the duration of its '75 leg. (There was a 1976 leg as well, which did not include her.) A song started "coming" to her, and she wrote pieces of it during the bus rides. Called "Coyote," it would be one of her wittiest, sexiest, and most un-self-pitying, telling the story of a woman in a transient situation who meets a stranger from a beguilingly different background: a cowboy. (What Joni was writing, of course, Carole was living.) A brief, humorous but avariciously erotic affair seems to ensue in funky roadhouses and hotels with lots of "keyholes and numbered doors."

For years, fans who loved the casual, devil-may-care-about-feminism abandon of the song, which would lead off her 1977 album *Hejira*, have wondered *who* "Coyote" was. Who was the man who has *two* other women but, Joni sang in a flattered flush, still wants her? And the one who inspired one of Joni's ten best lines ever: in a coffee shop in the morning, right after their tryst, the sexy brooder is "staring a hole in his scrambled eggs"; then he "picks up my scent on his fingers while he watches the waitress's legs."

"Coyote" was Sam Shepard.

Joni's breezy adieu of a hook—"No regrets, Coyote!"—is a sort of ten-years-later version of "Cactus Tree" 's "She will love them when she sees them." And it is how any sophisticated woman in her early thirties would want an affair to end. But whether or not that interlude with Coyote/Shepard was so blithely inconsequential is questionable.

Joni and John and her band embarked on the *Hissing* tour in mid-January 1976. Joni sang the deliciously suggestive "Coyote" on the tour and told audiences that it had come to her during Rolling Thunder. Before the end of the *Hissing* tour, for reasons that may or may not have had to do with the source of the song, Joni and John had such a big fight that the rest of the tour (including its international leg) was canceled. They broke up—this time (they thought) for good. His version of events: "I finally left. There was too much water under the bridge—I'm not gonna cite a certain thing, an 'I did this, she did that.' We had our differences, but it was a buildup."

Joni stayed with her friend Neil Young for a while to sort out her life; then, around late spring, she embarked on a cross-country road trip, traversing the northern part of America, west to east, with two male friends. One of her road mates, in the midst of a custody battle, was picking up his young daughter from the child's grandmother in Maine; the other, who was considerably younger than Joni and with whom she became briefly involved, was the inscrutable near-juvenile ("he lives with his family . . .") that Joni describes in "A Strange Boy."

After her road companions remained on the East Coast, Joni rented a white Mercedes, donned a red wig, renamed herself "Charlene Lattimer," and drove herself back across the country, this time taking the southern route. But the trip—her *hejira*—was undeniably symbolic, from the brassy red wig (denoting a female performance-art-like adventure) to the fact that she was undertaking it all by herself: the contemplation-breeding solitude; the arduous, unshared driving. To the fact that she was making it while America was celebrating the two hundredth anniversary of the Declaration of Independence: freedom for the thirteen colonies; freedom (yet again) for the Cactus Tree girl. The long trip seemed to highlight how out on a limb she'd chosen to climb. As with more than a few other women in their early thirties, the indecisiveness that had started as a temporary principled rebellion had become her life. Six years ago she'd journeyed through Europe—sleeping in Matala caves and Ibiza *fincas*—to shake off a relationship with Graham. Now, in shaking off John, cold-water interstate restrooms, blue motel rooms, and Winn-Dixie cold cuts formed the starker backdrop and sustenance for her advanced reflections.

As she drove and stopped and drove and stopped, she wrote song-postcards from the road, many of them puzzling out the breakup. The half tongue-in-cheek 1940s torch-style "Blue Motel Room" mused about getting back with John. In the title song, "Hejira" (literally, "Mohammed's flight from danger"), Joni embraces her "melancholy," as she has so many times before, but this time—months from turning thirty-three—thoughts of mortality encroach; while she's visiting a church in one of the cities, the wax from the devotional candles "rolls down like tears." Continuing on, she falls "in with some drifters cast upon a beach town" on the Gulf of Mexico; "Charlene Lattimer" ends up making them dinner (it's not only the likes of Geffen, Dylan, Cher, and Sarah Vaughan that she'd cook for) and thinks fondly of them as she drives on. We eavesdrop as she seeks relief from her oppressive analytic thinking and her deep self-absorption. She is grateful when she succeeds at ditching the former (in a forest, she marvels at the "muscular" clouds and exhorts the sun to "shine on your witness!"). She also overcomes the latter: while gassing up at a service station, she is riveted by a tacked-up photo of the earth taken from the moon and by the fact that "you couldn't see a city / on that marbled bowling ball . . . [emphasis added] or *me here,* least of all." "Westbound and rolling," she's finding solace in the "refuge of the roads"—that line, the title of the song.

The trip's profound epiphany comes near journey's end. Nine years earlier, Roy Blumenfeld had thought of Joni as "Dorothy, trying to find her way home." Now a different storied female—not naïve, like the fluffy-dog-toting victim of the Kansas tornado, but rather a skilled woman who *chose* her risks—comes into play. Traversing a strip of highway "through the burning desert" of the Southwest, the silence is broken by an overhead burst of "six jet planes"—probably a test formation from a nearby military base. Those thin metal stripes in the sky remind Joni of "the strings of my guitar," and she—solo-piloting her vehicle across the perilously empty hot sand—feels a sharp kinship with another solo pilot: Amelia Earhart. Joni checks into "the Cactus Tree Motel, to shower off the dust" of all that journeying, literal and figurative; she sets her head on the "pillows of my wanderlust." The song she writes that night braids Earhart's disappearance with her own protracted wrestling with her vulnerability in affairs of the heart and her ever-reasserting need for independence. Six words about dashed anticipation—"It was just a false alarm"—end every stanza. For Earhart, the "false alarm"—the thing that never came—was a rescue vessel. Joni's "false alarm" is disproof of the fear she'd expressed in "River," that she is incapable of love, destined to spend her whole emotional life "in clouds at icy altitudes." "Clouds," "planes," "cactus tree," "wanderlust," "roads," "picture-postcard charms": ten years of her images and preoccupations woven into one penetrating hymn. Conceived at the end of the long drive that capped off six years of fraught relationships, the tour de force "Amelia" would be the last deeply soul-baring song the young Joni Mitchell would ever write. She'd said it all.

One day in late 1977, when J. D. Souther walked into Peter and Betsy Asher's house on Summit Ridge Drive, he was introduced by the Ashers to a trim black man, his face half-hidden by big shades and a wide, thick mustache. The dude's name was Claude, and Souther took him to be a pimp. He was nattily attired in dark creased pants, white vest, light, pointy-collared shirt, and white jacket. His fluffy Afro was topped by a slick chapeau. For ten minutes there was minimal small talk among the group—the Ashers, Souther, Claude, Danny Kortchmar. Claude didn't say much; yeah, well, pimps, y'know.

Claude took off his hat. And then he took off his *wig*. Claude was *Joni,* in blackface. Souther and Joni had been lovers, but he hadn't recognized her under the costume. This was her new alter ego, a character she would imminently name "Art Nouveau," her "inner black person," as her friend and archivist Joel Bernstein wryly puts it.

Like many young white people of her generation, Joni romanticized being black (without the disadvantages of being black, of course). She would increasingly insist that her music was "black" and that, as it progressed deeply into jazz, it should be played on black stations (it rarely was). "My harmonies were not very 'white,' like James Taylor's or Carole King's," she would later say (wrongly, in the case of Carole, whose music is largely R&B-based). "I gravitated toward . . . 'black' voicings out of gospel and jazz, because they mirrored what I was feeling." Joni has repeatedly said that she has already written the first line of her autobiography, and (perhaps referring to the day at the Ashers') it is this: "I was the only black man in the room."

It is easy to take the insistence by a blond granddaughter of Nordic-Scottish-French-Irish Canadian farmers that she is somehow "black" as an offensive delusion, or at best a dry performance art conceit. But such crossover hubris wasn't only quintessentially '60s-generation (à la Ellen Willis's remark); it was also timelessly *American,* in the opinion of cultural critic Stanley Crouch. The heroine of Crouch's novel *Don't the Moon Look Lonesome* is a young blond woman from (Saskatoon-longitude) South Dakota, whose jazz singing and long relationship with a black jazz musician represents both an attempt to embrace racial Otherness *and* a confrontation with the limits of doing so. When Crouch's novel was published in 2000, the character was compared to Peggy Lee. In a way, it is Joni—Joni from 1977 to 1980.

After *Hejira* was released in late November 1976 to good sales (peaking at #13 in *Billboard*) and reviews (with *The New York Times*'s Stephen Holden later noting that "Miss Mitchell refined Bob Dylan's elongated

narrative line into a folk pop poetry of unprecedented density and sophistication"), Joni discarded confessionalism. She picked up where *Hissing* had left off, with an album she called *Don Juan's Reckless Daughter,*
the cover of which bore, among others, the image of Joni as the black
pimp Art Nouveau. It was during the making of this album that Joni met
Don Alias, the jazz musician with whom she would have a serious three-
and-a-half-year relationship.

Born in Harlem and a pre-med graduate of Pennsylvania's Gannon
University, Don Alias was in many ways uncannily like John Guerin.
Both were almost exactly four years older than Joni; both were drummers and total jazzmen from whom Joni learned a great deal about the
idiom; and both were men of whom, despite having had "tempestuous"
relationships with them, Joni remained fond. (Another sad similarity:
both Guerin and Alias died, in 2004 and 2006, respectively, of heart
failure.)

A handsome, very tall, dark-copper-skinned man with a trim Afro
and a wide mustache, Alias was a percussionist who eventually specialized in an Afro-Cuban sound. He'd played with Dizzy Gillespie and with
Eartha Kitt's dance troupe in the late 1950s; then he'd been Nina Simone's musical director for three years. From 1969 to 1971, he'd worked
with Miles Davis—his congas can be heard on *Bitches Brew*—and he
toured with Miles. Jaco Pastorius, considered the best jazz bass player in
the business, was working with Joni on *Don Juan's Reckless Daughter.*
Pastorius's input was crucial on the album; in the same way she needed
a jazz drummer for *Court and Spark,* she needed a jazz *bassist* now. Pastorius had called in Alias. Don's reaction to the prospect of working with
Joni Mitchell was close to what Guerin's had been. "I thought, 'Oh, another one of those skinny-ass folksingers,'" he recalled, in an interview
he gave for this book, two years before his death. As with Guerin, once
Alias got into the studio, he was stunningly disabused of his condescen-
sion. "What a genius of a musician Joni was! And intuitive! And eloquent!" As she had to Wayne Perkins and Tom Scott on "Car on a Hill,"
she told Don, "Sound like a garbage can!" "Sound like something's falling down the stairs!" He quickly came around to viewing *Don Juan's* as

"just one of those great artistic Joni Mitchell albums." Winning over jazz musicians was now her point of pride.

Don remembered, "There was definitely a warmth being built up during the session, definitely a *thing*." One night Joni suggested going dancing at On the Rox, the Roxy's upstairs private club. "And it happened there; it happened there as we danced. I fell in love with her. I fell in love with her openness—what openness! I fell in love with her childlikeness, that wide-eyed childlike quality. And her independence and intelligence."

They became a couple. In a trip that Don said was "supposed to be our kind of honeymoon," he and Joni rented an RV and drove from L.A. to Albuquerque, New Mexico. Joni had found out the address of her hero, ninety-year-old Georgia O'Keeffe. As usual, she was going to just show up, uninvited, at a doorstep. Don hadn't heard of O'Keeffe before he met Joni, "and then she showed me some of those paintings—how naturally erotic those flowers were." On the drive down, Don wrote a song in honor of the legendary painter. "*Geor*-gia O'*Keeffe! Geor*-gia O'*Keeffe!*" he sang, rhythmically slapping the congas while Joni drove. And they both laughed when, finding themselves starved, in the desolate area of desert where the movie *Giant* had been filmed, it took them an hour to drive to the closest restaurant for some (very bad) Chinese food.

When they got to O'Keeffe's gate, "this was her moment," Don recalled. "I said, 'You go ahead, Joni.' I just nodded and went back to the RV."

Joni—who considered herself "a painter first" and who turned out paintings (which would soon fill numerous shows) as steadily as she did songs—walked to the compound's gate. Inside was not just a hero, but a kind of mirror. Like Joni, O'Keeffe was the child of a northern midwestern farm family (Wisconsin, in her case). Like the young Joni, the young O'Keeffe had been a beauty. Like Joni, who'd started painting when girls in art school (like her classmate Beverly Nodwell) were warned that they could merely *teach*, not *make* art, O'Keeffe had defied such an etched-in-stone fate. With her husband, photographer Alfred

Stieglitz, and their friends, such as Paul Strand and Edward Steichen, O'Keeffe was at the center of the Modernist culture of the 1920s and 1930s, in the same way that male-musician-ensconced Joni was at the center of the popular culture of the last ten years. And, like Joni, O'Keeffe had produced a paean to clouds, inspired by what she, like Bellow's Henderson, who had inspired Joni, had viewed from airplane windows.

Don sat in the car and played his congas. When Joni returned, "she was in heaven!" he recalled. She had not been turned away. (A correspondence would develop, and the following year, Joni would visit O'Keeffe for five days. During this talk, O'Keeffe mused to Joni, "I would have liked to have been a painter and a musician, but you can't do both." On the basis of her own life, Joni replied, "Oh, yes, *you can*!" only later realizing that it was *O'Keeffe* who'd "ploughed the grain" that had eased Joni's journey.)

When Joni told John Guerin about her unrebuffed visit to O'Keeffe, he smiled.

Joni wanted Don Alias to move in to her Bel Air home, but he refused. "I said, '*No* way!' That mansion was the princess's palace. I'd always be 'Mr. Mitchell' if I lived there. What was I going to do?—tell her maid, 'Do my shirts, Dora'? With all that money that was rolling around, I really fought hard not to get involved with that." Instead, he insisted that they divide their time between her Bel Air home and his apartment in a modest neighborhood—on Sepulveda, between National and Pico. Joni obliged. His not wanting to be "Mr. Mitchell" was a big issue in their relationship, she would tell friends. And on one of their first dates, he became incensed that a wealthy male fan, noticing her at the restaurant, sent a bottle of wine to their table. (Joni was hurt by his reaction, which he realized was excessive and gratuitously proprietary.)

Approaching Joni's lily-white social world, Don took a deep, wary breath. "It was a big, powerhouse scene of Jack Nicholson, of Crosby, Stills and Nash, of Linda Ronstadt—and here *I* am, the black guy coming into this thing." Even though her character Art Nouveau had nothing to do with Don, he was certain that "a great deal of those people thought that Art Nouveau had been based on me, that *I* was a *pimp,* and that I was using Joni—the black cat capitalizing on the white woman with the money." Since she was recently known to date musicians, such as Perkins and Guerin, who were lower down in the star hierarchy than she—something that, needless to say, wouldn't be an oddity for a male star—"it was 'Oh, here comes another one of Joni's toys,'" Don felt—made worse when the "toy" was African-American. Through their years together, even though Joni considered him, as one friend says, "the real deal: a brilliant musician who she learned from, and such a musically connected guy," Don had a seasoned skepticism about these supposedly black-music-worshiping rich white musical stars. His radar picked up their masked appraisals of him, and he was sensitive when he was not officially acknowledged as what he was: one of the major men in Joni's life.*

The "one guy" on the scene who Don felt never viewed him negatively was Jack Nicholson, who, from the first time they met, knew that Don had worked with Miles Davis and who, along with his girlfriend Anjelica Huston, unfailingly respected him as a social peer and a serious musician. With just about everyone else, Don felt he had to maneuver a little. "Stephen Stills was an asshole, unequivocally"—though not for any racial attitude. "Bob Dylan and Stephen Stills would be sitting around at Joni's house, talking mainly about themselves, their careers, and how good they were. Dylan was a quiet dude, but Stills was *always* talking about himself. Don Henley was also a real obnoxious guy—'me, me, me.' Graham Nash, on the other hand, was always a gentleman." Don said

---

* In 2003 PBS aired a documentary/musical tribute to Joni, "Woman of Heart and Mind." Several of Joni's past significant others were featured or mentioned as such. Don Alias was extremely hurt that he was not asked to participate and was not mentioned, and he strongly suspected that the producers left him out because of his race. (A white female friend from Joni's past also thought the omission seemed pointed.) Alias said: "Her relationships with Larry, and John, and Graham were mentioned, and I want to know *why* I wasn't there. *Why* did they take so lightly—as if it didn't exist!—a relationship with someone I loved so much? That bothered the hell out of me." He paused. "Well, when I talk to Joni again, I want to find out." He died before he could.

that Joni would protect him from having to endure the egomaniacal Stills and Henley. "I would be coming downstairs and Stephen would want to include me, and Joni would say, 'No, he doesn't get involved in stuff like that'—which I'm so glad she said; she kind of stood up for me."

Don viewed Linda Ronstadt as "the intellectual"; Betsy Asher, Joni's best friend, "was beautiful and in torment, always talking about Peter and [John Phillips's daughter] Mackenzie Phillips." The Ashers had recently ended their marriage. For the last eight years Betsy had been the L.A. rock world's premier hostess, mediator, and confidante ("Betsy knew about everything and could have *been* anything—she could have been a Sherry Lansing," says Danny Kortchmar), but now, alone, she fell into a downward spiral—cocaine abuse, paranoia, agoraphobia—that eventually resulted in years spent in a sanitarium, from which she is now fully recovered. (James Taylor's hit song "Her Town, Too"—written with J. D. Souther—detailed Betsy's emotional vulnerability during this time and the couple's divorce.)

As for Warren Beatty, Don marveled at what the others were long used to: "Every time I saw Warren, he was hitting on somebody." Don had a tactic when Beatty walked into Joni's house. "I used to always stand up—because, within that crowd, Warren was Mr. Man and he was the tallest, and," at six feet five "*I* was taller than him, so that way he wouldn't feel so kingpin-ish." (But at least one form of more blatant masculine one-upping Don Alias did *not* want, though Joni certainly did. As she had with Jackson and other lovers, Joni painted a portrait of Don. But this was a different kind of portrait: "It was me, with my bathrobe open with—bang! like this—a hard-on sticking out. I said, 'Joni, what are you *doing*?'" when she hung it "smack-dab in the middle of the living room" of the loft they would soon share in New York. Don was embarrassed. "My friends would come over and they'd go, *huh?* Joni said, 'What's wrong with it?'" He said she said it was a "testament to his sexuality," to which he replied, "It's not a testament to anything—it's annoying; it's an embarrassment!" Don wanted her to repaint it with the bathrobe closed, "and she fought me on it, all the way, *all* the way."

Finally, they compromised: She repainted part of the painting, making the penis tumescent, not erect.)

Released in December 1977, the double album *Don Juan's Reckless Daughter* was intensely ambitious and contrarian music: jazz-based, experimental. Its centerpiece was the sixteen-minute-long "Paprika Plains" (in which Joni reminisces about the prairies of her childhood), a Gershwin-like opera (with Laura Nyro–like turns at the piano)—part Philip Glass, part-melodramatic old movie score—with splashes of great risk and beauty. But what Joni's fans had always related to so deeply *wasn't* her trying to be Philip Glass; it was music that had made so many women say, as Danny Kortchmar puts it "'I was so depressed, I was going to slit my wrists, and then I heard one of your songs.'" With this album, people felt Joni deserved either applause for leaving the comfort of her feathered nest (one critic later called it a "masterpiece") or dismissal as cold, pretentious, and irrelevant. Years later, Steve Pond in *Rolling Stone* would recap its reception by calling it "four widely dismissed sides of sometimes forbidding jazz" and saying that Joni had become "a jazz dilettante." How the public was coming to feel is represented by a fan's recent confession on a Web site devoted to discussion of Joni's work: "I've struggled to enjoy much of Joni's output after 1977, but the albums prior to that were perfection."

Three months after the album's release, in March 1978, Janet Maslin, writing in *Rolling Stone,* delivered a review whose thrust was hinted at in its headline—"Joni Mitchell's Reckless and Shapeless *Daughter*"—only gently, for Maslin's opinion was devastating, and all the more so for being thoughtfully reasoned. Calling the album "an instructive failure," she said, "Mitchell appears bent on repudiating her own flair for popular songwriting, and on staking her claim to the kind of artistry that when it's real doesn't need to announce itself so stridently." That review, and others like it, would leave Joni angered and wounded. For a tough, confident woman who could dictate to and win over session after session of skeptical old-hand jazz musicians, and for a recording artist of whom studio executives would (having learned the hard way) sigh, "You don't tell Joni Mitchell what to do," she was surprisingly needy—she wanted her fans' love. And, like others who had (as she'd prophetically put it in "For the Roses") gotten "a taste for worship," she was presumptuous, expecting those fans to follow her away from the bargain they had struck: that she was describing life for both of them. The album reached only #25 in *Billboard,* but it went gold (as with Carole's *Simple Things* of that same year, her previous momentum assured as much); still, like Carole's, it would be Joni's last album to do so. Joni had been lacerated critically the same year as Carole—Carole for being too sappy and self-derivative; Joni for being removed and pompous. It wasn't just that staying at the top was harder than getting to the top; more to the point, rock and pop music belonged to shining youth, and they were no longer young.

In late 1978, Joni rented a New York loft on Varick Street, at the western juncture of SoHo and the Village, and despite his initial protests ("Joni, you know goddamn well I'm not going to be able to pay any kind of rent on this space!"), Don moved in with her. (It was on these walls that the argued-about bathrobe portrait of Don by Joni hung.) Don had a group called the Stone Alliance, and the loft was his base of operations. Joni wanted to go to Don's mother and grandmother's Harlem apartment for Thanksgiving, but Don was nervous. His family's knowledge of Joni Mitchell was "practically nil. I thought they'd think, 'What are you doing, bringing a white girl in here?'" On Thanksgiving Day, "Joni walked in and my grandmother wanted her to take off her shoes, and Joni did—and *right away* there was a love affair between my grandmother and Joni. She really, *really* loved Joni. My mom did, too. And . . . a black family in Harlem and a white woman?" Even well into the 1970s, Alias recalled in no uncertain terms that, at least within his family, that "was taboo. *Taboo!* But this thing between her and my grandmother was really special. It touches me now, just thinking about it. They *really loved* each other. We went there a lot. Joni loved being accepted."

As for Myrtle and Bill, they were "flabbergasted"—a confidante says—to learn their daughter had a black boyfriend. But Don didn't care. "I was so damn in love with Joni—so crazy about her—I was willing to meet Myrtle and Bill; I was willing to break down a wall." When the meeting did take place, "they never gave me the impression" they had any negative feelings about him, Don said. They ended up liking him just fine.

In late 1978, the legendary jazz composer, bassist, and orchestra leader Charles Mingus asked Joni to collaborate on an album with him (an honor that made John Guerin a little jealous). Mingus wrote six melodies (flatteringly, initially, called "Joni I" to "Joni VI") to which Joni would write the lyrics—a new situation, and one she would likely not have consented to from a lesser musician. Mingus was in the final stages of painful, paralyzing amyotrophic lateral sclerosis, and he was wheelchair-bound. He was lovingly tended by his wife, Sue Graham Mingus, who in a very real sense personified that "Americanness" of Stanley Crouch's novelized highplains-raised white jazz singer. A Martha Stewart lookalike, Sue was the debutante daughter of a Midwestern family so straitlaced that (as she put it in her memoir *Tonight at Noon*) "Desire was an undercurrent, folded away with the linen. We were a formal and modest family . . . The rawness of our bodies was barely acknowledged—soft mollusks safe inside our casing." A family, in short, like Joni's.

Sue had been drawn to the volatile, tempestuous, Watts-born Mingus, and their union was passionate and committed. Since Mingus's death, Sue has devoted her whole life to furthering Mingus's legacy and getting his music heard. Joni (often with Don) worked with Mingus in New York, and, later, in Cuernavaca, where Sue was nursing her frail husband through last-ditch faith healing. Here was Sue Mingus, the blond, pretty, heavily relied-upon behind-the-scenes spouse of her famous, divalike, and indulged black artist husband; and here was Joni Mitchell, the blond, pretty, famous, divalike, indulged artist (and jazz *novice*) who had an accomplished black male jazz musician boyfriend on whom *she* heavily relied behind the scenes. It's hard not to wonder how Sue and Joni regarded each other: as day-for-night opposites *or* sisters in spirit?*

Joni composed the lyrics for four of the pieces; recording commenced; then, after Mingus's death in early January, Joni fully com-

---

* This question was put to Sue Mingus, in an e-mail she invited. She declined to reply.

posed two other songs, "God Must Be a Boogie Man" and "The Wolf That Lives in Lindsey." In "Goodbye Pork Pie Hat," for which she wrote the lyrics (Rahsaan Roland Kirk had composed an earlier set) and Mingus wrote the music, Joni—utilizing images from Mingus's biography *Beneath the Underdog*—makes statements about the dangers to black men of interracial relationships. Joni had an all-star cast of jazz sidemen: not just Pastorius and Alias, but Herbie Hancock and Wayne Shorter. Released in June 1979, the album was obviously a risk—her fan base was already confused by *Don Juan's* (and, to some extent, *Hissing*). But, as she told Cameron Crowe in a long interview in *Rolling Stone:* "You have two options. You can stay the same and protect the formula that gave you your initial success. They're going to crucify you for staying the same. If you change, they're going to crucify you for changing. But staying the same is boring. And change is interesting. So of the two options, I'd rather be crucified for changing."

Reviewing the album for that same publication, Ariel Swartley didn't seem to know what to make of it and chose to focus on its well-touted riskiness rather than its satisfactions. Noting an "angry edge" to Joni's guitar and the "taste for dissonance" that make "it see[m] as if the tensions [that] Mitchell's courting [are] star[ting] to drive her crazy," Swartley concluded, "Joni Mitchell keeps asking the hard questions, touching nerves. And the pressure she applies is increasingly brutal, increasingly deft. It's been a long time since her songs had much to do with whatever's current in popular music." Reviewing it later, *The Village Voice*'s Robert Christgau called the album a "brave experiment" that had failed.

Joni launched a tour called *Shadows and Light,* for which Don—wisely taking control—played both drums and percussion. In the fashionably ripply perm that had for the last few years replaced her lank, straight hair, she performed with the neo-doo-wop group the Persuasions, and the live album included the beautiful tour-title composition, with its soul-stentorian refrain: "Blind-*ness*! *Blind*-ness, and sight!"

Joni had never really let go of John Guerin. Don said, "I think Guerin always knew that, deep down, there was an unexplainable love between him and Joni, and that nobody could break that. It took a while for me to acknowledge" that. Throughout her years with Don, John was always there in the background—her "friend of spirit." Don saw Joni's insecurities. "Deep down, she may have had insecurity about being able to hold on to a man." But more than that, "she was vulnerable about her art." She had always been an obsessed worker. She had claimed work as a necessity and key to her identity back when it was unusual for a pretty girl to do so—to wit, her days of hours closeted in the tiny room in Chuck's Detroit apartment. But in late 1980, at thirty-seven, her work ethic was different from when she was twenty-two; now, the perfectionism, intensity—and adulation—had shaped her. She was a self-absorbed artist: needy, entitled-feeling, idiosyncratic enough to believe she could impinge on the people she relied on for artistic counsel whenever she wanted (which, since she was nocturnal, was often in the middle of the night): an indulgence that a man in her position would, rightly or wrongly, be assured of.

Joni was in Canada writing the title song for a movie, *Love*, by Swedish actress-director Mai Zetterling, in which nine stories written by women were being filmed, anthology style. There was tension on the set, and Joni was having trouble sitting in her hotel room with the Gideon Bible, struggling to transform I Corinthians 13 into a love anthem. Anxious, she called Don in New York "and she said, 'Come up! Come up!'" he recalled. "So I went up to Toronto and *immediately* got swallowed up in the Mr. Joni Mitchell syndrome. At four, five in the morning, she's asking me, 'What do you think of this? What do you *think*?' I'm like, 'Jesus Christ, give me a break!'" Don decided to return to New York. "She says, 'Why are you going back?' and I said, ''Cause I want to rehearse my band,' but I *wanted* to say: 'Because you're fucking *killing* me. Gimme some air!'" Don's departure really upset her, he says. "The next day," after he left—as he soon found out—"Guerin flew in."

Not long after that, as Don recalled it, Joni gave him twenty-four hours to get all his belongings out of their New York loft, which he considered his home. "It was like a *guy* breaking up," he marveled, of her attitude. "It really hurt the hell out of me!" But, according to a friend of Joni's, her reason for the abrupt breakup was simple and more than justified: "They had what she called a fistfight. She told me that is why she ended it."

After the breakup, in 1981, Joni traveled to Jamaica. It was here, in this reggae-drenched land, that she fell in love not only with reggae but with what she'd call the "pop-rock polyrhythm" sound of some of the newer hit groups: Steely Dan, Talking Heads, and especially the Police. (Later, however, Joni would wryly take co-credit for the unique sound of the group's uniquely named lead singer, Sting, a.k.a. Gordon Sumner, often quipping that she and James Taylor had taken to addressing him as "Son" because he'd picked up so much vocal phrasing from them.) But something else happened in Jamaica: Joni developed a severe ovarian infection and arrived back in L.A. in crisis and pain. Guerin visited her in the hospital and was alarmed. "She got really sick," he said. "It was really rough." Around the same time she was also starting to be physically challenged by postpolio syndrome, the dismaying return of muscular weakness from the long-vanquished disease. There were other challenges, too. "A lot of people we knew were suddenly dying—overdoses and strange deaths," says record producer Dave Naylor, who ran with the *Saturday Night Live* writers (the deaths in this crowd included Doug Kenney and John Belushi) and who says that he and Joni started dating because "we were going to so many funerals together." But Naylor—a rich, hip, handsome confirmed bachelor (about whom she may have written the song "Ladies' Man," for her next album)—had a life that he says "was a complete mess at the time," while "I felt Joni really did want a real serious relationship," something he could not provide.

Joni was two years away from forty. After a string of conflict-filled romances, a hospitalization for a serious infection, and a loss of her fans, maybe it was time to choose the easy and nurturing way for a change. A whole new generation of women of varying degrees of merit on the shock-value-to-talent continuum—Rickie Lee Jones, Deborah Harry, Madonna, Pat Benatar, Chryssie Hynde, and Joan Jett (all of whom had essentially supplanted an interim generation that included Fleetwood

Mac's Stevie Nicks and the highly regarded Patti Smith)—were now the queens of the airwaves (and of that initially cheesy-seeming brand-new phenomenon that robbed records of their imaginative value: music videos), riding on the "ploughed dirt" (to use Joni's term for what O'Keeffe had provided her) that Joni, Carole, Carly, Laura Nyro, Grace Slick, and Janis Joplin had provided through a more concerted battle against the limits of being a young American female. The idea of living the hard and soulful life—the life that Joni and D'Arcy Case had sought, that she and Joy Schreiber had found they had in common, that she and Ronee Blakley followed, through Nietzsche and Van Gogh: maybe you could live it for just so long.

Joni's next album, *Wild Things Run Fast* (on her former housemate's new label, Geffen Records) was such a departure not only from her jazz albums but also from the confessional ones, that the critics noted that fact almost before anything else. Stephen Holden called it "the most ex-hilaratingly high-spirited album Miss Mitchell has ever made," featuring "several vibrant rock-and-roll performances that communicate a rare joy in being alive. The feeling of playfulness that runs through the album also makes *Wild Things Run Fast* different in spirit from [emphasis added] *all* of Miss Mitchell's previous records. It is as though, at 39"—the album was released in late 1982—"the preeminent confessional song-writer of her generation had finally faced down the romantic demons that haunted her earlier albums."

In fact, the exorcising of demons was literal. Though no one knew this at the time (including Joni's parents, from whom the secret was still firmly kept), it was in the first song on this album, the wistful "Chinese Café/Unchained Melody"—which, not accidentally, featured Joni "listen-ing" to "Will You Love Me Tomorrow" on a jukebox—that Joni explicitly confessed: "My child's a stranger / I bore her, but I could not raise her." No one picked up on this revelation—or on the fact that, despite the up-beatness in the rest of the album, this song was *purely* a woman bluntly (and half-unbelievingly) announcing a new phase in her life: "We're middle class, we're middle aged."

Similarly, the bebop-rhythmed, deceptively cool "Moon at the

Window"—in which she commiserates with Betsy Asher, then in the throes of her breakdown, and remarks on how hard women can be on themselves, and that "sometimes the light can be so hard to find"—has as its refrain "At least the moon at the window / the thieves left *that* behind." Self-evidently, and with deft sarcasm, the line means: any part of our soul and sanity that *isn't* pinned down can be "stolen." But according to Joni's confidantes, the song has a deeper, more literal meaning. When Brad MacMath split from Toronto in early autumn 1964, he left his pregnant girlfriend a painting of a moon out a window.

She could write about the baby now because she could finally see she'd had no choice back then. It was "the times" that made a single girl *have to* place a baby for adoption. That was what she always said to Don Alias whenever they talked about it. She had done what she'd had to do. Indeed, Georgia O'Keeffe's own musing about women's creative limits had made her feel extra-justified. If she'd kept the baby, there would have been *none* of her work.

The bass player on *Wild Things Run Fast* was a very tall, lean, darkly handsome twenty-four-year-old with tousled black curls and a rakish pirate's mustache. But Larry Klein's swashbuckling looks obscured the decency and psychological conservatism of a natural caretaker. (Klein's friend Dave Naylor thought of Larry as "someone with the perfect combination of patience and balls.") Larry Klein's father was a Jewish aerospace engineer and his stay-at-home mother was, he says, caught "in the pincers of the late 1950s–early 1960s housewife disease"—Betty Friedan's "problem without a name"—"which made for booming Valium sales." A female psychotherapist was a kind of "second mother" to him. Thus, Larry grew up ("in deep suburbia—in Monterey Park in the San Gabriel Valley") with a marriage model in which the man was the soother of the more complicated woman and therapy was a part of life. Emotional helpmate was the role he *expected* to fill.

Joni met young Larry Klein just as the nonfiction book *The Cinderella Complex: Women's Hidden Fear of Independence,* by Colette Dowling, was becoming a nerve-hitting best seller. For and about women in their thirties who had pioneered feminism, it addressed the unextinguished longing to be protected. Maybe, for women like Joni—so fiercely independent, they seemed intimacy-averse; so talented, confident, and accomplished, they routinely directed men in their workaday projects—that neediness took the form of the middle-of-the-night imprecations she'd made to Don Alias and the constant availability she'd relied on from John Guerin: both relationships, so frictional. Maybe it was time to find a more straightforward protector.

Over the year of the recording of the album, Larry and Joni developed a friendship, "getting into philosophical discussions" while playing pinball. He was besotted. "I had never met a woman remotely like Joan," he remembers thinking. "She was just a whole other species for me," able to hold "rambling discourses on everything from Beethoven to Nietzsche to politics to the environment. It was a level of interaction that was so far above anything I'd ever had with a woman, I was pretty stunned. Every conversation was so catalytic and cathartic for me because, aside from being the brilliant, prescient thinker that she was, she was *thirteen years* older than me. My most serious relationship was a high school romance. Here I was, twenty-four and thinking, What planet is this woman from? This is amazing!" It was "daunting" to feel a mutual attraction developing between himself—this provincial young man—and this much-older musical icon. "Moving forward to act on that impulse, I thought, This is either gonna be fantastic or the absolutely most embarrassing thing I've ever done in my life."

It turned out *not* to be the most embarrassing thing he'd ever done in his life.

The reggae-beat "Solid Love" is a euphoric testament to Joni's feeling for Larry—"Klein," as she called him. Larry moved into a house in Malibu with her (she kept the Bel Air house as well) and, as summer of 1982 turned to autumn, he recalls, "we would joke, 'Will you still marry me . . . ?' after knowing this and that about each other or enduring some difficult situation." Joni told Larry that, because of the infection she'd gotten in Jamaica, she probably couldn't get pregnant; he said he was okay with that.

John Guerin had recently married. "Now that you're married, *I* can get married," Joni told him. "I'd like to think we had a certain thing that she didn't have with most people," John mused, shortly before his death.

On November 21, 1982, a couple of weeks after Joni turned thirty-nine, about fifteen close friends and family members of Joni Mitchell and Larry Klein attended their wedding at Elliot Roberts's Malibu house. Joni wore a traditional wedding dress and a tiara of flowers. A New Age healer performed the ceremony; Joni's housekeeper Dora's daughter was the flower girl. Betsy Asher tried hard to make it, but at that point she had gotten too afraid to leave her Summit Ridge house. Joni and Larry limited the guest list because, as he says, "we didn't want any skeptics there, and, of course, a lot of people were skeptical" about "the discrepancy in our ages," among other things. How would this "solid love," this normal happiness, affect her writing?

carly

late 1973 – late 1987

Early in Carly's pregnancy, she and James and Ellen and Vieri Salvadori had traveled to Europe. After they returned to New York, James entered treatment, and Jessica remembers Carly "going to visit James in rehab when she was pregnant, realizing the depth of his problems and having to come to that understanding" that she had married a drug addict. "I think things were really difficult, and she worried—and felt insecure." Still, she was strong and nurturing; as someone who worked closely with James says, "Carly got James on methadone, and that was an achievement." Others, however, say that methadone would prove for him at least as difficult a habit as heroin.

Carly had seemed absolutely clear-eyed in her interview with James in *Rolling Stone*, pronouncing "junk" one of the addictions that was socially "unacceptable" as well as "self-destructive." She had spoken of how loving a man with an addictive personality had only made her see more keenly drugs' insidiousness. ("I snorted cocaine a couple of times, but it was never as bad to me as when I saw James getting into it.") But, as she would realize eight years later, "I didn't go into [the marriage] with a great deal of projection about the future. I was caught up in the moment. I just knew I was very much in love with James and

I wanted to be with him for the rest of my life." In that way she was typical of her times. Upper-middle-class young women, used to being airlifted out of dangers they were visiting as tourists, were apt to be hopeful that love could carry the day and that effort invested in a decent, striving man would be rewarded. And, thirty years before trailer-park methamphetamines sullied drugs' patina of elitism, addiction was a sign of sensitivity and vulnerability. James Taylor had always traded on that romance.

But now there was a child in the picture. Sarah Maria (Sally) Taylor was born on January 7, 1974; James audio recorded the birth of the baby girl who would inspire him to write a song named for her. "I was there at the hospital when Sally was born and I think I'd never seen James so happy," Ellen says. "I remember the two of them diapering her, the nurse teaching them how." Bringing the baby home, "Carly was just so happy," Jeanie Seligmann remembers. "It seemed as if her world had gotten smaller, but not in a bad way. She was really focused; she had found herself. She was still going to be very creative, but the part of her life that had been scattered for a while was coming into its own."

Hotcakes, Carly's ode to this season of contentment, had been recorded late in Carly's pregnancy. It was another Richard Perry production. (Because he'd pushed her so hard during *No Secrets,* he had to woo Carly—then, as he recalls, "full-on pregnant"—over lunch at Tavern on the Green, to get her to work with him again.) Released days after she gave birth to Sally, it sold nearly a million copies, peaking at #3. The album featured Carly and James having great fun with Charlie and Inez Foxx's rocking version of the old folk song "Mockingbird." Punctuated by their call-and-response on each syllable of the title word, and by punchy near-campiness (James doing a Yiddish "hoid" for "heard"), the Top 10 single was a smart way to have their cute couplehood both ways (wisely, they turned down starring roles in a remake of *A Star Is Born*), and the song became a staple of their joint appearances, with Carly jumping all over the stage with gawky abandon.

The jaunty, ragtimelike "Older Sister" was another one of Carly's songs about the sisterly awe and competition that had marked her childhood, as was the more darkly autobiographical "Grownup," about her inability to grow out of the insecure little girl in a "white nightgown . . . playing with her hair" while looking at her parents' friends assembled for cocktails. Her casual insistence on following the adage "Write what you know" had met with sneers (and sometimes still did), but little by little, as women woke up from the ultimately perishable conceits of the countercultural dream, the line she drew from a certain kind of childhood to a certain kind of womanhood made identifiable sense. Praising the album for being "not deep but . . . honest," Jon Landau in *Rolling Stone* wrote: "Carly Simon never apologizes for writing about herself or her well-to-do background that has been so gratuitously criticized."

"Mind on My Man" was as smooth a standard as any her friend Jonathan Schwartz would spin. "He's a gentleman lost at the fair / He's a lotus that opens and closes, notice he won't always let me in": she locates James. More, those last phrases describe what women find attractive in men—vulnerability, abandon, mystery, but with decency—in the voice of a woman who is not at all self-protective but is very self-aware.

The album's hit single, "Haven't Got Time for the Pain" (#2 in the adult contemporary market) with its operatic, string-infused interlude—which she wrote with Jake, and which Landau called "her best single to date"—underscored her current life: Enough self-obsession already! ("You showed me how, how to leave myself behind / how to turn down the noise in my mind.") Enough existential angst! ("Suffering was the only thing made me feel I was alive.") But Carly's bleating voice undercuts her vow of emotional peace—she's too passionate to stay unpained—and gives the song its edge. "Think I'm Gonna Have a Baby," her snapshot of the era of platform shoes and strident autonomy-professing, made up in mischief for what it lacked in grace, and it introduced in this most urban but visceral of writers what would be her affecting motif: the idea that a woman—fluid, absorbing, eternal—is a "river."

The *Chicago Tribune*'s Lynn Van Matre (in her joint Joni-Carly review, headlined "A 'Spark' of Strengths, with 'Hotcakes' of Humor") got at something important: Carly's songs "are stamped firmly with her own personality, yet the personal touch doesn't go so deep that listeners can't borrow a little from the music to apply to their own situations." Carly would continue to ply this identifiability. For almost twenty years after *Court and Spark,* Joni would largely abandon that territory (which she had pioneered) to stake her claim as a risk-taking musical artist.

The joint review was ironic because Carly felt competitive with Joni. Jac Holzman had left Elektra to research video and audio development for Warners; Elektra merged with Asylum, and Carly felt herself to be "the ugly stepdaughter" thrust into Joni's sponsor's stable. Carly heard that Geffen had said things about her; "I don't know if any of it is true," she would later say, "but they seemed vitriolic." Because *Hotcakes* was released close to the same time as *Court and Spark,* Carly and her manager, Arlyne Rothberg, felt that Joni's album was given priority.*

Six months after *Hotcakes* and Sally were born, James released his fifth album, *Walking Man,* his first without Peter Asher, Kootch, and others in their recording family. Despite seven weeks of promotional touring (and the achingly lovely title song), it sold surprisingly poorly, ending up as his lowest-selling album. When Carly had had her double #1 with *No Secrets* and its "You're So Vain," James's almost simultaneously released *One Man Dog* had peaked at #4, its single "Don't Let Me Be Lonely Tonight" at only #14. So now Carly had two albums and several singles that bettered her husband's—and handily. "And not only were Carly's doing better, but their albums were always released

---

* "The comparisons to Joni were a terrible thorn in Carly's side at the beginning," Jake Brackman says. Between Joni having been James's girlfriend and Joni's high esteem as a songwriter, "both of those things formed two blades of a single sword into her heart. She wanted the respect that Joni got. When Carly sold the rights to 'Anticipation'"—to Heinz Ketchup, for a popular commercial—"and appeared on the cover of *Playing Possum* in that little teddy, people would say to her, 'Joni *wouldn't* do that.' And that hurt her."

at the same time," Arlyne laments today. "You have to think back and say it was bad planning on everybody's part, including mine. Why didn't we have the good sense to say, 'Let's put at least eight months between them'?"

The disparity was "hard" on Carly's marriage, Arlyne says. "We hadn't come that much into female liberation—not that it's even easy today." Steve Harris recalls that now, during James's solo performances (he toured all the time, whereas Carly had stopped touring), "People in the audience would cry out, 'Where's Carly? Where's *Carly*?! Sing "Mockingbird"!' I don't know if James liked that." To appease his fans, James would bring his wife out from the wings and they'd duet on that cut from her album. Arlyne says that Carly "always, *always*" minimized her success in front of others, especially when James was around. "It became so natural that I did it automatically with James," Carly says. "She would never take a compliment without saying, 'I'm married to one of the world's great musicians,'" says Jessica.

Carly fell madly in love with Sally, and, like many upper-middle-class women in the new earthy-mom age who'd been raised with household help assisting social, distracted mothers, she was wrestling with a task that seemed as daunting as any other breakthrough. Ellen says that, for both of them, a big question was: "How can you carve out your own life, your own way of *being* in the world, that is radically different from the mothering that you had—and *become a different kind of mother*?" Even though she had her son, Niccolo, first, Ellen says, "I learned from Carly that you *could* consciously become someone different. She was a relaxed, spontaneous, loving, giving mother—so different than my own upbringing with nannies and formality."

Consciousness raising had exposed the mother-daughter knot. So many women were obsessing—to themselves, their friends, their therapists—over that relationship's seemingly inescapable imprint that author Nancy Friday was, shrewdly, writing a book (*My Mother/My Self*) that, upon its publication, would become a massive best seller. Carly had a mother's helper, but she did the day-to-day work herself and—to the horror of Trudy Taylor ("who," says Arlyne, "would tell *ev-*

erybody how to live their life; I think she criticized Carly a *lot.* I can't imagine anyone *not* being scared of her")—she was breast-feeding Sally. Using her body to nurse her baby—feeling "essential to someone else's life"—was, she said, as "heavy" (the then-favored word for "profound") an experience as "a woman could feel."

The young family moved to L.A. for a few months so James could record his sixth album, *Gorilla* (its title track named when James, after a fight with Carly, went to the Central Park Zoo, saw a gorilla, and imagined that that's how his angry wife viewed *him*), and Carly her fifth, *Playing Possum.* Carly's album cover was a provocative statement, that being a wife and mother didn't mean you gave up any hot-chick rights.

At Norman Seeff's studio in L.A. Carly took off her dress and started dancing around in a little black teddy and knee-high black boots. When she and Arlyne saw the contact sheet, they both zeroed in on a profile shot of her: she was on her knees, with her long, muscle-thighed legs apart, and her fists clenched at her side. It seemed as if she had nothing on under the teddy, which stopped mid-buttock. The photo was artily cropped so her head was half cut off, her hair springing down her back, her lips parted. It was an image of a beautiful, half-undressed, erotically charged young woman. In 1975, it stood to be the most explicitly sexual photograph ever chosen for the cover of *any* woman's album. Carly and Arlyne usually disagreed on cover shots, but on this one they were joined at the hip. "We both *knew* it was a great picture, and we were prepared to fight for it," Arlyne says. They didn't have to; "the record company never interfered."

That new mother and "erudite Simon & Schuster heiress" Carly Simon would use such a photograph caused a sensation; Sears Roebuck, the Wal-Mart of its day, banned the album; perfect strangers came up to Carly at Bloomingdale's and told her she was obscene and disgusting. But the album cover (which went on to adorn almost as many male dorm walls as the Betty Grable poster had adorned barracks walls in World War II) sent a welcome signal in that winner-take-all feminist moment. Carly was calmly defiant that being treated like a "piece of meat" by *others* was entirely separate from asserting her *own* carnality. "There's a great deal of difference," she informed *Rolling Stone's* Ben Fong-Torres. "Being attractive sexually is not something which I feel guilty about or embarrassed by in any way. I feel that it's *great*. I felt very sexy when I wrote most of the songs" on *Playing Possum*. (As if to underscore the point, she conducted part of the interview with Fong-Torres in an erotic art gallery, where she was selecting a painting—"Quite nice, but not erotic enough," she casually opined to the dealer—as a present to producer Richard Perry.)

Cueing off on the album's unavoidable talking point—its cover— Stephen Holden said that *Playing Possum* was a "celebration of the body at play" and that with it "Simon has largely abandoned plaintive balladeering for a blunt style that means to be aggressively sexy." Holden thought she tried but mostly missed the mark, except for what was supposed to have been the hit single, "Attitude Dancing" (it made a disappointing showing, peaking at #21). Actually, Holden had it backwards: "Attitude Dancing," an unmelodious gimmick song about a kind of precursor to "vogueing," was one of the least interesting songs in the album. The title song, "Playing Possum," a too wordy and too obvious bit of sociology inspired by her brother, Peter—about politicos becoming communards becoming Eastern-religion spiritualists—came in a close second in an album otherwise overflowing with songs that are rawly and elegantly all about sex. "After the Storm" takes on the impact of sex after an argument, from stimulation to appeasement. In the traditional, folky "Look Me in the Eyes"—with its delicate melody and celestial chorus—she's rubbing a lover's "limes" all over her body and "climb[ing] on you like a tree." The song's hook—"but I *beg* you when you love me, look me in the eyes"—poignantly joins the sexuality to intimacy. And despite the sometimes quotidian lyrics and an uninspired melody, "Waterfall" (with James humming in the background) seems to be about orgasm. "Are You Ticklish?" is a woman at a dinner party coming on to a man she wants to bed. In "Love Out in the Street," Carly is a *noir* hussy having a public sex spat with her lover. (She and James did have fights. During the production of *Playing Possum,* in March 1975, a twenty-seventh birthday party she hosted for him at their rented Coldwater Canyon house turned so unpleasant for her—Jake recalls it had "something to do with Joni"—that she ended the evening by checking into a hotel.)

The album's controversial centerpiece—Arlyne was nervous about Carly's insistence that it be released as its first single—was "Slave." The song was Carly's way of lamenting that, despite the rhetoric of feminism, acculturation and psychology were hard to change: "I'm just another woman, raised to be a slave." James's withholding nature, his lack of enthusiasm for her music, and her need to minimize her success around him: all of this kept feeding her desire to win him, a prize as elusive as her father had been. The song's candor is devastating.

The unsettling, politically incorrect song caused Arlyne to publicly break ranks with her client. "I don't like 'Slave,'" she told Fong-Torres, "not because of its music but because of its point of view." Arlyne, a rare female manager in rock music, had bristled when, during an early Central Park concert, the male stars had a trailer to dress and relax in, while Carly was made to change in the public ladies' room. But Carly held firm. Yes, she said, she expected the song to elicit a "little scurry of female hair on the back on first hearing, probably because [women will] take the song at face value," but she said that it was *actually* a "pro-high-consciousness" song because it identified a stubborn relic of female behavior that she was "angry about—goddamnit, sometimes I actually *still* feel like a slave!"—enough to want to alter. In retrospect "Slave" is apocryphal. Even decades after she and James divorced and remarried (and divorced those second mates), Carly Simon's inability to stop loving James—her involuntary fixation on their time together—is right up there with her great generosity, her sophisticated wit, her almost dangerous candor, and her joie de vivre as one of the most noticeable things about her. "James!" she exclaims in an e-mail. "What a clenched fist of hard love!" For years, with few exceptions, he has declined contact with her ("He's not going there—guys don't," one male friend says)—and about this willed avoidance she muses, with the pain that one hears in her songs: "There is no exit from that silence."

* * *

During the headily feminist/Me Decade years—when *New York* magazine's cover featured a picture of a smiling mother of three who "ran away" from her family and when Avery Corman was writing his soon-to-be-best-selling novel, *Kramer vs. Kramer,* about a custody fight between an oppressed wife turned self-actualizer and a sexist husband turned full-time father—the female partner of (as *Rolling Stone* had called them) the Simon-Taylors was dealing with the reality beneath the new fairy tale.

First, there was her commitment to being a mother. She was so wrapped up in Sally, for a while she thought she'd never record again. Second, there was her terror of performing. Fame—"that's been my viper, my devil, my iguana," she says—had exacerbated her stage fright; her "panic attacks" (which biofeedback, est, and Transcendental Meditation couldn't quell) were manifestations of her guilt at being the one Simon sister who *wasn't supposed* to be a star but became one. "Every minute of her career was drama," Arlyne recalls. For years to come, whole days before her performances would be devoted to her trying to calm herself, sometimes with the full-time help of loved ones.* Carly was literally hypersensitive. The lights, crowds, and loud noises of a large venue led to a condition called "flooding"; she would experience palpitations, feel as if she were going to have a heart attack. She stopped touring. Third, there was deference to James. This time around, his *Gorilla* and her *Playing Possum* were more evenly matched in sales, and James's hit from that album—the delicious "How Sweet It Is (to Be Loved by You)," which was a remake of Holland-Dozier-

---

* Jake reels off: "I've done it, Jim [Hart, her second husband] has done it, [friend] Tamara [Weiss] has done it, Sally's done it . . ." Leah Kunkel remembers Carly throwing up backstage before the 1979 No Nukes concert and thinking, "She's a little . . . *crazy!*" Carly took to wearing too-tight shoes, so the discomfort would preoccupy her out of her stage fright, and before performing at President Bill Clinton's birthday, she had her whole band take turns spanking her so the pain would knock out her fear of going on after Smokey Robinson.

Holland's Motown hit for Marvin Gaye—shot to #5. "There have been moments of terrible friction based on who is higher on the charts," Carly admitted a few years later, "and it's more comfortable if James is more successful than I am." At the same time, Carly controlled most of their day-to-day life. "He completely went along with her life," says Jake. "That's the thing with a junkie: They've got a secret;* they've got a little other life—*that's* what *they* control. But their outward life, they give *you* to control." The men around Carly saw her changing. "She went into this myth of being a wife and mother so strongly, even when James was on the nod," says Jake. On James's tour of Japan, Russ Kunkel recalls, "Carly came along and she was like anybody's wife." Russ adds, "They seemed, as a couple, very much in love."

The early to late-middle 1970s was one of the worst times to be married to someone with an addictive personality. Hard drugs, especially cocaine, were now considered "recreational," and celebrities were always plied with them. "James would get a lot of free dope because people wanted to spend a little time with him and that was their ticket to an hour or two," Jake says. "They'd say, 'I just got a little China white' or 'I just got a little Mexican brown.'" "I'm ashamed to say that I was really in cahoots with James," Betsy Asher says. "I was in trouble myself—doing coke, way too much." "It wasn't a strange time for [addiction] to be happening in the music business—it was almost unheard of for it *not* to be happening," Carly says. At the same time, much less was known about spouses' roles in addiction than is known today, and the addict's desperate-to-help partner had to make do with guidance that had barely moved beyond the pot-and-psychedelics days. "Colleagues of mine who were practicing in the 1960s and 1970s tell me that the concept of 'codependency' didn't come in until the *end* of the 1970s," says Dr. Terry Horton, medical director of Phoenix House, the largest and one of the oldest nonprofit substance abuse

---

* James enjoyed hiding references to heroin use in his lyrics, he once told one of his dope dealers (who was interviewed for this book) during a dressing-room hand-over of some balloon-bagged product in the early 1970s.

services organizations in the country. Al-Anon, Alcoholics Anonymous's spouses' group, was known only to people in "the program"; this did not include James, who utilized private treatment (at a facility on York Avenue, and through talks with Dr. Andrew Weil, and others) but was not in AA.

Thus, in a hedonistic, drug-friendly time, couples outside of the small addict-and-partner help community were left to their own naïve devices. James was a young, lifelong-privileged man, able to feel he could beat the odds. During his marriage to Carly, he did *not* reach the point "where you say," as Peter Asher puts it, "'either I quit or I die.'"

Carly was at a loss for how to help James. "She'd get hysterical at his disappearance," says Jake. "She'd find the dope and flush it down the toilet." Carly says, "I lived in a state of fear for years. Addiction really takes over everything, and we were in its power. When James walked in the door, I was overly sensitive in examining his expression, examining the size of his pupils, looking for evidence—*always* looking for evidence. I was so nervous every time he went in a bathroom. I was incredibly naïve. I thought I could actually stop his addiction. Who was I kidding?" Still, she says, "like all difficult situations," James's addiction was "something we got used to. Generally there were not emergency situations"; rather, there were "ones where he had to sleep something off or the regular methadone delivery [was late]."

Yet there *were* other times. "James was a very active addict in those years," says one who worked with him. Peter Asher says, "You rapidly learn, about druggies: they will lie; they will cheat; they will do all kinds of despicable things. Carly and James would have rows quite often. They were two talented, neurotic, very interesting people, which made their relationships difficult," even apart from James's addiction. ("I got him with all his baggage, and he got me with all of mine" is how Carly puts it.) Asher continues, "She was justified in ordering him out of the house a couple of times. During one of those archetypal moments I got a call from the Westbury Hotel, where we had an account. The desk clerk said, 'There's a man here—he's shown up, he's kind of disheveled, he's got no shoes on and no identification, and he claims to be James Taylor.' My assistant, Gloria, said, 'That's him!' She didn't need to talk to him." It turned out that "Carly and James had had a huge row, and he left the house and made his way to the Westbury, shoeless. Obviously, it had been an altercation of some vehemence."

On the other hand, James's effort to quit drugs made him tremendously poignant to Carly. "James was very, very rigorous at fighting his addiction, and it was very moving to see his fight," she says. Jake, who is seasoned in AA talk, says, using a term that wasn't known back then, "Carly was an enabler." As Carly explains, "A lot of James's relationships, including with me, fed into his addiction. When you're an addict, if you decide you're seeing, say, maple trees, then seeing one leaf fall from the tree is going to get you to need the drug. A lot of what I became to him became what he had to go get the drug to avoid.

"So I became very much the enemy, and it fit into the way I had been treated by a lot of men in my life, especially my father. It's so hard to break those patterns! I found James incredibly intoxicating and brilliant and funny; what was devastating was how he turned so many of those things against me. And you feel so responsible! 'What did I do wrong?!'" James's drug addiction, exacerbating his withdrawing nature as it did, stimulated Carly's neediness, just as her father's silences had, years earlier. What the needle-and-guitar was for the one, the infirmity-and-piano had been for the other. In both realms was a girl hungry for love and a mother pained that her husband wasn't more present with their children. "It became a cat-and-mouse game," says Carly. Tim White expressed it this way: James was "clever, shy, reckless, aloof, gentle and romantic in his own unreliable way; he was as casually self-absorbed as a man hooked on heroin for the better part of nine years could be. Drawing him out of that relationship and into hers, Carly found, was like pulling a grown man through a knothole." More bluntly, Arlyne says, "It's impossible to have a relationship with a junkie; there's no 'there' there!"

While trying to rescue her husband and caring for Sally, Carly continued to write and record. She put her complaints about James's absent parenting and their fights over the parental double standard into the sarcastically sweet-sounding "Fairweather Father" (in the liner notes, she denied the song was about James) for her 1976 *Another Passenger*. Though the album, produced by Ted Templeman, didn't sell well, it was praised by *Rolling Stone*'s Ken Tucker. Still, that review and others reprised some old cliché complaints about her.

By now, the hard-core rock press had gotten over their enthrall-ment with "You're So Vain" and were back to dismissing Carly as slick and pop. Even some women reviewers disliked Carly for a life that seemed too easy, straight, and connected.* Yet the women's movement was encouraging college girls to apply to law and med school; to be a young *woman* was to recast as *correctly* "political" those things (acquir-ing professional status and one's own money) that had been disdained as bourgeois—and were *still* bourgeois if you were male. Whether they were slightly younger women who were embracing currently-NOW-blessed, once-thought-"straight" ambition, or ex-wild-children Carly's

---

*   Local women were especially harsh, since late 1970s Manhattan was exceedingly down at its heels, and downtowners had a cockeyed pride in living closer to its filthy curbs than, say, a Central Park West penthouse. Two female *Village Voice* reviewers took gentle to not-so-gentle aim at Carly's May 1977 appearance at the Other End (the re-named Bitter End), which was attended by Diane Keaton, Warren Beatty, and Art Gar-funkel. Susin Shapiro derided the "culturally privileged turnout" filled with "record honchos" who "cooed and purred," along with "Carly's family, friends, some select press, plus a few paying customers in the spirit of token democracy." M. Mark started her review by declaring, "Carly Simon has been getting on my nerves for years"; harrumphed suspiciously through Carly's performance; opined, of her romantic-pain songs, "She's too sleek and well-adjusted to be a credible victim"; and assailed her for being more cotillion than feminist. "Although she's begun to consider the injustices of the prom world, she apparently hasn't thought about walking away from that old demeaning dance of courtly love. It's way past time for Carly Simon to define herself. She'll always get asked to the prom, and she doesn't have to say yes." Steve Harris remembers that evening—including the fact that Mick Jagger slipped into the club (somehow, over these years, he was always subtly circling Carly) and sat down in the back booth with him, Arlyne, and Diane Keaton. The presence of the sexy lead Rolling Stone made Keaton so unbalanced, she called him "Mike" instead of Mick all night.

own age made suddenly sensible by having babies, young and young-ish women *were* becoming more "middle-class."

From *Passenger,* Carly had a hit with a Michael McDonald song, "It Keeps You Runnin'," and its "Libby" celebrates her new close friend-ship with songwriter Libby Titus, "a charming, funny, vivacious hell of a woman," as Danny Kortchmar describes her, whose lovers or hus-bands included, in said order, the Band's Levon Helm, Dr. John, and Steely Dan's Donald Fagen.

Another new friend was Mia Farrow, Carly's neighbor in the Cen-tral Park West building that she and James moved into as renters after selling their brownstone. "I wanted to *be* Carly," Mia says. "I would see her walking down Seventy-second Street smiling, with a big bunch of flowers and her coat almost to the ground—the woman can *stride!*—and I knew all was well with the world. Even though she was riddled with phobias and she was always running herself down about her stage fright, she's also fearless with love and life." The two women created, in their floors-apart twelve-room spreads with Central Park views, a cup-of-sugar-borrowing friendship that spanned the 1970s and 1980s. And Carly visited on Mia the kind of solicitousness she lavished on her other women friends: Carly would make Mia her special red wine pasta; Carly was Mia's son Moses' godmother; when Mia's mother took a fall in the building, Mia came home to find Carly and Jake standing over the older woman with a first-aid manual. Carly fixed Mia up with a male friend of hers, dressing Mia for the date "in an antique lace blouse from out of her closet," Mia recalls, "and introducing me to the man with lights down and candles burning." They would spend hours comparing money problems and shortcomings. "Not that we weren't *both* paralyzed with fear, but I'm more repressed, and Carly seemed so strong in my life—like a warrior, and the most loyal person I know. And she has a childlike quality of being unbuffered by her accomplish-ments. I've spent my whole life around celebrities in one way or an-other, and I've never known a celebrity *less* likely to get any safety and comfort from her success; it's like she's nine years old sometimes."

And Mia noticed, of course, Carly's trademark quality: "She is the most romantic *and most indiscreet* person I know."

The demureness of the photos (emphasizing Carly's face and long legs) for *Another Passenger* was due to the fact that she was pregnant through much of 1976. On January 22, 1977, she gave birth to a son, Benjamin, by natural childbirth. James timed Carly's six hours of contractions and, charmingly, made up a story to try to preoccupy his wife during each one. It was Carly who'd endured the horrendous labor pains, yet she told a reporter that James's help and his lack of flinching had led the impressed doctor to "let him stay 'til the end"; in this she was displaying the pride and optimism of the bad-boy-taming woman, reveling in the reliability she had gently coaxed out of her rebel. She was naïve, of course. A friend who himself had a drug problem remembers how Carly would tell him about James's rehab efforts, hopeful each time. The friend was dubious. "James would go in detoxes; then he'd come out and something would happen and he'd go back to drugs. He had the junkie mannerisms, the junkie gait: things he didn't lose. If you keep those attitudes, after rehab, something gets you uptight and you're back on drugs again."

The focus of Carly's worried vigilance shifted off James's physical signs and onto the baby's: Carly felt sure that something was wrong with their son. "He was hardly a sick-looking child, but he would run these high fevers; Carly would have to put him in a tub to get them down," says Arlyne. "All the doctors were saying, 'There's nothing wrong with him, there's *nothing* wrong with him,'" but she continued to take him to doctors. "She persisted; she was like a mother possessed."

Carly's seventh album, *Boys in the Trees,* produced by Arif Mardin, was released in June 1978. (In the meantime, she had had a #1 adult contemporary hit singing the Carole Bayer Sager–Marvin Hamlisch song, "Nobody Does It Better," the title song of the James Bond movie *The Spy Who Loved Me.*) Carly posed for the cover photo, by Deborah Turbeville, sitting, bare-breasted, in an empty ballet studio, rolling a silk stocking up one leg. But she and Arlyne ended up thinking that, as Arlyne puts it, "the picture didn't lend itself to the sensationalism of having her naked" so they had it retouched to add a silky camisole. The album, which went platinum, gave Carly a Top 10 hit with the bouncy, torchy, loving "You Belong to Me," which she cowrote with Michael McDonald, and which, like so many of her songs—including another on the album, "In a Small Moment" (and "In Times When My Head," in the previous one)—was about cheating, jealousy, and temptation: the adult preoccupations she had witnessed in her childhood and which were dancing around the corners of her current life. The title song—the reverent, eerie "Boys in the Trees," in which she relives her sexual awakening in the bosky secret garden of the Simon beauties—is one of her most personal and haunting. It showcases her mainstay themes—pounding lust, high anxiety, female competition—and in the same way that endearingly clunky lines have become her signature, so, too, now is a kind of unique geography. The place "where the boys grow on the trees"; the woman-rivers; the lovers who become each other's West Indies; men becoming oceans: all dot a sensual interior map as pungent and viney as a Rousseau painting and as quirky as Dr. Seuss land.

The five-and-a-half-year marriage of James and Carly seemed at a point of sublime equilibrium. They had their son and their daughter, and the Vineyard house that James (who would rather be up there fixing a carburetor than going to one of Carly's Manhattan fundraisers for *Ms.*-supported political candidates) was working on. And, for all Carly's angst about their competition over pop-chart standings (she had recently talked to her brother's guru, Ram Dass, about the sticky situation), this new album of hers involved more of James's input than any previous one. He *la-la-la*'d on "Boys in the Trees." Carly sang his self-mockingly bluesy "One Man Woman" and a disco song—"Tranquillo (Melt My Heart)"—that they had written together, which was unabashedly derivative of the year's musical smash hit, the Bee Gees' *Saturday Night Fever* soundtrack. Most affecting was their duet on the Everly Brothers' "Devoted to You." On it the two "lanky aristocrats" sounded as stirringly pious—as poor-white-soul—as if they were sitting in an Appalachian church pew.

It had been a good couple of years for James Taylor. His *Greatest Hits* album had been released, and after moving to Columbia he'd enjoyed, in the album *JT,* a full-scale comeback. The rocking "Your Smiling Face" was his biggest self-written hit since "Fire and Rain," and he had another hit in his inspired remake of Jimmy Jones's slyly boastful pop soul "Handy Man." But it was not a good time at home. Carly was still desperately searching for the cause of Ben's fevers. Arlyne, who had a son with a medical condition and who knew how a child's health could overtake one's life, was awed by her friend's refusal to take no for an answer. Because so many doctors were saying that despite the fevers, the child was fine, "even James said, 'Leave him alone!' and I could understand anybody saying that, because the doctors had been so reassuring," Arlyne recalls. "But Carly's attitude was, she was going to save that kid, no matter what! She was the best mother of anyone I knew—and that was before the parenting books; you had to do it by instinct." Carly was still breast-feeding Ben;* despite Trudy Taylor's very vocal disapproval, she would do so for three and a half years.

The strictures of Carly's complicated domesticity were making her work harder than ever. While taking care of a baby, a toddler, and an addict husband (who was touring many months of the year, leaving her functionally as a single mother), she was writing songs for *Come Upstairs,* her eighth album of almost totally original songs in as many years. She who (as opposed to Joni and Carole) had floundered in her free-as-a-bird early to mid-twenties—writing unsuccessfully; taking lowly jobs; unable to marshal the ambition that her boyfriends (disapprovingly) saw in her but her girlfriends didn't—discovered something

---

* Breast-feeding was still considered downscale, weird, or "hippie" in the late 1970s, especially to high-born women from a different generation and men from the provinces. When Joe Armstrong, the new *Rolling Stone* bureau chief, came over to Carly and James's apartment for dinner one night, he was stunned when Carly whipped out her breast to nourish Ben while passing the salt and pepper. "I was this kid from West Texas! You sort of want to watch, but you don't want anyone seeing you watching," he recalls.

that other women of the I Am Woman, post-hip era were discovering: that limits and responsibilities could actually discipline and focus you. "I've gotten to know myself much better in the context of marriage," she told *Rolling Stone*'s Charles Young, who seemed shocked by that women's-magazine-like admission. "Everything was amorphous before," Carly continued. "Now I know what I can do and what I can't. Too much freedom doesn't help you artistically." Young tried to shake some proper I'd-die-for-my-art! statements out of this too-sensible realist, asking Carly what she'd do if her "muse" told her she'd have to move to a "grungy small town in the Midwest" for artistic inspiration. She replied, "I would have to see if they had good schools, good drinking water, good playgrounds." A really *grungy* town, Young prodded. But he wasn't talking to muse-directed Joni. "Then I couldn't go," Carly said. "My children need me here." Yet all this groundedness didn't keep her from *also* saying, when Young asked why so many of her songs seemed to be about adultery, "I've never bought that open-marriage thing—I've never seen it work—but that doesn't mean I believe in monogamy. Sleeping with someone else doesn't necessarily constitute an infidelity." Rather, she said with a laugh, infidelity was "having sex with somebody else and telling your spouse about it, anything you feel guilty about." She concluded, as many in the decade had concluded: "I don't think anybody has any idea what sexual morality is anymore."

Despite his success, James was not in control. He was binge drinking—going on benders with his friend Jimmy Buffett, blacking out at parties. ("I don't have much moderation in my drinking," he would soon admit to his friend Tim White, in *Rolling Stone*; "I get intoxicated, I lose control, and I've sometimes made mistakes when I was too high that I deeply regret.") Jessica remembers visiting Carly in a Boston hotel room, and "James was sitting back in the shadows in his white pajamas, in and out of being present. He was a very nice man when he was present, but he suffered from his addictions all the time."

Soon after, the couple was visited at their Vineyard house by a coked-up John Belushi and his wife, Judy. When Judy, whose tough, cool manner had led Carly to believe that she didn't share Carly's angst and worry, confided to Carly that *she* didn't know how to keep *her* husband from doing drugs, Carly burst out in tears at the futility of her own more earnest efforts. By the winter of 1979–1980 "Carly was very long-suffering," Betsy Asher says. Betsy recalls "one outrageous night" in New York when she, James, and others "had been out at a Cuban restaurant and walking with Eric Idle and his now-wife, Tina, and Richard Belzer, who was over the line. We went back to Carly and James's place—it was two or three in the morning—and Richard was yelling obscenities out the window and Carly came out and said, 'The children are asleep.' Poor thing! She was carrying the whole load alone." Jake agrees: "Betsy and James were snorting together. *So* many people were. People that Carly considered her friends, me included, were at cross-purposes with her; they were turning on with James." Still, "James *was* trying to figure his addiction out. He would profess a desire to change; he would say that *very* sincerely and Carly would be full of hope." "And," Carly says, with admirable honesty, "in *not* knowing *how* to help, I became even more helpless and foolish and more of a deterrent to his stopping. In my very small and genteel and tidy way, I was trying to make up for the explosion of a city"—James's addiction, abetted by their friends—"by cleaning up one small block": throwing away the drugs, examining his pupils.

In 1979 Carly wrote and recorded one of her most candid albums: *Spy.* Taking the fraught secrecy and erotic betrayals of her childhood (which now had counterparts in her marriage), she set out to "spy on myself." Other than a minor hit with the hard-rocking "Vengeance" (about a man and woman out-betraying each other)—full of her signature belting—no one seemed to notice the heartfelt album, which, in retrospect, sounds like a zero-hour bid to save her marriage. In "Just Like You Do," she makes common cause with James's vulnerability—her fears and phobias the equal to his addiction—begging him "to return to that brave innocence we once knew." "Love You by Heart," which she wrote with Libby and Jake, is a plea for James to get off junk. "We're So Close," which announces its significance with stark piano chords, serves up a therapy session truism with elegance and surprise. Using, as a vehicle, the skilled Vineyard architectural work that James had thrown himself into for escape (and using her favorite narrative story form*), she has the man in the song say, "We're so close, we can dispense with houses": in the rush of love and avoidance, even what is being (or *needs* to be) built can be brushed aside. She closes by learning that an overinvested-in re-bound that's meant to *repair* only worsens the problem: the man ends up saying, "We're so close we can dispense with love." From houses to love, from symbol to essence. To this day, Carly believes "We're So Close," through which she acknowledged her marriage's dissolution, "is the saddest song I ever wrote." The betrayals that the album hints at were real. "The 'jungle'—the basic reptilian brain—took over" in terms of temptations, Carly says. "There were admissions of infidelities and things you try to do"—confessing, apologizing—"with all the amount of love surrounding it." When male rock stars were on the road, there were girls—it came with the territory—and James was not immune. Meanwhile, James, as some-one who worked with him thought, still harbored suspicions that Carly and Mick Jagger were continuing contact. Finally, as 1979 turned to 1980, James became involved with a Japanese dancer named Evelyne and Carly drew very close to studio engineer Scott Litt.

Carly and vibraphonist Mike Mainieri began to write together: she the lyrics, he collaborating with her on the music, "and in the slow weeks of winter we rented a small house in Vineyard Haven on the beach." Of their efforts, collected in *Come Upstairs*—songs that represented Carly's new desire to "get there faster, without so much intellectualization"—*Rolling Stone*'s Ken Tucker said her "instincts are bold, but her music betrays her. Confronting a self-imposed semi-retirement [not evidenced in her album output, just her performing],

---

* Carly once described this form thusly: "I wra[p] the story line in four simple verses (ABAB) with a bridge just before the last chorus . . . It's like the ballads I used to sing that reach a climax somewhere around the fourth stanza, and then the final chorus has a kind of irony, meaning something different when all the facts are on the table."

declining disc sales and the pervasive peppiness of the new wave, Simon has responded with a comely perversity by writing a batch of new songs that are either loose and trashy or tight and morose." The title song was a new wave–beated riff on Carly's franchise subject, seduction and sex; it was likable, but some of the others had a faux-B-52's feeling that brought out her shrillness without her melodiousness. Having gotten a late start on her career, she seemed to be in overdrive now, both missing *and* hitting. With her infectious "Jesse"—utilizing the full arc of her plea-to-rocking-growl range—she hit #11, her first big score in a little more than two years. (Meanwhile, James's album *Flag* was going platinum due to its single of Carole and Gerry's "Up on the Roof.") Barely noticed on *Come Upstairs* was the song she titled "James." On it her voice is so meek, she—the brassy-classy queen of indiscretion—seems to be asking permission to name him. Strikingly, she uses the same images (a seashell pressed to the ear; the younger James slumped soulfully over his guitar) that Joni had used in her songs about him.

On the strength of her hit with "Jesse," Carly planned a *Come Upstairs* tour, pushing herself back on the road. All of this—the writing and recording, the time with Scott Litt, the James separation that wasn't a separation, the planning of the tour—was wrapped around her life's core: Sally and Ben. Carly was the over-the-top mother she'd become ("She's like me," says Arlyne, of their mothering of their once-infirm adult sons: 'You'll do your own laundry when I'm *dead!*'") because of her memory of her own childhood. Perhaps it took a former child hypochondriac to obsess about Ben's fevers, despite doctors' telling her he *wasn't* sick.

In summer 1980, before the tour was to start, came Carly's "worst day of my life."

It turned out she had been right in her insistent hunch about Ben. As Arlyne recalls, "She found a doctor who said, 'Look at this—his *kidney!*'" It was dysplastic (abnormally formed). "One kidney was totally diseased; it had to come out immediately. The other was partially diseased; it would be regenerated. Carly's finding that doctor was one

carly

Carly's goofy behavior, at eight, was her way of getting attention as the youngest in a trio of sisters. *(Photo by Richard Simon, courtesy of Carly Simon)*

When Richard Simon died, high school senior Carly was comforted by Harvard freshman and budding novelist Nick Delbanco. Soon they would play house, expatriate style, in the south of France. *(Peter Simon)*

Carly (far right) was a bridesmaid at the June 1964 wedding of her best friend, Ellen Wise (center), to high school sweetheart Vieri Salvadori. Shortly afterward, Carly went off to England and met decadent, witty lady-killer Willie Donaldson. *(Courtesy of Ellen Questel)*

Carly's opening for Cat Stevens at L.A.'s Troubadour in April 1971 debuted her eponymous first album and made her a star. Cat became the first of her many rock- and movie-star romances that spring and summer. *(Peter Simon)*

Carly's very private wedding to James Taylor, in November 1972—just before "You're So Vain" was released (and just after Bianca Jagger told James she suspected Mick and Carly had been lovers)—found them waxing somber. (*Peter Simon*)

But a honeymoon pose captures them as rock's blithely glamorous First Couple. *(Peter Simon)*

An addict virtually all through their marriage, James looks slightly uptight while frolicking with Carly and preschooler Sally in their Central Park West apartment. (*Peter Simon*)

Carly and James belt out "Mockingbird" at James's concert at the Universal Amphitheater in L.A. in August 1975. (© *Sherry Rayn Barnett*)

Carly marries poet, insurance man, and ex-priest-in-training Jim Hart on Martha's Vineyard in November 1987. *(Peter Simon)*

One of the first celebrities that newly elected Bill Clinton wanted to meet was Carly. In the summer of '93 the Clintons and the Harts got together on the Vineyard. The president's hand tight around Carly's bathing-suited waist and that familiar, slightly-more-rakish-than-Oval-Office smile speak volumes. *(Peter Simon)*

A mutual friend thinks Carly's lack of inhibition enabled Jackie Kennedy Onassis (here with Carly in the early '90s) to vicariously be the person she might have been without the burdens of tragedy and hagiography. *(Peter Simon)*

At a 2006 concert in Boston (where Carly performed with Ben and Sally), Carly and lifetime close friend Jessica Hoffmann Davis celebrate the camaraderie that began when they were awkwardly tall preteens in Riverdale. *(Peter Simon)*

of the most miraculous things I've ever seen." However, according to
Timothy White's book, James's father, Ike Taylor, was crucial in secur-
ing the doctor.

Ben was rushed to Columbia Presbyterian Hospital for emergency
surgery. Carly waited through the surgery, distraught. James was not
there. "Here was Ben—very, very sick—and instead of showing up at
the hospital, James was out on the street; Carly couldn't understand it,
couldn't deal with it," recalls Steve Harris. According to Carly, James
wasn't there with Ben because he was driving his girlfriend Evelyne to
the airport.

After Ben was wheeled out of surgery, "Carly was at his bedside
and she was losing it," Arlyne remembers. Andrea Simon urged propriety and stoicism upon her highly emotional daughter. "She was saying,
'Remember who you are, conduct yourself well.'"

When James finally arrived at the hospital, he didn't go in right
away. "He was sitting on the stoop outside while I was screaming at
him to go upstairs," Arlyne says. "He didn't react to anything I said."
Eventually, he went upstairs—and as Ben was waking up from the anesthesia, a touching scene ensued. The little boy's penis had been protectively taped against his body for the surgery, "but Ben thought,
'Where *is* it?!'" Jake says. When Ben couldn't find his penis and started
crying, James pulled down his own pants and "tucked his own penis
under" some material "to say, 'It's still here; it's just under the ban-
dages.' James really rose to the occasion, and it was very sweet."

Still, touching scene or not, Carly couldn't get past James's absence
during the surgery. She knew he loved the children, but to disappear
during the direst emergency, at the very moment his presence was
most needed? That grievous act of self-absorption became the point of
no return in their crumbling marriage. James could ignore *her*, but ignoring *Ben* at his most vulnerable was unforgivable.

In this, she was bolstered by the climate. The consciousness-
raising groups of nine years earlier had evolved into tough girlfriend
talk against men behaving badly. Women had bills of rights, lists of
what they shouldn't and wouldn't take anymore. Over the last few

years, during Ellen's now-rocky and unhappy marriage to Vieri, "I would tell Carly my woes and she would commiserate. One day she said to me, 'You know, you said this five years ago to me and I'm really afraid you're going to say this five years from now.' That was my wake-up call." Divorce came to be seen as a necessary righting of a danger-ously compromised disequilibrium that would only continue to hurt the woman. The belief, introduced by Carly's first song, that a barely independent woman could best strengthen herself *alone* had mush-roomed into orthodoxy. In the recent *An Unmarried Woman,* Jill Clay-burgh's character broke up with an "ideal" man (played with rumpled charm by Alan Bates) because she still had "work" to do on herself after her recently ended marriage. Carly—and Clayburgh, and Arlyne's other client Diane Keaton, and Meryl Streep—represented all those brainy, likably neurotic women who'd *just* learned to stop taking crap from men, while other women cheered them on.

Arlyne now wonders if Carly should have listened so much to the empathic outrage at James's behavior that came her way during those months. "Having a sick kid is different than any other situation. There wasn't a chance to let them recover from the ordeal without making judgments. It's like saying, 'Dad just died; shall we sell the house?' You can't decide life-changing things when you're in the midst of *another* life-changing thing."

Carly lost twenty-five pounds from her thin frame during Ben's convalescence. Despite her anger at James, "there was a great attempt" for them "to be solid and get back together around Ben," she says. Mia Farrow knew something "horrific" had befallen her neighbor's son; but, she says with regret now, she couldn't be of much help because "the children and I had moved into Woody Allen's sphere and my friends were not welcome by him there. That doesn't speak very well of me, but that's the way I was then."

In the fall, with Ben strong enough for her to leave his bedside, Carly embarked on the rescheduled *Come Upstairs* tour. Her son had conquered a degenerative kidney; well, then, *she* could conquer her fear of large concert halls. Later she realized that "the very idea of the tour was foolish," given Ben's illness and the deterioration of her marriage, but the colliding crises had stripped her of perspective. The first five dates went well; she had triumphantly staved off the "flooding." But then, in Pittsburgh, "she just gave in," Jake says. Soon after the fateful night, she described to Tim White what he then termed the "grotesque denouement" of her ten-year-long performing career: "I felt as if I couldn't stand up straight—and then I couldn't catch my breath. When I got out onstage I was having such bad palpitations that I couldn't breathe at all and I couldn't get the words to the songs out. I seemed to go to pieces in front of the audience."

As she later told Stephen Holden, Carly realized she had a choice. "I could either leave the stage and say I was sick or tell the audience the truth. I decided to tell [the truth and say] I was having an anxiety attack, and they were incredibly supportive. They said, 'Go with it— we'll be with you!' But after two songs I was still having palpitations. I suggested that I might feel better if someone came on the stage. About fifty people came up [onstage] and it was like an encounter group. They were massaging my back and legs and saying, 'Hey, Carly, we're with you—take your time.' They rubbed my arms and legs and said, 'We love you.'" With her fans' help, "I was able to finish the first show. But I collapsed before the second show, with ten thousand people waiting." She cried her eyes out at the failure and humiliation.

Carly came home and tried to sort things out. Though she was giving up performing (at Lucy's behest), she continued to record. She put together an album—*Torch*—of classic torch songs (adding a song of her own) and a blues number. Mike Mainieri arranged and produced it. Its cover showed Carly in a low-cut gown, writhing in pain and longing, grasping the arm of a tall, dark—James-like—man who, his back turned, is pulling away from her. She dedicated the album to her parents, her uncles, and Jonathan Schwartz, all of whom had ingrained in her a love of standards. She added: "Also to those who made me cry." A gold-card member of the sexual revolution, a pop goddess, Carly had been in love so many times you'd think she'd have hardened by now. "But some of them," she says today, as she felt then, "just *last*, like motherfuckers . . ."

Carly took the album to L.A. in mid-1981. She tracked down Danny Armstrong, who was living there. "I don't know how she got my number," he said, "but she said, 'Why don't you come over; I'm at a friend's place and my friend isn't here.' I said, 'I'll bring my wife'"—he had recently married, and he was still in payback mode— "and she asked, 'Oh, do you *have* to?' I said, 'Yes. I do.'" He paid Carly a visit.

Danny, who had thought that Carly "followed directions on life's box," and who had smoothed the ruffled feathers of his class resentment with the consolation that she could never achieve any of her idol Odetta's soulfulness, was stunned by the pain she was in. As they talked, he saw a woman far deeper than the jaunty girlfriend he remembered. "She was so unhappy; after me, she'd been through a lot of crap. She'd changed a lot." Danny had assumed that fame had made the uptown girl *more* uptown; this was a reversal of expectations. She put the album on the record player. "You'll like this; it's right up your alley," she said. They listened to her sing "I Got It Bad and That Ain't Good"—"and," Danny recalled, "it was so good—so moving—it upset me."

James and Carly officially separated. "James would never have left; he's not the type. He would never leave anybody—*never*; he makes the women leave; they have no choice," Jake says, echoing Susan Braudy's perception of his passive-aggressive nature. So Carly made the move, which meant she shouldered the responsibility, and risked any remorse, for their marriage being over. James took a small apartment in the neighborhood to be close to the children. "James and I had had other [lovers], but we hadn't split, and when we split, he took it terribly; I didn't take it well, either," she says.

The children were deeply affected. Eventually—one might say inevitably—came regret, and Carly begged James to come back. "I beat my head against the wall so many times," she says. "'Please! We're af-fecting two children's lives—let's reconsider!'" But James had moved on from Evelyne. The new woman in his life, who was not happy with Carly's entreaties (nor Carly with her), was actress Kathryn Walker. Carly's particular view of things then is that "when James met Kathryn Walker, he was happy for a moment because I loved somebody else"—Scott Litt—and now he was tended to. (Kathryn Walker's comments to Tim White, in the biography *Long Ago and Far Away: James Taylor, His Life and Music,** indicate a much closer, more sincere meeting of the souls between the two: "James and I met at a point in both our lives when we were open to a fresh start, to the need for a new begin-ning . . . We also just fell in love.") In Carly's view, Kathryn was deter-mined and predatory. "She was a fierce, fierce woman who wanted James at all costs. She knew exactly what she wanted."

Kathryn Walker was an actress of the most serious sort. She had taken graduate classes at Harvard, been a Fulbright scholar in dra-matic arts in London, and her résumé featured theater work and work in Emmy-winning PBS and other quality TV productions in New York. She was fresh from a wrenching (and, no doubt, guilt-inducing) trag-edy. In August 1980 her fiancé, Doug Kenney, the Harvard-educated cofounder of the *National Lampoon* and cowriter of *Caddyshack,* a brilliant, unstable thirty-two-year-old cocaine abuser who had joked about suicide, died from a suspicious fall from a cliff in Hawaii right after Kathryn had left him on the island to return to work. (Kenney's was one of the funerals that had occasioned Joni's relationship with Dave Naylor.) Among Kenney's last jotted writings, which his friend Chevy Chase found, were declarations of his love for Kathryn. If there was anyone motivated to *save* a man, it might be a woman who'd en-

---

*   For the book, which was published in 2002, White (who died of a heart attack just after its completion) was forbidden by Trudy Taylor from interviewing Carly and obtain-ing her point of view. White's portrait of Carly is neutral to negative; his portrait of Kath-ryn Walker, whom he interviewed, and who was by then divorced from James (James had married his third wife, Kim Smedvig, the public relations director of the Boston Symphony Orchestra), is almost obsequiously positive.

dured the suicide of a man who'd signaled that he'd *needed* saving from her.

In 1982 and early 1983, two avoidable deaths stunned James Taylor. His friend John Belushi died of a cocaine-heroin speedball, and his acquaintance Beach Boy Dennis Wilson drowned while swimming drunk. These tragedies issued that "either I quit or die" message that Peter Asher always knew would be the only hope of salvation for James. At almost the very time that Carly's divorce from him was filed, James checked into a detoxification clinic; he had cleared four months for the process. "You don't '*get* someone straight'; the addict has to do it himself," says a person who was with James "the night he went into rehab. He went there by himself. You hit bottom, you wake up, you make that decision."

Kathryn Walker helped James Taylor through it. Susan Braudy ran into her in the midst of James's detoxification—which included night sweats, outbursts, nightmares—and "Kathryn said, 'This is too much! This is impossible!' She couldn't deal with it anymore." But, says the friend who was with James when he entered rehab, "Kathryn was powerful." She was also that rare thing in 1982: "a practiced Al-Anon member."

After detoxification, James funneled his energy into exercise. He worked out five days a week at a gym and jumped rope hours a day. "It's hard to stay sober," the friend, who often worked out with him, says. "He's done an amazing job." He never relapsed.

That Carly should have spent nine years doing everything she could think of to try to get James over his addiction (while some of her friends undercut her by partaking of drugs with him); that she had to painfully watch his addiction detract from his parenting of their children—and *then* for him to get clean so quickly and thoroughly after their divorce, with another woman's help—"this was the *absolutely crushing irony*," Jake says. "Carly was trying to do this the entire time she was with him, then Kathryn comes in and—boom!—he's Mr. Twelve Step." A friend who met Carly in the early 1980s recalls, "She said, 'It's not fair! When I had him he was a heroin addict and now Kathryn gets him and he's healthy!' She talked about James obsessively. It was clear to me that she was profoundly in love with him, and that she certainly hadn't settled certain issues about this. A great deal of what was left needed emotional cauterization; that wound seems, to me, to be open still." The person continues, gingerly: "You take heroin, you're escaping from some pain; you're able to stop taking it, maybe the pain's gone. Carly never drew the connection: James clearly was not prepared to walk away from drugs when he was married to her. I didn't see the two of them together so I didn't know the dynamic, but," the person is implying, maybe there was something *in* the fabric of the relationship that made it hard for him to stop. As Carly herself said, "I very much became the enemy." "What a hard thing for her to have to bear," Jake says, "whether it was the fault of their dynamic or not."

According to Carly, her divorce from James, which she did not want, "was totally orchestrated by Kathryn Walker." Carly remembers their last moment as man and wife: "He was sitting in front of me in the courtroom and I just have a picture of his ankle that will stay with me forever. I remember *every* way his ankle bone turned and where his pant leg stopped, and his sandal—it *stays* with me." Not with a bang but a whimper.

When Ellen told Carly she was divorcing Vieri, Carly—who'd given Ellen that valuable wake-up call a few years earlier—"just kind of sat back and smiled and said, 'You don't think that's going to solve anything, do you?'" Enlightened talk among women about what they *deserved* from men made such fair-sounding good sense; to educated, privileged women who'd ridden the wave of liberation with élan— who'd done "work" on themselves, who'd *scienced* love, whether as Jungian Ph.D.s or pop star feminists or anything else—that talk was supposed to be the beginning of self-esteem (a concept that was not yet a cliché). If only that righteous empowerment you were supposed to feel could lead to something other than irony and regret, or could change things. "Years later," Ellen says, "I told Carly, 'You were right; that was no easy solution.'"

Carly released her eleventh original album, *Hello Big Man*—its title tune, homaging her parents' romance—the year of her divorce, 1983. She was in the shadows; it was the era of Madonna and Cyndi Lauper. Carly and Carole and Joni's generation—their bulging emotional dossier, all those lessons learned—was irrelevant. History was CBGB's; history was Sid and Nancy. *Real* history was Stevie Nicks. Unnoticed in *Hello Big Man* was "Orpheus," one of Carly's favorites of her own songs and a personal signifier in her current life. It's an obvious melodrama, but, to her, a real one. Giving James the name of the ancient Greek poet of the lyre (and, by implication, making herself into his adored wife, Eurydice, whom he lost, tragically, twice), she sings of how James first drove her away, then when she took the bait, closed the door to their relationship and moved on, even though she was more than willing to return. Her pleading refrain—"But it was *there* for us . . ."—movingly expresses her regret for ending the relationship, a move he had essentially forced upon her by his behavior.

Carly had a new man, Al Corley, a handsome blond actor from the Midwest over a dozen years her junior who'd been the original Steven Carrington on *Dynasty*. Corley (who eventually became a director) would inspire Carly's taunting, defensive "My New Boyfriend," on her next album, in which a woman declares her rebound romance with a younger man to be not as shallow as it seems. Al was great with Ben and Sally, "teaching them how to dive off a diving board; teaching Ben to play basketball; he was youthful and very active athletically," Carly says. In the boundaries-demolishing tradition of her family, in the mid-2000s Carly's son, Ben, would be romantically involved with Al's post-Carly girlfriend.

The Peyton Place–like incestuousness of their lives was never more evident than on one night in 1984 at an Upper West Side restaurant. Carly (now broken up with Al Corley) was there with friends while James, Kathryn, and Russ Kunkel were seated at another table. James and Russ had met and bonded fifteen years earlier at that first "Fire and Rain" session. They were virtually best friends, but there was also a power and status difference—James was Russ's "boss" (Russ uses that word, unironically); they were recording star and drummer. Russ was the person who, on April 6, 1971, had come into Carly's Troubadour dressing room and made her even more stage-frightened than she already was by exclaiming (as he recalls his words): "Dig this! James Taylor's coming to see the show!"

"Carly came up to the table," Russ recalls, of that evening in 1984. "Being around Carly was uncomfortable for James because it was uncomfortable for Kathryn, but Carly said 'Hi!' And"—in hearing range of James—"she gave me her number and said, 'Call me if you're going to be in the city for a while.'" Carly remembers the atmosphere being so awkward that the candle on the table fell over, "and"—she exaggerates—"Kathryn's sweater went up in flames."

Russ continues: "Carly looked great, so, what the heck—I called her. I went to see her, and we had lunch, and there was an attraction there." In a matter of weeks, Russ leased out his L.A. house, came to New York, and moved in with Carly—he and his boss's ex-wife became a couple. Someone who knew them all at the time says, "James was over Carly; he didn't care that Russ was *with* her, but he didn't want her backstage at the shows." Carly says, "Russ and I fell in love, and he was trying to work with James, but I wasn't allowed to go to the performances. It was very awkward and devastating." One night Carly challenged that ban. When a person who worked with James ran into Carly and Russ walking into the backstage area before a concert, "I looked at Peter Asher," the person says, "and he looked at me and we *ran* to the elevator and pushed the down button to get the hell out of there." James Taylor got *angry*. "In hindsight," Russ says today—with a session player's sense of "knowing his place"—"maybe" the romance with Carly "wasn't the best idea because it made my boss feel uncomfortable."

The relationship with Russ was very good for Carly. While he was indeed a simple man ("There were no conversations with William and Rose Styron about the German philosophers," Jake would say to Russ's eventual replacement, Jim Hart, who *did* make such repartee), he was "loving, kind, and guiding," Carly says, "and he was more important than anyone else in my musical education. He taught me to be self-taught. He was the most enthusiastic and knowing audience I ever had and he wasn't competitive with me."

That influence had to wait for an album to manifest itself. Carly had her twelfth album, *Spoiled Girl*, pretty much mapped out when she started living with Russ. Stephen Holden generously called the August 1985 release a "spicy, lighthearted romp," but Carly admits she lost her judgment when making it. Indeed, she used nine different producers, it hewed to the trendy dance music sound that was not her natural métier, and though the album may have *sounded* "lighthearted," she'd approached it with desperation. She unloaded her worries on Don Was (the producer for the B-52's, who later produced Bonnie Raitt's Grammys-dominating *Nick of Time:* its wonderful title song, a woman's contemplation of aging) right after they met. "She said very candidly that she was afraid of not having a place in music anymore," Was says. Joni and Carole were in similar situations: Joni had made, with husband Larry Klein, a synthesizer-driven album, *Dog Eat Dog,* which the radio stations were ignoring; Carole made the synthesizer-driven *Speeding Time* (her husband, Rick Sorensen—still known as Teepee Rick in the hills of Idaho—cowrote one of its songs, "Chalice Borealis"), which also fared poorly. All three were women past age forty. Joni and Carole were married; Carly was regretfully divorced and involved with her ex-husband's drummer, and both she and Russ had been put in their "place" by James. Hardly an ego-enhancing situation.

The only song, aside from "My New Boyfriend," that Carly solely wrote on *Spoiled Girl* was "The Wives Are in Connecticut," about an executive whose own cheating on his wife first fills him with macho pride and then makes him wonder if his cuckolded wife's amorousness is *really* directed at him or has been inspired by a secret affair with any number of local young studs. Listeners didn't know it, of course, but that witty song had Richard Simon and Auntie Jo and Andrea Simon and Ronnie Klinzing written all over it. Still, the album, for the most part, tanked.

By the time *Spoiled Girl* was released, Carly and Russ were officially engaged. Carly contends that her engagement to her ex-husband's friend and drummer is what made James ask Kathryn to marry him. Others might disagree, but most agree that the Carly-and-James story didn't end when their marriage did. For James, his almost exaggerated avoidance of Carly was in keeping with his confrontation-ducking personality, and almost surely influenced by his strong new wife and even stronger mother.* (Says one who knew all parties well during that time: "It was very difficult for James to have Carly in his life—to communicate with her at *all*—when he was taking on new relationships. It just didn't work for him. He had to cut himself off.") For Carly—Leah Kunkel recalls James's brother Livingston first expressing this widely shared feeling—"her divorce from James was just another chapter of their relationship." In any case, says the close friend, "the children were wounded by that divorce. They deeply and passionately love their mother and father."

James and Kathryn were married in December at New York's Cathedral of St. John the Divine. Carly moved Russ into the romantic Vineyard home—with its beautiful fields, woods, and ocean views—that she'd lived in with James and which became hers in the divorce (she lives there, to this day). She told reporters who inquired that, though they had postponed it because of scheduling conflicts, "at some point there will be a wedding . . . I'm in love with someone I want to marry. He has children** and I have children and we want to

---

* "I think Trudy eventually ruined *all* her kids' marriages," says a person who worked with James. "She couldn't help it. She loved her kids too much. She was married to a madman herself, who left her." Ike Taylor had an affair and then divorced Trudy to marry and have two children with a much younger woman; eventually both Ike and his wife died and the children were orphaned. "Trudy was going to do everything she could to 'save' those kids of hers," says James's colleague.

** Russ and Leah had a teenage son, Nathaniel; Leah was also raising her deceased sister Cass's daughter, Owen.

combine them and make a family." (Not everybody believed a wedding would take place. "Russ was in over his head with Carly" is how Leah puts it.) Free from James's aversion to the soirees that Carly favored (even though, as Jake notes, every woman James married "was an 'uptown girl' who dragged him into a life of cultured cocktail parties—he seemed to want or expect that"), she cultivated friendships templated on her parents'—with the Styrons, with Art Buchwald, and directors Mike Nichols and Nora Ephron, whose turning of contemporary urbane love stories into movies would give Carly a second musical life.

But the ultimate of these new friends was Jackie Kennedy Onassis, who, as an editor at Doubleday, had approached Carly to write a memoir. Carly hesitated (and eventually turned the offer down), but a connection flourished. In Carly, Jackie saw someone "who was uninhibited and free-spirited, like *she* had been when she was running around Washington as a single girl with a camera and taking all those exotic trips and writing those diaries," says their mutual friend Joe Armstrong. "Because of the life she had, Jackie had to be so controlled; she was only *thirty-four* when her husband's brains were blown out while she sat next to him. But Carly got to *stay* that way. She was the most open, honest, colorful whirlwind of energy." In Carly, the former First Lady glimpsed the person she "couldn't be anymore."

Carly sang at Caroline Kennedy's July 1986 marriage to Edwin Schlossberg, doing a rendition of the Dixie Cups' "Chapel of Love" and her own first song for James, "The Right Thing to Do." At the wedding party, the mother of the bride—usually perceived as one of the most untouchable women in America—cheerfully used the same Portosan as the band members. Jackie gossiped like a schoolgirl with Carly about men and love and conquests. (And politics: John Kerry would probably be thrilled to know that, Carly says, during his years as Massachusetts senator, "Jackie loved him and always remarked on the fact that he had the same initials as JFK.") And the elegant Jackie was no slouch in the practical jokes department. One time Carly and Jackie went backstage after a Placido Domingo concert, and Domingo

flirted profligately with Carly, as was his wont. The next day a messen-
ger arrived at Carly's door with a gift-wrapped framed photo of Domingo, autographed, "My darling Carly, I will adore you forever."
Beside herself with surprise and glee, Carly called Mike Nichols, and
Lucy and Joey, and gloated about the memento. Then she called Jackie
and said, "Can you imagine? He sent this to me! I think he's in love
with me." Jackie roared with laughter, and confessed, "*I* signed and
sent that picture to you."

"You do the bass part—you *can* do it," Russ told Carly, when she
started writing her thirteenth album, *Coming Around Again*. He was
her coach and support system (as well as, on one track, her producer).
She credits Russ with returning her to her true musical self after a few
years in the trying-to-be-trendy wilderness. The title song originated as
an assignment: Carly would write the music for the Mike Nichols–
directed film version of Nora Ephron's novel *Heartburn*. Meryl Streep
was playing a fictionalized Ephron, dealing with being dumped, mid-
pregnancy, by a fictionalized Carl Bernstein (played by Carly's long-
ago one night stand Jack Nicholson). Character, writer, actress, and
singer-songwriter formed a perfect storm in proffering the cynical but
hopeful postforty female: a slightly more bedraggled, domesticated
(and tarter) eight-years-later version of Jill Clayburgh's plucky self-
sufficiency seeker in *An Unmarried Woman* and Diane Keaton's cerebral *and* bubbly heroines in *Annie Hall* and *Manhattan*.

Thanks to Russ, Carly jettisoned the disco touches and some of the
new wave sound that had colored her last two albums. She went back
to what she knew best: a ballad with romance and worldliness.
"Coming Around Again" was an announcement of both the phenomenon (unimaginatively named serial monogamy) launched by this
cohort of women and the fluctuation of feelings within a marriage that
might or might not be worth saving. The lyrics of the song niche it as
by and for a woman of a certain age and set, with no apologies. The
nicely ironic hook—"So don't mind if I fall apart / There's more room

in a broken heart"—is a thumbnail autobiographical sketch, as is the lingering plaint—"I believe in love . . . It's comin' around again." Carly popped the children's song "Itsy Bitsy Spider" (with Ben and Sally singing on it) onto the end of the song. Ephron and Streep cried when they heard it. Released as a single along with the movie, it hit the #18 spot and was Carly's biggest hit in six years.

Another song, the fetchingly arranged "The Stuff That Dreams Are Made Of"—in which a restless wife envies her friend who's "moving out to Malibu" with her "bright new shiny boy"—goes at the album's title theme from the opposite direction. In the song, Carly takes the role of long-married Lucy or long-married Jessica ("How have you been able to stay faithful to *one* man for so long?" Carly once marveled admiringly to Jessica; "Who says I *have*?" Jessica shot back, implying that her college-beau-husband had evolved into different "men" throughout their long marriage), giving women like herself advice to make a familiar man sexy and new. Now that it was *always* possible to break up with your mate and look around again, you had to talk yourself into the *artificial* conservatism and placidity that earlier generations of women never had the luxury of rejecting. Two classic Carly lust songs, "Give Me All Night" and "All I Want Is You," became minor hits, and the album went platinum. *Coming Around Again* was Carly's comeback. Stephen Holden said it was "the pop-music equivalent of the diaries of Anaïs Nin or Erica Jong's autobiographical novels."

Just about the time, May 1987, that the album was released, Carly's relationship with Russ had run its course. He says, "The relationship was like a cruise. It had a point of demarcation and it just ended." Russ's ex-wife, Leah, is more cynical. "When Carly decided they were breaking up, boxes of Russ's clothes arrived at his house," she says. Carly calls Russ "absolutely precious—a pure and incandescent generous soul. He's like the most innocent Thoroughbred who doesn't want to win the race because he doesn't want to make the other horses lose. He was caught up in the bigger dramas. He's been hurt by both me and James. If he had been smart, he'd have put up a Do Not Enter sign."

But Russ insists, "I have no regrets. I'd do it all over again. Carly and I had some wonderful times; she's a very loving, generous, incredibly kind woman—and she's as funny as a loon." As for James, "he and I have been through really high times and low times, but it doesn't matter; we're all still here; it's great. And I feel the same way about Carly." (Russ would eventually marry singer Nicolette Larson and they'd have a daughter, Elsie. Nicolette would die in 1997 from a sudden brain disorder. Russ remarried in 2004.)

Shortly after the breakup from Russ, Carly's face was featured all over Manhattan on bus shelter ads for *Redbook* magazine, announcing her as "Another *Redbook* Juggler." (Women "juggling" work and family was the late-1980s media version of self-congratulatory mainstream feminism). During this moment of peak visibility, Carly took a trip to visit Jake at his new house in Hudson, New York. Earlier that same day, a thirty-seven-year-old Mutual of New York insurance salesman and amateur poet (in the John Ashbery/Frank O'Hara mode) named Jim Hart had impulsively decided *not* to drive to his usual Sunday custody visit to his ten-year-old son, Eamon, but to take the Metro North Hudson Valley train. Jim Hart isn't sure why he made that decision. Maybe it was the gods.

Hart was a very tall and nicely built man with a broad, genially handsome face framed by a gently receding hairline. He emanated self-confidence and empathy; and this was odd because, on paper, the mediocre-to-grim details of his life would promise neither charisma nor magnanimity. First, there were his present circumstances: Hart lived in a modest apartment in Manhattan's drab middle-class housing project, Stuyvesant Town. He worked out of MONY's New Jersey office. He had only $50,000 in the bank. He was the divorced father of a severely disabled child (Eamon was born with infantile myoclonic seizure disorder, leaving him seriously mentally retarded and very physically challenged), and he and his ex-wife, Alannah Fitzgerald, had declined to have Eamon institutionalized. They cared for him themselves.

Jim was in "the program," AA. Before getting sober, he'd been, as

Jake (who knew him from his own time in the program) puts it, "a bad drunk." Then there was his background: unprepossessing, from a Manhattan-eye-view. He had spent most of his life in the pine-paneled provinces, growing up in Queens, attending nondescript Siena College, doing his first AA time in Rochester, living during his marriage near Albany (his wife was the daughter of the mayor of Troy, New York). Yet Jim Hart was a *naturally* urbane man. He exuded the literateness found at the tables of Elaine's. (One of his good friends was Pulitzer Prize–winning novelist Bill Kennedy, the author of *Ironweed* and *The Cotton Club*.) Better yet, he was a rapt, soothing listener.

There was a hidden wellspring for Hart's unplaceable air of casual gravitas and self-confidence. He had studied for the priesthood for six years. From the age of fourteen to twenty, he'd been a "fervently religious" black-cassock-wearing novitiate of the Franciscan Friars of the Atonement, known as the Graymoor Friars. He had lived in their seminary in Garrison, New York. "If you meet people in religious orders—people who have spent their time in contemplation of what life is all about—they are not impressed with anybody *ever*," Jim explains. "We"—he's including himself in this group—"know that you're a sinner and we're going to give you all salvation. And we know that we're all equal and that everything else is bullshit. And that is deeply, *deeply* in me. And if you think some other way—that a new hairdo, or a new car, or a new house on Martha's Vineyard is going to change your world—then you've wasted your life."

Hart's spiritualism outlasted his traditional religiosity. Just before he was twenty-one, he told his superior, Father Juniper, "I have to leave because I don't believe in God anymore." Father Juniper mused, "You know, some of our most important saints—Augustine, Francis, et cetera—had that problem. *I* don't think you have a faith problem; you have a *celibacy* problem." This proved true by default. Thrust into the noncloistered world, Jim Hart developed a happy attribute that would have been lost had he continued in the priesthood. "I'm incredible in bed," he says, without modesty or irony. "This is true. I have a long list of references." He came to think of himself as a "stallion."

And so, on that spring day in 1987, Jim Hart was standing at the Hudson, New York, station with his ex-wife, Alannah (a beautiful blond singer of Celtic music), and Eamon, waiting for the train back to the city. Walking to the same station eaves were Jake and Carly. The two old AA buddies, who'd kept in touch over the years, met up and Jake made introductions all around. Even though Jake assumed that Carly's first name alone was sufficient, "I introduced her as 'Carly Simon.'" But, amazingly (or, perhaps, strategically), Jim didn't know that Jake's friend was a famous singer.*

Jim kissed his child and bid his ex-wife good-bye when the train arrived, electronic horn sounding. Carly got in one car; Jim got in another, distant one. Then Jim (mentally erasing the fact that he had a girlfriend) raced through the clattering cars to find—and flirt with—Jake Brackman's sexy friend.

From Carly's point of view, Jim's not knowing who she was was more intriguing than insulting; he was so handsome and charming. Jim figured he had a shot with her when (he sensed) she *said* she was seeing someone but he could tell that she wasn't. He had the two-hour ride to woo her, and he shrewdly used his chits: his utter exoticism to this city girl's experience and what Jake had always admired as his conversational "silver tongue, his gift of gab."

Jim told Carly about his years studying for the priesthood in the Franciscan order, in which priests worked with AIDS patients and addicts. He zeroed in on her romantic streak by unfolding the two-hankie turn-of-the-century origins of the Graymoor Friars: an Episcopalian nun and a Catholic priest fell in love and vowed, as a sign of that love, to never so much as touch each other—and then they founded the first ecumenical order of the Catholic church. As the train rumbled its

---

* Shortly after he was elected president, and while he was vacationing on the Vineyard, Bill Clinton, with Hillary in tow, came to visit Carly, ostensibly to seek her celebrity's-eye-view counsel on how to assure that Chelsea would have a normal life—but also because he was a huge fan of Carly's. According to Jim, the first words out of the president's mouth to him were a mock-scolding, incredulous "What tree were *you* under, not to know who Carly Simon was?"

way to Penn Station, Jim also told Carly how he had come to be divorced. His wife had left him for a fellow Celtic musician, a man who was one of the rare practitioners of strictly classical bagpiping, the plaintive-sounding *plebra*. And he told her how his father had been, in his youth, a virtual member of the notorious Irish gang the Westies of Hell's Kitchen (according to legend, the Westies, among other things, left decapitated human heads in kitchen freezers) and had been criminally or psychiatrically institutionalized "fifty-five times before he was thirty-five years old" but was *also* one of the wisest men he knew.

As he was proffering this unique biography, Carly was enraptured by Jim's milieu and experiences. She had spent every one of her over-forty years of life in the worldliest of circumstances, yet "there were worlds that are *not* about Carly Simon. I understood that," Jim says. He could give this to her. And he wanted to. "Within twenty minutes of talking to her, I knew this was going to be a very significant relationship."

Carly felt the same way. "I met a handsome man on a train," Carly enthused to Jessica after she got home. "He was a priest and he's a writer." "What has he written?" Jessica asked. Carly indicated that he hadn't exactly published yet, "but he's writing a book," she said brightly. True, Jim had a novel about himself and his father mapped out in his head. It was just a matter of putting it down on paper. He even had a title for it, *Spike and Dive*. (The title referred to the measures of a rock face, and it was also slang for the angle of entrance into a woman's vagina.)

A romance quickly developed. As Jessica viewed it, "Carly found in Jim a great intellectual partner. She loved talking to him. She thought of him as a philosopher, and she valued his opinion on things. They could speak for *hours*. It was an immeasurably close relationship, very different from what she had with James."

Jim held his own in Carly's high-powered social world. Jackie Onassis found him absolutely fascinating. Andrea flirted with him. Mike Nichols became his chum. ("Fake it 'til you make it," Jim says, of his ability to mix with this crowd.) And he possessed two qualities that made him a perfect match for Carly: a grandly romantic perspective and high sexuality, a combination of qualities he would later express in his dedication to her of his 2004 self-published volume of poems, *Milding*: "If a stallion had a goddess . . ."

One day in fall of 1987 Jim called Jake, saying, "I need to talk to you—you're the only one who knows both of us. I want to ask Carly to marry me. What do you think?" First, Jake told Jim that he would have to consider it during lunch and for Jim to call him later. When Jim did so, Jake hesitated; then he said, in his slow, low voice: "She's the most neurotic woman in the world." He paused, then added, "But she's the only one who's worth it."

Jim proposed and Carly accepted. Jim quit his job at MONY; he would write *Spike and Dive* full-time now. They estimated it would take a year, maybe two, for him to complete the novel. She had faith in him.

They had one "huge" fight, Jim says, just before the wedding. Carly wanted Jim to sign a prenuptial agreement. Such documents were now being recommended when, among other things, people of different economic levels were marrying. "I was furious," Jim says, "because the prenup elevated one aspect of the relationship—and *not* the most important one—over all others." Jim asked his father's advice. "Do you love her?" Hart the elder asked. His son replied, "I *adore* her!" "Well, she's dead wrong," the wise crook said. "But apologize to her for fighting with her—and sign it. Because if you love someone, apologizing when you're *wrong* doesn't count. Only apologizing even though you're *right* counts." Jim signed the prenup.

Two days before Christmas 1987, as a light snow drizzled the Vineyard, Carly's and Jim's families gathered in an Edgartown church for their wedding. "Carly looked like a Russian heroine" in her fur-cowl-necked, tight-bodiced white dress, Jim says.

As the pair ferried off to their honeymoon in Nantucket, Carly's loved ones were delighted that she was happy. They hoped that *this* mutual caretaking would work, permanently.

PART SIX

"in the river i know
i will find the key"

CODA

the middle '80s to the present: three women, three endings, one journey

reuniting

Joni came into middle age with Larry Klein by her side. Their relationship spanned the ten years from her thirty-eighth to her forty-eighth birthday, never an easy juncture for a woman—and no less so for one who assumed that she was venerated as a questing artist (to be embraced by her fans *wherever* her musical journey took her), rather than one whose greatest bond with her public lay in how radiantly her internal life reflected their own.

During the nine years of her marriage to Larry, Joni's career, already derailed during her jazz experimentation, went deeper into a trough by way of her collaborations with her young husband. There are some who believe Klein's synthesizer-heavy, drum-machine-based music hurt her career; that she had yielded to modishness at the expense of her true spirit. Others believe that, however off-mark their musical collabora-

481

tions, Larry patiently absorbed and managed the anger that Joni increasingly felt. "Getting older was hard for Joni," says Larry. She saw an injustice. "Men around that age"—Jagger, McCartney, Eric Clapton—"are still considered vital in pop music, but women aren't. Joni is someone who's stuck to her guns artistically, and I told her repeatedly that the way she pursued her career, with such single-minded devotion to artistry and holding on to her integrity so intensely, not chasing after commercial success, she had carved out a fantastic path for herself to grow older and still be vital."

If it sounded as if Larry was tending to Joni a bit, he doesn't deny this. And although there are those who feel that he (so little known before their marriage) benefited tremendously, financially and otherwise, by being married to a legend, the relationship took its toll on him. "It was a real test for me to be that grounding influence to a person who was going through some really intense stuff, and who was flying around in a pretty wide swath. I hadn't developed the ability to deal with conflict in a completely mature way—to not just sublimate my anger internally."

The first album of her songs that they produced together—her fourteenth album, 1985's *Dog Eat Dog*—was political in spirit. Having her romantic life settled gave Joni the luxury of thinking about politics, she has said. In it she exhorted against televangelists (presciently, it would turn out; the hypocrisies of Jim and Tammy Faye Bakker in the 1980s were nothing next to the grip on Republican politics that fundamentalist churches would exert twenty years later), and also Wall Streeters and advertising hucksters. *Dog Eat Dog* was poorly reviewed and her poorest-selling album in eighteen years. And though her next album, 1988's smoother and more listenable *Chalk Mark in a Rainstorm,* was enthusiastically received (*Billboard*'s Timothy White called it "lucid" and "sublimely sung") and sold better (reaching a respectable #45), it didn't touch the luster of her early albums, nor did the songs have that personal ache. Her 1991 *Night Ride Home,* whose title song honored Larry ("I love the man beside me, we love the open road"), was, as Stephen Holden said, "closer in spirit to her 1970s albums"; still it did about the same business as its predecessor. During these and subsequent years Joni bewailed what she called her banishment from the airwaves, spoke of her disdain for MTV, and tendered the opinion that she had been "blacklisted" from *Rolling Stone* because she had once thrown a drink in Jann Wenner's face and told him to "kiss my ass."

Larry coached Joni through several concerted attempts to stop smoking, but all of them failed. Once, he drove her to Palm Springs after she'd received an injection that was supposed to relieve the pain of withdrawal. He had left her alone in her hotel room and driven back to L.A., but then, unable to reach her by phone, he got in the car and drove back to Palm Springs. Joni hadn't answered the hotel room phone because she had borrowed a bike from the desk clerk and pedaled to the nearest cigarette machine, thirty miles away. During another ill-fated cold turkey attempt, "Joni got so ill-tempered, I ended up saying: '*Please* smoke. Or else we're both going to end up dead.'"

At some point in her early forties Joni discovered she was pregnant—a surprise, since she had assumed that the infection she'd suffered in Jamaica had left her infertile. She would later tell a friend that "she wanted the baby, badly." Larry was excited to be a father, although things were still so preliminary that they hadn't gotten to thinking of names.

In her first trimester, Joni miscarried. Larry had a recording date in England; musicians were waiting for him. He delayed his departure, then he asked Joni if it was okay for him to go and fulfill his commitment. She consented. In an act more naïve than callous, but with a devastating effect on Joni, he did leave. "In retrospect, it was really a bad thing," he says today. "I didn't know very much about what happens to women when they miscarry—the potential psychological problems, the depression. Knowing what I know now, I wouldn't have gone. It really damaged our relationship; she saw it as me putting this job higher in importance than her health." A friend of Joni's says, "She was really sick, in a lot of pain, after he left." Not only did she suffer the physical and psychological symptoms alone, but a line had been crossed: "Larry's leaving broke her trust in him." In two very different ways, over twenty-plus years, she had lost two babies, and in both cases men had profoundly let her down by failing to hear what she wanted but did not say, instead of what they wanted and she agreed to.

Joni took what she would come to feel as Larry's betrayal stoically. "She had been through so much by the time I met her, it had produced a certain resilience in her," Larry says. Consequently, the Joni who was his wife was "not an overly sentimental person. She's got a bit of a hard edge in a certain way when it comes to existential events, whether it's death or children or illness. The flip side of that was a kind of fatalistic attitude toward these things."

By 1991, the eighth year of his relationship with Joni, Larry had sunk into a deep, serious depression. "I was starting to come apart," he says. Larry thinks that Joni had been "looking at me to be the ideal person, to be the patient person who's there when she was angry; the calm, reassuring person when that was needed, and the childlike person who could relate to her on the most innocent level." The need to keep filling those shifting roles had worn him out. "She was as helpful as she could be" with his depression, "having wrestled with those kinds of demons herself," he says, but Joni, who's been called by some a "narcissist," would tolerate only so much. Larry wanted them to go into couples therapy, but Joni expressed disdain for Western psychology. "So we had a pattern of her saying, 'I'm just not able to be in a relationship; I'm not *made* for this,' and me responding, 'Oh, come on, let's *make* this work.'" Twenty-one years earlier she had told Graham Nash, "If you hold sand too tightly, it will run through your fingers." Larry was now in Graham's place, his earnestness and neediness driving her away. Besides, when your best work has energized from intense relationships with edgy men, the normalness of marriage to a man who is a soother deprives you of prime material. As Dave Naylor, who remained close to both Larry and Joni, puts it, "It wasn't just the miscarriage" that marked the end of the marriage for Joni. "She needed some inspiration, some play—she needed some interaction with men."*

Joni and Larry spent Thanksgiving 1991 at his aunt and uncle's. "Then we came back to Joni's house in Bel Air," Larry recalls, "and—to her credit, for being honest—she said, 'Listen, Klein. I am who I am. I'm not going to be changing a lot.' So I said, 'I've got to go. This is killing me.'"

Larry moved to a house in Venice and "spent five years—probably the most difficult period of my life—completely reconstructing myself. The relationship with her was the most valuable thing for me, but it had ended in failure. I felt, Wow, who *am* I again, now?" He was left with the stereotypically female task of extricating an autonomous *self* from the emotional mesh of a marriage dominated by *her* identity. And Joni? Joni was alone again. But fate works with its own symmetry. Although Joni Mitchell had no idea of it now, across the country, in Florida, a conversation was occurring that would set in motion the most profound imaginable end to her existential void, to her haunting aloneness.

The Gibb family of Don Mills, Toronto—parents Ida and David and now-grown children David and Kilauren—always went somewhere warm for Christmas vacation, and this year, 1991, they chose Miami. Kilauren, twenty-six, had something to tell her parents: she was pregnant. She was having a baby with her boyfriend, local rock-group drummer Paul Kohler.

Kilauren had always been so different from her parents. They were timid and uncharismatic; she was headstrong and self-possessed. They were bookish; she was artistic—she liked to paint (and did so in a colorful, realistic style). While they were prim and dour, she was, as a friend calls her, "a renegade spirit, a girl who hung out with the band." They were not very attractive, but she was, as one beau put it, "unapproachably beauti-

---

* At least one friend of Joni's believes that Larry exacerbated Joni's insecurity by "flashing younger singers in front of her all the time" and that she (continuing to work with him as she did, after their divorce) never entirely got over him.

ful." (She had been discovered by Ford Models when she was in high school in Toronto and had done runway modeling in France and Australia before coming back to Canada. She used the money earned from her modeling to buy fashionable clothes.)

Yet so many of the things Kilauren *was* made her a kind of errant jigsaw piece that didn't fit in her family's cardboard puzzle board. Adventurous and bohemian, headstrong and stubborn; a music lover, a dreamer, a low-level model dressed better than her peers; a painter, a traveler; a tall, blond, high-cheekboned girl who melted men's hearts. *Whose* puzzle board *did* she fit in?

Seeking answers, Kilauren called Canada's Children's Aid Society. She was told that there was something called a Non-Identifying Background Information form that every relinquishing birth mother in the 1960s had to fill out. Even nearly three decades later, it was hard to obtain this information, and the bureaucratic delays varied from province to province.

Kilauren had her baby, a son. She named him Marlin. She broke up with the baby's father and was kept intensely occupied as a single mother. Four years passed.

In early 1995, the phone rang in the Toronto apartment of a young man named Tim Campbell. Tim had grown up with Kilauren and was a friend of Ted Barrington, who was now Kilauren's boyfriend. Tim had been adopted himself. When he was nineteen, something called the Match Program came into being across Canada. If you were an adoptee who wanted to find your birth mother, you put your name in a registry, which was checked against a registry of birth mothers who wanted to meet the children they'd relinquished. If a match was found, both parties would go into separate counseling and then be given each other's contact information. Tim signed up for the Match Program right away. Four years later he got a registered letter: "There's a match!" When he and his birth mother sat down at the coffee shop, face to face, "we were both so excited, it took us five hours to order anything more than a Coke." The importance of that reunion led Tim to become a volunteer counselor for

Children's Aid, spending his spare time imploring skittish birth mothers to add their names to the registry.

Now, in January 1995, Tim was listening to Ted's girlfriend Kilauren Gibb, who seemed "frantic and desperate," Tim recalls. "She said, 'I still haven't heard anything and I'm at the breaking point. I *have* to know who my birth mother is by my thirtieth birthday or . . .'" Tim knew that not knowing "is a big black hole that can consume" an adoptee. He took Kilauren's desperation very seriously because he'd had a friend who was adopted and in response to that unfilled "black hole" had hanged himself. Tim used his Children's Aid affiliation to get Kilauren's name to the top of the Match Program list. Even with that boost, months went by; more months; then *more* months.

Finally, in 1996, Kilauren received her registered letter, revealing the Non-Identifying Background Information. She and Ted called Tim and he was read these words (as Tim distinctly remembers them): "Your mother was from a small town in Saskatchewan and left for the U.S. to pursue her career as a folksinger."

And this is where serendipity came in. As Tim was hearing Kilauren's excited recitation through the phone wire, he repeated the words aloud. His girlfriend, Annie Mandlsohn, was in the room. Annie, a photographer, was older than Tim. Eight years earlier she had been a graduate student at Canada's York University, getting an advanced degree in Canadian/Native relations. She had befriended another, older graduate student, a poet and member of the Ojibway tribe, Duke Redbird. The two had become confidants, and they talked about the 1960s, an era that Annie romanticized and Duke had lived through. In the course of their talking, Duke broke a secret he'd been keeping for twenty-four years. In 1964, he'd lived in a tumbledown rooming house in Yorkville, Toronto's bohemian quarter. His floormate there was a blond girl from Saskatchewan, the future Joni Mitchell. The secret part of the story was this: Joni had been *pregnant* at the time; she was going to give up her baby once it was born. This bit of gossip was something Annie had never shared with Tim. As soon as Tim repeated the words of Kilauren's letter, Annie grabbed the phone and informed Kilauren, "Your mother is Joni Mitchell!" Tim recalls, "Kilauren said, 'No way!' She was speechless."

Annie took control. Kilauren had to go to see Duke Redbird and ask him what season he was in the rooming house with the pregnant Joni. Kilauren was born on February 19, 1965. If Duke said summer, then Kilauren couldn't be Joni's daughter. But if he said that Joni had been pregnant in early winter . . .

Kilauren tracked Duke down at the Coloured Stone, the Toronto restaurant he owned. Redbird recalls, "Her attitude wasn't like she'd won the lottery. She wanted to connect with her birth mother, no matter *who* her mother was." Duke answered her question: it was just before Christmas 1964 that he'd known the pregnant Joni.

Kilauren now had her answer. Duke suggested Kilauren try to contact Joni through Canada's Society for Composers and Performers.

By now, Joni's patch of being ignored had ended. Her 1994 *Turbulent Indigo*—the startlingly husky voice refracting her tart, mature complexity—was touted as one of her finest albums in years. (Tim White, now the editor of *Billboard,* called it "one of the most commanding statements of a peerless, seventeen-album career" and praised its "rare blend of romantic faith and fervid realism.") Joni used a self-portrait depicting herself as her hero Vincent Van Gogh as the cover. Her characters had ripened to a *noir* sheen. The female recluse in "Sunny Sunday" (who could be "Marcie," all these life-dented years later) "dodges the light like Blanche DuBois" and fruitlessly shoots at lampposts like some menopausal Quixote. Situations of former earnestness now provoke a cranky realism: "Sex Kills" has Joni driving a car just as "Refuge of the Roads" did, but *this* Joni's not the reforming narcissist awed at her humble place in the universe; she's a pissed-off social critic deriding "all these jackoffs at the office." Long-brewed hurts make their way into the album; "Not to Blame" excoriates Jackson Browne, but nobody knows why; and, in the album's most transcendent piece—and one of Joni's finest songs ever—the cruelty and humiliation she suffered as an unwed mother is transmuted into a searing imagining of life in an historically real Irish home for fallen women called the Magdalene Laundries.

By now, Joni's having given up a baby was a whisper of a rumor bobbing under the surface of public acknowledgment. She had confessed (in a 1990 gotcha! exchange with a London radio interviewer) that she'd had a baby; that fleeting broadcast moment on the faraway shore had not made it to North America, except to provide the basis for a mostly unnoticed, small April 1996 *Globe* story in which a supposed art school friend talked about Joni having had a baby and having put it up for adoption. The brief article in the sleazy tabloid was rife with errors, saying, for example, that Joni was nineteen, not twenty-one, when she gave birth.

For years Joni had kept the possibility of the search for her baby in a kind of locked box. She still had not told her parents, and with every year the secret seemed more trouble to uncover. Larry Klein, Don Alias, and John Guerin all remembered her having fleeting pangs to try to "find my kid," but they were just that—fleeting. However, 1996 was an affirming year for Joni. Late-in-coming awards started flooding in all at once: *Turbulent Indigo* was the surprise winner of Best Pop Album Grammy (Joni's unexpected selection may have been partly compensation for the Grammys she *should* have won years earlier), and she won *Billboard*'s newly instituted and very prestigious Century Award. In addition, Stephen Holden publicly criticized the Rock and Roll Hall of Fame's "antifeminine" bias for their failure to honor Joni (she was inducted the next year, as well as into the Songwriters Hall of Fame); the National Academy of Songwriters and the National Songwriters Association each awarded her a Lifetime Achievement Award; BMI gave her their one-million-performance certificate for "Big Yellow Taxi" and "Woodstock," their two-million-performance certificate for "Help Me," and their four-million-performance certificate for "Both Sides, Now"; and she won Canada's prestigious Governor General's Award. There were perks to being fifty-three years old.

In addition, her personal life had come satisfyingly full circle. She was now in a relationship with Canadian poet Donald Freed, a Métis (half Indian) who traveled around Canada's remote areas, teaching children to turn their lives into poetry. Her friends approved; one called Freed "a one-hundred-percent great person, with boundaries; a really together man." The fact that he and Joni had been introduced by Myrtle, and that the two had grown up on the opposite shores of the Saskatchewan River, made the union seem like a destined homecoming. Joni wrote a song with an explicitly midlife-female title ("Face Lift") about Freed; ringing through it is her abiding tussle with Myrtle's unflinching propriety. (Joni's Myrtle character angrily demands, "Did you come home to disgrace us?" when Joni and Freed stay at a local hotel together; Joni cries, "I'm middle-aged, Mama! . . . Why is this joy not allowed?")

Like many women her age, who'd by now hacked at the quandary of love vs. freedom from a dozen different angles, Joni found the long-distance relationship a good solution. When the now happily married John Guerin asked, "But, Joan, isn't that guy *in Canada* all the time?" she answered, "Yes, but it's *better* that way. I see him when it's cool." After all that emotion spilled for so long, by the mid-1990s "I don't think Joni could *be* head-over-heels anymore," John surmised. Then Joni saw Don Alias for the first time since their abrupt breakup a decade and a half earlier. Alias dropped by her house one day, hoping to rekindle the romance. "We danced around a little bit, happy to see each other, and then Joni said, with a smile, 'I thought you were mad at me'"—for giving him twenty-four hours to get his possessions out of Varick Street—"and I wanted to say, 'You're goddamn *right* I'm mad at you!' but I said, 'No, I'm not mad.'" Alias asked Joni if she was seeing anyone; she mentioned, as Alias came away thinking of him, "the cowboy," Freed. They parted, friends. As for other exes: Graham Nash sent Joni flowers every year on her birthday, and James Taylor sang her praises ("He seemed to look back on their relationship more positively than she did," says a friend). With Jackson Browne she remained angry.

Joni's decision to search for her daughter had started in 1996, as a result of that early tabloid article. The foster mother who had cared for Joni's baby for seven months contacted Joni's managers, sending photos. When Joni received the pictures, she reportedly said, "My daughter . . . my baby . . . my child," as if the sheer ability to mouth those words was intensely relieving. She marveled at how the baby resembled Sadie, her musically frustrated maternal grandmother. "She must be a really strong woman," Joni said, of her adult daughter.

By the end of 1996 (concurrent with another article in the *Globe*), Joni announced that she was searching for her daughter. In an interview with the *Calgary Sun*, Myrtle (after offering lip service to the appropriate reaction with "We would have been supportive if we had only known" about the baby back then) proved that Joni had in fact judged her mother's reaction accurately all along. "It's Joni's fault this is coming out now; she's too open and frank about it. This is really embarrassing," Myrtle fretted.

Joni's Vancouver-based managers, Steve Macklam and Sam Feldman, handled the responses; hundreds of thirty-one-year-old adopted women wanted to be Joni Mitchell's baby.

Knowing she was the one, Kilauren contacted and recontacted Macklam and Feldman, but "the first e-mails went unanswered for six weeks," a friend recalls; Kilauren felt frustrated. By the early weeks of 1997 she was calling or e-mailing almost every day. Finally, the Gibbs located a long-buried photograph of Kilauren, in their arms, taken the day she left her foster mother. In early March Kilauren sent this photo to Macklam and Feldman; they matched it against the ones Joni had been sent one year earlier by the foster mother. To Joni's protectively skeptical managers, there could be no doubt now.

Joni was on vacation with Don Freed, in Santa Fe. There she was: on that "burning desert" in cactus tree land, her self-anointed locus of female solitude and independence, where she'd imagined a heart-to-heart with Amelia Earhart and had a real one with Georgia O'Keeffe. Returning to her hotel after an outing with Don, she received Macklam and Feldman's message with the phone number for one Kilauren Gibb. Joni called, and into the voice mail exclaimed, "It's Joni. I'm overwhelmed."

Days later, on March 11, Duke Redbird got to his Toronto restaurant and found this note: "Hi, Duke . . . I went to see you today because I'm on my way to L.A. on Thursday, March 13, to visit Joni. She remembers you and your brother and your kindness [bringing her apples] during her time of need. She couldn't believe that I had met you. She is my mother and she has sent my son and me to visit her . . . Thanks for being so kind. Love, Kilauren Gibb."

Kilauren and Marlin flew, with first-class tickets from Joni, from Toronto to L.A. They were met by a limousine and driven to Joni's house. Kilauren didn't know to go to the side entrance; she rang at the (mostly unused) front entrance. Joni came out onto the balcony to redirect Kilauren—mother looked down and daughter looked up, awkwardly, comically Romeo-and-Juliet-like. Joni raced downstairs and opened the door. And, as she would later write it, in her abashed, eloquently measured song about the occasion: "In the middle of this continent, in the middle of our time on Earth, we receive one another." Here was her Kelly Dale—here was her Little Green—thirty-two years later.

Turning themselves into a family was, while euphoric, mined with dangers, as Joni's own words in "Stay in Touch" predicted: "But our roles aren't clear / So we mustn't rush." For Kilauren, the contrast between glamorous Bel Air with Joni as her mother and, as a friend says, "dreary suburban Toronto" was dizzying. There was the matter of their strong similarities—Kilauren and Joni "are both brutal to argue with; they've got excellent selective memories," says one who knows both, "and they're both feisty, like Myrtle. They're three birds of a feather." There was also the matter of their equally strong differences. As Dave Naylor puts it, "It drives Joni crazy, 'cause she's Kilauren's mom and she can't understand why this daughter of hers doesn't have this work ethic that she has." "Joni has Kilauren on a short leash," says a friend, using, figuratively, the same word, "leash," that Joni had once described Myrtle *literally* using on her as a child. How strong, these generational echoes! Joni and her daughter and mother *were*, indeed, as she had so early written, "captive on the carousel of time."

American articles somewhat reverentially praised Joni's dutifulness to her new family. Joni told *The New York Times* that, for the sake of her grandson, Marlin, she was now watching network TV. The *Times* quoted Marlin's sweet comment about Joni's steadfastness in his life, that he "couldn't imagine . . . Joni going away."*

Meanwhile, Joni's eighteenth album, *Taming the Tiger,* was released in 1998. It included "Stay in Touch" as well as "Face Lift"; a paean to lust (Joni told friends she was on the now-popular-with-her-cohort elixir, hormone-replacement therapy) that she wrote with Freed, "The Crazy Cries of Love"; and "Lead Balloon," which parlayed her spat with Jann Wenner into an apt jab at society's approval of angry men and scorn for angry women. In the title song, "Taming the Tiger," Joni took another broad swipe at the music industry: the radio serves up "formula music, girly guile, genuine junk food for juveniles." So reuniting with her daughter *hadn't* scratched every itch, and receiving the flood of awards two years earlier *hadn't* bought her silence. Once the pert, fragile, bell-voiced pleaser (and jelled in aspic as such in much of the public's mind), she'd evolved into a prickly, husky-voiced straight shooter; her songs still (but from that *other* "side now") as astringently unphony as they had always been.

Joni and Donald Freed broke up. Like Don Alias, he objected to her calling him in the middle of the night.

Kilauren had a second baby—a daughter, Daisy, with Ted Barrington—in 1999. And then—on a good day for emotional clean sweeps, the first day of the new millennium, January 1, 2000—came an almost inevitable blowout.

Kilauren and Marlin were visiting Joni in Bel Air. Kilauren was excitedly preparing to go with Joni to a party given by Michael Douglas and Catherine Zeta-Jones. While she was dressing, she let Marlin sit in front of the TV. The movie *The Green Mile,* which featured a torture scene,

---

* The Canadian press was more skeptical, with some columnists noting how long it took Kilauren to prove she was Joni's daughter, and harshly saying that Joni had given her daughter to another family to raise and then, as a celebrity, with fanfare, claimed her when she wanted to.

was on. Joni heatedly objected: it wasn't appropriate for Marlin to be watching a violent movie. Kilauren heatedly rebutted: the movie was fine for Marlin.

Joni shot back: "Don't talk back to *me*—I'm your *mother*!"

Kilauren shot back, "What do *you* know about being a mother? You gave me away!"

And then Joni slapped Kilauren's face.

Kilauren called the police, but when the officers arrived, she declined to press charges. Kilauren and Marlin spent the night at the house of a friend of Joni's.

Since that time, Joni Mitchell and Kilauren Gibb have made their way through a thicket of complicated emotions to arrive at a relationship that feels like real life. Joni visits her daughter and grandchildren in Toronto; they visit her at her houses in L.A. and near Vancouver. When Kilauren said she wanted to have an evening with her birth mother and birth father together (Kilauren had also reunited with Brad MacMath), Betsy Asher had Joni, Kilauren, and MacMath (the bestower of Kilauren's deep-set, up-slanted eyes) over for dinner. In a photograph taken that evening, Joni, her long-ago art school boyfriend, and Kilauren are smiling as easily as any long-married middle-aged couple and their adult daughter.

Joni's nineteenth album, 2000's *Both Sides, Now,* and her twentieth—2002's double-disc *Travelogue*—both feature her singing her songs in her new, life-deepened voice.

In 2003 Joni was the subject of a PBS *American Masters* tribute-biography, "Woman of Heart and Mind." James Taylor was among the participants honoring Joni in word and song. She unappeasedly continued to call the recording industry a "cesspool," railing, of the pop landscape: "What [should] I do now? Show my tits? Grab my crotch? Get hair extensions and a choreographer?" Danny Kortchmar puts the complaint thusly, referring to rap music, "Today, people write love songs to their jewelry."

Joni has essentially asked, thought-provokingly: *Do we* destroy the female artists among us? She concedes that since so many people have said her early work was her best, maybe it was time to believe it herself. In 2004 she ran into Jackson Browne in a grocery store. He told her he couldn't bear the animosity between them and the two reportedly buried the hatchet. A more momentous milestone: Myrtle Anderson, whose high standards had shaped Joni, died at the age of ninety-five on March 19, 2007.

As for Joni and Kilauren, they are close and they have their ups and downs. "You know what?" a friend of Joni's says. "With all Joni's exasperation over Kilauren, and her worries about Kilauren, and their back-and-forth hurts; and her time, happily, spent with Kilauren and Marlin and Daisy: like it or not, Joni's become a mother, after all."

And an artist, first and foremost. Joni spent the summer of 2007 recording her twenty-first album, *Shine,* a bravura effort of electric music, every track of course produced by Joni, who also supplied virtually all of the instrumentation. James Taylor added his guitar to the title song. The album tackles grand themes—not just environmentalism, the smart set's cause du jour, but the problems of organized religion. She dedicated it to her grandchildren, Marlin and Daisy. It was released, on Starbucks's Hear label, in late September 2007, heralded by a full-page ad in *The New York Times:* "A Timeless Voice Challenges Today's World." Joni was reportedly annoyed that her proposed cover—the arched backs and bulbously muscled thighs of leaping male dancers—was not thought to be the best signifier for a Joni Mitchell album, artists' faces, not strangers' buttocks, being considered more congenial. But there those muscled buttocks were, on the counters of those thousands of serene, glossy, ubiquitous heirs to her feisty, funky, hidden-away Louis Riel. Starbucks surely learned what everyone knows: She is Joni Mitchell and she isn't backing down.

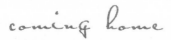

coming home

Throughout the 1980s, there were two Carole Kings. To the wider American public there was Carole the beloved singer-songwriter, about whom people in their thirties and older affectionately but briefly wondered, "What happened after *Tapestry?*"—and whose Brill

Building hits were increasingly being marketed as what would be called "classic rock." This Carole King was a genial legend and a good-works activist. She gave ten performances, around the country, to fund-raise for her friend (and, though few knew this of her, fellow Western statesman) Gary Hart during his presidential bid in 1984. Briefly thought to be the "new Kennedy" that Americans were still wistfully determined to uncover, the handsome, square-jawed—and, of course, married—Colorado senator self-destructed by daring the press to follow his every move, only to wind up with a blonde on his lap on a boat called *Monkey Business*. This Carole King also performed at Willie Nelson's first Farm Aid concert. In image and, increasingly, in real life, she was an environmentalist, taking her earth-motherliness to the next—political—stage.

The other Carole King—Carole King Sorensen—was known only in Custer County, Idaho, and there she was very much disliked. She was considered a combative, wealthy interloper with a New York accent (a "city slicker from the Bronx [sic] and Los Angeles," as one local paper put it), who, even while genuinely embracing ranch life (Carole *did* milk her cows and chop wood for her stove; she and Rick *did* run a livestock operation; and their ranch house was, by musical star standards, almost threadbare), didn't quite get Custer County's values. Says a woman who is married to a seventh-generation mountain Idahoan (and who, as a newcomer herself in the early 1970s, learned the code when she pulled a cake-mix box from the grocery store shelf—only to have another customer disapprovingly pluck it out of her hand, put it back on the shelf, and say, "*I'll* teach you how to bake that cake from *scratch*"), "You don't wear dirty jeans to a community meeting, like Carole did—that's what *rich hippies* do. You leave your ranch work clothes at home and you wear pressed, proper clothes." Besides bucking convention, Carole and Rick were pursuing their closed-road case against her neighbors, the French and Schoonen families; against Custer County; and against the U.S. Forest Service. Says someone who was a party in her legal battle: "There are *two* things in this state that people fight over: water and access." She'd picked one of them.

Both sides had merit: Carole had purchased the Robinson Bar Ranch only after doing research to determine that a road that ran very close to their living quarters was their private property. In neighborly fashion, they gave the people whose ranch abutted theirs—Thorlo and Dorothy French and David and Helen Schoonen—the combination to the lock on the gate, so they too could make use of the road. However, the Sorensens' research did not take into account local custom: as long as anyone in Custer County could remember, that road had been used by *everyone* in the county; it had been treated as if it were a public road, and during the winter months, it was often the only alternative to a circuitous—and dangerous—mountain pass. So, at the urging of the neighbors and the U.S. Forest Service, in September 1981 Custer County had declared the road public, and its sheriff issued Carole a *criminal* citation for placing a locked gate on her road. (One independent-minded deputy sheriff, having heard from his colleagues no "justifiable rationale" for criminalizing the civil complaint, later said that he believed the act was "carefully planned to harass and intimidate" Carole.) Carole fought back; the forest service, county, and her neighbors counter-fought,* and, while no one outside the state knew of this feud, the Idaho papers were full of stories (at least twenty-six, by one count), for the next six years.

Carole and Rick approached their shared battle from opposite political perspectives: she, the left; he, the right. He was the survivalist, angry at and deeply distrustful of the federal government, seeking privacy and freedom at all costs. She soon melded the anger about privacy and property rights that she'd originally picked up from him with the environmentalist and communitarian perspective that was more her

---

* In November 1981, Carole and Rick filed action in federal court, claiming their right to due process had been violated, and they asked that the road be declared private. In early 1982, a judge dismissed criminal charges against Carole. In January 1983, a federal judge ruled that her rights had not been violated and that the road issue was for the state to decide. In June 1985, Carole's neighbors and Custer County sued her and Rick in state district court, seeking an order declaring the road open. In August 1986, the district court ruled for Carole; the neighbors appealed the ruling. In June 1987, the district again ruled for Carole; the neighbors appealed.

style. The battle with the U.S. Forest Service led her to research, discover, and become appalled at that agency's plans to build roads
throughout Idaho's 20 million acres of wilderness so that logging companies could cut down and profit from the unprotected trees. (Idaho and
Montana were the only states at the time that didn't have wilderness
protection laws, and, in pro-business Reagan America, they weren't
likely to get them.) A participant in the legal fight remembers their different miens: "Teepee Rick showed up in federal court for depositions
with a buck knife on his belt, trying to be threatening." Carole, who the
participant remembers as being "pretty hard-nosed," nonetheless retained humility, and humor. When a court worker (who knew Carole
was *some* kind of female music star but didn't know which one) asked
her to sing a few bars of "You're So Vain," Carole obligingly delivered a
rendition of Carly's song.

During the seven years that the case bumped along, in and out of
courts, "Carole was very unhappy; she was in a deep, deep depression," a confidante says. "Did she have good times with Sorensen? Yes,
sure, she did—she has all the frailties of any woman and maybe more
so. I think she was desperate to find somebody who would love her for
herself," and the reclusive Sorensen, who (unlike Rick Evers) had no interest in her connections to the music industry, must have appeased her
fear of being used.

Living with this wary warrior at their Robinson Bar Ranch, Carole
lost touch with her *Tapestry* friends like Stephanie Fischbach, and she
was doubly isolated from her Brill Building friends. Cynthia Weil understood that "obviously Carole wanted to be in Idaho and [Sorensen]
wanted her to be there, and he didn't like us very much." After their
closeness in New York and their benign distance from each other from
1967 on, this Rick One/Rick Two period (as Cynthia would come to
view the years from the late 1970s to the late 1980s) seemed a chasm,
despite their occasional bouts of writing together. "I just felt that Carole
and I were so different, I had no insight into what her direction was. I
didn't understand" her life and "I thought, Who am *I* to tell her anything? I'm probably living a life that she wouldn't want." Besides, "I

think when Carole falls in love with somebody, she can't see quite clearly, and I can understand that—it happens to the best of us. So I just backed off. But Carole knew if she wanted me, I'd be there."

Actually, Carole had, on her own, come to the same conclusion— that she hadn't been seeing clearly: at least in terms of her approach to city-vs.-wilderness. "I jumped; I cast off everything; I ran away from this town," she admitted to the *Los Angeles Times*'s Charles Champlin at the dawn of 1984, with the failure of her fourteenth original album, *Speeding Time,* fresh behind her. "I have a way of not doing anything in the middle when there is an extreme available. And I realized I'd thrown away good things with bad—the energy and the people who were doing good things. I have to admit it; I write better in the city, but the rest of your life suffers." Over the next three years, though she made forays into New York and L.A., performing in an off-Broadway play in 1987 and acting in and writing the score for a minor movie, *Murphy's Romance* (starring Sally Field and James Garner), in 1986, most of her time was spent in Idaho with Rick. It was hard not to think she *was* out to pasture, amid the horses and cows in her pine-ringed mountain fortress. In 1987 she and Gerry were inducted into the Songwriters Hall of Fame, and a year later they received the National Academy of Songwriters Lifetime Achievement Award. That was what happened when you started writing as a teenager, became a seasoned pro before you could vote, and a superstar in your twenties, then slowly dissolved over ten years: a *lifetime* achievement award at age forty-six. Carole was determined to not be "honored" into irrelevance.

In the meantime, she was developing a second career as an environmental activist.

On February 10, 1988, Carole finally won her bruising locked-gate case. Idaho's Supreme Court upheld the district court's 1986 ruling, declaring her road private. The victory allowed Carole to widen her focus from her—not particularly sympathetic—personal situation (which had fostered the image of, as even one supportive report conceded, "an outsider coming in and locking up a piece of Idaho") and to come out swinging against the new logging and access-road-building on *all* the land of her adopted state. As she succinctly put it: "I protected my rights and now I am working to protect *everyone's* rights." "The destruction of wilderness is a form of corporate welfare which is costing taxpayers money, says singer and wilderness advocate Carole King," an Idaho newspaper wrote, paraphrasing her rousing speech to an audience of one hundred members of the Idaho Conservation League in May of that year. (The Conservation League was outnumbered by pro-loggers in the conservative, timber-industry-dependent state.) "Timber companies want Idaho's roadless land released from wilderness consideration so they can harvest additional board feet. But before the companies can reach the trees, the U.S. Forest Service has to build expensive roads at public expense, King says."

By now an Idahoan at least halfway to her bones, Carole knew that the case had to be made not with liberal-speak but with dollars and cents. Clearing the wilderness was costing people money that could be better spent on schools. She didn't oppose logging or mining, Carole said, just deficit timber sales and tax write-offs for strip mining, which were returning to the public a mere nine to thirteen cents for every taxpayer dollar spent on the preparation for timber sales. "She was very savvy," says Rocky Barker, an environmental reporter (and native Idahoan), who saw that "she was on her way to becoming a leading voice in the national wilderness-protection movement. Carole was not a dilettante. She was a true believer and dedicated activist."

Barker had first "met" her on the phone, when he'd been hired on the environmental beat of the *Idaho Falls Register*. An agitated Carole had called the paper from Washington, during the middle of a big Reagan-supported logging initiative. "She said, 'I'm back here working with Congress to try to convince them to stop spending money on roads that destroy our national forest and are costing more money than the timber brings on the market!'" She was meeting major workers in the wilderness-protection movement, and, in late 1988, joined with Cass Chinsky, a Montana city councilman, and Mike Bader, an ex-Yellowstone ranger, to form the Alliance for the Wild Rockies. Within two years, she would come up with what local environmentalists considered "an extremely unique" view, says Rocky Barker. "She wasn't calling for stricter provisions against trucks and trail bikes on the unprotected land in Idaho and Montana—she wasn't calling for turning all of the region into wilderness. She just wanted to 'leave it as it is,' which mirrored the view of a majority of Idahoans. They didn't want more restrictions, but they didn't want it logged."

Carole continued to speak at public hearings ("You combat ignorance by education, and that's where I can use my role as a famous person," she said. "While I'm not a walking encyclopedia, I know a lot about this issue"), even amid angry dissent. At one October 1990 hearing, the Idaho Trail Machine Association bused in a large group of motorbikers and snowmobilers to try to drown out Carole with jeers.

In the same way that living in the mountains had balmed Carole's post-*Tapestry* fall from grace and the shock of Rick Evers's self-destructive death, fighting for the wilderness enabled her to feel close again to her native metropolis. In 1989, when she recorded her next album, she named it (and its title song) *City Streets*. For its cover she was photographed against a graffiti-streaked brick building: eyes closed, head high, wild haired, an adamant, sensual expression on her face. An internal shot showed her in leggings, long boxy jacket, clunky shoes, and big late-'80s hair, slouched inside a funky loft: the costume and setting suggestive of *Flashdance,* Madonna videos, and the like.

Four of the album's ten songs she wrote herself; two she wrote with Gerry, and the rest with various new cowriters. Capitol promised her—and delivered—major promotion. *City Streets* was her strongest-sounding and strongest-selling album since just before the two disasters she'd lovingly produced with Evers. Hard rock, Broadway, and country influences abound on it, smartly and zestily produced by Carole and her new guitarist and musical partner, Rudy Guess (Rudy's wife, Lorna, became Carole's manager and friend). Carole's voice is lusty and aggressive, 180 degrees from the terse, muted melancholy on *Rhymes & Reasons* (which may have reflected her ambivalence at the mixed-blessing hugeness of *Tapestry*). In *City Streets,* she is a middle-aged, mountain-life-idled superpro who knows there are no more laurels to rest on. "Ain't That the Way," which she solely wrote, is an almost-two-decades-later reprise of her beloved themes of connectedness, but with an older and wiser edge. "Whenever you think you're in control / Everything turns around . . .": the lyrics didn't have to be eloquent; the post-*Tapestry* critical drumming, the divorce from one man she loved and the drug-fueled death of another, the years of depression—this hidden history was eloquence enough. After writing for years for soul artists but respectfully refraining from using black parlance, she'd earned the right to insert a blues call—"Ain't that the way . . . "—between every stanza.

Rolling Stone praised the album's good intentions and acknowledged the buzz of "comeback" expectation, but then leveled that familiar verdict: "King has yet to re-create the chemistry of her work with producer Lou Adler in *Tapestry* and its immediate follow-ups in the early Seventies." The album reached #10 on the adult contemporary chart.

Carole had formed the group The City, with Danny and Charlie, when she'd left New York for Laurel Canyon and changed her life. Her new album, reinvoking New York, heralded a kind of twenty-two-year-later return. With her youngest child, Levi, about to graduate high school and go off to college, she had more freedom; she acquired an apartment in Manhattan and began testing the waters of living there again. Carole had done children's theater, playing the mother to Tatum O'Neal's Goldilocks (John Lithgow was the father) in a 1984 staging of the fairy-tale-turned-play of that name. At some point around 1990 she did another children's play. A handsome young actor named John Bennett—he went by the name Johnny B—had a bit part in the production. "And they got together," says Roy Reynolds. "He was a young, good-looking guy. But he was too young for her." Nevertheless, she fell for him.

It felt safe for Carole to have this split life; Rick *never* left the mountains.

Except when he did. Trading his animal pelts for inconspicuous blue jeans, one day Rick drove to Boise, then boarded a plane to Salt Lake City and then another to Kennedy Airport.

The buzzer rang in Carole's apartment. She was stunned to see him at the door.

Her fourth marriage was over. As she complained at the time to a confidante, "Every time I divorce another husband, it costs me a million dollars."

Carole released her sixteenth original album, *Colour of Your Dreams,* in 1993. On the cover—and possibly inspired by her relationship with the much-younger Johnny B—she, at fifty-one, stands splay-legged and challengingly pigeon-toed, like a blue-jeaned street kid (the taut-chinned face in an accompanying video suggests she had a face-lift), in front of another graffitied wall, and she uses Guns N' Roses's Slash prominently on her rocking "Hold Out for Love." But those apparent symbols of a concerted youth consciousness aren't borne out in the music, which reflects a naturalness and comfort, starting with the beautiful, soulful "Lay Down My Life."

Reviewing the album for *Rolling Stone,* Kara Manning put Carole into historical context, stressing her contributions (she "shattered sales records with her transcendent second solo album *Tapestry* [and] the giddy success of King's refined collection . . . paved an open road of possibilities for her and her contemporaries Joni Mitchell, Laura Nyro, and Carly Simon") and saluting Carole for pushing her reinvigorated landmark style despite being what one was not supposed to be in pop music: "a woman over forty-five." Hailing Carole as "one of the spiritual forebears of the softly subversive underground of young female songwriters"—Sheryl Crow, Ani DiFranco, Tracy Chapman, Natalie Merchant, Sarah McLachlan, Shawn Colvin (who was being produced by Joni's ex-husband Larry Klein), Melissa Etheridge—who were "trying to break into the boys' club of the FM band," Manning wryly noted that, "ironically, King's battle for renewed recognition is frustrating testament to the bullheadedness of today's radio programmers—who no doubt grew up owning a well-worn copy of *Tapestry*."

A song from *Colour,* "Now and Forever" (Carly had written a differ-

ent song with the same name about Russ Kunkel), became the theme
of the movie *A League of Their Own*. Like Carly, Carole saw that scoring
films for congenial peers (Penny Marshall, a Bronx-to-L.A. girl, was to
Carole what Mike Nichols and Nora Ephron were to Carly) was a way
to extend her reach beyond the age-ceilinged limits of radio. Carole
went out on tour for the new album and her 1994 live album, *Carole
King in Concert,* was the result.

By now something else, significant to Carole's second career as an
environmental activist, had happened: the Reagan era was over, and
Bill Clinton was in the White House. (Carole had performed at his Ar-
kansas inaugural ball.) Environmentalists rejoiced. "It felt like our generation had taken charge," says Rocky Barker. Carole started working
with Brock Evans, the longtime Sierra Club leader who'd gone on to
become the National Audubon Society's lobbying director. Her Alliance for the Wild Rockies was now—quite radically—calling for protect-
ing 16 million acres ("That was twice as much as anybody, even in the
environmental community, had suggested," says Barker) of wilderness
in Idaho, Montana, and parts of Wyoming, Oregon, and Washington.
In May 1994, Carole testified for the plan, the Northern Rockies Ecosystem Protection Act (NREPA) at a hearing called by U.S. House of
Representatives subcommittees.

Foes came out of the woodwork to assail her. Montana Republican
senator Conrad Burns called her "a washed-up rock-and-roll singer."
"This millionaire recording star has absolutely no sensitivity to the
working men and women of the state of Idaho that she now so proudly
calls her residence," sneered Idaho Republican senator Larry Craig,
who would—thirteen years later, in 2007—find *himself* sneered at (and
then some) after his Minneapolis men's room arrest.

But one man was listening: Bill Clinton. Carole King and Bill Clinton became friends. At the beginning of his second term, Clinton, while
not formally taking a position on NREPA, was said to have been suffi-
ciently inspired by it to use his power of "administrative rule" to par-

tially protect all roadless areas.* "I would argue that Carole King is the earth mother of the roadless area initiative," Barker says. Michael Garrity, the Alliance for the Wild Rockies executive director, adds that, from the 1980s to the present, "Carole King has always been our hardest-working, most effective lobbyist."

In April 1997 Carole took a Grand Canyon river trip with elderly conservationist Martin Litton and Ric Bailey, of the Oregon Hells Canyon Preservation Council. As the canyons loomed on either side of the ribbon of rapids they were navigating, a dream came into focus: a superorganization that would bring the now-hundreds of environmental groups into one fold. Five months later Carole and Ric Bailey assembled dozens of environmental leaders in the White Cloud foothills behind her Robinson Bar Ranch. The White Cloud Council was born, with the mandate "to protect what is wild and to restore what should be [wild]" through "big dreams" and "bold plans." Carole remains one of a half dozen leaders of the thriving group today.

If only love could come, and stay, as easily as work.

At some point in the mid- to late 1990s Cynthia heard from Carole. "She was in distress. Another relationship"—with Johnny B—had ended, Cynthia recalls. "It was the first time she called and said, 'Can I come and spend time with you?' So Barry and I said, 'Please, stay with us.'" Cynthia had met Johnny B once, "and he didn't impress me." She knew that Carole understood that their great age difference made a breakup inevitable. "There's a realistic part of Carole, and I think she always knew this guy should be with someone who could give him children." Still, she'd gotten "very invested" in the relationship "and she cared for him deeply. When the breakup came, there was just a lot of pain."

Carole stayed with Cynthia and Barry for several weeks, during which time Cynthia had the idea of fixing her up with a screenwriter-director friend of theirs, Phil Alden Robinson. Alden Robinson, who

---

* President Bush has tried to rescind Clinton's roadless rule, but has been kept from doing so by the courts. NREPA continues to be reintroduced in Congress, year after year.

was eight years younger than Carole and bore a casual resemblance
to Steven Spielberg, was born in Long Beach, California, grew up in
far upstate New York, attended Union College in Schenectady, began
a TV and radio broadcasting career, and then spent the Vietnam War
as a member of the motion picture unit of the air force. After his discharge from the air force, Alden Robinson moved west and broke
into screenwriting in the early 1980s, writing the television drama
Trapper John, M.D. and the screenplays for the movies *All of Me* (which
starred Lily Tomlin and Steve Martin), *Rhinestone* (which starred Dolly
Parton and Sylvester Stallone), and, most famously, Kevin Costner's
baseball epic, *Field of Dreams,* which Alden Robinson also directed.
Cynthia thought Phil "*so* smart and *so* funny that, though he's not traditionally handsome, he becomes handsome because of his mind and
his sensitivity."

When Cynthia contacted Phil to tell him that she wanted to fix him
up with Carole, he called back from Bosnia, where he was researching
a movie. "I'd love to meet her," he said, enthusiastically, "but I won't be
back in time." Cynthia persisted; once Phil was back in L.A. and Carole
was again staying with Cynthia and Barry, Cynthia engineered their
meeting at a dinner party through her friend Beth Rickman. "I told
Carole, 'This guy could be for you!'" Phil had arrived with a date, but
Beth diverted Phil's date's attention, and Carole and Phil "spent a lot of
the evening together," Cynthia recalls. The next night he came to our
house and picked her up for a real date. Barry and I said, 'Oh, you
kids! Be sure to be home by midnight' and 'No necking in the car.'"

In a week or so Cynthia got a call from Carole *and* Phil, who announced to their matchmaker, in unison, "We are madly in love." "They
were even righter for each other than I ever imagined," Cynthia says.
"They like the same movies, they like the same food, politically they're
on the same wavelength." But those similarities paled next to the point
that Cynthia next makes: "Phil is the first guy who has ever taken care
of Carole the way she should be taken care of, and who appreciates her
in the way she needs to be appreciated." Interviewed for this book in
2003, Cynthia said, "She seems so happy, and I'm happy for her."

Roy Reynolds–having lived through Rick One and Rick Two and Johnny B with his friend–felt just as euphoric about Phil. "Carole is with the man she should have been with her whole life!" he enthused, in 2003. "She told me she's happy *for the first time*."

With Phil, Carole returned to her Brill Building social set after decades in self-imposed exile. She and Phil spent time with Barry and Cynthia and with Jerry Leiber and Mike Stoller and their spouses. Mike sat next to Carole at the wedding of Cynthia and Barry's daughter Jennifer, and–his mind racing back forty years, to when Carole and Gerry used to try out their new songs for the Drifters–he sheepishly confessed, "I always loved the way you sang. The only reason I never recorded you was that you weren't black."

Carole's 2001 album, *Love Makes the World*–of mostly new songs she wrote with others–radiated her new sense of satisfaction. The title track is as infectious, whole-hearted, and commercial as any of her Brill Building or early-1970s hits, but the album implicitly acknowledges that the music scene has moved on, and Carole seems willing to make do with her slightly patronized but affectionate placement in the baby boomer* legends market. Her voice is warm, slightly hoarse, earnest but *natural*– the theatrical and accentless *Tapestry* enunciation has given way to the soft, frank Brooklyn vowels that survived thirty-five years' diaspora. There is a sense of tying up life's loose ends, as she sings her and Gerry's deliciously mournful "Oh No Not My Baby" with only her ex-husband Charlie on bass. Charlie had since remarried, had another son, and divorced, but he was still family, and the intimacy of the collaboration honors the significance of their marriage. (Not that everything is down-memory-lane; she also performs a duet with Kenny "Babyface" Edmonds.) One year before her sixtieth birthday, settled in with Phil, Carole seems in this album to be celebrating her sophisticated maturity:

---

* The term "baby boomer" by now had come to refer to anyone who had lived through the 1960s, even as a child. It literally refers to the broad population of people born between 1946 (after the end of World War II) to 1964.

on the cover, in a chic, low-cut black sweater dress and Glenn Close–in–*Fatal Attraction* curls, she's hugging herself and smiling.

Carole was a grandmother of three now, by way of her daughters with Gerry. Sherry a producer of children's records, and her husband, Robbie Kondor, had two children; singer-songwriter Louise and her husband, Greg Wells, would soon have their second child. As for her children with Charlie: Levi, a University of Texas Ph.D. in cognitive science, would soon marry his girlfriend, Bina, and Columbia University–educated Molly was a sculptor; her large, bold, angular, painted wood pieces have been featured in gallery shows.

After having been the first female rock star to actively campaign for a president (back when she and James starred in the 1972 McGovern fund-raisers), Carole had never stopped being political: campaigning for Gary Hart in 1984, and working with her good friend Bill Clinton on wilderness issues throughout the 1990s. For the 2004 election, she actively campaigned for her friend and Idaho neighbor John Kerry, traveling the country and giving intimate concerts in donors' living rooms. The next year she held a concert in Hyannis, capturing the spirit of the campaign. The 2005 live double-CD *The Living Room Tour* (which became a strong seller through the new boomer merchandising godsend, Starbucks) is Carole's retrospective of her forty-year career. In her fans' yelps of joy at her candor (she shout-sings: "I'm *sixty-two* . . . and there are so many [songs] I'd like to do") and in their sing-alongs on the gems of her oeuvre, they're pronouncing her a national treasure. She's finally stopped trying to beat that mixed-blessing verdict and seems content to join it.

Her voice on the album is Brooklyn-cadenced and emotional. It's a voice that says, "It's too late, baby, whoa, it's too late": too late for her old ambivalence about fame. Among the tracks, she treats fans to a medley of songs that she wrote, she says, "with Gerry Goffin?"—the gentle interrogative is contempo-speak—and *also* asks her fans to *honor* him: "my first husband, my first lyricist, and still a very dear friend," understating the tenacious bond that had withstood their early angst and their combined six marriages to subsequent spouses. Even today,

Gerry, his fourth wife, and most of Carole's and Gerry's collective children, including Dawn Reavis Smith and her children, spend Thanksgiving with Carole.

At the live performance's close, she hoarsely shouts, "I love you!" and the crowd whoops: *Likewise!* But it is another exhortation of hers—"We're *Am-ER-ica;* we're *gonna make* it!," ad-libbed into the refrain of "Sweet Seasons"—that lingers. That hope-against-odds sensibility had permeated *Tapestry,* and it had gained fresh necessity in the post-2000-election culture war, which the song was now addressing. And its spirit had been born on that long-ago day when, with friend Camille Cacciatore at her side and the Brooklyn phone book in hand, Carole Klein of Sheepshead Bay became Carole King of America.

In March 2007, the National Association of Record Merchandisers and the Rock and Roll Hall of Fame voted *Tapestry* #7 on a list of two hundred albums that every music lover should own (*Sgt. Pepper* was #1). *Tapestry* had inched out Dylan's celebrated *Highway 61 Revisited.*

In late November, James Taylor joined Carole in headlining for three nostalgia-filled sold-out nights at the Troubadour. Danny Kortchmar, Russ Kunkel, and Leland Sklar backed them up; Gerry was given props from the audience.

Carole is no longer with Phil Alden Robinson. By age sixty-five, she was single again. Danny had bemusedly noted that the responsible, conventional girl he'd first met as the "Brill Building pro" had—surprisingly—gone on to live "three different lives; maybe *four* different lives." To which one might add: "And counting."

surviving

Jim Hart seemed to provide just the right mesh with Carly. "He was so attractive, and very smart, and well read—and Carly is high-maintenance," says Jeanie Seligmann, voicing a widely held opinion. "Not just anybody would want to take on this very complicated person. So it had to be someone where their needs coincided. It seemed that Carly both needed to *be* taken care of and needed to take care *of* Jim.

She had the money, for one thing, and she was eager to encourage him to reach his potential as a writer, while he could tend to her emotionally." Jim actually relished that latter task; he found Carly's efforts against her phobias touching and heroic. "Fifty percent of Carly's day is spent warding off the fear that something is going to kill her—imagine having to live that way!" he says. "But she lives in a kind of hopefulness that I've seen very few people live in. She wraps her heart around her craziness and she does it in a way that's genius; she outfoxes her own neuroses."

Jake Brackman agrees. "Jim is very steady. He may be in a kind of low-grade depression all the time, but it works for him; it makes him mellow. Carly is an emotional roller coaster. Jim will listen to Carly's slight-of-the-day; he's not entitled to his own drama, he's not competing with her. *She* can take the stage all the time. And he has that social quality that James was totally lacking: you can take Jim anywhere and he won't look at his shoes; he'll look at *you,* and he'll say he had a wonderful time and mean it." Of Carly's celebrity-studded world, "where he was constantly hobnobbing with Bill Styron and Art Buchwald and Mike Wallace and John Updike"—not to mention Jackie Onassis—Jake says, "Jim completely held his own with these people—he can carry on a literary conversation as good as they're gonna get. His social relations are extremely smooth. He'd learned from a very young age how to ingratiate himself with the Jesuit priests. He became best friends with Mike Nichols, independent of Carly. When Carly and Jim were having problems, Mike would take *Jim's* side."

Her new husband's eloquent poetry lifted Carly's romantic heart. Soon after they married, they traveled to Quebec, and he took from their intimacy there the sense of being "north on the plain of Abraham / cupping these few droplets of flame / as for the first time." Theirs was "a love," he wrote, "that has searched for its landscape," that "pierces a new air, kisses your face / and changes it after all these years." He awaited his wife and lover's "breath once more / to light the flesh of this day."

Carly worked with Jim on the theme song for Mike Nichols's next movie, *Working Girl*. Viewing the opening footage of the movie—the Staten Island ferry gliding past the Statue of Liberty toward Manhattan's skyscrapers—Carly knew she wanted to score it with "a hymn with a jungle beat." It was Jim who turned to *Finnegans Wake* to come up with the first line of the soaring anthem, "Let the river run / let all the dreamers wake the nation." Carly and Jim together turned to the poets William Blake and Walt Whitman,* and came up with the hosanna "Come, the New Jerusalem," the song's emotional fulcrum. "Let the River Run" is one of Carly's most stirring songs; and when she was named Best Song winner at the 1988 Academy Awards, she took the stage and said, "Thank you to my husband, Jim Hart. You wrote the best lines of the song—thank you, sweetheart."

Still, Jim says he lost his temper a lot that first year and a half of marriage. One blowup occurred in October 1989, when Carly and Jim were set to attend a Rolling Stones concert at Shea Stadium with Carly's twelve-year-old son, Ben; John Kennedy Jr.; and Allen Ginsberg and his partner, Peter Orlovsky. It was shortly after a New York tabloid headline blared "The Hunk Flunks," about Kennedy's second failure of the state bar exam, and the humiliated young man didn't want to be seen in public. But Carly took him in hand. As Jim recalls, "She picked up the phone and said to John, 'You listen to me! This is *not* open for discussion! You are *going* to that concert and you are *going* to have the time of your life and there's no argument about it!' She was 'Auntie' with him."

Carly was right about Kennedy having a great time at the concert, but she hadn't predicted the trouble she'd have with her husband's jealousy. A preconcert meeting between Carly and her party and Mick Jagger was arranged—but Jim was left out of it. As he recalls, "We get to the stadium, and I'm aware that I'm excluded from the meeting. It's made to look like an accident but—I have *really* good radar—it's *no* ac-

---

* Whitman had appropriated the idea of New York as a modern-day biblical capital from William Blake's urbanity-venerating words ("And was Jerusalem builded here / Among these dark Satanic mills?") in Blake's poem "The New Jerusalem."

cident." As Carly, Ben, and John went backstage to greet the rock icon who had been a seductive presence in Carly's life since 1971, "I went *bat-shit*," Jim says. "I was out-of-my-mind jealous about Carly being with Jagger." When everyone was back in their seats and Jagger was onstage, "I just *glowered* through the whole performance"—so intensely that "John got scared; he was thinking, 'Jesus, who *is* this guy?'" Later, back at the apartment, "I blew my top." Jim was so enraged at Carly for what he felt were her lingering feelings toward Jagger that Ben, alarmed, called the police. Later, Carly screamed sense into Jim: "Don't you see? I could have married those people! I *didn't want* those people! I wanted *you!*"

True to the promise of their marriage—and to Carly's faith in Jim's talent—Carly supported Jim while he plugged away at his novel, *Spike and Dive*. The expectation was clear: "'Jim, write the Great American Novel.' And Jim tries to write the Great American Novel, and it's a really tough road," he says. Being married to Carly and being close friends with Bill Kennedy opened doors. But the writing itself went slowly, and, as Jim says, "people of integrity and credibility and professionalism don't mess around" with unmaterialized books, so the connections only went so far. The novel he and Carly thought would take a year and a half was not completed in two years, nor three, nor four. Carly's friends worried that her faith in Jim's ability to turn his desire to be a writer into published work was now like her faith in James's ability, during their marriage, to turn his stated desire to quit heroin into actually quitting. Jim felt tremendous pressure. "I said, 'Am I nuts at my age'—forty-two—'to try to write a novel?'" His friends had varying opinions. One said, "Look, Jim, I wrote for twenty years and no one knew who I was—you gotta keep doing it." Another said, "Do you want to be a failed novelist, or a successful insurance man?"

During these same years that Jim toiled and stalled on his novel, Carly was very productive. Jake had once seen her as having two roads to choose from: either being an arts-and-cause maven like Andrea or being an artist and presence in her own right. Now, moored in a marriage to a man who tended to her emotionally, and at the same time anxiously mindful that the career revived late in the game through *Coming Around Again* and "Let the River Run" wouldn't stay afloat forever, Carly became both the social maven *and* the workhorse. She began writing the first of what would be four children's books, *Midnight Farm,* and working with Jake on an opera, *Romulus Hunt,* as part of a collaboration between the Metropolitan Opera and Washington's Kennedy Center; she opened a small Manhattan art gallery named (after her Academy Award–winning song) Riverrun; and she would eventually open, with her friend Tamara Weiss, a boutique, Midnight Farm, that is still thriving on Martha's Vineyard.

Most important, she released two albums by the end of 1990 and one in 1992. One of the 1990 offerings was *My Romance,* in which she wisely renewed the standards franchise that would serve her well in years to come, this time interpreting a group of wistful torchers— "My Funny Valentine," "In the Wee Small Hours of the Morning," "Bewitched," and "Time After Time," among them—like the kind that she and Tim Ratner had fallen in love to when Jonathan Schwartz played them on his all-night radio station. She also included the Irish ballad "Danny Boy": the first song she had ever learned to sing, courtesy of her "good" nanny, Allie Brennan (as opposed to her mean nanny, Nancy Anderson), to whom she dedicated the album. The other album, *Have You Seen Me Lately?* featured her new original compositions. It was a pressing midlife quest; as she frankly described it to *The New York Times*'s Stephen Holden, she was "middle-aged and feeling a decaying process starting." Having been "brought up nonreligious" (yet now married to a former seminarian), Carly was finding that "I have more questions and am trying to find answers more concentratedly than I've ever had to in my life." But the album, in which (as Holden restated the now-tedious trope) her "white, upper-middle-class adult sensibility" was trained on "the longings and insecurities of people who have it all, with wrenching honesty"—and which was delivered in Carly's typical "at once open-hearted and high-strung" voice—didn't catch on like its predecessor, *Coming Around Again,* had. But the

1990s would produce so many life-and-death challenges that Carly's palette of concerns—expressed in her songs of (as Holden put it) "anxious desire and erotic competitiveness"—would give way to more primal issues.

Carly's next album, the soundtrack for her friend Nora Ephron's 1992 directorial debut, *This Is My Life* (about a single mother raising two daughters), gave her a minor hit (#16 on the adult contemporary chart). "Love of My Life" came to her one night when Sally and Ben were going to bed. Sally, eighteen, would soon be off to Brown University, but Ben, fifteen, had had a bumpy boyhood. Between his dyslexia, his bouncing around to various schools, and a character much like his father's (but warmer), Carly had always been anxiously enmeshed with him. As the youngsters strode to their bedrooms that night, Carly impulsively called out: "You are the love of my life!" The angst of motherhood—both prosaic *and* operatic ("My heart is riding on a runaway train!")—illuminated the song.

Since 1981, Carly had avoided playing large venues. Her fear of flying and her anxiety disorder hadn't receded. Now she had Jim drive her and her backup band to local concerts in a Winnebago. Carly used her affliction to bond with and help others. The singer-songwriter Marc Cohn (who'd just had the hit "Walking in Memphis") became one of the young male friends to whom she would also become a big sister. "We had soulful conversations" during the early 1990s, Marc recalls. They shared "extremely debilitating disorders where you have to function despite being in a very anxious place." Carly took matters in hand. "She wrote me a contract for getting over my writer's block: I would sit down at the piano for an hour a day. She gave me a long list of things I couldn't use to keep from writing—I couldn't use my divorce; I couldn't use my anxiety. Then she made me sign it. It was incredibly Carly-esque: generous, understanding, and funny." Marc did such a good job of overcoming his anxieties "that when things got easier, I almost didn't want to tell her; there's a part of that symbiotic friendship when it's easier to be equal." But he did tell her—"and she was thrilled for me."

Toward the end of 1992, Jim's inability to complete his novel after four years of effort—and four years of Carly supporting him, emotionally and financially—was eating away at their marriage. He gave up on the novel entirely. Despite being "madly in love" with each other, as he puts it; despite a personal intimacy that seemed to have nothing to do with money and résumé, sadly, "the world couldn't go away in our heads," he says. "When you marry a famous, relatively wealthy woman and you don't have money of your own, you're a bounder. With any relationship that's this unbalanced, you both withstand a psychological barrage." Jim moved into a small apartment in a tenement building on the Upper West Side—"the move showed I was a man of integrity"— and went back to selling insurance.

Carly deeply missed the man who soothed her through her anxieties, and Jim wrote of now being "a spoon without a mate," aching "for your melody and musk . . . a tad of linen next to your skin . . . the timbre of your voice close to my breath."

The separation only lasted a few months. Emergency intervened: Andrea Simon was diagnosed with lung cancer. Jim returned to Carly, while Carly cared for her mother on the Vineyard. He secured a position teaching poetry at Harvard with Robert Coles, the noted child psychologist. Eventually, when Coles started a quarterly magazine on the arts and humanities called *Double Take,* Jim was made editor.

Carly's relationship with her larger-than-life mother had always been complicated. She had both rebelled against Andrea (becoming a hands-on, breast-feeding mother rather than relying on nannies, for one thing) *and* become *like* Andrea: the witty seductress, the stylish life organizer. As with many psychoanalyzed, feminist women, she had come to view her mother both sympathetically—as a victim of an earlier, sexist age, doing what she *had* to do to escape husband-borne indignities—and also critically, angrily. One day (before Andrea's cancer had been diagnosed) Carly dashed off a lyric-metered letter to Andrea about the unresolved issue of Ronnie Klinzing. "Why can't you apologize / You say it was all Daddy's fault / He loved Auntie Jo and treated you like a scullery maid . . ." Still, Carly contended, the victims were her and her sisters. She considered mailing the letter—getting one's true feelings out was the orthodoxy of the day—but was stopped by a remembered bit of Andrea's advice: never mail a letter composed in strong emotion. The wise demurral would inspire an album (and title song), *Letters Never Sent*.

Even as Andrea's cancer advanced, "she was still indomitable," Jim says. "She said, 'You've gotta do this! You've gotta do that!'" Carly cared for her frail mother—"carrying Andrea to the ferry," Jim says, "taking her to the bathroom—this woman who had been such a giant and such a tremendous influence on her daughters." When Andrea resisted radiation treatment, Carly hired two handsome young actors to escort her mother to the hospital; Andrea rose to the occasion. As 1993 turned to 1994, Andrea's prognosis dimmed. Carly, Joey, Lucy, and Peter decided not to tell their mother that she was dying. "We knew it was a truth that she did not want to know," Lucy has said. Instead, they gathered around her bed in the Grosvenor Avenue house and sang to her. In February, she succumbed; Carly was at her bedside, and "I wanted to crawl under the covers with her and go back to the womb," she told a confidante.

Instead, she wrote:

> *I fought over the pearls*
> *With the other girls*
> *But it was just a metaphor for what is wrong with us*

Those three lines are resonant for any adult sisters for whom arguments about material things are merciful proxies for the hurts, hierarchies, and guilts of childhood, which indelibly animate their sisterhood. In the alternately solemn and buoyant "Like a River," in which she invokes the grand nurturance of the mother she cannot believe is dead, Carly returns to the simile (female = river) she'd coined twenty-two years earlier in "Think I'm Gonna Have a Baby," but now she shears it of its breeziness. "I'll wait no more for you as a daughter," she sings, then turns around and vows, "but I will wait for you for-*e*-ver, like a river."

Immediately after Andrea's death, Carly's friend Jackie Kennedy

Onassis took a turn for the worse in her battle against lymphoma. Carly had a lunch for Jackie on April 14, 1994—"the last day that Jackie was leading a normal life," says Joe Armstrong, who was present. "Jackie was just finishing a round of chemo; she was wearing a wig, which was very upsetting and jarring to Carly and me, because we hadn't seen her in a month or two and she was no longer the strong, vibrant person we knew." Still, Jackie was upbeat. "She said, 'Just four more weeks and I get my life back.'" As Carly's two guests were putting on their coats and leaving, Carly said, "I have something for you," and she put a tape of a song, "Touched by the Sun," into Jackie's hand, explaining that she had written it for her. The song, delivered with Carly's "You're So Vain" ferocity, was about a woman living in proximity to greatness—as women of Jackie's (and Andrea's) era did—but also living daringly, even foolhardily. ("I *need* to let them say, 'She must have been *mad*.'") People had thought Jackie Kennedy "mad" when she married homely, crass, foreign Aristotle Onassis and fell off her young-widow-of-Camelot throne. But her quieter audacity was in being, for twenty years, a regular Manhattan working woman, strolling alone through Central Park; trying, with any editor's limited effectiveness, to get celebrities to pen tell-alls; living happily with a man she wasn't married to; standing in movie lines like any ticket holder.

Jackie, Joe Armstrong says, "was bowled over by Carly's song."

At the beginning of the third week of May, when the Central Park outside their windows was freshly abloom, Carly and Joe knew that Jackie was dying. They were on their knees, praying, in Joe's Upper West Side living room, when the phone rang. It was Marta, who'd been Caroline and John's nanny, saying, "Come right over." Jackie wanted to say good-bye. The Fifth Avenue apartment was mobbed with friends, but only women, and few of them, at that, were allowed into the bedroom. "Madam wouldn't want a man to see her like this," Marta told Carly, so Joe hung back as Carly entered the bedroom of the most queenly woman in America.

A day or so later, Carly and Joe returned to the apartment—for

Jackie's wake. "We were just shattered," Joe recalls. They hadn't expected "a big cocktail party, people with drinks in their hands, all this
noise—and there was Jackie, in the corner, in the casket." At the funeral, Ted Kennedy humorously orated about his brother—"Jack" this
and "Jack" that. It seemed odd to many that the woman who had for
decades led such a singular, self-powered life was, in death, reduced
to that long-ago stage of her life she had surpassed—being the orna-
mental wife among young lions. The Camelot images that filled the
nation's TV screens during the tributes to her seemed as knee-jerk and
unrepresentative as Joe and Carly felt the wake had been.

Letters Never Sent was released in 1995, with Carly's songs to her
mother and Jackie on it. But there were no singles, no hits. Carly was
now called a "heritage"—read older—artist by Arista. She had passed
the fifty-year mark.

Carly loved Jim; her charming poet was the stallion who thought
her a goddess. But for all of that romance, issues remained in their
marriage, and Carly and Jim did what so many verbal, middle-aged
married people now did: threw themselves into couples therapy. "Carly's attitude was: 'I don't give a shit how much this hurts! We're gonna
get an answer!'" he says. But "two or three" therapists later, they felt
fatigued and disheartened. "The last counselor—we're both crying,
walking down the street . . . and she says, 'I'm not doing this anymore.'
And I say, 'I'm not either.'" They made one last—inventive—stab at
counseling. Carly had read that in China, when married couples have
problems, they enlist another couple to counsel them. They chose
Jim's good friend, TV writer David Black, and Black's wife, Debbie, to
perform this function. Through their "sessions" with the Blacks—with
David heatedly taking Carly's side and Debbie heatedly taking Jim's
("she, like me, was trying to be independent within a marriage")—they
realized one root of their problem: "Carly thinks and feels symbolically,
while I think and feel literally."

Still, that abstract revelation didn't solve things. In 1997 Carly and
Jim moved into an arrangement they would occupy for the next eight
years: they would stay married, remaining "madly in love," talking many

times a day like best friends, keeping the future of their relationship open—but mostly living separately. Of those "many ways to touch," they'd found an imperfect version they could live with. Carly recorded another album of classic torch songs ("Spring Will Be a Little Late This Year," "Ev'ry Time We Say Goodbye," and more) with one original composition, *Film Noir*. Steeped in emotion over the limbo state of her marriage, she put her heart into the songs; *Film Noir* is her favorite of her albums. Then again, perhaps all that emotion was her body warning her mind that, after her mother's death and Jackie's death and the separation from Jim, an even bigger blow was coming.

In October 1997, Carly felt a lump in her breast; she went in for a mammogram. Breast cancer awareness was on every woman's radar screen now. Pink ribbons in October, support groups and foundations abounded; you knew your chance was one in eight. Especially if you were over fifty and thus had beaten those odds for so long, and if you had, as Carly had, thirty-five years earlier, taken those high-dosage Enovid birth control pills, then every time you donned the paper exam gown, your heart skipped a beat. "We all felt, 'Is *this* mammography the one?'" says Mia Farrow.

Carly was scheduled for a biopsy.

Jim (who now had a public relations job in Manhattan) had been ready to dash out to the airport for a business trip when his secretary stopped him and said, "Carly's on the phone, hysterical." The tumor was malignant. "In the initial shock of diagnosis, I banged my head against the table and said, 'No! No! No! You're wrong!' to the doctor on the phone," Carly says. Later she e-mailed Mia: "The anvil has fallen."

Once the shock wore off, "I just gathered my forces together," Carly says. "It felt like little people coming out inside me—a phalanx, a Roman army, saying, 'We're going to do what we need to do to make you well! Of course, you're going to beat this!'" "She was remarkable, she was amazing—there was no self-pity; she just said, 'Let's go!'" Jim says, adding, "Women are amazing." Indeed, Carly discovered that breast cancer was "something you pass on, like a sorority sister. Within hours, all these women began to appear—my neighbor Anna Stras-berg, and Lucy and Joey and Blue, my assistant, and Marlo Thomas—so many women wanted to support me. Gloria Steinem"—who'd had a lumpectomy—"called me and said she'd been through it and she'd gone dancing afterward."

With Lucy's help, Carly secured the noted oncologist Larry Norton.* The mastectomy was scheduled for November 12. The cru-cial thing was the sentinel node test that followed, to see whether the cancer had spread. As Carly was wheeled into surgery, she says, "I felt I was under a guillotine." Waiting for the results, Jim raced to the church across the street from Memorial Sloan-Kettering Cancer Insti-tute, fell to his knees at the Shrine for St. Jude, "and prayed my ass off." Everyone's prayers were answered. "The words 'no nodes' were so powerful—that was my rescue," says Carly.

After the surgery Carly took Sally and Ben for a trip to the island of Tortola. Then she started chemotherapy—her hair did not all fall out—and she struck up a telephone friendship with Trish Kubal, a Bay Area–based venture capitalist and mother of four who'd had a mastec-tomy the previous year. Trish had first spoken to Carly right after her diagnosis, when "she was scared, very frightened, but hungry for knowledge," Trish says. Now, the two women—survivor and patient—talked almost daily, and Trish passed on to Carly her breast cancer so-rority sister life lessons. "One: forget public health statistics; you are a sample of one. You only have your own life; save it. Two: you need to be able to fall apart; you need the emotional freedom. Forget about being a 'good patient.' Three: some people are going to be jerks when they hear you have cancer; this is a good opportunity to prune people you don't need in your life any longer. Four: if you don't take care of yourself, you're going to end up resentful. On days you don't feel like

---

* Needless to say, this is a different Larry Norton from the hippie preacher who per-formed Carole King's third wedding.

it, don't get out of your pajamas! Five: *you will learn from this*. You will realize how important regular life is. In a split second your world has changed," Trish told Carly. "People will say, 'Do you want to see the Taj Mahal? Do you want the Hope diamond?' And you'll say: 'No! I want to have a cup of tea at my kitchen table and love my loved ones.'"

The rules went just so far. After the chemotherapy, Carly entered a depression deeper than any she had ever known. Jim helped her through it, and it was grueling. "We had a lot of trouble," he sighs. Ironically, or fittingly, in helping Carly through her depression, Jim would prepare for his own, which beset him several years later and which Carly helped him through. "Styron said it well," Jim says. "Depression is the wrong word—it should be called a shit storm."

Carly, who had always leaned on her friends (and *given to* them), was now in new, dark territory. She'd always been anxious and phobic, but before she was young, and healthy, and famous, and living with a lover— or, at any given time, at least *some* of those things—when her demons descended. Now she had none of those props. She says, "The one thing anyone knows who has been through a hefty bout of melancholia is that you think it will never end and, therefore, you can't use up your dance card with your friends. You get good at avoidance and denial and the fake smile." Only with intimates, like Jim, could she be herself. During this time, Jim says, "She would often say, 'Why do you put up with me? I'm such damaged goods! What are you doing with me?' And I would say, 'Don't you see? I'm not in love with your success! I'm in love with your *struggle*.'" Poignantly, he was echoing what she had shouted to him after the Mick Jagger incident at Shea Stadium: *I love you for you*. Yet the idealistic innocence of that sentiment was hard to maintain in the trenches of complex midlife reality.

One day, after an appointment with Dr. Norton, Carly met Ellen for a drink at the Carlyle Hotel. She was planning on getting breast reconstruction (she eventually did), her depression had lifted, and she felt buoyant and hopeful. As if on cue, who should enter the bar but Mr. "You're So Vain" himself: Warren Beatty! "Oh, how wonderful that you're in town [from the Vineyard]," the charming lothario said. "Why are you here?" Carly told him: for an appointment with her oncologist. "And she felt the warmth in his voice disappear," Ellen says. Beatty quickly exited. Trish had been right—cancer involved pruning people from your life on the basis of character.

On the other hand, James had come through. One night, when Carly was midway through her chemo, he'd visited her in her New York apartment. As he was leaving, she said, "If you ever think of me, just give me a call. Even if we're just silent on the phone together, that would be so nice." Carly remembers that he replied, "If I called you every time I thought of you, there would be little time for anything else."

Still, despite that sweet exchange, in late 2000, Carly was without a record label, hitless, motherless, a breast cancer survivor, and past fifty-five. Her grown children were off on their own. Jim was living apart from her, and James would soon marry his third wife, Kim Smedvig. Carly was at a point in her life when, she has said, "I had to fight being discarded like an old dog." She moved a drum machine into Sally's old bedroom at the Vineyard house; she taught herself how to lay out eight tracks and mix them. And, working from nine p.m. until dawn, she self-recorded an album of songs that came from the heart, *The Bedroom Tapes*.

She wrote and sang about her deep depression and about her fear that she was viewed as a has-been, with her big hits and glamorous men all in the past. The centerpiece of the album was the song "Scar," about the lessons that breast cancer had taught her. Though she didn't name him, Warren Beatty's recoiling at the news of her cancer was a "gift in disguise," she sang, implicitly revealing how much more usefully brambled her journey was than his emotionally cosseted one ("that poor little puppy, so scared of misfortune and always on guard"). Women of her generation *had* had the more challenging journey—and that had paid off in wisdom.

Don Was, who'd had such success with Bonnie Raitt's *Nick of Time,* and who'd been one of Carly's producers on 1985's *Spoiled Girl,* visited her during this time. When Carly had entered his life at the beginning of the 1980s, she had taken him—"a bum with bad credit from Detroit," as he puts it—under her wing. She had helped him pick out a present that would make the woman he was in love with agree to marry him, and she had used her charm and connections to install him into David Susskind's old apartment. Now he listened to *The Bedroom Tapes,* and, he recalls, "They were incredibly personal and unslick. With her unfounded humility, Carly doesn't know how magnificent she is."

The album wasn't perfect. Other than the wise, forgiving "Scar," with its great hook line, "And a really big man / loves a really good scar," most of the songs were subpar for Carly, but they were a hand grenade against profound despair. That's what counted.

After her chemotherapy was finished, Carly sprang to the rescue of Ben's close friend and Exeter classmate John Forte. Forte, the Fugees' producer, had been staying with Carly during the recording of *The Bedroom Tapes.* Like Marc Cohn, John Kennedy Jr., and Don Was, Forte became one of the younger male mentees in her life. He called her "Mama C." In the same way that Andrea had been infuriated by the inability of her friends Jackie and Rachel Robinson to be able to buy a house in Connecticut, Carly was infuriated by how John—black and dreadlocked—was always getting stopped by cops for no reason. (Once, only her presence in the car spared him a bogus interrogation. "I look so damn above-the-law—an older white woman who couldn't be hiding anything more interesting than a thermos full of lemonade.") In July 2000, John Forte was arrested at Newark Airport, where he'd agreed to pick up a package (he thought it contained cash) that proved to be full of narcotics. He was sentenced to fourteen to twenty years in prison. Carly put up $250,000 of Forte's $650,000 bail—and she made justice for John Forte her personal mission. She has bankrolled his appeal and has spoken out against the onerous Rockefeller drug laws. Over the last seven years, a good hunk of her time has been spent meeting with Orrin Hatch, Ted Kennedy, and anyone else of influence to get John's conditions improved (she managed to have him moved from a Texas prison to a Pennsylvania prison, so his family could visit him) and to try to get his sentence reduced.

In 2005 Carly recorded her fourth album of standards, *Moonlight Serenade*. It became a huge adult contemporary hit. Many older artists—Rod Stewart and Linda Ronstadt, among them—recorded standards. But for Carly alone they were not a warmed-to novelty, but rather a plumb line to her childhood. She followed up that success in February 2007 with *Into White*, which also invoked the past, its title song written by her old friend Cat Stevens. The most arresting track consists of Carly, Ben, and Sally singing a slow, spectral version of James's achingly beautiful "You Can Close Your Eyes," which he had written for Joni. James had been a drugged-out, absent father during Sally's and Ben's childhoods, and that fact had anguished Carly. Now, like so many second-chance older dads, the decades-straight-and-sober James Taylor was earnestly arranging play dates for his and wife Kim's young twin sons. A woman *did* have to have the placidity of a river to put up with life's stream of ironies.

In early 2007, Carly and Jim Hart finally divorced. Ending her second marriage, to a man she deeply loved, was crushing. Still, in time, as ever, a new man emerged in her life. Richard Koehler is different from the others: not a musician, not a writer. Rather, he is a (handsome, blond) laparoscopic surgeon and former combat Marine, some years Carly's junior. Additionally, Sally and her husband, Dean Bragonier, moved onto Carly's Vineyard compound, where Ben, too, lives. In early autumn 2007, while Carly was recording a new album of almost all-new songs, Sally gave birth to a son, Bodhi. Thus Carly is now a grandmother, as are Carole and Joni. And so the river flows, the circle game repeats, the rutted road gets easier to walk down.

And that is how it is for all three of these women—all three of these girls like us—who were born into one female culture and changed it—year by year, song by song, risk by risk—so sweepingly and daringly.

Most of this book was reported through interviews that were conducted in person, by phone, and via e-mail. The majority of sources were interviewed numerous times. My list of interview subjects appears, alphabetized, in the Acknowledgments; my articles and book sources appear in the Bibliography. Here is a nonalphabetized rundown of the sources I most relied on for each specific chapter. A few sources spoke only on condition of anonymity, an accommodation I agreed to only after feeling confident of the respectability of the source's motive for the request. In other cases, people who were elsewhere named in the book requested anonymous sourcing for one or two particular anecdotes or opinions. In these cases, "a confidant" or "a friend" is used in the text, and the person is generally *not* re-enumerated as "Anonymous" below.

The following publications are abbreviated thus: *Chicago Tribune: CT; The Idaho Statesman: IS; Los Angeles Times: LAT; The New York Times: NYT; Rolling Stone: RS; The Village Voice: VV; The Washington Post: WP.*

OVERTURE: THREE WOMEN,
THREE MOMENTS, ONE JOURNEY

naming herself

AUTHOR INTERVIEWS with Camille Cacciatore Savitz, Barbara Grossman Karyo, Leslie Korn Rogowsky, Joel Zwick, Al Kasha, Danny Kortchmar, Roy Reynolds, Jerry Wexler, and two anonymous sources.
BOOKS: Rosen, *White Christmas* (for the anecdote about 1906 Lower East Side

settlement worker). Brownmiller, *In Our Time*. Brooklyn (New York City) telephone directory, 1955.

ARTICLES: General reading throughout Carole articles bibliography.

exposing herself

AUTHOR INTERVIEWS with Duke Redbird, Nicholas Jennings, Jeanine Hollingshead, Betsy Siggins, Richard Flohill, John McHugh, Martin Ornot, and Larry Klein.

BOOKS: Jennings, *Before the Gold Rush*.

ARTICLES: Bayin, "Joni & Me," *Elm Street*, 2000. Crowe, "Joni Mitchell," *RS*, 1979.

OTHER: Author heard the recording of Joni Anderson's October 21, 1964, performance at the Half Beat on Chuck Mitchell's reel-to-reel tape recorder at Mitchell's home in Iowa, and tape-recorded it.

daring herself

AUTHOR INTERVIEWS with Steve Harris, Jac Holzman, Jim Hart, Ellen Questel, Leah Kunkel, Russ Kunkel, Jessica Hoffman Davis, Mia Farrow, Tamara Weiss, Betsy Asher, Jake Brackman, and the then heroin-dealing Beverly Hills doctor's son.

BOOKS: Holzman and Daws, *Follow the Music*. Thom, *Ms.: 25 Years of the Magazine and the Feminist Movement*. Brownmiller, *In Our Time*. Carabillo, *Feminist Chronicles*. Heilbrun, *The Education of a Woman*.

ARTICLES: "James Taylor," *Time*, 1971. Braudy, "James Taylor . . . ," *NYT Magazine*, 1971. Dunbar, "Making It in Low Key," *Look*, 1971. Van Matre, "Singing-Songwriters," *CT*, 1971. "Rock: Year of the Woman?" *NYT*, 1971. Brenner, "I Never Sang . . . ," *Vanity Fair*, 1995. Hilburn, "Cat Stevens and . . ." and "Carly Simon Has . . . ," *LAT*, 1971. Crouse, "Carly Simon Review," *RS*, 1971. White, "Carly: Life Without James," *RS*, 1981. "Sony/ATV Music Publishing . . . ," *Business Wire*, 1997.

OTHER: Author conducted e-mail correspondence with numerous significant second-wave feminists, including Kathy Amatniek, Roxanne Dunbar, Gloria Steinem, and Jacqui Ceballos.

CHAPTER ONE

AUTHOR INTERVIEWS with Gerry Goffin, Camille Cacciatore Savitz, Barbara Grossman Karyo, Joel Zwick, Jerry Wexler, the late Jack Keller, Beverly

Lee, Mike Stoller, Donny Kirshner, Barbara Behling Goffin, Cynthia Weil, and Al Kasha.

BOOKS: Guralnick, *Last Train to Memphis*. Branch, *Parting the Waters* and *Pillar of Fire*. Emerson, *Always Magic in the Air*. Wexler and Ritz, *Rhythm and the Blues*. Whitfield, *A Death in the Delta*. Salamon, *Facing the Wind* (about Willowbrook). Madison High School 1958 yearbook.

ARTICLES: Kamp, "The Hit Factory," *Vanity Fair,* 2001.

OTHER: "Hitmakers: The Teens . . . ," A&E, 2001.

CHAPTER TWO

AUTHOR INTERVIEWS with Frank McKitrick, Sandra Stewart Backus, Marie Brewster Jensen, Bob Sugarman, Joan Smith Chapman, Henry Bonli, Elsa Boni Ziegler, D'Arcy Case, Graham Nash, Chuck Mitchell, Dave Naylor, the late John Guerin, Luc Dagenais (archivist of the Grey Nuns of Montreal), and Christopher J. Rutty, Ph.D. (founder and president, Health Heritage Research Services, Toronto).

ARTICLES AND TRANSCRIPTS: Matteo, "Woman of Heart and Mind," *Inside Connection,* 2000. Edmonton Press Conference, 1994. "My Top Twelve," BBC-1 Radio, 1983. "Rock Master Class Interview," 1985. Enright, "Words and Pictures," *Border Crossings,* 2001. "Biography," Jonimitchell .com. Jacarello, "Both Sides, Now," BBC-2 Radio, 1999. Lydon, "In Her House, Love," *NYT,* 1969. McFayden, "The Teacher and . . . ," *The Age,* 2002. Crowe, "Joni Mitchell," *RS,* 1979. Various short articles, *The Regina Leader-Post,* 1955–57. Bayin, "Joni & Me," *Elm Street,* 2000.

OTHER: Personal diaries of the Grey Nuns of Saskatchewan.

CHAPTER THREE

AUTHOR INTERVIEWS with Jeanie Seligmann, Lucy Simon, Jessica Hoffmann Davis, Tim Ratner, Nick Delbanco, Ellen Questel, Jake Brackman, and Jim Hart.

BOOKS: Delbanco, *Running in Place*. Schwartz, *All in Good Time*.

ARTICLES: "Carly Simon," *Current Biography,* 1976. "Richard Leo Simon . . . ," *NYT,* 1960. Brenner, "I Never Sang . . . ," *Vanity Fair,* 1995. "Timeline," CarlySimon.com. PeterSimon.com. Fong-Torres, "Carly" *RS,* 1975. Young, "Carly Simon's Land . . . ," *RS,* 1978. White, "Carly . . . ," *RS,* 1981. Tosches, "Free, White, and Pushing 40," *Creem,* 1984.

CHAPTER FOUR

AUTHOR INTERVIEWS with Cynthia Weil, Barry Mann, Gerry Goffin, Brooks
Arthur, Marilyn Arthur, Mike Stoller, Jerry Wexler, the late Jack Keller, the
late Al Aronowitz, Donny Kirshner, Al Kasha, Camille Cacciatore Savitz,
Barbara Grossman Karyo, Jesse Goffin, Jeanie McCrea Reavis, and Dawn
Reavis Smith.

BOOKS: Emerson, *Always Magic in the Air*. Gitlin, *The Sixties*. Gould, *Such Good
Friends* (and author's own interview with Lois Gould in the early 1970s).
Raskin, *Hot Flashes*. Bosworth, *Diane Arbus*. Adams, *Superior Women*. Branch,
Parting the Waters and *Pillar of Fire*. Posner, *Motown*. Accessed through Web
site only: The Civil Rights Movement: A Photographic History ("The
March on Washington, 1963: We Stood on a Height"), by Steven Kashen.
Jones, *How I Became Hettie Jones*.

ARTICLES AND DOCUMENTARY TRANSCRIPT: Lichtenstein, "Carole King Steps . . . ,"
NYT, 1970. "Louise Goffin Interview," Rock Electronic Telegraph. Kamp,
"The Hit Factory," *Vanity Fair,* 2001. Fox, "Betty Friedan . . . ," *NYT,* 2006.
"Hitmakers: The Teens . . . ," A&E, 2001. "The Mad, Happy World . . . ,"
Life, 1961.

CHAPTER FIVE

AUTHOR INTERVIEWS with Bob Sugarman, Joan Smith Chapman, Sandra Stewart Backus, D'Arcy Case, Colin Holliday-Scott, Shawn Phillips, Deborah
Symonds (about Child Ballads), Betsy Siggins, Chick Roberts, Gene
Norman, Neil Norman, Beverly DeJong, Bruce Sterling, George Mihalcheon, Walt Drohan, Doug Bovee, Eric Whittred, Sandra Jarvies, Duke
Redbird, Jeanine Hollingshead, John McHugh, Martin Ornot, Larry Klein,
and Nicholas Jennings.

BOOKS: Students' Association of . . . , Tech Record. Van Ronk with Wald, *The
Mayor of MacDougal Street*. Von Schmidt and Rooney, *Baby, Let Me Follow
You Down*. Dylan, *Chronicles*. Symonds, *Weep Not for Me*. Phillips, *California
Dreamin'*. Petrie, *Gone to an Aunt's*. Fessler, *The Girls Who Went Away*. Jennings,
Before the Gold Rush. Hadju, *Positively 4th Street*. Gruen, *The Party's Over Now*.
McLauchlan, *Getting Out of Here Alive*.

ARTICLES AND TRANSCRIPTS: Charles, "The Joe & Eddie Story," *Goldmine,* 1993.
Joe & Eddie album liner notes. Lacayo, "What Women Have Done . . . ,"
Time, 2007. "Coffee Houses" and Fowell, "Fowell on the Coffee House
Beat," *The Telegram,* 1964. White, "Joni Mitchell," *Billboard,* 1995. Crowe,
"Joni Mitchell," *RS,* 1979. Enright, "Words and Pictures," *Border Crossings,*
2001. Edmonton Folk Festival, 1994, www.jmdl.com. Yee, "Songwriting

and Poetry," *WP*, 1969. Brand, "The Education of . . . ," *Co-Evolution Quarterly*, 1976, and a general reading of all Joni's interviews.

CHAPTER SIX

AUTHOR INTERVIEWS with Carly Simon, Lucy Simon, Helen Whitney, Lanny Harrison, Ellen Questel, Nick Delbanco, Mia Farrow, Jessica Hoffmann Davis, Danny Kortchmar, Jake Brackman, Al Kooper, Arlyne Rothberg.
BOOKS: Holzman and Daws, *Follow the Music*. White, *Long Ago and Far Away*. Delbanco, *Running in Place, The Martlet's Tale*, and *Grasse 3/23/66*. Asbell, *The Pill*. Blacker, *You Cannot Live As I Have Lived* . . . . Donaldson, *The Big One* . . . . Cohen, *Beautiful Losers*.
ARTICLES: Braudy, "James Taylor," *NYT Magazine*, 1971.White, "James Taylor," *RS*, 1981. CarlySimon.com. Blacker, "Sex Addict, Crack Fiend . . . ," *The Independent*, 2005. Hawtree, "William Donaldson . . . ," *The Guardian*, 2005.

CHAPTER SEVEN

AUTHOR INTERVIEWS with Gerry Goffin, the late Al Aronowitz, the late Jack Keller, Cynthia Weil, Barry Mann, Donny Kirshner, Stephanie Magrino Fischbach, Danny Kortchmar, Charlie Larkey, Abigail Haness Marshall, Roger McGuinn, Connie O'Brien Sopic, Joe Butler, Steve Katz, Michelle Phillips, Lou Adler, Russell Banks, Jerry Wexler, Billy James, Michael Schwartz, John Fischbach, Toni Stern, Ralph Schuckett, Peter Asher, Betsy Asher, Madeleine Wild, and Richard Corey.
BOOKS: Spitz, *The Beatles*. Aronowitz, *Bob Dylan and the Beatles*. Katz, *Home Fires*. Tamarkin, *Got a Revolution!* Walker, *Laurel Canyon*. Davidson, *Loose Change*. Kort, *Soul Picnic*. Phillips, *California Dreamin'*. Hoskyns, *Hotel California*. Holzman and Daws, *Follow the Music*. Biskind, *Easy Riders, Raging Bulls*. Bergen, *Knock Wood*. Gitlin, *The Sixties*. Crosby and Gottlieb, *Long Time Gone*.
ARTICLES: Perusal of *Eye* magazines, 1967–69. Braudy, "James Taylor," *NYT Magazine*, 1971. Larocca, "The House of Mod," *New York*, 2003. Miles, "The Ultimate Carole King Interview," Rock's Backpages. Lichenstein, "Carole King Steps . . . ," *NYT*, 1970. Echols, "Thirty Years . . . ," *Los Angeles Weekly*, 1994.
OTHER: Author's personal memories of U.C. Berkeley and the Bay Area 1964–67. Authors' interviews about Jim Morrison in the mid-'60s, with various surfers, for 2006 *Vanity Fair* article "Malibu's Lost Boys." Liner notes of CD reissue of *Now That Everything's Been Said*.

CHAPTER EIGHT

AUTHOR INTERVIEWS with Chuck Mitchell, Eric Andersen, Tom Rush, Armand Kunz, Jeanine Hollingshead, Henry Bonli, Jane Bonli, Elsa Bonli Ziegler, Larry Klein, Tim Campbell (re Canadian Match Program), the late Estelle Klein, Joy Schreiber Fibben, Gene Shay, Steve Katz, Roy Blumenfeld, Al Kooper, Mort Rosengarten, Joe Boyd, and Estrella Berosini.

BOOKS: Hemenway, *The Girl Who Sang with the Beatles*. Roiphe, *Up the Sandbox*. Spitz, *Dylan*. Hajdu, *Positively 4th Street*. McKenney, *My Sister Eileen*. Kooper with Edmonds, *Backstage Passes*. Collins, *Trust Your Heart*. Holzman and Daws, *Follow the Music*. Cohen, *Beautiful Losers*. Crosby and Gottlieb, *Long Time Gone*. Hoskyns, *Hotel California*. O'Brien, *Shadows and Light*. Fleischer, *Joni Mitchell*.

ARTICLES AND INTERNET-FOUND TRANSCRIPTS: Astor, "Songs for Aging Children," *Look*, 1970. Patterson, "The Boy on . . . ," Rock Radio Scrapbook. Jacarello, "Both Sides, Now," BBC-2, 1999. Fawcett, "A Search . . . ," *California Rock, California Sound* (via Internet). Ward, "The Queens of Rock," *Us*, 1978. Smith, "Off the Record," 1988. Small, "Joni Mitchell," *People*, 1985. "Joni Mitchell," *RS*, 1969. "Rock 'n' Roll's Leading Lady," *Time*, 1974. Flanagan, "Secret Places," *Musician*, 1988. Brand, "The Education . . . ," *Co-Evolution Quarterly*, 1976. Crowe, "Joni Mitchell," *RS*, 1979. Didion, "Goodbye to All That," in *Slouching . . .* , 1967. Iyer, "Leonard Cohen," *Shambhala Sun*, 1998. McClain, "Two Single Acts . . . ," *Detroit News*, 1966.

OTHER: Tape of Chuck and Joni Mitchell interview with Murray Burnett for Philadelphia Radio, 1966. Tape of Joni Mitchell at the Second Fret, 1966. Author heard both at Chuck Mitchell's house and recorded and transcribed them. Personal letters of Chuck Mitchell. Author's personal knowledge of downtown New York scene in 1967.

CHAPTER NINE

AUTHOR INTERVIEWS with Carly Simon, Ellen Questel, Jake Brackman, Jessica Hoffman Davis, Jeanie Seligmann, Myron Yules, the late Danny Armstrong, Arlyne Rothberg, and (for domestic violence law) Patricia Barry, Esq.

BOOKS: Gitlin, *The Sixties*. Indian Hill Camp 1967 yearbook. Biskind, *Easy Riders, Raging Bulls*. Holzman and Daws, *Follow the Music*. Katz, *Home Fires*.

ARTICLES AND TRANSCRIPTS: Sexton, "Carly Simon," *The Independent*, 2006. "Timeline," CarlySimon.com. PeterSimon.com. Christgau, *Christgau's Record Guide*, 1981.

OTHER: Author's experience working at *Eye* magazine from September 1967 to

August 1968. Author's conversation with Jill Clayburgh, during an interview for *McCall's* magazine, in 1978.

CHAPTER TEN

AUTHOR INTERVIEWS with Estrella Berosini, Salli Sachse, Russ Kunkel, Graham Nash, Ronee Blakley, Nancy Carlin, Trina Robbins, Cary Raditz, Debbie Green, the late Estelle Klein, Peter Asher, and a friend of the Gibb family from Don Mills, Toronto.

BOOKS: Crosby and Gottlieb, *Long Time Gone*. Holzman and Daws, *Follow the Music*. Zimmer, *Crosby, Stills & Nash*. Fleischer, *Joni Mitchell*. Cross, *Room Full of Mirrors*. Hoskyns, *Hotel California*. Paglia, *Break, Blow, Burn*. Nietzsche, *Thus Spake Zarathustra*.

ARTICLES AND TRANSCRIPTS: Brown, "Joni Mitchell," *RS*, 1968. Dunn, "Question and Answer," *RS*, 1994. "Diary of a Decade," Greater London Radio, 1990. "Joni Mitchell," *RS*, 1969. Ruhlman, "From Blue . . . ," *Goldmine*, 1995. Houston, "Joni Mitchell," Salon.com, 2000. "Joni Mitchell's New Album . . . ," *RS*, 1970. James, "Joni's Miles . . . ," *Circus*, 1975. LeBlanc, "Joni Takes . . . ," *RS*, 1971. "Joni . . . Interview," *Details*, 1996. *Dick Cavett Show*, 1969. Hilburn, "Crosby, Stills . . . ," *LAT*, 1969.

OTHER: Recording of Joni Mitchell and James Taylor at Royal Albert Hall in London, October 1970. Author's own experience in Ibiza and Morocco, and writings published in *Rolling Stone* from 1969 to 1970. Author's post-Woodstock interview with Jimi Hendrix, which turned into "I Don't Want to Be a Clown Anymore," for *Rolling Stone*, October 1969. James Taylor quote re Carole King: liner notes of CD reissue of *Tapestry*.

CHAPTER ELEVEN

AUTHOR INTERVIEWS with Charlie Larkey, Stephanie Magrino Fischbach, John Fischbach, Danny Kortchmar, Graham Nash, Gerry Goffin, Leah Kunkel, Russ Kunkel, Abigail Haness Marshall, Lou Adler, Toni Stern, Madeleine Wild, Ralph Schuckett, Michael Schwartz, Betsy Asher, Peter Asher, Connie O'Brien Sopic, Richard Corey, Susan Braudy, the late Estelle Klein, Estrella Berosini, Kris Kristofferson, Cary Raditz, Jerry Wexler, Barbara Behling Goffin, Ronee Blakley.

BOOKS: Kort, *Soul Picnic*. Roszak, *The Making of a Counter Culture*. Reich, *The Greening of America*. Katz, *Home Fires*. Hayden, *Reunion*. Gitlin, *The Sixties*. Thom, *Ms.: 25 Years of the Magazine and the Feminist Movement*. Brownmiller, *In Our Time*. Heilbrun, *The Education of a Woman*. Beattie, *Chilly Scenes of Winter*.

ARTICLES: Maynard, "Visiting Ann Beattie . . . ," *NYT,* 1980. Miles, "The Ultimate . . . ," Rocksbackpages.com. Braudy, "James Taylor," *NYT,* 1971. Crouse, "'Blue,'" *RS,* 1971. Crouse, "'Carole King Music,'" *RS,* 1972. Ward, "Carole King," *WP,* 1976. Landau, "'Tapestry,'" *RS,* 1971. Hilburn, "Times Woman of the Year," *LAT,* 1971. "What's Playing in . . . ," *O, The Oprah Magazine,* 2006. Hilburn, "Music Review," *LAT,* 1971. Heckman, "Joni Mitchell . . . ," *NYT,* 1971. Daum, "My Dinner . . . ," *LAT,* 2006. Heckman, "From Songwriter . . . ," *NYT,* 1971. Hilburn, "Carole King Sweeps . . . ," *LAT,* 1972. Garbarini, "Joni Mitchell Is . . . ," *Musician,* 1983. Miller, "In Search of Love . . . ," *Being There,* 2004. Flanagan, "Joni Mitchell Has . . . ," *Musician,* 1985.

OTHER: CD of Carole King at Carnegie Hall, June 1971. Personal e-mails from early feminists: Steinem, Ceballos, et al.

CHAPTER TWELVE

AUTHOR INTERVIEWS with Carly Simon, Jake Brackman, Ellen Questel, Kris Kristofferson, Jac Holzman, Arlyne Rothberg, Jessica Hoffmann Davis, Steve Harris, Russ Kunkel, Danny Kortchmar, Abigail Haness Marshall, Leah Kunkel, Betsy Asher, Richard Corey, Tamara Weiss, Richard Perry, and (re marriage statistics) Stephanie Coontz.

BOOKS: Holzman and Daws, *Follow the Music.* Braudy, *Between Marriage and Divorce.* Coontz, *Marriage, a History.* O'Reilly, *The Girl I Left Behind.* Dormen, *The Best Place to Be.* Yetnikoff with Ritz, *Howling at the Moon.* Finstad, *Warren Beatty: A Private Man.*

ARTICLES: Jahn, "Carly Simon Sings . . . ," *NYT,* 1971. "Carly Simon Concert Is Off," *WP,* 1971. Holden, "'Playing Possum,'" *RS,* 1975. Hilburn, "Carly Simon Has . . ." and "Cat Stevens and . . . ," *LAT,* 1971. Davis, "'Anticipation'" *RS,* 1971. Heckman, "Carly Simon Sings . . . ," *NYT,* 1971. Crouse, "'Carly Simon,'" *RS,* 1971. White, "James Taylor," *RS,* 1981. Werbin, "James Taylor & Carly Simon," *RS,* 1973. Fong-Torres, "Carly," *RS,* 1975. Hemphill, "Kris Kristofferson . . . ," *NYT,* 1970. Leavitt, "She," *Esquire.*

OTHER: Karen Durbin's posting on *The Nation* Web site after Ellen Willis's 2006 death. Author's experience as part of the *Ms.* family in the early 1970s. Robert Christgau, via Internet, 1981. Ellen Willis's *New Yorker* review, quoted by Christgau via Internet.

CHAPTER THIRTEEN

AUTHOR INTERVIEWS with Danny Kortchmar, Stephanie Magrino Fischbach, John Fischbach, Charlie Larkey, Camille Cacciatore Savitz, Roy Reynolds, Joy James, Randy Stone, Mike Stanger, Bruce Stanger, "Cassie," Cynthia Weil, Brooks Arthur.

ARTICLES: Lichtenstein, "Carole King Draws 70,000 . . . ," *NYT,* 1971. Zito, "King's Soggy Do" and "The Silent Side . . . ," *WP,* 1973. Crowe, "A Child's Garden . . . ," *RS,* 1974. Hilburn, "Another Winner . . . ," *LAT,* 1971; "The Return of Carole King," *LAT,* 1973; and "King's 'Tapestry' Wearing Thin," *LAT,* 1977. Alterman, "A Bland Carole King," *NYT,* 1973. Van Matre, "Carole's a Nervous . . . ," *CT,* 1973. "Q & A with David Palmer," accessed through Internet. Rockwell, "A Sweet New Record . . . ," *NYT,* 1975, and "Friends of Carole King . . . ," *NYT,* 1976. "Carole King Signs . . . ," *LAT,* 1976. Daley, "Carole King," *WP,* 1978. Emerson, "Pop: Carole King . . . ," *NYT,* 1978. "Richard Evers," *Post Register,* 1978. Singular, "Trouble in Paradise," *Denver Post Empire Magazine,* 1984. "Just Married," *IS,* 1982. Strauss, "Carole King," *IS,* 1984. Holden, "'Fantasy,'" *RS,* 1973, and "'Thoroughbred,'" *RS,* 1976. Woodward, "The Earth Moved," *IS,* 1995.

OTHER: Copy of Rick Evers's prison record e-mailed by Idaho Department of Corrections. Liner notes written by Carole King for *Welcome Home* album.

CHAPTER FOURTEEN

AUTHOR INTERVIEWS with Larry Klein, Salli Sachse, Danny Kortchmar, Roy Blumenfeld, Russ Kunkel, Billy James, various friends of Joni Mitchell and Jackson Browne, the late John Guerin, the late Don Alias, Wayne Perkins, and Ronee Blakley.

ARTICLES AND TRANSCRIPTS: Crowe, "A Child's Garden . . . ," *RS,* 1994. Ruhlman, "From Blue . . . ," *Goldmine,* 1995. "Jackson Browne," *Detroit News,* 1972. Davis, "Joni Mitchell's 'For the Roses'" *RS,* 1973. "Biography," Joni Mitchell.com. Robert Christgau, on Internet. Hoskyns, "Joni Mitchell," *Blender,* 2003. Van Matre, "A 'Spark' . . . ," *CT,* 1974. Landau, "A Delicate Balance," *RS,* 1974. Echols, "Thirty Years . . . ," *Los Angeles Weekly,* 1994. Kot, "Joni's Jazzed," *CT,* 1998. Strickland, "Joni Dances . . . ," *Calgary Herald,* 2007. Hansen, "Music Icon Joni . . . ," NPR, 1995. Maslin, "Joni Mitchell's Reckless and Shapeless . . . ," *RS,* 1978. Swartley, "The Babe in Bopperland . . . ," *RS,* 1979. Holden, "A Summer Garden . . . ," *RS,* 1976; "High Spirits . . . ," *NYT,* 1982; and "Joni Mitchell Finds Peace . . . ," *NYT,* 1991.

CHAPTER FIFTEEN

AUTHOR INTERVIEWS with Carly Simon, Jake Brackman, Ellen Questel, Arlyne Rothberg, Peter Asher, Betsy Asher, Mia Farrow, Jessica Hoffmann Davis, Tamara Weiss, the late Danny Armstrong, Russ Kunkel, Leah Kunkel, Marc Cohn, Don Was, Joe Armstrong, Jim Hart, and Dr. Terry Horton, medical director of Phoenix House.

BOOKS: Andersen, *Sweet Caroline*. White, *Long Ago and Far Away*. Hart, *Milding*.

ARTICLES: Alterman, "Carly's Happy . . . ," *NYT,* 1974. Cohen, "'Spy,'" *RS,* 1979. Considine, "'Spoiled Girl,'" *RS,* 1985. Hoerburger, "'Coming Around Again,'" *RS,* 1987. Hilburn, "Carly Simon Will . . . ," *LAT,* 1980. Holden, "The Pop Life: A Spicy . . . ," *NYT,* 1985, and "Carly Simon's Emotion-Laden . . . ," *NYT,* 1987. Hunt, "What's a Wife . . . ," *LAT,* 1977. Landau, "'Hotcakes,'" *RS,* 1974. Christgau, "Carly Simon Is Not . . . ," *VV,* 1976. Mark, "Carly Simon," *VV,* 1977. Rockwell, "Carly Simon: The Fans . . . ," *NYT,* 1977; "Pop Comeback," 1977; and "Carly Simon at the Bottom Line," *NYT,* 1978. Shapiro, "I Bet You Think . . . ," *VV,* 1977. Shewey, "'Hello Big Man,'" *RS,* 1983. Van Matre, "Carly's Still Anticipating," *CT,* 1972; "A 'Spark' . . . ," *CT,* 1974; "Bold Plans for . . . ," *CT,* 1980; and "Carly Simon Carrying . . . ," *CT,* 1982. Wadler, "Carly Simon: Anxiety . . . ," *WP,* 1983. Werbin, "James Taylor . . . ," *RS,* 1973. White, "Carly," *RS,* 1981, and "James Taylor," *RS,* 1981. Young, "Carly Simon's Land . . . ," *RS,* 1978. Simon, "How Lyrics Work," DoubleTake, 2006.

OTHER: Web site of the Graymoor Friars.

CODA:
THREE WOMEN, THREE ENDINGS,
ONE JOURNEY

AUTHOR INTERVIEWS with Larry Klein, Duke Redbird, Annie Mandlsohn, Tim Campbell, Dave Naylor, friend of Gibb family, the late John Guerin, the late Don Alias.

ARTICLES: Bannister and Lai, "Songbird Joni Searches . . . ," *Globe,* 1994. "Heartsick Joni Mitchell . . ." and Gould, "Joni Mitchell's Life and Death . . . ," *Globe,* 1996. White, "Joni Mitchell's Many Shades . . . ," *Billboard,* 1995. Fulton, "Alberta Native . . . ," *Calgary Sun,* 1996. Arnold, "The

Reunion . . . ," *National Post,* 2001. Holden, "Joni Mitchell Finds Peace . . . ," *NYT,* 1991, and "Too feminine . . . ?" *NYT,* 1996.

coming home

AUTHOR INTERVIEWS with anonymous party in King/Sorensen–Custer County locked-gate dispute, Roy Reynolds, Rocky Barker, Joy James, Mike Stoller, Michael Garrity (executive director of the Alliance for the Wild Rockies), Cynthia Weil.

ARTICLES: Abe, "Carole King to Star . . ." and "Carole King's Attorney . . . ," *IS,* 1985. Barker, "Singer Uses Fame . . . ," *Post Register,* 1990, and "Carole King Lobbies . . . ," *Times-News,* 1991. Bradley, "Carole King Emerges . . . ," Gannett News Service, 1994. "Carole King Wins . . . ," *IS,* 1986. Champlin, "Singer Carole King Opts . . . ," *LAT,* 1984. Ellsworth, "Carole King Blazes . . . ," *IS,* 1989. Hernandez, "Road on King's Land . . . ," *IS,* 1985. "Career and Causes . . . ," *Idaho Press-Tribune,* 1984. Peterson, "Ruling Put Off . . . ," *IS,* 1986. Pratter, "Carole King," *Times-News,* 1988. Singular, "Trouble in Paradise," *Denver Post Empire Magazine,* 1984. Strauss, "Carole King," *IS,* 1984. "The Singer and . . . ," *Wall Street Journal,* 1984. "Trial Date Reset . . . ," *IS,* 1986. Stuebner, "Jones Calls Road . . . ," *IS,* 1988, and "Singer Carole King Wins . . . ," *High Country News,* 1988. Hoerburger, "'City Streets,'" *RS,* 1989. Manning, "'Colour of Your Dreams,'" *RS,* 1993.

surviving

AUTHOR INTERVIEWS with Carly Simon, Jim Hart, Jeanie Seligmann, Jake Brackman, Marc Cohen, Don Was, Ellen Questel, Jessica Hoffmann Davis, Joe Armstrong, Trish Kubal.

BOOKS: Hart, *Milding.* Davidson, *Leap!*

ARTICLES AND POSTINGS: Brenner, "I Never Sang . . . ," *Vanity Fair,* 1995. "Timeline," CarlySimon.com. Howe, "Working Girl . . . ," *WP,* 1988. Holden, "The Pop Life: Carly Simon, Again," *NYT,* 1989; "Pop Music's Romance . . . ," "Carly Simon: Have You . . . ," "The Pop Life: A New Album . . . ," and "The Pop Life: Carly Simon Looks . . . ," *NYT,* 1990. Carly Simon interview with Paula Zahn, CNN.

ACKNOWLEDGMENTS

I felt my own longing mirrored by the Shirelles singing "Will You Love Me To-morrow." I moved from California to New York for life because of "Up on the Roof." I became a young woman in that city—living just like Joni in "Chelsea Morning"; feeling just like Joni in "Both Sides, Now"—as Aretha belted "Natural Woman." In 1969 my sister, Liz—in her long hair, long skirt, shawl, and guitar, bound for a cottage in Laurel Canyon—told me about someone who expressed life for her. "And she calls him Willy," she said, of Joni and Graham. In early 1973, I sat in my still-tie-dyed-curtained walk-up and devoured every word of the *Rolling Stone* interview of Carly Simon-Taylor, and I knew that this peer, who I might have bumped into at Bendel's or Zum Zum or the *Ms.* party, was the first feminist rock star and that we were taking the ride together.

When I conceived this book, in 2003, I went to the representatives of Carole, Joni, and Carly, and asked not to interview them, but to be able to talk to their closest friends. I set my limits first of all out of realism and also because I didn't want my shaky author's objectivity (I was *starting out* admiring) to be undermined by access to my subjects. Besides, I had written a number of books in the chorus-of-voices style, where friends tell the story of a person and a world, and that form had worked well. One day, Carly Simon appeared on my voice mail and, later, in my e-mail in-box, and over the many months of this project, I took judicious use of her generous candor, which was always offered without strings. "I'm not expecting deference. I'm expecting to have my feelings hurt," she wrote me, early on—one of the many reasons to like her. Joni sent word that she did not want to be grouped in a book with two others, but my access to her friends proved undiminished. Carole, through her representatives, had been the first to approve this project, but later told people not to speak to me. By then, people *wanted* to speak—it was their journey, too. Last summer I made a concerted effort to interview Joni but was turned down (she was busy recording *Shine,* among other things). I didn't try with Carole because I knew she was trying to write her own autobiography and was unhappily aware of this book. I sincerely hope that all three women will feel, despite whatever misgivings, that I have captured them and honored the significance of their body of work. At the risk of sounding gratuitous, I thank them from the bottom of my heart for their unsurpassable music, and for the soundtrack it provided for my youth.

Special thanks to Tisha Fein, childhood friend and peerless Grammy producer, for her initial guidance in the world of the music business; to Bobbi Andelson, for that outstanding, heartful research—six fat scrapbooks of clips; to Laurie Sarney and Jennifer Jue-Steuck for similar research brilliance. My agent, Ellen Levine, never stopped believing in this project; my publisher, Judith Curr, waited for it through several missed deadlines; and my editor, Malaika Adero, not just graciously but enthusiastically accepted a manuscript that was over *double* the contracted length. Elisa Petrini was a valuable sounding board; Sybil Pincus, an expert shepherd of the manuscript. Patricia Romanowski, Robert Legault, Tina Peckham, and Annette Corkey went above and beyond the call of duty in beating into submission all those errors that originally pocked this manuscript, despite what I thought was my own rigorous fact checking. Thank you to indexer Nancy Wolff. The musically way-cool Ben Umanov created the discography.

My husband, John Kelly, while immersed in detailing the agonies of the Black Death and the Irish famine for his own publisher, lived with me during all my verbosely expressed worries and obsessions, and he said the magic words: "You're writing social history." Ever-so-talented rising young writer and editor (and accidental über-"in" restaurant booker extraordinaire) Jonathan Kelly made me proudly known as "Jon's mom" by his family at *Vanity Fair*. *Glamour* editor in chief Cindi Leive gave me six months off to break the back of this book; it was working with Cindi, and the other terrific women at *Glamour,* that sharpened my desire to tell the story of this *other* generation. My sister, Liz Weller, my friends Eileen Stukane and Carol Ardman—and *you,* Mrs. Katz. We all lived these years—oh (Mrs. Katz . . .), did we ever.

Thank you to the people who patiently spoke to me:

Lou Adler, the late Don Alias, Eric Andersen, the late Danny Armstrong, Joe Armstrong, the late Al Aronowitz, Brooks Arthur, Marilyn Arthur, Betsy Asher, Peter Asher, Sandra Stewart Backus, Russell Banks, Rocky Barker, Joel Bernstein, Estrella Berosini Cory Bishop (formerly Elyse Weinberg), Ronee Blakley, Roy Blumenfeld (special thanks), Henry Bonli, Jane Bonli Boone, Doug Bovee, Joe Boyd, Jake Brackman (special thanks), Susan Braudy, Kerri Brusca, Joe Butler, Leslie Butler.

Tim Campbell, Nancy Carlin, D'Arcy Case, Joan Smith Chapman, Marc Cohn, Richard Corey, Jessica Hoffman Davis, Beverly DeJong, Nick Delbanco, Rick DePofi, Henry Diltz, Walt Drohan, Cliff Fagin, Mia Farrow, Joy Schreiber Fibben, John Fischbach, Stephanie Magrino Fischbach (great thanks, and affection), Richard Flohill, Mel Futorian, Barbara Behling Goffin, Gerry Goffin, Jesse Goffin, Debbie Green, the late John Guerin.

Steve Harris, Lanny Harrison, Jim Hart, Mac Holbert, Colin Holliday-Scott, Jeanine Hollingshead, Jac Holzman, Billy James, Joy James, Michael Jared, Sandra Jarvies, Nicholas Jennings, Marie Brewster Jensen, Leilani Jones (special thanks), Barbara Grossman Karyo, Al Kasha, Steve Katz, the late Jack Keller, Donny Kirshner, the late Estelle Klein, Larry Klein, Kris Kristofferson, Al Kooper, Danny Kortchmar, Trish Kubal, Leah Kunkel, Russ Kunkel, Armand Kunz, Charlie Larkey, Beverly Lee, Ed Lee, Mike Mainieri, Anne Mandlsohn, Barry Mann, Abigail Haness Marshall, Jim McCrary, Roger Mc-Guinn, John McHugh, Frank McKitrick, George Mihalcheon, Chuck Mitchell, Patti Mitsui, Jenny Muldaur, Graham Nash, Dave Naylor.

Martin Ornot, Miranda Parry, Alan Pepper, Wayne Perkins, Jim Perrone, Richard Perry, Michelle Phillips, Shawn Phillips, Ellen Questel, Cary Raditz, Jeanie McCrea Reavis, Duke Redbird, Roy Reynolds, Trina Robbins, Leslie Korn Rogowsky, Chick Roberts, Mort Rosengarten, Arlyne Rothberg, Tom Rush, Salli Sachse, Camille Cacciatore Savitz (great appreciation), Ralph Schuckett, Michael Schwartz, John Sebastian, Jeanie Seligmann, Gene Shay, Betsy Siggins, Lucy Simon, Peter Simon, Dawn Reavis Smith, Connie O'Brien Sopic, Bruce Stanger, Mike Stanger, Bruce Sterling, Toni Stern, Mike Stoller, Randy Stone, Bob Sugarman, Deborah Symonds.

Russ Titelman, Ezra Titus, Matt Umanov, Don Was, Cynthia Weil, Tamara Weiss, Jerry Wexler, Helen Whitney, Eric Whittred, Madeleine Wild, Ben Yarmolinsky, Myron Yules, Larry Yurman, Elsa Bonli Ziegler, Joel Zwick. And a few who wish to remain anonymous.

We wove the tapestry together; this song *is* about you; and if you want me, I'll be in the bar.

—New York City, January 2008

BIBLIOGRAPHY

ARTICLES

Among the many articles and transcriptions of TV and radio broadcasts perused and utilized for this book are these, divided by the woman to whose sections of the book they pertain:

carole king

Aarons, Leroy F. "McGovern Begins Buildup for Campaign in California." *The Washington Post and Times-Herald,* April 8, 1972.

———. "Singing and Ushering for McGovern." *The Washington Post and Times-Herald,* April 17, 1972.

Abe, Debby. "Carole King's Attorney Seeks Release of Documents." *The Idaho Statesman,* January 5, 1985.

———. "Carole King to Star in Film; Suit Goes On." *The Idaho Statesman,* March 1, 1985.

Alterman, Loraine. "A Bland Carole King." *The New York Times,* July 15, 1973.

Barker, Rocky. "Carole King Lobbies for Wilderness." *Times-News* (Twin Falls, Idaho), November 18, 1991.

———. "Singer Uses Fame to Tout Wilderness: Carole King Makes Case for Her Outspokenness." *Post Register* (Idaho Falls), November 5, 1990.

Bradley, Carole. "Carole King Emerges as a Strong Voice for Wilderness." Gannett News Service, May 3, 1994.

"Career and Causes: Carole King's Privacy Issue Becomes Public Brawl." *Idaho Press-Tribune* (Nampa), June 3, 1984.

CaroleKing.com.

"Carole King Signs with Capitol." *Los Angeles Times,* December 8, 1976.

"Carole King Tops Grammy Winners." *Los Angeles Times,* March 16, 1972.

"Carole King Wins Round in Suit over Road." *The Idaho Statesman,* June 25, 1986.

"Carole King Wins Top 3 Grammy Awards." *Chicago Tribune,* March 15, 1972.

Champlin, Charles. "Singer Carole King Opts for Joy in the Country." *Los Angeles Times,* January 1, 1984.

Crouse, Timothy. "'Carole King Music' [review]" *Rolling Stone,* January 20, 1972.

Daley, Steve. "Carole King." *The Washington Post,* November 21, 1978.

Dove, Ian. "Music: Carole King's Casual Journey." *The New York Times,* May 27, 1973.

Ellsworth, Mark. "Carole King Blazes a Comeback Trail Through Boise." *The Idaho Statesman,* August 11, 1989.

Emerson, Ken. "Pop: Carole King at Palladium." *The New York Times,* November 20, 1978.

Feather, Leonard. "Established Signers Bucking Trend." *Los Angeles Times,* January 7, 1973.

"Four Sing for Politics at Forum." *Los Angeles Times,* April 17, 1972.

Fox, Margalit. "Betty Friedan, Who Ignited Cause in 'Feminine Mystique,' Dies at 85." *The New York Times,* February 5, 2006.

"Grammy Awards: 3 for Carole King." *The Washington Post,* March 15, 1972.

Heckman, Don. "Carole King Wins 4 Grammys as Record Industry Lists 'Bests.'" *The New York Times,* March 15, 1972.

——. "From Songwriter to Song Singer in a Leap." *The New York Times,* August 22, 1971.

Hernandez, Angel. "Road on King's Land Ruled Private." *The Idaho Statesman,* November 1, 1985.

Hilburn, Robert. "Another Winner for Carole King." *Los Angeles Times,* October 8, 1974.

——. "Carole King Sweeps Recording Honors with 4 Grammys." *Los Angeles Times,* March 15, 1972.

——. "King's 'Tapestry' Wearing Thin." *Los Angeles Times,* August 16, 1977.

——. "Music Review: Carole King in Greek Bow." *Los Angeles Times,* August 20, 1971.

——. "The Return of Carole King." *Los Angeles Times,* April 7, 1973.

——. "Review of 'Simple Things.'" *Los Angeles Times,* 1977.

——. "Times Woman of the Year: Carole King: Return to Simple Values." *Los Angeles Times,* December 13, 1971.

"Hitmakers: The Teens Who Stole Pop Music," A&E, 2001.

Holden, Stephen. "Carole King: Thoroughbred: Music Reviews." *Rolling Stone,* March 25, 1976.

——. "Carole King Performs at Town Hall." *The New York Times,* February 20, 1984.

——. "'Fantasy' [review]." *Rolling Stone,* August 2, 1973.

——. "Pop/Jazz: Back for Night at Town Hall, Carole King of Idaho." *The New York Times,* February 17, 1984.

Hoerburger, Rob. "'City Streets' [review]." *Rolling Stone,* May 18, 1999.

"Judge Takes Suit against King under Advisement." *The Idaho Statesman,* August 24, 1985.

"Just Married: Composer-Singer Carole King Weds in Sunrise Ceremony at Idaho Ranch." *The Idaho Statesman,* August 3, 1982.

Kamp, David. "The Hit Factory." *Vanity Fair,* November 2001.

Landau, Jon. "'Tapestry' [review]." *Rolling Stone,* April 29, 1971.

Larocca, Amy. "The House of Mod." *New York,* February 17, 2003.

Lichtenstein, Grace. "Carole King Draws 70,000 to Central Park." *The New York Times,* May 27, 1973.

——. "Carole King Steps into the Limelight." *The New York Times,* November 29, 1970.

"Louise Goffin Interview." Rock Electric Telegraph, 1016 (Web site).

"The Mad, Happy World of the Surfers." *Life,* September 1, 1961.

Manning, Kara, "'Colour of Your Dreams' [review]." *Rolling Stone,* June 24, 1993.

Maynard, Joyce. "Visiting Ann Beattie." *The New York Times,* May 11, 1980.

Miles. "The Ultimate Carole King Interview." Rock's Backpages, www.rocks backpages.com.

Murphy, Jean. "10 Honored in Ceremonies as Times Women of the Year." *Los Angeles Times,* December 7, 1971.

"'Only Love Is Real.'" *Chicago Tribune,* May 9, 1976.

Peterson, Anne. "Ruling Put Off in Suit Filed by Sorensens." *The Idaho Statesman,* December 20, 1986.

Pond, Steve. "Louise Goffin: Rebel from a Rock & Roll Family." *Rolling Stone,* October 4, 1979.

"Pop Music." *Los Angeles Times,* July 11, 1971.

"Pratter, Mark. "Carole King: Timber Policy Amounts to Corporate Welfare." *Times-News* (Twin Falls, Idaho), May 22, 1988.

"Profiles of 1971 Women of the Year." *Los Angeles Times,* December 7, 1971.

"Q & A with David Palmer: Carole King." Online, December 5, 2002.

"Richard Evers [obituary]." *Post Register* (Idaho Falls), March 24, 1978.

"Rock Edges into Mainstream Politics." *Los Angeles Times,* April 11, 1972.

Rockwell, John. "Friends of Carole King Fill the Beacon Theater." *The New York Times,* March 7, 1976.

——. "The Pop Life: A Sweet New Record by Weaver of 'Tapestry.'" *The New York Times,* March 14, 1975.

——. "The Pop Life: Carole King's Tapestry of Success." *The New York Times,* February 5, 1976.

"Rock: Year of the Woman?" *The New York Times,* June 6, 1971.

Rohter, Larry. "Still the King." *The Washington Post,* March 10, 1976.

Segal, David. "The Rock Journalist at a High Point in Music History [obituary of Al Aronowitz]," *The Washington Post,* August 3, 2005.

"Singer's Suit against Custer Postponed." *The Idaho Statesman,* May 7, 1987.

Singular, Stephen. "Trouble in Paradise." *Denver Post Empire Magazine,* July 1, 1984.

Snyder, Rachel Louise. "Will You Still Love Me Tomorrow?" Salon.com, June 19, 1999.

Strauss, Gary. "Carole King: All She Sought Was Peaceful, Secluded Life on Her Ranch." *The Idaho Statesman,* May 27, 1984.

Stuebner, Stephen. "Attorney Says Sorensen Did Nothing Capricious." *The Idaho Statesman,* February 15, 1988.

——. "Jones Calls Road Ruling Troublesome." *The Idaho Statesman,* February 13, 1988.

——. "Singer Carole King Wins Her Locked Road Case in Idaho." *High Country News,* April 11, 1988.

Supree, Burt. "For Young Readers: Maurice Sendak's Really Rosie." *The New York Times,* February 29, 1976.

"The Singer and the Forest Rangers." *The Wall Street Journal,* May 30, 1984.

"Trial Date Reset for Suit Filed by Carole King." *The Idaho Statesman,* November 30, 1986.

Van Matre, Lynn. "Carole's a Nervous Queen." *Chicago Tribune,* May 21, 1973.

——. "Singing-Songwriters: 1971 Is Woman's World." *Chicago Tribune,* July 4, 1971.

Ward, Alex. "Carole King: Creativity in a Cautious Comeback." *The Washington Post,* March 9, 1976.

"What's Playing in Lionel Richie's Ear?: Carole King, Tapestry." *O, The Oprah Magazine,* October 2006.

Woodward, Tim. "The Earth Moved." *The Idaho Statesman,* July 27, 1995.

Zito, Tom. "King's Soggy Do." *The Washington Post and Times Herald,* May 25, 1973.

——. "The Silent Side of Carole King." *The Washington Post and Times Herald,* May 24, 1973.

joni mitchell

"A Conversation with Joni Mitchell." *Grammy Magazine,* March 1997.

"Alberta-born Singer Gets Raves in London." *Alberta Herald,* November 25, 1970.

"An All-Star Tribute to Joni Mitchell," *TNT,* April 2000.

Aquilante, Dan. "Back to Woodstock." *New York Post,* August 15, 2006.

Arnold, Tom. "The Reunion, from Both Sides, Now." *National Post* (Toronto), 2001.

Astor, Gerald. "Songs for Aging Children." *Look,* January 27, 1970.

Atlas, Jacoba. "Unique Interpreters of Pop: Leonard Cohen." *Playboy,* November 1968.

Bannister, Paul, and Lo-Mae Lai. "Songbird Joni Searches for Love Child She Had at 19." *Globe,* July 12, 1994.

Batten, Jack. "Can.Pop," *Chatelaine,* September 1969.

Bayin, Anne. "Joni & Me." *Elm Street,* November 2000.

"Both Sides, Now." BBC-2, February 20, 1999.

Brand, Stewart. "The Education of Joni Mitchell." *Co-Evolution Quarterly,* June 1976.

Brown, Les. "Joni Mitchell." *Rolling Stone,* July 6, 1968.

Christgau, Robert. *Christgau's Record Guide,* 1981 (online).

Charles, Don. "The Joe & Eddie Story." *Goldmine,* February 5, 1993.

"Coffee Houses." *The Telegram* (Toronto), July 9, 1964.

Crowe, Cameron. "A Child's Garden of Jackson Browne." *Rolling Stone,* May 23, 1974.

———. "Joni Mitchell: The *Rolling Stone* Interview." *Rolling Stone,* July 26, 1979.

Crouse, Timothy. "'Blue' [review]." *Rolling Stone,* August 5, 1971.

"Cyber-Talk, America Online." January 26, 1995, www.jmdl.com.

Daum, Meghan. "My Dinner with Joni: A Fan's Notes About Conversations with Mitchell on Art, Politics, and Music." *Los Angeles Times,* December 9, 2006.

Davis, Ella. "Amelia." *The Regina Leader-Post,* May 15, 1957.

Davis, Stephen. "Joni Mitchell's 'For the Roses': It's Good for a Hole in the Heart." *Rolling Stone,* January 4, 1973.

"Diary of a Decade." Greater London Radio, June 1990.

The Dick Cavett Show. August 19, 1969.

Didion, Joan. *Slouching Towards Bethlehem: Essays.* N.Y.: Dell, 1967.

Dunn, Jancee. "Question and Answer: Joni Mitchell." *Rolling Stone,* December 1994.

Echols, Alice. "Thirty Years with a Portable Lover." *Los Angeles Weekly,* November 25, 1994.

Edmonton Folk Festival, 1994, www.jmdl.com.

Enright, Robert. "Words and Pictures: The Arts of Joni Mitchell." *Border Crossings: A Magazine of the Arts,* 2001.

Fawcett, Anthony. "A Search for Clarity." *California Rock, California Sound* (Reed Books, 1978), www.jmdl.com.

Feather, Leonard. "Joni Mitchell Makes Mingus Sing." *Down Beat,* September 6, 1979.

Flanagan, Bill. "Joni Mitchell Has the Last Laugh." *Musician,* December 1985.
———. "Secret Places." *Musician,* May 1988.
Fowell, Jake. "Fowell on the Coffee House Beat." *The Telegram* (Toronto), July 9, 1964.
Fulton, Laila. "Alberta Native Gave Up Daughter." *Calgary Sun,* December 1996.
Garbarini, Vic. "Joni Mitchell Is a Nervy Broad." *Musician,* January 1983.
Goddard, Peter. "Joni Mitchell: All Sides Now." *The Telegram* (Toronto), June 5, 1969.
Gould, Martin. "Joni Mitchell Life and Death Hunt for Baby She Gave Up 33 Years Ago." *Globe,* December 31, 1996.
Hansen, Liane. "Music Icon Joni Mitchell Discusses Her Music." *NPR Weekend Edition,* May 28, 1995.
"Heartsick Joni Mitchell Hunts Baby She Gave Up." *Globe,* April 16, 1996.
Heckman, Don. "Joni Mitchell at the Crossroads." *The New York Times,* August 8, 1971.
"Her Back Pages." *HotPress,* March 30, 2000.
Hilburn, Robert. "Crosby, Stills and Nash at Greek Theatre." *Los Angeles Times,* August 30, 1969.
———. "Crosby, Stills Voted Top Rock Group." *Los Angeles Times,* October 5, 1971.
———. "Joni Mitchell's New 'For the Roses.'" *Los Angeles Times,* November 21, 1972.
Holden, Stephen, "A Summer Garden of Verses." *Rolling Stone,* January 15, 1976.
———. "High Spirits Buoy a Joni Mitchell Album." *The New York Times,* November 7, 1982.
———. "Joni Mitchell Finds Peace in Middle Age." *The New York Times,* March 17, 1991.
———. "Too Feminine for Rock? Or Is Rock Too Macho?" *The New York Times,* January 14, 1996.
Hoskyns, Barney. "Joni Mitchell." *Blender,* June–July 2003.
Houston, Frank. "Joni Mitchell." Salon.com, April 2000.
Iyer, Pico. "Leonard Cohen: Several Lifetimes Already." *Shambhala Sun,* September 1998.
Jacarello, Roland. "Both Sides, Now." BBC-2, February 20, 1999.
"Jackson Browne [review]," *The Detroit News,* 1972.
James, Viola. "Joni's Miles of Aisles Breathes New Life into Her Legend." *Circus,* March 1975.
Joni at Edmonton (Canada) Press Conference, August 5, 1994. www.jmdl .com.

"Joni Mitchell." *Broadside,* April 26, 1967.

"Joni Mitchell." *Rolling Stone,* May 17, 1969.

"Joni Mitchell." *Rolling Stone,* October 15, 1992.

Jonimitchell.com.

"Joni Mitchell Hangs It Up." *Rolling Stone,* December 13, 1969.

"Joni Mitchell Interview." *Details,* July 1996.

"Joni Mitchell Is 90% Virgin [advertisement]." *Rolling Stone.*

"Joni Mitchell: The Isle of Wight Music Festival." www.jmdl.com.

"Joni Mitchell's Daughter: Chatelaine Model." *Jam!* (online), 1997.

"Joni Mitchell's New Album Will Mean More to Some Than to Others" [advertisement]." *Rolling Stone,* May 14, 1970.

"Joni Mitchell: Woman of Heart and Mind: A Life Story." PBS.

"Joni Rocks Again." *Chatelaine,* June 1988.

Kot, Greg. "Joni's Jazzed." *Chicago Tribune,* September 9, 1998.

Lacayo, Richard. "What Women Have Done to Art." *Time,* April 2, 2007.

Landau, Jon. "A Delicate Balance." *Rolling Stone,* February 28, 1974.

LeBlanc, Larry. "Joni Takes a Break." *Rolling Stone,* March 4, 1971.

Lydon, Susan Gordon. "In Her House, Love." *The New York Times,* April 20, 1969.

Maslin, Janet. "Joni Mitchell's Reckless and Shapeless Daughter." *Rolling Stone,* March 9, 1978.

Matteo, Steve. "Woman of Heart and Mind." *Inside Connection,* October 2000.

McClain, A. L. "Two Single Acts Survive a Marriage." *Detroit News,* February 6, 1966.

McFayden, Warwick. "The Teacher and the Debt." *The Age* (Australia), December 15, 2002.

Miller, Adam D. "In Search of Love and Music: Joni Mitchell's Musical Exploration." *Being There,* December 2004.

"My Top Twelve." BBC-1 Radio, May 29, 1983.

Patterson, Dale R. "The Boy on the Couch: B. Mitchell Reed." Rock Radio Scrapbook: Canada's Aircheck Archive (online).

Personal correspondence of Chuck Mitchell, 1964–1967.

Personal records of the Grey Nuns of Saskatchewan, by Luc Degenais, archivist of the Grey Nuns of Montreal.

"Pop Music." *Los Angeles Times,* July 11, 1971.

"Review of 'For the Roses.'" *The New York Times,* 1972.

"Rock Master Class Inerview." Capitol 95.8 FM, December 29, 1985.

"Rock 'n' Roll's Leading Lady." *Time,* December 16, 1974.

Ruhlman, William. "From Blue to Indigo." *Goldmine,* February 17, 1995.

Small, Michael. "Joni Mitchell." *People,* December 16, 1985.

Smith, Joe. "Off the Record." 1988.

Sony/ATV Music Publishing and Joni Mitchell Enter into Worldwide Agreement." *Business Wire,* August 26, 1997.

Strickland, Eugene. "Joni Dances into Hearts of New Generation," *Calgary Herald,* February 9, 2007.

Swartley, Ariel. "The Babe in Bopperland and the Great Jazz Composer." *Rolling Stone,* September 6, 1979.

Ward, Ed. "The Queens of Rock: Ronstadt, Mitchell, Simon and Nicks Talk of Their Men, Music, and Life on the Road." *Us,* February 21, 1978.

White, Timothy. "Joni Mitchell: A Portrait of an Artist." *Billboard,* December 9, 1995.

——. "Joni Mitchell's Many Shades of Indigo." *Billboard,* August 27, 1994.

Wild, David. "Joni Mitchell." *Rolling Stone,* October 15, 1992.

Van Matre, Lynn. "A 'Spark' of Strengths, with 'Hotcakes' of Humor." *Chicago Tribune,* February 17, 1974.

——. "Singing-Songwriters: 1971 Is Woman's World." *Chicago Tribune,* July 4, 1971.

Various short articles, women's pages, *The Regina Leader-Post,* 1955–57.

Yee, Min S. "Joni's Love of Words Turns into $500,000 Bonanza." *The Washington Post,* August 29 1969.

——. "Songwriting and Poetry." *The Washington Post,* September 14, 1969.

carly simon

Alterman, Loraine. "Carly's Happy About Being Happy." *The New York Times,* April 21, 1974.

Blacker, Terence. "Sex Addict, Crack Fiend and Moralist." *The Independent,* June 28, 2005.

Blinder, Elliot. "Carly Simon Rides Again." *Rolling Stone,* February 4, 1973.

Braudy, Susan. "James Taylor, a New Troubadour." *The New York Times Magazine,* February 21, 1971.

Brenner, Marie. "I Never Sang for My Mother." *Vanity Fair,* August 1995.

"Carly Simon." *Current Biography,* August 1976.

"Carly Simon Concert Is Off." *The Washington Post and Times-Herald,* November 25, 1971.

"Carly Simon on Bill." *Los Angeles Times,* November 18, 1971.

"Carly Simon: True Confessions." *The Independent,* 2006.

CarlySimon.com.

Christgau, Georgia. "Carly Simon Is Not a Folksinger." *The Village Voice,* July 5, 1976.

Christgau, Robert. *Christgau's Record Guide,* 1981 (online).

CNN interview with Paula Zahn, 2005.

"Concerts Today." *The New York Times,* June 18, 1971.

Cohen, Debra Rae. "'Spy' [review]." *Rolling Stone,* October 4, 1979.

Considine, J. D. "'Spoiled Girl' [review]." *Rolling Stone,* September 26, 1985.

Crouse, Timothy. "'Carly Simon' [review]." *Rolling Stone,* April 1, 1971.

Davis, Stephen. "'Anticipation' [review]." *Rolling Stone,* December 23, 1971.

Dunbar, Ernest. "Making It in Low Key: James Taylor." *Look,* 1971.

Fears, Stephen. "For the 'Real' Carly Simon, Living a Quiet Life Is the Right Thing to Do." *Chicago Tribune,* October 2, 1983.

Fong-Torres, Ben. "Carly: There Goes Sensuous Simon." *Rolling Stone,* May 22, 1975.

Hawtree, Christopher. "William Donaldson–Satirist and Writer Who Made His Name with the Henry Root Letters." *The Guardian,* June 25, 2005.

Hemphill, Paul. "Kris Kristofferson Is the New Nashville Sound." *The New York Times,* December 6, 1970.

Heckman, Don. "Carly Simon Sings at the Bitter End; She's Flying High." *The New York Times,* October 30, 1971.

Hoerburger, Rob. "'Coming Around Again' [review]." *Rolling Stone,* June 18, 1987.

Hilburn, Robert. "Carly Simon Has Impressive Album." *Los Angeles Times,* March 9, 1971.

——. "Carly Simon Will Raise the Roof." *Los Angeles Times,* September 26, 1980.

——. "Cat Stevens and Carly Simon Sing." *Los Angeles Times,* April 10, 1971.

Hinckley, David. "Looking at Hell: No Nukes, 1979." New York *Daily News,* July 8, 2004.

Holden, Stephen. "Carly Simon: 'Have You Seen Me Lately?'" *The New York Times,* September 23, 1990.

——. "Carly Simon's Emotion-Laden Self-Portrait." *The New York Times,* May 3, 1987.

——. "Carly Simon Triumphs over Her Own Panic." *The New York Times,* June 17, 1987.

——. "'Playing Possum' [review]." *Rolling Stone,* June 19, 1975.

——. "The Pop Life: A New Album of Popular Standards by Carly Simon." *The New York Times,* March 7, 1990.

——. "The Pop Life: A Spicy New Album by Carly Simon." *The New York Times,* August 7, 1985.

——. "The Pop Life: Carly Simon, Again." *The New York Times,* February 22, 1989.

——. "The Pop Life: Carly Simon Is Planning Feature-Length Videodisk." *The New York Times,* October 12, 1983.

——. "The Pop Life: Carly Simon Looks at Middle Age and Lost Pleasures." *The New York Times,* October 31, 1990.

——. "Pop Music's Romance with the Past." *The New York Times,* April 29, 1990.

Howe, Dessan. "'Working Girl': A Bull Market." *The Washington Post,* December 23, 1988.

Hunt, Dennis. "What's a Wife, Pop Star, Mother to Do?" *Los Angeles Times,* September 21, 1977.

Jahn, Mike. "Carly Simon Sings at the Bitter End." *The New York Times,* May 22, 1971.

"James Taylor: One Man's Family of Rock." *Time,* March 1, 1971.

Jordan, Rosa. "Kris Kristofferson." *Progressive,* September 1991.

Kaye, Elizabeth. "Just Another Word for Nothing Left to Prove: Kris Kristofferson." *The New York Times,* August 16, 1998.

Kors, Michael. "Carly Simon." *Interview,* July 2004.

Lahr, John. "Petrified: The Horrors of Stagefright." *The New Yorker,* August 28, 2006.

Landau, Jon. "'Hotcakes' [review]." *Rolling Stone,* February 28, 1974.

Leavitt, Leonard. "She: The Awesome Power of Gloria Steinem." *Esquire,* October 1972.

Mark, M. "Carly Simon [performance review]," *The Village Voice,* May 1977.

McKenna, Kristine. "Carly Simon: Pretty and Unabrasive." *Los Angeles Times,* April 30, 1978.

PeterSimon.com.

"Richard Leo Simon, Dies at 61, Co-Founder of Publishing Firm." *The New York Times,* July 30, 1960.

Rockwell, John. "Carly Simon at the Bottom Line." *The New York Times,* May 6, 1978.

——. "Carly Simon: The Fans Don't Scare Her Anymore." *The New York Times,* June 12, 1977.

——. "Pop: Comeback." *The New York Times,* May 15, 1977.

Rubin, Stephen E. "No Sad Songs for Carly." *Chicago Tribune,* August 5, 1976.

Sexton, Paul. "Carly Simon: True Confessions." *The Independent,* January 13, 2006.

Shapiro, Susin. "I Bet You Think This Piece Is About You." *The Village Voice,* May 23, 1977.

Shewey, Don. "'Hello Big Man' [review]." *Rolling Stone,* November 24, 1983.

Simon, Carly. "How Lyrics Work." www.DoubleTakeMagazine.org, November 9, 2006.

"She's Got Her Nerves." *The New York Times,* May 17, 1992.

Tucker, Ken. "'Another Passenger' [review]." *Rolling Stone,* August 12, 1976.

——. "'Come Upstairs' [review]." *Rolling Stone,* September 4, 1980.

Tosches, Nick. "Free, White, and Pushing 40." *Creem,* January 1984.

Van Matre, Lynn. "A 'Spark' of Strengths, with 'Hotcakes' of Humor." *Chicago Tribune,* February 17, 1974.

——. "Bold Plans for Stage-Shy Carly Simon." *Chicago Tribune,* July 20, 1980.

——. "Carly Simon Carrying a 'Torch' for the '40s Sound." *Chicago Tribune,* March 7, 1982.

——. "Carly's Still Anticipating." *Chicago Tribune,* April 17, 1972.

——. "James Taylor's Circle of Friends." *Chicago Tribune,* March 15, 1971.

——. "Singing-Songwriters: 1971 Is Woman's World." *Chicago Tribune,* July 4, 1971.

——. "Some Sweet Baby James." *Chicago Tribune,* October 12, 1971.

Wadler, Joyce. "Carly Simon: Anxiety & Essence." *The Washington Post,* October 30, 1983.

Ward, Ed. "The Queens of Rock: Ronstadt, Mitchell, Simon and Nicks Talk of Their Men, Music, and Life on the Road." *Us,* February 21, 1978.

Werbin, Stuart. "James Taylor & Carly Simon." *Rolling Stone,* January 4 1973.

White, Timothy. "Carly: Life Without James." *Rolling Stone,* December 10, 1981.

——. "James Taylor." *Rolling Stone,* June 11, 1981.

Willis, Ellen. Remarks on "You're So Vain" from *The New Yorker* quoted by Robert Christgau on Web site.

Yorke, Jeffrey. "Carly Simon's Sudden Serenade." *The Washington Post,* April 17, 1987.

Young, Charles M. "Carly Simon's Land of Milk & Honey." *Rolling Stone,* June 1, 1978.

BOOKS

Some of the books I used as sources, context, and inspiration were:

Adams, Alice. *Listening to Billie.* New York: Simon & Schuster, 1975.

——. *Superior Women.* New York: Alfred A. Knopf, 1984.

Andersen, Christopher. *Sweet Caroline.* New York: William Morrow, 2003.

Aronowitz, Al. *The Best of the Blacklisted Journalist.* Bloomington, Ind.: 1st Books Library, 2003.

——. *Bob Dylan and the Beatles.* AuthorHouse, 2004.

Asbell, Bernard. *The Pill: A Biography of the Drug That Changed the World.* New York: Random House, 1995.

Beattie, Ann. *Chilly Scenes of Winter.* Garden City, N.Y.: Doubleday, 1976.

Bergen, Candace. *Knock Wood.* New York: Ballantine, 1985.

Biskind, Peter. *Easy Riders, Raging Bulls: How the Sex-Drugs-and-Rock 'n' Roll Generation Saved Hollywood.* New York: Simon & Schuster, 1998.

Blacker, Terence. *You Cannot Live As I Have Lived and Not End Up Like This: The Thoroughly Disgraceful Life & Times of Willie Donaldson.* London: Ebury Press, 2007.

Bosworth, Patricia. *Diane Arbus: A Biography.* New York: Avon, 1985.

Branch, Taylor. *Parting the Waters: America in the King Years, 1954–63.* New York: Simon & Schuster, 1988.

——. *Pillar of Fire: America in the King Years, 1963–65.* New York: Simon & Schuster, 1998.

Braudy, Susan. *Between Marriage and Divorce: A Woman's Diary.* New York: William Morrow, 1975.

——. *Family Circle.* New York: Alfred A. Knopf, 2003.

Brownmiller, Susan. *In Our Time: Memoir of a Revolution.* New York: The Dial Press, 1999.

Carabillo, Toni, et al. *Feminist Chronicles: 1953–1993.* Los Angeles: Women's Graphic, 1993.

Cohen, Leonard. *Beautiful Losers.* New York: The Viking Press, 1966.

Collins, Judy. *Trust Your Heart: An Autobiography.* Boston: Houghton Mifflin, 1987.

Coontz, Stephanie. *Marriage, a History: From Obedience to Intimacy or How Love Conquered Marriage.* New York: Viking, 2005.

Crosby, David, and Carl Gottlieb. *Long Time Gone: The Autobiography of David Crosby.* New York: Doubleday, 1988.

Cross, Charles R. *Room Full of Mirrors: A Biography of Jimi Hendrix.* New York: Hyperion, 2005.

Davidson, Sara. *Leap!: What Will We Do with the Rest of Our Lives?* New York: Random House, 2007.

——. *Loose Change: Three Women of the Sixties.* Garden City, N.Y.: Doubleday, 1977.

Delbanco, Nicholas. *Grasse 3/23/66.* Philadelphia: J. B. Lippincott, 1968.

——. *The Martlet's Tale.* Philadelphia: J. B. Lippincott, 1966.

——. *Running in Place: Scenes from the South of France.* New York: Grove Press, 1989.

——. *Spring and Fall.* New York: Warner Books, 2006.

Didion, Joan. *The White Album.* New York: Simon & Schuster, 1979.

Donaldson, Willie. *The Big One, the Black One, the Fat One and the Other One: My Life in Showbiz.* London: Michael O'Mara Books Limited, 1992.

Dormen, Lesley. *The Best Place to Be.* New York: Simon & Schuster, 2007.

Dylan, Bob. *Chronicles: Volume One.* New York: Simon & Schuster, 2004.

Emerson, Ken. *Always Magic in the Air: The Bomp and Brilliance of the Brill Building Era.* New York: Penguin, 2005.

Fessler, Ann. *The Girls Who Went Away: The Hidden History of Women Who Surrendered Children for Adoption in the Decades Before Roe v. Wade.* New York: Penguin, 2006.

Finstad, Suzanne. *Warren Beatty: A Private Man*. New York: Harmony Books, 2005.

Fleischer, Leonore. *Joni Mitchell*. New York: Flash Books, 1976.

Fong-Torres, Ben, ed. *The Rolling Stone Rock 'n' Roll Reader*. New York: Bantam, 1974.

Friedan, Betty. *The Feminine Mystique*. New York: W. W. Norton & Co., 1963.

Gitlin, Todd. *The Sixties: Years of Hope, Days of Rage*. New York: Bantam, 1987.

Gould, Lois. *Such Good Friends*. New York: Random House, 1970.

Gruen, John. *The Party's Over Now: Reminiscences of the Fifties: New York's Artists, Writers, Musicians and Their Friends*. New York: The Viking Press, 1967.

Guralnick, Peter. *Last Train to Memphis: The Rise of Elvis Presley*. New York: Little, Brown and Company, 1994.

Hajdu, David. *Positively 4th Street: The Lives and Times of Joan Baez, Bob Dylan, Mimi Baez Fariña and Richard Fariña*. New York: Farrar, Straus and Giroux, 2001.

Hart, Jim. *Milding: Poems*. West Tisbury, Mass.: Yark Press, 2004

Hayden, Tom. *Reunion: A Memoir*. New York: Random House, 1988.

Heilbrun, Carolyn G. *The Education of a Woman: The Life of Gloria Steinem*. New York: The Dial Press, 1995

Hemenway, Robert. *The Girl Who Sang with the Beatles*. New York: Alfred A. Knopf, 1970.

Holzman, Jac, and Gavan Daws. *Follow the Music: The Life and High Times of Elektra Records in the Great Years of American Pop Culture*. Santa Monica, Calif.: FirstMedia Books, 1998.

Hoskyns, Barney. *Hotel California: The True-Life Adventures of Crosby, Stills, Nash, Young, Mitchell, Taylor, Browne, Ronstadt, Geffen, the Eagles, and Their Many Friends*. New York: John Wiley & Sons, 2006.

Jennings, Nicholas. *Before the Gold Rush: Flashbacks to the Dawn of the Canadian Sound*. New York: Viking, 1997.

Jones, Hettie. *How I Became Hettie Jones*. New York: Grove Press, 1996.

Johnson, Joyce. *Minor Characters*. Boston: Houghton Mifflin Company, 1983.

Jong, Erica. *Fear of Flying*. New York: Holt, Rinehart and Winston, 1973.

——. *Fruits & Vegetables*. New York: Holt, Rinehart and Winston, 1968.

Katz, Donald. *Home Fires: An Intimate Portrait of One Middle-Class Family in Postwar America*. New York: HarperCollins, 1991.

Kooper, Al, with Ben Edmonds. *Backstage Passes: Rock 'n' Roll Life in the Sixties*. New York: Stein and Day, 1977.

Kort, Michelle. *Soul Picnic: The Music and Passion of Laura Nyro*. New York: Thomas Dunne Books, 2002.

McDonough, Jimmy. *Shakey: Neil Young's Biography*. New York: Random House, 2003.

McKenney, Ruth. *My Sister Eileen*. New York: Harcourt, Brace and Company, 1938.

McLauchlan, Murray. *Getting Out of Here Alive: The Ballad of Murray McLauchlan*. New York: Viking, 1998.

Nietzsche, Friedrich. *Thus Spake Zarathustra*. New York: Dover, 1999 (republication of 1911 Macmillan translation).

O'Brien, Karen. *Shadows and Light: Joni Mitchell: The Definitive Biography*. London: Virgin, 2001.

O'Dair, Barbara. *Trouble Girls: The Rolling Stone Book of Women in Rock*. New York: Random House, 1997.

O'Reilly, Jane. *The Girl I Left Behind: The Housewife's Moment of Truth and Other Feminist Ravings*. New York: Macmillan, 1980.

Paglia, Camille. *Break, Blow, Burn: Camille Paglia Reads Forty-three of the World's Best Poems*. New York: Vintage, 2006.

Perrone, James E. *Carole King: A Biblio-Biography*. Westport, Conn.: Greenwood, 1999.

Petrie, Anne. *Gone to an Aunt's: Remembering Canada's Home for Unwed Mothers*. Toronto: McClelland and Stewart, 1998.

Phillips, Michelle. *California Dreamin': The Music, the Madness, the Magic That Was*. New York: Warner Books, 1986.

Plath, Sylvia. *Ariel*. New York: Harper & Row, 1961.

Posner, Gerald. *Motown: Music, Money, Sex, and Power*. New York: Random House, 2002.

Raskin, Barbara. *Hot Flashes*. New York: St. Martin's Press, 1987.

Reich, Charles A. *The Greening of America*. New York: Random House, 1970.

Roiphe, Anne Richardson. *Up the Sandbox*. New York: Simon & Schuster, 1970.

Rosen, Jody. *White Christmas: The Story of an American Song*. New York: Scribner, 2002.

Roszak, Theodore. *The Making of a Counter Culture*. Garden City, N.Y.: Doubleday, 1969.

Salamon, Julie. *Facing the Wind: A True Story of Tragedy and Reconciliation*. New York: Random House, 2001.

Schwartz, Jonathan. *All in Good Time: A Memoir*. New York: Random House, 2004.

Silber, Joan. *In My Other Life*. Louisville, Ky.: Sarabande Books, May 2000.

Spitz, Bob. *The Beatles: The Biography*. New York: Little, Brown and Company, 2005.

———. *Dylan: A Biography*. New York: McGraw-Hill, 1988.

Stansell, Christine. *American Moderns: Bohemian New York and the Creation of a New Century*. New York: Metropolitan Books, 2000.

Stone, Irving, and Jean Stone, eds. *My Life & Love Are One: Quotations from the Letters of Vincent Van Gogh to His Brother, Theo*. Boulder, Colo.: Blue Mountain Arts, 1976.

Students' Association of the Southern Alberta Institute of Technology. *64 Tech Art Record*. 1964.

Symonds, Deborah A. *Weep Not for Me: Women, Ballads, and Infanticide in Early Modern Scotland*. University Park, Pa.: Pennsylvania State University Press, 1997.

Tamarkin, Jeff. *Got a Revolution!: The Turbulent Flight of Jefferson Airplane*. New York: Atria Books, 2003.

Thom, Mary. *Ms.: 25 Years of the Magazine and the Feminist Movement*. New York: Henry Holt and Company, 1997.

Van Ronk, Dave, with Elijah Wald. *The Mayor of MacDougal Street: A Memoir*. Cambridge, Mass.: Da Capo Press, 2005.

Von Schmidt, Eric, and Jim Rooney. *Baby, Let Me Follow You Down: The Illustrated Story of the Cambridge Folk Years*. Amherst, Mass.: University of Massachusetts Press, 1979.

Walker, Michael. *Laurel Canyon: The Inside Story of Rock-and-Roll's Legendary Neighborhood*. New York: Faber and Faber, 2006.

Wexler, Jerry, and David Ritz. *Rhythm and the Blues: A Life in American Music*. New York: Alfred A. Knopf, 1993.

White, Timothy. *Long Ago and Far Away: James Taylor: His Life and Music*. New York: Omnibus, 2002.

Whitfield, Stephen, *A Death in the Delta: The Story of Emmett Till*. Baltimore: Johns Hopkins University Press, 1991.

Woodward, Bob. *Wired: The Short Life and Fast Times of John Belushi*. New York: Simon & Schuster, 1984.

Yetnikoff, Walter, with David Ritz. *Howling at the Moon: The Odyssey of a Monstrous Music Mogul in an Age of Excess*. New York: Broadway Books, 2004.

Zimmer, Dave. *Crosby, Stills & Nash: The Authorized Biography*. Boulder, Colo.: Da Capo Press, 2000.

. . . plus the yearbooks of Madison High School in Brooklyn; the Riverdale School in the Bronx; and Indian Hill Camp in Stockbridge, Massachusetts; and the 1955 Brooklyn phone book.

carole king

1970 *Writer* (Ode)
1971 *Tapestry* (Ode)
1971 *Music* (Ode)
1972 *Rhymes & Reasons* (Ode)
1973 *Fantasy* (Ode)
1974 *Wrap Around Joy* (Ode)
1975 *Really Rosie* (Ode)
1976 *Thoroughbred* (Ode)
1977 *Simple Things* (Capitol)
1978 *Welcome Home* (Capitol)
1978 *Her Greatest Hits: Songs of Long Ago* (Ode), compilation
1979 *Touch the Sky* (Capitol)
1980 *Pearls: Songs of Goffin and King* (Capitol)
1981 *One to One* (Atlantic)
1983 *Speeding Time* (Atlantic)
1989 *City Streets* (Capitol)
1993 *Colour of Your Dreams* (Rhythm Safari)
1994 *Natural Woman: The Ode Collection (1968–1976)* (Ode) compilation
1994 *Time Gone By* (Priority), compilation
1994 *In Concert* (Rhythm Safari)
1996 *Carnegie Hall Concert: June 18, 1971* (Ode)
1997 *Goin' Back* (Sony Special Products), compilation
1998 *Pearls / Time Gone By* (MCA International), compilation
1999 *Her Greatest Hits: Songs of Long Ago* (Ode/Epic/Legacy), compilation
1999 *Tapestry* (Ode/Epic/Legacy), reissue
2000 *Really Rosie / Music / Tapestry* (Ode/Epic/Legacy), reissue
2000 *Super Hits* (Ode/Epic/Legacy), reissue
2000 *Really Rosie / Her Greatest Hits* (boxed set) (Ode), reissue
2001 *Love Makes the World* (Rockingale Records)
2002 *Wrap Around Joy / Thoroughbred* (Sony International), reissue

2002 *Writer / Rhymes & Reasons* (Sony International), reissue
2002 *Music / Fantasy* (Sony International), reissue
2005 *The Living Room Tour* (Rockingale Records)
2007 *Welcome to My Living Room* (DVD) (Rockingale Records)

1968 *Joni Mitchell* (aka *Song to a Seagull*) (Reprise)
1969 *Clouds* (Reprise)
1970 *Ladies of the Canyon* (Reprise)
1971 *Blue* (Reprise)
1972 *For the Roses* (Asylum)
1974 *Court and Spark* (Asylum)
1974 *Miles of Aisles* (live) (Asylum)
1975 *The Hissing of Summer Lawns* (Asylum)
1976 *Hejira* (Asylum)
1977 *Don Juan's Reckless Daughter* (Asylum)
1979 *Mingus* (Asylum)
1980 *Shadows and Light* (live) (Asylum)
1982 *Wild Things Run Fast* (Geffen)
1983 *For the Roses / Court and Spark* (Asylum), compilation
1985 *Dog Eat Dog* (Geffen)
1988 *Chalk Mark in a Rainstorm* (Geffen)
1991 *Night Ride Home* (Geffen)
1994 *Turbulent Indigo* (Reprise)
1996 *Hits* (Reprise), compilation
1996 *Misses* (Reprise), compilation
1996 *Dog Eat Dog / Wild Things Run Fast* (Geffen), compilation
1998 *Taming the Tiger* (Reprise)
2000 *Both Sides, Now* (Reprise)
2001 *Girls in the Valley* (PopToones), compilation
2002 *Travelogue* (Warner Bros.)
2003 *The Complete Geffen Recordings* (Geffen), compilation
2004 *Supergold* (Galaxy), compilation
2004 *The Beginning of Survival* (Geffen), compilation
2004 *Dreamland* (Rhino), compilation
2005 *Songs of a Prairie Girl* (Asylum/Reprise/NoneSuch/Rhino),
     compilation
2005 *Artist's Choice: Joni Mitchell* (Hear Music), compilation

2005 *Songs Chosen by Her Friends & Fellow Musicians* (Live More Musically/Hear Music/Rhino), compilation
2006 *Woodstock* (Luxury), compilation
2007 *Shine* (Hear Music)

carly simon

1971 *Carly Simon* (Elektra)
1971 *Anticipation* (Elektra)
1972 *No Secrets* (Elektra)
1974 *Hotcakes* (Elektra)
1974 *No Secrets / Hotcakes* (Asylum), compilation
1975 *Playing Possum* (Elektra)
1975 *Carly Simon / Anticipation* (Elektra), compilation
1976 *Another Passenger* (Elektra)
1978 *Boys in the Trees* (Elektra)
1979 *Spy* (Elektra)
1980 *Come Upstairs* (Warner Bros.)
1981 *Torch* (Warner Bros.)
1981 *You're So Vain* (Pickwick), compilation
1983 *Hello Big Man* (Warner Bros.)
1985 *Spoiled Girl* (Epic)
1987 *Coming Around Again* (Arista)
1988 *Greatest Hits Live* (Arista)
1990 *My Romance* (Arista)
1990 *Have You Seen Me Lately?* (Arista)
1992 *This Is My Life* (Qwest)
1993 *Carly Simon's Romulus Hunt: A Family Opera* (Angel)
1994 *Letters Never Sent* (Arista)
1995 *Clouds in My Coffee 1965–1995* (Arista), compilation
1997 *Film Noir* (Arista)
1998 *The Very Best of Carly Simon: Nobody Does It Better* (Global/Warner)
2000 *The Bedroom Tapes* (Arista)
2002 *Christmas Is Almost Here* (Rhino)
2002 *Season's Greetings from Room 139* (WEA)
2002 *Anthology* (Rhino), compilation
2003 *Platinum & Gold Collection* (Arista), compilation
2003 *Great Hits Live / Working Girl* (BMG)
2004 *Reflections: Carly Simon's Greatest Hits* (BMG Heritage), compilation

2004 *Reflections: Carly Simon's Greatest Hits* (bonus track) (WEA International), compilation
2005 *Moonlight Serenade* (Columbia)
2007 *Into White* (Columbia)
2008 (as of January 2008, untitled)

INDEX